THE SONS OF NIGHT

Antoine Gimenez & The Giménologues

Advance praise for *The Sons of Night*:

"The publication in English of Antoine Giménez's memoir is a fantastic addition to Spanish Civil War literature in that language. Giménez was one of countless anonymous anarchists who fought for the Spanish revolution and this charming and moving account of his adventures deserves to be widely read. Its publication alone would be worth celebrating, but the accompanying text—an extraordinary labour of historical detective work by the historian affinity group The Giménologues—makes it essential reading for anyone concerned with the recovery of the libertarian and cosmopolitan tradition that shaped Giménez's generation. Taking the memoir as a starting point, the authors strike out into some of the most obscure corners of civil war-era Spanish anarchism and shed light on some of its most complex and controversial aspects. By turns unsettling and inspiring, it is never less than fascinating. Paul Sharkey, the Kate Sharpley Library and AK Press deserve great credit for bringing this treasure trove to an Anglophone readership."—Danny Evans, author of *Revolution and the State: Anarchism in the Spanish Civil War, 1936–1939*

"The Gimenologists—whoever they are—deserve our thanks for this wonderful book, clearly a labour of love. Not only are Giménez's memoirs a gripping and often moving read, but the Gimenologists' extensive notes (along with Dolors Marín's very useful foreword) are a treasure-house of information about the innumerable, mostly still anonymous people who did their bit for the construction of a libertarian socialist society. This is a good example of collective (even anonymous) history from below that is as rigorous in its scholarship as any work produced by academics. The enthusiasm the Gimenologists brought to their detective work (and to the fight to get the memoirs published in the first place) is infectious."—David Berry, author of *A History of the French Anarchist Movement, 1917–1945*

"The astonishing memoirs of 'Antoine Gimenez' (the pseudonym of Bruno Salvadori, an Italian adventurer who joined the international section of the Durruti Column) have been reconstructed and validated by the French collective Les Giménologues. Adorned by their scholarly apparatus, Salvadori's memoirs now provide an invaluable internal account of the role and internal difficulties of the libertarian forces in Aragón. Unmissable!"—Paul Preston, author of *The Spanish Civil War: Reaction, Revolution, and Revenge*

THE SONS OF NIGHT

being

BOOK I:

Memories Of The War In Spain (July 1936–February 1939)

by Antoine Gimenez

plus

BOOK II:

In Search of the Sons of Night

by The Giménologues

Antoine Gimenez & The Giménologues
Foreword by Dolors Marín Silvestre
Translated by Paul Sharkey

Published by
AK Press and the Kate Sharpley Library

The Sons of Night

© 2019 Antoine Gimenez & The Giménologues
Translation © 2019 Paul Sharkey
Foreword © 2019 Dolors Marín Silvestre
This edition © 2019 AK Press (Chico, Edinburgh)

ISBN: 9781849353083
E-ISBN: 9781849353090

Library of Congress Control Number: 2017957074

AK Press	AK Press
370 Ryan Ave. #100	33 Tower St.
Chico, CA 95973	Edinburgh EH6 7BN
United States	Scotland
www.akpress.org	www.akuk.com
akpress@akpress.org	ak@akedin.demon.co.uk

The above addresses would be delighted to provide you with the latest AK Press distribution catalog, which features books, pamphlets, zines, and stylish apparel published
and/or distributed by AK Press. Alternatively, visit our websites for the complete
catalog, latest news, and secure ordering

Kate Sharpley Library
BM Hurricane
London WC1N 3XX
UK
www.katesharpleylibrary.net

Originally published as *Les fils de la nuit. Souvenirs de la guerre d'Espagne* (Montreuil,
France: Libertalia, 2016)

Special thanks to Vincent Roulet and Myrtille Gonzalbo for their translation assistance
Also, please visit www.gimenologues.org

Front cover design by John Yates | stealworks.com
Printed in the USA on acid-free, recycled paper

Dedication
from the Libertalia French edition, 2016

This republication is dedicated to Ascen Uriarte, a Giménologue from the outset, who has left us for the company of the sons and daughters of night …

Just as the second Spanish-language edition of this book was going to the presses, Viviane, Pilar's daughter and granddaughter of Antonia from Peñalba, passed away at the age of forty-eight.

In a sense, she had inherited from her mother "the blows sustained during the war and later, by the wretched life in the refugee camps." Like her, Viviane ran away from real life a few years ago.

It was thanks to Viviane that Antoine Gimenez, her adoptive grandfather, proffered us these memories.

CONTENTS

Book I

Memories of the War in Spain (July 1936–February 1939)

by Antoine Gimenez

Book II

In Search of the Sons of Night

by The Giménologues

Endnotes On Antoine Gimenez's Memories

Biographical Notes

Appendices

ADVISORY   *bizarre methodology?*

We appreciate that the book you have in your hands is not going to make for very easy reading, as its critical apparatus is longer than the manuscript that was its starting point.

For this reason we venture to recommend that you read Antoine Gimenez's text (and the few footnotes attached to it) through once, and then, if your heart is in it, read it a second time making the forwards and backwards leaps that we suggest to you by means of the endnote numbers placed in bold ornamental brackets throughout the text (each page with an endnote has its corresponding page number from Book II at the bottom of the page as a navigation tool).

We have written this book the way it pleased us to imagine it being read, which is very selfish of us but primarily reflects the manner in which our research was conducted.

We started off by using the singular testimony from a leading character unknown even in anarchist circles, in order to deal generally with the war in Spain, following the various phases of the Durruti Column's International Group and the many ups and downs of life on the Aragon front.

The endnotes that run from page 207 to page 545 are, on occasion, quite substantial, but our hope is that you will bear with us here, for what is brought to light there is hard to find and, in most instances, beyond the reach of the average reader and sometimes hitherto unpublished.

To complement this battery of endnotes, we have added individual biographical entries, found between pages 549 and 646, which readers are urged to refer to, in that they contain clarifications likely to make the endnotes more readily understood.

The bracketed notations are ours throughout.

—The Giménologues

PREFACE

"In 1936 I was what is conventionally referred to nowadays as a 'marginal': someone living on the edge of society and of the penal code. I thought of myself as an anarchist. Actually, I was only a rebel. My militant activity was restricted to smuggling certain pamphlets printed in France and Belgium over the border without ever trying to find out how a new society could be built. My sole concern was living and tearing down the established structure. It was in Pina de Ebro and seeing the collective organized there and by listening to talks given by certain comrades, by chipping into my friends' discussions, that my consciousness, hibernating since my departure from Italy, was reawakened."

— ANTOINE GIMENEZ

The lines that follow are an invitation to step inside the life of a young Italian, a bit of a hobo, who was toiling in the fields near Lérida when the military coup d'état erupted on July 18, 1936. From the very outset, the reader is gripped by the heady atmosphere of those events of July 1936 in Catalonia, as the military and church structures teetered. Then we follow the narrator as he volunteers for service as a militiaman with the anarchist Durruti's column, newly arrived from Barcelona to wrest Zaragoza from the reactionary coalition. To be more specific, Antoine Gimenez then joined one of the bands of international volunteers that were set up along the Aragon front, long before any International Brigades were raised. This International Group was launched by the Frenchmen Berthomieu, Ridel, and Carpentier.

The pace of the writing, the switch from one scene to another, the bitterness of the fighting, times spent with the village collective, the impassioned arguments, the author's personal reflections, the depictions of the male and female militia members, speak of a world turned upside down. What we have here is the earliest document of such comprehensiveness related to the inception and activity of the anarchist militias and, more particularly, to those units of irregulars that were referred to at the time as the "Sons of Night."

Our Italian, who once upon a time had gone by the name of Bruno Salvadori, offers us a rather original touch as well where this sort of testimony is concerned:

"Not for a second does Antoine hold back from incorporating into his account those moments that cannot be unraveled from our everyday lives, like complementary aspects of the revolutionary transfiguration under way at that critical juncture. Just as he regales us with every detail of a meal, so he matter-of-factly recounts his amorous relations," wrote Paco Madrid in November 2004 in his foreword to the Spanish-language edition of the *Memories*.[1]

This aspect of his writing, as precious to him, we know, as the gaze of his lovers, was to be behind the scandalous contempt in which certain publishers who were approached held Gimenez's manuscript. These old-fashioned prudes in France and Spain, some of them styling themselves "libertarians," had the gall to suggest to the author that they might indeed publish, as long as he would agree to the removal of certain "scabrous" passages.

Like most of the protagonists of the war in Spain, Antoine kept the keynote moments of that experience to himself. He kept his distance from the anarchist movement and over the years penned only short poems and texts. Then in 1974 a thaw set in, and, in order to satisfy the curiosity of his adoptive granddaughter Viviane, he threw himself into the writing of his *Memories* over the next two years. At the same time, this Spanish-Italian-accented old chap in the beret looked after the premises of Marseille's little libertarian group, premises that were frequented by young folk who, to this day, have fond memories of him. He had this

---

[1]   Operating in perfect liaison with publisher Julián Lacalle and his friends Jorge Montero, Pablo Jimenez and Federico Corriente, Paco Madrid also saw to the translation of the *Memories* (which was published under the title *Del amor, la Guerra y la revolución* by Pepitas de Calabaza, Logroño, La Rioja).

way of capturing their attention with his simple, colorful expositions on anarchist theory, punctuated with his own personal recollections.

Once the manuscript was complete, Antoine had it read by those closest to him before touting it unsuccessfully to publishers, as we have said. When he died in 1982 only a few copies of his *Memories of the War in Spain* were run off, until the day when the Giménologues made up their minds to take it upon themselves to publish.[2] They set to work, trying to identify the names of the main characters in his account, starting with the members of the International Group:

> "The [International] Group was formed prior to there being any question of paying militia members a wage.... most of its members had given up their careers and normal occupations to scurry off to Spain. Some came from Italy, like young Giua, others from the Ruhr and the Saarland, some from the political or social underground, like that remarkable 'burglar' from the Romagna who, having resolved to die fighting, put up all of the loot he had amassed in France in order to buy weapons." —Mercier Vega, 1975

> "To Bianchi, Staradolz, Bolchakov, Zimmerman, Santin aka le Bordelais, Conte, Jimenez, Scolari, Balart, Barrientos and Cottin, comrades in the nameless cavalcade." —Mercier Vega, 1970

> "We have set our sights on a dialogue with them, a dialogue with the dead, so that something of their version of the truth might survive that might be of assistance to the survivors, to the living.... All that remains of them and of thousands of others, are a few trace chemicals, the residue of bodies doused in petrol and burnt, and the memory of brotherhood. We have had our evidence that it is possible to live collectively, with neither God nor master, which is to say, alongside men as they actually are and in the circumstances of a world such as they made it."—Mercier Vega, "Refus de la légende," 1956

These extracts testify to the fact that Louis Mercier Vega never forgot the "Spanish squabble" that had touched him to the quick, albeit that he scarcely ever talked about it. Wasn't his being himself

---

2   "Giménologues" meaning the sweet fools who had fallen for Gimenez and spread the word.

one of those "survivors" a prerequisite for his being able to invoke in such detail the members of the International Group, of whom "our" Gimenez was one?

We quickly came to understand that Charles Ridel—the young man in the helmet who spoke to Gimenez at the close of that day in September 1936 in Siétamo—and Louis Mercier Vega were one and the same person.

With that in mind, the Giménologues could see things more clearly, or at any rate so they thought, and off they set on their orienteering exercise, sticking closely to the clues left behind by activists from another era. Ridel and his friends of yesterday and today were their most consistent guides, for they steered us in the direction of men and women who were already working on the International Group and related topics: men and women like Marianne Enckell, Freddy Gomez, Phil Casoar, David Berry, Charles Jacquier, Abel Paz, Miguel Amorós. … Obviously, this opened up fresh perspectives and further complications. Excitement growing as we explored fresh avenues on the basis of surnames and first names or odd situations thrown up in Antoine's narrative, the Giménologues then came to realize that the seemingly superficial *Memories* were furnishing data that, once expanded by and set alongside other sources, had much to say about lots of little-known, indeed unknown aspects of the Spanish revolution.

By that point we needed to drink directly from the well: the archives at the International Institute for Social History in Amsterdam holds documentary sources from the CNT and FAI regarding, say, foreign volunteers, the day-to-day life of the fighters on the Aragon front, and the frictions that erupted between the latter and a section of the anarchist leadership. The cherry on the top of the cake was when Kees Rodenburg, who at the time was in charge of the Latin department, steered us toward the photograph and the file on Mimosa, a female member of the militia. Then, on the advice of Eric Jarry, we stumbled upon the Italian Central State Archives in Rome where the file on Bruno Salvadori, a file opened and "fed" by Mussolini's political police, popped up before our startled eyes at the eleventh hour of our final day's research.

We might add that a slightly more deeply embedded trail kept us with bated breath for months on end. It afforded us the opportunity to exhume a few dead bodies, like those of Lucio Ruano and Justo Bueno, CNT action men whose chaotic and highly colorful careers provided insight into some of the arcana of the anarcho-syndicalist organization in the 1930s.

Our third qualitative boost, and by no means the least, came thanks to the successful search for Antoine's French-Iberian family that had moved away from Marseilles following Antoine's death. Rather enthused by our venture, which stirred precious memories, Viviane and Frédéric delved into the back of a garage to retrieve dusty boxes left over from their relocation from Marseilles; several of them were packed with snapshots and writings by Antoine. Bitten by the bug, Frédéric set off for Aragon to winkle out Antoine's "second" family in Pina de Ebro, the Valero Labartas. And lo and behold, some of the protagonists of this story, Félix and Vicenta and their descendants, welcomed us into their homes, whereupon further accounts and photographs were added to our harvest.

There was no way that the Giménologues could have kept all this treasure to themselves; which is why Antoine's *Memories* have been issued with annotations that have become rather substantial as the months have gone on. We indulged ourselves by expanding upon our discoveries with insights into the Spanish libertarian movement, thereby inviting less-well-read readers to dip their toes for a moment into the ever-shifting and (as we would argue) infinitely rich world of the anarchist milieu.[3]

⸙ "No historical event set against the backdrop of the 1930s spawned as many lies as the war in Spain." —Paul Johnson, 1981

⸙ "The things I saw in Spain brought home to me the fatal danger of mere negative 'anti-Fascism.'" —George Orwell, 1938[4]

3   A good glimpse of the Giménologues's efforts can be found in the form of the radio broadcast we made of a part of Antoine's narrative, after one of our number had a good idea. That sound recording, broken up into twenty half hour installments, was broadcast, on a trial basis in January 2005 over Radio Fanzine in Forcalquier. Later it continued on its sweet way from one French-language radio station to another, in France, Belgium, and Canada.

We might also mention the happy initiative of the Djauk Populovitch theater company based in Saint-Romain-des-Îles (Saône-et-Loire department), with its adaptation of Antoine Gimenez's manuscript. The show was entitled *Del amor, la guerra y la revolución*.

4   *New Leader*, June 24, 1938.

Nostalgia & memory

"Being built on men, the Spanish Revolution is neither a perfect construction nor a castle of legend. The first thing we need to do for the
sake of balance is to reexamine the civil war bit by bit and on a factual
basis and not turn it into a source of nostalgia through our praises.
This is something that has never been conscientiously and courageously
done, for it might have resulted in exposing not just the weaknesses and
treacheries of others, but the delusions and shortcomings of us libertarians as well." —Louis Mercier Vega, 1956

This latter consideration, phrased by Mercier in his inimitable
style, seems to us to match up pretty well with the spirit with which
Antoine's narrative is shot through. In his *Memories* we find chronological mistakes and sweeping generalisations, but our author definitely belongs beside Ridel-Mercier in that "spiritual brotherhood of
lie-resisters" that emerged during those ghastly 1930s and that was
hailed by André Prudhommeaux.[5]

But if we want to map his progress through the Spanish labyrinth,
we will find nothing but lies in need of exposure and legends in need
of discarding. And we must still, unfailingly, dig down into the hold
and unearth the steps, sayings, and writings that lie hidden there and
the men who have been forgotten. For many of the protagonists in and
commentators upon that conflict were consummate camouflage artists
and counterfeiters, most especially at the heart of the incipient revolutionary process. The need for concealment was even acknowledged
at the time of the revolution by a faction of the anarchists who chose
the believe—were they being realistic?—that the capitalist democracies
would deliver arms to the Republic if only libertarians would enter
the government. One might be tempted to speak of the Foolish Years
apropos of 1936 and 1937, when we see how that social warfare was
progressively scaled down to a positional war pitting fascists against
antifascists.

"For many of the revolutionaries flooding into a Spain that was all fire
and fighting, it represented not hope but the death of hope, the ultimate sacrifice savored as a gauntlet thrown down to a complicated and

5   See the extract from a letter sent by André Prudhommeaux to Helmut
     Rüdiger in 1959 reprinted in Nico Jassies, *Marinus Van der Lubbe et l'in-
     cendie du Reichstag* (Paris: Éditions Antisociales, 2005), 155–56.

nonsensical world, as the tragic outcome of a society in which human dignity is held up to ridicule day in and day out. Fully committed to the pursuit of their personal fate in a context where total commitment was a possibility, few of them had any thoughts for the future." —Mercier Vega, 1956

Plainly we have had to reserve a special place for the writings of the Spanish militia members and "foreigners" who, in an unheroic but decent way, acted out their understanding of history.[6] It seemed to us that they were relatively badly treated by all representatives of the antifascist camp, not to mention the constant denigration they endured in the days of front lines and farming collectives in Aragon.[7] Libertarian communism had been enshrined in the CNT's program in 1936. In the collectivized countryside and in most of the militia columns it looks like this was taken seriously by men and women who thought one either took part in a revolution or refrained from doing so, but one did not put it off until later … especially when the tramp of jackboots was echoing throughout Europe and every frontier was turning into a barred cage. Anti-militarists, revolutionaries, Jews, exiles, escapees, everyone who knew persecution by the state flooded into the peninsula to drink in what it was like to live like fully fledged men and women. These beings, often characterized by the populism that was in the air as the scum of the earth crossed the Pyrenees to become

6   We have worked against the backdrop of the writings of one-time militia members such as Paul and Clara Thalmann, Simone Weil, Juan Breá, Mary Low, and Georges Sossenko and would give a special mention to the testimonies of Albert Minnig, Edwin Gmür, Helmut Kirschey, and Franz Ritter, into which we have delved aplenty, thanks to the kindness and helpfulness of Marianne Enckell from CIRA Lausanne, who saw to the translation of the last three mentioned. And we might add the testimony of the Swede Nils Lätt, translated by Pierre Enckell.

7   Recent publications by Miguel Amorós in Spain and by François Godicheau in France have largely afforded a voice to those anarchists who refused militarization, the historical compromise with the bourgeoisie and subservience to Stalin and who had a hard time making themselves heard when not blackguarded or dumped in the dungeons of the Spanish republican state. Here let us single out the publication of an anthology compiled by François Godicheaux, *No callaron. La voces de los presos antifascistas de la República (1937–1939)* (Tolouse: Presses Universitaires du Mirail, 2012).

practical internationalists. Which is also how the Spanish revolution lit up the world, for a brief while at any rate....

> "Memories are not just material facts, battles fought, adventure, but also the more or less conscious motivations that prompt us to act."
> —Antoine Gimenez

Thanks to his seven lives, Antoine managed to make it through the entire period between the first days of revolution and the collapse of the Aragon front in March 1938, then the awful *retirada* in February 1939. Unintentionally, the Giménologues have also spent three years following the meandering causes and character of the Spanish revolution and, by implication, the counter-revolution's as well. We have tried to adhere closely to the facts, while making no secret of our own opinions. Anything we have not managed to establish we have dealt with by way of leads that need to be chased up, in the hope that we may have whetted other aficionados' appetites.

In previous editions we said that we might naturally feel the need to add to our critical apparatus in possible future editions. Well, that time has come.

*

It seems to us that Antoine has managed to render palpable part of what was at stake during the years 1936 and 1937 in Catalonia and Aragon. There, in that crucible of anarcho-syndicalism, where young boys and girls were most often banding together on the basis of their affinities in their districts, that proletarians passionately yearned to bring down capitalist society while at the same time making free men and women of themselves.

So, in memory of what they set out to do and because it pleases us to think that there is some thread connecting us to their revolt, what we have done is recapture some glimmer of their spirit through the practice of affinity and freely circulating documents. The Giméno-logues have not come away disappointed, with the odd, rare exception; some of the protagonists (some who are still with us), some eyewitnesses, and researchers of every persuasion added their morsel to the exchanges of which this book is the fruit. Right to the very last, it has benefited from the collaboration of all the people mentioned earlier in this foreword, plus many others, whom we warmly hail here: Rolf

Dupuy, Claudio Venza, Gioivanni Cattini, Octavio Alberola, César M. Lorenzo, François Godicheau, Édouard Sill, and Vicente Martí (some of whom are no longer with us), José Morato, Alex Pagnol, Josep Lladós, Pierre Sommermeyer, Furio Lippi, Gianpiero Bottinelli, Tobia Imperato, Raúl Mateo Otal, Enrique Tudela Vásquez, Víctor Pardo Lancina, José Luis Ledesma, Nico Jassies, Eduardo Colombo, Paul Sharkey, Luis Bredlow, Robert Chenavier, Michel Léger, Reinhard Treu, Liliane Meffre, Marianne Kröger, the' Association Carl Einstein-combattant de la liberté, Manel Aisa, Pere López, César Benet, Marisa Fanlo Mermejo, Costán Escuer, Pepe Maestro, Anselm Jappe, Francisco Pérez Ruano, Nieves Borraz Martín, Peter Huber, Dieter Nelles, Carlos García, Harald Piotrowski ... and more besides.

May these few pages conjure up an appetite within you for diving headlong into those tragic 1930s and lead to your sharing our opinion that the history of the social war in Spain will never be over until we have done with the world that made it a possibility, and a necessity....

And now, off we go to Zaragoza!

The Giménologues

FOREWORD

Memories of the War In Spain: An Impressionistic Portrait of the Aragon Front

What the reader is holding is a splendid book of memoirs from one of the many anonymous individuals who passed through during the Spanish civil war and revolution of 1936–1939.

The Spanish civil war drew in countless antifascists from all around the globe, aghast at the craven European agreement not to intervene in Spanish affairs. This agreement was breached by Mussolini and Hitler, who used their air forces and troops to help the Francoist army to victory in 1939.[1]

In July 1936, some of the athletes who had arrived in Barcelona to participate in what came to be described as the Counter-Olympics stayed on in Spain. All these male and female antifascist athletes had come to compete in the celebrated People's Olympics in 1936, a counter to the Berlin Olympics celebrated against the backdrop of Nazi euphoria. Many of those athletes took part in the fighting in Barcelona in July 1936 and later marched off to the Aragon front with the columns raised in Barcelona. The Swiss Clara Thalmann and her husband Paul were two of the athletes who enlisted in the Durruti Column and, later sympathized with the "Friends of Durruti"

---

[1]   That help carried on even after the members of the International Brigades had been compulsorily repatriated on September 23, 1938.

Group.[2] Clara Thalmann competed as a swimmer and her husband, Paul, was a journalist.[3]

The very first columns bound for the front were organized shortly after the initial fighting in Barcelona in July 1936. Three anarchist columns called after the best-loved activists in the proletarian imagination—Durruti, Ortiz, and Ascaso—set off, full of enthusiasm, on July 23 and 24.

Other antifascists from all over the world just happened to find themselves on the peninsula or had rushed to Barcelona, Valencia, or Madrid, keen to fight for the Republic and to try to conjure up within it the revolution sought by the anarcho-syndicalists who had gained the upper hand on the streets right from the outset. Within a week or two they had signed on with the columns and were off to the front.

By August, a further two anarchist columns would be raised—the "Los Aguiluchos" and the "Roja y Negra."[4] A lot of these volunteers were to perish in the fighting.

2   They were to leave behind their memoirs in German, *Revolution für die Freiheit* (Hamburg: Verlag Association, 1977), in which they also describe how they were arrested in the wake of the May Events in 1937 and how they then left for Paris, as well as their part in the German resistance. In the 1960s they lived in a commune in the south of France. Clara took part in a documentary featuring Augustin Souchy (*The Long Hope*, 1981) about their experiences in Spain.

3   After May 1937, Clara and Paul Thalmann spent seven weeks in detention in the Santa Ursula prison in Valencia, accused by the communists with being "counter-revolutionaries." See Peter Huber, *Les Combattants Suisses en Espagne Républicaine* (Lausanne: Antipodes, 2001).

4   Officially, the very first anarcho-syndicalist column, the Durruti-Pérez Farrás Column, set off on July 24 with some 2,000 volunteers, many militia women among them. But a day earlier a lot of lads from the Barcelona affinity groups had impatiently set out for Aragon. The Ortiz Column, made up of 2,000 anarchist militia members and soldiers from the Thirty-Fourth Regiment, would also set off; this column would swell to 6,000-strong, absorbing the (anarchist) Hilario Zamora and (Catalanist) Peñalver columns. The third column was the Ascaso Column, with its 3,000-some volunteers; it absorbed part of the (Esquerra Republicana's) Villalba column. Toward the end of August, the volunteers from the "Los Aguiluchos de la FAI" set off, with García Oliver along, and so did the "Roja y Negra"; both these columns were anarcho-syndicalist and made up of residents from the districts of Barcelona and its industrial satellite towns (Hospitalet, Santa Coloma, Badalona, Prat de Llobregat, etc.). Each of these had around 1,000 members.

Later, weeks after the anarchist columns had set off for the front, Bayo's expedition bound for the Balearics (August 16 to September 12, 1936) would be organized; this included a *centuria* made up mostly of French, Cuban, and Argentinean volunteers of both sexes, albeit there were also Germans, Poles, and Austrians. The attempt to liberate the Balearic Islands culminated in a ghastly failure, and on their return to Barcelona the militia members reenlisted for the Aragon front to carry on with the fight, where many of them would perish within just weeks.[5]

Within the Durruti Column, what came to be called the International Group was raised: its members included Antoine Gimenez, our protagonist. As he himself was to explain years later: "In 1936, I was what is conventionally described nowadays as a 'marginal': someone living on the edge of society and the penal code. I thought of myself as an anarchist. Actually, I was only a rebel."

Gimenez was the alias assumed from 1935 onward, by Bruno Salvadori, an Italian anarchist who had been living in France for several years. From that point onward, "Gimenez" would be the name he went by. It was a very commonplace name that solved a few little scrapes he had been having with the police. Bruno Salvadori (b. Chianni, Pisa,

If we try to quantify their strengths we find that the anarchists were overwhelmingly in the majority on the front lines as compared with the Del Barrio–Carlos Marx Column of the Partido Socialista Unificado de Catalunya with its 2,000 members who set off on July 25. Two sizable columns were raised by the POUM (the Workers' Party for Marxist Unification) the Lenin-Maurín Column with its 2,050 members (50 of them foreigners), and on August 29 a second POUM column set off with another 1,000 members. The Catalan nationalists raised the Macià-Companys Column, with 2,000 men from the Esquerra Republicana, and the 3,000-strong Villalba Column. There was also the much smaller "Pirenaica" Column, made up of highly radicalized Estat Catalá personnel well versed in mountain warfare and sabotage operations. For the working-class makeup of the anarchist columns, see José Luis Oyón and Juan José Gallardo *El cinturón rojinegro: Radicalismo cenetista y obrerismo en la periferia de Barcelona, 1918–1939* (2004) and Abel Paz's *Durruti in the Spanish Revolution* (Oakland: AK Press, 2007), and *The Story of the Iron Column* (Oakland: AK Press, 2011) for the story of the anarchist resistance to militarization among the members of that column, raised in Valencia.

5   One of the first be killed in Barcelona was an Austrian athlete by the name of Mechter. He would soon be followed by many more, some of whom had interesting life stories yet to be brought to light by collective history.

1910, d. Marseilles, 1982) was a bricklayer, a stateless libertarian, jack-of-all trades, committed enough to have risked his life opposing fascism. He left behind a poetic scrapbook containing his musings and jottings from the war and the revolution in Spain.[6] The outbreak of the war caught him unawares, working in Vallmanya in the El Coscollar highlands in the townland of Alcarràs (Segrià-Lérida), from where he headed for the front line, and in Pina de Ebro he embarked upon that stage in his adventures that would alter his life once and for all.[7] As he explained: "It was in Pina de Ebro and seeing the collective organized there and by listening to talks given by certain comrades, by chipping into my friends' discussions, that my consciousness, hibernating since my departure from Italy, was reawakened."

The International Group, so-called, in which Gimenez's comrades served as part of the Durruti Column, was divided into three. Each unit had its own designation: the "Sébastien Faure" (made up mostly of Italians and French), the "Erich Mühsam" (Germans, Prussians, Poles, and Russians) and the "Sacco and Vanzetti." All in all, this added up some four hundred men and women who, after militarization was imposed, came to make up the Twenty-Sixth Division, or switched to other units.

Our Italian-born protagonist shared experiences with a sizable group of stateless persons from all over the world who had come to fight the fascist plans of the Spanish so-called Nationalists. From them we need pick out only a handful of names to show that they represented a kaleidoscopic vision of the Aragon battlefront. A ragbag of

---

6   For a good biography, see Myrtille Gonzalbo and Rolf Dupuy in *Dictionnaire des Anarchistes*, April 2014 (http://maitron-en-ligne-univ-paris1fr./noticeGimenezAntoine).

7   He was to fight on until demobbed in 1938, when we find him working in Barcelona until he was obliged to flee into exile via Portbou, and he was interned in the Argelès-sur-Mer concentration camp, sharing the same fate as hundreds of his comrades. There he was part of the Libertà o Morte group, made up of some 117 Italian internees and intended to ensure their survival. After the Liberation he was to live in Limoges until he made up his mind to return to Marseilles in 1951, where he had lived in his younger days, and there he died, having mingled with anarchist circles in the 1970s and promoted talks and debates. On the French Argelès-sur-Mer concentration camp, which held some 100,000 prisoners, see John Andrés García, *The International Brigades and the Refugee Camps of the South of France* (Forrest, Australia: Manning Clark House, Inc., 2008).

men and women activists, of varying ages and backgrounds and a motley range of experiences and working histories, such a sample as had appeared but rarely in the history of humanity and into which we gain a firsthand insight through Gimenez's vivid memories; without circumlocution and with the sap of youth and no Catholic-bourgeois moralizing, he regales us with the varying fortunes over a few months when life and death danced in and out of the destinies of these men and women, cast by fate on to the inhospitable, arid lands of Aragon.

Gimenez was to share battles, meals, rest periods, and sabotage operations with Émile Cottin, aka Milou, who perished in the battle of Farlete in Huesca, with the historian and ethnographer Carl Einstein,[8] with Carl Marzani,[9] with the Belgian Louis Mercier Vega,[10] the Algerian Saïl Mohamed,[11] and not just with them but also with Marcel Montagut, Lucien Chatelain (killed in action in 1937), Simone Weil,[12] Georges Gessaume (who also died in action in 1938), Georgette Kokoczinski, aka Mimosa,[13] the Argentinean Lucio Ruano, Carlo Scolari, Pietro Vagliasindi, the German Helmut Kirschey,[14] Pierre Odéon,

8   Much documentary evidence about him has surfaced in recent years, ranging from a Spanish-language anthology of his writings from the Column to a biography in French and a number of collections of his writings. Translations of his writings about art have appeared in Sebastien Zeidler, *Form as Revolt* (Ithaca: Cornell University Press, 2016), and *Bebuquin* has appeared in translation.

9   Marzani left behind five volumes of memoirs, one of them devoted to Spain. See *The Education of a Reluctant Radical* (New York: Monthly Review Press, 2002).

10   This anarchist, Charles Cortvrint, was to use a wide range of pseudonyms, one being Charles Ridel. Mercier Vega himself admitted: "I, on my own, am a veritable federation of pseudonyms." His life story and record of activism are outside of the scope of this foreword, although there is plenty published about him in French, including a special edition of *A Contretemps* (No. 8, June 2002) devoted to his career.

11   Wounded in November 1936, he returned to France: his busy life as an anti-colonial anarchist activist awaits exploration. For further information, see www.libcom.org.

12   Weil sent her dispatches from the front to *Le Libertaire* in 1936. See her enlightening *On the Abolition of All Political Parties* (New York: Penguin Random House, 2014). For more about her, see the notes in Book II below.

13   For more about her, see the notes in Book II below.

14   After service in the front lines, he left for Barcelona on furlough and was arrested along with several other Germans by the Stalinists and taken to a

Jean Mayol,[15] the sixteen-year-old French youth Georges Sossenko, aka Georges Jorat, plus, of course, a legion of Spanish anarchist comrades from the most combative groups from the years of the Republic, people like Justo Bueno,[16] Antonio García Barón,[17] a great pal of Gaston Leval's, the still little-known Pepita Inglés and many others whose names crop up throughout his narrative.[18]

Let us point out that, besides these libertarians and communists at odds with Moscow who had mobilized and been active right from the earliest days of the revolution, from October 1936 onward, at the behest of the Communist Party, some 40,000 men and women, marshaled into what came to be called the International Brigades, were mobilizing for Spain. They made their way to Spain to fight on behalf of the Republic and, uneasy at the turn of the self-managerial developments being put into effect in Spain, to try to bring the revolution to heel. They made up a colorful, lively amalgam of idealists, workers, literati, miners, political activists, antifascists, Jews, artists, journalists, and freedom lovers. They were drawn from more than fifty-five countries, and it is estimated that some 10,000 of them perished on the battlefronts since they lacked military training and were facing the terrifying *africanista* army. From the war in Spain onward, some of them were to voice criticisms of Stalinist orthodoxy and would reexamine where they stood, let down by the turn that the war in Spain and world geopolitics were taking.

Of course, the English-language reader is already widely informed about all the personal testimonies from the various protagonists who hastened to Spain to fight on behalf of the republican camp and to defy General Franco's horrifying fascist intentions. The propaganda

---

"*checa*" during the May Events of 1937; he would be removed to the prison in Segorbe, from which he managed to escape, and he left Spain via Switzerland for the sake of survival after several months spent in France and Holland.

15   On the French volunteers, see David Berry, *French Anarchist Volunteers in Spain, 1936-1939: Contribution to a Collective Biography of the French Anarchist Movement.*

16   This book contains one of the finest biographies of this militant.

17   Barón was to survive Mauthausen camp to die in Bolivia. See Alfonso Daniels, *Meeting Spain's Last Anarchist*, on BBC World online.

18   For an account of the females lives invisible even to their own comrades in arms, see Lola Iturbe's *La mujer en la lucha social* (1974). Not yet available in English.

later peddled by the Communist Party and the outcome of the Second World War made best-sellers of such accounts, overshadowing more critical accounts and those from the least mainstream quarters. In the new world order with its two blocs, these were squeezed out.

From the world of academia, outstanding English-speaking hispanists, most of them sympathetic to the legitimate cause of the Spanish Republic and opposed to the Francoist dictatorship in place until 1975, toiled in the struggle against the shroud of oblivion settling upon the Spanish war and revolution and, in tough times, they amassed testimonies and documentation and established archives. They were not alone in this, but their dedication and commitment deserve to be highlighted. Even as war was raging, books midway between testimony and erudition appeared, Peter Chalmers Mitchell's *My House in Malaga* (1938) and that important fresco by the adopted Andalusian Gerald Brenan, *The Spanish Labyrinth: An Account of the Social and Political Background of the Civil War* (published in 1943, the fruit of his lived experiences on the ground).

Later came the classic studies by Hugh Thomas, Raymond Carr, Gabriel Jackson, Anthony Beevor, Stanley G Payne, the upward of three hundred interviews conducted by Ronald Fraser for his *Blood of Spain* (1979), Angela Jackson's work, and the encyclopedic output of Paul Preston, one of the most learned writers on contemporary Spanish history.

Some fine archives have been preserved in Britain, containing war memoirs and testimonies.[19] It is estimated that around 2,500 Britons served as volunteers in Spain. Many of them came to Paris from Great Britain under the auspices of the Communist Party, as well as the Labour Party, to be organized by the French CP and posted to its headquarters, which had been set up in Albacete. Among them were a large number of idealists interested in fighting the fascism by which Europe was being overrun at the time. They were poets, writers, journalists, miners, manual workers, adventurers, and much more, all well documented thanks to the efforts of foundations, archives, libraries, and universities which collected their precious testimonies

19   We have in mind the Working Class Movement Library, the Imperial War Museum Sound Archive, and the International Brigade Memorial Trust. See too the Spanish sections of the Marx Memorial Library and Workers' School and the People's History Museum, plus the relevant historical records of the British Labour Party and Communist Party.

for upcoming generations. Most of the Britons described the war from a communist vantage point, and from among them we should single out a cluster of publications contemporary with the conflict, some of which appeared in the 1970s, by which time the war was back in the public eye, coinciding with the period of the Transition in Spain and the return [to Spain] and tributes paid to the protagonists of the war.[20]

Let us briefly review a few of these contributions, with absolutely no pretense of being exhaustive, since the output has been prodigious. The works of John Somerfield, *Volunteer in Spain* (1937), Kenneth Scott Watson, *Single to Spain* (1937), and Claud Cockburn (writing as Frank Pitcairn) *Reporter in Spain* (1936)[21] were published early on. Let us single out Esmond Romilly's impressive *Bobadilla* (1937). A year after that came the aristocrat Katharine Atholls's book *Searchlight on Spain*. In 1938, the journalist William Rust published *Spain Fights for Victory* and a year after that, his *Britons in Spain: The History of the British Battalion of the XVth International Brigade*. We must give a mention to John Langdon-Davies and his classic testimonial *Behind the Spanish Barricades* (1936). The battle of Jarama, of course, left an important impression in the British collective imagination regarding the war in Spain, and here we should mention Ben Hughes's *They Shall Not Pass! The British Battalion at Jarama—The Spanish Civil War*, and Frank Graham's classic *The Battle of Jarama: The Story of the British Battalion of the International Brigade's Baptism of Fire in the Spanish Civil War* (1987). T. C. Worsley's *Behind the Battle* would see publication in 1977.

It is worthwhile pointing out fine reference holdings of such autobiographies and memoirs that recount much of the day-to-day events on the battlefields and in the urban rearguard. As early as 1965, there was Vincent Brome's anthology of interviews with Internationalists,

---

20   Let us single out Bill Alexander's crucial testimony *British Volunteers for Liberty—Spain 1936–1939*, plus upward of forty autobiographies, ranging from anonymous contributors through to books by John Angus (1983), Tommy Bloomfield (2006), George Green (1986), Peter Elstob (1939), Thomas Wintringham (2009), David Guest (1939), Laurie Lee (1996), Maurice Levine (1984) or Alun Menai Williams (2004), and many others yet to see publication of their original manuscripts.

21   Cockburn was criticized by Orwell who looked upon him as a Stalinist spy because of his dismal and blatant involvement in the May 1937 events in Barcelona.

The International Brigades: Spain 1936–1939. And in 2004, Richard Baxell published *Unlikely Warriors: The Extraordinary Story of the Britons Who Fought for Spain*.[22] In 2010, Angela Jackson collected the trajectories of many of the female antifascists in *Las Mujeres Británicas y la Guerra Civil Española*. Not to mention monograph studies such as Jackson's (2010) *British and Irish Volunteers in the Spanish Civil War*, co-authored with Jim Jump and Richard Baxell.

Lots of local monographs have afforded the protagonists a voice. Take Ian McDougall's *Voices from the Spanish Civil War: Personal Recollections of Scottish Volunteers in Republican Spain, 1936–1939* (1986) or Daniel Gray's 2009 study *Homage to Caledonia: Scotland and the Spanish Civil War*, in which several protagonists, orthodox and heterodox, get to have their say. The actions of the Welsh miners are set out in Hywel Francis's 1984 study *Miners against Fascism: Wales and the Spanish Civil War*, as well as in Robert Stradling's *Wales and the Spanish Civil War: The Dragon's Dearest Causes* (2004). We are indebted to Valentine Cunningham for his splendid book on writers, *Spanish Front: Writers on the Civil War*, published in 1986. Also deserving of mention here are Chris Arman's 2015 study *No Other Way: Oxfordshire and the Spanish Civil War, 1936–39* and the 1996 study by Don Watson with John Corcoran, *"An Inspiring Example": The North East of England and the Spanish Civil War, 1936–1939*, plus the Edmund Frow and Ruth Frow study *Greater Manchester Men Who Fought in Spain* (1983) and the Mike Cooper and Ray Parkes study *We Cannot Park on Both Sides. Reading Volunteers in the Spanish Civil War 1936–1939*, and finally, Bernard Barry's *From Manchester to Spain* (2009). A few journalists were caught wrong-footed by the war, as was the case with Laurie Lee, who had been in Vigo and Almuñecar in 1935 and, when trapped by the war, was evacuated on board the HMS *Blanche*, only to return as an International Brigader in 1937. His memories are set down in his autobiography.[23]

As time wore on, the great communist propaganda drive mounted at the end of the Second World War, glorifying the efforts of the internationals in Spain and in the resistance to Nazism across Europe, ensured that in the publishing scene and, more so, in certain academic

---

22   He had earlier published *British Volunteers in the Spanish Civil War: The British Battalion in the International Brigade* (2007).

23   See *Moment of War*, published in 1991.

circles, huge emphasis was placed on the wartime effort of the communists ousted from Spain. That effort was certainly not to be sneered at, but theirs was not the only effort, and it overshadows the contributions of others who shunned the Stalinist project. Some anarchists ran into difficulties getting to Spain under their own steam, and so they enlisted in the Brigades being raised in such faraway places as New Zealand.[24] The Canadians and Americans would go through the same thing.

Not all the memoir writers sang the praises of the communism that was carrying out the notorious "purges" of its own leadership apparatuses in the USSR. For some antifascists, the war in Spain proved an important catalyst making them rethink their ideas. We have in mind George Orwell and Arthur Koestler who left us their testimony and their indispensable books. With regard to Orwell, we would single out his *Homage to Catalonia* (1953), and in Koestler's case there is his *Spanish Testament* (1940), in which he recounts his activities as a spy, his being sentenced to death in prison, and later the concentration camp world of Le Vernet d'Ariège that he shared with the vanquished Spaniards, the model for what would be replicated throughout Nazi Europe during the 1940s. Koestler went on to publish *Darkness at Noon*, an indictment of Stalinism, in 1941. Emma Goldman too would express her unease, dating back to her visit to the USSR, where she paid a visit to the isolated Kropotkin, a malaise sadly borne out by her Spanish experience when she was even fearful for his life. On her three trips to Spain she sampled firsthand the experience of the anarchist rearguard, citing the collectivizations and the anarcho-feminist Mujeres Libres organization and its teams of nurses and its handling of social and hospital care. Goldman showed her solidarity by backing the libertarian revolution at rallies and in a range of articles.[25]

The English poet and journalist Stephen Spender (1909–1995) found the strong communist beliefs that had prompted him to risk his life in Spain as a newspaper correspondent rattled after visiting the front lines and cities. He published *Forwards from Liberalism* (1937) and *The God That Failed* (1949) with notes critical of the International

24   As we learn from Mark Derby's book *Kiwi Comrades: New Zealand and the Spanish Civil War* (Christchurch: Canterbury University Press, 2009).

25   On Goldman and her dealings with the anarcho-feminists and visits to Spain, see Dolors Marín, "Mujeres Libres: el derecho al propio cuerpo," in *Mujeres Libres*, (CGT Madrid, 2018). In English, see D. Porter (ed.), *Visions on Fire: Emma Goldman on the Spanish Revolution* (Oakland: AK Press, 2006).

Antifascist Writers' Congress held in Valencia and Madrid in 1937 because of the soviet delegates' arrogant treatment of the rest of those attending. Spender sided with the view of the Soviet Republic that André Gide and some European writers shared.

Some books on the war and revolution were written from vantage points close to anarchism, and we shall mention these since their dispersion over time and space presents an unreal picture of the anarchists' abundant and prolific contributions on this period. From among the texts written in or translated into English, we would single out the work of the Scottish journalist and activist Ethel MacDonald (1909–1960)[26] who came to Barcelona and worked for the CNT-FAI radio station. MacDonald arrived in Spain with a bunch of anarchist volunteers who were close to Guy Aldred and who included her comrade Jane H. Patrick (1884–1971), who worked in Madrid on the English-language version of *Frente Libertario* before relocating to Barcelona where she lived through the May Events of 1937.[27]

The East Prussian Jew Hans Erich Kaminski, an anti-Nazi activist and a member of the IWA in the 1930s, enthusiastically relocated to Barcelona as a journalist and would soon have his testimony to offer regarding the early months of the war. In 1937 he published, in French, *Ceux de Barcelone*, a book consulted and cited by most libertarian researchers.

In his books, Burnett Bolloten came close to the anarchists' viewpoint and to their disappointment at the role played by the Communist Party.[28] Murray Bookchin also wrote about Spain,[29] and John

26   See Chris Dolan, *An Anarchist's Story: The Life of E. MacDonald* (Edinburgh: Birlinn, 2009).

27   See John Taylor Caldwell, *Come Dungeons Dark: The Life and Times of G. Aldred* (Barr: Luath Press, 1988) and *With Fate Conspire: Memoirs of a Glasgow Seafarer and Anarchist* (West Yorkshire: Northern Herald Books, 1999). Their records and personal testimony are housed with the Mitchell Library of Glasgow.

28   See *The Grand Camouflage: The Communist Conspiracy in the Spanish Civil War* (New York: Praeger, 1961), *The Spanish Revolution* (Chapel Hill: University of North Carolina Press, 1980) and *The Spanish Civil War: Revolution and Counter-Revolution* (Chapel Hill: University of North Carolina Press, 1991). The interviews he recorded and materials he collected in Spain are housed with the Hoover Institute at Stanford University.

29   See *The Spanish Anarchists: The Heroic Years, 1868–1936* (Oakland: AK Press, 2001) and *To Remember Spain: The Anarchist and Syndicalist Revolution of 1936* (Edinburgh: AK Press, 1994).

Brademas conjured up eclectic books that came even closer to the anarcho-syndicalists.[30] Sam Dolgoff penned his own study of the collectivizations, *The Anarchist Collectives: Workers' Self-Management in the Spanish Revolution, 1936–1939* (1974), complementing the classic on-the-ground appreciation of the observer Gaston Leval, *Social Reconstruction in Spain* (1938), which has been published over and over again. From within the anarchist camp, Rudolf Rocker offered us his first impressions in *The Tragedy of Spain* (1937).

We would highlight the work of the London-based Italian Vernon Richards, *Lessons of the Spanish Revolution* (1953), and the publications of one of the protagonists of those events, the self-educated tilemaker José Peirats. In 1952, commissioned so to do by the CNT in exile, Peirats produced a trilogy that set out to relate the history of Spanish anarchism and that complements the (by then) classic works of Buenacasa, Santillán, Foix, Lorenzo, and others. His three-volume *The CNT in the Spanish Revolution* is now available in English translation (volumes 1–3, 2001, 2005, and 2006, respectively). His popular reference work *Anarchists in the Spanish Revolution* was translated and published for the first time in England in 1990. That book is not free of self-criticism since the writer had gradually been distancing himself from the organization in exile. Again from Peirats, we would single out his autobiographical notes, appropriately revised and redrafted, which present us with a fine study of the very model of the self-educated libertarian militant and advocate of self-management. Chris Ealham has presented us with *Living Anarchism: José Peirats and the Spanish Anarcho-Syndicalist Movement* (2017).

Here too let us mention Robert Alexander's *The Anarchists in the Spanish Civil War* (1999). And how could we forget to highlight Stuart Christie's book *We the Anarchists! A Study of the Iberian Anarchist Federation (FAI)* (2000), for its appreciation of the anarchist groups that preceded the revolutionary endeavors of 1936. Plus Chris Ealham's rigorous and insightful *Class, Culture and Conflict in Barcelona, 1898–1937*.

In the United States, thanks to conversations with female anarchists

---

30   See "A Note on the Anarcho-Syndicalists and the Spanish Civil War," *Occidente*, 11, no. 2 (1955): 121–35, and "Revolution and Social Revolution: A Contribution to the History of the Anarcho-syndicalist Movement in Spain, 1930–1937" (PhD, 1953), first published as *Anarcosindicalismo y revolución en España (1930–1937)* (Barcelona: Editorial Ariel, 1974).

exiled in Canada, Martha Ackelsberg has produced her splendid book *Free Women of Spain* (1991), focusing on the work of the Mujeres Libres, the first European anarcho-feminist organization, which had significant ties to Emma Goldman.

And now, to this essential bibliography must be added the notebooks penned by Gimenez, an unknown anarchist militant who sprang into action to fight on behalf of the social revolution and the recasting of relations between the individual and the powers that be. This was a brand-new conception of life, an opportunity to carve out different means of communications and relations between people, as well as genuinely dismantling the capitalist economy, in addition to representing a refusal and resistance directed at the state-planned economy. Gimenez depicts himself straightforwardly as a humane anti-hero, with all of his contradictions, grappling bravely with contradictions that also affected a fair proportion of the anarcho-syndicalist membership, which was obliged to explore new thinking that sometimes ran counter to their own authoritarian and archaic education, inculcated over centuries of exploitation.

As one of his comrades was to write in 1956: "We have tried to enter into a dialogue with them, a dialogue with the dead in order to preserve, from their truth, whatever is left that might be of assistance to the survivors and the living…. All that remains of them and of thousands of others are a few trace chemicals, the remnants of bodies doused in petrol and the remembrance of brotherliness. We had been given proof that a collective existence with neither God nor master, but alongside men as they actually are and in the context of a world such as men have made it, is feasible."[31]

The Giménologues Phenomenon:
Taking Back Anarchist History from the Libertarian Perspective

Allow us just a few short notes to set in context the historical juncture in which it fell to Gimenez and his comrades to find themselves in Aragon, because we need to be mindful of what life was like in the Spanish countryside in 1936; it was very different from life in many

---

31   Louis Mercier Vega: "Refus de la légende," *Témoins*, nos. 12–13 (1956). Available in English as "Rejecting the Legend," www.katesharpleylibrary.net/573p98.

of the European countries of its day. We have one example of this in the Aragonese filmmaker Luis Buñuel, who explains in the very first chapter of his memoirs: "There is a case for the argument that in the village of my birth (Calanda), the Middle Ages lasted right up until the First World War. It was an isolated, stagnant society, where class differences were very pronounced. The labouring people's respect and deference toward the *grands seigneurs*, the landowners, roots deep in the old ways, seemed immutable."[32]

This is the backdrop against which the deeds, or, why not come out and say it, adventures of our protagonist Antoine Gimenez were played out. The arrival of the anarcho-syndicalist columns in the villages of Aragon brought with it modernity and the discarding of tradition, as part of the new libertarian scheme of things. This anarchist scheme, previously trialed over years of industrial cooperativism in Catalonia involved the entire collectivity in the making of decisions affecting them all, and the immediate banishment of all those who had, down through the centuries, monopolized political and religious discourse.

What Gimenez has written shows us a new order in Aragon, built upon many "anonymous" individuals: Barcelona workers, quasi-urban farmers, internationalist volunteers, journalists, Italian and German exiles, Latin American proletarians, plus, of course, antifascist women, arriving with the columns to live cheek-by-jowl with the local inhabitants, joining with the most impoverished and worst-off locals to build, albeit briefly, a brand new social project. A social project that, of course, involved plenty of contradictions and resistance that crop up in our protagonist's memories as he grapples courageously with hindsight.

Here we might define what goes under the name of *Gimenology* as "the science that studies the deeds of nameless illustrious utopians"; according to the original group, "It is a science that just ranges wider and wider." The name *Gimenez*, a happy-go-lucky name to be sure and one commonly found in Spain, informs an enthusiastic pursuit of a history made "from below" by a group whose work is skilled and rigorous, but who are not rooted in the world of academia. Meaning that what we have here is a *Gimenological* approach to the study, reclaiming, and narration of the libertarian past.

32   Luis Buñuel, *Mi último suspiro* (Barcelona: Plaza y Janes, 1982).

The phenomenon teased out by this band of Gimenologists began in 2005 with a twenty-episode radio show that has been broadcast in Canada, Belgium, Switzerland, and France. Shortly after that came a Spanish-language edition of Gimenez's memoirs, one having failed to appear in the 1970s due to some bickering over that maverick and certainly peculiar set of memoirs. In 2006 we saw the publication of the French edition, complete with a wide-ranging volume of notes setting Gimenez's claims in context and putting names and faces to his front-line male and female comrades. The effort to contextualize all these anonymous protagonists has bestowed upon the Gimenological project a historical rigor and literary vitality rarely found in contemporary studies and accounts. The group's web page is interconnected with a multitude of projects that are retrieving part of our collective trajectory as people with libertarian affinities and pursuits. Web history and webs that weave history—this is the real work of those of us who devote ourselves to seeking to shed some light upon the past so as to transform our present.

We therefore hail this English-language edition of a collective effort that, very much in his spirit, embraces Gimenez's narrative as a simple tribute to his trajectory and that of thousands of anonymous fighters on behalf of social revolution. Thus far, the Gimenological approach has been self-management and the reclaiming of our own history, to an accompaniment of enthusiasm, plus, of course, a little dash of humor. Because, as Emma is said to have said: "If I can't dance, then it's not my revolution." anti· profesorial work(?)

This is a healthy intention when it comes to narrating today's history, as our collective history is too important to be left solely in the hands of the university professionals. The rigorous, exhaustive endeavors of the Les Giménologues affinity group set a splendid example.

Dolors Marín Silvestre
L'Hospitalet, July 2018

BOOK I

Memories of the War in Spain
(July 1936–February 1939)

Antoine Gimenez

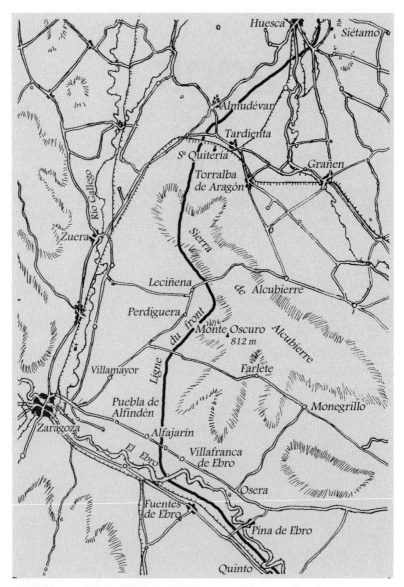

Map of the Aragon front in October 1936

TERESA

For some months past, the priest who came at regular intervals to say Mass at the Santa Clara convent had been portraying the Reds as merciless ogres, out-and-out demons spewing from Hell itself to spread murder, rape, and a thousand other atrocities across the entire world. He had been urging the sisters and novices to write to their families and tell them brace themselves for a fight to the death on behalf of "Christ the King" (*el Cristo rey*). The first rifle shots and the explosions of the first grenades had thrust Teresa into such a funk that, prone at the foot of a crucifix in her cell, she had not even heard the peals of the bell summoning them all to the chapel.

Half a dozen Falangists and priests had taken shelter in the convent, and they shot at us from there. Supporters of the *pronunciamiento* (coup) were now reduced to the fort in Lérida and the seminary. Women and children were strolling around, eager to see the signs that the revolution had left on the walls of their town, at which point well-aimed shots fired from a small opening, a sort of embrasure, wounded two or three passersby. Within minutes, about a hundred armed activists had gathered outside the convent door; one stick of dynamite was enough to give them access. They rushed inside: the Falangists and arms-bearing clergy had retreated onto the top floor, where they were slain on the spot.

As for me, I was not there, which is a matter of some regret, for I would have liked to see how those men who purported to stand for a god of love and justice met their ends with their weapons at the ready. I had stopped off at the chapel where the entire flock of sisters and novices was huddled, awaiting who knows what horrific end in the midst of torture and rape … but what they had feared didn't come to pass.

One CNT member stepped up and said to them: "*Señoras, no tengáis miedo* (Don't be afraid, ladies). You are to leave this place and you will be free to go wherever you please, be it to France or home."

And, surrounded by armed men, they left the convent behind.

The next day, the majority of the sisters caught a train to the border. A few, the Catalan ones, opted to stay until they could rejoin their families. After the nuns were gone, the mob invaded the convent and ransacked it. The motliest collection was stacked up in the little square: paintings, rosaries, crucifixes of every size, art books, profane and sacred items, even collections of some photographs that one would never have expected to see in the possession of the mother superior of a congregation of young girls.

A hand on my shoulder drew me away from my contemplation of the flames that were consuming all these items, a few of which may well have been works of art. It was Miguel, a young member of the Libertarian Youth who I'd met overnight in the course of the Spanish people's response to the coup attempt by Generals Mola and Franco. We'd hit it off immediately, and he insisted that he introduce me to his sister and his mother. Afterward, we were all but inseparable. I turned and asked him if he had had any news of his older sister, who had been with us when we broke through the convent door. Juanita was not far away and she was not alone; with her was a young girl, little more than a child. Miguel explained that his sister had found the girl in one of the convent cells, prone on the floor, half dead with fright, in front of a crucifix. Overcome with pity for her, Juanita decided to lead her out of there to bring her back to their mother, until she could be reunited with her own family. He wasn't happy with Juanita's decision and would have rather that the girl rejoined her own companions. He asked me to help him talk his sister out of the idea. Whether the little nun looked like she needed somebody to look out for her or whether it was because I liked Juanita, my advice to Miguel was to do as his sister wished.

The girl's name was Teresa; she was seventeen years old, and she had been in cloisters since she was seven. Her parents had decided that that was how it should be, so that all their assets should pass to her younger brother. Slated for a life of the cloth, all she knew of the world was what the priest had said about it in his sermons or what she had gleaned from tales of novices returning to the convent in later life. One evening, unprompted, she told us her story. When she lifted her eyes, her gaze drifted, almost in spite of herself, in the direction of Miguel; as for Miguel, he had eyes only for her.

The rebellion in Lérida was over in less than twenty-four hours; on July 18, 1936, the army had taken over strategic points around the city. That day I happened to be in the township of Alcarràs, helping out a friend on a farm in Vallmanya, when a friend from the village came to warn us that there was fighting in town.{1} I set off for Lérida with him right then and there. Along the way, other young people joined us. We were a good dozen strong by the time we reached the outskirts of town. The fighting had already ended, and there was utter silence. One kindly woman, recognizing one of the youths, told us that Falangists guarded the approaches to town. We decided to split up and meet up again later at the CNT local. Being an Italian national and unfamiliar with the terrain, I told my companions that I would carry on down the main road. I had an idea in mind: to get back to town I would have to have the permission of the Falange, but in order to move around freely I would need its blessing. Once in sight of the first houses, I started singing "Giovinezza" in such a tuneless voice that all the birds in the vicinity took flight. The words, if not the tune, echoed through the Catalan countryside like a gauntlet flung down. The street was deserted. Singing, I turned into it and was just beginning to think that the guard had been lifted when a raucous voice erupted behind me:

"*Alto! Donde va usted?* (Halt! Where are you going?)"

I turned, taken aback. An army officer had his revolver trained on me.

"Where are you going?"

"To Lérida," I replied. "*Italiano*, tourist."

A civilian, also armed, then stepped in and asked for my papers. I handed him my passport.

"*Italiano*, eh?"

"Yes."

"Fascist?"

"*Avanguardista*."

"*Viva Mussolini!*" he said, as he gave me back the passport.

I gave him the Roman salute and said "*Eia, eia alala*" before resuming my journey, mumbling the fascist anthem.

The CNT local was in the ruins of a building, which had once been occupied by the offices of the CEDA, a right-wing group led by Gil Robles. Fifteen or so people were loitering around the entrance. I had made up my mind to go into my act again if I needed to, and I wove my way through those gathered outside. To this day, I wonder why those guys let me through without a word.

How many comrades were there? Groups of them were coming and going, deep in conversation. Others, sitting on the floorboards around a pile of some sort of yellowish-red sand, were packing tin cans and bits of pipe. There were a few preparing cartridges with all the diligence of hunters on the eve of open season. And others still who were attaching detonators to bits of fuse. Everybody kept himself or herself busy while two or three young women did the rounds, handing out cups of coffee. Manuel, who I had left three kilometers outside of town, was already there, chatting to a young man who, even as he was talking, was sketching portraits of those present in a notepad. Manuel beckoned me over to marvel at the talent of his friend Miguel. I promptly advised him to burn these masterpieces, for if they were to fall into the hands of the Falange or the police, they would help them identify the comrades who were there. I told him that if he wanted to while away his time he could draw a fine landscape with a pretty girl, and he could use as his model a young woman who, at that precise moment, was coming our way to offer us a coffee. She turned out to be his sister, Juanita. He introduced me to her, saying that I had fallen for her and had asked him to do a portrait of her. Out of that we struck up a friendship; we were virtually inseparable after that throughout the entire time I spent in Lérida.

On July 19, to shouts of "UHP!" (*Uniós, Hermanos, Proletarios*, Unite, Brother Proletarians), the men of the CNT, FAI, UGT, POUM, and Socialist Party took to the streets. The troops garrisoning the town mutinied. The supporters of Generals Mola and Franco who managed to get away together with what few soldiers were still loyal to them, had retreated into the castle and into the seminary. A few isolated individuals sought the shelter of the Santa Clara convent and the churches.

When a society falls apart, there are always excesses; like an animal long penned up and suddenly released back into the wild, freed of all restraint, man, enslaved down the centuries, strives to quench his thirst, satisfy his desires and grudges; and so he loots and torches and kills. In the first few hours of freedom, he turns to looting; first, from the gun dealers, in search of weapons, and then from various food, clothing, and furniture stores. I remember seeing the door of an ice cabinet carried away by a guy dressed in patched-up trousers and an old shirt, even as an adjacent tailor's shop was being ransacked. Intrigued, I offered to help him carry off another item of furniture. His answer was that the only thing he needed was ice, as his wife had wanted nothing else ever since they were married. That said, I am forced to concede that the unions and other revolutionary organizations quickly accepted their responsibilities, and order was completely restored. The workshops and factories resumed operations, and businesses were turned into distribution centers. As in every popular uprising, the gates of the prisons were thrown open, but not all the inmates were political prisoners, so a watch service was set up; there was no need for what now belonged to everyone to be siphoned off for the benefit of the few. The word went out, not to specially formed groups but to every worker and activist in town. Taking turns, volunteers would stand guard or patrol the streets.

In Spain and elsewhere, the priest has always been capitalism's unfailing ally; *cura* (priest), *cacique* (political boss), and Civil Guard—these were the three mainstays of Spanish society. The workers and peasants were slaves to be used and abused by this trinity howsoever it chose. One had only to come into conflict with one of those three representatives of the ruling class, even over something trivial, and the offender was obliged to bend the knee or clear off. And if he resisted, it was unemployment, poverty, and imprisonment for him.

The gunshots fired from the bell towers and cloisters revived hatred and a thirst for revenge; a priest-hunt began. How many were killed? I have no idea.{2} I can still remember one of them, an athletic build of a man, walking ahead of two peasants, saying over and over again: "For pity's sake, don't kill me. I'm the father of a family."

Two barrels left him face down in the dirt. One of the murderers gave him the coup de grâce, saying: "*Tóma, cabrón!*" (Take that, you bastard!)

As for me, I was watching what was happening all around me. I was unarmed. In the looting of an armory, I easily made off with a hunting rifle. Unless memory fails, it was a .16 caliber, with a handful of cartridges that I had used up outside the seminary. Once my ammunition ran out, since I'd never had much appetite for hunting and found the rifle an irksome encumbrance, I passed it on to a comrade who traded me a magnificent dagger for it. So, with my hands free and as light as air, I was strolling around watching these people, intoxicated by a newfound freedom, trying to build society on new foundations.

When somebody asked me to come along on an expedition to some village or neighboring township where the presence of Falangists had been reported, Miguel and Juanita, who were working at the union, lent me their pistol. On those expeditions, I was lucky not to walk into an ambush or the lone snipers who targeted packed vehicles carrying men on their running boards and even on their mudguards.

As a general rule, by the time we showed up, matters had been sorted out by local residents, and there was nothing left for us to do—once the enemy's losses and ours had been counted, if there had been any fighting involved—other than celebrate their success by toasting the *revolución*.

On one such occasion, I witnessed a genuine tragedy. We were passing through a village quite some way away from Lérida. We were stopped in the square by an agitated mob; the richest landowner in the district, who they had thought had taken off for Huesca or Zaragoza, had been hiding in the cellars of his home. After he was found, the women and children of his family surrounded him, creating a human shield. Mother, wife, daughters, nieces, female cousins, and so on. About ten people of every age huddled around a purple-faced man, preventing him from budging. Around that human cluster stood five or six persons with their guns trained but not daring to open fire. That was the scene that met my eyes when I stepped into the yard, a poignant scene, with everyone shouting and weeping and wailing. Then it all happened so quickly: one woman ran up and cried out:

"*Padre, padre!*" (Father, Father!)

In her right hand was the butt of a .9 mm. The man looked at her, his face emblazoned with a bloodstain: "*Consuelo, sálvame, hija mia!*" (Save me, Consuelo, my daughter!)

The women and children parted before the newcomer who raised her arm and fired.

"*De la parte de mi madre*" (That's for my mother), she said.

Consuelo and I had arrived in the village in the same car. I knew her by sight, having previously spotted her during the earlier expeditions, always carrying her revolver, a mane of dark hair spilling over her shoulder, carefree and laughing, heedless of danger.

Prior to the revolution, she had plied the oldest trade in the world in the most poverty-stricken part of town. Together with her mother, she ran a sort of a dive where customers could assuage their thirst for alcohol and sex for around five pesetas. Since then, she had been fighting, seeking any opportunity to hear the bullets whistle past her ears and feel the kick of the gun in her wrist. Last time I saw her, she was clambering aboard a truck bound for the front lines.

Odd how the memories come to me even as I write: like a ball of wool locked up in a box, one reaches for an unruly thread, and lo and behold the whole thing unravels.

Despite their newfound freedom, looseness and debauchery held no sway over revolutionary youngsters. They preferred to spend their time away in discussion, probing and devising solutions to the everyday problems they faced in organizing the new way of life. Amorous entanglements were something of a rarity. During a stopover in a village where we spent the night, some woman to whom we had offered a few words of admiration of her beauty would join us from time to time, but that was a rare occurrence—an all too rare occurrence.

I remember one evening as if it were yesterday. I had gone to relieve Miguel, who was on night duty in an administration building, and had scarcely arrived when the rain began. A storm erupted, a real downpour complete with thunder and lightning and a wind that would rip the horns off an Andalusian ox. Eager to get back to Teresita, my friend dashed into the street and vanished after a "*Salud amigos, buenas noches!*" I was about to shut the door when a woman took shelter in the doorway. I took her for a grandmother, given that she was dressed in an old sopping wet black dress, her head wrapped in a scarf, and I invited her to step into the concierge's lodge. There was a fireplace there, and I could light a fire. Once the door was closed, off I went to the cellar to fetch some kindling. I was familiar with the place, having visited it with Miguel during an earlier stint of evening duty. When I returned, laden with wood, you could have knocked me down with a feather: there was no sign of the grandmother. In her place was a woman in her thirties. Her hair was trimmed very short, she was praying on her knees with her hands clasped, and water was dripping from her sodden scarf, which she'd placed on the back of a chair. My first thought, I will admit, was to show her the door, but there was the rumble of thunder, the rain was still pelting down, and I hadn't the heart. Without saying a word to her, I started the fire and sat on the cot that had been put there so that the watchman might get some rest during the night, because once the door was closed from within, there was no way of opening it from outside.

She was still saying her prayers. I gazed at her, unsure of my next move, and then I noticed that she was shivering and that the water saturating her clothes was forming a tiny pool around her. I went off to see if I could find something dry to put around her shoulders. The concierge's apartment was up a short flight of stairs. I dashed up there and was lucky enough to find in the closet a skirt and a blouse, not overly shabby, as well as two or three towels. These were for the only reasonably wearable items. Going back downstairs, I saw the door was open.

"*Merde!*" I exclaimed in French. "She's gone!"

But she was not gone. The violence of the storm had stopped her on the threshold. A blast of wind and rain had driven her back inside. I took her by the shoulders and said, "Come on, let's go back inside. You can't go outside, as you can see. I've found you a change of clothes."

I closed the door again. Once back in the lodge, I tossed the items I had found on to the cot and stepped outside again after telling her to change. In the hall, I drew my pistol. I removed the bullet and locked the safety catch. My idea was to get her to trust me and reassure her as to my intentions. About ten minutes passed before I knocked on the door again. No answer. I stepped inside. She was still standing in the same place, her arms crossed over her chest, quivering like a leaf. All of a sudden, I was angry. One stride and I was on top of her. I undid the top of her chemise, and slid it down to her feet along with some sort of a hair shirt she had been wearing next to her skin. I grabbed a towel and began rubbing her furiously. By the time I was finished, she was stark naked, her body as red as a beetroot from head to toe.

"Go on! Get dressed! What are you waiting for? For me to ravish you?" I shrieked at her and, stooping to gather up her soaking clothing, I added, in softer tones: "I'm not one for the rough stuff when it comes to love-making."

Miguel had left me his lunch-box. His mother, knowing that I would often be in her son's company, always made enough for two. I emptied it of its contents and laid out a bottle of wine, a flagon of coffee, and some ham on the table. His mother had done a good job, and there was enough there for two healthy appetites. While I was setting the table with a glass and a tin mug, the girl had dressed. The paper in which the ham was wrapped did double duty as napkin and plate. The shirt and top I had brought were too big for her but suited her better than that black chemise. As we ate, I told her that I had been raised in France and that woman was not made to dry up inside some convent but to live life and love and have fun. She listened in silence, her eyes downcast. What I was telling her did not interfere with her appetite for she was helping herself as if she had been on a fast for a month. After I had talked about myself, I asked her name.

"Encarnación," she replied.

Since she was answering now, I put a few more questions to her, which is how I discovered that she'd been born in Manresa and was eager to rejoin her family. She had been en route to the railway station when the storm broke. Once the meal was over, I slipped around behind her to get the coffee I had set on the coals to heat, and, once I had set the little pot on the table, I bent over to kiss her on the ear while my hands, sliding under her arms, brushed against the roundness of her breasts. A tremor went through her. I thought it was fear that was making her shudder. She already held my knife, which I had lent her so that she could cut some bread: I drew my 9mm. and placed it gently in her lap as I told her:

"Encarnación, you're a pretty girl, too pretty for a man not to want you. Let me caress and make love to you. I am weaponless, so there's no need to be afraid of me anymore."

Once again, I fondled her; I had opened her blouse and my palms could feel the warmth and firmness of her breasts while my tongue flicked at her earlobe. I had expected her to bridle at this and to object by word or deed. Nothing. It was as if she was made of marble; then, slowly, I felt her nipples grow erect and her breasts harden under my caresses. Her head rested against my chest.

By the time I woke up, she was fast asleep, her head in the crook of my arm. The crackle of gunfire reached me. I scrambled to get dressed, scooped my weapons off the table, and raced for the door, sliding the breech of my pistol to put a bullet in the chamber. The gunfire was drawing nearer all the time. Some of the reports were from very close by, and then silence descended. I opened the door; two men were sprawled in the road and some others were racing up.

"What happened?"

"Falangists! They tossed a bomb at the union hall, but it didn't go off. What are you doing here?"

"Sentry duty. *Salut.*"

After a few words with my friends, I darted back inside. I was afraid that Encarnación, roused by the gunfire, might venture out into the street. The scene there was not very appetizing, especially as one of the men shot was not quite dead. From the gap between the cot and the door she was just staring out at what was happening. I slid the bolt and the chain home again and gathered her into my arms to lay her down on the cot again.

"Are they dead?"

"Yes."

"And you could easily have been killed yourself?"

"That could happen any day. Such is revolution...."

She threw her arms about my neck. My mouth locked on her lips. Everything else receded: the fear, the danger, and the death that might well be waiting for us just around the corner. Later I walked her to the train station and watched as the train pulled away.

A few days later, at dusk, I was out strolling with Miguel, Teresa, and Juanita. My friend knew all about my little adventure with Encarnación; the *compañero* who had relieved him that morning told him that I'd spent the night with some woman who was certainly no comrade prior to her encounter with me. But he thought I'd indoctrinated her, judging by the way her arm was linked with mine. Miguel told his sister and Teresa what he knew, while making fun of me and my discretion. The girls guffawed like lunatics, adding their own comments to Miguel's. All of a sudden we heard shouting in the street:

"The Durruti Column! The Durruti Column!"

And in fact, the Durruti Column, having set out from Barcelona, was arriving in Lérida on its way to liberate Zaragoza.{3} Shouts of "Long live the FAI! Long live the CNT!" alternated with couplets from anarchist anthems like:

Arroja la bomba que escupe metralla (Throw the bomb that spits shrapnel)
Coloca petardos, empuña la Star (Place the petards, pick up the Star)
Acudid los anarquistas (The anarchists rally round)
Empuñando la pistola hasta el morir (Holding the pistol right to the death)

… or the Libertarian Youth's anthem:

Hijo del pueblo. Que oprimen cadenas (Son of the people, bounden in chains)
Antes que esclavo prefiere morir (Better death than slavery)

Truckloads of men and women added their own cries and songs to those from the crowd as they rolled through.

Fists in the air, we watched the trucks roll by and vanish into the descending night. It was at that point that I decided to set off the following morning for Zaragoza with Durruti and my comrades. I told one of my friends, and there was an eruption of objecting voices; I had no right to leave them just like that. I could just wait two or three days.

Miguel assured me that he would be going with me as well but needed at least forty-eight hours to sort out some family arrangements. Teresa was crying, for she thought that if I went Miguel would definitely be going with me. She would have renounced every revolution in history, past or yet to come, if only Miguel would stay. She already loved him with a love exclusive and absolute, even though the young man himself, in thrall to his ideal of righteousness and justice, had never tried to prey upon the girl's feelings. My friend was also fond of the young nun and behaved toward her like an older brother, affectionate and attentive to her every whim.

When we were on our own, Miguel used to talk to me about his love and the dreams that he felt were unattainable because of the revolution. Indeed, should the revolution succeed, it would not be without losses, deprivation, and suffering galore, and, in spite of my advice to him, he refused to make the young girl his partner.

After her initial surprise, Juanita said nothing. She said nothing, but she was the one who got us to come to agreement by pointing out to us that it was getting late, and I had to get some rest if I meant to set off early in the morning, and we should have supper together before that. Her mother had had no warning of our imminent departure. Once coffee had been served, it was Juanita that spoke up to give us her decision: she would be going with her brother and me. Nothing we said could budge her, and the subject was dropped. And then Teresa asked if I might do her one last favor before going. When I agreed, she asked me to get her a visa for France, and added: "Fighting and dying for your beliefs is all you think about. As for me, I'm heading back to the convent, and I'll be praying for you all from there. Forgive me."

And off she ran to her room to hide her annoyance.

The union local was open around the clock, and off I went immediately, in the hope that the fellow in charge of the visas might not be too much of a stickler. Juanita caught up with me on the street and linked her arm through mine:

"Tony, you do realize that the *niña* is in love with my brother?"

"And?"

"She mustn't go to France, because Miguel is in love with her. If she reenters the convent, they'll have a life of unhappiness ahead of them."

When the young girl had talked to me about going to France, I'd come up with an idea: I'd escort Teresa as far as the border, talk her into staying with some trusted friends of mine living in the Perpignan area, and wait there for her sweetheart to come and get her. I explained all this to Juanita, without mentioning that my plan was to make my way to the front without passing through Lérida again. So Miguel would be waiting for me in vain and might well not be leaving. As a long-time activist who, for nearly eight years had been involved in all the meetings and activities an intelligent, action-minded woman could take part in, Juanita had no difficulty getting a pass for Teresa. On her return, she asked if she could ask me a cheeky question.

"Go ahead," I answered, "no need for us to fall out."

"Do you love Teresa?"

"Yes, I love her as if she were my own little sister."

"And what about me? Do you love me?"

"If you weren't Miguel's sister, I'd have taken you as my mistress a long time ago."

"You reckon I'd have agreed to that then?"

"Gasping for it!"

"*Presumido*! [Big head!] A woman has only to look your way and you think she wants to bed you. You're all the same."

And off she ran, laughing. Miguel was waiting for us outside the house. María, his mother, and Teresa were in the room they shared with Juanita.

I could not sleep, and I was mulling over the arguments I might use to convince the young girl to forget about the convent and head for my friends' place. Those friends were a couple of dyed-in-the-wool pacifists, childless despite their twenty years together. I was just beginning to doze when the door to my room opened. A naked Juanita slipped in, her finger to her lips and a candle in her hand. I sat up in the bed: "Are you mad? What do you want?"

She set the light on the table and lay on top of me, casting aside the sheet I had over me and murmured: "*Cállate … te quiero … soy tuya.*" (Don't say a word … I love you … I'm yours.)

We locked lips, and she straddled me. Her body was hot and smelled of lavender.

By the time we emerged from our room, the sun was high in the sky. María had rustled up four bowls and some slices of bread for breakfast. She looked at us and said: "*Habéis bien dormido?*" (Sleep well?)

Then she came over to kiss me on the cheeks and added: *"Ahora tengo un hijo más."* (Now I have another son.)

As I returned her kiss, I asked her: "Where are Miguel and Teresa?"

"Here we are!"

Right on cue, Miguel and the *niña* walked back into the kitchen, standing lovingly side-by-side. He was naked to the waist, and she was in a dressing gown. I burst out laughing.

"So you finally made up your mind! You took your time about it. Congratulations!"

I was speaking to Miguel, but it was the girl who answered in reproachful tones contradicted by the glint in her eye: "That was your fault. Yes, Juanita's to begin with but then yours.... You're so indiscreet; we could hear everything coming from the room, right down to the heavy breathing ... not to say what we heard from you."

"Yes, and off you went for a word with my brother. You did the right thing, *querida*, because he's such a slow-coach he'd have let you go back to France before he'd ask you to be his girlfriend. And this one here is even worse than Miguel (where I am concerned), and would have taken off without so much as a kiss. Now I'll never be parted from him again."

Poor Juanita, not knowing that she had but a few more hours to live. Why didn't I let her follow me? Why, over the three or four days we spent together, did I talk her into staying at home with Miguel, who Teresa would not let go, and with her mother?

The CNT was recruiting volunteers to make up a *centuria* that would join the Durruti Column. Juanita walked me as far as the departure point for the convoy, and after one last kiss I clambered onto the truck and away we went. That was to be my last sight of her. She perished under strafing by some Francoist planes while out in the fields with some other comrades gathering the remaining sheaves of wheat.

THE WAR

Indifferent to the shouting and singing of my fellow travelers, I hadn't slept all night. I nodded off only to wake up in Alcarràs where the population gave us presents of some full wineskins. I availed of the chance to say hello to a few youngsters I knew. When the truck pulled out again I dozed off. I had caught the very last truck in the convoy, just so I could spend a few more minutes with Juanita. The others on the truck were all peasants from the vicinity of Lérida. Some of them I knew from sight, but most of them were strangers to me. A sharp application of the brakes woke me up: we had arrived in the vicinity of Fraga, a sizable town nestling on the banks of the Cinca River. Barked orders:

"Everybody off!"

We deployed in firing positions, our guns trained on the village that we overlooked from far higher ground. Not yet fully awake, I went through the motions: firing position, on my knees, clutching the butt of my 9mm. I could see two motorcycles hurtling down the slope toward the pueblo and the bridge that spanned the river. By my reckoning, my gun was totally useless at that range, even if I was shooting downhill. The motorcycles reached the village, crossed the bridge, and vanished, but then the riders reappeared, gesticulating frantically with their arms. Everyone raced for the trucks.

The village, Fraga, is located on the border of Catalonia and Aragon, and is renowned through all of Spain for its excellent figs. We received an enthusiastic welcome, and though the column had passed through a few days ahead of us, there were still some dried figs left. Each truck received its quota, supplemented by butifarra, chorizo, and other pig meats. Sustenance was assured. After a brief stop, we moved on: I watched my traveling companions, a dozen or so men between thirty-five and fifty years of age, the rest of us youngsters, I being probably the oldest of those. Our weaponry consisted of hunting rifles and handguns of varying caliber, and only one of us had a carbine that he was forever aiming this way and that. Afraid that he might shoot somebody, I advised him to quit swinging it around, which he did immediately. He handed me the gun and asked, "Do you know anything about using it?"

"Of course I do. Don't you?"

The Durruti Column in the square in Bujaraloz

"No. I took it off my uncle just before we set off. He must be searching everywhere for it. Care to show me how this thing works?"

"Sure. Watch. It's straightforward."

I pulled back the breech; the magazine was full but there was no cartridge. After removing the clip, I taught him how to handle the rifle. The others were watching me, drinking in the advice I was giving the lad. When I had finished, one of the boys seated closest to me said:

"Hey, *compañero*! You're from Extremadura, right?"

On my travels around Spain I had often been taken for a Spaniard; mistaken for a Catalan in Extremadura, or for a Navarrese or a Basque in Andalusia. If I admitted that I was a foreigner, then they were certain that I was French. Once, in Madrid, I had presented myself at a Civil Guard post to report the loss or theft of my papers, as they had disappeared from my wallet. Half an hour later, I was transformed into Pablo Esquerra, native of Pueblo Nuevo, home address in the Calle Principal in Barcelona. Those papers enabled a friend wanted by the police to carry on living in Spain up until the *pronunciamiento*.

"No, I'm not Spanish."

"French?"

"Not French either. Italian."

"*Anda, los Italianos son todos fascistas.* (Come on. The Italians are all fascists.) What's your name?"

"Gimenez, Antoine. And yours?"

"Gimenez? You're a Spaniard. You must have been pulling our legs!"

At this I drew out my passport and CNT membership card:

"Can you read? Look."

Of the twenty-five men there, only two of us could read: me and the young lad with the carbine who, after glancing at the union card, burst out laughing. He reached to shake my hand, saying:

"You're right. Anybody who fights at my side is my brother, no matter where he's from. So, you're Antonio? My name's Pedro." After his, every other hand reached out to shake mine.

When we arrived in Bujaraloz, the *centuria* delegate told us to choose a group leader. We needed one for every twenty-five men, and whoever was elected had to report to the column's command post (CP) at 8:00 p.m. Groups were quickly formed, the men getting together naturally on the basis friendship, neighborhood or blood ties. The oldest person in the group was appointed to take charge. The following day, we pulled out of Bujaraloz, bound for Pina de Ebro.

PINA DE EBRO

Pina de Ebro presented some difficulties; about twelve kilometers from town there had been a firefight with a gang of Falangists guarding the Gelsa crossroads. None of us was hit, though, and it all went fine.{4} The 2nd was put in charge of the junction and of conducting house searches.{5} We found no one suspicious. Because of their curiosity, the children were first to interact with us, though most—all those not already involved in social struggles—were scared. Nearly all the kids were barefoot or had on *abarcas* (a sort of homemade sandal made out of an old car tire). No one we asked had ever had a proper shoe on his feet, so we took them to the shoe store in the church square. The shop owner started handing out slippers to one child and then to another, since they needed to try them for size first, and he called for our help. Five or six of us then turned into shoe salesmen, and I recall that the youngest ones were asked for a kiss and the bigger ones for a hand-shake in return. This was quite a high price to ask of the younger ones since we had a three-day growth of beard!

Durruti had the townspeople assemble on the main square where he delivered a brief address.{6} He said that the land belonged to the people and that they needed merely to work it together, as a collective, but that any who would rather carry on with family farms were free to do so. He also said that money no longer had value and that work was all that mattered.

While we searched the houses for anyone in hiding, every religious object we came upon was taken out. Spaniards are very devout without actually being lovers of church and clergy, and I have often noted in the peasants a queer blend of Christian belief and avant-garde ideas—things that, looked at in the right way, are not incompatible. Be that as it may, the fact is that every time these devout Catholics had revolted against the established order, they burned down the churches and slaughtered the priests. The church in Pina was no exception to the rule.

Inside every house, on the walls and on the furnishings, there were crucifixes, pictures of saints, and rosaries. In certain homes, the women helped us rip them down and burned these objects, symbols of ignorance and slavery, in their very own fireplaces; elsewhere, where old folk pleaded with us or tried to hide such things, which they held dear, our task was lousy. I realized that day just the extent of the tolerance of these uneducated men; they stood ready to kill every priest on earth with a laugh and at the same time, in order to please some old man or elderly woman, were ready to help them hide a crucifix or blessed virgin. I remember seeing one out-and-out priest-slayer (I had seen his handiwork in Lérida) popping back into the room where an old, bed-ridden woman, was struggling to take down a crucifix from the wall above her bed. The man stepped back inside, detached the crucifix, looked at the old woman curled up under the covers, lifted the sheets slightly, and quickly slipped the crucifix underneath. He the scooped up two or three saints' pictures from the bedside table and turned to leave, catching sight of me on the threshold. He realized I had seen, and shrugged his shoulders.

"*Compañero, podría ser mi abuela, y tuya también.*" (Comrade, she could have been my grandmother or your own.)

We left together, pondering the stupidity of all who let themselves be bamboozled by the wind-sellers who promise paradise after a life of hellishness.

A few days slipped by uneventfully as we tried to break down the last remaining barriers that fear had erected between the most refractory souls and us. Then, one night, the alert was sounded: some Falangists and *requetés*[1] were gathering on the far bank of the river between Pina and Osera and were about to attack.{7} Silently, we took our places, about fifteen meters from the river's edge, in the foxholes we had dug over the preceding nights. Herrera and I were in a foxhole about one meter long and about fifty centimeters wide. Herrera was in his forties. On July 19, he had been in Barcelona's Modelo prison, staring at fifty or sixty years, I can't quite remember which. Freed, he and two of his usual accomplices had commandeered a car to get to Lérida,

---

1 "The *requetés* or "red bonnets" were the militia of the Traditionalist Communion, a far-right party, led by Manuel Fal Conde and the Count of Rodezno. They were veritable crusaders fighting for "God, Fatherland, and the King" and their officers were drawn from the Military Academy in Pamplona, a private institution launched at the beginning of 1935. Recruited from among the peasants of Navarre, the *requetés* were well-trained and disciplined. These Spanish equivalents of France's Chouans made up the core of the rebel army along with the Moroccan tabors and the Foreign Legion."— César M. Lorenzo, *Le Mouvement anarchiste en Espagne. Pouvoir et révolution sociale* (Saint-Georges-d'Oléron: Editions Libertaires, 2006), 200.

their birthplace. Ever since his adolescent years, he had survived on the proceeds of thievery and plunder, except during the intervals when the government had housed and fed him free of charge.

I am telling you all this because two days after that, during a patrol behind our lines designed to thwart potential enemy infiltrations, we stepped inside an abandoned monastery. We checked every floor and found nothing of interest, and then Herrera and one other guy peeled off to check out the cellars, while another comrade and I stood guard outside. I was beginning to tire of waiting; though the cellars may have been huge, time was dragging. Finally they came running out.

"Antoine," Herrera said to me. "Come take a look."

"What? What is there to see?"

"I don't know what it is, but it's definitely something not very Catholic."

Our other comrade, Herrera, and I went below, via the courtyard. Herrera grabbed a pick that was lying around, and once we reached the cellars he pointed to a stretch of wall where the stones had recently been cemented over.

"And? Is that what you wanted to show us?"

"Listen, the cemetery is at the far end of the garden. If the monks sealed up this rubble they assuredly had their reasons for doing so. This is a tomb, or a hiding place. Listen carefully."

Using the pick handle he gave a few taps to the wall. It was solid throughout, except where it had been rebuilt.

"You're right," I said. "It does have a hollow ring to it."

"So? Shall we take a look-see?"

"Go for it."

He started to work on the top line, which was the widest. The first stone finally gave way, after which it was child's play widening the fissure. Light from a torch then shone into the cavity, which held nothing but an old-fashioned strongbox bedecked with elaborate locks. It took only two or three minutes to lift it through the gap and break it open; it was jam-packed with gems and coins, several hundred years old. Herrera darted off to call the comrade posted outside. The moment he got back, we came to our decision; I would wait with two others while the fourth man went to get a car. By that evening, the strongbox and its contents were in the union local. If memory serves and my information is correct, the matter was reported in a number of French newspapers at the time.

It was around 2:00 a.m. when Herrera whispered to me:

"*Oyes?*" (You hear that?)

The faint hiss of running water had actually been added to a second rustling sound, itself very faint to begin with, drawing closer and closer: the sound of paddles in water. My heart began to pound so strongly that it felt as if it was about to burst through my chest. Stooped down in the bottom of the foxhole, my comrade handed me the tinder. My rucksack held two tin cans packed with TNT (tolite). I set one down in front of me on the sand and clutched the other in my left hand. A rifle shot rang out. A dark mass loomed in the darkness in front of me. I flexed my knees, edged over to the fuses whilst blowing on the tinder and started counting: one, two, three, four. Then came a blinding flash and an explosion, and the entire riverbank was ablaze. It was hell.

Behind me, I saw shadows looming out of the nothingness, jumping and running in my direction, then vanishing amid the deafening racket of rifle and revolver fire and exploding bombs. I hurled my last can at a shadow that had just appeared out of the night. Bullets buzzed through the air like angry wasps. The shrieks and sobbing from the wounded mingled with the hellish orchestra of weapons of death. Then the firing eased up, and very quickly a silence descended that was broken only by the moans and screams of the wounded. The two boats that had come ashore opposite our foxhole bobbed, splintered, and were all but submerged on the river. The boats' former occupants had not all had time to disembark, and most of them had been catapulted by the explosion into the water and drowned.

LA MADRE

It was early in the afternoon of that same day that I first met "La Madre." Kneeling beside a stream that snaked its way through tall clusters of poplars (I think they were poplars but can't be sure, for botany was never my strong suit), I was beginning to do my laundry.

"*Que haces, hijo*?" (What are doing, son?)

I lifted my head to see a woman of a certain age beside me, a huge basket under her arm. "Washing my shirt," I told her.

"There is no shortage of women in Pina to do the menfolk's laundry. Give me that, and you can collect it this evening."

"Where? I don't know where you live."

"Come to the Calle del Pino and ask for Tía Pascuala."[1]

Whenever I think of all the people I met in Spain before and during the war, and all the folk I lived alongside, mixed with, and had dealings with, the sweetest memory, the one closest to my heart, is of this Aragonese peasant woman who, amid the mayhem, opened her home to me and welcomed me like a once lost child. Tía Pascuala. La Madre.

Madre, you have long since departed this world, but the memory of you and the memory of my own birth mother ... to this day, after all these years, those are the memories I hold most dear.

At dusk I headed for the street she had mentioned. The heat had been fierce all day, so all of the residents were sitting on their doorsteps enjoying the cooler evening. Some were sitting on the ground itself; others on chairs or benches or nonchalantly leaning against the wall chatting about the previous night's fighting.

"*La casa de la Tia Pascuala, por favor*?" (Which is Tía Pascuala's house, please?) The elderly man to whom I was speaking had no time to answer me, for a boy of about ten took my hand and told me:

"*Por aquí, compañero*." (This way, comrade.)

And for the benefit of the others, as if revealing a secret, he said:

"*Es el francés*." (It's the Frenchman.)

I burst out laughing and followed on, with a general greeting of "*Hola, compañeros y compañeras!*" Her house was quite close by, and a tall girl answered the door, looked me over, and raced back inside.

1   In Antoine's original, he has her name as Pasquala—his Italianized spelling of La Madre's first name.

Left: Pascuala Labarta, at the end of her life. Right: Félix Valero Labarta, age 28

"*Madre, el miliciano.*" Then, returning to me: "*Entre, señor.*"

I never dreamed when I stepped across that threshold that this house would become my mooring, my haven of peace. For almost two years, I was made welcome every time I returned to the calm and affection that helped me forget the tough times and dangers I had been through.

On entering, one stepped directly from the street into a huge room equipped with a table and some chairs, plus a sideboard known as a *macia*, which served as a kneading table. Opposite the front door there was the door to the kitchen and a flight of stairs leading to the bed-rooms. La Madre came to greet me:

"Have a seat, boy. Here's your shirt. Vicenta, *trae el porrón.*" (Bring the *porrón).*" The girl set down on the table a sort of a jug with a spout at the side, which enabling one to drink without using a glass.

The family was made up of two girls and two boys. María and Manuel were not at home;[2] they were trapped in Zaragoza where María had been working as a maid. Vicenta and Paco[3] helped their mother work their plot of land. I was with them when the letter notifying me of Juanita's death arrived. La Madre and Vicenta found the words needed to ease my pain and remorse—yes, my remorse. Actually, had I agreed to Juanita following me, maybe she would still be alive. From that day on, I knew that I had found a family.{8}

---

2   Manuel was María's husband, not her brother.
3   Paco was actually named Félix and was La Madre's second eldest. He died in Pina de Ebro on January 14, 2008. (See Book II for the biographical note on the Valero family.)

BERTHOMIEU AND THE REST

It was around then that a band of French and Italians arrived in Pina. Their leader was an officer of the French colonial army who had gone off the rails, a man well versed in all the tricks of guerrilla warfare. With him were two Frenchmen, Ridel and Carpentier, both named Charles, and a guy from Savoy by the name of Affinenghi.{9} (I never bothered to ask whether he was Italian or French, for he switched easily between the two languages), an Italian by the name of Scolari[1] and a wee Spaniard, La Calle. I have forgotten the names of a few more who were there as well.{10}

I joined their group the day after they arrived. The local residents were curious but welcomed these folk who spoke languages that were incomprehensible to them (apart from Berthomieu and La Calle, none of them spoke Spanish). There was a bit of standoffishness, but that only lasted a few days.

On the day we took over the town, the sheep flocks that belonged to the peasants of Pina were on the far side of the river, and that is where they had stayed. We used to see them every day trotting out to graze two or three kilometers beyond the opposite riverbank. The river level had fallen, and there was a ford in Pina that allowed us to cross the Ebro and mount foot patrols to survey the terrain in anticipation of an advance. The river crossing and the patrols were Louis's idea. Every night, it fell to four of us, taking turns, to ford the river. Two of us remained on the bank to give cover to the pair scouting the interior. The others stood guard, ready to give the patrol back up in the event of any trouble.

One day, just as I was into the final part of my watch, I felt very uneasy because the guys, who would normally be back well before daybreak, were not back as the sun was coming up. I had clambered up to the highest branch of a poplar to give myself the farthest field of vision possible, and all of a sudden a tiny cloud that seemed to be coming from the ground drew my attention. I grabbed my binoculars:

---

1   Carlo Scolari arrived in Spain on August 28 with Michele Balart. Taken under the wing of the Durruti Column, he was then posted to Pina. He was thirty-eight years old. According to Carpentier's evidence, as gathered by Phil Casoar, the two friends would become the mainstays of the International Group along with Ridel, Berthomieu, and Carpentier himself up until late October 1936.

"Shit! What is that?"

I shinnied down the tree and woke Berthomieu.

"Louis, I reckon I'm seeing things."

He followed me back up to my perch. I hadn't been seeing things: there was actually a flock of sheep making its way across the plain, heading for the river. Four men—one on each side of the flock and two bringing up the rear—were running, waving, and shouting.

Affinenghi and Scolari had stumbled upon the pen where the sheep spent the night. Affinenghi had first stabbed the watchman and then his sleeping comrade; both were members of the Civil Guard. The shepherds were resting in the farmyard, and Scolari talked them into guiding the flock back to Pina. More livestock for the collective. The shepherds were reunited with their families. From then on, my colleagues were the focus of everyone's attention because everybody was keen to learn what had happened.{11} Since neither of them spoke any Spanish, I was obliged to act as their interpreter.

Scolari came from Toulon where, he told me, he had been working in the shipyard. He was a pacifist, a supporter of nonviolence, and he never carried a weapon. He had come to Spain not to fight but to see for himself a struggle he found utterly intriguing in terms of reforming society. He was a man of courage. Whenever a wounded man needed somebody to brave the gunfire and bring him safety, Scolari knew no danger. I once saw him retrieve a wounded man under machine-gun fire. The bullets were whizzing everywhere; it was a really hellish hail of gunfire. The enemy, overlooking us from the crest of a hill, had stymied our attack, forcing us to fall back to our original positions. The man was brought down about a hundred meters from our trenches. Scolari, bare-chested, hopped over the parapet and took off at a run for the wounded man. His madcap act caught everyone by surprise, even our opponents, who abruptly ceased firing and did not resume until Scolari was safely back in our camp.

Affinenghi, a mountain man, a farmer and woodcutter in the Alps, loved hunting, wrestling, and any sort of violent or dangerous activity. He was tall (standing about six feet), broad-shouldered, and as strong as an ox. Brave? Even now I wonder if we can call anyone brave when he does not know the meaning of danger. The missions I saw Affinenghi carry out were accompanied by unprecedented good luck, and he came though without a scratch, except for the last one, in which he was wounded. But that was a stroke of luck for him too, for the wound was minor, and he was evacuated. That may well have saved his life.

Our cosmopolitan band was growing day by day. Ridel and Carpentier, back from a trip to Barcelona, arrived with a young woman with long dark hair. I discovered later that her name was Simone Weil and that she claimed to be a syndicalist.{12} Little by little, our unit was growing. Volunteers were flooding in: French, Italians, Germans, Russians, Cubans, and an Algerian, named Ben Sala.{13}

When the Durruti Column set out from Barcelona, nearly every prostitute in Catalonia followed in its wake. Venereal infections wrought havoc in the ranks of its *centurias*. "Gori"[2] sent all these packing, except for the ones who had come with their partners and whose conduct was beyond reproach. But even among the ones who stayed, many left the front lines for work in the rear guard. It was not long before our group was the only one in Pina with female members. Six women looked after our nursing and kitchen needs: Marthe, Madeleine, Simone, Augusta, Mimosa, and Rosaria.[3] Marthe and Madeleine were partnered with Pierre and Hans respectively.[4] With the exception of Simone Weil, who headed back to France, all the others remained in Spain for good; Marthe, Mimosa, and Augusta perished in Perdiguera.{14}

We used to spend all our time training in crawling, moving noiselessly through the undergrowth, throwing grenades, as well as handgun and rifle shooting. We were organized into completely autonomous assault teams, or commando units we would we call them nowadays. {15} Captain Berthomieu was a stickler for dress standards in town and for how the men conducted themselves in war. One morning, two men were missing from assembly; where could they be? There had been no patrol the previous night, and besides it was not their turn. Enquiries were made in town; no one had seen them. At around 10:00 a.m., they turned up, looking very pleased with themselves, as if they had had a great time. Attendance at morning roll call was not mandatory, but there was an unspoken understanding that anyone could be called upon at any time of the day or night for any operation, and the

2   Gori was one of Durruti's nicknames, dating back to the time when he had been a refugee in Paris. Probably short for "Gorilla."

3   Rosaria should most likely be spelled *Rosario*, as the forename *Rosaria* does not exist.

4   Actually, Hans's first name was Hermann and his surname was Gierth. (See Endnote 10 of Book II, below.)

ENDNOTE {12}: 234; ENDNOTE {13}: 235; ENDNOTE {14}: 239; ENDNOTE {15}: 243

Louis Berthomieu making notes prior to an attack

command post needed to know where to find us. They apologized to their comrades and to Louis because, they said, they had been caught short, having decided at the last minute to volunteer to take part in the execution of some prisoners captured on an earlier patrol. (In the early months of the war, neither side took prisoners. Those who surrendered were shot more or less immediately.)

Louis flew off the handle, his jaw clenched. He paced backward and forward in the room he used an office and bedroom. Then he snapped:

"General assembly, and look lively about it!"

Half an hour later, we were all standing in front of the CP, and Louis addressed us:

"Compañeros, we have come from all over the world to fight for a just and humane cause. We fight, but we do not murder. I don't want anyone to be able to say, tomorrow, that the International Group led by Louis Berthomieu was a unit of executioners. Two of our number voluntarily served on the firing squad that shot prisoners we had taken. If you agree with them, let me know, and I'll go. Otherwise, I am asking you to exclude them from the group. The decision is yours to make."

We unanimously voted to exclude them, following a lengthy discussion as to what right we had to forbid them from doing what they had done, if that was their pleasure. We found a basis for agreement by

The Durruti Column's International Group

acknowledging that we had a right to live and die alongside folk who saw eye to eye with us on how one's actions in life should be viewed and evaluated.{16}

CONCHITA

On the far side of the Ebro River there was an abandoned farm whose inhabitants had fled to Pina for safety. The family was composed of father, mother, a son who was about eighteen, and a sixteen-year-old daughter, who, as was often the case in peasant families, had been placed in service as a maid for a wealthy family three or four years earlier. One day, smoke was spotted belching from the chimney. The son, Manuel, told us that his parents reckoned that Conchita, his sister, was back home again. Berthomieu asked me if I was willing to go and see what was going on. Manuel would gladly have gone with me, but Louis emphatically opposed it. As for me, I stated that I would pop over by myself to check things out The farm was upstream from Pina and too far away for Conchita to be brought over using the ford. It was also too far to walk (more than an hour), and there was the chance of being intercepted by an enemy patrol, so the decision was made to travel over by boat. Once the girl was on board, I was to make an incursion as far as the railway line a few kilometers from the river. Everything went well. I hid my skiff between some brambles and a pile of vine shoot kindling, then glided into the vineyard adjacent to the farmhouse. The sun was already coming up and lit up the roofs of the buildings. The fire had been lit again, for there was a streak of smoke floating skyward. Lying amid the wild shoots of a fig tree whose broad-leafed branches shielded me entirely from view, I mulled over some questions that remained unanswered.

"Who was living inside? Was it Conchita or some runaway? Or maybe fascists, who had set a trap for us? Either way, those inside were living the life of Riley! I might get a glimpse of them if they step outside to take a piss (if they are men) or when they fetch some wood or draw water from the well."

I carried on with my soliloquy so as not to dwell very much upon my situation, for I was not, repeat not, at all happy about it.

"Unless somebody comes out in the next five minutes, I'm going in."

That was the third time I had set myself that five-minute deadline to break cover, and still I could not make up my mind, for fear of walking into a trap. I couldn't hang around much longer without doing something, though. I had to come to a decision. I stood up, still hidden by the foliage, not taking my eyes of the door of the house. Finally it opened. A low-set girl walked in my direction. She paused by the vines growing closest to the house and plucked a bunch of grapes. It was indeed Conchita, Manuel's sister. Just as I was about to part the branches of my hiding-place, a voice called out:

"*Niña*, what are you doing here?"

I felt my blood run cold and the sweat bead on my forehead. Slowly I settled back down to the ground:

"Shit! That's all I need!"

I had not noticed the arrival of the five soldiers who were now standing at the corner of the building, their rifles trained and ready to fire. Unable to do anything else, I listened. The one who seemed to be in charge repeated his question:

"What are you doing here?"

"I live here."

"How many of you are there?"

"I'm on my own."

"Where are the others? You must evacuate this house; the Reds might come and slaughter you all. Are you sure there's no one else here?"

"No, sir."

The fellow issued an order. His men went off to search the outbuildings. The girl and the officer went inside. I had regained my composure and now just had to wait for them to leave. I returned to my musings: would they be taking the girl with them when they left? If so, then I had to come up with some way of getting rid of these five men. But how? I had no idea. I would come up with something when the crunch came. As I was mulling this over, I watched the soldiers, their search complete, enter the main building where the patrol commander and Conchita had gone. Quite some time passed before the girl reemerged, one of the soldiers in tow. She was carrying two small jugs; they were off to fetch some wine from the cellar. There was no coldness in the girl's eyes. Finding her home deserted, she must have realized that her parents and brother had crossed the river to join the republicans. Eventually everyone came out of the house again. I overheard the one who was giving the orders say:

"That's agreed then; you pack up your things and we'll drop by this way this afternoon to fetch you. We can load it all up on the cart and you can come to Quinto with us."

I was afraid he might tell one of his men to stay behind on the farm, but he didn't, and off they all marched, back to their base. I waited until they had disappeared from sight then approached the farmhouse, weaving a passage through the vine roots. In the meantime, the girl had gone off to fetch some water from the well. I was behind her now and I said:

"Conchita, your mother sent me to fetch you."

Startled, she half turned and—seeing me stripped to the waist with my three days old stubble, two grenades dangling from my belt, and pistol in hand—dropped the pail she was carrying.

"Not a sound. Your mother and brother Manuel asked me to look for you."

She quickly overcame her fright and said:

"We mustn't stay here. Come on. Let's get indoors."

Once inside she bombarded me with questions about her parents and her brother and folks she knew in Pina. My having answered this deluge of questions as best I could, she told me that the soldiers would be coming back with a cart to strip the farmhouse and ferry everything to Quinto. There was only one thing to do: to cross the Ebro before they got back, because later on the riverbanks might prove dangerous. Less than half an hour after that, part one of my mission was complete. Now all that was left for me to do was to scope out the territory between the river and the railway line, which I did without coming upon a living soul. It was a real cakewalk, with stop-offs at the foot of fruit trees that allowed me to assuage my hunger while indulging my taste buds. From atop these trees I scanned the area, searching for any unwelcome presence.

On the way back, it occurred to me that, by way of a souvenir, I should leave my two grenades in the farmhouse. With the girl no longer there, the soldiers would be very disappointed not to find something. I planted the first grenade behind the door; after removing the firing-pin, I jammed the safety catch with a coffee pot before legging it out through the window. The second grenade I set in a hole alongside a barrel, puncturing the safety catch and holding it in position with a jug half full of wine.

I had barely finished that little job when I heard the shouts of the carters in the distance behind the house. They were almost upon us. I took off, darting through the vines before lying down beside the fig tree. There were eight of them on the cart, which was drawn by a couple of mules, and they were calling out:

"*Niña, mujer, guapa!*"

Five of them ran ahead and entered the farmhouse like a whirl-wind. There came an explosion, followed by a rattle of broken tiles and shouting. One man staggered out, his hands over his belly and blood trickling down his face; he took a few steps and then down he went. The panicked mules took off at a gallop. The three men who had remained outside had sought cover among the vines. My booby-trap had worked perfectly.

For five or six minutes, there was no movement, except for the injured man who was groaning and from time to time calling out:

"*Madre … Oh! Madre!*"

One of them got up and went over to the injured man, said something to him, unhitched his water canteen, and after, giving it a shake, reattached it to his belt; it must have been empty. The other two stood up and were looking at their comrade who was begging them to get him something to drink. One of the soldiers then headed toward the cellar; some barrels could be seen through the open door. He was hesitant about going inside. I never took my eyes off him. After a good look around, he went inside, emerging after a few minutes with a canteen glued to his lips. The bastard had topped it up from the tap.

In the meantime, the wounded man had died. I saw one of his comrades swipe a hand across his eyes before standing up and heading for the farmhouse. He came out again almost immediately, had a word with his colleagues, and, after passing the canteen around, two of them left. The third man, gun at his feet, leaned against a wall. I thought he could see me, that he was keeping an eye on me. I could have run away, escaping by crawling on my belly in the direction of the riverbank and making it back to the river, but curiosity had me pinned to the ground. What was going to happen? Would they go back into the cellar? Had the others gone in search of reinforcements? No. Back they came, leading their mules by the bridle and hitching one of them to one of the rings installed in the walls of barns and stables for that very purpose. From the way they were acting (they were speaking too low for me to make out the words), I guessed that the cart had overturned not far from there. They must have been thirsty, for after draining that canteen, all three of them popped back into the cellar. There was no reason for them to be on their guard. One of them had already drunk some of the wine and was none the worse for it. But as far as I was concerned, the suspense began again: what was going to happen next? A shout went up:

The Ebro and a farm across the river at Pina

"*Cuidado!*" (Watch out!)

I saw one man leap away from the door, trip, get to his feet, and make a run for it. There was an explosion. A second body was sent sprawling in the dirt. The panic-stricken mules reared and tugged at their tethers in an effort to break free. The sole survivor fled in the direction of Zaragoza as fast as his legs could carry him, utterly terrified. I hadn't the stomach to go and take a look. I had but one thought: getting out of there. As I reached the riverbank and was now in sight of the homes of Pina on the far side of the river, I was overcome by a quivering that shook me from head to toe. My teeth were chattering like castanets; fear, sure, retrospective fear to be sure, but fear it was. There was only one idea in my head now: getting across the Ebro, getting back among my own, taking a seat in La Madre's kitchen with my feet under the table ... and still I was quivering. I have never quite worked out why. Subsequently, I had other hairy moments when I was actually in danger and face to face with the enemy. My reflexes have always been keen, and, in the wake of dangers braved, once in a place of safety again, I have been overcome by the same quaking that shook me like a prune bush. It wasn't a civilized man who worked matters out and weighed up the dangers and organized the approach and the attack. It was the animal, whose instinct for self-preservation revived the sure movements and shrewd wits of primitive man determined to survive, and bound to kill for that very reason.

One hour later, daylight was fading, and I turned up a hundred meters from the ford. I had crossed the Ebro on four vine branches that I had tied together with the rope that never left my belt and that I had used to secure myself on the upper branches of trees during all my watch duties. The noise of the grenades had been discernible from Pina, though not the gunfire, and they were wondering what could have happened. They reckoned I was dead or captured, which amounted to the same thing. Berthomieu told me that upward of an hour and a half had elapsed between the last explosion and the point where the lookout, up in the bell tower, saw me appear on the riverbank. To me it had seemed a much shorter time.

Friends, villagers, and militia members, women and children, had strung themselves out along the riverbank to intercept me as I passed. My paddle had yet to touch dry land before I was grabbed and carried along as folk raced and clustered around us until we could barely get through. In the end, I was set down at the foot of a tree and was bombarded with questions. Fortunately, La Madre showed up, plunged into the crowd and hugged me in her arms, sobbing:

"*Hijo mío, hijo mío, déjadlo vosotros, no véis que está cansado?*" (My son, my son, now you leave him be. Can't you see that he is worn out?)

Back home, La Madre bathed me in a big tub and put me to bed like a child, and I fell asleep in the room that was mine throughout the time I lived in Pina.

I slept rather late the following day. Augusta was there when I woke up. Louis had charged her with checking me over and asking me to go and brief him on what I had seen during my reconnaissance.

Augusta was twenty-two or twenty-three years old. After her parents were put in a prison camp, she left Germany and fled to France. It proved impossible for her to continue her medical studies, and she found herself jobless, so she came to Spain. A sporty type with a physique worthy of posing for Michelangelo or Cellini, she was the bane of the entire male population of Pina. I say bane because it was as if she was made of ice, so cold that no human warmth seemed to be able to thaw her. However, she was kind-hearted, always smiling, ready to help at every opportunity, which is to say, would as readily patch some torn trousers as cook a meal out in the open countryside with whatever ingredients came to hand.

I found Conchita's entire family gathered in the CP building, together with two recently arrived comrades who were chatting with Louis. One of them was the Russian Alexander Staradoff (we were to become good comrades later) and the other one was French, a Parisian by the name of Georges. Conchita's mother rushed up to hug and thank me. Conchita did not recognize me and watched these tokens of friendship wide-eyed. It was her brother who asked her what she was doing just standing there, motionless. At which she realized that the shaggy, bare-chested, bristle-chinned individual she had met yesterday and the close-shaven young man done up in well-ironed shirt and trousers before her were one and the same. All she could think of to say was:

"Ah! So it was you?"

Everyone burst into laughter.

After briefing Berthomieu and others on what I had been up to since Conchita and I had parted, we all went off to celebrate the girl's return.

THE COLLECTIVE

The days went by, and the column was still on the banks of the Ebro. A collective had been set up: the peasants (Pina being an exclusively agricultural village) plowed and sowed in preparation for the coming harvest. Lots of militia members joined the work squads to pass the time and keep busy.

The workday was eight hours long. In the evening, the peasants would gather to report on the work done in the fields that day and to discuss what needed to be done the next day. Nearly every evening, on my way home to Tía Pascuala's, which had become my home too, I used to drop in at the meeting hall.

One time, my attention was caught by raised voices. I paused, straining to understand what was behind the stormy argument. Somebody happened by, and, seeing that he was on his way home, I asked him what the reason was for all the brouhaha. He answered that he had no idea, given that he was a late-comer himself, and he asked me to follow him inside. Silence descended as they caught sight of an outsider at the meeting. I apologized, explaining what had happened, and made for the exit. A chorus of voices stopped me:

"Stay. No need to leave. Take a seat."

Someone took me by the arm, and somebody else brought a chair, and I found myself sitting around the table with the bookkeeper-secretary of the collective. He gave me a rundown on the argument and asked me to settle the dispute:

"We couldn't agree on the number of sacks of wheat stored in the warehouse during the day. There was a discrepancy: we are two sacks short."

His arithmetic was right; of that much he was sure. The error was traced to a clumsily scrawled figure. An eight had been misread as a six. Remember that 95% of Spanish workers and peasants were illiterate. A few could write their names, but that was it. On the other hand, they could nearly all count without any need for pencil and paper. They had a calculator inside their heads for adding, subtracting, multiplying, and dividing.{17}

Classes were held for those eager to learn to read and write. Those classes were held in the evenings, after work. Take it from me, it was a weird and—why not admit it?—a moving sight to behold. These men sat hunched over their books, focused on writing out the alphabet or struggling to hold the frail stem of a pen, which their callused hands, better used to handling weighty field tools, crushed into the paper. Some of them looked very old. Working the land had hardened their hands and stooped their shoulders; poverty had hollowed their cheeks and lined their foreheads. They might well have had only a few years left to live, yet there they were, every evening with a day's work over them, sitting on their benches in class.{18}

Occasionally, an impromptu talk might be given at some random meeting. Among the Spanish militia members there were a few schoolteachers and students who, when the opportunity arose, turned public speakers as they spelled out their ideas or outlook on life. In the Second Centuria there was a young schoolteacher who had taught at Francisco Ferrer's Modern School in Barcelona. He had the gift of the gab and liked talking about all manner of subjects, just as long as they held his listeners' interest.

One evening he was asked to tackle the subject of marriage and love. The room was packed. The youngsters were glad to attend these meetings because of the laughter and wisecracks, even though the topics might be serious ones. I can pretty much recall his speech, especially since his way of thinking was my own at the time and has not altered over the years since.

OF LOVE AND MARRIAGE

The speaker opened with something along these lines:

"Comrades, my apologies in advance to those who are going to be shocked by what I am about to say to you. Marriage, an institution—I was about to say, is several million years old but actually less than that, being a few dozen centuries old, since the arrival of Christianity.... Well, marriage, as we know it today, is love's graveyard. Woman must obey her husband and submit to his will, he being the master. In return, it falls to him to feed and protect her, the same as he would protect his livestock, for she is his chattel. She belongs to him. I am talking about all women, the ones born in gilded cradles and the ones who have been lying in makeshift beds ever since their very earliest infant cries. In this society, which we are out to destroy, the proletarian often marries just to get himself a housekeeper, a bedmate for the night, someone with whom to perpetuate the race of slaves and wretches whose clogs shuffle along every street in the world. And all for the greater benefit of the ruling classes who grind us down.

"The womenfolk of the working class are worn out by toil, weakened by inadequate nourishment, misshapen from too many pregnancies, are old by the age of thirty. You don't believe me? Take a look around you. Yes, I know what you say to yourselves; a girl has to marry, a woman with no husband is a plant with no leaves, a tree that bears no fruit ... and in order to break free of the supervision of her father or her brothers, in the hope of gaining a morsel of freedom, you are ready to give yourselves in return for a name. NO. I am against all forms of prostitution, even the ones legalized by the mayor and blessed by the priest. It is because of such prejudices, handed down to us through the ages and since the dawn of time that the female of the species, burdened by pregnancy, weakened by childbirth that prevents her from securing her own livelihood, needs somebody who can hunt and fish and climb trees in search of food; someone who can protect her, her and her offspring, against attacks by wild animals, should the need arise. So she was compelled to defer to the crude rule of nature, which requires that anything is acceptable as long as the survival of the species is assured. And survive the species has.

"Over generations, mankind had multiplied, spread to every corner of the globe, invented the machine, tamed lightning, and domesticated fire. The male of the species has enforced the law of might and turned woman into a chattel, a servant, or a beast of burden. Through centuries of subjection she was so conditioned that to this day there are countries where the man buys his wife, or where parents swap their daughter for goods, livestock, or some other crop. In our so-called civilized society, marriages are often—not to say always—based on the property, capital, and wealth of the parents, and not at all on the affectionate preferences of the engaged couple. If a man has several mistresses, they say admiringly of him: 'He's a real stud.' If a woman takes a lover, they say, 'She's a slut.' I demand—on behalf of woman, on behalf of all women—the same rights as we all have. I demand on behalf of one half of the human race the right to freedom in matters of love and motherhood."

The speaker's success, especially among the older portion of the male audience, was less than massive. In Spain, girls were a long way from the sort of freedom their sisters in France or elsewhere in Europe enjoyed, and so they said nothing, so as not to scandalize their parents.

The boys and grown men argued furiously, some agreeing with the speaker, some not. A few women contributed to the discussion. The speaker was asked how he would react if, supposing he was a married man, he was to discover that his wife had taken a lover.

"Listen, *amigo*," he replied. "If my wife is also a libertarian, that is, has the same regard for her freedom and for my own as I do, and she were to let me in on her desire to sleep with another man, setting out her emotional or physical case, we would decide between us how to proceed from there. If my wife is not of the same persuasion as me, she will not say a word to me, and if I find out I'm going to have to put a few questions to myself:

1) Have I failed to live up to her erotic requirements? If so, it is only fair that she should look elsewhere for what I cannot give her. Take an example: I invite you to dinner at my home. You are still hungry when you leave. Should I be angry because you leave my place and go looking for a sandwich? No, right? Sexual needs are comparable with nutritional needs. They vary from person to person. Some have big appetites and others are content with very little. So I just have the right to hold my tongue; at best, I might chide her for not having told me first.

2) She seeks a lover to meet her material desires, be they sub-sistent or extravagant. Again, the fault is mine in that I cannot earn enough money to provide her with what she wants.

In both instances, how should I react? In the first, there is nothing I can do about it; nature hasn't endowed me with enough strength to meet the shortfall, and I would be an arrant shit if, taking advantage of the power accorded me by the written law and mores, I were to stop her from indulging in the pleasures of the flesh on the basis of merely my own self-esteem. In the second, what could I do? Grin and bear it? No … for I'd be cashing in on her beauty, her elegance, her allure, all for my own benefit, to be sure, but I'd feel like the moral equivalent of those pimps who live off the earnings of prostitutes the way capitalists do off the earnings of workers, for prostitution is the oldest trade in the world. In which case, no matter how great the affection, love, and friendship I might feel for her, I would leave her."

"So you are a stranger to jealousy?"

"I am jealous of my mistresses. There is no contract binding me to them. The only thing that holds us together is erotic pleasure. It is only natural, if that pleasure should diminish or disappear, that one would go and look elsewhere, with new partners, for the pleasures that, as part of the natural order, are vital to the psychic equilibrium of every human being. I am jealous of my mistress because I abhor lies and hypocrisy. I abhor needless, pointless lies, told just for the pleasure of concealing what we have done from those around us, as if the belief were that one had no right to do it. As if we were not free and answer-able for what we do."

It was silent from the moment he began his response. One young woman had come over to him and listened without taking her eyes off him. Dolores, a young woman of about twenty-five, seamstress by trade, then asked him:

"Pedrito, what would you make of a woman who was to tell you right here, right now 'I love you'?"

"I'd think she was a clever, free young woman. I'd think she was way ahead of her time, on which grounds I'd admire and respect her, even if she were speaking to someone other than me. Is that what you wanted to hear?"

"Yes, but also, what motives could possibly have led to her making such a declaration?"

"There's a wide variety to choose from. You'd be able to list them as well as I can. Broadly speaking, they are the same for the man as for the woman; desire, curiosity about how someone will behave in a given situation, the itch to discover just how virile the person selected may be, and all of that may, ultimately, be muddled up with the love that prompts us all to believe that we seek the happiness of our beloved, when in actual fact we are only out to give expression to our own subconscious selves. And since our outlooks are nearly always different, they clash and pull in different directions and run up against one another ... and then we have the marital hell with sobbing and whining and grinding teeth; hence the need for a parting of the ways, a need, frankly, to look elsewhere for the realization of our dreams and the materialization of the chimeras that haunt us."

"So you don't believe in lifelong love?"

"Yes, I do; if it is founded upon openness and understanding and toleration of all the things that can drive a couple apart; differences in material or aesthetic tastes, or in intellectual or moral aspirations. It is very rare for two people having the same tastes and the same aspirations to find each other and form what is described as a 'family.'"{19}

The conversation carried on until it was very late. All of those who had to start back to work the following day had long since turned in for the night.

THE GORROS NEGROS

We were all tired of the monotony of our patrols, hardly ever inter-cepting the enemy, so Berthomieu decided to venture across the river to establish a bridgehead there. It was a real picnic; we set up around Manuel's home. All day long we took turns digging, widening and deepening the ridges that surrounded the house, and marked out the fields and vineyards or those that served as irrigation channels. We dug these trenches to allow us to shoot from a kneeling position. Come nightfall, we set off in small groups to stroll in every direction for two or three hours at a time.

Some of us ventured as far as the houses in Quinto de Ebro but didn't go into the village. A few did, though, pay the henhouses a visit, bringing back hens and eggs for us. That detail has stuck in my memory for it was the reason we lost one of our female comrades, Simone Weil, who scalded herself with boiling oil while frying up some eggs for lunch. She was evacuated to Barcelona and, from there, made her way back to France, having spent around about a month with us.[20]

A day or two after her accident, we received orders to fall back to Pina. Time was wearing on and we were no longer referred to as "*los internacionales*" but as "the *gorros negros*" (black bonnets). As head-gear, the *centurias* had adopted a beret known in French, I believe, as "*bonnet de police.*" It was shaped like an upturned boat. The Spaniards had them made in whatever colors they preferred; some were even multicolored. Louis advised us to wear the black ones, since a lighter color might give us away in the dark. Dressed in a jerkin belted at the waist, dark trousers, and the black beret, we were invisible once the sun went down, and we began to make our way through the rosemary and broom thicket in the fallow fields or the vineyards, olive groves, and orchards of the Aragonese countryside.

One of the operations I took part in was intended to open one sluice gate and close off another to ensure that irrigation streams reached the *huerta* in Pina. The locks were located far behind the enemy lines. Twelve of us, including Louis Berthomieu, were along on the mission, and, in addition to our weapons, each of us was carried a special little bag of cement. There was no guard on the locks, so it was a clean job. We shut off the open sluice gate, and an expert in such mat-ters sealed the whole thing off with a bag of cement. As for me, I was on stakeout some way from the work group so I can't really say how they pulled off the job. After we had wandered a fair distance from the sluice gates, we had a quick chat. Based on the time until daybreak, we could not take the same route back and be unnoticed. We decided to go for a shorter route, straight ahead. The front was not a continuous line; on the map, it looked like a dotted line, the dots being separated by spaces that varied in size depending on the nature of the terrain.

After an hour's comparatively brisk walking, Louis signaled us to stop at the foot of a small hill. Using sign language, he indicated what we needed to do and then started creeping up the slope, with five comrades deploying behind him. The last six, of whom I was one, were to follow them up after five minutes, as long as everything stayed calm.

Dawn was breaking, and in the distance we could just make out the peaks of the sierra above Alcubierre. We were halfway up the hillside when Louis's whispered call came:

"Hurry! Get up here!"

They had stumbled upon some sleeping Falangists. The one keeping watch, knocked out by the butt of a rifle, hadn't made a sound. The others didn't wake up: *navajas* and daggers alone had done the job.

Their post was crescent-shaped. The top of the little hill had been flattened out so that it resembled a hat-box about a meter deep and four or five across. Some bodies were laid out along the wall as if they were sleeping. We scooped up the post's weapons; six rifles, a machine gun, and a pistol, and, with those and the ammunition, we were more heavily laden going back than coming. Once out of sight of the enemy positions, I noticed that Berthomieu was frequently looking at his watch; when I asked him about this, he said that there was a dynamite charge due to detonate with a two-hour delay, and it was almost time to listen for the explosion. A few minutes later, we heard, almost at the very same instant, a deafening explosion in the distance and the challenge "Halt! Who goes there?" from our own outposts.

By the time we arrived back in Pina, water was flowing through the irrigation channels. We were exhausted; our outing had lasted almost twenty hours. La Madre brought me my supper in bed.

We crossed the river again a few days later, but this time on orders from HQ. Our mission was to engage the enemy and pin down some of their troops in order to facilitate the column's advance on Zaragoza.

We weren't regular soldiers; it was our job to swoop in on a target, hit hard, and disengage immediately. But "in war you just can't tell," and we might have to get down to it despite our lack of enthusiasm for trench warfare. Berthomieu, Ridel, Carpentier, and I, plus a few others who happened to be in the CP when the order came down made up our minds to cross the river in broad daylight. If we were spotted, so much the better. The troops stationed in Quinto would come out to attack us or would hold their positions and wait for us. In any event, they would not rally in support of the ones under attack from the republican units; in which case, we would achieve our purpose and our mission would be accomplished.

I said that Berthomieu, Ridel, a few others, and I had decided how our mission would be tackled. You must not think that I was part of the group's staff (actually, it had no staff). When any operation needed undertaking, it was discussed between us, with everyone putting in his two cents, and the best ideas, or what seemed to us the best ideas, were taken on board, or else some synthesis of the different suggestions was arrived at. Since its formation, the group's strength had increased tenfold. We now numbered a little over a hundred. With the Spaniards from Pina who joined us, we crossed the river that morning sometime between 9 o'clock and 10 o'clock with a group of about 120 men.{21} Manuel, who knew the area like the back of his hand—having been born and raised there—followed us across. Since Simone's departure, he had been a bit out of sorts; they were great friends, and she used to say that he was as handsome as a Greek god.

At the beginning, everything went off without a hitch. It wasn't until the second night that things went awry. A sentry alerted us to some suspicious sounds. In silence, we scuttled to our posts. It was as dark as the inside of an oven, and the sky was overcast. On other occasions, I would have been happy enough with a late-rising moon or its not showing up at all, but now I sorely missed *la blonde Phébe* (the moon). We had laid some barbed wire with tin cans and tiny bells, which Manuel had fetched from town, in some long grass about fifty meters from our lines of defense. My fear was, though, that the vanguard might not set off the trap, in which case they might be on top of us before we noticed, and then we'd be unable to stop them before they reached our dugout. Our bridgehead was shaped like a trapezium, with the farmhouse halfway to the top and the riverbank as the base.

Berthomieu had assigned us our positions: five men inside with the machine gun, twenty to the right of the outbuildings, and the same number to the left. Sixty were there to protect our flanks, with the remainder held in reserve as reinforcements for the hardest-pressed points in the event of an attack. In addition to the machine gun, we had eight automatic rifles and a few cases of French-made Lafitte grenades, plus our personal armories: rifles, handguns, daggers, and *navajas*. Tense and given away only by the odd dull snap of breaking twigs, we bided our time, peering through the darkness, our eyes peeled for the invisible enemy edging slowly and silently onward. Wild animals on the prowl, hoping to swoop upon other wild animals in their lair; the latter in turn, lurking in their foxholes, also biding their time, having sensed the danger.

Men confronting one another, some of them championing principles, ideas, and beliefs that had been around for upward of two thousand years. Others fighting to put an end to ignorance and man's exploitation of his fellow man and class privileges so that Freedom, Equality, and Love might finally prevail throughout the human race. Which of them was right? The champions of the past? Or the ones fighting for the future? The combatants of the present or the combatants of the future?

All of a sudden a bugle sounded, but the metallic noise was promptly drowned out by a call issuing from the shadows, tearing the night: "*Adelante! ... Arriba España!*" (Ahead! ... Spain, arise!)

There was a series of lightning flashes ahead of me, immediately followed by the sharp report of rifle fire, the explosion of grenades, and the crackle of automatic rifle shots mingling with the whizzing of bullets. Fire! The din grew deafening. The sour whiff of burnt powder made our heads spin. Affinenghi was on my right hand, on his feet, emptying the clip of his automatic rifle, then crouching to reload before standing up again to carry on with his deadly handiwork as if in a display of marksmanship. Then I watched as the flashes died away, the gunfire lost intensity, and silence descended once more upon the night. In the room where the machine gun had been set up and that was used as a command post, everything was topsy-turvy; a grenade had gone off inside, but no one had been injured. A real stroke of luck.

I came upon Berthomieu, Ridel, Carpentier, Mendoza (a Cuban), and Otto (a German), all there, as I was, waiting to report back. Our losses were light—to use the military jargon—with one dead and two slightly wounded but still capable of fighting. Louis urged us to remain on our guard because he was expecting a follow-up attack heavier than the first, and he told us that we had to hold out to the last man.

I remember saying to Ridel as we stepped outside, "Just as long as the second wave isn't a tidal wave."

To which he replied: "Bah! You can only die once."

We returned to our posts, and the comrades all seemed happy. We had seen the enemy off once, so there was no reason to quit now. If they came back, they'd get a hot reception. As far as I could tell, if there was anyone there fearful of our enemies' possible return, it was me.

About ten men climbed out of the trench to go retrieve some weapons and ammunition from the dead. It was a great harvest: they brought back rifles, grenades, and quite a lot of ammunition. We had barely finished dividing the booty when we had a pleasant surprise followed by a much less welcome one; the golden crescent moon had risen high in the sky, shedding its pale light over fields, vineyards, and woodland. A hundred meters ahead of us, we could now see a mob closing in on us, silent and terrifying. They stopped, caught suddenly by the moonlight's abrupt exposure of their presence (there wasn't a sound from our trenches), before resuming their progress, reassured. Eighty meters away now; in my head I calculated the distance between us: seventy ... sixty ... fifty-five ... fifty. Gunfire erupted from both our flanks simultaneously. The shadowy mass in front of me broke into a run, spitting flashes of lightning and lead. *Fuego!* (Fire!) The automatic rifles and grenades scythed down the front ranks but others stepped forward. They were getting nearer every second.

There wasn't a rational thought in my head now. It was as if I was having an out-of-body experience, but I could still feel the kick in my wrist as my finger squeezed the trigger. My eyes picked up on every movement around me, and with terrifying precision they trained the barrel of my pistol on the chosen target. Empty of a single speculative thought, my brain now was no more than an electromagnetic apparatus steering a killing machine. At one point, I thought I saw a giant leaping in my direction, about to fall upon me. I emptied the chamber and stooped to reload. He slumped across the trench, in between Affinenghi and me. How long did the firefight continue? I have no idea.

The sun was coming up when a bugle blew from far in front of us; the enemy withdrew, and we had won. I had lost ten men. Had the Falangists given it another quarter of an hour, I wouldn't be here to tell the tale, for we were out of ammunition. On average we had only one or two clips left for each combatant. Having assessed our losses, which amounted to nearly one in four of us, Berthomieu sent me off to request reinforcements to make up our losses and replenish our ammunition.

I was en route to the ford—where the boats were being used to evacuate the wounded—when I came upon a friend who would later prove of great service to me. Cowering over the body of a Falangist, a dog was fending off two stretcher-bearers intent on taking its former master away for burial. The bearers were unarmed, and they called me over to get me to shoot the thing. The beast was black from head to tail, and all you could see through its long fur were its eyes and teeth, behind curled back lips. I hadn't the guts to shoot it. I admired the dog's courage and loyalty and that, despite the stones thrown by the two men, it stood its ground beside the man who had been its friend and master. Using the rope I always carried around my waist, I finally managed to slip a noose around its neck, and so was able to drag him into Pina. There, after tethering him firmly in the yard, I handed him over to Vicenta's care.

Long before the sun was directly overhead I was on my way back to the farm; everyone was busily working to bolster our entrenchment in anticipation of the next attack. We were just about to sit around the table and open a few cans of corned beef when a whistle killed our appetites.

"Incoming!" yelled Berthomieu, heading for the door.

The blast sent us racing after him. There was a second shriek and another explosion.

"One short, one long. Watch out for number three. Evacuate the trenches and scatter!"

The third shell struck the barn. They might have had only one gun, but they knew how to use it. The farmhouse and the trenches were well peppered. The shelling lasted for about an hour. Thanks to Louis's initiative, we'd made it out of the danger zone in time. Hidden among the vines, lying on our bellies among the hazel trees, stretched out under the olives, we watched as the farmhouse and our fortifications were demolished. At dusk, a courier brought us the order to return to base; our mission finished.

Any army that does not advance retreats—even if it holds its position. We were definitely retreating. For more than a month[1] we had

---

1   We should point out that here is a significant inconsistency in the chronology of the manuscript: the capture of Siétamo on September 12, 1936, which

been ensconced on the Ebro's eastern bank.{22} Sure, we were organizing the revolution and giving some structure to a libertarian society. The collectives on the Aragon front were functioning in exemplary
fashion.{23} Durruti was uncompromising about the behavior of the
men under his supervision. He had had one *centuria* commander, Carrillo—a FAI member—shot because he withheld some jewelry and
then given it to his partner. The latter, a real glamor girl, had decided
to pay her man a visit, all decked out in the jewelry he had given her.
When quizzed, she admitted that Carrillo had found them in some
high society home in Barcelona and, instead of turning them over to
the union, had passed them on to her instead. The vast majority of us
were straightforward, honest types. We could see thievery as acceptable as a means of social struggle, without ourselves being capable of
carrying out a robbery or grabbing anything for ourselves. We used to
marvel at those who had the gumption to brave the dangers of living
outside of society in order to serve the Idea, stripping the mighty of
this earth of a little of their surplus so as to meet the needs of workers on strike or of prisoners and their families. For Spain's prisons
were filled with political prisoners. I believe I have already mentioned,
there were some thieves and thugs among us, but, as far as I could tell
from how they conducted themselves, they'd gone straight. They were
nearly all working, helping the peasants in the fields or the artisans in
the town.

Carrillo was tried before the delegates from the *centurias* and
sentenced to death. We were making a revolution and didn't want
to be driving out the bosses merely for others to take their places.
Gold, silver, and jewelry had to be used to obtain weapons for us—
for these were in short supply—rather than prettifying the wives of
those who maybe thought that they were within their rights to take
over the places and assets of the folks they had eliminated. Durruti
had his fellow fighter tried by those workers and peasants, and they
convicted him.[2]

Despite the calm that prevailed in our sector, from time to time one
us perished at the hands of lone snipers. That's how Émile Cottin who,

Antoine describes later in a chapter of that name, really should have been
mentioned here.

2   This may well be the incident to which Ridel is referring in the columns of
L'Espagne nouvelle in the summer of 1939 when he writes: "The unfortu-
nate militiaman was shot for having stolen a ring found in a village."

back in February 1919, had tried to shoot Clemenceau met his end. He was on guard, perched in a tree by the riverside, when one bullet, surely fired by an elite marksman, picked him off. He was a man of few words, a bit of a loner, always deep in who knows what daydream. We were sitting around the table in Tia Pascuala's, who'd agreed to cook something for about ten of us, when someone came in and announced: "They've killed Cottin."[3]

I barely knew him, and only later did I find out that he tried to assassinate Le Tigre (Clemenceau).

We had fun sometimes too. We told jokes. The comrades did what they could to distract themselves, when, for whatever reason, they weren't able to mingle with workers of the collective. One day, we were joined by two guys from Lyon. Since there were two empty spaces at my table, Louis sent them over to me. They were tall, broad-shouldered hulks, but above all they were loudmouths and never happy. They were always complaining about one thing or another. La Madre was over-oiling the dishes she was preparing for us, or they didn't like chickpeas. They could always find something that was not to their liking, but the thing they always came back to was the wine. A quart wasn't enough for them; they wanted at least a liter per meal. They assured us that back in Lyon they downed five or six liters a day, and that was not counting aperitifs.

One day, worn out by this, I had a word with Louis who advised me to give them a liter of a certain wine that La Madre had had him sample one evening when he had come to supper. This was flying in the face of normal practice among us, for we had agreed back in the early days that we would make a liter stretch to four people. I pointed this out to him, but laughed and said:

"Listen, Antoine, let them have a bottle apiece, on condition that they drain their bottles to the last drop unaided, each to his own. Make sure you have somebody reliable with you who can lend a hand."

That evening, I set the two liters in front of their glasses. As I began to eat, I told them that if they could drain their bottles without getting tipsy, they could have the same treat every day. They burst out laughing. Tipsy, on a liter of plonk? They could drink twice as much, no problem.

---

3   Emile Cottin was actually killed at the beginning of the battle for Farlete on October 8, 1936.

The entire meal was eaten amid sneers and jeers. Vicenta came to clear the table, and we got up. It was then that things went awry for our two chums. You'd have thought they were riveted to the bench they were sitting on; they just couldn't stand up. After a number of tries they struggled to their feet and managed to make it out of the room, unsteady on their feet.... The change in temperature between the heat of the dining room and the coolness in the street finished them. They leaned against the wall and dropped their heads. Vicenta had to swab down the area outside the door with water the next day, and we had to carry them to their beds. The wine must have been between 17 and 18 proof. It went down like mother's milk, as long as one sat still and didn't try to move or overdo it. Beyond a certain quantity, it cost you the use of your legs, as I knew from experience.{24}

ENDNOTE {24}: 283

FARLETE

I had just gone to bed when suddenly there was a violent pounding on the door, waking the whole house. "Action stations" was sounded. People were leaving. There were trucks waiting for us in the square. We reached Farlete at daybreak. We climbed down from the trucks and raced through the village to take up positions two kilometers beyond it in the northeastern sector of the township. We could hear the noise of battle in the distance. We could see the enemy arrive, advance, appear, and disappear depending on the lay of the land. We lay in wait for the enemy, lurking behind the sheaves of wheat, atop low hills that broke up the uniformity of the flatlands like dunes in the desert. About 150 meters from us, the opposition opened up with truly hellish gunfire. We didn't fire a single shot, not a cartridge. Taken aback by our lack of response, they stopped shooting and somebody called out to us, advising us to surrender and come over to their side. I can't remember now who it was that stood up and shouted: "Anarchists do not surrender."

They started shooting again, and we didn't respond. For two good reasons: we had very little in the way of automatic weapons, just one submachine gun and a few rifles, and the vast majority of us were armed with only handguns and grenades. Besides, we didn't have so much ammunition that we were in any position to squander it.

After quite a while, just as we were wondering why they weren't closing in on us, we spotted them withdrawing at a run. What had happened?

It was only after we were relieved that we found out that a number of my companions had glimpsed a silhouette looming over a hilltop flanking and to the rear of the enemy lines, a silhouette that had started waving its arms about. It was Georges, the little Parisian guy. I don't know why, but he had missed our departure. Arriving in Farlete on a munitions truck, he tried to catch up to us but had gotten lost. The sounds of gunfire had given him his bearings and brought him to that hilltop. Seeing a cavalry platoon heading his way, he had the idea of standing up so that he might be seen by the riders and waved his arms about as if urging them to hurry up. Believing themselves outflanked and wanting to avoid encirclement, the officers had given the order to retreat.

Farlete was saved.{25} The road that would take us to Perdiguera a month later was opened.[1] We had sustained one fatality and two wounded. The dead man was a Russian: as fate would have it, this fellow who met his end on the high plateau of Aragon had been born at the far end of Europe. A revolution had forced him to flee his native land. He was a White, part of the armies of Wrangel and Denikin. Having fled to France after the communists' victory, he had quit his job to come and die in Spain. Killed by the very people who just nineteen years earlier would have been his allies. What thought process, what brutal lesson taught by exile life had induced him to embrace our cause? That, we shall never know.

One of the wounded men was German; he had taken two bullets in the chest. We thought he was a goner, but he came through it after six or seven months in hospital. His partner, Madeleine, was able to travel down to Barcelona with him, and there she entrusted him to some friends.[2] After which she rejoined us in Farlete to carry on tending to our minor injuries.

---

1   This is a chronological error on Antoine's part: it was six days rather than a month later that the Perdiguera road was opened up as part of the same counterattack. The enemy was to mount a fresh assault on October 12 and would take Leciñena, inflicting heavy losses. In order to clear that section of the front, the Durruti Column and nearly one hundred men from the International Group were deployed on the Villamayor-Perdiguera-Leciñena road on October 15.

2   The couple were Hans, aka Hermann Gierth, and Madeleine Gierth.

ENDNOTE {25}: 284

MARÍA

Since leaving Lérida behind, I hadn't left the front once, whereas all my comrades had had one or more breaks in Barcelona, Tarragona, or some other Catalan town to restore their morale and help them forget the dangers of the war. I had made Pina my retreat. I had found myself a family, a mother and two sisters.

One fine day (or, to be more precise, one fine night) María showed up with a small bunch of comrades who, having previously been trapped in Zaragoza due to General Cabanellas's duplicity, had managed cross the lines in order to carry on the fight.{26}

Juanita's death had hit home with me; I had no interest in anything any more, beyond success in the missions assigned to me. Vicenta and María did all they could to bring me out of my depression. When they saw me deep in gloom, they could always devise some good excuse for asking me to accompany them somewhere or to lend them a helping hand. Very often we used to go and toil on the *huerta*, weeding and hoeing and digging for three or four hours at a time.

María told me of her life as a chambermaid; about all that she had had to endure from her bosses, their demands and their whims. She told me of her womanly dreams, what she planned to do once this war was over. And she spoke to me of her *novio* (sweetheart) who was still in the fascist zone and who she hoped to see turn up some day without a word of warning.

Vicenta, full of mischief and happy-go-lucky, with the insouciance of her years, used to tease me and stir up trouble and spend the entire outing laughing. She quieted down when there was work to be done, but once it was over (and with her it was over quickly) she would revert to teasing. She simply couldn't stay serious; I always wound up laughing and playing with her the way one does with a wayward, cheeky child.

La Madre, like any other mother, used to reason with me and strove to convince me that what had happened was not my fault and that nobody knew what fate held in store. Not that that stopped her from telling me on certain evenings when she watched me buckle up my belt and attach some grenades to it: "*Hijo*, take care and come straight back home. Don't do anything silly, son."

It didn't matter what hour I came home: I would always find her there, waiting for me. She kept a vigil for the return of this "son"

The Sébastien Faure Centuria of the Durruti Column's International Group, August 1936

who had arrived from nowhere, this boy that had no homeland and no family, no fireside, and no place of his own. Vagabond I may have been, but she had opened the doors of her home and her generous Aragonese peasant woman's heart wide to me.{27}

ENDNOTE {27}: 294

RETURN TO LÉRIDA

After that business in Farlete, Louis sent me on an errand to the CNT to sort out a matter that had created a rift between one of the youngsters in our group and his family. The boy was fourteen years old, really far too young to get himself killed. He had run away from home after a ferocious argument with his father and was reluctant to go back for fear of a severe beating. It was my task to get somebody from the office to approach his father about coming to reclaim the outcast, with a formal understanding that there would be no chastisement to follow. The youth came from a village in the Lérida area, and so I returned there after a two-month absence.[1] After making my way to the union and sorting the matter out with the secretary concerned, I set off for Miguel's home. I wanted to see him, my friend, and Teresa in order to wallow in their friendship again. But neither of them was around. Only Miguel's mother, María, was home.

María was very happy to see me and told me that her children were away in Sabadell for eight days and would return four or five days from now. I told her that I was looking for digs for the night, and she protested, saying that had Miguel been around I'd have been staying there, so there was no reason for me find somewhere else to stay that evening. My room was always ready for me. We sat down at the supper table. Neither of us had mentioned Juanita. I hadn't asked anything for fear of opening up old wounds. During our meal, María talked to me of Miguel and his partner. The little nun had proven to be quite the intelligent, busy housewife, and she was very much in love with him. Miguel was lucky when he fell in love with her and she with him. Everything was going fine until coffee was served.

When Juanita was still around, it had always been her that served coffee. Maria cleared the table and stood there, motionless, staring at the chair where her daughter should have been sitting. She began to cry. She wept with her eyes fixed, without making a sound. The tears rolled down her cheeks, cheeks scarcely marked by her troubles and

---

1   Here we have another chronological mistake on Antoine's part: his trip to Lérida definitely took place in late September, following the famous battle for Siétamo on September 12, 1936, which he has mixed up here with the battle for Farlete.

cares. I stood up and placed an arm on her shoulder (she was a lot shorter than me), obliging her to raise her face and I started kissing her to dry her tears. I covered her eyes and cheeks with kisses. I could taste the slight saltiness of her tears. And my mouth found hers.

I hadn't had any dealings with a woman since I had left Juanita behind. I forgot about everything, with a single thought in my head; I had a woman in my arms. She did not pull away and accepted my kiss. My tongue forced its way past her teeth and searched for hers. I could feel her fingernails dig into the nape of my neck. Like a wild animal carrying away its prey, I lifted her up to carry her to her room. In no time, she was stripped of anything that might hamper me; her breasts spilled out, as white as alabaster, the hardening nipples seeming to invite kisses. I leaned over her and felt her thighs close around my waist. From that evening I have stored away a series of images that revolve inside my head, mingling and melting together: a face, a belly, thighs, filmed from every angle as if by some mad moviemaker.

By the time I woke up it was broad daylight, and I was alone. I felt unburdened and glad to be alive. For a moment, I mulled over what had happened. I regretted that she was not beside me. Fearing she had gone out (for I couldn't hear anything in the apartment) I got up and, naked as a jaybird, made my way to the kitchen. She was sitting near the table, mending the tears made in our haste the previous evening. Startled to see me there, she stood up, letting her work fall, and turned her back to me. She was wearing a sleeveless blouse held up only by two straps knotted behind. I had a growing urge to take her and hear her moan and cry out with pleasure. I untied the knot supporting her blouse, sliding it down her arms and she stood naked before me, with only her hair to cover her. I kissed the nape of her neck, her shoulders and her back as my hands stroked her body from her chest to her hips and the silky triangle of her pubis. She stayed flattened against me for a long time, then slowly she crossed her arms, leaning then on the table and hiding her face away. She arched her back and her backside was offered to me like some enormous fruit set atop the columns of her quivering thighs.

That entire morning was spent between embraces and conversation during which we renewed our strength by eating fruit and eggs. These didn't require a lot of time to prepare and, so as not to waste time, we did not bother getting dressed in between.

She was a treat to the eyes, somewhat on the short side, her breasts proud and tipped by a very deep pinkish bud. I asked her how she had managed to retain such a splendid bust after two pregnancies, and she told me that her milk was not good for her children; she hadn't breastfed them. She admitted that when she woke up she had felt like kissing me awake but then felt ashamed of that urge. She said that my love-making the previous evening had ignited in her the fire to which she was now in such thrall that she was frightened of ending up alone again once I left.

We both knew well enough that nature and her laws had thrown us into each other's arms, shattering at one stroke all the boundaries erected over two thousand years of Judeo-Christian civilization by society's hypocritical morality. She knew, as I did, that we were just two creatures thrown together at a specific moment when we needed each other, creatures who were happy to have their minds and flesh melted down in the crucible of pleasure.

I left early that afternoon. We shared one final kiss on the doorstep. She had wanted me to carry away the image of her unclad body. Naked, erect, eyes slightly moist, maybe on account of the pleasure she had just sampled or maybe from the tears that she was holding back, she spun around and said to me:

"Look, I'm no beauty, I know that, but you said I was and I want to believe it. We may never see each other again. Remember me just as I am. I'll never forget you."

MONTE OSCURO

I returned to Pina and to garrison life, dividing my free time between the house, strolling with Tarzan (my dog), and conversations with friends on the best way to use the weapons we had. By the end of September our group's numbers had swollen considerably. We numbered about 150 when we were dispatched to Farlete to see if we could hold a position that had never been occupied before. At daybreak, after a night's walk through the rain, across cornfields where our espadrilles sank into the dirt and refused to come out again (so much so that most of us removed our shoes), we arrived at the foot of Monte Oscuro.

We clambered up to the summit, as Berthomieu, a career officer, had quickly sized up the strategic locations. Under his direction, we promptly set to work on fortifying the positions, installing posts, advance posts, and entrenched machine-gun or automatic rifle nests. We were there for some days. Even in Spain, at 800 meters above sea level, it is not very warm, so we returned to Farlete, and the Spanish *centurias* finished off the work we had begun.

We, the group's elders, were very glad for a change of garrison. Pina was like home to us; there we had our families and ate and spent the nights with them. We didn't know anyone in Farlete. We were billeted in barns and ate our meals together in a big hall. Augusta, Mimosa, and Marthe did the cooking. Madeleine, whose partner was that wounded German, served us at the table, helped by two women from the village.

In Farlete, I began to chat with Madeleine. I'd seen her almost everywhere I went for some time, and honestly before my trip to Lérida I hadn't paid attention to her. Sometimes the way she did things annoyed me. I'd changed, but she was still forever annoying me with her little kindnesses, kittenish ways, and the way she had of always fussing over me. La Madre had noticed the change in me and as soon as she saw me joking with a girl, she would make fun of me. One day, I said to her:

"Madre, you have two good-looking chicks in your henhouse. Aren't you afraid of somebody stealing them?"

She looked me straight in the eye and replied:

"Son, I know that if you were to have a word with them, you could have them both. But I also know that you won't do anything of the sort and that if anybody pesters them you'll protect them more

View of the barns in Farlete where militia members were billeted (2009)

than their brothers. So you see, *hijo*, I know you better than your poor mother does."

I gave her a hug and went off for guard duty.

We had come to the end days of September and I was itching to spend a day with just the family. After informing Louis, I climbed aboard a truck bound for Gelsa de Ebro. Augusta shared the same craving as me; she was keen to see the girlfriends she had made in the little town.

Throughout the journey, I chatted her up and she laughed heartily at all my jokes. I knew that I had no chance of getting anywhere with her; she was renowned for her coldness. We used to say that she had an allergy to love; she was a kind-hearted friend, devoted, and she'd do anyone a favor, but no one got anywhere with her. I think I tried every piece of nonsense a boy could possibly say to a girl and made every proposition there was to be made to any bride. I never took it seriously. Augusta use to dissolve into tears of laughter, and I with her. My memories of that trip are full of tenderness and purity, despite the lascivious and verging-on-offensive tone of our conversation.

Poor Augusta. She had only a few days left to live. A one-time student of medicine, she had made some friends among the women she had taken care of. We were glad to be on our way to see the regular people that we loved. Before I climbed down off the truck, I tossed her one last remark:

"Augusta, don't forget that I am quite capable of forgetting my sex, and if you ever need a playmate for a bit of fun some day, keep me in mind."

She thumped me and burst into laughter as she said to me:

"Tony, my boy, you're a complete nut-case."

She was still laughing as we parted.

MADELEINE

September was drawing to a close,[1] and Berthomieu was making frequent visits to HQ, but contrary to his normal practice he'd never tell us what was behind his trips. There was unease in the little band of us veterans; something was going on, but what? One evening, Louis asked me to fetch Staradoff, a Russian, and Lino, an Italian-born naturalized Frenchman who had served under his command in Africa. Once we were all together, Berthomieu told us bluntly: "Starting tomorrow you are to remain in ongoing touch with the CP.... I'll be needing you...." He was careworn and edgy. I had never seen him in that state before.

In Farlete I had chosen a billet in an unused building. Part of the roof had been demolished by a shell and showed a patch of sky. To get to it, I had to pass the cemetery. On my way to bed I could see, through a gap, the dead bodies disinterred by the shelling. There was one that, by some freak chance I can't explain, was intact and looked like a mummy. The coffin had partly fallen away but the cadaver was dried up and mummified. The soil was most likely so rich in arsenic or something else that prevented putrefaction.

I had just stretched out on my bed, a straw and hay-filled plank framework. It was firm and smelled good. Two bedcovers that La Madre had given me took the place of the mattress cover, and a soldier's cape, a gift from an elderly Farlete peasant, served as my blanket.

I had been out walking all afternoon with Louis, Lino, and Alexander. Out in the field, Louis explained what it was he was expecting of us. On paper, it was all very straightforward: three machine guns required knocking out so that the guys could take the enemy position. He had divided the job up between us; Lino would take the one on the left, Staradoff the one on the right, leaving me to handle the middle one. The problem was the timing. Between 9:30 and 10 p.m., we couldn't count on the sentries being asleep or worn out. We had scanned our route through the binoculars, identified the bushes that might help us conceal our approach, and picked the spot from which we had to throw our bombs. With the binoculars glued to our faces we had spent over an hour scanning the hillside that we'd need to

---

1   Again, this was between October 8 and 16, 1936.

climb up nearly stone by stone. In answer to one point raised by Lino, Louis replied:

"This is war, and you're the only ones with any chance of pulling this off."

I thought about what Berthomieu had said; it was all well and good talking about a chance, but against what odds? Two to one or a thousand to one? I wasn't reassured. I strongly doubted my ability to play the warrior on the warpath, no matter what Louis might have thought. The sound of a footstep wrenched me away from my memories of the afternoon, and a voice called out to me

"Antoine!"

"Yes, who is it?"

"It's me, Madeleine!"

I thought she had come to fetch me, so I pushed off my cape and got to my feet. She was already at my bedside.

"Who wants me?"

"Nobody. I know you're heading off tomorrow...."

I lit the two oil lamps and looked at her:

"How do you know?"

"Louis told Augusta and Mimosa to hold the pharmacy in readiness.... I'm to stay with the reserves."

"And that's what has brought you here?"

"No, this is!"

She climbed on to the bed and embraced me with a passion that I wouldn't have expected from her. Her kiss drove away any unease I had been feeling. Not that I desired her, but, since fate had sent me a playmate, why not sit back and enjoy it? I undressed her without hurrying. First, I peeled off her blouse. She was wearing a lacy brassiere. Her chest had begun to arch slightly. Her skirt slid over her hips and she stepped out of it, pushing it to one side. I was startled; she seemed so much younger in the glow from the oil lamps. Only her breasts gave her away somewhat.

"Now you," I told her.

She unbuckled my belt, stripped off my trousers and shirt, leaned over to set them down at the head of the bed, and, as she straightened up again, she laid her hands on my legs and slid them from ankle to hip. The tip of her tongue traced a moist line from my penis to my throat. Clasped to me, her arms about my neck, she raised her face to mine, her pink tongue darting to her red lips.

I started kissing her neck, shoulders, and breasts, and then took one nipple into my mouth, and, while stroking the back of one hand, I slid the other between her thighs; she was moist and on fire. On contact with the fingers probing her flesh, her legs parted as if to allow deeper penetration, then closed again like a vise around my trapped hand. Her knees bent, and she turned around, dragging me with her, and stretched out, mumbling something I didn't understand. My mouth slid over her skin from chest to vagina and trapped her clitoris firmly between my teeth. A cry rose from her throat, and her entire body convulsed as if an electric shock had passed through her.

Her hands, clamped in my hair, held my face tightly between her gaping thighs. She remained braced like that for a second before falling back, exhausted. I carried on with my task. My hands kneaded her breasts as my lips and tongue persevered with their mission. I too was spent, and once I could feel that she was beginning to stir again, that her hips and belly had resumed the light rhythmic dance that is the prelude to ecstasy, I moved upward and lay on top of her. Madeleine grabbed my torso and with a wiggle of her hips she tumbled me over so that I found myself on the bottom. She rode me like an Amazon riding a wild stallion.{28}

PERDIGUERA—PART ONE

By the next evening, it was down to brass tacks for us. Berthomieu had taken half the men—about a hundred. In October night falls rather quickly, so while the afternoon may have seemed long to me, the dusk seemed very brief. Hunched over, knees bent, we moved ahead, testing the ground with the point of our shoes, careful not to make any noise.

Nearing the first machine gun, Lino dropped down, signaling to us to carry on. Then it was turn to head out at the bottom of the hill; Staradoff went on alone. I looked at my watch, worried that its luminosity might give me away farther uphill. I tied my handkerchief around my wrist to cover it. My hand was shaking. The minutes dragged by, and the chill night air went right through to my bones. The cry of an owl broke through the night. That was the signal; the Russian was in position.

I began crawling forward. This had to be done quietly; the hill was pretty steep and covered with rocks that were in danger of breaking free, with the slightest help, and rolling down into the valley below, making an infernal racket. My hands tested the ground slowly, moving aside stones that might roll away and draw the attention to me. My heart was pounding. Since I'd began ascending the hill, my mind had been blank. What meager gray matter I possessed had been poured into a sharpening of my senses of touch, sight, and hearing. It was as if I had some sort of a detector in my fingertips. My eyes, now used to the dark, could discern the smallest tuft of grass, the tiniest bump in the ground that might be a stone.

I halted, my path blocked by a huge rosemary bush. I recognized the scent of the lower branches grazing my nose. I groped the terrain and raised myself up on my elbows, straining to peer through the brush. Shit! I had advanced too quickly and gone too far. Berthomieu had warned me that distance is hard to figure out in the dark. I lifted my handkerchief to check the time: six or seven minutes ahead of schedule. From far away on my left flank there was a noise. A burst of gunfire, a second burst, then a third. Stretched out flat, my head against the bottom of the bush, sweat beading on my forehead. It was no good telling myself that the ground, turned over by the excavation of the trench and held in place by the bush, amounted to a sort of mini-parapet shielding me from the bullets. I was sweating and felt like there was a hand clutching my throat. Silence. Then a voice called out:

"Why were you shooting? We can't see a thing."

A different voice answered:

"I heard some stones rolling away, out there, in front of me."

"Did you see anything?"

"No...."

"Might have been a rabbit."

"Yeah, maybe."

Then silence once more. I was thirsty, my throat was dry. Mechanically, I swung the pouch filled with grenades around from my back to my chest. One in each hand, I grabbed two criss-cross-patterned metal "duck eggs." We had no assault grenades. Far behind me the owl hooted. One, two, three. I tossed my "pineapple" the way one would toss a ball in a game of *pétanque*. I was too close to do anything else. Off to my right, Alexander had beat me to it; I heard his grenade explode before my own. Off to the left, the machine gun went into action. There was a short burst, a scream, and the machine gun went silent. In between two explosions I heard Staradoff shriek something in Russian. Like him, I disposed of my load by targeting the trench. A scream erupted behind me, welling up out of the depths of the night. The patter of a running crowd, coming closer, all around me, moving past me. Onward! Freedom! *Adelante*! CNT! *Avanti!* Shouting in all sort of languages.

"You okay there, Tony?"

Somebody took me by the arm and held a bottle to my lips. I recognized it was Marthe.

"Thanks, Marthe. And is Lino okay?"

"That I don't know. Augusta went off to give him something to drink. You coming?"

She was in a hurry to get back to the group and to her partner.[1] I could understand that: they were virtually inseparable. I had often seen them out walking together, arms around each other or holding hands.

There was a comrade waiting for us beyond the parapet. Berthomieu told us, or to be more accurate, had someone tell us, that after an inventory had been made of the position we'd taken, we could rejoin them or start back for Farlete. Augusta turned up and announced that

---

[1]   Possibly a reference to Roger Baudart.

Lino was dead; after hurling his bomb, he had been mown down by a hail of gunfire. Once the women had left, Staradoff and I started scouring the trench. We were almost finished when Alexander came over and handed me a bottle:

"Here. Drink. It's good stuff."

It was a bottle of rectified spirits I could tell from the smell.

"Are you crazy, drinking that stuff? It's fuel—not a drink."

"Oh no! It's good stuff...."

He took the bottle back from me, raised it to his lips and gulped down—no exaggeration—three-quarters of it. I was expecting to see him fall down dead. But no! He saw that there was a little left, so he slipped it into his pouch and went off to complete his task. We were back in the barns around Perdiguera before midnight. The village was downhill from us, but I couldn't tell if it was a big settlement or a small one because it was too dark when we arrived. When the sun came up, I had better things to do than take in the scenery. Berthomieu had deployed his men along the crest of the hill that fell away to the highway and the village. We took shelter in the nearby barns. It was there, in that outbuilding filled with straw and farm tools, that I asked Louis why we had stopped so close to the village instead of mounting an immediate attack. He explained that Ruano's plan was to have us all slaughtered.

We had to switch positions in order to release our rear guard, while Durruti's *centurias* would simultaneously move out and cut off the road to Zaragoza—thereby cutting the garrison off from any reinforcements and from retreating toward Aragon's capital. Once the encirclement was complete, a squadron of cavalry was to feign an attack on the village from the hillside facing our position. That would be the signal for us to attack. We had pulled off stage one of the plan; now we had merely to hope that the cavalry would not keep us waiting too long.{29}

ENDNOTE {29}: 299

PERDIGUERA—PART TWO

There were about ten of us. Augusta and Mimosa had readied some bales of straw and opened up the pharmacy boxes. Their work done, they were lying down and chatting with Georges, a little Parisian who was whiling away the time opening and closing his *navaja* just for the pleasure of hearing the blade click. That strange music entertained him so much that even when walking around he would do it, slightly varying the speed at which the knife's blade opened and closed.

Mimosa called me over for a chat. The two girls had had no sleep, and there were about ten comrades all around us, resting up after their forced march. I found the girls charming little friends. Mimosa had shared my *chabola* (a hole dug in the ground and covered over with stubble and branches). She was Polish. Married to a brutal drunkard of a Frenchman, she had run away and crossed the border.[1] Her character was the very opposite of Augusta's; she was incapable of saying no, loved living, loving, and laughter. I remembered one evening on Monte Oscuro, too worn out to want to do anything other than grab some sleep, she had asked me to walk her in for the night and shield her from the desires of her admirers. I had agreed, and she had shared my palliasse just like a little girl might share her mother's bed.

I was sitting between the girls now. Mimosa was telling her girl-friend about the adventure we had shared the night before we were relieved. Berthomieu had dispatched me into Farlete to let the quartermaster section know that the group should be there by noon and that there should be a hot meal ready for the men. Mimosa had been unwilling to stay in the *chabola* on her own and had climbed out and tagged along with me. There was no way of getting from Monte Oscuro to Farlete other than by the ruts the carts left in the fields during fieldwork and at harvest times. We were lost.

I listened as she recounted how, after walking for two hours, she had had to stop to regain her strength and how angry I had been that I had could not quite get my bearings in the night, which was as black

---

1   Mimosa was actually not Polish, but she'd married a French socialist by the name of Kokoczinski, the son of Polish refugees. The "brutal drunkard of a Frenchman" was not her husband but her father-in-law. (See the biographical note below.)

as the inside of an oven. And then it had started raining, to make matters worse, soaking us to the bone. By the time we reached the *paridera* (shepherd's hut)—where, at the risk of giving away our position to some enemy patrol, I had started a blazing fire to help us dry out—she had been overwhelmed by a crazy urge to make love.

Mimosa spoke softly and laughed quietly so as not to wake our comrades. She had taken my hand and clamped it between her thighs. Augusta had grabbed the other one and clutched it to her breast. None of us knew that they would soon lose their lives. After giving me a kiss on the cheek, she had carried on with her story: her craving for kisses outweighed her fear of a patrol stumbling upon us. As she talked, I watched her undress. I could see her skinny body, tiny breasts and their pink buds.

The sky was beginning to lighten. We were all ready to fall on our prey. On our feet near a low wall that followed the summit of the hill, we scanned the hillside opposite for signs of the cavalry, ready to launch our attack on the garrison dug in in the village. In front of the wall, Alexander had set up one of the machine guns captured from the enemy and was training it in the direction of the outlying houses. A dark silhouette against the gray sky drew our eyes; a rider, followed by a second. Then the whole squadron profiled against the hilltop. Each of the horses bore two men, one mounted behind the other, and shooting broke out immediately. Bullets were flying around us from every side, mowing down the men who had not taken cover in time. Berthomieu told me to hold my position for fifteen minutes to allow him to give the order to fall back and return with more comrades. Once that time was up, we were to withdraw to another *pajar* (barn), which was not far to our rear and quite near the center of our deployment. Standing against the wall, I waited for Louis to return. I had scoped up a rifle and mechanically fired over Staradoff's head at anything that moved. He had skipped over the low wall after the initial shooting. It impeded his efforts to reach the hillside that swept up toward us from the highway. He was on his own. The two men who had been feeding his machine gun lay upon the ground, dead.

Inside the barn, some nurses were fussing over the wounded and dying. Eventually, Berthomieu reappeared. He gave me a quick breakdown of the lay of the land; the Spaniards had not mounted the scheduled movements, and we were all but surrounded. We needed to begin falling back. He showed me where our meeting point had to be—a

The hayloft today, with some of the Giménologues

building about fifty meters behind us. He left me to go and brief the remainder of the group. The man who had gone to tell Staradoff to pull back fell down, dead. Now there were only a half a dozen of us, and two female nurses. I told them to leave but they refused to abandon the wounded. I stepped outside just in time to see Alexander throw his arms in the air. Taken aback, I watched him; his fists were clenched, and he hurled one grenade and then another. He ducked down, grabbed his rifle, brought the barrel up to his mouth and squeezed the trigger. His head was catapulted backward, and he fell backwards A voice called out to me:

"Shake a leg, Antoine!"

Georges, sheltering behind the corner of the parapet, beckoned to me to pull back. The building had two levels. Down below, the peasants stored their tools, and up above they stored the straw and hay and sometimes also part of their harvest. A wooden ladder connected the two floors.

Cartagena, one of the very first Spaniards to have joined our group, had, together with some other comrades, loosened stones all around the building to create loopholes. By the time I got there, they were just finishing off the last one. Thanks to these holes, we could defend our position on all sides. Arranged at two different heights and staggered, the loopholes at ground level left no blind spots across which the enemy might slide along the walls. The lowest level had been installed at twenty to thirty centimeters above ground level and the higher one at the meter mark. Cartagena told me that Louis had advised him to carry out the installation in anticipation of the possible failure of our attack and to help us hold out until reinforcements came.

Slowly, our men peeled off and fell back toward our stronghold, and we strove to give them cover with our firepower. We numbered around forty men, able-bodied or wounded to some degree or another. Little by little, the gunfire grew less intense. We could see the barrels of enemy rifles trained on us from the low wall across the hilltop, and we knew that enemy forces were massing on three sides, mustering for one final onslaught. All of a sudden, there was a shout from up above: a lookout had spotted someone sliding through the grass. It was one of ours; someone had recognized him. We began shooting again, to cover his approach. He got to his feet unsteadily and then fell in front of one of the loopholes. Luckily that loophole was wide enough to allow us to reach for his legs and drag him inside. He was German, and he had been hit in the belly and chest. We wondered how he could have made it to us. He signed to us that he had something to say. We approached him to ask what had happened.

"You, get out quickly. Captain shot. *Frau Martha* shot. Comrades all dead. You leave. Quickly!"

We looked at one another and we asked ourselves; what should we do now? Should we hold out there until our ammunition ran out or until there was no one left? Or hoist the white flag, or wait to be killed on the spot? A minority of us argued that we should surrender.

We were just taking a head count of those who were opposed to surrender when we were interrupted by a deluge of curses and oaths accompanied by gunshots.

"Bastards, *hijos de puta*, murderers, *verdugos, figli di puttana!*"

We scurried to the loopholes. I thought I was losing my mind, shut my eyes again, and felt my stomach churn. I wanted to vomit. Down below in the dust lay two bloodied bodies, bellies torn open, entrails spilling from gaping wounds exposed to the sun. The two women were naked but clinging to life. Their hands struggled to hold in their intestines. Augusta and Mimosa. Somebody pulled me away from the loophole; it was Cartagena. I watched him shoulder his rifle, then heard gunshots. It was over. I was crying. And I wasn't the only one. Georges came over to tell me that the German had committed suicide by putting a bullet into his own head.{30}

ENDNOTE {30}: 304

LA CALLE

After that there was no more talk of surrender from anyone. We were all convinced that we were goners. We could expect no mercy. Man is a gregarious beast, and in certain situations the majority of people acknowledge the need to let themselves be led by the man or men they think best equipped to work out a solution to their problems.

Cartagena, Georges, La Calle, and I made up the quadrumvirate constantly bombarded by questions from the remainder of the besieged garrison. Cartagena was Spanish, originally from the city of that name. Tall and thin and as swarthy as any gypsy, with very pale eyes, he was not much of a talker. Given to acting first and explaining later. He always went for the radical, no-going-back solutions. No one knew a thing about his past, except that he must have spent a long time in France, for he spoke the language perfectly. He must have been in his forties.

Georges was a pal. He was French (Parisian), highly cultivated, light-hearted, had a devil-may-care attitude, and was given to telling funny stories. His parents, so he said, were professional thieves recognized and protected by the government, in return for the tithe they paid it. In actual fact, his parents were in business.

As for La Calle, his temperament was the very opposite of his countryman's. A Barcelona-born Spaniard, he had never known his parents. He had been brought up on the streets and grown up there; hence his name, La Calle (Street). Short (under five feet), La Calle suited his name: he was sometimes noisy, sometimes quiet and sombre. Candid, he didn't hold back about his hatred or contempt for anyone who bowed down or knelt before the holy pictures of any religion. In his view, all the earth's woes flowed from the priests, monks, pastors, or rabbis who cashed in on the ignorance and innocence of people and lived lives of depravity and extravagance.

I often heard him recount his life story or tell anecdotes when, in the course of conversation, somebody advocated that one should be free to believe in whatever religion one chose, if one felt so compelled. He would explode; his voice growing louder, cold, and cutting.

"Sure, I don't give a damn if you want to believe. Believe then! But no priests and no monks, pastors, or rabbis, because you don't know what they are hiding behind their unctuous ways and benevolent smiles. But I do."

Raised by who knows who, he could remember having begged on the city streets when he was still very young. Beggar and shoe-shine boy, those were his first two callings. As he got older, he wanted to learn to read and write. He practiced his penmanship by imitating the pages of the newspapers dumped on the streets, using a piece of coal for a pencil and the pavement for his paper.

One evening, the parish priest discovered him in the act of copying a page on to the church wall and suggested that he would teach him to read and write. He accepted the offer, glad to see his dream becoming a reality. He was about fifteen at the time, but, because he was so small, nobody could have guessed his age. The priest invited him into the presbytery and gave him food and drink; in short, bought his trust. He also gave him some lessons. Everything had gone great for a few days. Little José La Calle was walking on air.

One evening, after class, his teacher invited him to spend the evening there so that he might keep him company, for his housekeeper was to be away for a while. After the housekeeper left, the holy man felt the need to take a bath and suggested that José follow suit. The youngster suspected nothing; a priest was chaste, and God's earthly representative couldn't be given to vice. He stripped and stepped into the little room where a shower had been installed. The man of God stepped in with him to help him lather up. On the pretext of soaping him down, he groped and caressed every part of him, from calves to buttocks, back, belly, and chest. He lathered his penis while rubbing at his foreskin. José hadn't liked that at all but didn't dare say anything.

Once he was as clean as a new penny, his host put an arm around his shoulders and steered him toward the bedroom, while telling him all about what a joy it was to have such a kind young friend and one as bright as José was as well. It was in the bedroom that things went from bad to worse.... The priest started kissing him and running his hand down from José's nape to his buttocks; after some initial surprise, José broke loose, grabbed an oil lamp from the bedside table, and brought it crashing down on the priest's head. Then, dressing quickly, he made a break for it. He left Barcelona without a word to anyone, not even Angelita, a little girl, his long-time friend, just a year or two older than him. Three years passed before he returned to the city of his birth. He sought out his girlfriend. Naturally he wasn't expecting to find her still unattached. He was hoping that she was happy with her husband, and he would be glad at her happiness. If she was still free and was not betrothed, then he would ask her to become his partner. He came upon her one evening in the Barrio Chino, outside the Criolla,[1] her lips and eyes made up. Having become a prostitute. I can still hear the tremor in his voice as he clenched his fists and sobbed as he declared:

"Had she told me that that line of work was to her liking, that she was doing it of her own volition, I'd have said nothing and would have suggested that she come away with me and live with me off the money I would earn from working. But Angelita had a *chulo* (pimp) who used to thrash her when she didn't earn enough and who had forced her, by means of blows and threats, to prostitute herself. So, off I went, leaving her to her work, and I laid low. I waited nearly the whole night through … and then he showed up, seizing her by the arm as if she had never been anything else but his property. I stepped out of my hiding place and went up to him. I asked Angelita if he was her man. She answered: "He is, José." My *navaja* plunged into his heart without further ado. He said not one word. He stood there for a moment, popeyed, then fell facedown on the ground. And that's why I hate priests, why I fight against capitalists, because the priests and capitalists all pimp upon the people. They force us to toil for them the way the pimps force women to prostitute themselves; by dint of beatings and threats and the poverty in which they hold those who work."

---

1   This was the name of a famous nightclub located in the heart of the Barrio Chino, in the Calle del Cid. Jean Genet had been a regular customer there in 1932 and he mentions it in his *Journal du voleur* (1949). The club had lots of rooms to hire for prostitutes of either sex, while the top floor of the building housed dormitories for immigrants arriving in Barcelona in search of work.

PERDIGUERA—PART THREE

That is as much as I know and can remember about my three comrades. We were the oldest members of the group that were there. Cartagena was the one everyone paid the most attention to. As he was the most determined, his opinion, spelled out in concise terms, was generally accepted by all. La Calle, Georges, and I were all for mounting a sortie to try to extract ourselves from that hornets' nest. Cartagena told us to hold on. He had seen two or three of our guys running toward our lines, and his hope was that reinforcements were on the way. But the morning wore on, and nothing appeared on the horizon.

We were completely pinned down. We had seen the fascists taking up their positions so as to cut us off from the road to the sierra. A hundred or 150 meters from the barn there was an almost flat wheat field that stretched away to the foot of Monte Oscuro. There were some bunches of wheat between us and the plain. We had done our best to avoid being encircled completely, but we were running low on ammunition. And were now only firing targeted shots. They were trying to get us to use up our ammunition by means of decoys: caps and berets held out on the ends of rifles, but we just let them carry on and only opened fire once we were certain that the hat in question had a head under it.

It was around eleven o'clock when, having abandoned all hope of a republican attack to help us out, that we made up our minds to be done with it. La Calle, nerves raw from the waiting, as all our nerves were, said something along the lines of:

"They won't attack until after nightfall. They hope to be able to get close enough to set the place on fire. Which is what I would do if I were in their shoes. And what should we do? Wait for them to come and find us and roast us? When it comes to ways of dying, I'd prefer to go down fighting. We venture outside, and if we're all killed, at least we'll have the satisfaction of taking a few of them with us."

We spelled out our decision to the comrades. They all agreed to mount the sortie. Otherwise, we were like rats caught in a trap. One of the wounded suggested that those who were not up to running or walking and who therefore had no option but to stay behind could fire through the ground-level loopholes to draw off the full brunt of the gunfire from those venturing outside. All we needed to do was help

Militia members on the attack on the Aragon front, summer 1936

them get into the firing positions. The seriously wounded and dying begged us not to let them fall, alive, into the clutches of the enemy. Three or four of them, who had held on to their weapons, committed suicide. The remainder were finished off by Cartagena using a knife.

I was watching all of this as if it had nothing to do with me. I was an indifferent onlooker watching an absurd tragedy that was taking place outside of time … and in which there was one actor who could have passed for my twin. Using a piece of string that I had found in a corner, I had attached one of my handguns to my neck, making myself a lanyard that dangled down to the sheath of my dagger. The other end was tied to a buckle around my wrist. Kitted out like that, there was no chance of either being dropped while I was racing along, tossing grenades.

Everything was ready. Cartagena explained our plan in Spanish, and I did likewise in Italian and Georges in French. We were to split up into two groups, one on each side of the door. We were to open it and make a break for the sierra while those left behind gave us cover using the automatic rifles. If we stayed there, we were all effectively goners. If we surrendered then, at best, we would be shot. So it was in our interest to go down shooting. We had an example in front of our very eyes: the bodies of Mimosa and Augusta were proof that nothing and no one could expect mercy from the other side.

Our little lecture over, everybody positioned themselves facing the door: Cartagena and Georges on one side, La Calle in front on the other. I was to take my position near José, but at the last moment, for a few seconds, I found it impossible to move. Fear? Maybe so. What I do know is that, abruptly, up from the deepest recesses of my memory came the memory of my mother, dead some eight years or so, and for a short space of time it was as if she was standing in front of me. Then everything vanished, and I took my place in the middle of these men who were going to their deaths and knew it.

"*Vamos!* ... Let's go! ... *Andiamo!* ... *Adelante!* ... Forward! ... *Avanti!* ... Long live freedom!"

These cries erupted from our chests even as the barn door, forcibly thrown open, revealed a sunbathed plain.

PERDIGUERA—PART FOUR

It is all but impossible to tell what happened after we stepped out-side. Launched like arrows amid the screaming and the explosions and making off in two different directions, we put some distance between ourselves and the barn, but the element of surprise was short-lived. I was one of the last across the threshold. I ran, and as I ran I could see the comrades ahead falling down. How many times did I drop to the ground to reload my weapons? I cannot tell. I remember seeing Cartagena stop, raise his pistol to his temple, and collapse. Some men were fighting hand-to-hand, their weapons glistening in the sunshine. I saw Georges leap over a bale of wheat and a bayonet gleaming behind him and thrust into his chest. I fired at the man on his knees who had wielded the rifle. They both fell, one after the other.

As I kept moving I could feel the bullets whistling past me, close to my ears. In front of me lay the plain and, further off, La Calle, his auto-matic rifle clasped under his arm, running for dear life. The rifle slipped from his grasp and down he went. Tiny little dust clouds were churn-ing all around me the way the first drops of rain raise them as they slam into a dusty road in summertime. There was another machine gun up in the steeple. I started running in zig-zags. José, flat on his stomach, aimed his gun and fired. I saw the barrel shudder in time to the bursts issuing from it. I wasn't the target any more. The rain started falling thick and fast all around him. He called out to me: "*Más de prisa* (step it up), Antonio, faster!" and he raised himself up on his hands as if to get to his feet again. Only to fall back down to lie motionless, with one hand clutching his rifle. I took off on my run and took a punch in the kidneys. I could no longer see the dust clouds dancing in front of me, but I could still hear the angry burst from the machine gun far behind me. In the end, it fell silent. I broke down, rolling along the ground and falling into a bottomless abyss.

I woke at the bottom of a *barranco* (ravine). I had lost my foot-ing and passed out on stepping over the edge of that natural trench. It was still daylight. Two horsemen on patrol dragged me onto a path and brought me back to Farlete. I was utterly exhausted.

Once I had satisfied the natural curiosity of the comrades assem-bled in the command post and having gobbled down a fair bit of grub, I asked Madeleine to fetch a pack of cigarettes from the cartridge belt that I had cast aside, because the pocket in my jerkin was empty. The ammunition pouch served as a spare smoking kit. An exclamation in her native tongue made us turn around: she was staring at the leather as if she had never set eyes on one before:

"What's up?"

"See for yourself!"

As she said that, she emptied the contents onto the table. There was a hole on the outside of the pouch. The pack of cigarettes had been punctured by a lump of copper. Spotting that my left sleeve was torn, Madeleine raised me up for a closer look along with the others. Fortune, misfortune? Who can say? Not I. If living is a blessing, then I was blessed that day. Three bullets had come so close that they had punctured my jacket in two places: the sleeve and the side, in the case of the third, the bottom of my trousers. All three on the lefthand side. For a long time I carried that little cone of lead-filled copper around with me as a lucky charm.

PABLO'S ARRIVAL

The next day I was informed that I was the sole survivor of the massacre. Overnight, Ben Sala, an Algerian, and Manuel turned up; the sangfroid and camouflage skills of that son of the Maghreb, plus Manuel's knowledge of the terrain had enabled them to evade the attentions of the fascists and return to our lines once darkness had fallen. From their hideout they had seen Berthomieu, Marthe, and many another meet their ends. What they had to say confirmed what that German comrade had told us before he died.

No one in Farlete knew why the *centurias* had not budged from their positions. Swift enquiries made of the different sectors involved revealed to us that no orders had reached them. The people in charge had reckoned that we were merely mounting a straightforward raid, like we had before.{31} At Durruti's headquarters, Ruano, who had been in charge of implementing the plan, was nowhere to be found. Buenaventura himself knew nothing of the origins of the affair that had cost the lives of 120 of us.{32}

That day, I witnessed something that showed me another side to the character of Gori. Three or four peasants had been caught the previous night trying to close in on the tent where Durruti was resting, meaning to butcher him. They came from the Sierra de Alcubierre and were poor shepherds who the priests had turned into fanatics. Old before their time from hard toil and poverty, they resignedly awaited their death sentence. The firing squad positioned itself about ten meters from and facing the condemned men. "Take aim!" I saw the poor buggers make the sign of the cross. "Fire!" The twelve rifles all fired as one. All the condemned men fell, except for one who remained on his feet staring uncomprehendingly at the squad, his eyes wide with surprise. It has to be said that the revolutionaries must have been very poor shots to miss with a rifle at that distance. I was stunned myself. I listened for a second volley and the sight of one of the men stepping up to give them the coup de grace. Instead of which, I saw two guys carrying buckets filled with water that they conscientiously poured over the supposed dead. The rifles had been loaded with blanks. Gori let them go once he told them that we were at war with ignorance and slavery and not with poor devils who did not understand where justice and freedom lay.

The Durruti Column's International Group had been dealt a death blow in Perdiguera, but it was not entirely finished. A former Italian army colonel arrived to step into Berthomieu's shoes. We called him Pablo. I never knew his real name or the underlying reasons why he wound up in the company of revolutionaries. He was quite old. An officer in the 1914–18 war, he was not what would be described these days as a "*baroudeur*" or guerrilla leader, like Louis had been. Under him, we began to sample life in trenches or mass attacks as shock troops.

Everywhere he went, Pablo had with him a young woman who went by the name Louise. Slender, with a crumpled doll's face and quite easy on the eye, she had a soft, musical voice that was charming to hear. Since she was the very opposite of Madeleine, being quite small and chubby, I fell in love with her, so much so that Pablo noticed this and, in order to keep me away from her, awarded me a few days' furlough in Barcelona.{33}

BARCELONA

Another fellow, Lorenzo Giua, was on leave with me. His father was a teacher at some school I have long since forgotten the name of in Turin, Italy. He had been banished into *domicilio coatto* (assigned residence) on some Mediterranean island by Mussolini. Being a student himself, he had left for exile in order to get away from Italian fascism's goons.{34} We quickly hit it off. On our return to the front we became virtually inseparable, and for many a long months we shared everything we had. On our way through Bujaraloz, we were handed a substantial sum of money. Three months' pay. Ten pesetas a day for trying to get ourselves killed. Not too bad as pay went.

I had heard that, so as not to spook the governments of the democracies that might come to our aid by selling us arms, the Revolutionary Committee had been obliged to put the peseta back into circulation. But as far as I was concerned this was an eye-opener: the revolution had failed. As in Russia some time after the victory of the worker and peasant masses, the Communist Party bosses announced that they had to take a step back and restore the value of the currency. That initial step had been followed by lots of others and the Russian people had simply traded one master for another; the tsar, father of all the Russias, had been replaced by the little father of the people, Stalin.

Barcelona merely added to my sourness; the Ramblas were packed with people,[1] prostitution was rampant throughout the great city. Militia members on leave, identifiable by the overalls (*mono*) they had adopted, filled the streets with their singing and laughter, unable to see that their cause had been betrayed and that the revolution was defunct. Now all that remained was the war against fascism, the war between two forms of slavery.

Money, that blight, was back in play. Following a short visit to the union, Lorenzo took me to the home of some friends where I met Francisco and Emilio Ferrer, grandsons of the founder of the Modern School who had been shot in Montjuich, prior to the 1914–18 war, for his beliefs.

Francisco decided that he would come to Aragon with us. His partner, Giuditta, an Italian, a veteran anarchist militant driven out of

---

1   The original manuscript uses an Italian term, equivalent to "spewed forth."

Italy by Mussolini's accession, would come too. She had known Francisco since he was just a child, had latched on to him and not been parted from him since, acting throughout as his governess-cum-mistress. A fine woman, convinced of the correctness of her beliefs, she was always ready to lend a hand and make any sacrifice for the success of her ideals and the sake of her Francisco's happiness.{35}

In Barcelona I had the good fortune to meet the sort of person one doesn't easily come across in contemporary life, even if one is aware that they exist. Lorenzo had invited me along on an evening with two girls; they must have been sixteen or seventeen years old. That day was a delight; the girl who had picked me as her partner was likable, witty, given to laughter, and quite pretty, which did no harm either. I was spending recklessly and urging Lorenzo to get rid of the wad of notes in his pockets, so much so that he decided to confess to me that the girls were two pros who he had hired for the evening, and for the night, if I liked.

I have always had a soft spot for women, and ever since puberty my sole preferred pastime has been the game of love. But I have never been able to have a good time with a prostitute I am paying for; the very thought that she has the meter running even as I am caressing her is enough to kill any urge I might have had for a dalliance.

Discreetly, I put it to my companion that we shake Lorenzo and her girlfriend loose. She agreed, and, capitalizing on the milling crowds, we shook off our companions. Seated on the terrace of a café, I asked her to tell me what prompted her to turn to the world's oldest profession. Frankly, I had been expecting the usual, classical line about the sick mother, the family needing fed, the little brothers needing reared. She told me that she had been in the trade forever. Even as a girl, she had let herself be groped by the local grocer in return for candies, then, when she was older, for dolls and paste jewelry. At twelve she had surrendered herself to a guy who, in return for her cooperation, had offered her a gold necklace that she still wore around her neck. I listened to her recount all this, surprised at the open, serene look on her face and in her eyes, as if all of this was only natural. I thought back to the courtesans, to the priestesses of Venus, to ancient Greece and Rome.

Once she had finished her narrative, I let her in on how I thought of relations between a man and a woman, and then I spoke to her of La Calle and his little Angelita. I did not look in her direction as I spoke

Endnote {35}: 337

of the man whose death had allowed me to escape from the hell of Per-diguera. Emotion left me with a frog in my throat, and tears blurred my vision. I was reliving what had been a tragic time for me. In the end, I lifted my eyes to look in her direction; elbows on the table, her face held cupped in her hands, it was as if she had her eyes fixed upon some far-off vision.

I stood up and walked away, leaving a handful of pesetas in front of her. I had not gone very far before she ran to catch up; taking my arm, she thrust the notes back into my pocket and said:

"Don't leave me yet; it's not as if you have to be anywhere."

Her eyes were red, her voice quivering like a little girl denied what she wants and scolded. We strolled late into the night, and then I walked her home. Just as we were parting, she asked "When do you leave?"

"Maybe tomorrow, definitely by the day after tomorrow," I replied.

"This is my parents' place. Thanks. *Adiós!*"

"Thanks for what?"

"For not wanting to sleep with me and having been kind enough to keep me company."

She then closed the door and disappeared. I hadn't even asked for her name or told her mine.

DURRUTI, ASCASO, AND THE OTHERS

Giuditta and Francisco Ferrer introduced me to María, the sister of Francisco Ascaso, killed on July 15 during the storming of the Atarazanas barracks.[1] Durruti, Ascaso, Jover— three men renowned in Spain and across Europe.{36} All of the press had talked of their deeds and exploits in the wake of the murder of Cardinal Soldevila and the attempt on the life of King Alfonso XIII.

Francisco was the first to die, Buenaventura died some months after him, and Jover alone was to survive to seek refuge in France.

At María's home I was told this anecdote about Ascaso that testifies to his bravery and determination. In a café in a little Catalonian town, some Falangists, seated around a table, were arguing about the FAI and the CNT and bragging about giving a sound beating to any CNT member who might turn up. The establishment was almost exclusively the haunt of Falangists. I say "almost" because on this particular evening there was someone there who went and reported what he had heard to Francisco who was nearby. Ascaso strode into the café, walked up to the table where the four pals were still immersed in their bragging, gave his name and history and opened fire without removing his gun from his pocket, and then vanished before those present could collect their thoughts.

In every village, town, and hamlet across the Iberian Peninsula Durruti, Ascaso, and Jover were spoken of with admiration and respect. I remember one time in 1935, in a railway station where the ticket inspector had ejected me because I'd forgotten to buy a ticket, some peasants offered to put me up for the night. This was in Castile, between Madrid and Toledo, and their hamlet lay about ten kilometers from the station where these peasants had gone with a donkey laden down with two barrels to replenish their drinking water supply from a tanker. The beast knew the route so well that it needed no watching; one had only to follow it and even through the darkest of nights it would guide us home.

En route, we talked about the CNT, and Durruti's name came to my lips; it was as if I had name-dropped a hero of legend, a knight of the

---

1   In fact, he perished on the morning of July 20, during the second day of the storming of the barracks.

Ascaso, Durruti, and Jover in the offices of *Le Libertaire*, Paris, July 14, 1927

Round Table who roamed the byways of the world, hunting down the mighty and bringing relief to the wretchedness of the common people. In their eyes, I, who subscribed to the same beliefs, had turned into some sort of an apostle. Sound people, poor peasants from Castile. Out of that family of more than ten, only one barely knew how to read and write, a young woman, crippled by a kick from a mule when she was still a child and who lived in an institution where she was under care.

BERNERI

My short stay in Barcelona taught me that the social revolution was at a disadvantage; the overriding need to win the war was pushing the reforms we so cherished down the list of priorities. For the anarchists, prosecution of the war took precedence over all; they had agreed to enter the government of Catalonia in order to ensure the unity of proletarian forces. Already there was talk of reorganizing the army and structuring it along the lines of divisions, battalions, and so on.

At María Ascaso's place, very heated arguments between those who were for this and those who were against it lasted into the small hours of the night. I opposed a reversion to the classic army model, but my adversaries had an argument that carried some weight: first we had to win the war. Confident in their fighting prowess and in the justice and righteousness of their ideal, and sneering at the very idea of taking power for themselves, they reckoned that once peace had been restored, the worker and peasant masses would organize themselves along the lines of the Aragonese and Catalan collectives that we'd set up wherever we went. They paid no heed to the fact that all the parties and organizations fighting against the fascists had thrown open their doors to just about anybody, simply in order to inflate their own numbers. So, in numerical terms, the balance of power had altered, switching from one side to the other.{37}

In certain towns, the Communist Party, virtually nonexistent before July 19, was now the majority. Other political factions also saw their membership grow but to a lesser extent. The power struggle was obvious to all, even those like myself who had no truck with the upper echelons of politics.

On the same day that I first met Francisco Ferrer, I also made the acquaintance of Camillo Berneri, a philosophy lecturer whose opinion carried a lot of weight among libertarians of Italian extraction. I bumped into him again at María's. As we chatted, we took a shine to each other. I genuinely relished listening to him, and he would chuckle when, in reply, I would take my line of argument to absurd lengths.

One evening, the conversation turned to the chances of a libertarian's going self-employed and opening a workshop. I chipped in, trying to show him that, over time, if the business prospered, the libertarian would be inclined to expand his workshop and hire additional staff to meet the demand and keep the customers happy. And one fine day the erstwhile anarchist would find himself a member of an employers' association and an honorary partner in police efforts to protect his factories and capital from the demands of his workers and staff. The anarchist is only human, prey to all the same temptations and all the foibles of the society in which he finds himself. The greatest demand he makes of himself is the effort it takes to remain, if he is a worker, peasant, or clerical worker, what he is. If fate has blessed him with all the wealth in the world, he must summon up the strength to walk away from his rank and wealth and take his turn at being someone who works for a living, which is to say, is exploited.

My tirade had earned me the sympathy of a professor who, on discovering that I was eager to get back to the front as I had begun to weary of city surroundings, suggested that I make the trip along with him. Berneri had no illusions as to how the struggle between the various factions competing to win power in republican Spain was going to turn out. When I quoted him a splendid phrase from Louise Michel— "Power is cursed; its turns all who wield it rotten"—he responded that Louise was right but that, despite the shortcomings of certain of her most cherished comrades, she had carried on with the fight up to the very last day of her life, faithful to her ideal. He also said that one must never lose hope, in spite of setbacks, shortcomings, and betrayals. Humankind is on the road to anarchy, meaning on the road to absolute freedom for every person, to a form of society in which there will be only two articles in the law book:

> 1. Freedom of one individual ends where the freedom of another begins.
> 2. Everyone must produce according to his ability and consume in accordance with his needs.

Then he reminded me of this dictum of Elisée Reclus: "Anarchy is the highest expression of order."

It was Camillo Berneri who painted me this picture of social progress; he said to me:

"The wanderings of humanity resemble the swarming of red ants through tropical forests; they advance in tight ranks, destroying all other animal or vegetable life in their path in order to feed themselves. The natives set fires and dig ditches to divert them and stop them in their march and thus protect their fields and crops. The ants go marching on. The front ranks smother the fire and block the water-logged ditches. The rest march over the calcified or drowned corpses of those who have sacrificed themselves so that their breed may reach the spot where they can build the new city. Anarchists have always been the spearhead of society's progress toward absolute freedom of the individual. Compelled by reactionaries to resort to violence to champion or win the right to life, we stand fast by our ideas, but we always refuse to use force to impose them."{38}

THE SIERRA DE ALCUBIERRE

At Bujaraloz, we went our separate ways after promising to meet up again some time.

The group in Farlete was no longer what it had once been; many of the older hands had left. Some had left Spain entirely, others had joined different units (the ones that were referred to as the "International Brigades").{39}

After I got back, Pablo called all the veterans together. There were about ten of us; where were all the others? The vast majority had perished in Perdiguera. The remainder, disgusted with what had happened, had packed up and left.

Affinenghi, Scolari, Otto, Jacques, and a few others whose names I cannot recall, had formed a little group, which the colonel held in readiness at his CP for reconnaissance missions and mounting raids. {40} Among the most recent recruits, there were certain persons who I suspected were attracted by money rather than anything ideological. They were loudmouths, pretentious types always ready to brawl with one another at the drop of a hat, and they forced Pablo to press for us to be sent up the line. And so it was that, instead of operating as a flying column, we began to turn into a unit just like any other.

We were dispatched to the Sierra de Alcubierre to relieve a *centuria* there. The CNT comrades had done sterling work. The trenches were dug and extremely well planned and I might even say comfortable. Covered access corridors connected the firing positions to a troglodyte city, which housed the units holding the position. These caves, out and out subterranean homes, hacked into the mountainside, offered us perfect shelter against the rigors of winter. It was actually quite chilly at that altitude, especially at night.

I shared my dugout with Affinenghi and two Spaniards, as well as Tarzan, my dog, who used to sleep at the foot of my bed. Anticipating a lengthy absence, I had taken the example of a number of comrades and brought my four-legged friend along. Tarzan fit right in on every count: he was black, with long, curly hair, which all but covered his eyes, and his paws were strong and muscled. All of which set him apart from the other canine personnel sharing our lives. The other dogs were greyhounds from the whippet family, bred for chasing down hares on flat ground; their paws were long and twitchy, their coats short and light in color. Tarzan never barked. Wherever I went, he stayed close by. On patrols, he kept a few meters ahead of me, muzzle in the air, ears cocked, vigilant for all sorts of smells, all sorts of sounds undetectable by me. Sometimes he would halt, and a soft growling sound would come from his throat like a whispered warning to me that there was a strange presence nearby. I reckon dogs are blessed with some sort of intelligence and that certain specimens of the canine variety can size up a given situation and act accordingly. To me, Tarzan was a clever dog. My evidence? Here goes: It had snowed all night and all through the day. The sierra was blanketed in snow. At about 1:00 a.m., I left my post after passing on the watchwords to the comrade who had arrived to relieve me. It was as cold as Siberia, and once beyond the communication trench I found myself in a lunar landscape of blank whiteness. Snow was still coming down. I was following Tarzan, trying to set my feet down in his paw prints, for the thick blanket of snow had obliterated any trail. We were almost back to my billet, but he stopped, pointing his head down into the valley below and growling softly. I patted him to calm him down, but the growling persisted, and his lips curled back as if to bite, and then he moved on ahead. I had no idea what was happening. I thought maybe he had picked up the scent of some hefty game bird and that that had roused his hunting instinct. Curiosity impelled me to follow behind him just to see how the hunt turned out and, if need be, to help out. Noiselessly we edged forward. Seeing that I was following him, Tarzan stopped growling, and everything was silent. At the bottom of a tall pine tree, he stopped and crouched down, ready to leap on his prey once it was in range. I was straining to see if there was anything moving nearby, in the gaps between the trees. What sort of game was he stalking? It was not long before I had my answer.

After a little while, I saw a dark shape emerge from cover, skip across the blanket of snow, and disappear behind a bush. Then one, two, three, four dark shapes skipping after the first one. A commando team trying to catch us unawares, capitalizing on the snowstorm and freezing cold. They had skirted around our lines by slipping in between two posts and planned to ambush us from behind, perhaps in the hope that if they were spotted before the attack, they might pass themselves off as republican strays.

At that moment, though, I was still figuring this out. After lobbing a Lafitte behind the bush, I opened up with my pistol. The exploding

The Col de Alcubierre, viewed from a position close to the one occupied by Orwell

grenade and gunshots woke everybody in less time that it takes to write as much. Armed men surrounded me now. My bomb and pistol shots had killed no one, but they were stopped in their tracks. We took five prisoners who were dispatched to HQ.

That wasn't the first time that dogs had gotten wind of the approach of enemy snipers, but they used to bark, warning us that they had scented the enemy, who then withdrew before we could strike. If I have dwelt at such length upon the intelligence and capabilities of my four-legged friend, it is because I cannot claim any of the credit for his education. But his first master must have been an ace trainer. I was astounded to discover his intelligence, bravery, and also his loyalty. Several Spanish comrades assured me that Tarzan was a poacher's dog. Now, never having been keen on hunting, I had never bothered to put that to the test. It was only six months after the military feat that I just described when Tarzan revealed his talents as a hunter. For almost a month we had been in a position that was, to say the least, not comfortable. Franco's artillery and aircraft had sworn to starve us out, and, with shelling and keeping us pinned down, they prevented food supplies from reaching us as normal. When the quartermaster corps did manage to get its chickpeas through to us, they were so undercooked that we had gotten into the habit of saying that we could fend off any attack successfully, using slingshots and chickpeas alone.

One morning, a chorus of exclamations drew my attention:

"Look, down yonder, that's a rabbit, no, a hare…. *Es demasiado lejo para tirar* [It's too far away to shoot at]…. Shall we let the dogs loose? Yes, yes, the dogs…."

Gaps were opened in the barbed wire defenses, and a yapping pack took off after the quarry it had smelled or seen. I had Tarzan on a leash, for he had developed the habit of sometimes going missing for hours on end, and I was afraid of his finishing up in the pot, as mincemeat, something that had already befallen some of his ilk.

One of my friends advised me to let him loose so that we could see how he performed in the coursing now underway. I removed his collar and, after a look at me, off he went like a lightning bolt … only to stop about a hundred meters from us. This was ridiculous: sending a dog of his caliber out hunting with beasts bred for that specific purpose, some of them with plenty of experience behind them. The hare, for hare it was, fled, leaping over tufts of thyme and rosemary, with the whole pack in his wake. My dog, after gazing at the quarry and the pursuers for a moment or two, seemed to lose interest in their frenzy and took off on a parallel course at a gentle trot…. I was gutted; I knew that my pal could not outrun hares. That is not what nature intended him for. I regretted having sent him off on this adventure in which he had no part to play. I was about to head back to my tent when a shout made me stop:

"Bravo, Tarzan! Bravo!"

Someone filled me in: instead of chasing after the hare, Tarzan had trotted off to position where he reckoned the hare had to pass by. And he was not mistaken. He grabbed it as it passed, and, with the quarry now between his teeth, he was running flat-out to seek my protection, for the entire pack was on his tail. My entire section went out to meet the dog and protect him from the others who might have turned on him just to recover their sought-after quarry.

But back to the sierra. Over the two months we spent there, aside from a few alerts during which we had to repel some minor raids, the days passed peaceably and uneventfully. Our task boiled down to standing guard and keeping our weapons in good order. Our free time we occupied as best we could: game players played endless games of cards, checkers, or chess; others whittled at blocks of wood; but the majority opted instead to listen to the lessons in history, geography, or sociology delivered by impromptu lecturers during the afternoons and evenings in a cave quite roomy enough to hold about thirty people.

The lecturer dealt with the same topic over several days and took questions, trying hard to get his message across to his audience and only moving on to another topic when there was no one left with queries. How often had I heard these words?

"For millennia now, those who did the producing had been rebelling against their exploiters. From Spartacus's rebellion up to the Russian revolt, workers and peasants have always fought to build the City of Happiness and have always been betrayed by those in whom they have placed their trust when they were lucky enough to have routed their enemy. Two instances of this; everybody is familiar with the French Revolution; as far as the French people, ground down by the nobility and clergy, were concerned, the Republic was synonymous with freedom and social justice; 'Men are born free and equal before the law.' Ah, but what law? The law laid down by the bourgeoisie in alliance with the clergy: 'The employer had supplanted the aristocrat. The working man and the peasant slave on.' But in spite of equality in the realm of economics and society having fallen through, humankind had smashed its strongest bond, belief in the divine right which made it feasible, with God's help and by his almighty will, for the people to be ground down and exploited. With the French Revolution, humanity embarked upon one of the final stretches on the road to freedom and equality between men. In Russia, the worker and peasant soviets drove out the nobles, the clergy and the Russian bourgeoisie, but they then placed their trust in a political party and its leaders, who, once ensconced in power, overhauled the machinery of the state by making it more efficient and more ruthless. Thanks to that, they robbed the workers' councils of all their prerogatives. Russia has succumbed to the rule of a new tsar who has emerged from the very ranks of the revolution. Capitalism goes by a different name. The nation's wealth is no longer the property of a few families. It belongs to the state, meaning that it is the property of the party dignitaries in power. In Russia, the dictatorship of the proletariat is in actual fact the dictatorship of the Communist Party; dictatorship means oppression, slavery, informers, violence, murder for those clamoring for the right to freedom and economic and social equality."{41}

And so we whiled away our time, trying to better our education and trying to share our knowledge with those who had not had the opportunity to sit at a school desk.

And then one find day, it was back to Farlete for us.{42}

LA NIÑA

Madeleine had taken off for Barcelona to see her husband and son.{43} I returned to Pina, where there too a certain change was discernible. The populace had moved on. The smallholders had voluntarily joined the collective. Huge tracts of land were now being farmed.{44} The girls and boys had shrugged off the yoke of the old morality, which had forbidden them to speak with one another without a chaperone.

I had evidence of this change right from the very first days that I was back in the *pueblo*. I was out strolling with Tarzan when someone called out to me:

"Stopped talking to people, have you, Antonio?"

It was a young girl with whom, prior to Perdiguera, I had had long conversations, along with La Calle, on the subject of woman's rights and obligations in the libertarian society, as we envisioned it. She was between twenty and twenty-five. Small, skinny, with a tanned triangular face like a gypsy's. She was no beauty but the moment one looked at her all one could see was her eyes and her mouth. Long, long lashes around her eyes made her dark pupils look even darker. Her full red lips were perfectly shaped—and all of this without the aid of any makeup, of course.

"Hi! I thought you'd be out in the garden. Where are you headed?"

"Just out for a bit of a stroll. I'm on leave. Fancy a glass of warm wine?"

"I'll take anything offered by a pretty girl."

"Come in now, and stop your nonsense."

The fire was smoldering in the hearth. The scent of mulled wine was coming from a saucepan set on the coals. I took a seat in one corner of the room, surprised not to find her mother or some neighbor woman there. I asked her:

"Where's your mother?"

"She's out in the fields with Father."

"So you're all on your own?"

"Yes."

"In that case, I thank you for your kindness, but I'm going to leave, because I don't want you to be the subject of gossip. Your fiancé would be none too happy to find out that you'd welcomed a man into your home and had been there alone with him."

"Changed times, Antoine. No one will say a word. I'm a grown-up. After seven years of engagement, Francisco has gone off to war and I haven't heard a thing from him since. Sit down and tell what has become of the comrades; we never see anyone here in Pina any more."

As she chatted, she poured the wine and sat down beside me on the bench. As I brought her up to date, I watched her; I found her altered, not physically, for she was still as spindly and thin as ever. Picking up on the fact that I was sizing her up, she asked me what I was thinking about, looking at her like that.

"Do you know, you've grown prettier than before I left?"

"You liar. I'm not blind. Nobody else has ever, ever talked about finding me pretty."

"And what do the lads say to you?"

"Nothing."

"And your fiancé?"

"He's gone."

"Yes, I know, but before he went didn't he ever tell you that you have the most beautiful eyes in the world, that anybody seeing your mouth has the urge to nibble it?"

She started laughing and said:

"Feel like a nibble at me, do you? Didn't you have any lunch?"

I set my glass down on the hearth stone. I took her face between my hands and kissed her on the lips. She pulled back.

"Forgive me, niña, I've been wanting to kiss you for a long time; but don't be afraid, I'm leaving now."

"Why? I'm not afraid of you."

There was a twinkle in her eye and her mouth partly opened in a smile affording a glimpse of the pink tip of her tongue. Her hands pressed on my shoulders to stop me from getting to my feet. By common accord, our lips met once more. Her trousers were open by the time I left, but she was still a virgin. On the doorstep, she asked me, in a whisper:

"Will you be back?"

"Yes, *querida*."

"*Mañana*?"

"Yes, tomorrow."

The following day I went back, as much to keep my promise as to let her know I was due to leave. That very morning I had been warned that my leave was over. I was to return to my unit in Farlete that night.

CNT militia members in Barcelona

As I stepped back indoors, all hopes of flirting with her evaporated; her mother was there, in front of a huge stack of laundry needing ironing. After the usual pleasantries, I told her that I would be leaving. In alarm the girl asked me:

"Right now? "

"No, tonight."

"Then we still have some time. You'll have supper with us. My mother will let Tía Pascuala know."

Taken aback at the snap decision making, which was not customary in Spanish families at the time, I suggested that she should deliver the message, as her mother was very elderly. The old woman beat her daughter to an answer:

"Son, you have only a few hours left to chat together. Don't waste them."

And in a voice laden with sadness, she added:

"Enjoy life while there is still time."{45}

The girl took my hand and said:

"Come along, Antoine, come along."

"Where?"

"Upstairs!"

ENDNOTE {45}: 375

I followed her. I was bewildered. I had helped Vicenta and Maria move some furniture in their bedrooms, but this girl had not led me up to her room for my strength, as she hadn't asked me to help with anything with her mother present. At the top of the stairs, now out of earshot of her mother, I asked her:

"What are doing up here, *niña*? It's risky, your mother being downstairs, She might walk in on us."

"*Tonto* (Dummy)," she replied, "I've told her everything. My mother has stayed home so that we can be free to do whatever we want." Then, pushing at one door, she said:

"And this is my room."

As she said, it she bolted the door and turned the key. I was astonished, I'll freely admit it. I must have looked like a duck that had stumbled upon the knife. Luckily, the confidence she had been displaying till now evaporated; she was as troubled as I was. For a moment, we just stared at each other in silence. I remember asking her to let down her hair, which she wore in a large bun. I felt silly and awkward. I no longer wanted to have fun with her. Seeing her there so tiny and fragile, I was afraid of hurting her or damaging her. I would have walked away had I been able to so without shocking her, without telling her that I did not think she would be up it. Her disappointment might well have been more hurtful than anything else.

I went over to her and began unbuttoning her dress. Her hair hung almost to her ankle, providing her with a shifting black cloak that she threw behind her once the final item of clothing had been cast aside to display the tiny model of her lovely female form. The top of her head reached only as far as my chin and her breasts were like two medium-sized pears, each tipped with a pale pink nipple. She could easily have been mistaken for a young girl of thirteen or fourteen had it not been for the dark patch of her pubic hair spilling out and overshadowing her upper thighs. I lifted her up to place her on the bed; slipping her arms about my neck, she took my mouth in a kiss that took my breath away. When I came up for air, she murmured:

"*Ponte en cuero también.*" (Now you get naked too.)

In a single bound, she was off the bed to helping me peel off everything that might get in her way. In less time than it takes to tell it, we were both in our birthday suits: Adam and Eve before the original sin. She clambered back onto the bed, which was very high, and stretched across it, her legs dangling, her thighs slightly parted. I leaned over her;

my mouth clamped to one breast and a hand on the other. I spent a long time caressing her like that. I knew that she was a virgin, and I was afraid, not of any consequences, for she was willing enough, but of my hurting unduly and ruining her appetite for love-making and men. My hand left her breast, sliding down her belly, skimming the dark patch and slipping between her thighs where my fingers began to play. My mouth in turn abandoned its prey and, bending my knees, I kissed her clitoris. Startled, she arched her back and said:

"*Tómame, tómame toda.*" (Take me, take me all.)

After the first spasm she remained still, as if asleep. My tongue and lips carried on with their caresses and again her belly started quivering slightly. With my palms, I could feel her nipples stiffening and my fingers were sensible of the heat from her breasts, hardening with pleasure.

When I entered her, she cried in pain. Then, taking me by the shoulders, she drew me to her and held me while her legs encircled my kidneys as if to stop me from withdrawing. Only her belly danced to the rhythm of pleasure. For a brief moment we remained entwined, saying nothing. I was gazing at a face that I no longer recognized. A face that seemed younger and almost beautiful.

The first thing she said filled me with unease:

"Darling, thank you for having made me a woman ... your woman."

I felt myself blanch. Astounded, I stared at her. All of a sudden, I felt as if I had walked into a trap. I started laughing:

"My woman! But don't you know that I'm already married? As far as I am aware, I made you no promise of marriage."

"No, you don't understand. You can go; this very night you may go who knows where. You may never return, but I am and will be your woman. Yesterday, you pleasured me with your caresses and refused to take advantage of me. Which is why I asked you back again. I shall never marry."

"Are you crazy? What about your fiancé?"

"My fiancé was marrying my father's land, not me. The other boys talked to me like I was a sister of theirs. But they all found me too small and too weak to make a proper wife capable of bearing children while helping them with their work."

I enfolded her in my arms again, but she broke away and said:

"Augusta told me that after love-making, one should wash. Do you want to clean up?"

Augusta, La Calle, Louis. All the others. They were gone, but their lessons were bearing the fruit they had hoped for. Briefly, it was like I could see them again, spreading our principles and our beliefs, but the girl's gay laughter brought me back down to earth.

"Look, darling." She showed me the blood smears on the white sheets. "Come, take me again, *hazme gozar* (pleasure me)."

SIÉTAMO

At nightfall, we set off for destination unknown. By daybreak, the trucks had dropped us off in a field on the edge of an olive grove under the branches of which we sheltered in order to escape the eyes of the pilots of Francoist planes.[1]

As dusk fell, we set off on our march again. For hours, we marched single file, following barely discernible trails, weaving through the shadows of the hedges that marked the boundaries of the plowed fields, for the moon shed its light upon us like some lighthouse lost in space.

Eventually we came to an abandoned farmhouse. We were exhausted. There was only one thing I wanted: to get some sleep. Which is what I did. My little team followed suit. Stretched out on the ground, heads leaning on the kits that we never unpacked in case we needed to move off again, we sought the oblivion that, despite our weariness or perhaps because of it, was slow in coming. Then two gunshots erupted. We leapt to our feet and dashed outside. A Spaniard stopped us, calling out:

"*Calma, compañeros*; nothing serious. We killed that bastard Ruano."[2]{46}

Ruano, the man responsible for the butchery in Perdiguera, had just paid the price for his treachery. We surrounded the comrade, bombarding him with questions. Where were we? Was this a staging-post or journey's end? He informed us that we were just outside Siétamo, a village overlooked by a castle stronghold. It had been occupied by Franco's army and some Falangists but had been all but overrun by the POUM's columns. Pablo had just delivered the briefing we needed, plus the passwords and some advice that he thought we needed in the situation in which we found ourselves. Then, before the sun came up, he was off to make contact with the command of the forces surrounding the village.

---

1   Given the author's jumbling of the chronology, the entire next part of the text up to the chapter entitled "Sariñena" should have come before the chapter entitled "Farlete," earlier in this manuscript. As a result, we are now some time before September 12, 1936, and the International Group is still under the leadership of Louis Berthomieu.

2   The original manuscript has the name spelled *Roano*.

The first rays of the sun revealed the precariousness of our position. We were caught in the crossfire; on one side, the rifles lurking in the houses and in the fort; on the other, mortar and light artillery fire, as was obvious from the shell craters on the walls, on the roof of the farm, and all along the line of trenches trailing right and left of the outhouses.

The Spanish units had held the position before us; pinned down by the coordinated artillery fire and the guns spitting death from the fort and from the windows of the houses, they had abandoned their posts, leaving a gap through which reinforcements and fresh supplies could reach the garrison. That was made that much easier because the highway cut through our lines about fifty meters from where we now stood. From what Pablo told us, we had been sent there to close that gap and attack the village.

Otto summed up the situation:

"The second they get sight of us, they'll pound us with shrapnel. Then it's good night, company."

There were about twenty of us, twenty-five maximum. The veterans among us, the ones who had been with the group prior to Perdiguera and who had known Berthomieu, gave the newer recruits a quick rundown on the procedures to be followed. We made up our minds to play dead until night fell, then, before the moon could rise, to surge forward and go and dig in nearer the village houses. That maneuver had the advantage of dropping us out of reach of the automatic gunfire from the fortress and perhaps thwarting the artillery barrage that, in the adjusting of the guns, ran the risk of firing a few shells on Siétamo itself.{47}

We spent the entire day making plans. Louis had always told us that, when on a mission, it was up to us to devise the best solution to our problems, without waiting for some commander to hand us one. I remember that Affinenghi suggested we launch an attack as soon as the bombardment started and, if by chance a shell landed on the outlying houses, to capitalize upon the defenders' dismay and enter the village. All day long he pushed his plan and refused to concede to any other ideas. Luckily, events were not on his side. And we were not obliged to follow the example of Simple Simon and jump into the water in order to keep out of the rain.

When the moon rose, we were about fifty meters from the walls of the village's first house. A double line of trees hid us from view. Two

Siétamo village prior to the civil war, with castle on the left

small outbuildings—a barn and a stable—served as our support bases
and HQ. The entire area was checkered like a chess board, with each
field bounded by a hedge of tall trees and bushes. The field between our
HQ and the road that followed the contours of the village, passing by
the bottom of the castle, was also entirely lined with trees and bushes.
We capitalized on the denseness of that natural barrier and positioned
our guard posts within just meters of the very windows from which
our foes were sniping at us. It was risky, but, as long as we were quiet
about it and didn't talk while on guard duty, they had no way of guess-
ing that we were so close by.

The first action came toward midday. We had dispatched a runner
to let Pablo know about our forward surge. It was broad daylight by
the time he got back, and the snipers in the castle spotted him just as
he was crossing some open ground, greeting him with a few bursts
of machine-gun fire. We watched as he dived from tree to bush in an
effort to reach the huge hedge at right angles to the village, a hedge
that we had followed on leaving our initial position and that shielded
him from the enemy's eyes. At that point Affinenghi, with his typical
contempt for danger, broke into a run and, with his hands near ground
level, loped up the hill and disappeared into the curtain of greenery,
shaking the shrubbery and bushes. Our runner had now arrived and

delivered his report, but the machine gun was still directing its fire into the hedge where the branches were still shaking ever closer to our former position. It was after nightfall before Affinenghi reappeared. Chuckling, he said that from the moment the enemy learned that we were manning the hillside, there was nothing more to worry about. He had lit a good fire and covered it over with plenty of dead leaves in the hope that at dawn it might still be smoldering and suggesting our presence there. That would get them to squander a few shells and quite a bit of ammunition. A tide of criticism greeted these revelations. He alone was delighted with his idea. He went off, seething with anger, to relieve a comrade from guard duty, just so that he would not have to listen to us any more.

Every one of us was assailed by uncertainty and doubts. The word from HQ was straightforward, with no equivocation possible. The position was to be defended at all costs, and, until such time as the day came for us to attack, we were to look for a gap in the enemy deployment or discover his weak points.

We spent the night mounting patrols and doing the rounds of the guard posts we had set up all around our camp, and didn't turn in until the very early hours. I was woken by some explosions. Affinenghi had been right; they were pounding the entire lower slopes with mortar fire.

For ten days or so, we hid like foxes in their dens, coming out only at night and keeping to the line of the hedges, detouring dozens of meters in order to have the shrubbery for cover as we relieved our sentries. Crossing open ground by day or even on a clear night meant, at best, a visit to the hospital.

It was in Siétamo that I took my one and only war prize: my share of the loot for twenty-eight months of warfare, as well as a pair of binoculars that I still have at home. Otto and I were out doing the rounds. Everything was quiet; absolute silence. We had reached the furthest area of our deployment and were about to head back when the guy on guard signaled for us to stop. There was a faint noise coming from the road. And it was coming closer. Otto darted over to head off whatever it was. I followed. When we got to the end of the hedge we saw two shadows on the road about to climb the embankment into the meadow. Otto showed me his knife; I understood. I drew my dagger and waited. As supple as a snake, Otto edged a little closer to the embankment.

The first of the shadowy figures jumped, landing on his heels, but, having miscalculated the drop, took a spill and then got to his feet. My adversary was less than two meters ahead of me with his back to me. His comrade jumped in turn. My mouth was dry, my head about to explode. I could feel my heart pounding like a drum at a funeral march. I took a leap, my fist clutching my dagger, planning to the strike between the shoulders. He turned to face me. My arm fell, the blade plunging, up to the hilt, into his left shoulder. He slumped without a word. Otto had cut the throat of the other Francoist army soldier. We gathered up their weapons: a standard army-issue rifle and a regulation handgun carried by the one I had slain. He was an officer and also had some binoculars, which I hung on to as a souvenir, for up until that point I had not taken anything for myself.

BELIEF

Ten days there; a comparatively long time. The first days had been spent on the fortification of our position. Then, since patrols, stints on guard duty, and sleep left us some free time, we tried to pass our leisure time in whatever activity pleased each of us the best. In the early days, the motley personalities making up our unit banded together in according to their tastes and affinities and likes: card players, checkers players, domino players, or odd-job men who spent their time touching up our trenches. Finally, there were those like me, who wrote page after page in a notebook dallying with the muses or writing short stories or articles that were then read out.

Sometimes by day and sometimes at night one of us would cobble together a sort of talk on some topic; we used to refer to them as our "lullaby-singers" since most of us dropped off to sleep before they reached the end. Everything and anything was an excuse for such long speeches and more or less logical musings.

One afternoon, having just got back from doing the rounds, I decided to stretch out on the ground in the lukewarm sunshine (this was in winter),[1] with my knapsack and cape for a pillow. Scolari, Otto, and a few others were also basking in the sunshine until it was time for the relief, when Mario, who had been pacing the yard, immersed in some problem, came over to us. He showed us a small silvery cross, likes the ones young girls wear on a little chain around their necks, and said:

"*Compañeros*, here you have the instrument of the mighty works which, two thousand years ago, were enough to send condemned men to their deaths. If a fellow like the one they call Jesus were round nowadays, in Spain they'd have him garroted, in France, guillotined, in England they'd string him up and in two thousand years' time there'd be a little guillotine or tiny little gibbet adorning our partners' daughters' bodices. You see, my friends, my comrades, our society is the same as the one that was around back in the days when that vagabond, dreamer, and poet was tramping the roads of Galilee, preaching equality among men and calling for justice and freedom.

"If he ever really existed, Jesus was what would be described today as a revolutionary propagandist. Actually, who were his disciples and

---

[1]   In reality, this takes place in September.

from where were his recruits drawn? From the most wretched strata of the society of the day; from among the slaves, the fishermen, the laborers. Massacres and persecutions show that the ideas peddled by that dreamer, ideas such as freedom, equality, and justice, struck fear into the ruling classes of the time. The numbers of his followers were legion. Fleeing persecution, the militants took to every road in the world, preaching their impossible dream. Jesus, the troubadour who made a living telling his parables wherever the road led him, must have been a fabulous storyteller, intelligent, and sensible of poverty, to have struck such fear into the bourgeois, the clergy, and the Roman army occupying the land of his birth, so together they decided to make an example of him by crucifying him. In order to rule and tame and stymie the thirst for justice, which posed a threat to the very foundations of society, they made him into a god. Jesus was probably not the only one peddling such notions or the first. As I see it, he was the one executed with the greatest fanfare and the most cruelty. His death remains etched into the memory of his disciples who have told the story, embellished to suit the needs of the cause.

"Unscrupulous men, some of them clever and crafty, cashing in on the people's ignorance, assumed the leadership of that vast movement, turning it into the instrument of oppression and willing slavery by organizing the power of the Roman Catholic Church. Spiritual power, allied with temporal power; social order was salvaged as were the privileges of the ruling classes. Jesus, the shoeless, has become the very symbol of submissiveness, resignation in the face of wretchedness and slavery.

"And God? No, I am not a believer in God, for I don't like hatred. If God existed I would have to hate him for all the evil that he allows humanity to endure. The very same humanity that, according to the faithful, he made with his very own hands and in his own image. One cannot love a father who dooms his children to pestilence, cholera, tuberculosis, cancer, and all the other woes that afflict the world. This Almighty Father that allows the vast majority of his children to sweat so that a tiny minority can claim all the earth's asserts. Don't talk to me about free will, which he is supposed to have left men. An endlessly powerful, infinitely kind father looks on while his children so misuse the freedom he had accorded them, would, if he truly loved them, have quickly mended their shortcomings. If he cannot do so, he must be a poor fellow, or, if he will not, he's a bastard deserving only contempt and disgust.

"But there is no God; he sprang from men's ignorance and from the need to explain away the natural phenomena of the causes of which they knew nothing. Man is a queer sort of a beast: he needs to know the reason behind things, and in order to explain away the origin or cause of some phenomenon, when he does not know one, he invents one. When the intellect began to blossom, primitive man raised countless questions for which he could devise no answers. So he populated the whole environment with gods, spirits, and demons. As his knowledge expanded, these supernatural beings have departed this earth and sought refuge in the vastness of space. It is out of fear of losing their privileges that the churches have always been against the advances of science."

ATTACK

That was how we whiled away our free time between stints of guard duty and patrols. Death roamed around us, ever present. Sometimes one of our own perished, the victim of carelessness on his part or an urge to die. Yes, at least one of those who perished in Siétamo had taken his own life. I can no longer recall his name. He was about sixty years of age. He joined the group shortly after its formation, but he never spoke to anybody and was always standoffish. One day, on his way to guard duty, instead of keeping low and sticking close to the hedge, which screened us from the eyes of the snipers, he walked across the field diagonally. A bullet hit him right in the head. We discovered from some papers and press clippings that he was wanted by the police for something that was a far cry from the social struggle. He and two accomplices had killed two rentiers in the course of an attack.

Not that this was a surprise. We knew that many among us had unsettled matters with the police for things unrelated to social struggle, but as long as they abided by the rules we'd made for ourselves we gave them no grief. As I said, this fellow actively sought death, as openly crossing that meadow meant giving the opposition's best marksmen a target, and we all knew it.

One night, we decided to attack. We'd noticed a doorway without a shooter. A little further along to the left and to the right there were machine guns in the windows, meaning six or seven meters away from the spot. Maybe it was a trap. We'd find out soon enough.

We'd decided to wriggle across the gap on our bellies so as to give the snipers less of a chance of seeing us. Though there was no moon, "the white light falling from the stars" might very well give us away. Affinenghi was to cross first. Being the best built of us all, it would be easier for him to break down that unmanned door. Stubborn as a mule, he tried to cover the ground by jumping across the road. He stood on the embankment and collapsed with a bullet in his thigh. As luck would have it, I was supposed to follow him. With the Savoyard downed, it was now up to me to try my luck. Getting across a road isn't the greatest challenge, but the three-meter gap between me and my target seemed unbridgeable. I set off wriggling across the ground, jaws clenched to stop my teeth from chattering. The pick head in my waistband felt like a leaden weight against my back, and there was only one thought in my head: when you hear the report, the bullet will be a long way away ... the bullet will be a long way away.

I could touch the wall with the tips of my fingers. Gunshots were crackling all around, but they were too late for I was now across. I stood up, flattening myself against the wall. Dangling above the lock there was a length of rope tied into a huge knot: the latch. I gave it a tug; the door opened, it was unlocked. Maybe it was a trap. I removed the pin from a grenade, shoved the door as hard as I could, and hurled it inside. The shooting died down. Ritter's and Otto's automatic rifles had had the better of the enemy.{48}

Some comrades joined me and burst into the house. There were only two rooms; a ground floor and another that offered no access to the other buildings. Every man became a demolition laborer, and we brought down the partition walls. Daylight was beginning to break through by the time we had ensured complete control over the first floor of the building. We tried venturing onto the street, but it was impossible, due to a number of well-placed automatic weapons. With about ten comrades, I went out the way I'd come in, and we did the rounds of the block of houses. We found ourselves in a small square with one street leading away from it. One side was in our control, the other still in Falangist hands. The street led to the foot of the castle. The entire village looked abandoned; not a single shot greeted our arrival on the square. One of us took off running. A burst of gunfire dropped him. Another took off and was brought down as well. Getting through was proving a dangerous business. Scolari grabbed a rifle from the hands of one comrade and vanished into the house beside us. Jacques, the moviemaker, signaled to me that I should follow him.{49}

I did the rounds of the square, sticking close to the walls. When we reached the street, we took off running. A shot rang out, but we were through. We darted inside one building, climbed the stairs to the top floor and then out onto the roof. We broke quite a number of tiles but otherwise reached the church steeple without mishap. Jacques pulled a red and black flag out of his pocket and secured it to the steeple. We'd done it.

Surprised that no one was shooting at us, we calmly retreated back down into the deserted church; after making sure that no one was hiding there, we went down into the basement. There we were surprised to find three soldiers hiding behind a marble statue, waiting for us. They came out from their hiding place with their arms in the air.

ENDNOTE {48}: 385; ENDNOTE {49}: 388

The back of the church, from where Gimenez's group mounted its attack

We learned from them that the entire garrison had been ordered to withdraw into the castle and that the villagers had been held in the basement there ever since the beginning of the siege.

Having delivered these surrendered soldiers to our CP, I set off to systematically comb through every house in the village. They all looked like hastily abandoned homes; closets gaped open, beds were unmade, clothing was strewn around. There was only one thing that had been done meticulously: every morsel of food had been removed. Not a crust of bread or a handful of grain in the granaries. I will say nothing of the hens and rabbits, for they too were spectacularly absent. Only the condition of the dead showed that the village had not been deserted long. The blood was still wet. I remember because I stepped in one of the pools of blood, lost my footing, and stumbled against a little low door—previously overlooked—which led to stairs to a cellar.

The first thing I spotted down there was a ham dangling from the main rafter. Drawing my dagger, slicing off and gobbling down a morsel took less time than it takes to tell of it. Once I had collected myself, I drew up an inventory: there were a few hams and a barrel or two of wine. I unhooked the hams, refilled my canteen, and emerged from the house to be greeted by whoops of delight from my comrades who were surprised by this windfall. That day we ate like capitalists:

The central square in Siétamo during the fighting

plain ham washed down with a little local wine, which asked nothing more than to be drunk.

With the village now occupied, we gathered around the castle, calling on the garrison to surrender so that we could avert unnecessary bloodshed. No response but a volley of shots, so Otto, tired of waiting, walked into the open, planning use a grenade to blast a passage in. We watched as he pulled up short and then fell. Scolari and another guy darted out to get him. We let off hellish gunfire by way of covering them, all our weapons spitting death. Otto was dragged back to our cover. I was too far away to see for myself, but someone told me that Otto was dead; shot right through the heart. Other units arrived to relieve us soon after:

"They got Otto. He's dead."

The loss of my friend made our victory less sweet. Scolari, Affiinenghi, Ritter, and I accompanied the stretcher-bearers who went to get Otto. We wanted to see our comrade one last time. He was at the bottom of the stairs where Scolari had left him, lying on his back, his arms by his side like a horizontal sentry, but his big, wide-open eyes stared at us and moved. We rushed over to him. A stretcher-bearer undid his jerkin to inspect the wound, but there wasn't a drop of blood. On the left side of his chest, there was a bluish mark, a bruise about the size of a coin. That was all that was wrong with him. He had been unconscious for about two hours. When we showed up, he was just getting his bearings again in a world we thought he had departed forever. Mysterious quirk of ballistics? Defective bullet? Or was it the inscrutable law of fate? I only asked myself those questions much later—in 1944—when I discovered that he had died near Limoges, fighting in the ranks of the Resistance.[1]

At the time the only thing that mattered was that my German friend was still alive, that he could go on playing his harmonica to our great delight as he accompanied the singing of Mario, Ritter, or García. A couple of good swallows of cognac, generously offered by the stretcher-bearers, and Otto was nearly as good as new again. Still a bit on the weak side, he got to his feet, putting his weight on us, and asked "Have they surrendered?"

Those were the very first words he said. The bullet that hit him had smashed a pair of spectacles and lodged in his wallet.

In the village, there were three abandoned cars. We took one, and the five of us sped off for a spin around the castle. We were laughing and singing and yelling like kids with a day off or playing hooky. Only Ritter knew how to drive. He took the wheel, but after a few minutes someone else wanted to try. We were all a bit giddy and took turns driving. When it was my turn, the car, which had been rather compliant with others, began weaving around drunkenly. We were swinging from right to left and laughing like lunatics. In the end, annoyed maybe that it had failed to scare us, the car suddenly decided to leave the road behind and rolled over into the ditch. We made our way back on foot.

When we got back to CP, there was a surprise waiting for us. Aznar, one of the soldiers we had found in the church basement, had been able to prove that he had been active in a workers' organization before his military service, and he was granted the right to tag along with us. As we ate, he told us that every one of the village inhabitants was locked up in the castle dungeons, that the men of arms-bearing age had been forced into service and were defending the place. It turns out that he had been one of the men at the machine-gun post on the left side when I'd crossed the highway, and he told me that I'd succeeded because the machine-gunner was sure that, since there had been

I   We have discovered a German anarchist who served with the Durruti Column and fought in the French Resistance. This was Helmut Thomas, killed as part of the maquis in the Aude department in 1944. See http://www.gimenologues.org/spip.php?article626.

no patrol—and once Affinenghi had been brought down—no one else would try to cross for the rest of the night. By the time he'd scrambled back into position, I had already crossed and our automatic rifles had gone into action.

We went to bed very late that night. Mario sang his old Neapolitan songs, Ritter regaled us with Tyrolean songs, a Spanish comrade recited some of the poems of Federico García Lorca, all to the accompaniment of Otto's harmonica.

I have never been able to explain how the garrison we had under siege managed to escape. All I can say is that, in the early morning hours, the gates opened and the women, children, and old men of the village emerged, shaking with fear.

That evening, we left Siétamo forever to go and take up our positions about ten kilometers away in Loporzano.{50} As far as I was concerned, that village was nothing more than a few hours of stopover. It wouldn't be worth mentioning except that, after a good night's sleep, I had woken up with a slight ache in my jaw: it was the first time I'd ever had a toothache.

SARIÑENA

Typical of military logic, after telling us to move ten kilometers north of Siétamo, I was ordered to take a truckload of arms and munitions south. We were to head for Farlete on roads that followed the Sierra de Alcubierre, doing what we could to avoid the towns and villages occupied by POUM or PSUC units, which might have commandeered our truck.

Our newest recruit, Aznar, was at the wheel and telling me about life under siege and—for the tenth time—describing how, for ten days, their ears had been cocked for the slightest sound in the night; how, convinced that we were trying to starve them out, they'd relaxed; and how, once the patrols had passed by, they used to play cards, which is how I managed to get across. After opening fire at Affinenghi, they were convinced that, as had been the case on previous nights, we'd turn in for the night, taking our wounded comrade with us.

A few kilometers south of Siétamo we were intercepted by a group of irregulars who forced us to leave the passable trails and head cross country. The two comrades in the back were wounded during the shooting. Thanks to their courage and Aznar's cool head we managed to shake off our attackers, but in the course of escaping we got lost. Unfamiliar with the area, we were obliged to drive on pretty much blind, heading southeast.

A steeple loomed on the horizon just as the engine started to fail, and Aznar started cursing like a sailor:

"Me cago en Dios y en su puta madre, hijos de putas de todos los santos!"

The truck came to a halt; we'd run out of gas. Aznar and the two wounded comrades—whose wounds were slight—asked me to go and find help. According to them, I was the best marcher. Aznar had to stay behind to booby-trap the truck and blow it up if necessary.

It took me an hour to reach Sariñena, a little fiefdom of the POUM. The POUM's militias were organized in the class style of every army in the world; rank meant everything, and there was no arguing. At their HQ, I approached an orderly who referred me to the corporal, the corporal to his sergeant, and so on until I got to the captain who showed me into a large room, telling me I should wait there. The commanding officer was at a meeting, and the captain was not empowered to assign men with a car to bring out the required gasoline. My toothache was flaring again; it was as if needles were being hammered into my skull.

How long did I pace that room? I have no idea. I remember head-butting a door open and finding myself in a lecture room. A dozen people seated around a long table rose to their feet, startled by my intrusion. I shouted to them that I needed gas to get the truck rolling again and that I wanted to talk to whomever was in command there. They gathered around me, asking me who I was and where I'd come from. As if by magic, my toothache eased up. Orders were barked. I jumped onto a motorcycle, and the rider took off cross country, followed by a tiny car laden with gas cans.

By evening we were billeted in Sariñena, and I had lost my first molar. Our victory in Siétamo was nothing when it came to the progress of the war.[1] The news was not good; Durruti had set off for Madrid, which was besieged by Franco's divisions.{51} Franco had taken over following the deaths of Generals Mola and Sanjurjo. In Seville, Queipo de Llano was supervising the push against Málaga. Up in the North (Asturias and the Basque Country), the fighting was still going strong.{52}

In Pina, I'd finally admit to myself that "Gori" had been murdered by the communists in Madrid, outside the University City.{53} I had already been told about his death, but I had refused to believe it, because ever since I'd met him, I had thought he was a dead man time and again. This time, though, the news was true. The communists hadn't messed up. Manzana had replaced him at the head of the column, which they were beginning to refer to as a "division"—just the way our *centurias* had been turned into "companies."{54}

During the early weeks, we tramped the Aragon front from the Sierra de Alcubierre to Velilla de Ebro. Reconnaissance patrols and raids alternated with stays in Pina, where I had reoccupied my digs at Tía Pascuala's. She always delighted to welcome me in like the prodigal son every time I returned.

Madeleine was back from Barcelona. Her partner was still in hospital, making a slow recovery from his wounds. She used me as a sounding-board and would tell me that her countrymen didn't know how to satisfy her. Unfortunately for her, in Pina, I slept at La Madre's and she was billeted with a different family, and it was almost impossible for us to snatch enough time together to satisfy her. So she got back at me

---

1   Antoine's narrative is back on track here: we are now in late November 1936.

ENDNOTE {51}: 401; ENDNOTE {52}: 405; ENDNOTE {53}: 407; ENDNOTE {54}: 425

by not giving me any space the whole time I was in there. No matter where I went, she followed me around. I was often with Tarzan and Madeleine, and we looked like a couple out walking the family dog.

The news she brought back from the Catalan capital was depressing. The power struggle between the various factions in the republican camp was continuing. The CNT was now part of the government through García Oliver and Federica Montseny. Such partnership with the government, even if it was described as a coalition, amounted to treachery in my eyes and was proof that we hadn't been clear-sighted enough to know that we shouldn't be embracing the leadership style of the political parties and sitting at their table. But while doing our bit for the war effort, we had to retain our independence in social terms so that we could reject any law or systemic reform that might have flown in the face of the basic freedoms of the producer masses.

The reorganization of the column into battalions, companies, et cetera, was continuing. Gritting their teeth, the comrades were agreeing to be led by officers who were nearly always chosen by the troops or the union. These changes were most poorly received inside the International Group, so much so that a team of militants was sent down from Barcelona to persuade them to embrace the new arrangements, at least outwardly and on paper. María Ascaso was one member of that team. She dropped in to see me in Velilla de Ebro to give me a pack of French cigarettes and to take me to task for not coming to the meeting held at divisional CP, a meeting designed to persuade us to at least go through the motions of bowing to the demands of the restructuring of the republican armed forces.

We spent an entire afternoon arguing. She tried to convince me of the need for us to reassure the democracies, such as France and England, by making them believe that we were standing up for the Republic and had a strong, disciplined army ready to defend society as it stood on its territory. I tried to get her to understand that we were a group of irregulars with arrangements of our own and that we could be more effective by remaining outside of the army. I managed to convince her that I was right, but my success was short-lived. The majority of the group's members caved in to suggestions from the propaganda team, which returned to Barcelona proud of having accomplished its mission.{55}

The only tangible result from militarization was that nearly all the Germans and a sizable number of the French and Italians left us in order to swell the ranks of the [International] Brigades in Albacete.

ENDNOTE {55}: 428

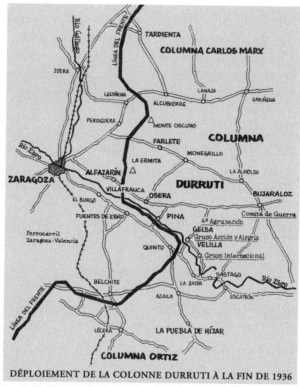

DÉPLOIEMENT DE LA COLONNE DURRUTI À LA FIN DE 1936

Deployment of the Durruti Column at the end of 1936

Durruti's murder had seriously shaken any appetite I might have had for the fight. My friends Scolari, Giua, Otto, Mario, and Ritter belonged, with me, to a small band unfriendly toward militarization and the discipline that it entailed. Pablo knew that he could rely on us when it came to the crunch as long as he didn't ask us to do things that we had always refused to do—even though they might cost us our freedom or material well-being. We were nearly all draft-dodgers or deserters.{56} The exodus of comrades toward the International Brigades had cost us half of our strength. Pablo decided to send me to Barcelona to recruit more Italians and French and others from the Catalan capital, volunteers to swell our ranks; Giua, Ritter, and Otto came with me.[2]{57}

2   Another chronological mistake on Antoine's part: he is not talking here about the April 12, 1937, battle of Santa Quiteria, as he plainly describes that fighting later on, in the chapter entitled "Rosario's Death."

ENDNOTE {56}: 440; ENDNOTE {57}: 447

BARCELONA: MAY 1937

The moment she found out that I was due to leave for Barcelona, Madeleine, unhappy with her stay in Pina (the group's constant redeployment had virtually stopped us from seeing each other face to face as we might have wished) announced to Pablo that her husband had called her to his bedside and that she was going with us. In Barcelona, the union had requisitioned an apartment for her in a street adjacent to the Diagonal,[1] the city's longest arterial route—before to the uprising, it had been the plushest quarter of the city.

It was in that apartment of hers that she talked me into staying there during my time in the city. That kept me out of the city center and away from the skirmishes that erupted a few days later between supports of the Communist Party on one side and of CNT and POUM supporters on the other.

As the door closed behind us, Madeleine set her luggage down and turned to me. She threw her arms around me and whispered, "Alone at last."

I often wondered back then what it was about her that made her crave caresses and kisses. Did she unwittingly sense somehow that her days were numbered? That she had only a few more months left in which to enjoy life? Whether or not she had a premonition of imminent death or something else, I don't know; I do know, though, that she was insatiable. Inside the apartment, we went around naked all the time; often, when we were in different rooms, she would call out to me:

"Come here, Tony."

"What do you want?"

"Come here!"

Then, once I was near her, she would say to me, breathlessly:

"Caress me, darling."

I would accede to her request with pleasure for I loved her moist skin, soft to the touch.

Those first few days flashed by. Then, one evening, the doorbell rang. It was her son, a young man about fifteen or sixteen; just in from

---

1   Possibly the Calle del Francoli (see below), though it does not intersect with the Diagonal.

France. His presence brought us back to reality and meant we had to venture outside and reestablish contact with the world.

Barcelona was in turmoil; the power struggle between the different factions was at its peak. The anarchists had been on edge following Durruti's murder. Shots were fired, and bombs exploded here and there around the city. Police personnel from the Communist Party, CNT, PSUC, and POUM criss-crossed the city, checking passers-by. I say "police" because the CP had its own secret police corps, modeled after its Russian equivalent, and the CNT and the other political factions had organized control patrols to combat the fifth column. Each faction had its private police force, and that did nobody any good.{58}

One morning, I bumped into Berneri at the union. Since we were under pressure to establish contacts, with an eye to recruitment of our volunteers, we arranged to meet up the next day, *a media tarde* (in mid-afternoon).{59} I would never see him again. That evening, I was told that the communists had overrun the Telefónica and that Berneri and his friend Barbieri had been summoned to the Generalidad and killed.[2]{60}

First Durruti and now Berneri. The communists, fans of absolute power, were teaching a definitive and radical lesson to anyone who might oppose their hegemony over the masses.

Communism, the new religion—with Marx and Lenin for its two-headed God and Stalin as its prophet—as fanatical with its ruthless police, as any medieval Christian or Muslim with their Inquisition. The communists would tolerate no argument with their dogmas, or support any ideas or views that were more liberal or more revolutionary than their own. They were always ready to end any movement once it was in danger of slipping out of their control and turning into a self-managerial revolution. (Just as Maurice Thorez had in the France of 1936 with his dictum: "One has to know when to halt a strike.") As far as the communists were concerned, the worker and peasant masses had just one duty: obedience to their directives, and individuals should not express views other than those consistent with the line drawn by the party leadership.

I knew that after Alexander Staradoff had sought an alliance with Nestor Makhno, who with his libertarian guerrillas had driven the

---

2   Antoine may be telescoping things somewhat since the news of Berneri's death did not break until May 6.

ENDNOTE {58}: 456; ENDNOTE {59}: 462; ENDNOTE {60}: 463

armies of Wrangel and Denikin out of the Ukraine, the communists had mounted a surprise attack on his camp. Makhno managed to get away and fled to France. Staradoff, taken prisoner, was banished to Siberia. He carried one memory from his days in the salt mines there: the shackles around his wrists and ankles. Deportees toiled in chains. The salt dust, slipping between the steel and the flesh, had burned the skin and left whitened circles where the shackles had been.

Madeleine and I set off to rejoin the comrades fighting in the city. Barricades sealed off certain crossroads. As we made our way toward the city center, we stopped off at the German "Spartacus" group's HQ, in front of which the pavement was being ripped up to build a barricade.{61} Madeleine knew quite a few people and asked if we could join that group. It made no difference to me whether we were there or somewhere else. Berneri's death had rid me of any inclination or urge I might have had to do anything, even fight. In my mind, the revolutionary war was over, lost.

Madeleine introduced me to a number of her countrymen. Since she described me as a Perdiguera survivor and told them of that I'd been in Siétamo (Jacques's movie about that had been screened in Barcelona's cinemas{62}), I received a friendly welcome from those of them who spoke French or Spanish. Among the names of the comrades she introduced me to, one of them caught my ear: Einstein. This was a middle-aged man with graying hair. We chatted for a while in front of a map of the city that he was scrutinizing, in a room that he used as his office. It was only as I was leaving that I remembered about the theory of relativity, and asked Madeleine if he was the one who had come up with it. She told me, no, that was his brother. Some years later I discovered that my Einstein had taken his own life to avoid being handed over to Hitler by Laval and Pétain's collaborators.{63}

One or two days were spent trading gunshots with Assault Guards manning a building opposite our trenches, listening to the wireless broadcasting speeches and appeals for calm from the leaders of the various political factions, arguing about the likelihood of the arrival in Barcelona of *centurias*, which, rumor had it, had begun to move from the Aragon front toward Catalonia in order to thwart the communists' bullying.

Then came the pathetic appeal from García Oliver and Federica Montseny, asking the libertarians of the CNT to stop fighting.

Endnote {61}: 473; Endnote {62}: 477; Endnote {63}: 479

SOLEDAD

I made my way home with Madeleine in utter disgust, downhearted and unsure of how to proceed. Should I return to the front or leave Spain? My girlfriend, alive to my dismay, used her rich imagination and well of affection to boost my morale and get me to stay with her. Afraid that I might be tempted to carry out some violent but pointless act, she never left my side.

To occupy my mind, she organized soirees attended by girlfriends who were nearly all employed at the hospital where her husband was being treated. She also bullied me into stepping out for long walks through the Catalan countryside, sometimes as part of a group, sometimes just the pair of us like two lovers seeking some time alone.

Among Madeleine's nurse friends, there was one who was really funny. She was forever giggling, always up for a joke; it seemed as if life, as far as she was concerned, was just an excuse for fun. She was no beauty; her dumpy figure was reminiscent of an unfinished sketch, with round, googly eyes and an ever so slightly upturned nose. Only her mouth with its lush, dark red lips looked beautiful. But I can't swear to that, as I don't recall ever having seen her mouth at rest; I reckon she must have laughed or talked even in her sleep. Her scathing wit spared no one, especially me; she saw me as a dreamer lost in the clouds and unable to see the sordid reality of life. Without our confidence in humankind, convinced that human beings were spineless and incapable of rational thought and intellectually lazy and always ready to blindly follow the first silver tongue that promised them the moon, like a flock of sheep follows the shepherd leading them to the slaughter, she showed utter contempt for all convention, scandalizing all around her with her repartee, which often wounded the listener's self-esteem.

She must have been between thirty and thirty-five years old, and her name was Soledad (Solitude). The name fit her like a glove. According to Madeleine, she was constitutionally single, highly cultivated, and spoke four languages in addition to Spanish. She split her life between her job and learning. She didn't care at all about material goods and most of the things that interest other women. Soledad used to say that the human animal's only cravings, its only needs, were the needs to eat, drink, sleep, and make love.

C.N.T.   F.A.I.

MILICIAS ANTIFASCISTAS

COLUMNA DURRUTI - CUARTEL GENERAL

¡VENGANZA!

Frente al enemigo, de cara, con el pecho henchido de generosidades, con el fusil en la mano, mano amplia de trabajador, ha sido muerto en MADRID nuestro amigo, nuestro hermano DURRUTI.

Ninguno vale más que otro en nuestras líneas. Pero cualquiera vale más que todos cuando sabe captarse nuestro cariño. Y nadie más querido, como ninguno más cariñoso, que nuestro DURRUTI. No lloraremos su muerte, pero nuestros ojos estarán turbios y nuestros puños apretados, hasta que no quede uno vivo de nuestros enemigos.

Atacábamos en defensa de un ideal de libertad; luchábamos por una vida mejor; no llevábamos en el pecho más que deseos humanos.

Pero a todo ello se une ahora una nueva consigna: LA VENGANZA.

Hermanados por DURRUTI en su Columna, hermanémonos para su venganza. LUCHÁBAMOS COMO HOMBRES Y VAMOS A LUCHAR COMO FIERAS.

¡MILICIANOS DE LA COLUMNA DURRUTI! ¡¡HERMANOS!! ¡HAY QUE VENGAR SU CORAZÓN ROTO! ¡HAY QUE LLEVAR SU NOMBRE POR LA ESPAÑA FASCISTA, COMO UN NOMBRE DE MUERTE!

EL COMITE DE LA COLUMNA

Durruti Column Committee proclamation calling for vengeance following Durruti's death in Madrid

One morning, Madeleine and two of her girlfriends had to leave very early to bring her son to some peasants on the outskirts of Barcelona. So I was by myself when a knock came at the door. It was Soledad.

"Madeleine's not here," I told her.

"I know. She's the one who told me you were by yourself today. I have some time off, the whole day to myself. Madeleine asked me to stop by and have a chat with you."

As she said this, she was closing the door and locking it.

"So we won't be disturbed," she said. "I want to speak candidly with you."

That took me off guard. I could hardly tell her to leave, and I didn't dare tell her to shut up and leave me in peace to enjoy a few hours on my own. She was a real chatterbox, the words just spewing from her. As she worked in the kitchen she brought me up to date on all the hospital gossip, the patients' state of health, the wounded arriving from the front. After serving up the coffee, she fell silent. Startled, I looked up. Her elbows on the table, Soledad was staring at me and grinning.

"Your turn to talk now. I'll bet you can't tell me what I've been saying, apart, maybe, from the fact that I've made your ears burn. I'm here to ask you something."

"Oh yes? What?"

"What did you make of last night's discussion?"

During a discussion on the topic of the young, Soledad had said that parents had no rights over their offspring, other than their duties, for parents never think about how their children's lives on earth will turn out. Her theory was that couples make love for their own pleasure and out of physiological necessity, nature having designed it that way in order to guarantee the survival of the species, the same as any other living creature on earth. Down through the millennia, man has evolved and broken free of many moral constraints and material dangers and designed and built today's society on the basis of survival of the fittest. All knowledge about birth control is banned and liable to punishment under the penal code and under religious dogmas. The more human beings there are on earth, the more poverty and the easier it becomes for the people in power to recruit cheap labor and police to control those who go barefoot and, if need be, crush attempts at revolt. We bring children into this world in order to perpetuate man's enslavement of his fellow man. And we'd like them to be grateful to us for a lifetime of slavery in a society founded upon the exploitation of the productive majority by a hypocritical minority that rules by relying upon ignorance and upon the force of its machinery of repression. The children of the proletarian classes owe their parents nothing, for their parents have never bothered to think about the living conditions they might be able to provide for them. All they thought about was sexual pleasure and pride in perpetuating the species.

Having considered for a moment, I answered her question:

"I strongly believe that you are correct, but I have to confess that I had never considered the matter before last night."

"Listen, Tony, Madeleine has told me that you want to leave Spain. The war isn't over yet. Despite all our setbacks, we may still win this war. I can understand your being disgusted by all these deaths and by the ruthless contest to take power. But you take your dreams of justice and universal love too much to heart. Remember that, through the history of humankind, all that revolutions have managed to do is secure recognition of a few rights for the individual. Whether we win or lose is not going to make a lot of difference to the structures of our society.

As long as ignorance remains the lot of the masses, Falangists, socialists, or communists all speak in the name of the people's freedom, but
really all they have in mind is their own interests and the chance of
their clinging to or earning privileges for themselves. Stay with us, but
don't delude yourself. The fight goes on and it will carry on forever,
no matter who emerges victorious. Since the dawn of time, men have
been fighting for freedom and justice. But the moment some faction
takers power, it instantly turns into a force for repression in order to
hold on to the privileges acquired by some individuals, and the fight
resumes, generation by generation, striving for the dream known as
Anarchy."{64}

The entire afternoon was spent deep in discussion. We had completely forgotten that Madeleine was due back mid-evening, and then a
voice called out from the vestibule:

"What are you two up to? Squabbling, are you?"

She had used her key to open the door and we hadn't heard a thing.

"Tony, assuming you have any strength left, give me a hand here."

Soledad giggled and protested:

"Tony's definitely more relaxed than he was this morning."

We relieved Madeleine of her parcels and she disappeared into the
bedroom, only to emerge a few moments later in the suit worn by Eve
before the original sin. She had been my mistress for months by that
point, but every time she appeared before me like that, naked, with her
face turned my way, her eyes full of tenderness, the eternal flame of
desire was stoked within me again and ran through my veins like a lava
stream down the slopes of a volcano.

Until then, I wasn't aware of the intimacy between my girlfriend
and Soledad. I looked at them, stunned, not knowing quite how to
react. Giggling at my surprise, she loosened the cord of my robe, sliding it over my shoulders while asking her friend:

"Who would you like to help you unwind this evening? Tony?
Or me?"

I'm no exhibitionist, and Soledad's presence cooled my craving for
Madeleine. Irked, I told her to stop it and not pester her girlfriend. I
turned to pick up my robe, but Madeleine held me back, saying:

"Look how beautiful she is, Tony."

Soledad had removed her top. She was not wearing a bra or slip.
Her skirt and tiny underpants joined the rest of her clothing on the
chair where she had tossed them. Sol was skinnier than Madeleine;

ENDNOTE {64}: 481

slightly taller, too, with long thighs, an athlete's flat stomach, and small breasts. Nature had scored a hit with the body but messed up the face. Arms around each other's waist, they looked at me, smiling. Madeleine broke free from her friend and taking me by the neck said:

"Caress me, darling, caress me."

I felt two arms around my waist and I wound up on the floor, lying on my back. That was one crazy night of erotic games, an orgy of caresses and kissing. My two partners were rampant and insatiable. From time to time Soledad would withdraw from the joust and get me a drink. When I woke up, Madeleine and Soledad were still sleeping. Their legs were thrown over my thighs and their arms imprisoned my chest. We were sprawled across the bed; I, and they, never did know when we had moved from the dining room into the bedroom. My efforts to free myself woke them up:

"Don't leave us, darling."

I had a headache and a dry mouth, and it felt like I had a hole in place of a stomach. I told them that as I freed myself and got up to go into the kitchen where they joined me almost immediately, forcing me to go and sit in an armchair in the living room. I was surprised because this was not like us. When something needed to be done, we would help each other if at all possible or necessary, or else one stayed by the other one to have a laugh. It was only after we ate that I realized that my girlfriends seemed worried. Sol was quiet and Madeleine wasn't angling for kisses or caresses, which was out of character for them both, as far as I could tell, anyway.

"What's up with you two? Are you sulking? Are you angry? What have I not done for you?"

Sol stood up without a word and went off to get a sheet of paper from the sideboard drawer. It was a letter from Pablo asking me to return to the group as soon as possible. Lorenzo Giua had given it to Madeleine after collecting it from the CNT headquarters where it had been sent. Instead of passing it on to me, she had mentioned it to Soledad and they had both agreed to treat me to the crazy night we had just shared.

"What are you going to do?"

I had no idea how to answer that. The thought of Durruti, Berneri, and Barbieri all murdered{65}, and of the dozens of comrades slain by the power fanatics{66} and those who had vanished into the GPU's jails{67} had destroyed my appetite for the war. What was the point of fighting? The masses were like flocks of crazed sheep slaughtering one another and incapable of using their own heads, as they trotted along behind the wind-sellers of politics, unaware that they were being used to win or cling to the power that allowed their exploiters to carry on using them. I felt the dreamy heat of the two female bodies against mine, and four hands brushing over my body covering it with caresses.

"What are you going to do?"

"I'm staying here."

The day slipped by uneventfully. Soledad admitted to me that she had mixed an aphrodisiac in with the Málaga wine she had served me between escapades. I now regret losing the list of ingredients to that erotic stimulant, which Soledad had invented and was made entirely of herbs and roots. Because I believed that the revolution was over, as far as the libertarians were concerned anyway, I made up my mind to stay in Barcelona with my girlfriends and look for a job (there was no shortage of work) so that I could support myself.{68}

Giua's unexpected arrival with Georges and Alfred, two friends of mine who he had bumped into at the union, where they had been waiting to leave for the front, called everything back into question. Jo and Fredy had arrived with a convoy of volunteers for the Brigades, but knowing where my sympathies lay, they had tried to get news of me through the CNT. When they found out that Lorenzo was part of the International Group of the Durruti Column, they asked him if he knew me, and he saw no problem with bringing them along to Madeleine's in the hope of finding me there.

Two days after that, we were on a truck hurtling toward the high flatlands of Aragon. They had countered every one of my arguments with their determination to find out all about the revolution's achievements and the republican militias' fighting style. They had brought the discussion to a close by declaiming Cyrano's tirade:

"*What say you? That it is futile? I know.*
But one does not fight in the hope of success.
No. No, it is all the finer when futile."

QUINTO DE EBRO

For ten months—ever since the outbreak of the war—we had held Franco's men outside Madrid and had won the battle of Guadalajara, but, overall, the fascist armies occupied three-quarters of the country. Italian and German weaponry, infinitely better where land forces were concerned, was backed up by Italian and German airpower that nearly always tilted the scales, despite the courage and initiative of the republican fighters.

On our side, there was much talk of Russian arms and munitions, but I have to say that, by the end of July 1937, in my sector of the front, we still had not seen any of that. There were only a couple of changes: hunting rifles had been put back into storage and replaced by military-caliber Winchester and Lebel rifles. The Winchesters came from Mexico and the Lebels from France. Our machine guns dated from the 1914–18 war.

Not that any of his stopped us from feeling confident. The revolution might have been over, but we could still hope for victory in the war. Besides that, for many of us, there was another reason to carry on fighting: the hatred we felt for the people behind the massacres in Badajoz and Málaga, for the people who had leveled Guernica and were bombing towns and villages with planes supplied by Hitler and Mussolini.

Returning to the Aragon front with my friends plunged me back into the climate of aggression and restrained fury that one obtained among the militia members manning the front lines. The upshot of the militarization of the *centurias* was that the sector was entirely uneventful. The only moves made by the regularized units were those carried out under orders from HQ. What with stints on guard duty and training marches, everybody was restless and waiting for the moment when we would surge forward.

My group were slight exceptions to the general rule: we were quite often entrusted with reconnaissance missions, and once we mounted an attempted push against Quinto de Ebro. From Velilla, where we crossed the river, we made for the village, hoping to catch them unaware, but failed. The only lingering memory I have of those twenty-four hours is the cry that went up from one man fatally wounded, a cry I think I can still hear when I am watching a war movie showing men falling on the battlefield. "*Mama, Mama,*" her name echoing through space like a final appeal for help or, rather, mumbled with his last breath. How often have I heard it? I don't know any more. But I do remember it, maybe because it was such a beautiful day. Maybe because we thought that, following the initial skirmishing, which had long since ended, we were out of danger and the noise of battle had ceased. Slightly to the rear of our lines, Lorenzo and I, flattened against the ground, were observing the enemy's positions. There was no sign of movement. The sun, almost directly overhead, was bathing the flat-land with its scorching rays and bringing drowsiness to men worn out by a sleepless night. Then that shriek erupted, violent and hopeless, shattering the spell and jerking us back to reality. A mantle of silence descended upon us once more, a silence heavy with menace and danger. A man had died; he had made his way through Italy, France, and much of Spain to meet his end on the soil of Aragon.

I said that it was my sole memory of that expedition, but I was wrong. There is another memory that comes flooding back. A few hours later, after we had been relieved at our observation posts, we were stretched out prone, unwinding, doing a few physical exercises, when we heard engines off in the distance: aircraft. Three planes were drawing nearer, *las tres Marías*, coming from Zaragoza. They were coming to support the infantry defending Quinto. This was the first time I had seen planes in operation. I had, of course, heard of the "three Marias," which patrolled the skies and occasionally bombed our lines, but I had never seen them close up. Lying on our backs with our eyes riveted on the three planes, we watched as they closed in. After wheeling in a wide circle overhead, they set to work. They began at the far end of our line. We could see the bombs gleaming in the sunshine as they fell, before they exploded with a thunderous boom as they landed. In tri-angular formation, the planes were coming our way and shedding their heavy load. Now they were on top of us. A silver flash hurtled toward us with a shrill whistling sound. I shut my eyes and heard a dull thud.

When I opened my eyes, I saw Lorenzo looking at me and then turning to look behind us. I did the same. The bomb lay there, less than a meter away, stuck in the dirt and with its fins still trembling. Not a word passed between us before we were overcome by blind panic and leapt to our feet. We ran as fast as our legs would carry us. The next day, back in Velilla, we recounted our tale to our comrades, laughing like lunatics at how terrified we had been. Lorenzo told Pablo that the group's mounted runners and motorcyclist should be replaced by a couple of couriers capable of fighting on the run because, he argued, we had beaten every race record set since antiquity. The way he told our story and made fun of the situation was such that I was the first to break out laughing.

That operation was the only one of any note that Pablo mounted within days of our rejoining the front, and it resulted in failure.{69}

CONCHITA, ASUNCIÓN, ROSITA

We returned to Farlete where we reverted to living high on the hog; it was a holiday, punctuated from time to time by nocturnal visits to the folks across the lines. My two friends and I felt as if we were blessed by outrageous good fortune. We always made it back from our sorties without loss and sometimes brought back some prizes of war, weapons of German or Italian manufacture.

Once we brought four young people back with us. We had set out with a young Spanish lad from the Zaragoza area, our mission being to reconnoiter the position and gauge the strength of an artillery muster of which HQ had gotten wind. Everything went well, except for one hitch: we were still on our return journey when the sun came up. We had no option but to hide and wait for nightfall. Our guide led us to a little mesa covered with thyme and rosemary and broom; off in the distance, we could see the roof of a farmhouse. The comrade told us that he wanted to drop in and give his mother a hug (she lived in one of the houses we could see), and he'd be back by nightfall. He left us after dumping his heavy armaments: rifles and grenades.

I had never known a day to drag so long. All our senses were elevated. The slightest sound or bird's shadow made us start. Our nerves were stretched to breaking point. But everything as uneventful. The sun continued to climb toward its highest point, rather too slowly for our liking. The afternoon went by somewhat better, as far as I was concerned anyway, for after eating few biscuits and draining my canteen, I dozed off.

By the time I woke, the sun was low in the sky and nearly setting; the day was drawing to an end. Soon we could resume our journey. The night draped the countryside in shadow. Somewhat reassured, we decided to give our comrade another hour to show himself before we set off. We were going to leave as soon as he arrived, but when he reappeared he was not alone; he had four adolescent boys in tow, each with his bundle. Our guide explained that they wanted to cross our lines and were relatives of his. Before dawn, we were on the way back to base.

The following day, we were startled to see our guide out strolling around as proud as peacock with a fabulous looking girl who he introduced to us as his wife. There were another three young girls as well:

two sisters-in-law and a cousin. The youngsters we had assumed were boys had in fact been women; they had kept their sex a secret from us in case we might refuse to take them along in view of the dangers we might run into along the way. We toasted the success of his scheme, chuckling at the subterfuge and at our naiveté, for none of us had had the slightest inkling as to the real identity of our last-minute companions.

We quickly became inseparable from the girls. An odd friendship grew between us, composed of tenderness, trust, and, on our side, respect for their tender years. In what we said and did we strove not to upset them or lead them to believe that we thought of them as women; we treated them as if they were just girls. Conchita, Asunción, and Rosita were sixteen, eighteen, and nineteen years old.

Right from the first days together, we came to a joint decision; the girls were to be nothing more than friends, young pals to us. We pledged not to exploit the genuine, touching, and unsolicited attachment they displayed toward us, especially since they'd been joined by Francisco, their brother-in-law, and cousin and his wife Pilar. Sometimes they'd hang around us all night. When we were on duty, they'd tag along with us to training, trying to keep up with the same exercises with such determination that soon they knew how to handle a rifle or handgun, how to throw grenades and creep around under cover of the bushes. During working hours, they were level-headed, serious, and diligent, though, once training was finished and we were on the road home, they would become light-hearted and fun-loving, giggling at everything and nothing. They would bicker with one another just for the fun of snuggling against us and dragging us into their squabbles. How often did we go for strolls around Farlete or Pina? On occasion, Otto, Ritter, or Mario would join us. The girls would bombard them with questions about their homelands and their families. The lads would answer with a laugh and sometimes tease them—especially Mario. One of them—I can't remember now which one—had asked him what he called himself. Mario replied, "Niña, I don't call myself. When they need me, people call me Mario."

On another occasion, we were chatting about the sincerity of one comrade's views. Having listened quietly to our line of argument, Mario extracted a carefully corked bottle from his knapsack and asked us what it contained. The label read "Cognac" and there were three stars. The bottle looked new. The cork barely protruded from the neck and our answer was: "It's cognac."

As humorless as any pope, he uncorked the bottle and passed it to the girls, saying, "Ladies first."

Conchita, quickest off the mark, grabbed it and raised it to her lips, "It's water!" she exclaimed.

"Yes, it's water. You see, men are like this bottle. Once upon a time it held cognac, then wine and right now, water. The label has stayed the same but might easily have been changed. It's the same with men. Over the course of their lives, they change. Some of today's revolutionaries will turn into conservatives tomorrow if their economic circumstances change. Some will swap labels, others their ideological contents if their own personal interests are at stake. Before he dies one can never tell whether or not a man has kept faith with his primary ideal. Only at that point will it be apparent whether he has betrayed or respected his beliefs, for then one will know how he lived. Among humankind there is a breed that poses a great danger to the working and peasant classes: the left-wing politician, who seeks our support in winning power and who, once he has his seat in government, forgets his promises and turns into the most dogged champion of the privileges he once upon a time fought against. A proletarian who participates in a revolutionary movement with an eye to securing his entitlement to an easier life turns, once he gets his chance to become boss or rentier, into a conservative bourgeois.

"The same goes for political parties; be they republican, socialist, or communist. Once they win a majority and take over the leadership of some country, they forget about their initial purpose and turn into the toughest defenders of a regime they used to combat when they were on the outside of the leadership. In a hurry to take power, the socialist Mussolini sold out to capitalism and, thanks to the spinelessness of those elected by the people, imposed his dictatorship in Italy. Léon Blum, a socialist heading up the French government, pushed the Non-Intervention Law through, but lets Hitler and Mussolini dispatch their armies to Spain. Power is corruptive of men and ideas. Jaurès's socialism wasn't the socialism of Blum. The republicans of the Commune do not have the same aims as the aims of the Third Republic. Revolutionaries turn into wild-eyed conservatives or reactionaries. The peasants and workers have to extract their rights to well-being and freedom from them one by one. Kropotkin, Reclus, and Pietro Gori abjured the privileges of their class in order to champion and spread the same ideal of equality and total freedom as we are trying to accomplish here."

Mario loved to talk. For fifteen years, he had mulled things over in a prison cell. He was making up for those fifteen years of silence, and we used to hear him out without saying a word, for what he said had a curious and deep resonance within us.

As I say, he loved to talk, and he did talk, but only when invited to do so. We used to enjoy urging him to expound upon his ideas and his viewpoints and his outlook on life and the resolution of certain social problems. Somebody (I can't remember who) argued once that social differences would still be exist even in a freer society. In economic terms, a laborer would be inferior to an engineer, the necessity and education of the two not being the same. Helped by a few comrades, I tried to demolish his arguments by staking a claim to the strictest equality, but my opponent was able to come with more arguments to see me off. I was on the point of conceding when Mario, who had been listening to us without breathing a word, stood up and said:

"Comrade, we are all at liberty to believe what we choose. You're an intellectual and have studied. Here we are all drawn from the 'people' … shepherds, laborers, peasants; not many of us can read and write. In their eyes, you appear cleverer because you have had more schooling. Allow me to tell you that humanity has less need of you than it does of the shepherd who fetches you the milk for your break-fast every morning. The structure of society is the same as it was back in prehistoric times. It is founded upon the force that was vital to the survival of the species. Over the centuries, as consciousness and knowl-edge expanded, religious power was conjured up so as to consolidate the might of the warrior chief, and, to cap it all, it was propped up by the most corrosive of psychic poisons: money and its corollary, private property. Slowly, over the centuries, humankind has made progress: the slave of earlier times has been replaced by the wage-slave.

"Back in the days of the Roman Empire, the slave's dream was to be able to buy himself back and become a free man again. These days, the proletarian's dream is to climb the rungs of the social ladder. If not for his own sake, then for that of his offspring. A laborer dreams of his son becoming a workman, and the latter that his son will, some day, make an office worker or teacher. All the so-called political parties claim to want to invert that ladder and turn everything upside down. Like it or not, I am fighting. Not to turn it around but to lay it flat so that all rungs are on the same level. Yes, on the same level, for I find it nonsensical that the most useful trades, the ones people cannot live without, are the ones most sneered at and least regarded. That the classes that produce nothing, the ones that today sit at the top of the social ladder and whose usefulness is artificially contrived, rule over and grind down all the rest. In order to live and prosper, humanity needs no bankers, lawyers, soldiers, or policemen. It does need farmers, miners, workers to start, and then engineers, chemists, and physicists. For millennia now, there has been an ongoing struggle between those who hold power and the outcasts who work so that humankind may make strides in the direction of justice, equality, and love between all individuals. Even Christianity in its early days was communitarian; wealthy converts had to surrender their assets to the community. As it grew, and built up enough strength to take power, it was corrupted, and these days, with its spiritual power founded on the ignorance of the masses, it is a brake upon men's march to freedom.

"How come every philosophy, every revolution driven by the right to equality, justice, and freedom of the individual has failed? For one very simple reason: they have always sought to combat "facts" without enquiring into and eliminating "causes." That cause goes by the name of property and its virus is money in all of its guises: whether hard coin or paper bills. Until such time as property is eliminated, whether individual ownership or state ownership, there will be neither justice nor equality among men. I am fighting for a society wherein only the toil of each person will have any value and will allow us all to live free and equal. From our earliest years onward, we are all used to thinking, not about that which is most useful in life but about what will bring us in the most money so that we can satisfy our whims or quite simply better our lifestyle. Nothing—be it murder, thievery, prostitution, or fraud—is off limits as long as it is an avenue to wealth. The society in which we live today is a jungle, even though we claim to be civilized. We will only truly be civilized when everybody can choose from among those trades required by the collective, whichever one pleases him the most, in the knowledge that it will allow him to live a fully free life as the equal of everybody else."

Thus spake Mario. We heard him out, endorsing his line of reasoning. Sometimes one of those present would put the case for the opposition, more to spur him into expanding upon his reasoning than to rebut his arguments. In actual fact, as far as we were concerned, what he had to say invoked the striving for a world from which poverty and social inequality would be banished.

Much later, while cutting back some woods on the banks of the Vézère, my friend came to mind. I acknowledged that, like a wood-cutter, he had removed the clutter from my mind and patiently cleared away all the thorns that were smothering the craving for freedom, which drive the young and spurred us into revolt, albeit often blind and unconscious revolt, against social injustice.

OFFENSIVE

Time passed. In August, rumors started to circulate about the International Brigades being due to arrive to man positions on the Aragon front. Then we discovered that an airstrip had been set up in Candasnos. Pablo asked us to stand by our posts and hold ourselves in readiness for any eventuality. Those orders had consequences; our little girlfriends Rosita, Asunción, and Conchita never left our side now, and, for all our good intentions, the inevitable happened.

I can't recall now which of us was the first to succumb. What I do remember is that one evening I found myself alone with Conchita. I was just back from the CP where I had met up with all the group's old hands—Otto, Ritter, Mario, a Swedish comrade, and two Frenchmen and somebody else whose name I have forgotten. Pablo briefed us that the Brigades were on their way and that we should make ready to infiltrate the enemy's rear guard. We were in a state of permanent alert.

As ever, Conchita was waiting for me. According to her, the others had turned in for the night a good while before. I watched as she spoke to me. My facial expression must have mirrored the sudden urge I felt to sweep her into my arms and nibble at her lips, for she giggled and asked me what was up with me and if I was sick. The sound of her voice cleared my head again and I told her to go to bed. She refused, on the grounds that it was still too early. To get her to go, in the hope that her upbringing would move her, I admitted to her that I was a married man but that she was too pretty and I wanted her. Her reaction surprised me: she stepped up to me, her face radiant with joy, and she burst out:

"Es verdad? Me quiere? Antonio, quiere que sea tu querida? (Is that the truth? That you love me? Antoine, do you want me as your sweetheart?)

Snuggling into me, her arms about my neck, her mouth was close, all too close to my own. Conchita had not yet turned seventeen. By telling her I was a married man, I had honestly hoped that she might go away so that I could wriggle out of the yearning I had for her. I had been mistaken. My admission had merely accelerated matters. She was already a woman, so why disappoint her? My mouth touched hers and her body grew heavier in my arms. Closely entwined, we retreated into the room. Once near the bed she stepped away, unbuttoned her *mono* and slowly slipped it down. Smiling at me with her eyes and lips. I just

On the front, December 1936

watched her without moving, as if scared of seeing her vanish upon my waking out of a splendid dream. I watched her undoing her bra even as she stepped out of the overalls. Her legs, her thighs, the dark pubic mound, then her high breasts, small and hard and tipped with two pale pink roses with the nipples barely discernible. She shuddered when my fingers skated over her chest in order to slide under her armpits and my mouth began to nuzzle at her breasts. At which point the thought that she was probably still a virgin crossed my mind. My lust evaporated, giving way to the fear that I might hurt her and damage her.

To conceal my reticence from her, I was about to bend at the knee when, leaning on her elbows she hoisted herself onto the bed before turning over with her legs dangling down, thighs parted, affording me sight of a fig, its flesh swollen and fit to burst with sap, the red pulp of the fruit was visible. Conchita called out. Her hands grabbed the nape of my neck as my lips closed over her clitoris, as if she was afraid that

I might break off. Her body shook and writhed. I could feel her nails scratching my skin, and then, after one last contortion, she fell still. I carried on caressing her; my hand lightly rubbed the nipples that I could feel erect and hard against the palms of my hands, and I carried on licking at her, especially as my lust was on the rise again and I had only one ambition now, to bring her to an ecstasy of pleasure. Her hips now began to quiver slowly, and her hands clasped my head again. Her bodily movements gathered speed. When I entered her, a muffled cry of pain or surprise escaped from her lips. Her legs crossed around my thighs, her fingers dug into my shoulders and drew me closer to her, seeking to render the contact between us all the closer.

We were awakened by some pounding on the door. It was my friends, coming to warn me that one of the International Brigades was camped nearby. Seeing the two of us emerge from the bedroom, they erupted into laughter. Rosita and Asunción were with them. Then they congratulated us after their fashion; Jo and Fred by teasing me and the two girls by bombarding Conchita with questions and giggling.

The area was teeming with armed men, volunteers drawn from all directions. The 15th Brigade was raring to go. There were a lot of Britons and Americans, as well as Italians, French, and some Cubans with whom we might strike up a conversation.

I invited one Italian communist to pay a visit to the collective in Pina. Despite the front's being so close, the village's peasants had made such strides that even the three or four small landowners in the township who, only a year earlier, had preferred to carry on working their land on an individual basis, had realized that by working in concert they might spend less time in the fields and turn to whatever other pastimes they might prefer, and so had applied to join the collective. The entire village was now inhabited by one big family, with everything shared in accordance with the inclinations and needs of each individual. Land that had never, in living memory, been farmed had been cleared and planted. Families were eating meat two or three times a week (prior to '36 they had only tasted it once or twice a year, and, even then, not every year).

The comrade, who was keen to convince me that dictatorship of the proletariat, like they had in Russia, was a necessary way station on the road to achieving libertarian communism, honestly acknowledged that the libertarian experiment in Aragon was encouraging, but he had his doubts about the chances of it spreading further afield to an entire country. As he saw it, Russian communism, being highly centralized and enjoying absolute power, was what was needed in order to tackle the countless enemies of proletarian revolution. He was reluctant to accept that the new ruling class would not be willing to give up the power it had won and that it would do whatever was required in order to stop the masses from dwelling on injustices and individuals from demanding their rights.

By the end of that morning, we parted as good comrades but neither of us had budged from our position. He had a blind trust in his leaders. From his company commissar up to Stalin himself, including the entire party hierarchy, they were all infallible and genuine.

That evening, Jo, Fred, and I arrived back to find our girlfriends fussing around the table where three places had been set. There was an out-and-out feast set out on the table: roast chicken, fried rabbit, ham, cheese, and red wine. We were all the more agreeably surprised when we knew that the very next morning we were due to move out on a mission that was more than straightforward reconnaissance. Three plates, three glasses, three chairs. I shall never forget that evening. We had laid everything out on the table so that no one need trouble themselves to go off to fetch more food or drink. The girls sat on our laps. We giggled and cracked jokes like lunatics. Conchita forced me to retrieve slices of meat from her lips and came up with other childish pranks that had her in gales of laughter. We had forgotten about the war and past dangers and any that might lie ahead of us in the near future. Now we were nothing but youngsters, full of life, love, and joy.

Toward the end of the meal, somebody raised the subject of our departure. After some initial surprise, Asuncion calmly stated:

"A wife should follow her spouse. Fred, *querido*, I'm coming with you."

Rosita echoed the sentiment:

"Me too."

"I," Conchita took up the refrain, "am nobody's wife, just *su querida*. I'm going wherever he goes because I'm a militia, and Tony has always told me that we are free to choose how we live and fight. I know he won't deny me the happiness of fighting alongside him."

The discussion was a very short one before I found myself in my room with Conchita. She was happy to be leaving with us the next day on this new adventure, which would prove to be her first real action.

SACRIFICED

We set off the following afternoon. We had spread the word that thirty of us were off on leave. The others would be relieved by the Brigades, so that they could head back to Cruce de Gelsa for some rest. In Bujaraloz, Pablo briefed us on our objectives. We were to infiltrate behind the enemy lines and delay or prevent the arrival of reinforcements during the push that was due to be launched overnight. We barely had time to return to our theater of operations. Five groups of six were spread out over a roughly twenty-kilometer front from Velilla de Ebro to Fuentes.

Our guide left us at the republican army's very last forward position after pointing out the trail we were to follow. After crossing a narrow valley and rounding a pine- and shrub-covered hill, we spotted lights shining on a hilltop far to our rear; we had successfully penetrated the enemy's defenses. We marched south, sticking to the edge of the wooded hills. A noise in the distance brought us to a sharp halt. A vehicle, maybe a car or a truck, was approaching. The truck, as it turned out, swept past about forty meters from where we were and pulled up a short distance further on. The men who climbed down from it spoke without any fear of being overheard; they were on their way to relieve their comrades.

Scampering like hares through the bushes, we closed in on them. Jo and Fred set the automatic rifles in position, and we opened fire. Screams of pain, shrieks of terror. Every sign of life was erased. The shooting ceased. We had taken them entirely by surprise. The enemy had barely had a response. The sound of engines informed us that other troops were coming, but they stopped before they came within range. We could not see a thing, and, like ourselves, the opposition took cover among the clumps of broom and rosemary. Fred was the first one to hear them. Someone was crawling in our direction. Firing almost at ground level, the automatic rifles swept the area while the girls and I let fly with some grenades. Once the rustle of the feet running toward us had ceased, calm descended once more.

Time wore on. Leaving our female comrades under cover, we scouted the area around us. We were at the foot of a very steep hill, which was initially hard to climb. Withdrawal was proving a bit tricky. In the distance we heard a muffled explosion, followed by a whistling noise and an explosion on the side of the hill. It rained stones all around us. Another explosion, right in front of our position. Then the night was filled by a shout welling up from who knows how many chests:

"*Arriba España!*"

Our last remaining grenades and the automatic rifles enabled us to fend them off, but Fred and Asunción lay lifeless, their hands clutching their weapons. The decision was made to beat a retreat. Too late: a deluge of shells bombarded us.

I came to on a sheepskin cot in a *paridera*, a dry-stone-walled, wattle-roofed hut where shepherds would shelter with their flocks overnight or during storms.

Every part of me ached. My head was by far the most painful part of me as it hurt me even when I remained motionless. I felt as if I had fallen down six flights of stairs. An elderly fellow approached me:

"*For fin te despiertas.*" [You're awake at last.]

He raised his canteen to my lips and had me drink. "*No tengas miedo* [Don't be afraid]. Drink, it'll do you good."

Before I could ask him anything, he told me that he had heard the overnight fighting. All the Francoist posts had been attacked, virtually simultaneously. Once the danger had passed, he had set off with his dog and donkey, homeward bound. He had stumbled upon me sprawled among my already cold comrades. A moan had attracted his attention. Spotting that I had no obvious injuries, he loaded me onto his donkey and retraced his steps. After offering to share his meal of bread, sausage, and dried figs, all washed down with a few swallows of red wine, he escorted me part of the way and pointed out a shortcut.

It was getting dark when I arrived in Cruce de Gelsa in an ambulance that had picked me up along the road. The Aragon offensive was spreading out toward Belchite, and, according to the driver, that town would very shortly be liberated. I had such a headache that I couldn't take in what he was telling me: I heard it and that was all.

The group was camped out at the crossroads on the Bujaraloz road awaiting the order to move up along the line. Somewhat farther along, a battalion from the Brigades was resting up from the rigors of a long journey by truck. I was making my way back from the CP when I bumped into Hans, Madeleine's partner. She too had gone off to try to find out what had become of me. As we waited for her to return, Hans told me what had induced him to enlist in the Brigades.

Ever since the May Events, POUM militants had been the prey. Andrés Nin had vanished and had probably perished in some Stalinist party jail. For a German Trotskyite, the Brigades were a safe haven as long as he held his tongue and accepted the discipline. At that point, Madeleine reappeared. I remember that she chatted with Hans in German for a moment. Then Hans bade me farewell and took off, saying:

"*Hasta luego!*"{70}

The night wrapped us in its shadows. The touch of my girlfriend's lips on mine banished the nervous tension that had sustained me ever since I woke up in that *paridera*. That tension was suddenly gone, and, burying my face in the hollow of her shoulder, I started to weep, bawling like a baby. Ridiculous, yes, I know. How can any man deserving of the name, a fighter toughened by nearly a year of warfare, dissolve into sobs, and in the presence of a woman, even if she is his mistress? Yet that is what happened. I broke down like a puppet whose strings have been cut.

Madeleine stretched me out on a blanket and all but lay on top of me, asking me what had happened that was so terrible. Whereupon I told her everything; about how Jo and Fred had met their ends, and Conchita and Asunción and Rosita who had wanted to share in our fate out of love for us too. As I talked I regained my composure. By the end of my account, I had recovered my composure and asked her to overlook my weakness.

The very next morning, I left. I was never to lay eyes on her again, nor she me, for she would not survive; Hitler's bombers slew her during air raids on Barcelona.

In physical terms, that was the busiest time of my life; the Republic's push in Aragon made us a flying column, forever on the move between the Huesca front and the Belchite-Teruel front.

Following an exhausting trek under a scorching sun, the very first operation brought us to the crest of a hill where we stopped. It was already after dark. I dozed off almost immediately under a tree and did not wake until the next morning when I was roused by Pablo, who shouted at me that we had to get out of there. Our position was too far forward, and we were in danger of being encircled.

That was the day I found out what a fighter plane was all about. We were walking, stretched out, through desert-like countryside with only sparse, stunted vegetation, when German fighters swooped on us, strafing us. And so the carousel of death rolled on, planting fear. Flattened against the ground, on my back as was my habit, I watched them dive out of the clouds as if they had to crash, only to pull out of the

ENDNOTE {70}: 500

dive, swoop upward, wheel around, and start all over again. After what was actually quite a long interval, I heard Pablo's voice, screaming at us to open fire at the planes:

"*Apuntad delante el aparato.*" [Aim in front of the planes.] On my command, open fire!"

All I had was a revolver. I refrained from squandering my ammunition, which allowed me to witness what was going on around and above me. The opening volleys had no appreciable impact. Between the pass made by the last plane in the squadron and the return of the first one, a few minutes elapsed, minutes that our machine-gunner used to dart with his weapon behind the trunk of a dead tree in the midst of the denuded wasteland; the ends of its main branches reached for the sky. I could see the small dust clouds kicked up by the hail of gunfire virtually make a beeline for the tree before the plane leveled out and climbed vertically with an angry humming sound, leaving in its wake a trail of black smoke before disappearing to the east, followed, after one final pass, by the others.

That same afternoon, I had the chance to see some Stukas in action. These bomber planes swooped almost vertically upon their target, dropping their payload from a distance of about four or five meters, maybe even less than that. And so I saw them demolishing and setting fire to the trucks that were coming to fetch us, rendering the road impassable. The bombs left craters two meters in diameter and a meter deep.

Not that I am the only one to have described the horrors of aerial bombing. Trucks and cars burning and exploding, people running, only to be mowed down by the shrapnel. The reason I bring it up is that that was the day I noticed that, myself being in no danger in that I was a few hundred meters away from the theater of operations, I was able to look on impassively, without quivering with impotent fury or out of pity for the fallen, at the apocalyptic spectacle being played out before my very eyes. That war had seen me lose all my friends and in just one night Jo, Fred, Mario, Otto, and Ritter had been swallowed up by the dark and I was on my own.{71} Juanita and Conchita, the women I had loved, had disappeared forever.

The slaughter left me indifferent. Had the war so hardened me that I now looked upon the loss of men fighting on the same side as me as something reasonable and natural? "That's war for you," Pablo told me. "Today it's their turn to perish, tomorrow it could well be mine or yours or someone else for whom you have some regard."

ROSARIO'S DEATH

Mario and Otto rejoined us in Tardienta. Swept along by the wave breaking over Belchite, they hadn't been able to catch up, and we thought they were dead. The republican offensive pressed on. Such were the losses we had taken that our group was now "international" in name only. About fifty men remained of its two-hundred-man complement, and the gaps had been filled by an influx of Spanish volunteers.

Pablo reorganized his unit into three companies of Spanish-speaking volunteers, plus two twenty-five-man groups; one was mostly Anglophone and the other mostly Latin, the object being to make the communication of orders that much easier in the field. And so my friends and I wound up as part of a unit of the line. No more one-man missions, raids, or reconnaissance work.{72} Not that it bothered me; quite the contrary. Rumors were rife that the Council of Aragon had been done away with and that the government was getting ready to assume direct control of the worker and peasant collectives in Catalonia and Aragon, which was the death knell for the libertarian experiment.{73} As in Russia, the assumption of power by the communists sounded the death knell of the soviets. The advent of the government under Negrín, their stooge, marked the beginning of the dismantling of libertarian achievements in Spain, which was only to be expected; same cause, same effect. No centralized government—of whatever hue—can leave trades groups a free hand to put their creative capabilities to the test. Indeed, that might afford workers an insight into the precise value of their efforts and into the pointless existence of all the idlers who purport to belong to the "liberal professions" (financiers, politicians, judges, and lawyers).

But the war raged on. One night, we relieved a battalion that had just captured an enemy position.[1] Rosario was from Andalusia, the widow of a driver shot by the Falange right at the beginning of the revolution. She had joined our team shorty after it was first formed and had taken charge of the most menial yet most essential business of the unit: the cooking and sewing for comrades who were clueless about

---

[1]   In view of Antoine's mistake with the chronology, the following account ought to be placed back in the context of the April 1937 battle for Santa Quiteria, as described in endnote 57.

how to sew on a button or how to darn a sock. Every time we moved on, she moved with us, her canteen always at hand if we were thirsty or if we fancied a crust of bread or a can of corned beef if our destination was still some way away and our bellies were rumbling.

When Pablo had reshuffled the unit, he had told her that she could be transferred to the CP, but she had rejected this, as she had no interest in officers. Rosario had picked up a rifle and joined a company. That very night, she took her turn on guard duty with the rest of the comrades, heedless, as we all were, of what awaited us in the hours ahead. I had eventually fallen asleep only to wake at first light, just in time to see some silhouetted figures go over to a cannon abandoned by the enemy about a hundred meters from our trenches and at the edge of the other side of the hill. Rosario was with them. Some fifty men and women in a huddle around the gun, intent on pushing it over to our lines. Every eye was on the profiled removal. In the pale light of the breaking day, that was all we could see. None of us had the wit to scan the terrain beyond the gun emplacement. Unsuspected, tragedy struck: we watched as shadows popped up from both sides at once and swooped, screaming, on our comrades. A general melee ensued, punctuated with the odd gunshot; the fighting was hand-to-hand. Then one voice rang out above the din of battle, like an order:

"*Matadme, compañeros, fuego!*" [Kill me, comrades. Shoot!]

The voice was Rosario's. Our machine-gunner adjusted the barrel of his gun a touch and opened fire.

It was daylight by the time the entire volunteer company moved out under covering fire to retrieve our dead.{74} Calm descended once again. My comrades, worn out, grabbed some shut-eye. A few read or spoke quietly in their mother tongues. I leafed through my copy of Cervantes's *El Quijote*.

The purr of engines made our eyes lift to the skies; there was a squadron, flying very high, coming in our direction. It made one pass over us, and then the air raid began. Zeroing in on our trenches, the bombs peppered our positions, demolishing our entire defenses and inflicting serious losses upon us, in terms of personnel and weaponry. Our telephone lines were cut, and the officer asked me to go and alert HQ to our situation and request fighter backup if possible. When I returned to the lines I brought with me the order to fall back. Our planes were busy elsewhere, and we did not have enough Mosquitos to cover all fronts.

The men began to succumb to panic. I will never forget the haggard face, complete with clownish chalky eyes and lips, of the man who scuttled down the slope in my direction; I swear he didn't even see me there. The dance of death played on. How I managed to make it to the trench without being hit I have no idea. Fear had me by the throat and by the belly.

We started evacuating the position. The able-bodied carried the wounded, dropping down and struggling upright again under a hail of bombs and shrapnel, for the enemy, noting the absence of republican fighter cover, deployed his fighters to blast us between passes by his bombers.

The injured man I was struggling to rescue from this hell with help from a comrade died before we could get him to the end of the dugout. We left him there, and I retraced my steps to look for my knapsack, which I hadn't managed to grab on account of the wounded man, when I passed it a few minutes before. I really treasured my copy of *Quijote*. I waited for the wave of aircraft to sweep past and then made a dash for where I had dumped my things. The ever-present fear that I had managed to bring under control gained the upper hand again at the ghastly sight that had me rooted to the spot: two bodies lay under my cape. One had half his face missing as if a blow from an axe had sliced his face into two neat halves. The other's belly gaped open, and his intestines were spilling out through the wound and looked as if they were still throbbing with some vestige of life. Horror, disgust, and fear made me forget everything else. Careless now of planes and shrapnel and bombs, I turned and ran until somebody stopped me by throwing their arms about my waist, making me take a tumble by the foot of a wall.

He handed me a bottle and said "Drink!"

I gave the bottle a quick tap against a stone, the cap flew off and I drank. By the time I pulled the bottle away from my mouth, it was empty, but I was thinking lucidly again.

"Feeling better?"

"Yes. What has you here? How come you didn't take off?"

"I'm here to show you the way and to give a drink to any who need one. You're the last of them, I reckon, but we can hang around a bit longer."

A track that snaked between the trees and brambles took us to the valley where I was reunited with what was left of my unit. Our strength had melted away like butter left out in the sun. Dead, missing, or wounded. More than half of my comrades were not there to answer the roll call. Pablo questioned us over and over again, having us start our report of events ten times over, taken aback by the precision of the bombing which every one of the survivors had brought to his attention.

Deep down, every one of us hoped that we might be sent back into the rear for reorganization and to wait for fresh recruits before rejoining the fighting. But our hopes were dashed; we were assigned to hold on to a forward position in a valley that, in peacetime, must have been pasture. Stretched out before us was a verdant plain and, off in the distance, the line of hills we had abandoned twenty-four hours earlier. With a pair of binoculars, we watched the Francoists repair the trenches destroyed by their aircraft. We were too far away to be in any position to hamper them in their efforts. Republican artillery and aircraft were spectacularly absent.

I have a sharper recollection of how many days we had been in that position before the lookouts sounded the alert; they had picked up the sound of voices ahead near one of their posts, one voice calling out something that nobody could understand. For a while we thought it might be Germans trying to pull a fast one, and then the voice called out again through the night: someone was yelling "Help!" in Swedish.

There were two Swedes in the Anglophone group. One had yet to rejoin his comrades, and we had all figured he was a goner. The poor wretch, both legs peppered with shrapnel and with a broken ankle, had dragged himself and crawled in his more lucid moments (as he simply had to have drifted in and out of consciousness and as the pain must have been atrocious), driven on toward our lines by the instinct of self-preservation. At the field hospital where I escorted him, the doctor told me that gangrene made anything that he might do pointless and that he was in urgent need of an operation if he was to stand any chance of pulling through. I shall leave you to imagine what that operation was like, carried out as it was under canvas with rum as an anesthetic. Both legs were amputated; a few days later he was shipped out to Barcelona. They tell me he returned to Sweden a few months after that.{75}

MILITARY CONTEMPT FOR HUMAN LIFE

There in that sector, I saw for myself what superior officers thought of the lives of their troops, or maybe the manner in which, in times of revolution, units made up of personnel who do not share the same ideology as the folks in the government. We had been relieved: a company of Libertarian Youth took our places on the parapets of the trenches.[1] My comrades and I waited to be sent back into the rear for a time, but all the rest we got was that they had us bivouac in a forest near the front line. We were held in reserve. Pablo warned us to expect a visit. As the afternoon wore on, a group of officers, their cuffs and caps resplendent with "scrambled eggs," showed up in the woods. Forming two ranks, we watched them walk past, fresh-faced and grinning, weighing us up in much the same way that dealers weigh up cattle at a fair. As they reviewed us, we flopped down on the spot without saying a word. By the time Pablo got around to telling us to "fall out" we were all lying down. I remember he was not happy because among the visitors were some Russian officers there to evaluate the republican army.

I don't know if that was really the case, but I know for certain that throughout the next night trucks kept on delivering men to the sector and that an attack was launched at dawn. A ferocious exchange of fire, punctuated by the explosion of grenades, woke me up. It was still dark. Only a faint lightening of the sky suggested that daylight was imminent. The hilltops off in the distance looked to us like a weaving line of lightning bolts, and the sudden flashes of grenades lower down gave us some indication of the rate of progress. From time to time, the whistle of stray shots made us duck instinctively.

Franco's troops had seen off the first wave of attack. Daylight was already reaching into the valley floor. The sun was warming the peaks of the sierra by the time the fighting resumed with its initial intensity. This time, though, mingling with the din of machine-gun fire and grenades, there was a song rising from a thousand chests, a choir, snatches of which reached as far as us:

> *Hijo del pueblo, te oprimen cadenas*
> *Antes que esclavo prefiere morir*

---

1   The narrative resumes: we are in August 1937 at this point.

Libertarian Youth battalions singing as they climbed the hillsides to attack. We watched them trying to dart uphill, only to be mown down by crossfire from automatic weapons. A voice close by said:

"That isn't battle; it's butchery."

To which Pablo replied, "Those are German tactics, massive attacks. Men count for nothing."

The advance posts of the position had fallen, but still the enemy held. Then out of the sky came the roar of an engine, which drowned out all the rest, enemy fighters coming to the aid of their hard-pressed infantry.

Hundreds upon hundreds of dead, an entire younger generation sacrificed for nothing. Under canvas that evening we chatted about what had induced HQ to commit these boys (some only sixteen years old), who had arrived virtually unprepared and with no military training, to a frontal attack upon an almost impregnable position. It was said—though it could not be said with certainty—that the government had disbanded the Council of Aragon, or meant to, and was out to take control of the collectives, that it was out to eliminate CNT forces and the forces of POUM, the members of which were being hunted down by the communists' secret police. At the front there was no need for police or for prisons. A few operations like the one we had just witnessed, and the members and sympathizers of the POUM and CNT would have been annihilated.{76}

It was now winter, and the theater of operations had moved.{77} Seconded as a liaison agent to a battalion of the line, I escaped the absorption into the Brigades that my pals had experienced. The battle for Teruel was at its height. The sector was quiet, and I whiled away my time by dabbling in poetry and strolling the length of our positions in the company of Bobini, a young captain, a music-hall performer who had kept his stage name as his nom de guerre.[2] We would chat all day long and, on occasion, very late into the night about the underlying

2   On March 15, 1939, Bobini was in the Saint-Cyprien camp, according to this testimony: "I joined the comrades from the Twenty-Sixth Division (formerly the Durruti Column). Among the comrades I knew there were Ginés Martínez (major), from the Las Corts Libertarian Youth, and (captain) Jesús Cánovas Ortiz, both of them from Barcelona; the latter had the nickname "Bobini" in CNT circles and was known to perform at festivals as a 'comic.'" (Taken from Jesús López Carvajal, *Mémoires de ma vie. Mémoires d'un ouvrier anarcho-syndicaliste dans l'Espagne du XXe siècle*, unpublished.)

ENDNOTE {76}: 527; ENDNOTE {77}: 529

principles by which our society should be governed. Bobini encapsulated his theory in a single sentence:

"The more extensive our rights, the greater our obligations. If I have an entitlement to consume I also have an entitlement to produce."

When talk turned to his livelihood, he used to say:

"I'm useless. I can sing and tell jokes and make people laugh. But this world of ours is a jungle. Those who produce have nothing or next to nothing. The layabouts, whether they are aristocrats, bourgeois, or military, enjoy the best of everything. In order to survive—and because I couldn't, by force or trickery, take a tiny bit of their surplus in order to meet my basic needs—I played the fool for them."

Sometimes he would talk to me about his children and the hopes he had for them. He used to say:

"I'd like it if they had freedom of choice, without any economic constraint, and were in a world free of corruption and hypocrisy, where *freedom* and *equality* are not empty, meaningless words, a world from which ignorance would be banished and where one could be an engineer and a peasant at the same time, or a philosopher and a miner or a doctor and a bricklayer, or whatever, in accordance with one's individual aptitudes and abilities. I have always hated violence; I have never liked fighting. Even as a youngster I avoided fighting; today, though, I fight in a deadly battle against the people with the power, the privileged and their guard dogs. And the most terrifying thing of all is that I bear no ill will toward the guys on the opposite side. I fight them without hatred since all they are doing is obeying their masters, the ones who have always exploited them in the name of some irrefutable and inhuman destiny."

It was Bobini's firm belief that all the political parties were in the pockets of high finance. Socialists, republicans, liberals … they were all led by bourgeoisie manipulated by international capitalists; even the communists were up for hire. And the proof? Look at how Thorez had called off the strike wave in France in June 1936 or Léon Blum's Non-Intervention Agreement regarding Spain.

Our winter passed without event. The fighting was taking place far away from us, and we were never called in as reinforcements.

The glorious days of spring found me overlooking a fractured, desert-like plain where Bobini's company was stretched over nearly two kilometers along the crest of a series of small hills, and, as far as the eye could see—even with binoculars—here were no signs of life.

This was where Tarzan, my faithful and devoted friend who had kept me company through the winter, revealed his talents as a hunting dog. I described this earlier.

Our trenches were protected by a network of barbed wire. Our days slipped by uneventfully, to the extent that even the artillery bombardments that were unleashed every time a supply convoy tried to reach us with our chickpeas were welcome a distraction. We used to count the salvos and the numbers of shells that didn't explode since there were always a few of them that thudded into the earth and stayed there until the bomb disposal unit showed up.

Everything went well until the day Bobini received the order to send out a patrol to map the enemy's forward positions. The liaison agents reached us late in the night. We set off at an easy pace at around 1:00 a.m., knowing that for the first three or four kilometers we were unlikely to run into anything other than another patrol. In fact, there was nothing that would slow us down other than the reconnoitering of a ravine that started fifty meters from the base of one hill and meandered southward, becoming deeper and steeper-sided. Tarzan was trotting around us, sniffing out all the smells of the land that was gradually coming back to life. We had stopped in order to decide whether we should keep going or turn around and head back, because the sun had come up and its rays were now lighting the peaks of the higher hills. We pushed for a return to base. Surveying our return trip, we noticed the profile of a horse and rider against the dark blue of the sky. One, two, three, four … an entire platoon of cavalry lay ahead of us. Our cover was blown. The riders were coming down the slopes. We made a quick decision to scatter and wait for them in the ravine. The race began. After a moment, I realized that I had missed the natural dugout. Bullets were whistling by. I ran, zigzagging to throw them off. I dropped down and fired. A horse buckled and fell. The race was on again. I heard the clatter of horseshoes on dry ground and wheeled around firing my .9 mm. The rider threw his arms apart and the spooked animal passed me. I set off again at a run, running like no man has ever run. I was out of ammunition. I realized that this was the end, that I was in the same situation as the fox in a hunt. Like the fox, I ran as fast as my feet could carry me. Mechanically, I stowed my pistol back in its holster and my fingers clenched the hilt of my dagger. They had stopped shooting. I glanced quickly behind me. My pursuer had unsheathed and with saber raised high was about to strike at me when

I jumped at him, grabbing his arm, which he had lowered in order to run me through. We both fell to the ground, but he had the blade of my dagger in his belly. I stood up and set off running again, and in the distance I could hear the rattle of machine-gun fire.

Shadows fussed around me. I was helped up, and somebody asked:

"*Estas herido? No parece. Mira como tiembla.*" (Are you hurt? Doesn't look like it. Look at how he's shaking.)

They gave me something to drink. In my headlong run I had landed in front of a position manned by some socialist comrades. Having heard the gunfire, the entire company was in battle stations by the time I came into view. Through his binoculars, the captain had watched the final stages of my race against death. It was he who congratulated me on my sangfroid and my reflexes, and in order to show me that I had no reason for false modesty, he recounted everything he'd seen with his own eyes. If it had occurred to him that fear had been the driver of my actions and that it was the reaction of a cornered animal that dictated my every move, his admiration for me would probably have evaporated. He wouldn't have believed me if I told him. I sat, patting Tarzan who was recovering at my feet, his mouth gaping open and tongue dangling.

MACABRE RECOLLECTION

If I remember correctly, it was at the beginning of March that the rout began. I had just about regained my strength when the group I had rejoined on the evening of my race was thrown into the fray. The Francoists were mounting attacks across the entire front.

How long did we stay in that position? Was it twenty-four or thirty-six or forty-eight hours? I have no idea. I remember that we arrived under a rain of shells just at nightfall. The Spanish comrades had just seen off an attack by enemy infantry. Teams of stretcher-bearers were bustling about, evacuating the wounded. Planes ... artillery ... infantry on the attack. The rattle of machine guns and rifle fire, grenades exploding, shells and bombs going off. We had lost all sense of time. Drunk from fatigue, gunpowder, and alcohol, we clung to that parcel of earth with a single thought in our heads: *no pasarán* (they shall not pass). Soon, night fell and we were no longer visible to the planes. Somebody jumped into the dugout and asked for the officer commanding. A voice replied:

"He's dead."

"Quickly!" the newcomer went on, his cap adorned by two gold stripes, "We have to evacuate this position, or we're going to be encircled. Look down there!"

The gunners had trained their sights on us. We scattered, fleeing from the pounding of the artillery units. One of my Spanish friends followed me, and we ended up, utterly drained, at the bottom of a sort of a cliff.

We couldn't see a thing. We were groping our way along the cliff face, searching for a way through, when my chum said to me:

"*Oye, hay cuevas*" (there are some caves here). I'm not going any further as this one isn't big enough to take two of us."

Before he could finish speaking, my hand felt a gap. Another small cave, the floor strewn with dead wood, twigs, and stones. This cave would do fine while I waited for the sun to come up. I cleared it of anything that might be in my way and slid inside, feet first. I used my knapsack, which I had placed between two large boulders, as a cushion.

I was woken up by a ray of sunlight and quickly realized where I'd spent the night: a graveyard torn up by bombing. The shattered headstones, the overturned figurines, the bones strewn around the bomb and shell craters revealed its intensity. The cave where I'd slept was a vault, and I'd cleared out its first and rightful occupant. I called out to my comrade:

"*Eh! Amigo!*"

I watched as he came flying out of his hiding spot like a cannonball, and he said:

"*Virgen santísima madre de Dios.*"

As he grabbed his rifle with one hand, he was blessing himself with the other. The shock of discovering that he had violated a grave was so severe that he had lost his grip on reasoned thought. It had revived an atavistic fear and the prejudice etched into his subconscious by two thousand years of Judeo-Christian belief. We didn't hang around.

THE BEGINNING OF THE END

Those final months were a genuine nightmare for me. We were moved from one place to another along the front line in an effort to spot the enemy breakthrough, which was still overrunning us, forcing us to fall back. We had come to such despair that some of my comrades, rather than retreat another step, chose to stand their ground and face slaughter on the spot. Certain rumors, rife among us, were the death blow to our morale. On their way up the Ebro, units from the Líster Brigade had broken up the peasant collectives that were still in operation after the Negrín government's deliberate dissolution of the Council of Aragon, and it was only a matter of weeks before the enemy's launching of his offensive. The word also was that FAI, CNT, or POUM personnel passing through sectors held by Líster or by El Campesino (both of them communists) were invariably being shot.

Some time after hearing these rumors, I had an opportunity to find out the truth. As I arrived in the Lérida area with a bunch of Spaniards, I was frisked and arrested by El Campesino's men who took me, and my comrades, to their HQ. En route, I asked my comrades to state that I was with the Brigades. An officer subjected us to close interrogation. One by one, we were put through the wringer, and I couldn't tell you how many times the whole process was repeated. After every appearance before our inquisitors, the numbers of us under interrogation dropped.

I had to go through my whole story: how I was French, attached to the Fourteenth Brigade. How I had been blown off my feet by an air raid and been hospitalized in the military hospital in Bujaraloz. How I knew none of the young men who were with me. In the end, they released me but ordered me not to leave the camp. By dawn, I was long gone.

Heading north, I was hoping to patch up with my group. I actually did track down Pablo, Otto, and a Cuban comrade. All the others had left for Teruel. Pablo handed me an envelope that Mario had asked him to pass on to me. It contained a notebook in which my friend answered a series of questions I had asked him one evening. My hasty departure on a reconnaissance mission had prevented me from hearing his responses, and we hadn't been around each other long enough to talk since then.

A few days later, I briefly bumped into Bobini again on the banks of the Segre; he wasn't well and was shipped out to Barcelona. The sector seemed fairly calm; the enemy was far enough away from the riverbank that, while on guard duty, we could forget that death and suffering lay around the corner for us, as time was passing and the war was still going on.

One morning we were woken up by the sound of an artillery barrage off in the distance to our right. We were unfazed, because as far as we could see—even with binoculars—there was no movement on the other side of the Segre.

I was busy reading through Mario's notebook for the umpteenth time when I was sent for. The new captain and the commissar had been seconded to us by a political commissar in order to boost our morale and convince of the need to embrace dictatorship of the proletariat as a staging post en route to the establishment of libertarian communism.

The commissar, Cathala, filled me in on the situation: the Falangists had crossed the Segre upstream from us. Telephone lines had been cut, and I was to get to HQ as quickly as I could and deliver a dispatch from the captain to the highest ranking officer I could find. Having followed the river for a kilometer or two, I decided to take the road southbound from Seo de Urgell to Lérida; its pavement ran about a hundred meters from the riverbank.

I had barely emerged from the cover of the reeds along the riverbank when I heard the characteristic whistling of an incoming shell dangerously close to me. The shell exploded between the road and me. I went to head back toward the river, and a second shell landed a fair distance ahead of me. I'm not sure how many times this was repeated. I had the probably mistaken feeling that some gunner was using me for target practice. His every shot dogged my movements as if he was determined that I was not going to make it to the highway. In my zigzag run, I was trying to reach my goal all the same. That goal was to get across that road and make it to HQ, which was located on the hillside behind the one where I was trying my damnedest to avoid being cut down by shrapnel. A jump made between explosions brought me to the edge of a gap below road level. I darted in there as fast as my legs could carry me and flopped down, gasping for breath, under the arch of a bridge.

I wasn't alone. A voice called out: "You wounded, *compañero*?"

It was a woman. Her eyes twinkled with a strange glint, and her entire body was shaking; she was afraid, terrified out of her mind. I was trying to catch my breath and in no position to answer her. The artillery barrage was growing in intensity. She came over and ran her hand very gently over my cheeks, shoulders, and chest and repeated her question:

"You wounded?"

Her hands were cold and her unearthly staring eyes seemed to want to delve into the very depths of my being. Then she withdrew her hand and reached for her neck and began quickly undoing her blouse; two marble spheres spilled out, the nipples pointing in my direction, erect and hardened by a surge of desire. She rolled back her skirt and, grabbing me by the shoulders, turned around to trap my legs between her own. With one arm around my neck, she pulled my head into her face while her other hand slid between my thighs to free my penis. Taken aback by the violence of this urge to make love, given the circumstances, and by the heat from her body, which was offering itself so unbelievably freely and impetuously, my thinking clouded by my recent exertions, I surrendered to the wave of eroticism radiating from her and permeating my every sense.

I came to lying on my side with one ear pressed against the dirt and I could hear a slight noise off in the distance. Like the vibration of tectonic plates. Suddenly, just the way a blast of wind drives away the mist of a summer's morning, my mind cleared and made me rush on to the roadside. Tanks were rumbling along the pavement, heading in my direction.

Within minutes I was back at HQ, where I was welcomed with open arms. The phone connection had been cut off by the Fifth Column (Franco supporters who had stayed behind in republican territory). Signals had repaired the sabotage and restored communications. After hearing to what I had to say about the tanks, the officer issued the order for us to fall back, and the base was promptly evacuated.

That evening I rejoined my company, and the marches and countermarches resumed; sometimes we stayed in a position for only a few hours before being relieved and moving on to somewhere else. I had the distinct impression that the high command was at a loss as to what to do next. Later I found out that the power struggle was raging on and that it was having an impact at staff level in the army.

CATHALA

It was during one of these unexplained relocations that I made my peace with Cathala, the political commissar. Ever since he joined the company, I hadn't spoken a word to him other than what was strictly necessary. I never went along to any of the talks he gave, which resulted in many comrades not attending them either. One day, he used the captain as a go-between in order to ask me what was behind my systematic non-attendance. I sent him word that it was because no counterarguments were entertained.

Anyway... we had reached this hill. We had positioned forward posts on the edge of a stream that snaked its way through the undergrowth a little lower down in the valley floor and we were busily digging foxholes with whatever we could find, when the order came for us to make a hasty withdrawal. I went off to tell the guys in the forward posts.

When I came back up the hill, everybody was gone, except for Cathala, who was waiting for me and scolded me for taking so long. I showed him my neckerchief, heavy with apricots. He took a handful, and, as he strode on to catch up with the others, he began chatting to me about the need to go through the dictatorship of the proletariat in order to one day arrive at libertarian communism. We had to be disciplined and strong to face up to the coalition of reactionary forces, whose representatives—even within the ranks of so-called leftist parties (he cited the Socialist Party, and the Basque and Catalan home rulers)—were the last to lift a finger on behalf of the working class, despite their holding government positions. Being bourgeois themselves, it was the leaders of that [Socialist] party who were championing capitalism's interests, and they had no hesitation in using the police against workers who were insisting on their rights to life, while the latter sort [the autonomists] were demanding their economic independence so that they might exploit natural and human assets for their own benefit, keeping the producer masses in thrall to the capitalists and the clergy.

There was a lot of truth in what he was saying. I had to concede that and I didn't hesitate to tell him so. We had come to the rearguard detachment. The comrades were walking nearby, listening to our conversation. Happy to hear that I was endorsing him, he was about to pipe up again when I said to him:

"I'm not done, comrade. Hear me out as I heard you out. I don't follow you. The criticisms you make of the socialists who were voted into power could maybe also be made of the communists, should they achieve power by the same means. History is awash with similar examples going back into darkest antiquity. So far the slaves have risen in revolt only to get themselves with fresh masters. Back in the dawn of the human revolution, revolt took on the guise of religion, ignorance working to the advantage of two sets of authorities, the spiritual and the temporal, which occasionally blended into one. Today it's the same story as two thousand years ago. Why? Because the men who hold or take over the reins of a society are corrupted, and, in order to assert their authority, they need some instrument of corruption that allows them to forge the tools of repression that prevent every attempt at revolt or rebellion. And that instrument is money. The Russian workers' and peasants' committees understood that well, and they did away with money. The Communist Party brought it back once it had taken power and, today, Russia kowtows under the jackboot of one man: Stalin and his police organization. The old masters have disappeared and been replaced by Party officials who are no better, because, man being what he is, a repressive agency—such as the CP is in Russia—would not be needed if freedom and equality applied to the various elements that make up society. "Power carries a curse," Louise Michel used to say, in that it turns any who go near it rotten. We are out to demolish the centralized form of government, change the structure of this so-called thousand-year civilization, which is rooted in force, hypocrisy, falsehood, and ignorance. Wherever society is organized into classes and castes, look closely and you'll find that the human condition hasn't changed: there are slaves, serfs, farmers, and workers. The terms used to describe that segment most vital to the survival of the human race may have changed, but the situation remains the same.

"You supporters of centralized leadership issue your directives to the various trades and claim to know what the collective body you lead does or doesn't need. You measure each person's efforts in cash, contriving so that those whose work is most essential for survival are the most poorly paid. We want every person to answer for the survival and well-being of the collective. Let him be alive to the fact that producing is a natural necessity and so a duty, but also that he has a right, in return, to consume whatever he needs without anyone being able to forbid him from it in the name of some established order of more or less divine origin.

"'Anarchy is the highest expression of order.' Those aren't my words; they are the words of Elisée Reclus, a history professor. I see them as true, for being an anarchist means precisely knowing where my rights end and what my duties are, without anyone able to assume that he has the prerogative of telling me, in the name of anything, what I am allowed to do and what I am forbidden to do. You want proof? Look at us; we are at war. We have accepted a minimum discipline. We don't march in step, we don't salute our *responsables*, but we obey during the fighting. Tell me, Commissar, how many times have we, of our own volition, retreated in the face of the enemy? Why? When we arrived in these hamlets and towns and villages, what did we do? We told them to carry on working their land just as before and that they could work them in concert with one another, if they wanted to, as well as the lands abandoned by the *caciques*, and told them that it was all theirs. The peasant collectives took shape, and the Council of Aragon was established. In the workshops, trucks were fitted with armor plates, and carts were repaired. In the countryside, folks cleared and hoed and planted so as to feed a whole unproductive army and the mass of the population in the rear. That struck fear into all the power-hungry politicians on every side, inside Spain and abroad. It would be horrific for them if it came to pass that the producer classes, united behind their trades bodies, and working on one another's behalf in complete freedom, rather than being herded and led by a swarm of drones, were to realize the freakish situation in which they've been held for millennia past. It would spell the end of every privilege, the end of man's exploitation of his fellow man. And that is something that no politician, right or left, wants to see, because he would have to return to the fields, the workshop, the mine, or the office to earn his fair share of everyone's labors. They would prefer that things stay as they are. Their masters in the world of high finance guarantee them wealth and honors and all sorts of privileges just as long as they keep the common folk in ignorance and subjection.

"Until such time as money and its corollary, property (be it state property or private property), are done away with, there will always be the rich and the poor, the exploited and the exploiters. And that, we libertarians refuse to countenance."

We had arrived at our destination. Cathala looked at me for a moment without saying a word, and then he said:

"You honestly mean that. But how many would be capable of living by your principles?"

He offered me his hand and, after shaking mine, went off. We had set up camp in the vicinity of a village swamped with Aragonese refugees, all of them originally from Bujaraloz, Pina, Gelsa, and hamlets in that area.

THEORIES

It was there that I found myself reunited with most of my friends; Tía Pascuala, her daughters, and one of the two lads from the household; and *la niña*, so tiny alongside a lad with corn-yellow hair, like a giant beside her. She introduced him to me with these simple words:

"*Mi compañero.*"

Some friends from Pina told me that the Líster Brigade had broken up the collectives in the Ebro valley, destroying all their records so as to remove all traces of the work they'd achieved, and resorting to armed force where they encountered substantial or better-organized opposition. There, among others, I reunited with a young woman and her daughter, originally from Peñalba. After my friends Jo and Fredy died, I had promised her that I would look out for her and her daughter if I came through this war alive and not unduly messed up. But that's another story.{78}

We were sent back up the line. After defending our positions in the face of two or three attacks and having beaten off the enemy, with some losses and mayhem, we were relieved and sent to Santa María de Molla. The battle of the Ebro was in full swing. The news reaching us was contradictory and vague, but there was one thing that every report said: it was out-and-out hell.

Our commanding officer had set up his command post in the out-buildings of a farm about two hundred meters from a cliff, which made me think of the prow of three boats washed up on a beach, but it was actually a meadow with a gentle slope.

Our sector was calm. I spent my days reading or sunbathing and my evenings chatting with one or other of the men on guard at the battalion's CP.

One day, Cathala met up with me in the meadow where, as usual, I had retired after the midday meal for a quiet read of a novel by Federico Urales, the father of Montseny; someone had just lent it to me. As I saw him approaching, I quickly pulled on my trousers for I was as naked as a jaybird. I called out:

"Good day, Commissar."

"Drop the "commissar." I haven't issued you an order."

"What's going on?"

"I'd like you to tell me how we could introduce a libertarian society these days without passing through the Marxist communist stage, so as to prepare men to live in a libertarian collective. How, without the use of force, could we require all men to do some work and to produce, like you said."

To be quite honest, his question surprised me and I struggled for an answer; I've never been a public speaker or a propagandist. When the revolution broke out in Spain, I was a "reb," a rebel, an outlaw sometimes, someone who these days would be called a "marginal." But rarely have I made it my business to try to persuade anybody of the correctness of my beliefs and dreams. I looked at him silently for a moment and then said:

"We expose our thoughts; we don't impose them. We resort to violence only when we have to, in order to defend our own freedom and the freedom of those we hold dear. When the system's moral and material violence become too much for us, when scorn and hubris mock wretchedness and suffering, then—driven to despair and finding death preferable to the life of a slave—a comrade stands up: the bomb explodes; the pistol cracks; and a king, a minister, a president is cut down. And then the talk is of terrorism. But we are not the terrorists. The real terrorists are those who, by fair means or foul, are out to keep the wealth of the earth for their own exclusive benefit. We are not asking anyone to put their trust in us and give us the chance to enact laws or give us the power to enforce them. We are not asking for what the politicians ask for, because we are men and every bit as susceptible to corruption as they are. We say that all the world's workers should wake up to their rights and should assume full responsibility for their production and the tools and materials they use in their labors. Getting rid of money means destroying the instrument of corruption that allows for social class distinctions. Our society is organized along the lines of a jungle: with the strongest and wiliest feeding upon the weakest. Men have always stood up to preach respect for life and for equality for all human beings. Buddha and Jesus are the best known of them: revolutionaries in their day, and one went missing and the other was put to death. Their teachings have been misconstrued and have become instruments of oppression thanks to the ignorance of the proletarian masses. How do we envisage the society of the future? To us libertarians, society should be an association of trades bodies essential to the life and development of every human being, with preference and privilege for none. As we see it, a laborer has the same rights as an engineer the moment they both place the fruits of their physical or intellectual capabilities in the service of the collective. Everyone should produce in accordance with his capabilities and should consume in accordance with his needs."

We parted at nightfall. Before he left, he smiled and said:

"Yes, it would be great if we could make a reality of what you say. But men are what they are, and your ideas are merely a dream."

I must confess that I didn't tell the commissar that what I said was set out almost word for word in the notebook that Mario had given to me. In that little book, my friend had set out the sum of his experience, his hopes, and his ideal.

Forgive me for the long exposition of ideas. As I see it, these memories are made up not only of material facts and fighting and adventures but also of the more or less conscious motives that inspired us to act.

DEMOBILIZED

I spent about a month in Santa María de Molla. One morning, I was called to the Second Army Corps's HQ, where I was told that I was to leave the front; I was being demobilized like every other foreign volunteer.{79} Two days later, I arrived in Barcelona. The city and its suburbs were swarming with refugees. Provisions were very hard to come by and hunger and misery added to the ghastliness of air raids. Despite that, in the midst of catastrophe, in the upper echelons of politics, people were still jockeying for some illusory authority, and the communist police were hunting down POUM members.

I found work in a warehouse that took delivery of packages sent by relatives and friends from France to help those on their side who were still fighting. Each party or trade union had its own aid organization taking delivery of collective or individual aid trucked in from France once or twice each week. In Moncada, I found my partner, who had fled to her parents' home, and for a while I commuted to and from work by train. Then Antonia rented an apartment in town, and we shared the life of all the old city's residents: a life divided between the quest for provisions and the fear of bombs.

Between October 1938 and February 1939, hope I had secretly been nurturing of meeting up again with some of my fellow combatants—Mario, Lorenzo, Ritter—dwindled. Otto was the only one of my friends that I saw again. Giua had been killed, and Mario and Ritter vanished forever on the banks of the Ebro. And Madeleine was killed by a bomb right there in Barcelona.

Death had created a void around me, and to this day I wonder why he spared me. I laid eyes on Soledad again toward the end of January. She scarcely ever set foot outside the hospital any more as her work afforded her no respite. That particular morning I had come to work early, and Soledad was picking up some packages for the wounded in her care. After some effusive greetings, she filled me in on the comrades from the group who had passed, more or less badly injured, through her hands: Pablo had been taken prisoner, and the Cuban, who had taken a bullet in the thigh, had seen him dragged away by some Italian soldiers during one counterattack. Others, lots of them, had vanished in the whirlwind, while, behind the lines, the political bigwigs argued over morsels of power, and the police hunted down POUM and FAI members, the incorrigible supporters of a fight to the bitter end.

In the first week in February, on the first of February to be precise, Antonia, Pilar, and I left our home for the Barcelona train station, where I bumped into some Italians: Lodovico Rossi{80}, his partner Louise, and their boy, Lina Simonetti{81}, Giuditta, the partner of Francisco Ferrer (grandson of his namesake who had been executed in Montjuich)—Francisco had been killed by the Cheka in Barcelona back in May '37—and Auguste Magnani, his wife, and their two children.

The station was crammed full of men, women, and children of every nationality, all uneasy, nervous, and fearful. Like every migration by peoples driven out by barbarian invasion, the huge exodus of the Spanish Revolution's defeated was starting.

The Fifth Column was stepping up its attacks and sabotage. Franco's armies were at the city gates. We were leaving Spanish soil in the hope of getting out to Mexico, Venezuela, or Chile. In my wallet, I had a paper from the Mexican consulate allowing me to travel there with my wife and family. Our train took us as far as a hamlet about twenty kilometers from the border, and we spent a few days there. Then, on foot along the railway tracks, we headed for France. Our progress was slow for several reasons: Italian and German planes sometimes bombarded us, forcing us to take cover in the wild, and there were children to be carried (due to the food shortages in Barcelona, they were all undernourished and didn't have the strength to walk).

We were near Culera,[1] a small railway stop, the last one before Portbou when death swooped in one last time for me in Spain. Picture a crowd of people—men, women, and children—walking through a tunnel. Now picture a locomotive, all fired up but with no one to drive it or slam on the brakes, hurtling at full speed into that long, dark tunnel crammed with bodies. My experience as a hobo had prompted me to recommend that everyone walk in single file as close as possible to the tunnel sides, and that's what saved us. The engine swept past us like a lightning bolt in the midst of a hellish screech of metal and the terrified and pained screams of the injured and dying

The Fifth Column was lashing out indiscriminately one last time at people who were fleeing the horrors of the reactionary dictatorship that was descending upon Spain.

---

1   Actually the town's name is Colera.

Portbou: the last stop for Iberian railway services. Every track was filled with vans filled with munitions, weapons, and provisions. For two or three days, or so the railway workers said, France had been delivering to republican Spain the convoys that she had been holding back in her yards for the previous two, four, or six months. France was actually handing them over to Franco and to his pals, Hitler and Mussolini.

In Portbou, the women and children and elderly men were loaded onto these vans heading back to France. Able-bodied men had to cross into France under their own steam.

One last time I climbed this familiar hill, having faced the customs officials and crossed it many, many times prior to 1936. As I walked, I drew my .9 mm from its holster. I took it apart with a pen-knife and dumped the various component parts around the hill. The gendarmerie and the French army were waiting to greet us.{82}

Marseilles, 1974–1976

EPILOGUE

I have now come to the end of my tale; I have tried to stick to the truth, such as I remember it. Certain things, important only to me and the truth of which I cannot be sure, I have kept to myself. In any case, the most important thing, as far as I am concerned, is not so much the hard facts as the motives that impelled these people to do what they did.

Barely out of my childhood, I lived through the advent of fascism. I saw the spinelessness of the politicians vis à vis the rolling-out of Blackshirt violence. Between twelve and fourteen years of age, I devoured the works of Kropotkin and Malatesta, the poetry of Pietro Gori, and countless pamphlets, retaining nothing from them all but a seed of revolt and a boundless admiration for those who stood up, with dagger, pistol, or bomb in hand, to the tyrants grinding people down.

In 1936, I was what is conventionally referred to nowadays as a "marginal": someone living on the edge of society and the penal code. I thought of myself as an anarchist. Actually, I was only a rebel. My militant activity was restricted to smuggling certain pamphlets printed in France and Belgium over the border without ever trying to find out how a new society could be built. My sole concern was living and tearing down the established structure.

It was in Pina de Ebro, seeing the collective organized there, listening to talks given by certain comrades, and chipping into my friends' discussions, that my consciousness, hibernating since my departure from Italy, was reawakened. Mario tried to give me the benefits of his experience and his knowledge, and to that end he had spelled out for me in black and white a number of ideas and facts for me to think about. His lines of argument and the clear, concise exposition of his thinking allowed me to give some cold consideration to the evolution of society, to register the accuracy of his appreciation of the facts when he argued that political groups of revolutionary derivation turn reactionary. Whether they are republican, socialist, or communist, on achieving power, their number one priority is to consolidate the machinery of repression and cling to or reestablish the very privileges they were supposed to do away with.

Conditioned by thousands of years of ignorance and slavishness, to heed and obey and believe, the toiling masses of humanity slowly awaken as their capacity for reason grows and as they demand the right to live free of all impediments.

Used to having a master, a manager, a shepherd, the individuals making up humanity together, depending on just how conditioned they are, follow society's professional fraudsters who promised them equality, freedom, and justice. Nowhere in the world is there equal freedom for all, any more than there is an independent court, for they are overseen by whichever faction holds power, and they are obedient to the high finance group that gives it the wherewithal to get that power. Money is not only the fuel of war, it is also the fuel of politics and the purpose of every human pursuit. Nowadays all efforts are inspired by the profit motive. People say, "There's profit in that, but not in this," and, in order to make money, ever increasing sums of it, they forget about what is required and what is useful to humanity, and, bit by bit, they turn the entire world into a prison.

Farmers and workers, engineers and scientists need to understand that they do not need financiers or bankers or politicians just to live freely and happily. But they do need one another if humanity is to survive and make strides toward universal happiness, and, to this end, they must first eliminate all the parasites that oppress them and exploit them and reduce them to the status of animals harnessed to this task or some other.

These days, and from earliest childhood, human beings are trained to appreciate the value of money. The entire educational system is predicated upon the possibility of the child's being able, upon achieving adulthood, to earn money to cover his needs. By my reckoning, it would be more rational and humane and serve society better if a child was allowed to select from among the collective's most essential trades the one that excites him most and that, more than any other, will allow him to enjoy life's pleasures. But that's possible only in a libertarian society from which private property has been banished, where money no longer circulates under any guise, where man, having been freed from his prejudices and patriotic and religious complexes, will finally have realized that, for all our physical or intellectual differences, we are all equals and mutually dependent upon one another, each of us with a duty to bring the collective the fruits of his labors in order to be able to help himself to what he needs.

We purport to be civilized beings. But that word means nothing, for we have slipped backward, in sociological terms; tribal society was fairer and more equitable in its structures than our super-civilized society. Most people lament the rising crime and violence and blame modern youth for all of society's woes, without realizing that the real culprits are those (I should say "we") who failed to ensure that their children and grandchildren were born into a truly just social organization founded upon equal shares in the tasks essential to the survival and well-being of all. Violence and crime are useful to the ruling classes for, on the pretext of stamping them out, they permit the police in their service to crush any revolt attempted by the producer classes and to recruit from the underworld henchmen to carry out the dirty deeds that even a police officer would refuse to carry out. There is a great effort to set the individual child or adolescent on the path to becoming an adult filled with admiration for murderers, thieves, and swindlers of every sort.

Literature, movies, and television in the service of the rich feed the human animal's primitive instincts so as to hold him in a state of semi-barbarism that keeps individuals apart, pits workers against peasants, laborers again skilled workers, and the latter against technicians, engineers, physicists, and chemists. Modern society, being founded on money, cares little for what's useful and beneficial to humanity, caring only for what is profitable. So-called consumer society is a vast, worldwide fraud; everything there is adulterated, falsified, and poisoned. Advertising impels people to buy just about anything, conjuring up new cravings that require even more money if they are to be satisfied. Human beings, mesmerized by the lust for money, fail to notice that this endless pursuit leads to all the catastrophes that will result in the destruction of life.

Those who hold power, the capitalists and rulers over us, in order to secure their hold over the producer masses, have always striven to pit the various families that make up humanity against one another; country, religion, ideals … anything is good enough to serve as a pretext for murder, looting, and the unleashing of hatred, for hatred is an impediment to people's thinking along wholesome lines.

Patriot, racist: same thing. Both imply the same notion of the superiority of one person over another, the same germ of hatred that will pit one person against another at a point chosen by whatever politician they appoint as their master. Contemporary society is built on violence, injustice, and hate, and its cardinal virtues are falsehood, treachery, and hypocrisy.

Nearly forty years have passed. For all the advances in science, and despite the monstrous slaughter that has stained the entire world with blood and that hints at the horrors of the next war, men and women refuse to understand that humankind will never enjoy peace, justice, equality, or freedom as long as money and its logical consequence— private ownership—endure. As long as capitalism (whether the private or the state variety) focuses all of its efforts on building and perfecting the instruments of destruction, maintaining a climate of permanent warfare, and until the masses refuse to play along and finally rebel, no salvation will be possible.

Those trades and professions essential for the survival and well-being of the collective must have the status to which they are rightfully entitled, and for that to happen we must do away with all the parasitical elements exploiting them.

All revolutions have failed. Despite its Declaration of the Rights of Man and the Citizen, the French Revolution preserved the social and economic inequality of the *ancien régime*. The Russian Revolution culminated in a dictatorship as bad as any other dictatorships of reactionary parties, and which retains the same economic differentiations. The Chinese Revolution is not yet over, but it has retained those factors that will, sooner or later, lead it to failure: money and private ownership, a centralized leadership, and a professional army.

Forty years on, as I look around me, I can see that the power struggle continues, as bitterly and as incoherently as ever. I can see workers, peasants, technicians, academics, blinded by money, turning on one another. Above them, the politicians and their masters look on, laughing and rubbing their hands.

I see the earth, my home, I see humankind, my family, slowly being entrapped by the profit motive, by the sordid interests of the few on the march toward death and utter destruction, and as my thoughts turn to you, my friends, who perished fighting for an ideal of absolute equality and total freedom, I say to myself that you had it right: only a libertarian society can save humankind and the world.

End

INITIALS AND ORGANIZATIONS CITED

BOC—Bloc Obrer i Camperol (Worker-Peasant Bloc), opposition communists

CAMC—Central Antifascist Militias Committee

CEDA—Española de Derechas Autónomas (Spanish Confederation of Right-wing Independents)

CGT-SR—Confédération générale du travail-syndicaliste révolutionnaire (revolutionary syndicalist CGT)

CNT—Confederación Nacional del Trabajo (National Confederation of Labor), anarcho-syndicalists

Comintern—Communist International, aka the Third International

DAS—Deutsche Anarchosyndikalisten (German anarcho-syndicalists)

DEDIDE—Departamento Especial de Información del Estado (Special State Intelligence Department)

ERC—Esquerra Republicana de Catalunya (Republic Left of Catalunya), left-wing Catalanists

Estat Català—Catalan State, party of the Catalonian middle class

FAF—Fédération Anarchiste de France (French Anarchist Federation)

FAI—Federación Anarquista Ibérica (Iberian Anarchist Federation)

Falange Española—Spanish Falange, a movement launched by José Antonio Primo de Rivera, modeled on Italian fascism

FAUD—Freie Arbeiter Union Deutschlands (Free German Workers' Union), anarcho-syndicalists

FIJL—Federación Ibérica de Juventudes Libertarias (Iberian Libertarian Youth Federation)

Generalidad (or Generalitat) de Catalunya—Commonwealth of Catalonia, Catalan home rule government

GPU—Gossudarstveynye Politicheskoye Upravlenye (Soviet secret police, subsumed into the NKVD in 1934)

IR—Izquierda Republicana (Republic Left)

IWA—International Workers' Association, anarcho-syndicalists

IWW—Industrial Workers of the World, anarcho-syndicalists and revolutionary syndicalists

KPD—Communist Party of Germany

LRWP—League for a Revolutionary Workers' Party, Trotskyists

LIDU—Lega Italiana dei Diritti dell'Uomo (Italian League of the Rights of Man)

NKVD—Nardodnyi Komissariat Vnutrennikh Del (Soviet political police)

OVRA—Organizazzione di Vigilanza e Repressione dell'Antifascismo (Organization for the Monitoring and Repression of Antifascism), fascist Italy's secret services

PCE—Partido Comunista de España (Communist Party of Spain)

POUM—(Partido Obrero de Unificación Marxista), Workers' Party of Marxist Unification, opposition communists

PSOE—(Partido Socialista Obrero Español), Spanish Workers' Socialist Party

PSUC—Partido Socialista Unificat de Cataluña (Unified Socialist Party of Catalonia), mainly communists

Requetés—Carlist military organization

SAC—Sveriges Arbetaren Central-organisation, the Swedish anarcho-syndicalist labour organization

SAP—German Workers' Socialist Party

SIM—Servicio de Información Militar, Military Intelligence Agency

SSI—Servicio Secreto Inteligente, the Generalidad's secret services

TEAT—Tribunal de Espionaje y de Alta Traición, Espionage and High Treason Court

UA—Union Anarchiste, France's Anarchist Union

UGT—Unión General de Trabajadores, Workers' General Union, socialists

UHP—*"Uníos Hermanos Proletarios!"* (Join forces, brother proletarians!), the rallying cry of the Asturian rebels in 1934

Unió de Rabassaires—Rabassaires' Union, small and medium Catalan peasants

USI—Unione Sindacale Italiana, Italian Syndicalist Union, anarcho-syndicalists

BOOK II

In Search of the Sons of Night

by The Giménologues

"By October, the militia columns [...] were faced with the
need to conjure up their own intelligence services [...]
At about the same time, night operations teams, known
as the Hijos de la Noche [Sons of Night], guerrillas
striking deep into enemy territory, were set up under the
authority and supervision of the columns alone [...]
Some of these teams and their leaders were surrounded in
Aragon by an aura of prestige and mystery, like the greatest
heroes in the war. We might mention, by the way, Gallart's
La Noche group, which struck across the Ebro at Fuentes
de Ebro; the Utrillas-based Los Dinamiteros group, whose
most celebrated leader was Batista from Valderrobres;
or Los Iguales, led by Remiro from Épila; not forgetting
Francisco Ponzán who, after a brief stint with the Council
of Aragon, proved to be one of the best guerrilla leaders and
intelligence agents on the Aragonese and Catalan fronts."

—RAMÓN RUFAT, *ENTRE LOS HIJOS DE LA NOCHE*

ENDNOTES ON
THE MEMOIRS OF
ANTOINE GIMENEZ

ENDNOTES 1 TO 32

The Activities of the Anarchist
Columns in Aragon

{1}

PAGE 30

This refers to the farmland of Vallmanya in the township of Alcarràs near Lérida. It still exists and belongs, just as it did back in 1936, to the family of the wife of the first president of the Generalitat of Catalonia, Francesc Macià.

Josep Lladós Tarragó (born on February 6, 1920, in Alcarràs, now living in France) confirmed for us this incident in Gimenez's life. We contacted him to interview him about his experience as a militia member on the Aragon front, and while reading through Gimenez's manuscript a tiny fragment of Josep's youth came floating back (he was sixteen years old in 1936):

> I remember Tony very well, as the name wasn't common in the region. He wasn't from the village [Alcarràs]. I had no idea where he came from. He had friends his own age, but I wasn't one of them. He was small, not very sturdy, and could get by in Catalan. He was something of an intellectual compared with the others and was a man of few words. He was what they refer to nowadays as a "marginal." One day, he disappeared, and that was definitely after the events of July '36.[1]

---

1   Josep Lladós Tarragó, "Mémoires et entretiens avec Frédéric Alémany," http://gimenologues.org.

{2}
PAGE 33

The most recent research has fixed the number of people murdered in Catalonia through the war at 8,352; upwards of 50% of these murders took place before September 30, 1936, and that percentage rises to 80% by the end of the year. Roughly the same percentages are found in militia-occupied Aragon, where the overall murder toll was 3,000. When it comes to the categories within the population worst hit by revolutionary violence, the highest toll was among the clergy, as 1,189 churchmen, 794 religious, and 50 nuns were killed in Catalonia. That figure accounts for nearly a third of the clergy slain in republican Spain—upwards of 6,800 in all.[2]

The term "repression" has become the conventional description for the spectrum of violent practices, in both camps, in which persons in the rear guard were targeted—apart from war-related incidents (air raids and such). The notion is greatly misleading in that it makes a straight comparison between the two camps by depicting them as equally beset by a sort of murderous madness. This is not without some sense when applied to the Francoist camp, which quickly set itself up as a mini-state, or even to the republican state reconstituted in September 1936. On the other hand, it is largely inappropriate when used to cover the spontaneous violence, laden with festering grudges, of the early weeks of the revolution.

After to the clergy, the rural landowner and industrialist sectors were the next sectors in society to be hit by the "repression." Bringing up the rear was the category that includes the right-wing judges, far right militants, and former *pistoleros* from the (employer-run) Sindicato Libre.[3]

Numerous acts of revenge carried out against law enforcement agents who had ferociously stamped out the attempted uprisings in December 1933 in Aragon should also be classified as grudge-driven.

---

2   See Santos Juliá (dir.), *Víctimas de la Guerra civil* (Madrid: Temas de hoy, 1999), 127.

3   See François Godicheau, *La Guerre d'Espagne. République et révolution en Catalogne (1936–1939)* (Paris: Odile Jacob, 2004), 111.

{3}

PAGE 38

Even as the Madrid anarchists were recapturing Alcalá de Henares and Guadalajara from the rebels on July 22 and 23, 1936, the Central Antifascist Militias Committee in Barcelona was laying the groundwork for an attack on Zaragoza.

The coup d'état had carried the day in what was one of the major anarchist strongholds in Spain, thanks to the treachery of the civil and military governors of the city and to the ingenuousness of the local militants. García Oliver launched a stirring appeal over the airwaves to the CNT militants in the Aragonese capital to rise up while columns of volunteers from Barcelona went to the aid of the working-class population. But the general strike was a failure, the population failed to rise up, and the rebel army began liquidating Zaragoza's best-known militants.

On July 24 and 25, Barcelona's population turned out to watch the departure of the fighters heading for Zaragoza. Nearly six columns, composed of one or two thousand men each, armed pretty much with rifles and the odd artillery piece, set off in trucks, buses, or trains. The anarchists of the CNT supplied the bulk of the personnel of the Durruti, Ortiz, and Ascaso columns. Members of the PSUC, the POUM, and the Esquerra Catalana parties, respectively, formed the Trueba-Del Barrio (later dubbed the Carlos Marx) Column, the Maurín Column (subsequently renamed the Lenin Column), and the Bueno Column.

Earlier, some Barcelona anarchist militants and Manuel Prieto García (nicknamed "El Cojo," this CNT member and Asturian miner had been actively involved in the Figols—(Upper Llobregat)—uprising back in 1932) from the BOC [Bloque Obrero y Campesino], set off by truck on their own initiative.[4] Reaching the outskirts of Pina de Ebro on July 22, they were ambushed, and all but one was killed. According to Vicenta Valero Labarta (see the biographical note below on the Labarta family), who was a young resident of Pina at the time, one of them managed to hide and survived. The Francoist press made much of the incident, depicting it as a notable military success.[5]

4   "Manuel Prieto minero asturiano apodado 'El Cojo'...," *El Blog de "Acebedo,"* http://elblogdeacebedo.blogspot.fr/2014/10/manuel-prieto-minero-asturiano-apodado.html.

5   See Graham Kelsey, *Anarcosindicalismo y estado en Aragón 1930–1938* (Madrid, Fundación Salvador Seguí: 1994), 73–74.

Other spontaneous departures by militants took place on July 22; the group of which Miguel García was a member commandeered a luxurious Packard and made a beeline for Caspe, where they were ambushed, losing some of their *compañeros*. Francisco Subirats's group joined García's on July 24. Together they attacked the military personnel ensconced in Caspe, but most of the assailants had no experience of warfare and none of the requisite firepower. Considerable further losses were sustained. They then sought help from a military officer in Lérida, Lieutenant Zamora, who had remained loyal to the Republic. Zamora took a hand in matters with some artillery pieces. Outriders from the Durruti and Ortiz columns then joined them.[6]

For more details on the taking of the town, see the book *¡A Zaragoza o al charco!*[7]

After Caspe fell on July 25 (only a small band of the Durruti Column militia members were involved), the Column occupied Bujaraloz on the 26th, before setting off on the 28th for the Osera plain. It spent the night 150 meters from the village.

Also on July 26, a team of scouts from the Durruti Column entered Pina de Ebro without firing a shot. According to the testimony of the Civil Guard José Colera Vidal, who was one of them, the group was made up of Catalan CNT personnel from the Metalworkers' Union ("Ripoll, Jimeno, Moreno, and Selles") plus some Civil Guards who had stayed loyal to the Republic; these were under the command of Lieutenant Pedro Garrido Martínez:

> Born in Cuenca in 1894 [...] Pedro Garrido served in the Civil Guard as a lieutenant [....] He is described as [...] "one of those rare Civil Guard officers with bona fide republican credentials." In his memoirs, Guarner [says that he] "kept us informed that the bulk of his superiors had, on their word of honor, signed up to commitments to assist the army revolt."[8]

On learning of the existence of the antifascist committee, of

6   See Miguel García García, *Miguel García's Story*, edited by Albert Meltzer (Orkney: Cienfuegos Press, 1982), 81–86.

7   Les Giménologues, *¡A Zaragoza o al charco!* (Montreuil and Lagarde: L'Insomniaque and Les Giménologues, 2016).

8   José Colera Vidal, *La Guerre d'Espagne vue de Barcelone: Mémoires d'un garde civil républicain (1936–1939)* (Paris: Cygne, 2008), 45.

which I [José Colera] was a member, he sought a meeting with me in order to place himself at the committee's disposal.[9]

This lieutenant set off at the head of the so-called "Black Legion" and thereafter had to join the Durruti Column.[10]

According to a report drafted by the Causa General after statements given by inhabitants of Pina:

> The Red vanguard that entered the village on July 26, 1936, was joined by one resident, Evaristo Aguilar Artigas [who pointed out to them the homes of the well-to-do who were then arrested] [...] and, at 15.00 hours, they were stood against the church wall [...] and were executed by firing squad.[11]

Arrested at the end of the war and charged with volunteering his services to the Durruti Column, Pedro Garrido pleaded that he had saved the lives of the doctor, the mayor, and a post office official in Pina. Nevertheless, he was sentenced to death and executed in the Campo de la Bota on November 14, 1939.

So, on July 26, Colera, who was standing guard at the entrance to the village, watched as a busload of CNT militia members, brought in as reinforcements, arrived. Shortly after that, the team of scouts set off again on patrol, joining up with the bulk of the Durruti Column, which had stayed at the Gelsa crossroads to brief it on the capture of Pina. Planning to head back there to spend the night, the group realized that the enemy had recaptured it. These events were described by two Pina residents when consulted by José Luis Ledesma in 1999:

> "On July 26, Jesús Salillas was threshing grain when, at around 20.00 hours, an avalanche of militants ran from their vehicle, shouting: 'From now on, no more work for you [...] They had arrived by bus, around twenty men, they burned the church, the archival and court records, and stormed the homes with any

9   Ibid., 46.

10   Pedro Barrachina Bolea, "La Guerra de columnas en el frente de Zaragoza (verano e invierno de 1936)," in Fernando Martínez de Baños Carrillo, (ed.), *Guerra Civil Aragón: vol. 7. Zaragoza* (Zaragoza: Delsan, 2010), 95.

11   Report dated March 23, 1943, Archivo Historico Nacional, FC—CAUSA GENERAL, 1425, Exp. 90.

money and seized everything ..." But the militia members made a mistake that day, "because they had forgotten that the enemy was very close by. They had built a crude barricade at the entrance, and got drunk, and one group from Zaragoza massacred them," that very night, the 26th (Jesús Salillas and Antonio P.).

Between July 26 and August "not a contingent remained, and that includes the Nationalists. And no one moved, neither on the Right nor on the Left." (Antonio P.).

In August, with the definitive arrival of the militia members "they entered with Durruti, without a shot fired" (Jesús Salillas).[12]

On the morning of the 27th, at 6:30 hours, once the scouting team had rejoined them, four enemy aircraft bombed the militias.

This led to panic among its personnel, who were mostly accustomed to street fighting with police but had had no military training and little in the way of experience when it came to fighting in open country. They suffered around twenty dead or wounded and many men broke and ran. The remaining militia members headed back in the direction of Bujaraloz, where Durruti gave the volunteers a severe reprimand in the town square:

> To those who ran today and stopped the column from advancing, I ask you to have the courage to drop your rifle, so that another, firmer hand can pick it up. Those of us who remain will continue our march. We will conquer Zaragoza, we will free the workers of Pamplona, and we will join our Asturian miner *compañeros*. We will win and give our country a new world. To those who return, I ask you not to tell anyone about what happened today, because it fills us with shame.[13]

While the other columns deployed facing Huesca and Quinto de Ebro and Belchite, the Durruti Column set up its headquarters in Bujaraloz, where it remained for a week. According to Miguel Amorós, summarizing Pablo Ruiz, an anarchist militant who was there, it was then that the Durruti Column proper came into being; its delegate

12   Communicated to the authors by José Luis Ledesma.

13   Abel Paz, *Durruti in the Spanish Revolution* (Oakland: AK Press, 2007), 484. (Abel Paz pieced the speech together based on eyewitness testimony.)

general managed to discipline a chaotic and enthusiastic mass without injury to the working-class and libertarian character of the struggle.[14]

Let us read the August 2, 1936, article dispatched from Bujaraloz to *Le Libertaire* by the Frenchman Charles Ridel who, within days, would be helping set up the Durruti Column's International Group:

> Full of good intentions, the guerrillas from Barcelona had obviously had to adapt to a new fighting style in what is now an out-and-out war involving aircraft and artillery. Here courage does not suffice; one has to gauge, organize, and plan ahead. Facing them, there are something like ten regiments holding Zaragoza and the surrounding areas [....] If the military factor were the only thing that mattered, the fascists would be strong. But there is a worm in the bud: their troops operate only under constraint and duress and may roll over on first contact with the revolutionaries. Among the revolutionaries, the initial shambles is being replaced by the requisite organization. There is no end of enthusiasm. The only problem is the procrastination on the part of the Generalitat: miserly with weapons, manpower, and equipment, slowing down, dragging its heels, and on occasion saying no. The government is cautious of victory in Zaragoza, which would be the deathblow to the army mutiny. It would be followed by a vigorous mopping-up of Navarra by confederal troops and the certainty that the CNT would see its influence become overwhelming [....] The purging of the areas under their control is proceeding according to regulation; revolutionary justice is the answer to fascist barbarism and cruelty. Priests and fascist officers are regularly paying the price for these.[15]

Some commentators and historians say that the inactivity of the columns facing Zaragoza over several days sealed the latter's fate in that it was never taken. This helped to feed a severe polemic targeting anarchist militants who are charged with incompetence, especially since the follow-up claim is that the city was poorly defended during

14   Miguel Amorós, *Pablo Ruiz de Galarreta: un sastre navarro en la revolución anarquista* (Vitoria: Asociación Isaac Puente, 2004).

15   Louis Mercier Vega, *En route pour Saragosse avec la colonne Durruti* (Lausanne: Ed. Noir, 1997), 4.

the final days of July. This matter by itself merits a more full exploration of the various degrees of responsibility at play.

For further information, see Miguel Amorós, *Durruti en el laberinto* (Barcelona: Virus, 2014), 31–38; Graham Kelsey, "El mito de Buenaventura Durruti," in Antonio Morales Toro and Javier Ortega Pérez
(ed.) *El lenguaje de los hechos: ocho ensayos en torno a Buenaventura
Durruti* (Madrid: Libros de la Catarata, 1996), 82–85; José Manuel
Martínez Bande *La invasión de Aragón y el desembarco en Mallorca*
(Madrid: Editorial San Martín, 1989), 81–86; Eduardo Pons Prades,
"Verano de 1936 ¿porque no se tomó Zaragoza?," *Nueva Historia* 26
(1979).

{4}

PAGE 45

Pina de Ebro is a farming town, which had around 2,380 inhabitants in
1936. In the February 1936 elections, 55.71% of the voters supported
Popular Front candidates, and 43.19% the right-wing coalition. There
was no local CNT union, but many CNT members have sour memories of Pina, having rotted in the ruined medieval convent there. That
former prison, the ghastly hygiene of which was still being denounced
in 1935, had been put into service again by the republican government
in early January 1933 in the wake of the mass arrests following the failure of the insurrectionist strike in Zaragoza.[16]

As to the absence of any local CNT branch in Pina, we should
point out what Alejandro Díez Torre revealed to us:

> The CNT militias from the Durruti Column reached Pina de Ebro
> on August 8, 1936, by which time that village had already begun a
> process of local upheaval, which involved a change in its political
> outlook. As on other occasions under the Republic—such as the
> installation of the Republic or the constituent phase and, above
> all, the Popular Front phase—events forced a change of local

16　Kelsey, *Anarcosindicalismo y estado en Aragón*, 114, 180–82, 252.

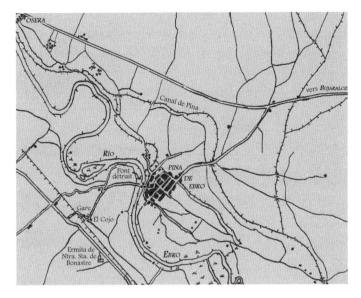

constituencies or leaders, which were now obliged to adapt to the new realities. So, whereas a local CNT union had been founded initially in 1931, its founders and members had had to alter their trade union view in 1932 when, in the wake of local pressures and governmental actions, the union was shut down. The upshot of this was that those affected by this launched a UGT-affiliated trade union as a local branch of the Land Workers' Union, which was tolerated up until the civil war.[17]

The same writer goes on to point out:

The same thing happened with many of the UGT's four hundred members—most of them formerly CNT personnel—who, as soon as the general strike was declared on July 21, fled eastward, without further support, looking for militia forces. The Durruti Column's arrival represented a fresh vista for the politically side-lined local left-wing leading groups, this time after ninety right-wing families had fled with the rebels. The rebel town hall was overrun, and—in the absence of any other organized local social or political force, except for former members and leaders of the

17   Alejandro Díez Torre, *Orígenes del cambio regional y turno del pueblo Aragón, 1900–1938, vol. 2. Solidarios* (Madrid and Zaragoza: UNED and Universidad de Zaragoza, 2003), 98.

Pina square and its church before July 1936.

UGT—they made up their minds, in light of the preceding organizational breakdown, to rebuild the old CNT union.[18]

And finally:

From that point on, and with a public proclamation in the village, the new Pina de Ebro CNT was launched: it was suggested that the population should join it (except for those who had thrown in their lot with the rebellion or involved themselves in the activities of the rebels during the weeks when the latter had occupied and lorded it over Pina). With 637 recruits to the Local CNT branch— 150 of them would join the militia units—the new organization oversaw social order within the village, where only those who had directly or indirectly aided and abetted the rebellion found their civil rights curtailed (and not because of any militia presence).[19]

At the beginning of August 1936, the Durruti Column resumed its push against Zaragoza. It had along with it young anarchists from the Metalworkers' Union, notably those making up guerrilla outfits of various description—the Hijos de la Noche, the Grupo Metalúrgico, the Banda Negra, et cetera. As for the last named of these, according to José Mariño, himself a member, it had initially been simply a picaresque title for a bunch of pals, the sort of thing the Libertarian Youth went in for in those days. At its head were the militants Pla, Sánchez, and Ripoll.

18   Ibid., 99.
19   Ibid., 100.

On August 8, 1936 preparations were made to capture Pina, and the presence of the Civil Guards was no longer seen as desirable. Having been stood down by "*compañeros* Sanz, Carreño, and Manzana,"[20] Pedro Garrido headed back to Barcelona, and José Colera followed. A *centuria* under the command of Francisco Carreño then headed for Gelsa; another two for Osera. Pablo Ruiz headed for Pina with two *centurias* plus the Banda Negra:

> When, on Saturday morning [August 8], the order came through to take the village where the fascists had sown terror [...] the latter were the lords and masters in Pina [...] The first ones in were the heroic guerrillas of the Guardia Negra, which is to say the "Bridegrooms of Death," as they preferred to be described. This group, made up of ten or twelve youngsters (earlier they had numbered nineteen or twenty) [...] made their way in, deploying in the village's narrow streets, inflicting numerous losses on the enemy who little by little retreated toward the center, albeit not without putting up some stiff resistance as they withdrew. But the "Bridegrooms of Death" pressed on and, having compelled them to fall back, in a stroke of daring, they positioned a machine gun on top of one building overlooking the entire village, forcing the rebels to flee across the Ebro.
>
> By the time the column entered Pina, all resistance had ended.[21]

Nevertheless, Gelsa, Pina, and Osera were left wide open to the Nationalists' fire from the river bank opposite, and the latter pounded them daily from their fortified positions on the hills above Quinto.

Further testimonies collected in the Centre Ascaso-Durruti in Montpellier, have made us aware of the existence of a small group of twenty-four youngsters from Madrid who joined the Durruti Column and played their part in the taking of Pina and Osera. One of them, Ángel Marín, has spoken of his meeting up with Carreño and Durruti and how the tag "The Madrid Group" was hung on them. Among the members of this group were Salvador Pobo Martínez (nicknamed El Practicante) and El Pinche (real name Francisco

20   Colera Vidal, *La Guerre d'Espagne vue de Barcelone*, 67.
21   *La Vanguardia*, August 12, 1936, 4.

Pérez). Ángel Marín points out that his group fought alongside other
groups including:

> Los Rebeldes, Los Somorrostros, La Banda Negra, Los Hijos de
> la Noche, etc., all of them dyed-in-the-wool militants, forged like
> Durruti in the crucible of anarcho-syndicalism. [They] were the
> column's elite and genuine defenders of the people armed against
> fascism![22]

According to Vicenta Valero Labarta, the inhabitants of Pina were
very frightened by the arrival of the anarchist militias. The Durruti
Column's militia members set fire to the archives, the church, and all
its precious contents. They carried off or ate all of the village livestock.
They killed between seven and nine people, including the priest and
the mayor—"This is all documented," she says. Besides, the Nationalists did the same things: raping and killing and burning. The villagers weren't used to war, weapons, and bombardments. The Durruti
Column assembled at the entrance to the village, on the Barcelona
road, on a hillside where there was a hermitage.[23]

Her account matches with that of Jesús Salillas Artigas, a Pina resident who—right up until his death in December 2005, according to
Jesús Inglada, who edited his memoirs:

> deplored the revolutionary violence used by the outriders from the
> Durruti Column. They were out to do away with all of the sym
> bols of military, political, economic, cultural, and religious author
> ity and had no regard for the lives of those who stood for them.[24]

In 1999, the very same Jesús Salillas told José Luis Ledesma:

> Those who did the killing were from Barcelona, but at the instiga
> tion of those from Pina.... They denounced fellow villagers who

22   Ángel Marín, "Hombres y hechos de la Guerra civil española," in Amedeo
     Sinca Vendrell, *Lo que Dante no pudo imaginar. Mauthausen-Gusen 1940–
     1945* (self-published, 1980), 51–58.
23   Vicenta Valero Labarta, *Entretien avec Vicenta à Saragosse*, May 11, 2005
     (sound recording).
24   Jesús Inglada, "Jesús Salillas Artigas: Un joven de Pina que ha vivido para
     contarlo" (Pina de Ebro: unpublished), 1.

they pointed out to the miliciens while the latter were searching for fascists. They were turned in "due to arguments and grudges."[25]

Another Pina resident, Valentín Gayán, stipulated: "Durruti was not the instigator of the repression in Pina."[26]

Over the days that followed, the columns pressed on toward Zaragoza and would overrun Farlete, Monegrillo, and Alfajarín.

For further details, see Miguel Amorós, *Francisco Carreño, el arduo y largo camino de la anarquía* (Vitoria: Asociación Isaac Puente, 2015), 30, 31.

{5}

PAGE 45

The reference here is to No. 2 *centuria*. The Durruti Column had set up its HQ in Bujaraloz and was organized into *agrupaciones, centurias,* and groups. One *agrupación* was made up of five *centurias*, each *centuria* comprising four twenty-five-man groups; there might be up to nine *agrupaciones*. The groups and *centurias* could choose their own delegates who, in principle, were liable to recall if they proved unsatisfactory.[27] According to a report by Ridel printed in *Le Libertaire* of October 30, 1936:

> in the villages occupied [such as Pina] a war committee was formed, made up, roughly speaking, of *centuria* delegates, a political delegate representing the workers' organizations and one or more local militants [...] Alongside the "military" setup, a series of ancillary bodies was created; supplies committees (ration committees, a transport oversight committee), etc. It took several weeks before the different columns on the Aragon front regularized their links, and longer still before a single command was introduced.

25   As communicated to the authors.
26   Ibid.
27   See Paz, *Durruti in the Spanish Revolution.*

Bujaraloz, August 14, 1936

In Barcelona, the Central Antifascist Militias Committee [...] was doing its best to coordinate the open-handed but scattershot initiatives from the revolutionary units. Liaison with Madrid was poorly handled and hobbled by the antagonism between the bourgeois democratic character of the central government and the social and revolutionary content of the Catalan organizations.

Among the membership of the Durruti Column's War Committee we find anarchist militants from the CNT and FAI including José Espluga, Miguel Yoldi, Francisco Carreño, Lucio Ruano, Francisco Mora, and Ricardo Rionda, but there were also servicemen who had stayed loyal to the Republic, men such as Enrique Pérez Farràs and Sergeant José Manzana, who became Durruti's righthand man.

Again, relying on Ruiz's testimony, Amorós explains that, in the beginning, militia members could float freely from one *centuria* to another depending on the affinities or frontline locations of their choice. Some treated themselves to leave in the rear guard. Others never returned to the front, causing the War Committee to issue a declaration, carried in the August 27, 1936, edition of *El Frente* (the war news of the column, printed in Pina from the 13th of that month onward):

We have come from Barcelona, and the road here is plain and clear-cut. Let anyone unwilling to pursue it by pressing ahead step off it once and for all. Of the absentees we shall say nothing, but it is our firm belief that those who march with us have but one idea in mind: pressing on to liberate our brothers and build a future.[28]

Organizing the militias was going to be time-consuming, but the main issue was the scarcity of arms, heavy artillery, and munitions. By mid-August the line of the Zaragoza front ran through Osera, Farlete, and Tardienta, and for weeks on end it would hardly move.

{6}

PAGE 45

As the state had been deprived of its prerogatives in Catalonia and Aragon—in the first few weeks of the war anyway—it fell to the local branches of the CNT to organize the population's new life. Contrary to what was going on in a number of still-republican villages in Catalonia—in Alcarràs or in Aragon, for example—there was no CNT committee in Pina to welcome the militia members. The Durruti Column's War Committee, established in Bujaraloz, then appointed Adolfo Ballano and Pedro Campón to form a revolutionary committee. Pablo Ruiz, who at one point chaired the Pina local committee, offered this description:

> Once Pina had been occupied, the militia members set up a Defense Committee that set about normalizing village life, commandeering the town hall as well as the assets and homes of the fascists. The lands belonging to the latter were handed back to the peasants. Provisioning was ensured by means of barter with the column, which received truckloads of foodstuffs dispatched by the unions back in Barcelona. In addition, the village was fortified.[29]

The property registers were destroyed. Small industries (like the flour mills) operated under the committee's supervision.

28   Amorós, *Francisco Carreño*, 31–32.
29   Transcription by Miguel Amorós, *Pablo Ruiz de Galarreta, el arduo y largo camino de la anarquía*, 9.

The Durruti Column then decided to collectivize the estates of the big landowners. Durruti arrived from Bujaraloz on August 16 in order to brief and reassure the people of Pina, which was now on the front line. Our "accredited reporters," Charles Ridel and Charles Carpentier, cited Durruti's speech the very same day in an article sent off to *Le Libertaire*, entitled "With the Durruti Column":

On Sunday August 16, the village square in Pina, located on the front lines and wrested from the fascists just a few days ago, is crammed with people. The big church is blackened by the fire that destroyed its furnishings and pious objects. No Mass today, for the priest has fled or been shot [...] A militant reads out the column's proclamation from the balcony. Just a few lines: "The assets of the local fascists have reverted to common ownership. All farm equipment is placed at the disposal of the township. The area is to be administered by the local committee elected by the village's general assembly. In exchange, the antifascist militia members ask for moral and material help from the populace." Once the reading had ended and the cheering abated, Durruti spoke: [...] "This is not Durruti talking to you, but the antifascist militias and the regionals of Catalonia, Aragon, and Navarra. We fight for you, for us, for the people. Once the campaign ends, we will have no stripes on our sleeves and no briefcases under our arms and will return to the factory, our rifles slung over our shoulders. We are workers just as you are. The revolution is only beginning, capitalist rule is finished, equality is to prevail, not the sort of equality that will cut all men down to the same size or to the same level of intelligence, but equality of rights and duties."[30]

In Pina, as in Gelsa and Bujaraloz, priority was given to harvesting the crops, which had been interrupted by the fighting. Tools were placed under common ownership, and machinery was introduced. According to the many announcements posted, private property and private businesses were done away with, as was money. Smallholders and artisans could only join the collective on a voluntary basis.

And how did the population react?

According to the recollection of Vicenta Valero Labarta:

30   *Le Libertaire*, September 11, 1936.

Young *pineros* enlist in the Durruti column

the decision to collectivize was never discussed [...] We were told where to go, and off we all went. They said we were to place everything *al montón* [under common ownership], so we did. We were so scared that we just did whatever they said [...] We were *ingénues*, didn't even known what rifle fire sounded like. [...] Everybody joined the collective, just like they said; after that it was off to the committee to apply for *vales* [vouchers], which were needed to make purchases.[31]

And here we also have Inglada's account, based on the testimony of the *pinero* [Pina resident] Jesús Salillas Artigas:

Jesús was one of those youngsters whose lives would remain marked by the revolutionary atmosphere that invaded the village of Pina. In the torrid summer of 1936 [...] he had no known political or trade union affiliations.[...] At the age of just seventeen and a half [...] Jesús Salillas enlisted in the Durruti Column as a volunteer, even though his parents disowned him. That was on August 24, 1936. Shortly after that, he would be but one of the roughly 1,500 militia members who left the Aragon front and went with the anarchist leader to rally to the aid of Madrid.[32]

31   Valero Labarta, *Entretien avec Vicenta à Saragosse.*
32   Inglada, *Jesús Sailillas Artigas*, 1.

Again according to Inglada's study, several youngsters from Pina like Jesús—about two hundred of them—joined the anarchist militias, and "the heads of the Durruti Column did not force anyone from Pina to sign up."

Simone Weil who showed up as part of the Durruti Column on August 14 jotted down a few curt, telegraph-style notes on a "conversation with some peasants from Pina."

Do they agree with farming everything in common?

First answer (repeated several times over): we will do whatever the committee says.

Old man: Yes.

　　–as long as they give him everything he needs.

　　–as long as he is not forever being pestered as he is today
　　　　with payments to the carpenter, the doctor ...

Another: he wants to see how it will work out.

Do they prefer farming together rather than separately?

Yes (none too categorical).

What did life used to be like?

Working day and night and very poor diet. Most cannot read [...]

And the priest?

They had nothing to offer by way of alms but used to give the priest poultry.

Popular?

Yes, with a lot of people.

How come?

No clear answer.

The people (all ages) talking to us had never been to Mass.

Had there been much hatred toward the rich?

Yes, but a lot more between the poor.

Surely that state of affairs might hinder their working together?

Not now; inequality is a thing of the past.

What if not everybody works the same?

Whoever does not work hard enough will have to be forced to do so. Only those who work will eat.

Is town life better than life in the countryside?

Twice as good. They do less work. They dress better, more diversions, etc. Town workers are more abreast of things ... One of their own who left to work in town came back after three months with a whole new outfit [...]

Many had been evicted for failing to pay rent. Forced into becoming farm laborers at two pesetas a day.

Rather pronounced sense of inferiority.[33]

For further details, see *La Vanguardia*, August 12 and 14, 1936; *Solidaridad Obrera*, August 11 and 13, 1936.

{7}
PAGE 46

On August 14, 1936, from their positions in Fuentes de Ebro and Puebla de Alfindén, the Nationalists tried to recapture Osera but failed.[34]

This is borne out by Ridel's testimony in his article for *Le Libertaire*:

Monday August 17: we are dug in in the village of Pina, which is located on the banks of the Ebro some thirty kilometers from Zaragoza. The area is under occupation by two *centurias*, a machine-gun team, the *Banda negra* (a dozen men plus one Italian ex-colonel), the International Antifascist Group, and the Red Cross. A few days ago, an attack mounted by the fascists on Obena [Osera], a neighboring village, was beaten off.[35]

For further information, see Alejandro Soteras Marín, *Mis Memorias* (Gúrrea de Gallego: Asociacion Casa Libertad, 2003), 52.

33   Simone Weil, "Journal d'Espagne," in "Écrits politiques et historiques," in *Oeuvres complètes*, vol. 2 (Paris: Gallimard, 1991), 374–82.

34   See Martínez Bande, *La invasión de Aragón y el desembarco en Mallorca*, 87.

35   *Le Libertaire*, no. 514, September 18, 1936.

{8}

PAGE 50

Let us look at a few extracts from a taped conversation between Antoine Gimenez and his adopted grandson, Frédéric, in 1982. All that has survived are these few minutes, thanks to which we have managed to identify the Valero Labarta family from Pina.

Antoine goes into greater detail of his second meeting with Tía Pascuala in Pina:

> She took me by the hand and led me a little further, and in the house she said: Tía Labarta, Tía Pascuala, the French guy is here! The Frenchman is asking for you.
> Show him in.
> And I saw someone appear in the doorway, a girl as skinny as her mother, young, about fourteen or fifteen.
> Are you?
> Yes, yes, that's me.
> Good, come in.
> I stepped inside.
> Wait a second. My mother is going to fetch the shirts for you.
> And she brought me a shirt, wow! Clean and well ironed. Oh my God!
> And so we began to chat. I speak a bit of Spanish.
> Fetch the *porrón*!
> The *porrón*. I don't know if you know what that is, what? The *porrón* is a sort of a bottle with a spout you can drink from without touching lips to it. Fetch the *porrón*, Vicenta!
> Up she came, and we had a bit of a drink and started chatting; where was I from, and have you any family? ... the sort of things that interest old women.
> Well, no, my mother's not around any more. Long since gone. There you have it.
> So you have no one?
> Well, no, no one.
> But how can you possibly get by?
> On this and that.
> Well, this evening you'll come here for supper.
> Wow!

Tía Pascuala's house today

Yes, yes, you'll come here for supper.

If you'd like, that is. As for me, I can't see any problem with it, right?

And so I began taking my meals at Tía Labarta's. She said: You'll be eating here.

I'm not sure if I can. I'll have to ask the group leader if I can eat in the homes of private citizens. Because, at the time, we didn't want to impose on people. If there were people offering us bed and board we would take them up on it, right? Now if no such invitation was made, well, we wouldn't take them up on it.

I said to her: I'll have to check.

She told me: Right, listen here; Vicenta, you go with the French *compañero* and explain to the chief, right, that starting this evening, he is our guest. He'll be eating and sleeping here.

Righto! Good, yes.

So I stood up and went with her. When Berthomieu saw me show up under escort from that … well, she was no beanpole, but she was on the skinny side, all the same … he looked at her, looked at me and said: Tell me, what do you think you're doing?

Me? Me? Not a thing. It's her. It's up to her to say what she means to do, right? As for me, I'm doing absolutely nothing. But as of tomorrow I am on guard duty, so this evening I need to get to bed early, and that's the whole of it.

Whereupon she said: *Señor, es mi madre que me envía a decirle que el compañero es que si no tiene ninguna oposición comerá y acostará en mi casa.* [Sir, I am here at the behest of my mother to tell you that, if it is all right with you, the *compañero* here will be taking his meals and sleeping in my home.]

What is your name?

At which she said to him: *Yo me llamo Vicenta Labarta y mi madre se llama Pascuala Labarta.* [My name is Vicenta Labarta and my mother's name is Pascuala Labarta.]

You're very young. And your mother and father are elderly.

And he said: I reckon I can grant him permission [giggles from Antoine].

Afterward, about two or three weeks later, when something happened that didn't go down well with the inhabitants of Pina, Berthomieu used to say: Listen, you are bastards and should take Pascuala Labarta as your example. There is a fellow who sleeps over at her house, yet we never hear a word of complaint. He doesn't create a problem. Could you people not do likewise? The fact that one of us comes from Germany and another from Cochinchina or Cuba does not mean that you have to act like ….

Because there were a few who were getting their hackles up, you see? Well, let me tell you, from then on, over the next two years I would get up in the morning, have a wash, pick up my rifle and cartridge belt, and throw open the door:

Vicenta, dile a tu madre que me marcho [Vicenta, let your mother know I'm off.] Right, off I go.

If by any chance I was leaving in the evening and would be back late [emotional silence], there was someone there who used to wait for me to come home. [Long silence.] Poor old woman!

[Frédéric speaking] She had her reasons for caring so.

Well, yes, because often I would go out and even more frequently would not return. That was what worried her. Once she knew that I had to go, and this happened to me one day—and that was the case one out of every three days—you could see the old lady melt because she had sons on the far side.

On the fascist side?

Yes, and a daughter, María, who was also over there. One of her sons plus María made it back across.

You went over and fetched them back, right?

Eh?

You went and fetched them.

No, that wasn't them. They crossed over all by themselves. María and her brother had crossed over alone. Seen alongside Maria's group, her mother was skin and bone, and Maria was a heavyweight. If she was to hit you with those breasts of hers she'd likely send you spinning back to Spain [laughter]. No, but she really was a sound woman. The whole family. The entire family. There were ... there was somebody [silence] We never knew ... the last time I set eyes on her was close to the Spanish border, I mean ... the French border, and she had had no news of her son who had stayed behind. And so, it was not . . . [silence] it was a pity . . . a sound woman, and her daughters were sound girls.

{9}
PAGE 51

The reference is probably to Arturo Arfinenghi:

Born on March 10, 1891 in Varallo Sesia (in Vercelli province), he was living in Paris when he set off for Spain, enlisting on October 18, 1936, in the Garibaldi Battalion. In November 1936 he was wounded during the early fighting on the Madrid front. Thereafter, the only record of him is in the hospitals of the city and in the ones in Barcelona. He left Spain in February 1939 and made his way back to Paris, where he lived until his death on March 4, 1963.[36]

{10}
PAGE 51

On July 31, 1936, the mouthpiece of the French Union Anarchiste, *Le Libertaire*, carried the headline: "The Spanish revolution is our

36   Centro Studi P. Gobetti and AICVAS (Associazione Italiana Combattenti Volontari Antifascisti in Spagna), *Sez. piemontese, Antifascisti piemontesi e valdostani nella Guerra di Spagna*, with introductory note by Anello Poma (Guanda: Parma, 1975), 4.

revolution!" The revolutionary retort to the Spanish army's attempted coup d'état was particularly electrifying for anarchist circles around the world. And from July to October 1936, before the International Brigades were set up, hundreds of volunteers were to head, singly or in small groups, for the Pyrenees.

Among them were many German and Italian refugees, as well as Hungarians, Bulgarians, and Yugoslavs, Poles, Ukrainians, and Russians and so on, extremely pleased at finally emerging from their enforced exile in many cases. Some of them were already in Barcelona when that summer came, including those who intended to compete in the Spartakiad, a sort of Olympic Games organized as an alternative to the official games in Berlin. Right from the start of the army revolt, there were *internacionales* fighting alongside the working-class population. When the time came to set off for Aragon, the first columns were joined by the Ernst Thaelmann group, which was set up by about ten Germans, most of them Jewish communists. Moreover, five Germans, the first three of whom were CNT members, were recorded on July 24 on the list of foreign militia members incorporated into the Durruti Column: the five were Robert Schreiber, Oskar Zimmermann, Jean Schwarz, Alfons Teschke—aged thirty, twenty-nine, forty, and thirty-nine, respectively—and Hermann Gierth.[37]

Some French volunteers approached the Fédération Anarchiste in Paris, which organized their dispatch by the truckload, or they enrolled through the UA and the CGT-SR. Others, libertarians and non-libertarians alike, made their own way to Spain. We don't always know their names, and their numbers have been estimated at between two hundred and several hundreds.

By the end of July, a French section had opened an office in Barcelona to welcome the volunteers and pass out CNT-FAI propaganda.

Armand Aubrion and a number of *compagnons* set off from Paris on July 22; Aubrion was to forward reports to *Le Libertaire*.

The UA's Saint-Denis chapter gave a send-off to Boudoux and several others. Mohamed Saïl (or, to use his full name Mohamed Ameriane ben Ameziane Saïl) was to send articles back to *Le Combat syndicaliste*. He was born on October 14, 1894, in Taourirt, Souk Oufella (Algeria). A heating mechanic and then earthenware repairer, he was an anarchist and anarcho-syndicalist militant affiliated with the CGT-SR. He left

---

37 See IISH, CNT, 63, II, 2.

for Spain as a volunteer and joined the Durruti Column sometime that September, it seems.

Georges Navel, a long-time draft-refuser, sometime shirker, and soon-to-be writer, had moved into a farmhouse in the Midi in 1935, eking out a living from a small garden and smallholding, a far cry from the greasy spoons and war-mongering atmosphere. However reluctantly, he boosted his income with seasonal jobs:

> In that region, the working day, when there was any work to be had, lasted ten hours, for wages were slashed to half of the levels of a few years before. My mind was made up not to put up with such conditions [...] I might grow vegetables, but never again would I work for the bosses.[38]

On July 29, he sold a few hens, jumped onto his bike, and headed for Perpignan: "For me, this was no 'pleasure trip'; I was going there to get in on the fighting on the barricades, unless it was already over, or make myself useful working at my trade."[39]

After many difficulties, he at last crossed over the Pyrenees: "I had struck out for the border-post [...] The initial response to my very first words, *soy francés* [I'm French], was *'Es igual somos todos hombres'* [We are all men equal] and that really appealed to me."[40]

Among Gimenez's soon-to-be friends, Charles Ridel and François-Charles Carpentier, members of the UA, took their pay and headed for the peninsula. In the 1980s, with his typical Parisian bluntness, Carpentier set the moment in its proper context:

> Previously we made mounted attacks on the trams in Saint-Denis, fighting with the cops, and we finished the night banged up in the Fort de l'Est ... Childish games. Now there were people fighting for freedom. We had to get in on it![41]

The duo arrived in Puigcerdà on July 29 and promptly penned some articles for their organization's newspaper, *Le Libertaire*,

38 *Les Révoltes logiques*, no. 14/15 (Spring 1981): 77–78.
39 Ibid., 77.
40 Ibid., 82.
41 Phil Casoar and Lucien Feuillade, "Itinéraire François-Charles Carpentier," *Le Monde Libertaire*, No. 708 (May 19, 1988).

reporting on the situation and on the establishment of the Durruti Column's International Group:

> Tomorrow we're off to Barcelona, then Zaragoza. There the fighting is bitter and bloody. The slaughter of anarcho-syndicalists inside the city has been terrifying, it seems. So the watchword of the FAI and CNT, "No quarter!" is understandable. Sentimentality has flown out of the window in the face of fascist savagery.
>
> From revolutionary Barcelona, July 30:
> [...] We are off to Zaragoza this evening to join up with Durruti who, at the head of one of the columns, is getting ready to storm the rebel city where, in spite of the horrific slaughter, teams of anarchists are still fighting, awaiting the revolutionary army that is to bring them deliverance [...].
>
> Bujaraloz, August 2:
> We have arrived in Bujaraloz, the seat of the Durruti Column's Military Committee. The official commanding officer, Pérez, is ensconced in Lérida, a hundred kilometers behind the front lines! [...]
>
> The militia members resemble Pancho Villa's men as popularized by the movies. No two of them wear the same uniform: blue overalls, civilian garb, motley uniforms, helmets, berets, Mexican sombreros, red and black police hats, etc. The only thing they have in common is the espadrilles. We bump into Italians, Frenchmen, Germans. Peasants mingle with workmen, and among them are some carabineers, Civil Guards, all obeying the FAI and CNT committees. [...]
>
> Saturday, August 8:
> [...] In nearly every one of the *centurias* one can find Italians, French, Germans, and even Belgians and Bulgarians. [...] They all mix well and make up a solid mass, despite certain language difficulties.
>
> A team of Italians and French has been formed with a one-time colonial officer [Louis Berthomieu] as its delegate; what he lacks in specific doctrine he makes up for in a very quick, unprejudiced intelligence. They are all lads from Paris, Toulon, or Grenoble. [...] Outlaws from Italy and victims of French imperialist exploitation have come to do their bit for the old dream of a libertarian society, a dream cherished for so long. The group

will grow bit by bit as fresh personnel come along. Confronted by the Legion from Morocco—that jumble of killers and thieves who have come to Spain to restore the bourgeois order—an international Legion of the stateless is emerging here in the peninsula to fight on behalf of revolutionary workers' order."[42]

For further details, see David Berry, *A History of the French Anarchist Movement, 1917 to 1945* (Oakland: AK Press, 2009); Jérémie Berthuin, *De l'espoir à la désillusion. La CGT-SR et la Révolution espagnole. Juillet 1936–Décembre 1937* (Paris: CNT-RP, 2000); Collectif, *Présence de Louis Mercier* (Lyon: Atelier de création libertaire, 1999); and *À contretemps* 14/15.

{11}
PAGE 52

Such action by the militia members was repeated elsewhere it seems, for in the testimony of column commander Antonio Ortiz we find the same sort of account:

> During the first few weeks of the revolution and the fighting in the Aragonese countryside, the militias lived off local resources. That meant a heavy toll taken from the flocks in the area, given that they wasted more meat than they actually ate. At the same time, the flock owners, the bulk of whom defected to the rebels, took their livestock with them to well beyond Belchite.
> A proclamation was issued banning the slaughter of animals [...] and then the guerrillas gathered intelligence as to the movements of 'enemy' livestock. One night when the latter were gathered into a pen near La Puebla de Albortón, some fifteen kilometers beyond the lines, a team of militia members rounded up the entire flock and brought it back over into lawful territory and "liberated" it. Thereby retrieving 4,000 livestock, sheep, goats, and cattle.

42 Mercier Vega, *En route pour Saragosse*, 1–5.

This formed the basis of the livestock resources of the south-Ebro zone [...] and within a few months those herds had grown to 10,000 head.[43]

{12}
PAGE 53

In Paris, in August 1936, the Comité pour l'Espagne libre (Committee for Free Spain) was formed with the pacifist Louis Lecoin as its spokesman. A series of meetings, exhibitions, and collections were held, and every week trucks left Paris laden with food supplies, clothing, arms, and ammunition. Such was the impact made by the revolution in Spain that even dyed-in-the-wool pacifists crossed the Pyrenees either to fight or to make themselves useful in some other way; or, quite simply, like Scolari, just to be part of things.

Simone Weil was a typical example:

I do not like war; but what has always horrified me most about it is the situation of those who find themselves in the rear. Once I realized that, no matter how hard I tried, I couldn't stop myself from participating in this war morally, which is to say, yearning daily, hourly, for the victory of some and the defeat of others. I told myself that Paris was the rear guard as far as I was concerned, so I caught a train to Barcelona, with the intention of getting involved.[44]

We know Simone Weil reached Pina de Ebro on August 14, 1936. She was an acquaintance of Charles Ridel and Charles Carpentier, having come across them during the strikes in Paris that June, and it was through them that she joined the International Group, a band of

---

43   Juan José Gallardo Romero and José Manuel Márquez Rodríguez, *Ortiz, general sin dios ni amo* (Barcelona: Hacer, 1999), 148.

44   Simone Weil, "Lettre à Georges Bernanos" in *Témoins, IIe année 7* (Zurich: 1954), 2–6.

irregulars charged with dangerous missions and made up mostly of foreigners. Ridel—who was later to adopt the name Mercier Vega—had this to say in 1975 of Simone Weil's arrival:

> She carried a rifle, wore the mechanic's overalls that served as a uniform, espadrilles on her feet, and a red and black bandana knotted around her neck, and on her head a cap in the same colors. She wanted to be and therefore was a militia member, contrary to what Gustave Thibon was to say in his foreword to *Gravity and Grace*, in which he depicts her as an observer.
>
> She was a militia member who was not without courage and who insisted on taking part in reconnaissance expeditions. Not that this didn't pose a few questions for the leading lights of the International Group: [...] Simone didn't have the foggiest idea how to handle weapons; furthermore, she was shortsighted and wore thick glasses. At first it was a matter of assigning her to rear-guard duties, such as setting up an outpost for the first aiders, but she kicked up a stink and insisted on running the same risks as the fighters. In the end, she got her way.[45]

For further details, see Charles Jacquier (dir.), *Simone Weil, L'expérience de la vie et le travail de la pensée* (Arles: Sulliver, 1998); Collectif, *Présence de Louis Mercier*.

{13}
PAGE 53

Among the foreigners who came to Spain as volunteers during the civil war, more than 250 French militia members have been identified, 150 of whom enlisted with the Durruti Column. Others set up the "Ortiz Column's International Sébastien Faure Group," which was to fight south of the Ebro.

45   Louis Mercier Vega, "Simone Weil sur le front d'Aragon," in Marc Hanrez (ed.), *Les Écrivains et la guerre d'Espagne* (Paris: Cahiers de l'Herne, 1975), 276.

The Michele-Schirru group, from the Italian section of the Ascaso Column

Enjoying comparative autonomy of action vis-a-vis the Durruti Column, the internationals made Pina their base. Their general delegate, Louis Berthomieu, was in direct touch with the War Committee. In the French newspaper *L'Espagne antifasciste*, no. 4, August 30, 1936, one can find this sort of small item:

Our postbag:
Our *compañeros* Carpentier and Ridel, Durruti Column International Antifascist Group, Pina de Ebro, ask French, Belgian, Italian, Bulgarian *compañeros* arriving from France to fight to write to them, with an eye to bolstering that group.

In August 1936, the very same group was to grow from twenty to about sixty individuals, and it would grow more over the coming months, with the regular arrival of Swiss, Austrian, and German personnel.

For the time being, most of the Italians and Germans who had come to Spain were on the Huesca front, serving in Catalan and Aragonese *centurias* attached to the Ascaso Column, or with the POUM column.

While a few Italians joined the Durruti Column in individual capacities, as Antoine or Scolari did, the sizable trans-Alpine refugee colony organized in France under the aegis of the Anarchist Revolutionary Committee came together in Barcelona from late July 1936 onward. The philosopher and anarchist theoretician Camillo Berneri, joined by Francesco Barbieri and many others, took charge of the influx of volunteers. They set up the Malatesta Group, liaising with members of the Catalan FAI and CNT, including Diego Abad de Santillán, who would become an active participant in the formation of the Italian militias. Here are some extracts from Berneri's correspondence:

> For the most part, the Italian antifascists who had come to Barcelona were drawn from every section of the anarchist movement [...]
> [...] Scattered across a number of hotels in the city, they were stirred and intoxicated by the spiritual rejuvenation resulting from the abrupt switch from the life of the hunted exile to that of the new citizens of a capital of the revolution, still bearing the stamp of the heady atmosphere of the formidable street-fighting. [...] Those anarchists who had not signed up for the Durruti Column's International Group were inclined to establish a strictly anarchist column and were itching to set off then and there. The impossibility of securing weapons immediately frustrated their plans, but they had already been mulling over enlistment in the confederal militias.[46]

Indeed, on August 5, the Italian anarchists agreed to overtures made by the dissident socialist Carlo Rosselli, from the Giustizia e Libertà group, regarding the formation of a mixed column serving as an umbrella for every part of the spectrum of Italian antifascists. And so was born the Italian Section of the Ascaso Column, which decided to abide by the political directives coming from the libertarian organizations. Its 120 men—Berneri, despite his being hard of hearing, was one of these—two-thirds of them libertarians, set off for the Huesca front and received their baptism by fire at Monte Pelato on August 28, 1936. Attacked by clearly numerically superior enemy forces, the section lost many of its men, including its commander, Mario Angeloni.[47]

46   Camillo Berneri, *Epistolario inedito*, vol. 2 (Pistoia: Archivio Famiglia Berneri, 1984), 268.

47   Gaetano Manfredonia, "Notes sur la participation des anarchistes italiens à la révolution espagnole" *La Rue*, no. 37 (Groupe Libertaire Louise Michel), (1986). For further details of the Italian volunteers and the relations between anarchists and socialists in Spain, see Alba Balestri, *La Section italienne de la Colonne Ascaso* (Saint-Georges d'Oléron: Éditions libertaires, 2015).

According to Enrico Acciai, the following Italian anarchists made the transition from the Durruti Column: Albano Bianchella, Mario Bellini, Giacomo Canepele, Mario Corghi, Filippo Lusvardi, Marcello Minello, Pietro Montaresi, and Carlo Moroni.[48] We will have occasion to mention some of these names again later.

As for the German and Austrian anarcho-syndicalists, they were part of the DAS (Deutsche Anarcho-Syndikalisten) group launched in exile back in 1933–1934 and headquartered in Amsterdam. Its Barcelona office (at 18 Calle de Aribau) was manned by about twenty people, including Helmut Rüdiger and Augustin Souchy, who took charge of the new volunteers. It should be mentioned that among the Germans and Austrians, only those who had previously belonged to some anarcho-syndicalist organization were actually members of the DAS (and so they, in many cases, were often Germans who had been living in Spain since 1932 or 1933). So the new volunteers were, for the most part, not DAS members, but the DAS group looked out for them. In all, nearly 200 German volunteers would enlist in the anarchist militias. A few joined the Durruti Column in an individual capacity, and others made up the Erich Mühsam group and joined the last anarchist column, Los Aguiluchos, to set off for the Huesca front in late August 1936. The Erich Mühsam group was made up of nine machine-gun specialists: Miguel (aka Rudolf Michaelis), its delegate; Pacha, an instructor; Kaenel, a technician; Winkelmann, Eberle, Aul, Christ, Laeubli, and Appel. The group went on to become a *centuria*, and it would fight as part of the Ascaso Column. After it saw action in the battle of Tardienta on October 26, 1936, it was reduced to just fifty men. On November 18, its delegate, Michaelis, sought to have them seconded to the Durruti Column's International Group. The members of the DAS wanted to join their fellow Germans who needed them for, among other things, a very specific task: the latter had pointed out the arrival over preceding weeks of:

> German authoritarian personnel in Spain. For the most part, they are Stalinists without any notion of what is going on this country. They blindly obey their communist bosses, and it is our

48   Enrico Acciai, *Viaggio attraverso l'antifascismo. Volontariato internazionale e guerra civile spagnola: la Sezione Italiana della Colonna Ascaso* (Viterbo: Università degli Studi della Tuscia: Viterbo, 2010), 49.

conviction that one day, once our common war against fascism has concluded, they will turn their guns on the Spanish anarchists, if the order comes. If this is to be averted, they must be targeted for special propaganda. This undertaking may well prove successful, insofar as those Germans do not act out of malice.[49]

For further information, see David Berry, *History of the French Anarchist Movement*; David Berry, *French Anarchist Volunteers in Spain, 1936–39: Contribution to a Collective Biography of the French Anarchist Movement*; Carlos García Velasco, Dieter Nelles, Ulrich Linse, and Harald Piotrowski, *Antifascistas alemanes en Barcelona (1933–1939). El Grupo DAS: sus actividades contra la red nazi y en el frente de Aragón* (Barcelona: Sintra, 2010), 91–198, and 405–426; Andreas Graf and Dieter Nelles, "Widerstand und Exil deutscher Anarchisten/Anarchosyndikalisten," in Rudolf Berner, *Die unsichtbare Front: Bericht über die illegale Arbeit in Deutschland (1937)* (Berlin: Libertad Verlag, 1997), 121.

{14}
PAGE 53

In an interview, Antonio Ortiz, general delegate of the Sur-Ebro Column, bragged about being the first to expel the women from his column. One of those women, Conxa Pérez, a young FAI member, who had gone up to the front at the same time as her brother and some friends from the Les Corts district of Barcelona, complained bitterly of the fact that female militia members had been dismissed that way and that no distinction had been made between them and prostitutes. She testifies that lots of young female activists from the districts of Barcelona had headed off to the front to pick up a rifle or to make themselves useful as nurses. She mentioned Libertad Ródenas who had had a hand in the taking of Pina, and the female guerrilla Carmen Crespo[50] from

49 IISH, FAI 1, November 18, 1936.
50 In Les Giménologues' *¡A Zaragoza o al charco!*, the reader will find fuller

the Sur-Ebro Column. This young Spanish woman [Crespo] had been living in France and had come to Barcelona in July 1936 to attend the antifascist Spartakiad games. From the moment the fighting erupted, she joined the militias and was nicknamed La Francesa (The French-woman). She was educated and shy but obviously of strong character. Far from wanting her expelled, Ortiz would rather have kept her on at his headquarters in Caspe by assigning her secretarial duties, but she wanted to fight alongside the guerrillas and made her own way to the front lines. She perished in an engagement in the Sierra de la Serna in December 1936, killed by a grenade.[51]

From the testimonies of the Swiss couple Paul and Clara Thalmann we know that few women managed to reach the front after October 1936. During their first stay on the Aragon front, Clara had no prob-lem enlisting as a militia, but on their second trip to Spain, in early January 1937, the pair searched for some way of getting back to the Aragon front:

> Then he [Souchy] advised us to approach the DAS (the German anarcho-syndicalist group), which had raised a hundred-man unit on the Aragon front. Souchy doubted whether women were still being granted permission to fight alongside the men: "As you know, the Valencia government has issued a decree to that effect. But here in Catalonia, it's the committees who make the decisions and, in your case, it will be up to the relevant military committee. Good luck!" [...]
>
> The group stationed in Pina gave us a warm welcome. They were all delighted by our arrival and eager for news from abroad and from Barcelona. [...] The men admired Clara on account of her courage, and promptly accepted her. There was still a woman in that group, the only one, a Spaniard known as Pepita who assisted a Spanish doctor in the infirmary. [...]
>
> Every appointment to any function within the group was made by means of democratic election, and the appointees could be replaced at any time should a general assembly so determine.

details about Carmen Crespo, notably the testimony from Emilio Marco, a former militiaman with the Ortiz Column.

51   See Ingrid Strobl, *Partisanas* (Barcelona: Virus, 1996), 354, 355. An English edition is available, *Partisanas: Women in the Armed Resistance to Fascism and German Occupation (1936–1945)* (Oakland: AK Press, 2008).

The first big argument revolved around the issue of whether Clara could stay with us. The issue had been raised by Michaelis. In our ten-man group, no one had a problem with it. Every evening, before the general assembly, Clara would flit from group to group, arguing her case. Come the meeting, she emerged the victor by a few votes, a remarkable outcome, given the government ban.[52]

Michaelis himself confirmed this in a letter dated February 3, 1937. He was writing from Bujaraloz to a "DAS compañero":

Manzana has issued a reminder that the women who have been on the front since the very beginning can stay there (unless the law changes) but the more recent arrivals must go. Clara Thalmann's case is not affected. The compañeros were induced to vote on the matter and, doubtless after influence was brought to bear, certain of them have voted against expelling the women. It is important that there should be no more women coming to the front.[53]

Antoine Gimenez refers to a Madeleine, an Augusta, and a Mimosa who stayed on with the International Group as nurses. He was referring to Madeleine Gierth and Augusta Marx, both Germans, who were later included in a list of DAS members in Spain. As for Mimosa, that was the nickname of Georgette Kokoczynski (see the biographical note below), a twenty-nine-year-old Frenchwoman who arrived in Spain on September 19, 1936. An activist since her adolescent years, she hung out in the libertarian circles around the newspapers *Le Libertaire*, *L'Insurgé*, and *L'En-Dehors*; she distributed *La Revue anarchiste* and its supplement *Choses d'Espagne*. In 1924, she met Fernand Fortin, with whom she shared the activist life in the Tours region. In 1928, she went back to Paris where she helped out with anarchist cultural events and demonstrations. She used to recite and sing with a group of friends, and it is at that point that she adopted the "stage name" Mimosa. She qualified as a nurse and decided to offer her services to the Spanish revolution after taking part in the August 28, 1936, rally in the Salle Wagram. Here is a letter that she sent to a French

52   Pavel (Paul) Thalmann and Clara Thalmann, *Combats pour la liberté* (Quimperlé: La Digitale, 1983), 136, 138, 140.

53   IISH, FAI, 1.

compagnon (no doubt Fernand Fortin) on the day she left Barcelona for the Aragon front, probably October 3:

> [On the letterhead of the Hotel Lloret at No 5, Rambla Canaletas]
> Barcelona, Tuesday
> Dearest Fernand,
> Having set off on September 18, I am still in Barcelona, though I think I am at last going to get to work this evening … setting off for the Huesca front. My thoughts of you are fond, as you know. I bumped into Arthur here; he of course was preparing to head back to France; I asked him to ask you for a collection of reviews for the very kind friend I mentioned to you. Arthur will very likely do no such thing, so be so kind, Fernand, as to forward the collection of reviews to Mr G. Mayer, 37 rue Davioud, Paris, as well as André's book which can be picked up for 2 francs on the *quais*, plus as many editions as possible of *Le Libertaire*. I will be very grateful to you if you would do this, and the gentleman for whom all this printed matter is intended will be obliged to spare me a thought and drop me a line. Is your mind still made up to come here? How's your morale … better I hope? Better than my own, which is very low. I was actually torn up about coming here, but I must. I would have liked to see you before I left, but I came to your place one day when you were out and never got the chance to try again.
> Lots of kisses, my darling old Fernand. Be happy; that's what I wish for you with all of the deep-seated fondness I have for you. I haven't seen the compañeros yet but I am to meet them for lunch. I think I've picked up Julien's trail. As yet, I have no idea what my address will be from tomorrow, but you can always write to the CNT-FAI, 32, 34 Via Layetana, Barcelona and they will forward it on to the … in all likelihood … Huesca … sector of the front.
> Georgette[54]

We have yet to identify Marthe with any certainty; she was, in all probability, Juliette Baudart. Unless she was Thérèse Bardy or Hélène Patou, the latter a French female worker mentioned by David Berry; she joined the Durruti Column along with Henri Charrodeau.[55]

54   IISH, FAI, package 50.
55   See maitron-en-ligne.univ.paris1.fr/spip.php?article73976.

As for "Rosario," we think Antoine is using it here as the first name of the combat militia-woman known as Pepita Inglés, of whom Lola Iturbe from the Mujeres Libres group has drafted a biography. Here is an extract from it:

> Pepita Inglés was born in Cartagena in the province of Murcia [...] On July 19 she was impressed by the enthusiasm displayed by the Barcelona libertarians who had taken charge of the situation in Catalonia, and on July 24 she set off for Aragon with the Durruti Column along with her partner, at cost to the well-being of their two children. Of the other women who also set off, I can remember the likes of Palmira Jul, Azucena Haro, and Durruti's partner, Émilienne Morin [...] When the column was en route to Pina, the fascists bombed it from the air. Some of the women, finding the harsh reality of war harrowing, turned tail for Barcelona. Pepita Inglés pressed on with the column. She lost her partner during the first attacks on Pina. She then joined the tank service [...]
>
> At first glance those armored trucks looked invincible but it was later realized that an ordinary Mauser round could penetrate them. [...] It required a cool head and determination to climb inside those sweltering, airless trucks![56]

{15}
PAGE 53

Let us take a look at Mercier Vega's account from 1975:

> The Durruti Column's International Group was in its infancy. It grew from the urge of a tiny core of foreign volunteers to raise a combat unit with a modicum of military training and, if possible, experience of warfare. Having taken part in a number of

56 Dolores (Lola) Iturbe Arizcuren, *La mujer en la lucha social y en la Guerra civil de España* (Canary Islands and Madrid: Tierra de Fuego and La Malatesta, 2012), 121–22.

operations (the advance on Osera, the occupation of Pina, the raid on Gelsa) the Berthomieux [*sic*]–Carpentier–Ridel trio realized that the Spanish *centurias* would need some time to learn the ABCs of fighting in open country and to get a grasp of the use of heavier weapons. Right from the outset, the group's function was plain and simple: to act as the spearhead allowing the militias to plow ahead.

The first mission entrusted to it was to sever the railway line in the Francoist-held territory. The two confederal columns [...] made uneven progress along the Ebro. Pina, on the left bank, was forward of the front lines manned by the Ortiz–Ascaso Column [Ortiz, in reality] on the right bank. The Falangist troops were kept supplied by rail convoys that left from Zaragoza and passed through Pina station on the other side of the river. Blowing up the railway lines would impede the shipment of food and munitions bound for the Francoist forces and would make a militia attack on Quinto that much easier.

Half a dozen volunteers, Simone Weil among them, carried out initial reconnaissance. The group established that there were irrigation channels, which might facilitate inroads and indicate the precise distance between the riverbank and the rail line.[57]

The testimony from the militiaman Soteras complements Mercier's account:

Up until then we hadn't had the slightest brush with the enemy. One day, we were told to make sure our weapons were ready for we were undoubtedly going to need them. In the middle of the afternoon, we set off in the direction of Osera [...] The centuria leader urged us not to spread out widely but to stick together and await our orders [...] Night had fallen by the time a big, high-sided but uncovered truck arrived and people started to climb down off it. It was a group that specialized in nighttime raids on enemy positions.

As they were in the process of dismounting from the truck, one of the leaders involved in the operation asked if there was a woman among the group. Nobody answered, but at that very

---

57   Mercier Vega, "Simone Weil sur le front d'Aragon," 276.

moment a woman appeared. She was armed like the rest of her compañeros. A shotgun with cartridges, or rather bullets in a bandoleer, and, around her waist, a belt packed with grenades. On her head she wore a black kerchief tied at the back, with the three letters FAI displayed in front.

Seeing her, he said that he was under orders not to let any women take part in the operation. Very sure of herself, she replied that whoever had issued the order should come and say that to her face: "Yesterday in Tardienta I lost my husband, and I am ready for anything." [This was definitely Pepita Inglés.]

The object of the operation was to mount a surprise attack on a Castillejos cavalry unit, which had settled into a farm on the far bank of the Ebro, outside Osera. A corporal and a soldier had defected from that unit and come over to our side during the night. With the intelligence they provided, the idea of mounting the raid had been devised.

This was this specialist group that had been commissioned to carry out the raid. We were not to intervene unless they needed some cover for their return journey. [...] The raid came off to perfection. No losses at all on our side.

The next day, I asked how the raid had gone: they had taken a number of soldiers and some horses prisoner. "Prisoner" is not quite the right word, for none of them stayed a prisoner. The men were asked if they had family in the republican zone and were given leave. Once the operation was over, the team brought in for the raid left and I never saw them again.[58]

{16}
PAGE 55

Again, in 1975, Mercier refers to what is undoubtedly the same sort of operation:

58   Soteras, *Mis memorias*, 52.

Neither collectively nor through a single one of its members had the Group been involved with any execution squad (two Spanish militia members were thrown out of its ranks when they admitted to having previously served on just such a squad). Louis Berthomieux [*sic*], as well as the delegates from the various sections, had consistently protected prisoners or harbored defecting servicemen from the threats of certain hotheads. [...]⁵⁹

It could be thought that Ridel is making things appear better than they were here since, if Gimenez is to be believed, those two Spaniards were indeed members of the International Group when they decided to serve on a firing squad.

For his part, Charles Carpentier, during the 1980s, recounted an affair that had made him furious:

Following the capture of Osera, we were sent back to Pina to be billeted in the notary's house [in the Calle Mayor]. It had been a very messy business; I was furious. For some reason or another I had gone off with Ridel to Caspe, and by the time we got back, the inhabitants of Pina had sentenced the notary to death and had asked the International Group to shoot the guy, and they had! I was really angry at this, really unhappy, and wanted to kick some guys out. Martínez and Ridel pleaded with me. Ridel said: "Okay, we'll say no more about it." But I wasn't happy with that. I said: "We came here to fight, not to shoot people. If prisoners are taken, we hand them over to the Spaniards and they can do whatever they like with them, but under no circumstances should we be shooting people."⁶⁰

Another prisoner execution involving the Durruti Column had led to the publication, in the Swiss review *Témoins* in 1954, of a letter from Simone Weil to Georges Bernanos sometime in 1938 (the letter had been made public in 1950 but had gone unnoticed at the time). Simone Weil mentioned certain tragic events that lingered in her memory and that Ridel had been witness to on the Aragon front: on August 22, 1936, the International Group beat off a Falangist attack; a sixteen-year-old

59   Mercier Vega, "Simone Weil sur le front d'Aragon," 278.
60   Collectif, *Présence de Louis Mercier*, 33.

prisoner was brought back, handed over to the Spaniards, and was shot. Carpentier says that they were all affected by the incident. Moreover, they had told Simone Weil about it when they paid her a visit while she was convalescing in Sitges in September 1936. She wrote to Bernanos that "the death of that little hero has been a burden on my conscience ever since, even though I only found out about it after the event"[61]

And she concluded:

> They set out as volunteers with notions about sacrifice, only to stumble into a war reminiscent of a war of mercenaries, but with added cruelty and less consideration shown to the enemy.[62]

Mercier Vega, who had always placed great value on Simone's involvement, responded to that letter in 1954, in a follow-up edition of *Témoins*:

> Denying or playing down the horrors of a revolutionary war do not come into it, any more than covering up for the instincts of certain militia members. The crucial thing is to convey a complete picture of the feelings or passions that can be given free rein, and not passing judgment upon revolutionaries en bloc.[63]

And twenty years later he added:

> Concern with striking a chord with Bernanos and coming up with a language they might both share seems to have driven Simone Weil to step outside of whatever experience she had herself. Her friends, who had accepted and adopted her, had, just as she did—if not earlier than her and against the very backdrop of civil war and on the ground—made a stand against the climate of needless violence.[64]

Regarding the matter of the "little Falangist," whose execution was attributed to Durruti, we have further details. In 2009, while

61   Weil, "Lettre à Georges Bernanos," 4.
62   Ibid., 5.
63   Louis Mercier Vega, "Lettre à Jean-Paul Samson," *Témoins IIIe année*, no. 8 (1954), 51–53.
64   Mercier Vega, "Simone Weil sur le front d'Aragon" 278.

consulting the files of the Pina de Ebro Causa General, we were surprised to stumble upon the tale of that young fellow, whose name was
Ángel Caro Andrés. He was a native of Tauste in Zaragoza province, a
village overrun by the Nationalists. Here is an extract from his father's
deposition:

> [...] on August 22, 1936, in the course of a nighttime battle around
> the township of Pina [...] he was taken prisoner by the reds from
> the International Brigade led by a certain Luis, a Spanish-speaking
> Frenchman. The reds brought this prisoner before Durruti [...].
> That great leader spared his life in light of his tender years [...]
> and ordered that he be locked up in the mayor's office in the
> town. But on learning of this, the reds who had fled from Tauste
> and who were in Pina asked Durruti to hand him over to them
> for execution, which Durruti refused to do; so they made up their
> minds to attack the town hall [...] the next morning (August 24)
> and they carried him off [...][65]

These men from Tauste, who had all witnessed the shooting of a
family member by Falangists, executed Ángel Caro near the Ebro.[66]

Robert Léger, who belonged to the same gang as Ridel and Carpentier in Paris, himself a member of the Fédération communiste libertaire and of the no less distinguished Jeunesses culinaires de France,
also set off for Spain in November 1936. He later spoke of his own
reluctance to kill, even when confronted by the enemy, and he recalled
that one day it fell to him to guard a young—fifteen- or sixteen-year-
old—Spanish prisoner charged with spying and destined to be shot.[67]

In a letter to the authors in 2007, his son, Michel Léger offers this
version of the incident:

> Resting up in a village near the front lines in Aragon, a CNT mili-
> tian spotted an adolescent, who no one in the village had greeted,
> "tagging along" with them. He was arrested and searched. His
> pack of playing cards was spread out on a table. Among the

65   Deposition, November 7, 1940, C.G. Tauste, 1425, Exp. 59.
66   On the basis of the details we passed to them, Phil Casoar and Ariel Cama-
     cho delved further into this matter: see Ariel Camacho and Phil Casoar, "Le
     petit phalangiste," *Revue XXI*, no. 12 (Autumn 2010).
67   Robert Léger, *Entretiens avec Phil Casoar, Paris* (sound recording), 1984.

The Ebro, through which the Sons of Night passed, at Pina

real ones were some blanks with sketches of the machine-gun emplacement, the reserve's equipment store, and the barn where they were staying, with personnel numbers and weaponry also noted. He was a fifteen-year-old spy from the Falangist Youth and the son of a wine merchant. "He was to be shot that very evening!" My father was chosen to guard him. The lad was in tears, and my father tried to lecture him and explain the right way of things. The boy was increasingly inconsolable and sobbing. My father said, "He looked like Arnaud [my son]. I was disgusted by standing guard over this poor victim of that lousy war, a child, a Francoist one to be sure but, still, a child and they were going to kill him!" Time passed and there were few people out and about in the sunshine but no one nearby. My father leaned over, grabbed the youngster by the shoulder and showed him the nearby field leading to the open countryside. "Off you go, quickly … quickly!" The lad was reluctant or did not understand, but in the end he took off. After he had gone far enough, my father shouted out: "Watch out! The prisoner is escaping!" A *responsable* appeared with his pistol in his hand to shout: "Then shoot, Robert! Shoot!" "*You* shoot! *You* shoot! Don't snap at me! I'm a cook, not a soldier!"

In a conversation with Phil Casoar, Robert brought up another anecdote:

On the Caspe or Belchite front, he and Maillol found themselves on guard duty and in charge of a machine gun. They spotted movement by young Falangists heading for a water source and planned to cut them down on the way back. However, neither of them could bring themselves to do it. They had no liking for killing and that, he said, was often the case.[68]

When class violence was unleashed, it was occasionally carried out by the population or was delegated to patrols of revolutionary "avengers." Sometimes, though, it was the local population or even the local revolutionary committees that protected persons likely to be executed, standing up to the *patrullas de investigaciones* and telling them: "No killing here!"

Here's an example from Alcarràs, Catalonia, in the dying days of July 1936; Josep Lladós recounts:

At the time, right-wing folks were in a very perilous situation. Not that the residents were out to do them the slightest harm, but the [CNT] Committee had, I think, twenty-six individuals locked up in the church, which was being used as a prison. In those muddled early days there were certain roving gangs enforcing "direct justice" and telling the inhabitants of the villages they passed through that right-wingers were bad people. Somebody leaked it to one such group that the Alcarràs committee was holding a number of people in the church, and one evening they showed up in the village. Somebody tipped off the young Committee, and the available members rushed off to the church a hundred meters away. Compañero Tudo, the chair of the Committee, posted himself in front of the door, and that was where an argument erupted between the village representatives and the avengers. The latter were out to take the prisoners away. The whole thing turned into a bitter argument, and luckily the residents and those militia members not guarding the road turned up. In the end, Tudo told them: "You're going to have to kill me before you can get to these people!" That night, the slightest spark could have turned into a bloodbath. The prisoners could hear every word. Among them was an elderly priest, who kept saying: "Take me and leave the

68   Ibid.

others alone!" After much hesitation, the priest was handed over. The gang calmed down and *mosén* Ramón [Father Ramón] was taken three kilometers outside of the village and gunned down by the side of the road. That was the sort of horrible thing that was going on in those muddled times. It's hard to imagine. Alcarràs should have erected a monument in honor of this young Committee that had the courage and humanity not to stand for an even greater crime. None of those families, right wing or not, deserved to die. Through his selfless sacrifice, *mosén* Ramón also helped calm minds and prevent a greater catastrophe. I feel compassion for him and his advanced years.

During those fiery times, three men were killed in Alcarràs. [...] That's three too many, but at the time there was no way to control what everyone was doing. Massive disorder and violence prevailed.[69]

For further details, see Casoar and Feuillade, "Itinéraire François-Charles Carpentier."

{17}
PAGE 63

Across Aragon, the population gathered in village general assemblies and didn't wait for anyone else to lay the groundwork for the new society. The local CNT militants reaped the harvest of years of the union's foothold there. We saw how, in Pina, the anarchist militias drove collectivization forward when the peasants had initial misgivings. Moreover, at the regional plenum of the Aragonese FAI, held in Alcañiz on September 20, 1936, a dispute erupted between those militants who, like Francisco Carreño, were talking about establishing libertarian communism in Aragon and those, such as José Alberola from Fraga, who had reservations:

69   Josep Lladós Tarragó, *Guerre et exil d'un républicain espagnol, 23 ans, apatride* (Bergerac: self-published, 2010), 28.

That, I say, is a war communism dictated by circumstances. By my reckoning, if libertarian communism is imposed, then it cannot be free.[70]

In Pina, the revolutionary committee, set up at the beginning of August, was composed of villagers, though its secretary, Juan Aris, was the political delegate from a Durruti Column *agrupación*. The membership figure for the newly established CNT union representing a number of trades was to swell considerably. For a variety of reasons, then, it's hard to gauge how much initiative the *pineros* [residents of Pina] brought to the growth of their collective. It could be that the overhaul of property rights was initially facilitated by the fact that much of the land had been abandoned by the owners. Before July 1936, in Pina—as in Fraga—land-owning aristocracy made up mostly of absentee landlords or foreigners, controlled one-third of the agricultural wealth.[71] This land was placed under common ownership from the start, without much difficulty. Later, as in other Aragonese villages, farming based upon individual smallholdings, to which the peasants were firmly attached, was turned upside down. As Eugenio Sopena, delegate from the Barbastro collective, told it forty years later:

> There were lots of peasants who thought that the collective meant that they were losing their land. [...] I'll take up a rifle, but I'm not prepared to pick one up to force peasants to work as a collective if they don't want to.[72]

The presence of armed men in the countryside posed problems, and on October 6, at an extraordinary plenum of CNT unions attended by some column leaders and representatives of collectives, "the Council of Aragon" was formed to "make sure that abuses are combated and that the villages where the columns are, are assured a free life," to quote the statement carried in *L'Espagne antifasciste* of November 14, 1936. Other items on the agenda, included various items ordering militia members to cease draining the assets (livestock,

70   Amorós, *Francisco Carreño*, 33.
71   See Julián Casanova, *Anarquismo y revolución en la sociedad rural aragonesa 1936–1938* (Madrid: Siglo XXI, 1985), 119–22.
72   Kelsey, *Anarcosindicalismo y estado en Aragón*, 405.

food supplies, etc.) of the villages and to not meddle in their sociopolitical affairs.

Antoine Gimenez tells of the close relations between militia members and peasants; many of the former labored in the fields when the front lines were quiet, sometimes eating and sleeping in villagers' homes. According to Víctor Alba and Graham Kelsey, relations between the collectives and the columns were consistent and close; the former largely feeding nearly 20,000 militia members, which is remarkable, given that 80% of Spain's wheat fields were in Francoist hands. They also note that between July 1936 and the Nationalists' entry into Aragon, thanks to the pooling of resources and assets, the prices of basic necessities did not rise in the countryside, whereas they were ballooning in Catalan towns. Thanks to the collective control of production, black-marketeering and speculation couldn't gain a foothold; the almost universal absence of money may also have been a factor. For while trade with the rest of Spain and with the outside world resumed, there was recourse to barter whenever possible, if only to prevent Aragon from being flooded by businessmen intent on buying up the wheat, pigs, and sheep, leaving local demand unsatisfied. The Aragon Defense Council, with the support of Antonio Ortiz, the general delegate of the Sur-Ebro Column, saw to it that up until July 1937—this being one of its leading functions—output was not diverted into any sort of trafficking. Ortiz himself recounts playing a trick on a businessman from Igualada who had come to see him with two suitcases full of paper money. He was required to abide by the collectivists' conditions and traded manufactured goods for the wheat he wanted—and paid the pre-war prices as well. Furthermore, in the early 1960s, Ortiz wrote an article analyzing the collectivization process and didn't hesitate to detail the mistakes or abuses, which were, he maintained, the result of improvisation in most cases. He was critical of the performance of groups of Barcelona militants who thought the peasants were immature types needing their hands held and who were, by late July, roving around the villages ordering "the implementation of libertarian communism." He stepped in when his own militia members called the peasants of La Puebla de Híjar fascists just because they didn't want to transfer their own smallholding *en el montón* (to common ownership). Later, Ortiz writes, things sorted themselves out, and collectivization proceeded through a blend of free choice on the part of village communities, intervention by column leaders, and intervention by the CNT Regional Committee and the Council of Aragon administration.

From July to October 1936, about 20,000 square kilometers was worked in common, and it was not long before the region was being referred to abroad as "the anarchist Ukraine, Aragon."[73]

Once the collective was up and running in a village, some thought was given to federating all the collectivized villages in the area (*comarca*). Next, every one of the twenty-five *comarcal* federations linked up with the rest. By September 1936, there were some 450 collectives. Pina de Ebro was one of them. Félix Carrasquer explains the next step in some detail: the formation of the regional federation of collectives at the extraordinary Congress of collectives held in Caspe on February 14, 1937. According to the minutes of that meeting, there were six hundred delegates there, representing five hundred collectives, drawn from twenty-five *comarcal* federations with 300,000 members (out of republican Aragon's population of 500,000). The Pina de Ebro delegate was E. Aguilar, who was prominent in the report dealing with "individualists," that is, smallholders who wanted nothing to do with the collective. To get some idea of the trend in collectivization in Pina, here are the membership figures from that time: six hundred in Pina, and 2,924 for the *comarca*'s six collectives. One month earlier, on January 3, 1937, a local assembly endorsed the points of agreement for the Pina collective:

> In the light of the above, the worker and peasant class, rising to the occasion, launches a voluntary Collective on the following bases:
> 1. Membership of the Collective is voluntary for all residents of the village, no matter their economic status and conditions upon their acceptance of the Regulation hereby laid down.
> 2. All members in agreement with the new social arrangement are to surrender all their assets to the Collective: land, work tools, working animals, money, and equipment.
> 3. Once circumstances permit, an effort will be made to build collective stables so that all livestock of use in farm work can be housed there; the same will go for cattle and sheep, and workers equal to the task will be selected.
> 4. All foodstuffs, grocery goods, and farm produce are to be warehoused in local collectives, so that they can be monitored; also, one or more cooperatives are to be launched to oversee the distribution of foodstuffs and various items that the collectivists need.

73   Gallardo Romero and Márquez Rodríguez, *Ortiz, general sin dios ni amo*, 138.

5. The amount of products distributed to collectivists may increase or decrease, depending on the collective's economic circumstances.

6. Work shall be carried out in teams, each one headed by an accountable delegate. An effort will be made to establish teams of cart drivers and ox-herders and workers with trades, so that *compañeros* with aptitudes can do these tasks in turns.

7. All persons of both sexes over fifteen years of age must work on behalf of the Collective. Persons over sixty years of age and invalids are exempted, unless their physical condition allows them to perform less demanding tasks for the good of the Collective.

8. The Collective cuts all ties with those who wish to carry on living the individualist lifestyle; so much so that they will not be able to look to the collective for anything. They will work their land without help; all unproductive land in their possession will pass to the Collective.

10 All exploitation of man by his fellow man is hereby abolished; as are, consequently, sub-letting, sharecropping, and waged labor. This measure shall be applicable to all local inhabitants, of whatever circumstances.

11. Sovereignty resides in the assembly, which shall operate by majority rule. Decisions about Collective members who upset its smooth running shall be made at assemblies."[74]

For a year, farming in Aragon resembled a mosaic of essays in libertarian communism, varying according to distance from the front lines, the presence of anarchist militants, the presence of columns, and the more or less explicit determination of each village to retain its autonomy, et cetera. In Ortiz's view, the experiment never had the chance to develop fully. As he put it:

> In Spain and in Aragon, it was not merely a matter of the "land's belonging to him that worked it." [...] It was a matter of satisfying ... ultimately the craving that runs deep in man... LAND AND FREEDOM.[75]

74   Gaston Leval, *Espagne libertaire* (Paris: Éditions du Monde libertaire, 1983), 234–36.

75   Gallardo Romero and Márquez Rodríguez, *Ortiz, general sin dios ni amo*, 150.

For further details, see Víctor Alba, *Los colectivizadores* (Barcelona: Laertes 2001); Kelsey, "El mito de Buenaventura Durruti"; Félix Carrasquer, *Les Collectivités d'Aragon, Espagne 36–39* (Paris: CNT-RP, 2003).

{18}

PAGE 64

On September 19, 1936, an Ateneo Cultural Popular [People's Cultural Athenaeum] was opened for use as a meeting-place with a library. *El Frente*, the Durruti Column's newspaper, reported it thus:

> [The peasants were called upon] to show up for lessons and lectures to equip themselves for the new life that is in sight.[76]

It must have been there that the evening classes Antoine speaks about were delivered. In the CNT paper, *Solidaridad Obrera*, of October 8, 1936, the Aragon correspondent wrote, somewhat disdainfully, of the peasants of Pina:

> The light of reason burst upon minds [...] rendered brutish by darkness, as the politicians and churchmen had impaired their understanding and muzzled their consciences.[77]

Lectures and public debates were held. On September 23, there was a big gathering instigated by the Kine filmmaking group, which showed a film about the Durruti Column. One of the most renowned of the CNT's public speakers and a member of the column, Francisco Carreño, took the floor to cite those

> CNT militants [who] are fighting for everyone's freedom and social and political equality [and urge them to] cut the ties that bind us to

76 Amorós, *Francisco Carreño*, 33.
77 Casanova, *Anarquismo y revolución en la sociedad rural aragonesa*, 122.

our families and our betrothed and our friends, and think solely of the struggle and the good of our wider family, Humanity.[78]

And as for *El Frente*, let us look at what Ridel had to say about it in *Le Libertaire*:

> Several militia columns have taken it upon themselves to launch their own newspapers, published by a team of printers serving in their *centurias*. The Durruti Column has its daily paper, *El Frente*, publishing out of Pina, less than a kilometer from the fascists. On a daily basis, this newssheet keeps combatants up to date with the situation on the front and on Spanish events overall. Likewise, the decisions of the War Committee, sanitary instructions, and other matters are covered by special features [...] There is nothing banal about seeing, around six o'clock, the peasants in the square and the sentries in their trenches devouring the pages of the little paper, every word, from first to last.[79]

{19}
PAGE 68

Members of the Libertarian Youth didn't wait until 1936 to rail against the narrow-minded mores of priest-ridden Spanish society. During the 1920s, a number of them had already turned to alternative lifestyles, according to their preferences: free love, naturism, pacifism, vegetarianism, and, often, individualism, under the umbrella of a rationalistic, naturalistic "new ethic" peddled by, among others, Isaac Puente. The reviews *Ética* and later *Iniciales* in Barcelona and Valencia gave wide coverage to such issues. After the advent of the Republic in 1931, almost everywhere, young boys and girls were already breaking free of the shackles of marriage and sexual chaperoning. Between 1932 and 1935, the writings of Amparo Poch y Gascón on the subjects of sexuality,

78   Amorós, *Francisco Carreño*, 34.
79   Mercier Vega, *En route pour Saragosse*, 8–9.

contraception, venereal disease, critiques of monogamy, prostitution, et cetera, were circulating in the *ateneos libertarios*. According to Martha Ackelsberg, Amparo Poch y Gascón stressed the fact that "sexuality was an important aspect of human identity and development."[80]

In Barcelona, the anarchist physician Félix Martí Ibañez, a pioneer in sexology with links to the review *Estudios*, opened a "psychosexual" consulting room. But not every woman had the courage to stare down society, as Thyde Rosell explains:

> Women workers (older women especially) rejected maternity leave even though it had been voted through by a "radical" government! In those days, women gave birth in the workplace. Many were afraid of being fired or feared that winning maternity leave would draw attention and popular disapproval to their sexuality.[81]

When the revolutionary process erupted, though little direct evidence has come our way, we can imagine how this mayhem in morals spread, within the republican camp and no doubt all the more starkly in the towns than in the countryside. The young Englishman Laurie Lee, on his travels through Spain, arrived after the Popular Front victory in a little fishing village called Castillo, about ninety kilometers east of Málaga in February 1936. He immediately noted that

> like a rush of blood to the head, this one [the spring] brought with it a curious relaxation of behavior and manner, a new freedom among the sexes.
>
> Jacobo and I still organized the hotel dances, but they were different now. Gone were the stiff and sweltering little marriage markets, with their chaperones and wax-haired suitors; now the floor was commanded by young fishermen and laborers, casual in sky-blue shirts [...].
>
> So the boys and girls [...] used our rackety dances to explore their newfound liberties. [...]
>
> [...] For a while there was a complete lifting of censorship, even in newspapers and magazines. But most of all it was the air

---

80   Martha Ackelsberg, *Free Women of Spain* (Oakland: AK Press, 2005), 167.

81   Thyde Rosell, "Femmes libertaires, femmes en lutte ... femmes libres!" in *Alternative libertaire*, no. 233 (November 2000).

of carnality, the brief clearing away of taboos, which seemed to possess the village—a sudden, frank and even frantic, pursuit of lust, bred from a sense of impending peril.[82]

Antoine's *Memories* are a unique testimony of this, as far as we can tell; he takes a mischievous delight in detailing for us what most libertarian women and, above all, men have omitted about this outbreak of libertinism. Even today there are those who would rather not hear about it …

Instances of nuns setting up homes with anarchists, just as Antoine recounts, should not have been all that rare; another foreign volunteer, the then very young Georges Sossenko, refers to some in his memoirs. In October 1936, he landed in the little town of Puigcerdà:

> There was also, in the vicinity, a small convent that was also in ruins, leaving the nuns to seek new lives. Some left the village, others set off to work at the hospital as nurses, while others went off to live with friends or relatives. There was even one that married one of the militiamen who had shut down the convent. We thought that was really interesting, and we'd joke that everybody was after a little nun of his own.[83]

{20}

PAGE 69

We can follow the activities of the International Group almost moment by moment thanks to the accounts of Charles Carpentier, Charles Ridel, and Simone Weil.

Let us look at the "travel notes" of the first pair, as published in *Le Libertaire* on September 18, 1936:

---

82   Laurie Lee, *As I Walked Out One Midsummer Morning* (Boston: Nonpareil Books, 2011),161, 162.

83   Georges Sossenko, *Aventurero idealista* (Cuenca: Universidad de Castilla-La Mancha, 2004), 109.

Monday, August 17.

[...] In the morning, around fifteen of us set off for the far bank of the Ebro and enemy territory, carrying with us a can of gasoline to burn the bodies of the two fascists killed a few days earlier by our sentries. In the clothing of one of them we found a travel diary cataloging the incidents in which he'd been mixed up since his campaign had begun.

The two bodies were dressed in uniforms much like our own, but they wore the red Basque beret, the identifying sign of the *requetés*—Catholic volunteers from Navarra and Aragon.

Our expedition then turned into a reconnaissance mission and took us as far as a little farm not far from a station on the rail line that leads to Zaragoza.

Our explorations gave us the idea of setting up an *avanzadilla* (outpost) in enemy territory, a position that would make it easier for us to support the column from Caspe that was pushing ahead along the opposite bank, bound for Quinto and Fuentes de Ebro. The return trip was without incident.

Tuesday, August 18.

The entire day was spent on a variety of preparations. We had to consider transport, bedding in, and feeding the International Group, which is to say about twenty-five men (including Simone Weil who has just joined us).

Tonight we will cross over to the far bank by boat.

Wednesday, August 19.

At 2.00 a.m., everyone is on his feet, each with a burden to carry in addition to his gear. These militia members, loaded down with cooking pots, provisions, rifles, cartridges, and shovels are an odd-looking procession.

Everything goes well, and by 4 o'clock our people have reached the far side without incident.

The morning and afternoon are spent reconnoitering the area, moving out the inhabitants from the "Durio" farmstead—sympathizers with our cause—looking for a spot to ford the Ebro and establish a bridgehead.

One young local resident—a pretty girl—a CNT member, gives us the lowdown.

Guards are posted and our new life begins, provisions being assured by a German compañero who has proven to be a gifted cook.

From the military viewpoint, we face around 112 fascists and three machin guns which hold Pina station and the grain silos that surround it. On our right lies Fuentes de Ebro, held by our adversaries, and to our left, Quinto, also in the hands of rebels and which represents a strategically important position, its fame dating back to the Napoleonic wars.

The big problem will be remaining undetected by the observers opposite.

Our delegate, who saw action in Verdun and, luckily, most of the French colonies, is wonderfully experienced, and his advice will prove vital to the survival of the little colony on more than one occasion.[84]

Looking now at Simone Weil's diary, we find that these events triggered quite different observations and thoughts from her:

Monday [August] 17.

[…] Louis Berthoumieu [*sic*] (delegate): "We are crossing the river." The purpose is to burn three enemy corpses. We cross by boat (a quarter of an hour of arguing. . .). We search around. Find a bluish cadaver, gnawed and ghastly. It is burned. The others search for whatever else is left. While we grab some rest. There is talk of a raid. The bulk of the men are allowed to cross back over. Then the decision is made (?) to put the raid off until the following day. We head back towards the river, without particularly bothering to hide. A house is spotted. Pascual (from the War Committee): "We're off on a melon-hunt." (Deadly serious!) We walk through the brush. Heat and a touch of anxiety. I find this nonsensical. All of a sudden it dawns on me that we are off on an expedition (to the house). There I am very emotional (I know nothing as to the purpose of all this and I know that if we are captured we will be shot). We split up into two groups. The delegate, Ridel, and three Germans crawl right up to the farmhouse. We watch from ditches (after the event the delegate screeches at us that we should have gone right up to the house). We wait. We hear talking … The tension is exhausting. We watch the compañeros return, not bothering to hide themselves; we join up with them and cross the river without mishap. This distraction could easily have cost them their lives. Pascual is in charge. (Carpentier and Giral are with us.)

[…] This sortie was the first and *only* time I felt afraid during my stay in Pina.

Tuesday [August] 18.

Many plans for the far bank of the river. As the morning is drawing to an end, the decision is made for the group and us to cross over in the middle of the night, to hold out for a few days until the column arrives from Sastano [Sástago]. The day is spent preparing. Worried about the submachine-guns. The Pina war committee has refused us them. In the end and thanks to the Italian colonel in charge of the "Banda Negra," we manage to get a hold of one—and then two. They are not tested.

The colonel was the first one to propose that we go in, but in the final analysis it was an official mission assigned by the War Committee in Pina.

Volunteers, to be sure. Last evening Berthoumieu gathered us around in No 18, and asked to hear our views. Utter silence. He then insists that we tell him our thoughts. More silence. Then Ridel piped up: "Okay then, so we are all in agreement." And that was that.

We go to bed. Male nurse wanting to lie-down . . . I sleep in my clothes. If it can be called sleep. Rise at 2.30 a.m. Knapsack packed. Emotional: glasses. Divvying up of tasks (I get map and basin). Orders. No talking while on the move. Somewhat emotional all the same. Crossing quickly. Louis was nervous for us, shouting (if they are over there …) We disembark. Wait. Daylight breaking through. The German is going to rustle up some coffee. Louis strips the hut clear, has the gear taken there and sends me there. I stay there for a bit then it's my turn to go get some coffee. Louis has posted guards. We set to work right away to sort out the kitchen and the hut and erect barricades to screen us. In the meantime, the others approach the farmhouse. Discovering a family there and a (good-looking!) seventeen-year-old boy among them. Intelligence: they had spotted us during the earlier reconnaissance. They had posted guards on the riverbank. Pulling them back when we showed up. 112 m[en]. Their lieutenant has sworn that he will have us. They are on their way back. I translate this information for the Germans. They ask: "Back across the river then?"—"No, rest assured, we're staying." (Shall we head back to Pina to telephone Durruti?) Orders: turn back taking the peasant family back with us. (While all this is going on, the German compañero appointed as cook is ranting because there is neither salt nor oil nor vegetables.) Berthoumieu, furious (going back to the farm yet again has its risks) assembles the expedition. Says to me: "You, kitchen!" I dare not object. Besides, my heart is only half in this expedition … Anxiously, I watch as they set off … (actually I am in almost as much danger myself). We grab our rifles and we wait. Soon the German is suggesting that we head for the little dugout beneath the tree occupied by Ridel and Carpentier (who are along on the expedition, naturally). We stretch out there in the shade with our rifles (unloaded) at hand. We wait. From time to time the German heaves a sigh. Probably afraid. I am not. But how intense everything around me is! War without prisoners. Anyone captured is shot. Our friends return. A peasant, his son, and the little boy … Fontana raises a fist as he looks at the lads. The son responds, but his reluctance is plain to see. Cruelly compelled … The peasant heads back to seek out family. We return to our respective posts. Reconnaissance plane. We take cover. Louis rails against carelessness. I stretch out on my back, gaze up at the leaves and the blue skies. Very fine day. If they capture me, they'll kill me … But deservedly so. Our guys have spilled quite a lot of blood. I am morally complicit. Utter calm. We regroup and then it starts up again. I take cover in the hut. Shelling. I step outside to head toward the submachine-gun. Louis says: "No need to be afraid (!)" Has me go with the German into the kitchen, our rifles slung over our shoulders. We wait. In the end, the peasant's family (three girls and one eight-year-old boy) turns up, every one of them terrified (there has been quite a bit of shelling). They are somewhat subdued. Very scared. Fretting about the livestock left behind on the farm (in the end we will fetch it back to them in Pina). Plainly not sympathizers.[85]

On August 20, 1936, Simone Weil injured herself. Her time in Pina lasted barely a week. Mercier described things in these terms in 1975:

At daybreak, the Falangists try to encircle the group, which is deployed around a small farm building. The Falangist attack is beaten off with some losses, one young fascist [this is the little Falangist referred to in note 16 above] is taken prisoner during a sortie. But the artillery positioned on the high ground picks out our militia members and adjusts its aim. By the third shell, the building is hit. The "internationals" having had time to pull back. The incident passes over. The fall back and crossing of the Ebro are completed without disorder.

Some hours before, Simone Weil, who had been posted to the kitchen—actually for her own protection—was evacuated: she had sustained a bad burn injury stepping into a pan of oil set on a blazing fire. After some first aid she had wanted to return to the group but we had to reason with her and talk her into being transferred to a *hospital de sangre* [field hospital].

In Sitges, where she is taken, she is visited by her parents who rush to her side. With the help of a few International Group militia members [...] they talk her into returning to France—temporarily—to complete her treatment there.

[...] On her return to Paris, she carries on ostentatiously wearing the colors of the FAI and CNT and takes part in major public gatherings in support of the Spanish Revolution. Even though she gradually drifts away from the revolutionary syndicalist movement in search of a different path [...] she will still show effective solidarity towards her former "compañeros."[86]

For further details, see Collectif, *Présence de Louis Mercier*.

{21}
PAGE 71

The *centurias* were flanked by special guerrilla teams whose mission was to attack the enemy's rear and gather intelligence. These were,

86   Mercier Vega, "Simone Weil sur le front d'Aragon," 276–77.

naturally, made up essentially of Spaniards and prominent among these was the Banda Negra, led—if Ridel and Simone are to be believed—by an Italian army ex-colonel, of whom more later. The dividing line between the *internacionales* and these autonomous flying squads must have been very fluid. More specifically, as this extract from the memoirs of Ramón Rufat shows, the term "Hijos de la Noche" (Sons of Night) had become a generic label:

So, by October, the militia columns […] were faced with the need to conjure up their own intelligence services […]

At about the same time, night operations teams, known as the Hijos de la Noche, guerrillas striking deep into enemy territory, were set up under the authority and supervision of the columns alone […]

Some of these teams and their leaders were surrounded in Aragon by an aura of prestige and mystery, like the greatest heroes in the war. We might mention, by the way, Gallart's La Noche group, which struck across the Ebro at Fuentes de Ebro; the Utrillas-based Los Dinamiteros group, whose most celebrated leader was Batista from Valderrobres; or Los Iguales, led by Remiro from Épila; not forgetting Francisco Ponzán who, after a brief stint with the Council of Aragon, proved himself to be one of the best guerrilla leaders and intelligence agents on the Aragonese and Catalan fronts. "In October, the militia columns […] found themselves faced with the need to set up their own intelligence units."[87]

Félix Valero Labarta sees Antoine as having been part of the Banda Negra. Antoine Gimenez himself mentions his group as having been known as the *gorros negros* (black bonnets): there is every indication that he was indeed one of the "sons of the night."

One *agrupación* delegate, José Mira, depicts them in operation:

During August 1936, our forces across the seventy-eight kilometer front, which stretched from Velilla de Ebro to Monte Oscuro (Leciñena), were at a standstill due to lack of munitions and war

87   Ramón Rufat, *Espions de la République. Mémoires d'un agent secret pendant la guerre d'Espagne* (Paris: Allia, 1990), 27–28.

materials. Faced with the unfeasibility of mounting big offensives, Durruti took the initiative by introducing warfare in small units, guerrilla warfare. The most intrepid personnel saw to the implementation of those proposals, by mounting surprise raids into the enemy's rear.

One day, it was the *internacionales'* turn, capitalizing upon a gap in the Aguilar area, to cross the Ebro and take the defenders prisoner; another day, it was the Banda Negra from the Grupo Metalúrgico that crossed the river at the same spot and attacked the rebel HQ in Fuentes de Ebro, taking fifty-nine prisoners and substantial war booty.

Later it was the Hijos de la Noche, striking several kilometers behind the rebel lines, who entered the enemy camp only to return, one fine morning, worn out but happy to have brought back thousands of head of livestock, which, with unparalleled altruism, they handed over to our general headquarters.[88]

Let us dwell for a moment on this somewhat curious offshoot of the CNT, in this instance of its Metalworkers' Union. It was one of the first providers of personnel of sound character to the *cuadros de defensa* (defense cadres) and other CNT action groups, which may have drawn a number of them into operations that ventured far beyond the boundaries of the law, up to and including murder.

We shall be dealing with this in much greater detail when we come to the biography of one of their most outstanding representatives, Justo Bueno Pérez, who was rightly commissioned by the high command of the Durruti Column, from the moment its reached Pina, to join with compañeros from the same sector such as Adolfo Ballano, Pedro Campón, Liberto Ros, José Martínez Ripoll, and others to set up a police unit, the so-called Investigation Squad. Its task was to purge conquered territory of all who might have posed a serious threat to the gains of the revolution. We are well aware that in such circumstances there is a tendency to see enemies everywhere and that there is no shortage of fingers pointed. It seems to be well established that the police unit sometimes equated with the Banda Negra executed several dozen people in the villages around Pina.

88   José Mira Martínez, *Los guerrilleros confederales. Un hombre: Durruti* (Barcelona: Comité regional de la CNT, 1938), 118–19.

According to José Luis Ledesma, author of a study of the violence behind the republican lines in Aragon, the numbers who fell victim to the "crackdown" in the Pina district covering the townships of Gelsa, La Almoda, Pina de Ebro, Quinto de Ebro, Velilla de Ebro, Osera, Fuentes de Ebro, Bujaraloz, Farlete, Alforque, Mediana de Aragón, Villafranca de Ebro, Alborge, Monegrillo, Nuez de Ebro, Rodén, and La Zaida were twenty-nine in July 1936; eighteen in August; twenty-nine in September; forty in October; and then two in November and December and zero in January 1937. There was a renewed spike in August 1937 with fifteen killings, following a rise to seven that June, and then six in September. The total figure for the period up to April 1938 was 162 deaths, twenty-three of them in the township of Pina.[89]

Looking again at the same source, we find the following statement regarding the township of Caspe:

Actually, the purge drive quickly became the domain of a few individuals serving on the local committees or on the columns' war committees. When the drive was under way, one or the other would set up "courts" to sit in judgment, without undue process, of "enemies of the revolution" and, not being given to half measures, would either acquit or sentence them to death. Again in Caspe, according to the sources available, denunciations were scrutinized by a sort of committee tribunal that initially drew a wide attendance but dwindled as time went on. In addition, there was a "column court," not "noted for its light touch." Elsewhere, the two were amalgamated into one, as happened in Azuara, Maella, Pina, and in Leciñena where, on September 9, following some finger pointing "a council of war was convened in the church." "The head of the occupying column [POUM], a fellow by the name of Grossi, took the role of prosecuting counsel, [...] and the remaining [eight] members were villagers." The charges against five of the accused were approved by the jury with a simple majority, and by the following morning the bodies were lying in open view in the graveyard. It was a fundamental difference from the early days; people were no longer killed in daylight

89 See José Luis Ledesma, *Los días de llamas de la revolución* (Zaragoza: Institución "Fernando el Católico," 2003), 340, 343.

but were, without exception, killed during the night hours of darkness and silence.

[...] Even though we can generalize about countless localized variations, the most common practice was for committee members, column councils, and investigation teams from outside the area to determine for themselves—without the benefit of any sort of trial or questioning—the fate of those who had been arrested only hours or days before, on the strength of denunciations or because their names were on one of the "blacklists" of "fascists" that were so widely circulated back then. After that, the main differences were how long it took before the fateful *"saca,"* whether they were to be put to death elsewhere, and what part would be played by the outsiders—ranging from executioners summoned by the committees, to groups and *"checas"* that showed up to demand that the "class enemies" be handed over to them. There was no shortage of these groups, like the "death cars" recorded as operating in the townships of Caspe and Sástago, or the Banda Negra, which did the same thing in and around Pina [...]

We can provide numerous examples here, beginning with Gelsa de Ebro or Fuendetodos—the bloodiest of the *"sacas"* incidents—and concluding with the incidents in Fabara and Plenas in mid-August and late September, respectively, which were each planned in such detail that every home and café stayed shut and no one was able to set foot on the streets by night.[90]

Later we find this:

Four days later, something similar happened in Lagata, one of the rare villages that had seen bloodshed under the Republic, as had previously mentioned [Letux]. With the war, however, there was no repetition, and later there would be blood spilled on just one occasion, during the republicans' retreat in March 1938. Nevertheless, on December 16, 1936, things took a different turn. It's hard to verify what happened, but the militias' losses in the aforementioned battle [the one in which Captain Jubert and many another guerrilla from the Ortiz Column perished], as well as the news that the rebels in Belchite had just shot the committee

90   Ibid., 141–43.

chairman's mother certainly played a part in it. Reprisals and personal issues were thrown into the mix with war and politics, and the result could hardly be mollifying. That evening, an "Hijos de la Noche *centuria* from the Durruti Column" (?) showed up (most likely called in for the occasion), and around 9 o'clock the heads of the committee summoned the *alguazil* and "handed him a list and two militia members and told him that he had a half an hour to bring in the persons named." So, having "silenced the village and posted guards at the entrances and exits of the streets, they went from house to house and arrested sixteen right-wing individuals," who they held for a half an hour in premises belonging to the Casa Consistorial while evidence was taken, and they were convicted in an adjacent room. You could easily guess what was about to happen:

At 10 o'clock, in a feigned removal to Lécera, they were loaded on to a closed truck, tied together in pairs. About three kilometers outside of the village, they were taken to a hill farm and, on the pretense that the truck had run out of gas, they were told to get out and then were lined up and gunned down …

At the last minute, two of them managed to escape by loosening their bonds and making a run for the hills, capitalizing on the darkness. They were arrested in the neighboring village, Samper del Salz, and later tried by the Caspe people's court. Tellingly, one was given a lighter sentence and the other acquitted.[91]

We should point out here that the information we get from historians specializing in acts of "repression" needs to be treated with the utmost circumspection, for they are very often reliant upon hastily drawn up prosecution files (hence the reference to their being *sumarísimo*), based upon denunciations extracted under terror or torture over the months following the Francoist victory or, speaking more broadly, upon a wide-ranging self-serving venture on the part of the new regime under the catchall designation of Causa General (General Enquiry), designed to prove that the "reds" had carried out massacres and on a much wider scale than the Nationalists. That effort fizzled, as, even by massaging the data and documentary evidence beyond all reason, the tame investigators could not come up with a figure in excess of 80,000 deaths; that was not enough to suit their bosses, and the matter was more or less laid to rest.

To illustrate this, and because it gives us some interesting insights into the situation in Pina during the first few weeks of the revolution, we've taken the following details from Justo Bueno Pérez's prosecution file:

• Justo Bueno Pérez's deposition made in the presence of Eduardo Quintela (a Barcelona police officer notorious as a ferocious anti-anarchist) on July 1, 1941:

> Questioned as to his wartime activities, he states that he remained at the front for just three months, at the end of which he returned to Barcelona and was commissioned by the "Organization" to set up the "Labora" workshops producing war materials [...] On the front he was in the police force set up there and led by Francisco Foyos [Foyo Díaz is the correct name].

• The deposition made by Caridad Martínez Hernández (a thirty-year-old married nurse) on July 1, 1941:

> She heard the anarchist Ballano recount how Bueno killed Silvio Sánchez in one front-line village, because the latter, in a conversation he'd had with [Bueno] had bad-mouthed Ruano [a close friend of Justo Bueno] [...] On several occasions she had heard that Bueno was killing persons inimical to the revolution by shooting them in the back of the head, after they were taken away by car, a murder method that became a veritable specialty of his, so it was said. And she is certain that he carried out many murders, several of them by himself, sometimes with Ruano, until he killed Ruano himself, after arguments about the division of the proceeds of their wartime thievery.

• The report forwarded by Barcelona Police Headquarters to the Captaincy-General (Court No. 2) sometime between July 16 and 19, 1941:

> [Justo Bueno] arrived in Pina village during the early days of August 1936 as part of the "Durruti" Column; his first act in the village was to burn down the San Gregorio hermitage. He went around with Adolfo Vallano [Ballano] Bueno, Liberto Ros Garro,

Pedro Campón Rodríguez, and a certain Federico; they made up a squad of the red police and set up offices in a house they had commandeered, and in which they were living. There, Justo Bueno received denunciations that made by different committees around the area against *personas de orden* [supporters of law and order], and then he and his compañeros traveled out to the location concerned and executed the individuals identified.

Here's an example: one night, Justo Bueno ordered the maid of the house where he stayed to get a meal together right away "for he was due at a feast in Gelsa that night." After the meal, they ventured to Gelsa. They returned to Pina early the next day, having shot twenty-nine people in Gelsa—the "feast" to which he had been referring.

All the murders carried out in Pina, Gelsa, Cinco Olivas, Alforque, Alborgue, Belilla [Velilla], etc., were at the hands of Justo Bueno Pérez and the members of his gang. They had access to a car and when someone was denounced as a "fascist," they set off immediately for the place and shot them.

• Cecilia Gracia Carreras's statement before the municipal judge in Pina on August 21, 1941:

In the house where she served as a maid, Justo Bueno Pérez, Adolfo Vallano, Pedro Campón, Liberto Ros, Juan Aris, and one Federico whose last name she does not know were lodgers and they were investigators for the army—or rather, for the anarchist government of Aragon. It is a fact that Justo Bueno, one day— the precise date she cannot remember—ordered her to prepare a meal immediately, for they were due that night to attend a feast in Gelsa, which is what they did, although she is unable to say whether they returned the same night or the following day [...] the following day, the word spread in Pina that the Investigations guys had killed upwards of twenty people in Gelsa. [...] She said that Justo Bueno and his compañeros were the masters of the village; they were in charge and gave the orders there.

• Report from Police Headquarters in Zaragoza on August 1, 1942, reproducing a report from the Pina Court dated January 14, 1942:

They had with them a woman named Pepita. She had poor vision and so wore eyeglasses, she was dark-haired, small and chubby, and was the "partner" of Roberto [Liberto] Ros, and went on to become that of Adolfo in Caspe. There was another woman named Pilar, Durruti's secretary, and a Lorenza who appeared at the same time, wearing blue overalls and armed with a handgun. It was Lorenza that murdered the village priest in the presence of all the *compañeros*, bragging of being very brave, and saying that the moment she spotted anyone wearing a scapular, she would put two bullets in him. This group operated with complete independence and never consulted with any superior before murdering anyone. They journeyed to Bujaraloz, Fraga, Gelsa, Cinco Olivas, Alforque, Alborge, Velilla, among other villages, where, in addition to killing people, they pilfered countless food items and valuables they found in the homes of those murdered. They took these back with them to Barcelona. It should be pointed out that in all these places they were in the company of the three women named above. With them there was also a midwife named Paquita who currently lives in Barcelona, having arrived with the very first advance party as the concubine of a captain from the Durruti Column named Collado. She initially moved on to La Retuarta hill, into the home of a guard named Marcelino [...] We haven't been able to find anyone in Gelsa capable of providing reliable information regarding the activities of José [sic] Bueno. His was a name they seemed to learn later and who they were unable to identify from a photograph. One gets the impression that there must be people in the village who witnessed crimes carried out by the person in question, but who, because of a lack of courage or some other inexplicable reason, refuse to make statements or detail acts when asked to do so.

• Deposition by Pilar Gracia Carreras, twenty-one, made in Barcelona on August 6, 1942:

This gang had a car it used to come and go from the village, although the witness has no knowledge of what activities they got up to. They were all armed, of course. She cannot remember if Bueno was the head of the gang, for in the opinion of the declarant, all those living at the house enjoyed the same powers

Justo Bueno

and authority. They never spoke of the activities in which they engaged during their incessant sorties by car. She never heard Bueno brag about murdering anyone in Barcelona or on the front. The role of the witness and her family was to act as the servants of the gang, which was in the family home; they prepared its meals, did its laundry, tidied its room, and other domestic chores. To her knowledge that gang was made up of *investigación* staff from the Durruti Column, it being said that the above-named was one of them. Of course neighbors from outlying villages would often show up at the house to talk to the occupants, without her being aware of the subject of their conversations as they locked themselves in one room, so that neither she nor her family members ever knew what was discussed. Even though she is asked repeatedly, she has no knowledge of the whereabouts of the midwife named Paquita, claiming she has never seen her in this city.

• Letter in his own defense from Justo Bueno, addressed to Court No. 2 on October 21, 1942:

> I arrived in the village of Bujaraloz with the aforesaid column. I was assigned to patrol—watch—duties, to prevent the commission of acts of reprisal or thievery but at no point was I required to intervene. After roughly three weeks, Durruti authorized anyone no longer wishing to remain with the column to return to Barcelona, and I took him up on it. That was the sum total of my activity with the Durruti Column, and if anyone saw me at the front it had to be in the village of Bujaraloz. [...]
>
> When I was arrested [June 29, 1941], with the police, there was a man named Sánchez, a metalworker who has a stand selling secondhand books in the San Antonio market on holidays, and also Caridad Martínez Fernández [sic], a one-time nurse at the Alianza Clinic, both having entered the service of the police for financial reasons. Caridad Martinez was aware that I had been extradited from France and moved to Madrid. She had traveled to France, and, seeing that I had been released without charges, she and her subordinate, Sánchez, concocted a whole series of sensational accusations, all of them false, since they all emanated from red personnel who were refugees in the camps in France, who could not forgive me for having held them up to disrepute every chance I got.
>
> [...] As to the incidents in the village of Gelsa, I have never been there, as was proved thanks to the photos my family sent your court so you could ask in the village if anyone had ever seen me. [...] As to Caridad Martínez Fernández, a nurse at the Alianza clinic, I met her sometime around 1931, and knew her as the married mother of twins. When I was held in preventive custody in 1934, I found out that she was visiting one Pedro Campón, who had been arrested over the raid on the "Oro del Rin." When I got out, I berated her for her behavior. I saw her again in 1935 [...] at No 25, Calle de Carretas. Manuel Escorza

[in charge of the FAI's intelligence service] lived across the street, and Caridad, who for personal reasons was not living with her husband, was staying there.

The Nationalist uprising erupted, and Caridad remained in the service of the fateful Escorza during that time. Come the retreat from Barcelona, Escorza, his mother, his wife, Campón, and Caridad crossed into France. Caridad set up house with Campón in Marseille, but something happened between Escorza's wife and Campón, and Escorza, his mother, and his wife left, leaving Caridad and Campón on their own and penniless. It was at that point that Caridad invented the story that she was Escorza's captive that entire time on; that she was the lawful wife of Campón, having divorced her husband. This is what she told the police, but, by consulting the Alianza clinic, and anywhere else she might be known—which is to say in the refugee camps—the truth might well shine through in all its splendor. I am confident that she won't be able to actually tell her husband's whereabouts, no more than she is going to be able to explain away her actions alongside the fateful Escorza throughout the whole of the *movimiento*.

Despite any threats she might make against me, she knows that I'm not about to keep a lid on the truth, and she is out to see me eliminated.

When Caridad saw me at large, she traveled to Pina de Ebro, and threatened my wife's family, the Gracias, telling them, for one thing, that she was Pedro Campón's wife; that I had been in Pina de Ebro; that the father of my wife's cousins, who is currently serving a thirty-year sentence, might get out if they would just say what she was telling them to say, since she was with the police and could pull a lot of strings on his behalf. My wife was told this by her cousins Pilar and Cecilia Gracia, who currently reside in Barcelona, from what I hear.

{22}
PAGE 75

The attempt by the International Group and some commandos to blow up the rail line and establish a bridgehead on the far side of the Ebro would fail. Let us look at Ridel's article in *Le Libertaire* of September 18, 1936, in which he says:

Sunday, August 25.

[…] We were finally roused by cannon fire from an artillery unit in Quinto
[…] Their fire was directed at us and was gradually zeroing in […]
We waited for a break in their firing in order to effect an orderly withdrawal from our positions.
Our artillery is too lightweight to be able to silence the Quinto guns and our planes are busy raiding Huesca.
[…] The order for a complete evacuation arrived from the War Committee.
By noon we were all gathered in the village.[…]
A red and black flag is still flying on the far bank.

So, from the end of July onward, the most daring militia members were embarking upon operations but not quite managing to accomplish them; villages such as Villafranca de Ebro and Alfajarín were taken and then lost for want of the equipment needed to defend them. Despite urgent appeals from the column commanders, echoed in the anarchist press, arms were still not reaching the Aragon front, and the militia members did what they could to arm themselves with weapons taken from the enemy. This largely accounts for the paralysis of the Aragon front, as the following excerpt from some correspondence from Miguel Amorós in 2005 makes clear:

The thwarting of the columns in front of Zaragoza was of concern to them all and not just the libertarians—even more so to the oversight body, the Central Antifascist Militias Committee [CAMC]. From the military viewpoint, there were not enough attackers (some of the militia members were serving in Majorca), not enough transport, no tanks or artillery, no heavy military equipment of any sort, much less aircraft. With three or four thousand militia members, entry could have been achieved into Zaragoza by surprise attack on July 24, but by August 10 they needed a lot more people. The vanguard of the Durruti Column was quite small, three or four centuries, no more. By August 10, General Cabanellas had received his reinforcements, the workers' resistance had been crushed, and the defensive arrangements around the city had been organized. They would have needed to knock out the artillery in Quinto and Fuentes de Ebro, neutralize the machine guns in Perdiguera, strengthen the trenchworks and fortifications, rebuild bridges, etc. Besides a few raids, none of that had been done. Logistics was still a problem. They could take a position, cross the river, approach a village and, at best, overrun it, but they could never hold on to it. They were short of reserve troops, fortification gangs, air support, bombs, and bullets. By September, the dearth of munitions was complete. And let us not even speak of winter clothing, boots, rain gear. By that point the Durruti Column had a few cannons but not enough of them, and just four *agrupaciones* in the lines (which is to say, two thousand fighters) plus another in the rear in Bujaraloz. And with those resources, it had to cover a front covering more than twenty kilometers. One does not need to read Clausewitz to know that an army finds itself increasingly neutralized the further it stretches beyond a critical point. The professional soldiers accompanying Durruti (Pérez Farràs and Manzana) knew that, but like Durruti himself there was nothing they could do about it. By mid-October 1936, the columns were in no position to mount any offensive. And a unified command brought no magic solution.[92]

The Ortiz (or Sur-Ebro) Column was stalled in Quinto and Belchite in the face of resistance coming from Nationalists armed with artillery. By the end of October, Ortiz himself was dispatched by the CAMC on a mission to Madrid to try to persuade Largo Caballero, the head of the government and minister of war, to fund a significant purchase of arms for the Aragon front. Here is the response he received at the end of their conversation:

92   Letter written in French.

Do you seriously believe that I am about to give you that money
to arm the FAI, which will mount a coup d'état against me?[93]

Durruti was also pestering the CAMC with demands for arms. On
September 6, he found out that some machine guns destined for the
front lines had been warehoused in Sabadell, near Barcelona, in some
UGT and PSUC buildings. The column's War Committee warned the
CAMC that Francisco Carreño and a *centuria* would be heading off on
an expedition to commandeer them. Santillán managed to get the PSUC
to amicably hand over the machine guns, which Carreño brought to
the front. Thanks to them, Fuentes de Ebro was captured on September
8, 1936, and sixty people pinned down in that village were freed. The
very next day, from Sariñena, Durruti delivered a radio address that was
printed in the September 12 edition of *Solidaridad Obrera*:

> Catalans! Count on us, the way we count on you.
> All arms held in reserve or in secret storage up to the front!

That same day, the Durruti Column and the International Group
played a crucial role in the capture of Siétamo near Huesca, and that
hammered home the message of the speech.

In Madrid, on October 2, Caballero and Durruti met with IWA
secretary Pierre Besnard, who was accompanied by arms dealers ready
to sell arms in large numbers. The same day, the cabinet decided to
fund this important arms deal, one-third of which was destined for the
Aragon front. The press picked up on the news. But two days after
that, the Russian ambassador Rosenberg sabotaged the deal; sure, Russian weapons were on their way, but no anarchist column would set
eyes on them, and with the weapons advisors to the great powers were
on their way. This was Stalin's first major venture into Spanish affairs.
Within a short time, the Soviet influence would gain ground, and the
anarchist leaders lobbying for entry into the central government would
switch to discourse revolving around unity, discipline, a unified command, and militarization. On October 25, the Republic would reduce
its ability to act even further by allowing the bulk of the Bank of
Spain's gold reserves to set sail for the USSR in payment for arms and
other supplies.

93   Gallardo Romero and Márquez Rodríguez, *Ortiz, general sin dios ni amo*, 117.

Thanks once again to Amorós's observations, let us turn back to one of the other factors behind the Aragon front being stalled. It relates to the disastrous Majorcan expedition (mid-August to early September 1936), which gobbled up men and materials at a point critical for the capture of Zaragoza.

From the moment the Generalitat government was spared, it relentlessly searched for ways to build its base at the expense of the Militias Committee. At the very beginning of August a new government was formed under Juan Casanovas. It included representatives from the PSUC and UGT. Though they had initially gone along with this reshuffle, the CNT demanded the immediate dismissal of the "Marxist" members of the cabinet, on the basis that they were already represented on the Militias Committee. The CNT, of course, abstained from joining the Generalitat cabinet and expelled the PSUC representative, Rafael Vidiella, from the Militias Committee for double-dealing.

That gambit by the Generalitat was flanked by the secret expedition to Majorca. The idea came from the government in Madrid; on August 8, Uribarry's Valencian troops, protected by two navy destroyers, came ashore in Ibiza, which had stayed republican. The Generalitat was out to seize this opportunity and threw its weight behind Captain Bayo, who enjoyed the obvious connivance of the PSUC and Estat Català and cooperation from "somebody" within the CNT (in August, absolutely nothing could be done without the CNT). The Generalitat's purpose in this entire episode was clearly to undermine the authority of the Militias Committee and thus of the CNT, through a victory that could be claimed for an official body (be it the Generalitat or the government of the Republic). This revealed the truth about the stance of one faction of the CNT (the sector influenced by the FAI Peninsular Committee), hostile to the influence and power wielded by García Oliver and the Nosotros group through the Militias Committee. When Bayo and Uribarry met up in Ibiza, Bayo staked his claim to the direction of operations in the name of the Generalitat (according to Uribarry) and also of the government of the Republic (there is a document dated August 10 from the Generalitat confirming Bayo's authority as the representative of both governments). Uribarry returned to Valencia with his column, and Bayo hoisted the Catalan flag on the island alongside the Spanish national flag. That a cruiser and two destroyers set off from Malaga on August 11, bound for Majorca, is proof that the national government was involved. Mahón (in Menorca) became the base of operations; 4,000–5,000 militia members landed on the 16th, and they ran into unexpected resistance. Although Bayo received reinforcements on the 22nd, his slow progress ground to a halt by the 25th. Majorca's defenders, though outnumbered, launched a counteroffensive on the 27th. They had six planes against one fighter squadron. Bayo sustained heavy losses and was pushed back. At that point the government began to lose interest in the matter, for it was short of men in Madrid and Malaga, and it apparently had misgivings about the Generalitat. The Militias Committee, still the main real authority in Catalonia, was all for a withdrawal, for its target was Zaragoza. The Generalitat began to fear that the failure of this operation, which it had sponsored, would only benefit those out criticized it, namely the Militias Committee. So it did its best to portray Bayo as being solely responsible: having gone behind its back, he should be shot!

At that time, in Madrid, the groundwork was being laid for Largo Caballero's socialist government. Two Catalan deputies made the trip up to Madrid and met with Juan-Simeón Vidarte, a socialist deputy at the Ministry of War and urged evacuation of the expeditionaries. On October 3, Bayo received his orders. Indalecio Prieto, the new cabinet's minister for the marine and air force urged Bayo on the 4th to wind up operations or he would be denied ships and planes. Bayo, crestfallen, returned from Majorca, abandoning a huge amount of equipment and hundreds of militia members, to face execution over the ensuing days. No one was willing to shoulder the responsibility for the catastrophe, and no one pointed an accusing finger at anyone else, given that the responsibility for it spread far and wide. Bayo was nonetheless called before a court-martial, which did not sentence him to death. We can read García Oliver's detailed account of the entire affair in his memoirs, for it is clear that he comes closest to the truth, though his account is tainted by his need to justify himself.

Ten days later, on September 15, a CNT national plenum drafted a report (endorsed by Federica Montseny, Juan López, and Aurelio Álvarez) insisting that Largo Caballero form a "National Defense Council." Many CNT leaders were now persuaded of the need to join the government of the Republic. The designation "Council" was a ruse to avoid the use of the term "government" and secure the approval of the membership without undue trauma. In Catalonia, the Generalitat talked the CNT into wrapping up the Militias Committee and joining *"el govern."* Santillán later explained—in *Por qué perdimos la Guerra*—that they went through with this to gain access to weapons and raw materials, although the real reason was most likely the urge to pave the way for the governmentalism that followed. What is certain is that the CNT acted behind the backs of its militants and that it had been doing so since August. It seems that the negotiations were conducted by two secondary individuals: Juan P. Fábregas, a right-wing Catalanist recently befriended by Federica Montseny, and José Juan Doménech. A regional CNT plenum was held from September 24–26, and on the 27th, García Oliver himself announced in *Soli* that the Militias Committee had been disbanded and that the CNT was entering the Generalitat government, "which represents us all." At the CNT's insistence, the government changed its name to "Council."

For further information, see Miguel Amorós, *Durruti en el laberinto*, 75–79; José Gabriel, *La vida y la muerte en Aragón* (Buenos Aires: Ediciones Imán, 1938), 50–70.

{23}
PAGE 75

On October 1, 1936, three anarchists joined the Generalitat, which then immediately issued a number of decrees: one on municipalization, the implication of which was that local revolutionary committees would have to disband, and another relating to militarization of the militias, which required civilians to relinquish their weapons. On cue, the PSUC press, while criticizing collectives on the grounds that "this is no time for utopian experiments in the realm of economics," laid into the "uncontrollables" who were accused of sabotaging the front and holding on to rifles and ammunition in the rear guard.

Durruti and other militia members were increasingly uneasy about the turn of events. Durruti rushed back to Aragon on October 5, because the Francoists were preparing a big push and the next day had a hand in the creation of the Aragon Defense Council. We have mentioned one of the council's functions before: managing relations between militia members and peasants. It also had to introduce some instrument for marshaling the creative urges of the Aragonese peasants and at the same time harmonizing and "steering" the economic and administrative organization of the region and of its collectives.[94]

Durruti hoped that the council would establish a local war committee overlooking all of the columns and that it would organize unified command for them all, so that they might shrug off the oversight from the Madrid government. He'd spoken of it in debates:

In order to defeat fascism, we have to put pressure on the central authorities, and, to get them to agree to our proposals, a council should be set up in Aragon to regulate all our activities.[95]

This new body would also take charge of policing duties, and bit-by-bit that would put an end to the autonomous groups, of which we have spoken, that were in charge of investigations. Soon a Security Junta (Council), entrusted to Francisco Foyo and Adolfo Ballano, took matters of public order in hand and created nine new commissar posts in Zaragoza province, one of them in Pina. In short, a sort of anarchist mini-government was being set up in Aragon. Félix Carrasquer observes:

It was obvious that the upkeep of a self-managerial collectivism and the defense of our regional autonomy fitted in with the performance of our duty of solidarity toward the government of the Republic, which all libertarians had taken on right from the outset with the loyalty and responsibility required of all by the common purpose: winning the war [...] Within the framework of such dependency and the violent situation all around us, how could we guarantee the order needed in the circumstances without ending up with a state structure?[96]

The Council of Aragon soon became the target of attacks by the central government, the political parties, and the Generalitat.

94 Antonio Ortiz in Gallardo Romero and Márquez Rodríguez, Ortiz, general sin dios ni amo, 130.
95 Paz, Durruti en la revolución española, 610.
96 Carrasquer, Les Collectivités d'Aragon, 72.

In December 1936, it deferred to certain pressures in order to be legalized.

For further information, see Ledesma, *Los días de llamas de la revolución*, 165–92.

{24}

PAGE 77

We think we have identified the two wine-guzzling guys from Lyon. They were Marius Brunand, bookkeeper, and Aimé Turrel, a bar-turner with Berliet, communist militants who set out for Spain at the end of July 1936. They made their decision individually but with the acquiescence of the Communist Party's regional federation.

These two volunteers were picked up in Figueras by a POUM recruiter and wound up in Barcelona in the POUM's headquarters in the Hotel Falcón. On August 10, they both applied for the Aragon front, but the column raised for that purpose was halted near Caspe by CNT-FAI forces, which enlisted the pair. They ended up in the International Group stationed in Pina de Ebro, where they found about sixty men, mostly French and anarchists, under Berthomieu's command. They saw action in the battle for Siétamo in mid-September 1936 and then in the fighting in Farlete and Perdiguera that October, returning safe and sound to the Durruti Column's headquarters. Durruti's partner, Frenchwoman Émilienne Morin, is said to have endorsed them by introducing them into the immediate entourage of the anarchist leader.

Wounded on active duty, Aimé Turrel sometimes attended the CNT-controlled "people's hospital" at No 388 Calle Provença, Barcelona. As for Marius Brunand, he was wounded in November 1936 and made his way back to France on December 4, 1936. He probably returned to Spain and bumped into his pal Turrel in February 1937 serving with the International "Anna Pauker" Battery, which operated under the orders of Gaston Carré on the Jarama front, in partnership with three Spanish brigades. By then Turrel was a gunnery lieutenant. Between spring and late September 1938, he took part in the battle of the Ebro before heading back to France that October, following the withdrawal of the International Brigades. In Lyon he returned to his activist ways as regional secretary for the PCF. On August 26, 1939, he was one of five militants who were outside the Berliet works handing out a PCF Regional Committee leaflet entitled "Long live peace," championing the validity of the German-Soviet Pact (signed on August 23). It was banned by the authorities, and he was prosecuted and convicted for defeatist activity. Called up after September 3, he was posted to the Luitel-Roybon camp in Isère, to the 5th Labor Company made up of persons to be kept under surveillance. Aimé Turrel went on to take part in the Resistance.[97]

{25}

PAGE 79

Here Antoine is telling us his version of the Francoist attack on Farlete at the start of October.

According to the report by Tranquillo (Giuseppe Ruozzi) published in Switzerland in the newspaper *Il Risveglio anarchico*, no. 959, and written in Pina on October 11, 1936:

> It is a rare day when cannon fire and shells from the fascists on the other side of the Ebro are not raining down on the little town of Pina. If it isn't Quinto, Fuentes is the source of the fire poured down on the poor, defenseless people. [...] A few weeks back, two hundred children from the area were sent away to Barcelona [...].
>
> September 27 was a horrible day; Quinto and Fuentes pounded us relentlessly all day [...]. This was a diversionary ploy meant to keep the militia forces pinned down, for, thirty kilometers further north, the fascists were mounting an offensive against Farlete [...]. The fascists had to fall back to their previous

---

97   Jean Maitron (ed.), *Dictionnaire biographique du mouvement ouvrier français* (Paris: Éditions de l'atelier, entries under Turrel and Brunand).

positions in a sorry state. October 4 proved another horrific day for Pina. The enemy returned to the attack in an effort to take Farlete and then pounded this martyred town.

As ever, the shells fell at random and caused injury neither among the inhabitants, nor in the ranks of the militia members.

In the Fonds André Prudhommeaux in the Gard departmental archives in Nîmes (AP 6J5) we discovered a handwritten text meant for publication in *L'Espagne nouvelle* newspaper. It is preceded by this introductory passage:

Letters from the Front
For understandable reasons, we are unable to publish the dispatch from the front insofar as the operations to which it relates are not yet over. Our readers will find here an account by *compañero* Tranquillo of the fighting in Farlete (October 8) and Perdiguera (October 15).

In Farlete
For some time now, the fascists have being showing signs of activity on the Zaragoza front. On October 4, a push against Farlete had been fought off. On the 8th, the fascists returned to the fray. Their cavalry, with 3,000–4,000 well-armed men behind them, got as far as the village gates. Their victory would have paved the way for a general advance by fascist troops, but on this occasion too it eluded them. Our militias weren't caught by surprise, but the outcome of the battle might have been unsure if a detachment from the Durruti Column hadn't come to our aid. The fighting lasted several hours and was very intense. In the end, despite his numerical and material ascendancy, the enemy was forced to withdraw in disorder in the direction of Saragossa, leaving many dead, wounded, and prisoners on the field. (Kindly translate the follow-up).

Alas, we have not been able to locate the "follow-up" in those archives.

So things were livening up on the "immobile" front. In order to put behind them a series of setbacks during September 1936, the

Nationalists' general staff laid on an offensive by a flying column led by Lieutenant-Colonel Gustavo Urrutia González. Its ultimate aim was to overrun Tardienta and the Santa Quiteria hermitage, and it was to begin on October 1, 1936. That operation was aborted, though, because of rumors of mass desertion by a section of the Palafox Bandera of the General Sanjurjo Tercio. In the end, the latter was disbanded and a very large number of soldiers shot without trial. Another attack was planned for October 4 in the Farlete-Osera sector, but the centurias of the Durruti Column pushed it back as far as the Los Calabazares position. A second attack was organized on October 8, 1936: a flying column of six thousand well-armed men, along with cavalry, artillery, and tanks launched an attack on the Farlete and Perdiguera sector. The response was orchestrated by the Durruti Column's War Committee: Durruti, Yoldi, Carreño, Flores, and Roda.[98]

Having studied the Francoist operations diaries, Barrachina is specific:

> From midday until 5 o'clock in the afternoon, the Alas Rojas (Red Wings) squadron flying out of the Sariñena aerodrome operated in support of the Durruti Column, with its ten planes and no opposition from enemy aircraft, bombing the attacking column from low altitudes with great effect. Given the troop density, defeat turned into rout. There were upward of a hundred losses (including eighteen fatalities). The Durruti Column took more than 150 prisoners.[99]

The same writer notes something that Durruti said, on October 13, 1936 in Sariñena, at a gathering of military forces in regards to setting up a unified command structure:

> If you are asking me how we defended Farlete and Monegrillo the other day, we defended ourselves as best we could, and at one point I could see us taking off at a run the whole way to Fraga.[100]

---

98   See Anonyme, *La 26 División* (Barcelona: Sindicato de la Metalurgia CNT, 1938).

99   Pedro Barrachina, "La guerra de columnas en el frente de Zaragoza (verano e invierno de 1936)," 140.

100   Ibid., 141.

In Farlete on October 8, 190 men effectively stood alone against the onslaught of thousands of their enemies along a seven-kilometer front line. The International Group, which didn't even have enough rifles to commit all its men, was called upon for the second time since September as a back-up force in a tough situation. One young Spanish militia member, Manuel Ramos, who died in October 2007, recounts:

> Ever since we left Barcelona, the enemy had kept out of sight, and we whiled away boring, monotonous days with no opportunity to get to grips with him, until the long awaited October 6, 1936. It was not quite daybreak when our lookouts reported movement on the fascist side [...] away in the distance, we were able to pick out the *Moro* cavalry, which Franco had brought over from Africa. We were told that we should be sparing with our munitions as we had only 150 rounds. We were the 26th *Centuria* and on our left flank was the 27th [...] with a mere two machine guns, we had no artillery [...] and the [enemy] infantry was advancing under the protection of a small tank [...].
>
> [...] The 27th was cut off from us and had only a small exit if it wanted to save itself, which is what it did before digging in in positions further to the rear; our centuria held its ground but was beginning to run low on ammunition, [...] we had been firing for seven hours, [...] the enemy was just a hundred meters away. We had the two machine guns evacuated lest they fall into enemy hands [...], and then reinforcements arrived, especially the internationals whose high fighting spirit gave us a great boost [...] the order now was to advance, and the enemy's resistance was starting to wane [...]. We were horrified to come upon a dead *compañero* who we were unable to evacuate and who had been beheaded by those barbarians. We knew what awaited us if we were to fall into their hands. [...] By 7 o'clock that evening [...] we were sure that the enemy had fallen back towards Zaragoza, the area ahead of us was clear, and we were wondering why we still there, [...] we could have laid siege to Zaragoza.[101]

The next day, their *centuria* was posted to Monte Oscuro. Ángel Marín, who was also there, offers a similar account of the battle:

101   Manuel Ramos, *Una vida azarosa* (self-published, 1993), 51–53.

I had never seen Durruti so serene. From his command post he was watching the enemy make preparations for a huge muster of Moorish cavalry. Because of the whiteness of their *djellabas*, they looked like a huge ice blanket covering the dried out soil of Mon-egros. This huge force advanced quickly, and it was very stirring stuff. It was only the fanned out deployment of our machine guns on our flanks that made success possible.[102]

Another eyewitness account, from Juan Sanz Martínez, notes the astounding outcome of the battle: the militias so often berated for their alleged incompetence and that would soon be systematically vilified had just successfully and with great coolness defeated an enemy far superior in manpower and equipment:

We arrived at the trenches defending the village of Farlete. Ear-lier, we came across a macabre spectacle: a huge plain strewn with men and horses. Some groups of militia members were carrying out the unpleasant task of shoveling them into huge pits [...] this spectacle was the result of the fighting that had occurred the day before between the Francoist army and militia members from the Durruti-Farràs Column.[103]

On October 21, 2009, the Giménologues were surprised to find ourselves contacted in these terms by the son of Isidro Benet, a former Spanish militia from the Durruti Column's International Group:

Hello, I would like to bring it to your attention that my ninety-three-year-old father fought on the Aragon front in 1936 as part of the Durruti Column's International Group. He was among the first to enter Siétamo and he fought in Perdiguera, Farlete, Pina, etc. He has read Antoine Gimenez's book [the first Spanish edition from 2005] and, while that he agrees with it overall, he takes issue with certain points regarding the battles. [...] If you are interested in contacting him, we live in Valencia. *Salut*. César Benet.

---

102   Marín, "Hombres y hechos de la Guerra civil española," 55.
103   Juan Sanz Martínez, *Vida y luchas de un idealista* (Valencia: Tetragrama, 1998), 148.

Interested? We should say so! … The meeting in Perdiguera with Isidro and César after months of warm and fruitful telephone chats was remarkable in every way.[104]

Here is what Isidro said about the battle for Farlete:

There were two centurias from the Durruti Column holding out against the Nationalists' offensive against Farlete. They were losing ground while under attack from Moorish cavalry when the International Group showed up to help them. I was in Pina with my *compañeros* when we were told to jump aboard the trucks that carried us out to Farlete. […] We were shelled en route and arrived just as the cavalry was attacking. We had just enough time to throw ourselves to the ground and take up our positions. On arrival, a French army captain [Berthomieu], tall, very brave, said to us: "Everybody hit the dirt. Do not fire until I give you the sign!" […] The Frenchman spoke flawless Spanish; he carried a Colt with a big false butt and he remained standing during engagements.

I was close to one of the two machine guns […] which were sweeping the flattened ground where lots of Moors and dead horses were strewn. All of a sudden, one horse, with its Moorish rider, his foot caught in the stirrup, swept overhead. I could see that the militiaman who had been firing was now dead (or at any rate wounded) and I took his place behind the machine gun. I did the firing, my friend Félix Bonells fed the munitions, and another friend of mine, Salvador Frasquet, lying on the ground, clung to the feet of the machine gun.

The battle took place close to an *embalse* [large water reservoir] near the A1104 road, a little over a kilometer from Farlete […]. The International Group took up its positions with the road to its rear, and the Moorish cavalry attacked from the Perdiguera direction. Near the village, but outside of it, there was a church. The republican artillery was shooting from point blank range, which is to say a very short distance away. During the battle, a transport plane, possibly a three-engined Junkers, swept over the Moors. It bore no markings, so we couldn't tell if it was republican or pro-Franco. It

104 We have published the entirety of his account, supplemented by maps, in our second book, *¡A Zaragoza o al charco!*

dropped a single bomb with great accuracy upon the Moorish cavalry. This is how the battle of Farlete was won, and it is confirmation that the International Group's intervention was crucial.

Another aspect of that day was underlined in *Le Libertaire* on October 30, 1936:

> Homeric battle! [...] The enemies of the people and of freedom have been forced to flee and this has been paid for in blood. Five of ours paid with their lives for love of brotherhood. Among them [...] Émile Cottin, big child and big of heart, Bianchella, Barriendos, Durruti's mess partner, Lemère, and a young Spanish soldier.

According to Barrachina, in the fighting in Osera and Farlete "many members of the International *centuria* perished."[105] But he gives no figures and cites no names. Concerning militia members killed during the battle for Farlete, the names J. Barriendos, Albano Bianchella, and Francisco Montés have indeed been found on the "List of the dead in combat in Perdiguerras [sic] and Farlete."[106] As for the Italian Albano Bianchella, all we know is that he is mentioned by Enrico Acciai.[107] One "Lemer Joseph, col. Aviateur" is listed in a roll call of "the French *milicianos*."[108] As for Antoine Gimenez, he refers only to the death of some "White Russian."

On the other hand, we can correct the death notice in no. 21 of *L'Espagne antifasciste*, which refers to the demise of "Louis Récoulis [sic] 24, and of his partner, Suzanne Hans, 22, volunteers with the Durruti Column, cut down by machine-gun fire in the attack on Farlete." Suzanne's nephew, Jean Boyon, has informed us that she had also signed on with the antifascist militias under the name Girbe (the surname of her mother's husband). This means that we can identify the fourth woman on the list of those who perished in Perdiguera on October 16, 1936.[109] Thanks to the five letters that Suzanne sent from the front lines to her parents, we know that she left for Spain in late September 1936, along with her partner Louis, and that they both actually took part in the

---

105 Barrachina, "La guerra de columnas en el frente de Zaragoza," 141.
106 IISH, FAI, 15.
107 Acciai, *Viaggio attraverso l'antifascismo*, 49.
108 IISH, FAI, 17.
109 See Appendix IV below.

Louis Recoule and Suzanne Hans

battle for Farlete, as can be seen in the last of the postcards sent from the "Durruti Column, Groupo [*sic*] international in Pina del [*sic*] Ebro"; it bears no date but must be from October 8 or 9. There, Suzanne writes:

> I have not been able to offer you any explanations so far, for there is censorship of every detail. We made a fair bit of ground today and are in Farlette [*sic*] and are going to attack. So far, everything is going pretty well....[110]

We shall speak of Suzanne and Louis at greater length in note 30. Finally, the book *Un trentennio di attività anarchica* mentions the death of one Italian:

> October 4—In Farlete (Zaragoza), death of Pietro Ranieri, serving in the Durruti Column. A well-known militant from Ancona who had played his part in the Ancona revolt in 1920.[111]

---

110   Communication from her nephew Jean Boyon to the authors, 2008.
111   Ugo Fedeli, *Un trentennio di attività anarchica 1914–1945* (Cesena (Forli): Edizioni L'Antistato, 1953), 185–86.

As for Ranieri, the *Biographical Dictionary of Italian Anarchists* suggests that he was killed in Perdiguera on October 16, 1936.[112]

According to the testimony of one of his friends, Frédéric Gascon from Marseilles, Émile Cottin perished during the battle for Farlete like this:

> lying flat on his belly on a slight rise, Émile Cottin was hit by a machine-gun bullet that struck him in the back of the neck and exited through his chest. Death was instantaneous.

In the *Dictionnaire biographique du mouvement ouvrier français*, we find this entry:

> Émile Cottin was born in Creil (Oise department) on March 14, 1896. "*I am an anarchist, which is to say an anti-authoritarian, anti-clericalist, anti-militarist, and anti-parliamentarist,*" Cottin announced at his trial, which began on March 14, 1919. A few weeks before, on February 8, 1919, he had shot at Clemenceau. Though Clemenceau was only slightly wounded, Cottin was sentenced to death by a Council of War, a sentence that was commuted to ten years' imprisonment plus a twenty-year banning order. He was supported by libertarians, the more so since Raoul Villain who had killed Jaurès on August 2, 1914 had been acquitted ... Incarcerated in Melun, he was held on death row for forty-two days. On August 21, 1924, he was released, deemed "severely defective," and assigned residence in Haucourt (Oise) where he was taken in by the anarchist Casteu. Cottin made twenty-franc bread-bins, which were advertised for sale in the weekly *Germinal*. Although under an assigned-residence order, Cottin nevertheless made his way to Paris where he met the woman who became his partner and with whom he had a son [or daughter]. But the couple parted. In 1930, while en route to Marseille to see his son, Cottin was arrested and jailed. By 1936 he was in Clichy, working as a cabinet-maker. That February he was arrested again and served three months in prison. In September

112   Maurizio Antonioli, Giampietro Berti, Santi Fedeli, and Pasquale Iusa (eds.) *Dizionario biografico degli anarchici italiani*, vol. 1 and vol. 2 (Pisa: Biblioteca Franco Serantini, 2003 and 2004).

1936, he left for Spain. The civil war had just begun, and he signed on with the Durruti Column's International Group. A month later he was killed on the Zaragoza front. "It was suicide," wrote Louis Louvet.

Cottin's last letter to his family dates from September 21, 1936. He gives his address as: "Émile Cottin—French committee CNT-FAI, Pedralbes Barracks, vía Layetana, 32, Barcelona."

For further information, see Abel Paz, *Durruti in the Spanish Revolution*, 549–51.

{26}
PAGE 80

This is a reference to Miguel Cabanellas, the general who placed his troops in the service of the Catholic-Nationalist crusaders and became chairman of the Burgos Defense Junta. He was even awarded the honor of investing Franco as head of state on October 1, 1936. Yet Cabanellas was a republican officer and a freemason. On July 18, 1936, General Núñez de Prado, who was on good terms with him, travelled up to Zaragoza from Madrid to persuade him not to join the rebels but to hand them over to him instead. He failed in this and found himself placed under arrest and executed. But it took some time before this became known. Contrary to the views of other Aragonese CNT leaders, Miguel Abós, a supporter of nonviolence, also gambled on Cabanellas's loyalty largely based on Cabanellas being a noted member of the masonic fraternity. Aware of the army ploy since February, the CNT more generally was relying on the Popular Front's ability to counter it. The civil governor, however, despite urgent lobbying from the anarchists, refused to arm the people. On July 18 and 19, confusion reigned, and activists waited in vain for weapons before taking to the streets. By the time the unions called a general strike, it was all over. On July 19, soldiers, Civil Guards, and Assault Guards were patrolling the working-class districts and smashing the strike through terror; day after day they rounded up, tortured, and shot known activists.[113]

And so Zaragoza fell almost without a fight, to universal disbelief, as the rebels easily seized control of Huesca, Jaca, Calatayud, and Teruel. Over the ensuing weeks, everyone who could do so fled the city and headed toward the Catalan columns. For months on end, the guerrilla teams from the Durruti, Ortiz, and other columns helped smuggle militants and their families across the republican lines while other survivors bided their time, hunted, in their hideouts. For instance, according to his daughter Engracia, Florentino Galván was smuggled out of Zaragoza by an "Hijos de la Noche" team and joined the Council of Aragon where he was the under secretary for agriculture. This is why and how recapturing Zaragoza became such an important gambit for the anarchists. According to a number of recent books, something like 2,500 people were executed without trial in Zaragoza in 1936.[114] Other works, which take into account the official executions, the numbers of dead discovered in common graves, and the evidence from family members, tell of 7,009 victims over the course of the war.

For further information, see Juan José Gallardo and José Manuel Márquez, Ortiz, *General sin dios ni amo*; *Andalan*, no. 294 (November 1980); "Florentino Galván Trias," http://gimenologues.org/spip.php?article375; and Giménologues, *¡A Zaragoza o al charco!*

{27}

PAGE 81

Vicenta Valero Labarta, Tía Pascuala's daughter, was twelve years old in 1936. She has clear memories of

the Italian militiaman, Antonio. When he arrived back from the front, filthy and lousy, my mother would heat some water and

113   See José Borrás, *Aragón en la revolución española* (Barcelona: César Viguera, 1983), 86–104.

114   Juliá, *Víctimas de la Guerra civil*, 66.

have him wash himself from head to toe—we had no electricity or running water; we had nothing. She would take his clothes, de-louse them and then it was—get to bed, you! She did whatever needed doing, as if he was another one of her sons. Which is what he was as far as we were concerned. [...] When he returned from the fighting, Antonio used to come to the house, and my mother would make him a meal. We used to boost his morale and say to him: "You're like a cat, nine lives! You come through it all and you'll never die." The house was tiny. Two rooms for four children. Antonio slept in the *pajar* [hayloft] with the livestock. [...] He used to bring us rice, chickpeas [...] because he would sometimes show up with seven or eight people in tow [...] grown men, and they had to eat. At first he used to ask my mother if he could have his meals at her place and then everybody started turning up, because my mother...[115]

And she offers the following portrait:

"Nobody stood on that woman's toes, not the Civil Guard or anybody else. She was very kind-hearted and if she had a crust of bread, she used to share it."

"No one came away from her house unfed," Vicenta's daughter María Jesús continues. "My grandmother was a real character! [...] She must have been quite terrifying. I was only young when she died. [...] There were lots of poor people in Spain; they would travel around the villages and ask for food, so my grandmother would invite travelers in and serve them up whatever she had. [...] There was some traffic through Tía's house. The maquis, the guerrillas, or the shock groups, all tramped through my grandmother's place. There were crowds in all the houses, as they used to drop off their clothing to be washed and the women used to help them out because they had no water and could not venture down to the river; so water was fetched from wells for every purpose..."

"The *internacionales* and the *regulars*," Vicenta pipes up "were in an empty house in the Calle Mayor—I can't remember now what the name of it was; it was near the Plaza de España. The owners are dead now. During the war they took off for Zaragoza,

115   Valero Labarta, *Entretien avec Vicenta à Saragosse.*

so the *internacionales* moved into the empty house. The Headquarters through which everybody tramped, the soldiers and the *internacionales*, were there; and it was from there that everybody emerged and set off to do battle."[116]

Vicenta remembers the story of Manuel, whose house lay on the far side of the river, and recalls how Gimenez fetched the sister back. When reading *Souvenirs de la guerre d'Espagne*, she was startled to find that Antonio doesn't mention her father, Tía's husband, Vicente, for he was around, and they had many conversations together; and her daughter María Jesús adds:

> My family was not very committed, it seems to me. My grandfather was a bit of a hot-head [...] he was more of a republican than on the side of the blues, the "blackshirts," as he used to call them.[117]

Vicenta remembers the arrival of her older sister, María:

> Back then, they were very tall, and María was tall, too, and good-looking, and I'm not saying that just because she was my sister.... She got married when the war started. Jacinto was born in May 1937. At the height of the war. Her husband's name was Manuel; he died young of throat cancer after the war.[118]

{28}

PAGE 90

There is no denying that contact with the *internacionales*, on the front as well as in the rear, had its part to play in the new relations between the sexes. It was not always easy for Spanish women, militiawomen or activist women to make eye contact with the men. Most of the latter

116   Ibid.
117   Ibid.
118   Ibid.

were not overjoyed at the sight of women—not to mention *their* own women—trying their hands at many jobs outside of the home.

The Basque anarchist fighter Casilda Hernáez Vargas stayed on the front until the beginning of 1937.[119] It was at that point that the equation of prostitute and militiawoman became widespread. This came as a big shock to her because in her view sexual relations in the front lines was a matter of natural and thoughtful choice:

> The days of women being confined to household chores and to the bed for the pleasure of her husband were gone. That women were going to the front lines to sleep with the men is a false claim. That said, when the two came into contact with each other, there was no avoiding certain affections and affinities, whether referred to as 'chemistry' or basic attraction, and relationships were formed, especially far away from urban areas, in places like Aragon. Physical, moral, and spiritual connections between men and women could take place on the front. Anything else would be a real aberration.[120]

Here is an extract from the testimony of the English woman Mary Low, an activist in Barcelona in late 1936:

> Spanish women were anxious to grab their liberty, but they had been closed up and corseted so long that they didn't know how much of it there was to be had. [...]
>
> The anarchist trade unions had begun a group, "Free Women," which issued manifestos and edited a splendid paper. I knew one of the girls on the editorial committee. [...]
>
> ... a French revolutionary fell in love with her and she loved him too. But when it came to bed, she refused with a comic and desperate virtue.
>
> [...] He was hurt by her attitude.
>
> "And why wouldn't you do it?" I asked.
>
> "Oh, because one hasn't time for all that during the revolution."

119 More of her in the chapter entitled "Militiamen, militiawomen" in Les Giménologues, *¡A Zaragoza o al charco!*

120 Luis Jimenez de Aberasturi, *Casilda miliciana. Historia de un sentimiento* (Donostia-San Sebastián: Txertoa, 2012), 66.

"It's not true," I said. "It's an excuse. You only say to hide your prejudices."

She looked at me and shrugged.

"Well, after all, one can't really be expected to change overnight, can one?"[121]

Contrary to what might be believed, the libertarian activists from the Mujeres Libres weren't leading the way in women's sexual emancipation; their educational mission and lobbying was limited to making sure the Generalitat of Catalonia legalized abortion "on therapeutic, eugenic, or ethical grounds," on making divorce easier, and broadening access to information about birth control:

> Sexual education didn't loom very large in its programs or in the journal. [...] The majority of articles related to sexuality concerned prostitution, analyzing its causes and efforts to eliminate it.
>
> [...] some groups [...] insisted that prostitution could not be eliminated; at best, prostitutes had to be protected from exploitation via unionization. In the early days of the revolution, there were attempts to organize prostitutes into a *sindicatos de amor* [love union].[122]

Mujeres Libres's most incisive writings, such as those coming from Lucía Sánchez Saornil, made fun at "libertarian marriages" at which trade unionists and revolutionaries stood in the officiating role instead of mayors and priests; she described this new public intrusion into private interpersonal relations as nonsensical and hypocritical.

The Mujeres Libres voiced no objection when militia women were banished from the front after October 1936; an article carried in their newspaper in July 1937 even found it understandable that "the woman [...] would rather swap her rifle for industrial machinery, and trade the fury of war for the softer side of her woman's soul."[123]

Sexologist Félix Martí Ibañez, whom we mentioned earlier,

---

121   Mary Low and Juan Breá, *Red Spanish Notebook* (London: Martin Secker & Warburg, 1937), chapter 14, "Women." Text available also at www.marxists .org/history/spain/writers/low-brea/red_spanish_notebook.html.

122   Ackelsberg, *Free Women of Spain*, 167–68, 169.

123   *Mujeres Libres*, July 10, 1937, cited in Mary Nash, *Rojas. Las mujeres republicanas en la Guerra Civil* (Madrid: Taurus, 1999), 168.

believed that the war had created brand-new biological and social duties for women. From here on they had to urge their men to conserve their physical and mental energy for battle. Their own duty was to facilitate "continence, sexual discipline, and harmony within erotic relations."[124] And so women should stay in the rear guard and stop insisting on their place in the trenches. He went so far as to berate the militiawomen who refused to act more cautiously:

> As for you mercenaries of middling virtue ... who, with the revolution at its height, have sought to turn the front, that holy ground impregnated with proletarian blood, into a bed of pleasure, away with you! If the militiaman comes looking for you, let him do so during his leisure hours, on his own moral responsibility, with strict hygienic precautions. But don't go leading him astray and turning his steely muscles into the mush of erotic lassitude ... you cannot wave goodbye to your former life by going around spreading venereal diseases on the firing lines ... Venereal disease must be eradicated from the front; and for that to happen, women must first be banished from it.[125]

{29}
PAGE 93

The massive push by the Nationalists under Lieutenant-Colonel Urrutia carried on through the anarchists' successful counterattack in Farlete.

A Francoist military telegram dated October 11, 1936 at 7:55 p.m. reports:

> With the same aim of breaking up the reported enemy attacks on Zaragoza, today we mounted an operation on Leciñena with an outcome favorable to our troops who have occupied a number of enemy trenches and the Virgen de Magallón hermitage

124 Ibid., 171–72.
125 Ibid.

overlooking the village [...]. At present, the operation is continuing.[126]

Here we have a POUM column experiencing a tough setback: the attack is recounted by one of the party's main militia organizers, Manuel Grossi, in his diary, first published in 2009. Here is an extract:

> The operation opens with a surprise attack on our right flank, moving from Perdiguera toward the upper part of the "Loma de Alcubierre," which is to say, out by the road-repairers' cottage that marks the boundary between Huesca and Zaragoza. The attack was mounted at night by Moors and some regular forces. Using prudence and strategy, they made it to the appointed elevation; they stormed the cottage and took Sitges *compañeros* prisoner, without any great resistance from them, due to the element of surprise. This will go down in the annals of crime as horrific; they hacked them to death with knives. They cut off their limbs, doused them in gasoline, and they set their bodies on fire. The two old folks who lived in the cottage received the same treatment.
>   So perished those sons of Sitges [...]. Those [fourteen] militia members of the POUM [...].[127]

The Nationalists had partly achieved their aims in that offensive and bolstered their position in Leciñena.

On October 14, 1936, the Durruti Column bolstered its defenses around Farlete and posted its *centurias* out toward Perdiguera; the thought was that it was seeking to engage the enemy. [128]

Let us take a look at various accounts and testimonials regarding the preparations for this battle:

To start, there's Lola Iturbe's:

> At headquarters an attack on Perdiguera, the last village before Zaragoza, was being planned. Durruti wasn't happy about the

---

126   AGMA, VZNC, 1299 Cp65.
127   Manuel Grossi Mier, *Cartas de Grossi* (Sariñena: Sariñena Editorial, 2009), 77.
128   See Anonyme, *La 26 División*; Martinez Bande, *La invasion de Aragón*.

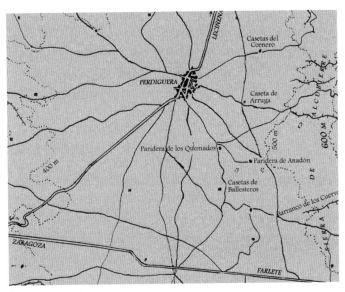

Perdiguera

idea for several reasons, but, because of the enthusiasm of his militia members and the International Group's confidence of victory, he eventually came around.[129]

And the account by Mathieu Corman, a Belgian journalist and communist sympathizer who was there and so understood the part played by the International Group:

> So far, the group has been familiar only with offensive operations, and its men think of that attack [on Farlete on October 8] as an insult. A little response is being prepared by Durruti's military advisors.[130]

From those two accounts one might think that the push against Perdiguera was some sort of a private initiative, the product of the impetuosity of the International Group's militia members, which is hard to believe. As Antoine points out, even though the group had up until that point been successful in nearly all of its assignments,

129 Iturbe, *La mujer en la lucha social y en la guerra civil de España*, 127.
130 Mathieu Corman, *"Salud camarada!" Cinq mois sur les fronts d'Espagne* (Paris: Tribord, 1937), 122.

Berthomieu was a thoughtful, painstaking type because they were in a difficult situation. And he was permanently in contact with the column's War Committee ensconced in Bujaraloz.

We also have the account of a participant, the Frenchman Charles Carpentier who returned to the front on October 14 on a truck full of provisions and clothing and driven by Pierre Odéon. The Union Anarchiste had asked Carpentier to bring Ridel back to France as it needed more able militants capable of orchestrating propaganda in support of Spain. But on that day, Durruti announced that the column was preparing a counter-thrust to drive back the Nationalists who had, for several days, been mounting mass attacks and threatening to break through the front. In *Le Libertaire* of November 27, 1936, Odéon described what followed:

> We were preparing for the return trip when *Gori*, as they called him, announced the next day's attack, which would attempt to capture Perdiguerra [*sic*].
>
> With his approachable and persuasive manner, Buenaventura asked Ridel to return to Farlete. Our friend readily acceded. Carpentier, not quite recovered from his wound, wanted to go with Ridel.
>
> I stayed at HQ, and Durruti [...] said to me: "It's now midnight. You'll sleep here and you can come with me at 2 o'clock tomorrow morning."
>
> Overnight the column's centurias mustered in Farlete. Throughout the 15th, they counter-attacked along the road that leads from Leciñena to Zaragoza and struck fifteen kilometers deep into enemy territory.

In 1986, in a letter to researcher David Berry, Carpentier wrote:

> I reached the group just before the order to attack Perdiguerra [*sic*]. Ridel and Berthomieu had set off on a little scouting trip. The order was passed to me and I sent a lad to ask what I should do, for I had just turned and was unprepared. Pending their reply, I tried to persuade five young women who happened to be there not to play any part in the attack, for no woman would have joined the group during my time there; they got irritated, so I let it drop. None of them turned back. We had had Simone Weil with

Carpentier (standing, center) and Odéon (wearing tie, left) in October 1936, just before Perdiguera

us for a few days and that had been enough. The runner returned to say that Ridel and Louis were waiting for us and that the entire group should follow.[131]

Clearly Carpentier hadn't taken part in the preparations, since he arrived the evening of the day Antoine describes—the day before the attack on Perdiguera. According to the plan Antoine describes, the International Group was there as a backup force. The story of the signal (the cavalry platoon) is a little hard to believe. Initially the War Committee's strategy was successfully implemented by Louis Berthomieu; they overran the designated position overlooking the hamlet. The question now is why Antoine (and perhaps other militia members) think that one member of the War Committee—in this instance Lucio Ruano—had planned to send them to their doom.

As far as we know, no other commentator on this battle—before or after the fact—said that the Argentinean played such a role. Ruano was quite well known and frequently mentioned in the anarchist press of the day; he was one of those trusted militants, close to Durruti, who

131   Communication from David Berry to the authors.

had been in action in Barcelona on July 19 and then had set off with him for Aragon. As well, Ruano was well regarded based on the recent capture of Siétamo, which had been achieved under his command. In their accounts, Ridel and Simone Weil mention the April 1936 execution of the one-time Barcelona police chief, Miguel Badía, that the CNT activist had taken part in.[132]

But because of later developments in Perdiguera, to which we will return later, Ruano fell into disfavor among the militia members and throughout the libertarian movement, so much so that his profile has been largely "vaporized" by partisan historiography. In short, Antoine has resurrected this "skeleton" from the closet in which it had been languishing for decades.

{30}
PAGE 97

In the weeks following October 16, the militant press in Spain and France published very emotional pieces on the tragic demise in the front lines of the International Group's nurses.

Augusta Marx, also known as Trude, was a member of the German Socialist Workers' Party (SAP) and had signed on with the anarchist columns. A handwritten document appears to relate to her:

> H. Diesel and Wolf. SAP delegation to the POUM Executive Committee. International Secretariat. Trude (female German comrade with Georgette). German Socialist Workers' Party.[133]

That young German woman features in an undated Spanish-language pass from the DAS stating:

---

132   We revisit that execution at some length in Les Giménologues, ¡A Zaragoza o al charco!

133   IISH, FAI, 50. The incident is also mentioned by Dieter Nelles in García, Nelles, Linse, and Piotrowski, Antifascistas alemanes en Barcelona, 144.

The DAS group supervised by the Regional Committee guarantees that *el* [*sic*] *compañera* Auguste [*sic*] Marx is an antifascist, which is why you should deal with her appropriately so that she may be incorporated into the International Column. The *compañera* is a qualified nurse.[134]

Lastly, there is a mention of her in the "List of German Compañeros from the Durruti Column's International Group mobilized on September 25, 1936,"[135] followed by the addresses of nearest and dearest to be contacted in the event of misadventure (say) confirming that Augusta had sought refuge in France:

a) Leo Cohn, 38 bis, rue Vital, Paris 19ᵉ.
b) 25 boîte postal [*sic*] Issy-les-Moulineaux (France).

Mimosa's death affected a lot of compañeros. The ghastly circumstances of her and Augusta's deaths, as related by Gimenez, do not seem to have been known to the group, who believed that they had been shot or perished in the dynamiting of a barn, in accordance with the report written with testimony from Francoist deserters. At the IISH archives,[136] we've been able to consult miscellaneous documents assembled by Georgette's friends in France and Spain following her death. Here are a few excerpts:

Dear *compañeros*: The notebook belonging to Georgette Kokoczynski who perished in Perdiguera has just been recovered.[137] We beg you to forward it to her husband or some reliable friend.

Anarchist greetings [signature illegible]
Grupo internacional de la columna Durruti

We have also found this letter from Mimosa's husband (the "Michel, my partner, my husband" cited in her journal):

134 IISH, FAI, 1.
135 IISH, FAI, Pe 1/C3.
136 IISH, FAI, 50.
137 Reproduced as Appendix VII.

Pedralbes Miguel Bakunin Barracks (French Section), Barcelona.
For forwarding to Georgette Kokoczinski
Paris, October 5.
My little Moute,

I thank you for writing to me so often and at such length. Your last letter reached me very quickly. I hope the same will be true of mine to you. My considered wish was that you'd stay longer in Barcelona. Since you have now gone, better in Aragon than in Madrid. The Huesca front is relatively settled since the beginning of the civil war, changes there are rare on either side and I hope the ambulances operate in better conditions there. We shall talk when we meet up again about what we are to make of the civil war. There would be no point in your laboring the subject in your letters. Is it really the case, as you write me, that there is a super-abundance of volunteers down there? If this applies to health staff and if you at any point become aware that others might take your place, then, I beg that you ask to be sent home. Had I realized that, I would not have advised you go. But *Vendredi* carried an appeal from Madrid for volunteer nurses. Can what abounds in Barcelona be in such short supply in Madrid? We get the impression here of a certain lack of coordination between the endeavors of the *compañeros* in Catalonia and those of the central government. I have been in Paris these past two days, utterly bewildered. I live in a sort of fog. There is too great an imbalance between army life and the life of a free man.

I sought refuge in the Bibliothèque Nationale, the only place where I can discover an atmosphere of serenity—it is where I am writing to you from—and my style certainly reflects the confusion of my mind. I don't know, petite Moute, what it was in my letter that you found cold—you know that I am not very talkative! And maybe the Spanish sun and the passions it unleashes made you find my usual tone chilly. However, ma petite Moute, how empty the house is without you in it! The only thing I can find there is your insufferable menagerie for which I am making efforts to find a home. It is really thriving and Mitsou has never been so fat. Maybe I will eat him, come the weekend. I haven't much else left to chew on. All I get from *Le Quotidien* is vague hopes of partial payments yet to come and I am impatiently awaiting an answer from Oran that should have come by now.

None of which is making me feel at ease (or putting any bread on my table). Meyer and the other *compagnons* are keeping well and have been asking after you. If your friend from Barcelona takes any photos of you, you should send them one.

A big, mushy hug to you, Moutiou. Keep thinking of me and writing to me. As soon as you can, send me your exact address and I will write you often.

Your Miecsezslaw

Several anarchist papers in France and Spain carried an insertion dated August 26, 1937: "*Mujeres anarquistas*-Georgette-Mimosa." People who had known her were asked to help put together a little book about her, an initiative dreamed up by her friends from the *Revue anarchiste*; articles in prose, poems, drawings, photos, etc, would be acceptable. They were invited to write to Spain, to Fernand Fortin, CNT-FAI French Section, Regional Committee, Barcelona. In France, the address was Marius Berger, 23 rue Croix-de-Bois in Orléans.

In addition, a text written as a tribute to Mimosa and drafted by one of the members of the Mujeres Libres group and signed *Kyralina* (Lola Iturbe) was distributed on July 19, 1937. Its opening lines read:

> On this, the anniversary of July 19, our thoughts are with the compañeros who fell in the struggle.[138]

As for Marthe—if she was Juliette Baudart—she was shot at the same time as her husband, Roger Baudart. Roger and Juliette were enrolled with the Durruti Column's "International Group" setting off for the front on October3, 1936. The same list contains the names of Louis Recoule, Suzanne Girbe, and Georgette Kokoczinski.[139]

In 2008, Jean Boyon, Suzanne Hans's nephew, informed us that Suzanne was born in Épinal on April 3, 1914. She had been active in the Union Anarchiste. Her parents hung out in libertarian circles; Jean emphasized that his grandmother was particularly active there. Louis Recoule was born around 1912; he was a militant of the Francophone Anarchist Federation, XIIIe arrondissement (Paris).

138   IISH, FAI, 50.
139   See IISH, FAI, 17.

Suzanne and Louis lived at 165 Rue Nationale in that arrondissement. Their two daughters, born in 1935 and 1936, died one after the other of meningitis and whooping cough.

Jean was born in 1935, the son of Suzanne's youngest sister. Suzanne would gladly have adopted him:

> Suzanne set off for Spain as much out of conviction as in a tantrum following her sister's refusal. She was a bit of a hothead.

After her death, Suzanne's parents raised Jean. They never found out where their daughter was buried. It was in memory of them that Jean was eager to find the location in Aragon.

On May 16, 2009, we were in Farlete and Perdiguera with Jean and Andrée Boyon. It was, no doubt, the first time that relatives of "internationals" had set foot in those villages. We had a conversation with a resident of Perdiguera named Costán Escuer:

> My uncle Mariano [who was fifteen years old back in 1936] recalls having seen two militiawomen arrested [Suzanne and Juliette Baudart, for sure] who were then flanked by soldiers and paraded through the village on foot. He believed that they were questioned at the command post. Every time he spoke of them, he mentioned that they were very beautiful women wearing harnessing (for their pistols, I imagine). He thinks, though he cannot be sure, that they were brought back outside the hayloft to be killed there, no doubt to show the residents that nobody would get out of this business alive. He insists that he never heard of them being disemboweled.

A year later, Costán put us in touch with Antonio Cugota, an eyewitness to the execution of one of the Perdiguera militiawomen:

> As chance would have it, my father has a friend the same age—he is eighty years old. Back then, he was just seven. My father can't recall the incident in any detail, but his friend has a very sharp memory, simply because he spent all his time hanging around the soldiers in the village. Near his home there was a camp where the soldiers did their cooking; across the way, there was the officers' camp and, a little further off, the headquarters. Well, Antonio was always hanging around the kitchen in the hope that they might

let him have a bite to eat—some bread, condensed milk, biscuits, some meat, some wine (at seven years old!)—and he was always listening to the soldiers' stories.

[...] He also told me lots of details about the day-to-day lives of the Francoist troops in the village: where they slept; the parapets that had been erected in the village; his recollections of village inhabitants who had been shot—among them his own pregnant aunt just about to give birth, whose fetus was discovered between her legs when they hoisted her out of the mass grave where she had been laid along with her husband and another thirty villagers—and such oddities as the three barrels of brandy and *anis* that stood outside his roadside home, which were referred to as the *"asalta parapetos"* [assault parapets]. When they were due to fight, the soldiers' canteens would be filled from them as a way of banishing fear [...] In all, over the period of the war, forty-one Perdiguera residents were shot, including the town hall clerk, the doctor, the schoolteacher, and one Popular Front councilor (one other councilor managed to escape, but the mayor was caught and made prisoner, escaping execution thanks to an uncle in the army). Taking into account that the population was only eight hundred, the number of shootings was massive [...] On the day of the nighttime assault [October 15] he was on the street and was told to get back home, as the reds were on the way. He told me almost exactly what my uncle had: the officer commanding the troops commanding from the village and the mayor fleeing to Valdelapez, Major Jérez flying off the handle when he arrived with the reinforcements and found the garrison unofficered, and later his death.

[...] On that morning [October 16] he heard that they had arrested a female militia member near the hayloft (he only ever mentioned one to me) and, as he was living in the heart of the operations command, once he saw someone moving, he sidled over with some other children [...]. Peering through the fissures in a huge wooden door in a stable near the post office, he could see the woman who was about to be shot. [...]

I asked him if he knew of another militiawoman, and he didn't; so the women were interrogated and killed separately. I also asked if it was possible that the two women had been disemboweled in front of the barn, and he had never heard that and said that if it had happened, he would have heard about it from the soldiers he hung out with all the time. I asked him again if he might be prepared to tell you this story if you were to come to Perdiguera, and he was agreeable.

And this is how we came to speak with Antonio Cugota and his wife Ofelia in their Perdiguera home in May 2010. We were very warmly welcomed, and Antonio told us:

> That night [October 15] the shooting was nonstop; the militia-woman was near the barn with a machine gun and the soldiers sneaked up behind her. They put her in a stable just here and, in the morning, they were ready to put her against a wall with three other militia members, dressed like hunters, and shoot her. She was a fair-haired woman, very pretty and well made. She was wearing a harness. She asked the captain in charge of the squad if she could fix her hair, and he said yes. Then he ordered them all to sing the *Cara al sol*. At which point the woman shouted *Long live communism!* and they were shot. If, or where, they buried her, I do not know. This has always been burned into my memory.

We showed him the only two photos we had of women serving with the International Group (and killed in Perdiguera). First, Mimosa's, since Antonio had mentioned a *rubia* (blonde), but he immediately said that it wasn't her. Next was Suzanne—though she was a brunette. After a lengthy silence, he became very emotional and said:

> Her face was round and full, quite like this one; it's the same woman, I'm telling you, it's her! She was a strong character!

Antonio enthusiastically agreed to have his photo taken.

In an article about Perdiguera in the Francoist newspaper *Amanecer*'s February 18, 1973 edition, they were still referring to

> "the Polish woman," a militia member who harassed Franco's troops for a time and who, thanks to the dauntlessness of a few brave men, was cornered, arrested, tried, and shot in the village.[140]

140   This source was passed to us by Costán Escuer.

Though we have confirmed that women from the International Group—besides the militiawomen Suzanne Girbe and Juliette Baudart—were arrested and executed, no one in the village heard about the demise of the nurses Mimosa and Augusta, as depicted by Antoine Gimenez. Maybe after they were shot their bodies were dragged and dumped in front of the last hayloft where the surviving internationals were holed up. Maybe they were dying, their bodies so battered that, from a distance, the militia members thought they had been disemboweled. Some Moors had arrived from Zaragoza as reinforcements on October 15. The cruel treatment of females meted out by Francoist troops (and generally ascribed to Moors) was known to their *compadres* and lingered in their minds. Alain Pecunia, the French translator of Ramón Rufat's *Espions de la République*, who had plenty of conversations with his author, told us that Rufat used to weep as he remembered the tortured female bodies he and his *compañeros* used to find in the front lines. Because of that, Rufat and other combatants used to insist that militiawomen should withdraw behind the lines.

{31}
PAGE 106

Now let us press on through the different accounts of the events of October 15 and 16. We have already mentioned the loss of the Col de Alcubierre and Leciñena, at some cost to POUM militia members. That opened a serious breach on the flank of the republican columns laying siege to Huesca, and the closest units promptly mounted counterattacks to recover the positions and stem the onslaught. This involved the reconstituted POUM forces, several *centurias* from the PSUC and the Macía-Companys Column, plus a further *centuria* from the Ortiz Column.[141] The fighting was very intense between October 12 and 20:

---

141 See Barrachina, "La Guerra de columnas en el frente de Zaragoza," 144.

In order to ease the pressure on the fighters in the mountains, on October 15, the Durruti Column prepared to move its lines forward from Farlete to Monte Oscuro and Perdiguera.[142]

While Durruti was trying to sever the highway to Zaragoza, as night fell on October 15, the International Group was attacking Perdiguera.

Martínez Bande, a Francoist historian, fails to mention that the October 8 attack on Farlete was a disaster. He says,

> there was a very strong attack on October 16, 1936 in Perdiguera. The enemy got a foothold in the outlying houses of the village and was then driven back; the attacks on the Col de Alcubierre, five kilometers east of the village; also took place over the ensuing days.[143]

In a footnote he stipulates:

> In the approaches to the Col de Alcubierre there lay 199 dead, 47 rifles, five machine guns, munitions, documents, and supplies, and a French officer was taken prisoner. We do not have the precise date on which the Col was occupied, but we imagine that it must have been on October 11 or 12.[144]

None of the Perdiguera witnesses (or their descendants) who we've spoken to ever heard of that French officer, which makes us think that Berthomieu may not have been killed in Perdiguera that day. More details emerge from this series of Francoist telegrams issued on October 16, 1936:

> 15.00 hours
> Departure of column which drives enemy out of Perdiguera and pursues him in the direction of Farlete: 60 dead counted, most of them foreigners, French, Russian, and some women. The column dispatched to the Col de Alcubierre to bolster the position has had contact with the enemy; the fighting continues."

142   Ibid., 146.
143   Martínez Bande, *La invasión de Aragón*, 136.
144   Ibid.

And, above all, the second telegram:

22.20 hours
To follow up the previous telegram: the news is that we have had
to abandon the Col de Alcubierre due to heavy pressure from the
enemy in great strength of numbers; what with Perdiguera and
the Col, we have recovered 110 enemy dead. A French officer has
been taken prisoner and a Spanish officer who was with the reds
has been shot.

At the bottom of the text there is a hand-written note added on
October 17, 1936, containing this order, issued to the 5th Division:

We require the name and photo of the French officer for publication.[145] (signature illegible)

What other French officer was fighting that day with the Durruti
Column, other than Louis Berthomieu?
Odéon was with Durruti on the morning of October 15:

We head for Farlete, arriving there about 4 o'clock. There was
great animation in the town, the men assembling in their *centurias*, red and black flags fluttering from the barrels of rifles. [...] At
6 o'clock the *centurias* moved off in the direction of Perdiguera,
and after two kilometers, they deployed the snipers.
    [...] Four kilometers outside of Farlete, they stop in their
positions [The *centurias* were bombed by two planes] [...] Gori
decided [...] to carry on with the reconnaissance [in a car with
Manzana and Odéon]. We hurtled along at 120 [km] an hour
and sighted Perdiguera on our right [...] We climbed to the
highest point of a hill and could see with our naked eyes the
Zaragoza-to-Leciñena road and the endless procession of fascist
trucks and cars. We had left the *centurias* three kilometers behind
us and Perdiguera's little church tower lay six hundred meters off
to our right [...] A motorcycle dispatch rider joined us, carrying
a message from the International Group, which was operating on
the edge of the Alcubiens [*sic*] highlands, about a kilometer from

145   AGMA, VZN 1299, Cp52.

Monte Oscuro, the view from Perdiguera today

us and off to our right. It was now 10:00 a.m. Durruti and Manzana put their heads together and decided to push the reconnaissance a bit further. The goal was to spot fascist machine-gun nests. [...] All of a sudden, the rat-a-tat of a machine gun [...] Impossible to raise your head; from Perdiguera off to our right not a single shot. Had the village been abandoned?[146]

Other anarchist chroniclers offer us this description of the sequence of events, highlighting a degree of recklessness on the part of the attack group:

That day (October 15, 1936) our militia members displayed cohesion and discipline in their movements [...]. But being overly eager for a fight, the forces drawn from the International Group, which was supposed to protect our right flank and was proceeding in the direction of Perdiguera, ventured too far forward and lost contact with the remainder of the force. On reaching the outskirts of Perdiguera, the group mounted a hand bomb assault and entered the village, scattering the enemy. But troops—upward of two battalions brought in from Zaragoza by truck—encircled the village where our Internationals put up a vigorous fight, successfully breaking through the cordon and

146   *Le Libertaire*, November 27, 1936.

falling back as far as our lines, in some cases. The rest had succumbed, holed up in a few of the houses in the village, where they fought to the end.[147]

In her article about Mimosa, Lola Iturbe added:

Georgette was among the International fighters. The attack failed. Fortune seemed to be favoring them at the beginning, the militia members mounting surprise attacks as far as the outlying houses in the village; but then they found themselves completely surrounded on all sides. Durruti gave the order to retreat but it proved only partially feasible, for they were swamped by very significant numbers of rebel cavalry.

Fifty fighters were left in the streets of Perdiguera never to return—Georgette was one. A group made up of French, Italians, and a few Germans held out, barricaded inside a house. They fended off the rebel attacks for as long as their supplies of hand bombs and ammunition lasted. Once these were exhausted, the fascists closed in on the house and called upon the besieged to give themselves up, or the house would be torched. Nobody took the offer. Every one of those heroes was burned to death, and Georgette (Mimosa) with them. She was twenty-seven years old.[148]

Corman regales us with a different, more epic account:

On October 17 [15], the column mounted an attack up the slopes of the Sierra de Alcubierre and, in a smartly implemented surprise move, made significant gains. When the first ranks of the International Group jumped into their trenches, the Moroccans fled in terror, screaming:

"*Alemanes! … Franceses!*"

Over the course of the afternoon, the head of the International Group managed to take up positions in the first few houses in Perdiguerra [*sic*], having covered ten kilometers of ground. But Berthomieu and forty of his men were too fearless. As a result of

147 Anonyme, *La 26 División*, 20.
148 Iturbe, *La mujer en la lucha social y en la guerra civil de España*, 127.

the impetuousness of their advance, they were left cut off from the bulk of the column. The enemy saw this and dispatched Moroccan cavalry from Zaragoza to cut off their retreat.

Encircled in a few houses, forty men stood up to a unit of Moroccans that was twenty times their size. Their ammunition is quickly exhausted by the repeated attacks of the Moroccans. Two militia members, Ridel and Charpentier [sic], then took on the dangerous mission to slipping through the Moroccan positions to go and notify Durruti of the situation. Of the men from the group that entered Perdiguerra [sic] that day, only two made it out. Most of those who stayed behind in their defensive posts were blown to pieces by grenades. Those killed included Berthomieu, Giralt, Trontin, Boudoux and a number of Germans I had come to admire.

The new trenches pass within fifteen hundred meters of Perdiguerra [sic]. The front has moved forward by eight kilometers. The territory gained is no compensation for the losses the column has just suffered. Berthomieu alone was worth more than that.[149]

Here, again, Carpentier gives his direct testimony:

After we met up [he, Ridel, and Berthomieu] we decided that about twenty of us would set off with grenades and I was handed a rifle, to capture the nearest positions overlooking the road. The rest of the group waited for someone to get them and we took those first positions ... two machine guns had been abandoned there. Ridel and four of the guys ventured somewhat further but did not get far before they ran into a cemetery where the enemy was dug in behind the walls. Ridel and the guys turned back and I fired two or three belts of machine-gun ammunition in the direction where they had come from. I had got the machine guns operational again, having seen service in the war in Morocco (the Rif) as a machine-gunner corporal with a Moroccan fusilier regiment. Night had fallen, and the three of us—Louis (Berthomieu), Ridel, and I—were talking; and Louis waited behind as we went off to fetch the remainder of the group (when I was wounded

149   Corman, "Salud camarada," 122–24.

the group had been about sixty strong; this time there were 240 of us) and Boudoux must have been there, but the situation was such that I could see [none of] the compañeros I had left behind. I was thinking about the attack and about the purpose of my being there: to bring Ridel back to France. The group reassembled and after yet another huddle with Louis [he] asked Ridel and me to get some gear, because he was sure that we would come back. We set off through the darkness and after quite a bit of trouble we were just about there when we bumped into a "liaison officer" who had lost his way while bringing [an] order to turn around since our troops attacking the banks of the Ebro had been pulled back. We turned around and covered a few kilometers before coming across the rest of the troops retreating, some seventy survivors … the rest—Berthomieu and the five women were among the 170 missing; the pressure off them, Franco's troops, including the Moors, had virtually wiped out the International Group. Needless to say, the 70 survivors were not very happy; there were a few compañeros from the beginning among them and they followed the advice we gave them.[150]

Phil Casoar, who interviewed Carpentier in the 1980s and to whom we put Antoine's account made a crucial point to us.

[At one point during the counteroffensive] Durruti had given the order to the *centurias* to withdraw and return to their previous positions. However, the runner dispatched to the Internationals to alert them to the overall withdrawal had gone astray in the countryside and arrived well after the battle. The Moroccans had no difficulty encircling the group, which was abruptly left without cover on its left and right flanks. Again according to Carpentier, after the massacre certain members of the International Group, mad with rage and convinced that they had been set up and dropped in it, wanted to head straight for column headquarters and give them what for. Yes, they felt betrayed. Perhaps some of them thought that Ruano, a member of the War Committee, was directly responsible for this bloody mess. Ridel and Carpentier had a lot of trouble persuading their compañeros that this was

150   Letter to David Berry, 1986, passed on to the authors.

all bad luck and they had to use their authority as founders of the group to stop them from seeking revenge.[151]

It is with this disaster that Ridel's service in Aragon ends. That very night, he and Carpentier traveled to Caspe by car; there a *compañero* working for the Ortiz Column's intelligence service secured them the requisite travel permits. From Caspe they headed for Barcelona and then on to France."[152]

In the village of Perdiguera, Scolari was the last to stay with Berthomieu. Of the seventy who survived, it was Scolari who told what happened to Ridel and Carpentier. In the FAI archives we came across these notes scribbled on some paper:

> Gimenez, delegate first gr[oup], eyewitness, stayed until virtually the last minute [and] Scolari (the last compañero with Georgette).[153]

And to finish, here is a report compiled right after in Spain by some members of the Union Anarchiste on the basis of information provided by survivors: it raises the hypothesis of a trap set by the enemy:

> Information concerning the death of four compañeros in Perdiguerras [*sic*]
>
> Wednesday October 14, the order went out that the village of Perdiguerras was to be attacked by the Durruti International Column. The attack occurred on the evening of the Thursday, October 15.

At the head of this group, there were four women:

> [...]. Entry into Perdiguerras proved very easy, the compañeros even got the impression that the rebels were on the run, for they discovered some spoils of war in the first houses. In reality, this was a trap. Moroccan cavalry cut the vanguard off from the rest of the group. They were swept by fire from machine guns posted

---

151   Correspondence with the authors, 2005.
152   Phil Casoar in Collectif, *Présence de Louis Mercier*, 17.
153   IISH, FAI.

The approach to Perdiguera from the Sierra de Alcubierre

in the streets. The survivors then took cover in the first houses of the village and defended themselves heroically, a handful against thousands. It was only on Friday October 16—at around 2 or 3 o'clock in the afternoon—that the rebels finished the job by blowing up the last two houses. The one where the women were (definitely Georgette and compañera Trude) was bombed by a plane. As for the other, it was dynamited.

[...] A counter-order, saying not to attack, was sent out but arrived too late (at 5 o'clock in the afternoon).

One version of this story says prisoners were taken, but that is unlikely as the information about the houses blown up has been confirmed by two (or three) soldiers [legionnaires from the Sanjurjo Tercio] who surrendered to the Durruti Column. These refugees have supposedly also stated that the women were shot(!)[154]

Antoine doesn't mention any counter-order not having been delivered, or a lost courier, or any sly maneuver on the part of the enemy. To him, it was obvious that the only explanation for the serious setback was treachery, for had the plan of attack merely been a bad one, someone would at least have come to their aid. Now, according to him, the "*centurias* had not budged from their positions." If it is true, as he says, that HQ didn't respond to the militia members justifiable request for an explanation, and that "Buenaventura knew nothing about the origins of the affair," one can readily understand the survivors' anger. It should be underlined that the anarchist militias, lacking in battle experience during the early months of the war, did make tactical mistakes,

154 IISH, FAI, package 50, box 521.

The cemetery in Perdiguera

and that the direction of the war also suffered from problems relating to communications and coordination.

Here Isidro Benet's account parts company from Antoine Gimenez's: they were not in the same location during the battle:

> There were four or five of us young Spaniards with the International Group with its 150–160 members. We were in Monte Oscuro in a spot overlooking the Perdiguera on one side and Farlete on the other, with the foreigners lower down. [...] Our custom was to proceed downhill along a ravine as far as Perdiguera [...]. It was already getting dark when we Spaniards rounded the Col del Maestro; the rest of the International Group was on its way from Farlete. Only those from the Durruti Column were involved. [...] We youngsters were always in a hurry and arrived ahead of the others and waited near the entrance to the village. Then the guys from the IG showed up. From a height of five meters, ten or twelve men, each with six bombs, attacked a trench [in which there was] a machine gun. [...] The Francoists took off. [...] We grabbed the machine gun and I swung it around to fire at the troops, but since I had no clue as to how to operate it, it wouldn't work; somebody else shoved me (amiably) aside and, shortly after that, it was working.[155]

By this point in Isidro's account, we note, part of the International Group, with Berthomieu and Antoine Gimenez, entered the village from one side and the group including Isidro was making inroads as far as the church. Consequently, he couldn't see what going on with the first group:

155   See above for Carpentier's testimony, in which he recounts a similar incident to David Berry.

So we were at the entrance to Perdiguera in a spot resembling a threshing-floor; at the far end there was a house and a street, quite close to the road from Zaragoza. We could hear the gunfire from fighting coming from 200 meters further into the village. We were keeping an eye on things as the flash of the gunfire allowed us to. I saw several members of the International Group die, like the Italian; plus another Italian who had gone crazy, in that he was closing on the soldiers and throwing his last remaining bombs; then down he went, dead. The fighting was essentially taking place inside the village. [...]

There were few people from the Group left, but how many of us there were and how many had perished, I don't know. Things had taken a bad turn; Moors and *regulares* had arrived from Zaragoza and they were firing down at us from the balconies and windows. They had us outnumbered. We should have all entered from same place; we had been caught wrong-footed and there was a lack of coordination. There was a German (I think, because he was speaking half in Castilian and half in German) giving the orders. We headed back in the direction of Monte Oscuro.

Our withdrawal was done at night, via that ravine again, and day was beginning to break [October 17] when we were 500 meters away. They stopped following us, afraid to go any farther and they let us go. We made it to Monte Oscuro. [...] Several Spaniards perished in the International Group; I have seen their names in the list of those who fell in Perdiguera. From our group of Spaniards, we were missing two or three; as to the fate of the rest, I have no idea. The missing went unnoticed because the Germans were mingling with them on one side; and the French from the other and it was the same with the Italians. Everyone was counting his own losses. I never saw Berthomieu in Perdiguera. [...]

After fifteen or twenty days, some militia members arrived to relieve us in Monte Oscuro and we headed back to Pina for a period of rest.

{32}

PAGE 106

From the testimony of the International Group's founders, Ridel and Carpentier, we figure that, out of the 240 men and women who belonged to it in late October 1936, almost 170 perished in Perdiguera. In 1972, Mercier Vega even referred to "200 deaths in the International Group out of the 400 who enlisted."[156] Now, in light of fresh evidence and examining things somewhat more closely, we are revising our figures. Close reading of Antoine's account highlights the fact that, prior to committing himself to the action, "Berthomieu had taken half of the personnel, which is to say, a hundred men...." Later he writes about the time in the famous barn: "There were around forty of us men, between the able-bodied and those wounded to one extent or another." The reader will have noted that Corman speaks of some forty "men with Berthomieu cut off from the bulk of the column" and Iturbe of "fifty fighters [...] who never returned."

David Berry, who has done a lot of work on the French volunteers serving in Spain in the anarchist columns, has compiled a list of fifteen who perished in Perdiguera.[157] We might add that the list "of the Perdiguera dead" drawn up quickly by members of the Barcelona-based French Section and of the Union Anarchiste names thirty-seven men and women clearly of a variety of nationalities.[158]

Georges Sossenko, a young Frenchman who left Paris on October 6 (quite possibly in the same truck as Carpentier and Odéon) and arrived on the front at Caspe where headquarters were, wrote a week afterward:

> We spent a week in Caspe, where our headquarters were, and the day after we got there we went to the restaurant where we were fed. We spotted great agitation among the military and civilian clientele and among the young waitresses. Since we spoke no Spanish, we didn't know why they were so upset. While we were eating, six to a table, Juan [Mayol] arrived, ashen-faced, and told us that the day before we arrived, October 16, there had been a

156   Bulletin du CIRA (Lausanne), No. 25.
157   See Appendix III.
158   See Appendix IV.

bloody battle in Siétamo [*sic*], Farlete, in which the sixty-man French detachment, commanded by the anarchist Louis Barthomieu [*sic*] had been wiped out, with no survivors.[159]

And, finally, this brief extract from a very rich article flagged up and translated thanks to the efforts of our friend from CIRA Lausanne, Marianne Enckell. It comes from the journal of Edi Gmür (a German Swiss who joined the International Group in late December 1936):

June 17 [1937].

Yesterday morning our company was loaded onto four big buses, which headed out to the front via Farlete. [...] Facing us, at the foot of the steep slope criss-crossed by little streams, was Perdiguera where forty-two men from the International Company had lost their lives.[160]

As we know, Carpentier left on the evening of the battle, with Ridel; they may not have known the exact numbers killed, especially if, as Antoine tells us, some survivors managed to make it back to HQ the next day. Since he is not sure that all of those in the group have been identified, or that all the survivors reported back to HQ, our provisional conclusion is that something between forty and fifty men and women perished during the International Group's attack on Perdiguera on October 16, 1936.

As well, we tried to identify some other of Antoine's *compañeros* on the basis of the list drawn up by the French Section. Listed there is a Simon Lacalle who caught our eye, and a Georges Chaffangeon (could he be "Georges, the little Parisian"?) who may, according to Ridel, have been a member of the Communist Youth in Lyon.

In his writings, Ridel often named some of his *compañeros* who perished in Spain; on October 23, 1936 in *Le Libertaire* he wrote:

Among those who perished defending the Spanish proletariat, we must mention Louis Berthomieu, the group's general delegate. An

159   Sossenko, *Aventurero idealista*, 115.
160   Edi Gmür and Albert Minnig, *"Pour le bien de la révolution": Deux volontaires suisses miliciens en Espagne, 1936–1937* (Lausanne: CIRA, 2006), 106–7.

The hayloft door, riddled with bulletholes

outstanding military expert, a true guide and friend, renowned for his bravery and calculating mind, his loss was sorely felt by us.

He had the soul of an adventurer, with all of the qualities that entails. Profoundly anti-fascist, he ignored the differences between this school of thought and that one, arguing that he knew nothing about them. Surviving on quinine, a dapper figure, he was forever on the move, watching and observing. Ensconced in one of the first houses in Perdiguera, he was cut off from the rest of the group after a flanking movement by the Moroccan cavalry and was blown up by dynamite along with a small band of compañeros.

Manuel Aracil, an FAI propagandist previously wounded by a burst of machine-gun fire in Siétamo, was killed by a bullet to the chest. He had returned that very day from convalescing, bringing back to the group a bunch of things he had bought with his own money and was delighted to be back with his old friends. A beautiful figure in the Spanish anarchist movement, he had several convictions from previous regimes. He was one of the men who built the libertarian movement with their faith and their lives.[161]

As for Alexandre Staradolz, Ridel and Carpentier mentioned him over and over again. In *Le Libertaire* of July 15, 1937, they wrote a lengthy article paying tribute to him:

161   Mercier Vega, *En route pour Saragosse avec la colonne Durruti*, 10.

He was Ukrainian, tall, straightforward, and gruff. We never found out much about him [...].

When volunteers who had come from the four corners of the globe complained about the naiveté of the Spanish fighters or grinned sadly as they watched peasant militia members firing at rebel aircraft with a revolver, Staradolz used to pacify them:

"Pay no heed to that. In '17, the Russian partisans were not much better. [...] Very rarely did we fight. Primarily we blew up bridges and railroad tracks. [...]

"Little by little we were trained, battle-hardened, organized.

"It'll be the same here."

Later he told us that he had been one of Makhno's men. [...]

He loved the "rough and tumble," gunpowder, terrain that needed exploring, raids to be mounted in silence, the machine gun that needed to make its presence felt when the right time came.

A new life was beginning for him with compañeros, something new, a free, sturdy existence, fresh air to fill one's lungs, a weapon to take care of and the feeling that we were fighting in everyone's cause, for the entire world, for something that was beyond him and that at the same time made him stand taller.

On a tour of Aragon by the Giménologues in May 2005, we came upon the son of the owner of the hayloft in Perdiguera where what was left of the International Group committed to the attack on the village had retreated on October 16, 1936. This individual, who prefers to remain anonymous, was aware of Antoine's account, a neighbor having recently shown him a copy of the Spanish first edition.

You can see the shrapnel in the door and the outer walls. That was where the fourteen [internationals] were encircled. They are buried quite close to here, and the place is marked, but I would rather not say where, for these poor wretches should be left to rest in peace. What would be the point of disinterring their remains? Some of them were burned indoors and those that ventured outside were gunned down.

He was greatly astounded that Antoine should have escaped once they were surrounded. His father had been there and saw the whole thing, as had some other elderly folks. He'd told him the whole story.

The hayloft and church today

In the 1950s there was much talk about it, but now there was not much left to talk about. His peasant father had stayed in the village all the time but never enlisted, and he was lucky. He passed away twenty years ago.

> The door is riddled with bullet and shrapnel holes. There was no urge to change that so it was left as a reminder [...] the roof was burned down; the hayloft itself was partly rebuilt after the war. Setting foot inside one has to go down a few steps; paving slabs have been laid, and the floor level raised; all of a sudden, there are no more dark patches at the foot of the wall; marks left by the bodies of the militia members that burned to death. And there is no sign left of the two holes [Berthomieu's loopholes]. I saw those things before the renovations were carried out. That made a big impression on me [...] The story about the deaths of the women, as recounted by the Italian militiaman, came as a big surprise to me; the village folk would have seen it; I never heard it mentioned.

Neither had he heard anything about the women's bodies being burned.

> The militia members must not have had too much intelligence about the garrison ensconced in the church and the number of soldiers in Perdiguera because otherwise they wouldn't have come near the place. But the people who were in the hayloft had

killed the garrison commander who ventured into the open at the head of his troops; Jérez, his name was.

Barrachina confirms that the fighting in Perdiguera was very tough and that the Segunda Bandera's commanding officer was also killed. Other officers were wounded and eight legionnaires killed. But the number of soldiers slain by the Francoist army itself was even higher: two brigades [officers], five NCOs and fifteen soldiers who had pulled out of Perdiguera on the evening of October 15, as well as ten cavalrymen, and three machine-gun feeders who had fled to Zaragoza were executed.[162]

The owner of the hayloft pointed out Monte Oscuro off in the distance:

The republican side was over there. You can still see trenches and shelters. There were many battles. The guys on this side used to mount attacks from Perdiguera and then there would be a counterattack and so on; and nonstop bombardments. The area was reduced to a wasteland. Long after the war there were houses still in ruins. [...] We were right in the front lines here. There were 800 to 900 inhabitants; the young ones were on the front, the oldest headed for Zaragoza. There was no plowing done, no horses, all of them having been commandeered; those who dared stayed on, and there were a few deaths. Above all, there were soldiers galore. Perdiguera was never captured. [...] Some years ago, while out plowing, we could still stumble upon bones and half a human skull. Bodies were strewn across the overgrown areas in the wake of the fighting.

162   See Barrachina, "La Guerra de columnas en el frente de Zaragoza," 147.

ENDNOTES 33 TO 50

The Resistance to Militarization

{33}
PAGE 107

Despite the Perdiguera disaster, the counteroffensive mounted by the Durruti Column made headway:

> In accordance with the orders from Operations at Column HQ, a continuous front was eventually established, extending our lines northward overlooking the Monte Oscuro massif, the highest point in the Sierra de Alcubierre, from which it was possible to dislodge the enemy, which resisted weakly. We made contact with the neighboring column, which counter-attacked via Alcubierre in the form of patrols.
>
> In all of the aforesaid operations, the enemy air force operated with what was, at that point, astounding intensity; for the very first time new German fighter planes appeared, swooping to under a hundred meters to strafe our forces.[1]
>
> On October 17 something very important happened: the second and third Heinkel 46 squadrons (three bombers apiece) arrived in Zaragoza [...]. Furthermore, on the same day, half a squadron of German Heinkel 51 fighter planes arrived from León [...] their presence would shortly change the odds in the skies over Aragon.[2]

But inaction soon descended upon the front once more; the militias still lacked the wherewithal for an attack on Zaragoza since Largo

1   Anonyme, *La 26 División*, 20–21.
2   Barrachina, "La Guerra de columnas en el frente de Zaragoza," 148.

Caballero had still not shipped them the weapons they had been promised. And there was another cause of tension and unrest: the militias
were to be militarized, military code and hierarchy restored.

Back in Barcelona, Díaz Sandino and García Oliver were in charge
of the Generalitat's Department (councilorship) of Defense since September 27, and, in theory, they were responsible for enforcing the
decree on militarization. The Durruti Column's War Committee held
a meeting and issued a statement about self-discipline, while staking a
claim to "freedom of organization":

> This column's militia members have every confidence in them-
> selves and in those of us who lead it through their express and
> unreserved delegation. Nevertheless, it is their belief, as well as
> ours, that the militarization decree cannot improve our chances
> in the fight and will, rather, create suspicion, reservations, and
> the aforementioned repugnance, leading to out and out disorga-
> nization [...] In light of which this Committee, acting as spokes-
> man for the loud objections raised by the column regarding said
> decree, finds itself compelled to reject it.[3]

Here is one of the rare eyewitness accounts of the International
Group at that point, as carried in *L'Espagne antifasciste* on November
4, 1936:

> Farlete, October 30, 1936.
> [...] I wrote to you recently to say that there was about a dozen of
> us compañeros from the CGT-SR in the International Group. We
> presently number fifty-two, coming from all over France [...] Oh
> yes! Here we are, and from our positions we can clearly hear the
> factory sirens of Zaragoza [...]
> As to the matter of militarization of the militias, shout it out
> loud to all who want to hear it: in every one of the columns led
> by anarcho-syndicalists, and they are the most numerous: 'Militia
> members, yes; soldiers, never!' Durruti [...] is neither a general
> nor a boss, but a militiaman deserving of our friendship. [...]
> Saïl Mohamed,
> no rank, no number, like all his compañeros.

3   Amorós, *Durruti en el laberinto*, 59.

There was a reorganization of the International Group. Pablo took over from Louis Berthomieu. Here again, Antoine's *Memoirs* rescue from oblivion a picturesque character whose trail we picked up in the FAI archives in Amsterdam, and on whom we found two fat files in the archives of the political police in Rome. Pietro Vagliasindi is the real name of this renegade from the Italian army. In his "Snippet from My Travel Journal," dated August 17, 1936 and published in *Le Libertaire* on September 18, 1936, Ridel spoke of the Banda Negra's being headed by a one-time Italian colonel. No doubt they are one and the same.

Vagliasindi was a fascist from Italian high society, charged with carrying out intelligence-gathering and spying operations in Europe during the 1920s and 1930s. After a conflict with his own party, he had been dropped from the Italian army in 1929, and he seems to have been out to settle scores with Mussolini. Over the course of 1934, now a dissident fascist, Vagliasindi settled in Sitges on the coast of Catalonia. He didn't want to give up military glory, and the Italo-Ethiopian war offered him a chance to request reinstatement in the army. In 1935, he took steps to put himself "under the orders of king and country":

> I told myself that it was better to perish on the field of battle than die some dismal, silly death in bed.[4]

But his application was turned down, and as far as Vagliasindi was concerned that represented "yet more proof of the cowardice of Italian governments, of whom Mussolini was, in the widest sense of the term, the sole master."[5]

And so, our ex-colonel found himself in Sitges at the time of the army's attempted coup d'état on July 18, 1936. The anarchists placed him under arrest and interrogated him. They consulted an enormous wealth of documentation (administrative, military, personal, correspondence, etc.) found during a search of his home, and, surprisingly, he went on to become one of the Durruti Column's military consultants, it being on the lookout primarily for experienced officers and inclined to welcome fighters with unusual pedigrees.

---

4   IISH, FAI, package 44. (Translated directly from the French by the unnamed anarchist author of the report drafted following a search of Vagliasindi's home.)

5   Ibid.

In a report dated October 2, 1936, signed by Pedro Bellver from the Defense section of the Sitges local antifascist committee and meant for Camillo Berneri, Vagliasindi is described as "compañero." The Investigation Department's inquiries had come to this conclusion:

> Close examination of papers belonging to Colonel Vagliasindi has produced no proof validating the accusation brought against him that he is a fascist agent, but there are several factors leading to the following conclusions: had Vagliasindi, rather than being in Sitges at the time of the fascist putsch, found himself in Zaragoza, he would presently be serving in the ranks of the fascists; had the Italian government agreed to readmit him to its service, he would presently be in East Africa.
>
> Papers show him to be a megalomaniac thirsting after military glory and an adventurer with a preference for the role of Don Juan.[6]
>
> [...] either Vagliasindi means to render great service to Italy by winning the trust of the antifascist militia just to betray it; or he is thinking of carving himself out fresh military glory and throwing down a gauntlet to Mussolini.
>
> [...] Vagliasindi is a nationalist-monarchist: there is nothing in his correspondence to suggest that he is anything other than a dissident fascist with a personal problem with Mussolini.[7]

His file was forwarded that very day to Lucio Ruano of the Durruti Column's War Committee, and Pablo went on to become a military advisor with the Column.

The International Group had been dealt a severe blow in Perdiguera, and nothing would ever be the same. The core of French founder members was no more. With losses and the departures of militia members who rejected militarization, the group was posted to Barcelona, no doubt with an eye to rest and overhaul. It was against this backdrop that Antoine took off on leave in late October or early November 1936.

A report dated October 24, 1936, emanating from the Italian intelligence services in Barcelona, tells us that the Italian ex-colonel also set

6   Ibid.
7   Ibid.

off for Barcelona, where he would meet with a representative of his former camp:

> I had a lengthy conversation with Pietro Vagliasindi on October 18.
>
> It turns out that he was made a commander (*comandante técnico*) in the Durruti Column. He has already taken part in fighting. He has seen action in Barbastro [August 1936], Siétamo [September 12, 1936], and on Monte Aragon.
>
> He is stationed on the Zaragoza front (but currently in Barcelona on leave and is to stay there for six or seven days).
>
> He heads an international column that currently has 180 men [which is yet another suggestion that the International Group was not decimated in Perdiguera], but according to Vagliasindi's categorical assurance, that number will grow to one thousand before November 15.
>
> Vagliasindi says that he had no option but to go over to the side of the revolutionaries; it was not what he wanted—he would rather have rebuilt his life in Italy. Vagliasindi blames the Italian authorities who have wanted nothing to do with him, despite numerous telegrams and letters.
>
> He says that he was faced with the dilemma: with us, or against us.
>
> One of Roselli's emissaries visited him at his home. He was initially curt with him but had to relent. Vagliasindi says that he came within a hair of being shot, because portraits of Mussolini, D'Annunzio, Starace, and other regime figures were found in his home.
>
> There is no doubt that Vagliasindi will do well on the front as he is a skilled and courageous commander. He is always being sent for and sought after in the most perilous situations. He says that he has some sympathy for the red fighters because they are brave and driven by a very lively fighting spirit. He declined to give an opinion as to the ultimate outcome of the civil war in Spain.
>
> He did tell me that the reds had significant war materials, arms and munitions. He states that the aid from the Russians and French is primarily moral, in that it is inadequate in terms of quantity. He tried to convince me that in the metalworking plants on the outskirts of Barcelona they are working night and day to churn out arms and munitions.

Getting back to "personal issues," he says with some bitterness that "they" have never been willing to take him into consideration. "I could not carry on forever living like a monk and letting myself be killed like a idiot. I could have been very useful to 'them' today, but it is too late now, for I cannot betray these 'people.'"[8]

{34}
PAGE 108

Lorenzo Giua was twenty-two years old. According to the biographical profile compiled by the prefecture in Turin in 1932, Lorenzo, while still at high school, had been

placed under arrest by the Special Court for the Defense of the State, for subversive propaganda and membership of the Giustizia e Libertà faction.[9]

Acquitted on April 29, 1932, on the grounds of insufficient evidence, he slipped out of Italy, crossing the border through the mountains on skis, mid-blizzard. Lorenzo took refuge in France at the beginning of 1934 and continued with his literary studies but became more and more involved in the antifascist struggle. His father, university professor Michele Giua, a well-known socialist activist in Turin, was arrested on May 15, 1935, and on February 28, 1936, was given a fifteen-year prison sentence for refusing to take an oath of loyalty to the fascist regime. On March 21 that year Lorenzo wrote to his mother from Geneva:

I see things as they are. I'm certain that they gave Papa the prison term they had had in mind for me ever since 1932. This hostage-taking policy, brilliantly introduced by Bolshevism and taken up by Hitlerism, is making further strides.[10]

8   ACS-CPC, 5281 86811.
9   ACS-CPC, 2413 13361.
10   Ibid.

On July 24, he set off from Geneva (where he was finishing his doctorate in philosophy) for Barcelona with anarchist Barbieri and other Italian refugees. Giua quickly made his way to the front and joined the Durruti Column, where he remained for seven months. He was wounded for the first time outside Huesca in September during the capture of Siétamo.

With Georges Sossenko's memoirs we find ourselves in Barcelona just as Antoine and Lorenzo ended up there. Having arrived on October 9, Sossenko and three other Frenchmen made for the Bakunin barracks where they joined hundreds of volunteers drawn from every nationality, including many Slavs and Jewish refugees in France:

> The Germans were the most numerous and it was immediately clear that they were well organized. [...] I later found out that they were not anarchists but communists, and that they went on to serve with the famous Thaelmann Battalion of the 12th International Brigade. [...]
>
> Our group joined other compatriots and soon we French numbered a hundred. Since we were free at the end of day, four of us who had quickly become new and inseparable friends, decided to head into Barcelona, this time decked out in uniforms and hats bearing the CNT-FAI insignia and with red-and-black bandanas around our necks. [...] We were all eager to get to the famous Barrio Chino which was said to be highly dangerous and disreputable [...] Juan had changed a lot since we arrived in Spain—he had grown more righteous and was always chastising us for being overly familiar with the Spanish: "They're not French and they don't like being messed with," he would tell us over and over.[11]
> I was already hugely disappointed on reaching the Barrio Chino because, in my naiveté, I thought that the revolution would have changed everything in a flash; now the militiamen were going with the prostitutes who were swarming in the area, as if it was the most natural thing in the world. The place was packed with people, and, in addition to the prostitutes, there were street-hawkers offering all kinds of junk, as if it was a holiday and not a country to which

11 Juan Mayol [Jean Maïllol], a Spanish refugee living in France, had set off from Paris by truck with them, serving as their interpreter and explaining lots of things to them. [Giménologues' note.]

we'd come to fight fascists and social injustice. Juan was much older than us, and though he disapproved of the situation, he went to great lengths to get it across to us that it wasn't that easy to do away with poverty at one fell swoop and that, gradually, through time, our anarcho-syndicalist ideals would triumph and then order would come to all of this [...] then these women could live with dignity in a just society [...] It wasn't that I wasn't tempted, but I didn't dare hook up with a prostitute, especially since the idea that a woman has to have sex with anyone just for money repelled me, and worse still, if she was forced to do so by some pimp. That was the first disappointment I felt in Spain, seeing that the vestiges of the ruling classes were so deeply ingrained in the order established by the capitalists.

Some days after that [mid-October 1936], our detachment, already one-hundred-men-strong, was ready to be moved up to the front. Our unit was known as the Sébastien Faure *centuria*, named after the French libertarian philosopher, and was made up mostly of anarchists, although there were some communists there as well. Although part of the Durruti Column, our *centuria* was seconded to the Ortiz Column [...]

Early on the morning of October 16, with our brand-new Spanish Tercio uniforms, about a hundred of us militia members were waiting on the platform at Barcelona railway station for the train that would take us to Aragon.[12]

In regard to Juan Mayol, we might add that his was Jean Maillol Ballester, mentioned in endnotes 16 and 32 above. His name, together with those of Georges Jorat (alias Sossenko) and Eugène Rappoport appears in a list of Ortiz Column International Group militia members leaving for the front on October 20, 1936.[13]

For further information, see *L'Adunata dei Refrattari*, April 9, 1938.

---

12   Sossenko, *Aventurero idealista*, 110–12.
13   IISH, FAI PE 15. For fuller details of Jean Maillol, see "Biographical Notices" in Les Giménologues, *¡A Zaragoza o al charco!*

{35}

PAGE 109

In the Barcelona-based Italian-language newspaper *Guerra di Classe* of July 1937 we find an article about the "Giuditta" whom Antoine mentions; here is an extract:

> The person speaking to us is an Italian anarchist. She was one of the first volunteers to follow Durruti into Aragon. For several months she fought against Franco's army in the trenches, rifle in hand. During a certain incident in the war, she was one of only three of her battalion to survive. We won't give her name. She is an anarchist woman! Her alias is: "*Yudith*."[14]

For more about Giuditta, see endnote 81 below.

Moreover, in *Mi Revista*, a Barcelona weekly movie magazine, we read that in January 1937 Francisco Ferrer was with the International Group stationed in Velilla de Ebro:

> [...] one of the *compañeros*, the group delegate, and grandson of Ferrer y Guardia told us:
> "In your report, emphasize the fact that our only aim is to participate in further swift attacks and that we are all ready to abide by the orders emanating from headquarters, which has at all times been deserving of the group's full confidence."[15]

{36}

PAGE 111

Antoine is referring here to the renowned action group, Los Solidarios. Let us read a few excerpts from the account in Garcia Oliver's memoirs

---

14   *Guerra di Classe*, no. 22, Year II, July 19, 1937.
15   *Mi Revista*, March 15, 1937.

of the creation of the group (we have added a few dates and clarifications inside square brackets):

> The CNT was coming out of the repression stronger than ever before. Sturdy branches from its trunk, like Archs [May 27 or June 25, 1921], the secretary of the Catalonian Regional Committee and Evelio Boal [June 18, 1921], secretary of the National Committee, and many others were murdered by *pistoleros* or by recourse to the *ley de fugas*. As far as the CNT was concerned, the loss of these valiant militants was like a pruning, after which fresh growth sprouted vigorously …
>
> The working class's enemies, the backward-looking right and the capitalists, the big landowners and the pro-monarch nobility, the higher and lower clergy, the Carlists and the *requetés*—everyone dependent for survival upon the robbery of the poor—were agitating too, but in the opposite direction.
>
> I received an anonymous letter that said: "We all know that ideas cannot be killed, but they can be bled. Which is what we are engaged in, bleeding them. And your turn is coming." […]
>
> "Ideas cannot be killed, but they can be bled": that spoke volumes for the direction in which the minds of those who had offered to assassinate us were moving. Salvador Seguí, accompanied by Paronas, had just been gunned down [March 9, 1923]. The city was convulsed because *El Noi del Sucre* was an institution. An unparalleled effervescence swept through CNT circles. There was talk of prestigious militants deserting […].
>
> Were Barcelona's anarcho-syndicalist militants about to buckle?
>
> […] In Manresa, the gunmen from the *"Libre"* [the bosses' tame union] tried to kill Pestaña, leaving him seriously wounded [on August 25, 1922]. […]
>
> Once again, taking to the streets was becoming inevitable. But nobody knew what to do. There was none of the decisiveness for which the local committee and regional committee had previously been known. […]
>
> Seguí and Paronas's murders […] jolted everyone. The union halls in Barcelona were packed again. Elderly anarchists, syndicalists old and young, people who we barely knew, turned out. They brought with them their handguns, freshly unearthed, and they

were up for a fight. No, they would not fall to their knees. They were up for the fight again. But how? [...].

[...] Word went out in a whisper. An important meeting of implicitly reliable militants was about to be held, convened by the regional and local committees in Barcelona. It would meet the very next day, before Seguí and Paronas's funerals. The meeting place was a shrub-covered island in the Besós.

There was no speechifying. There was agreement on the fact that we were not about to surrender, that we would try to answer back with a wide-ranging revolutionary uprising [...]. An action committee, referred to also as the Executive Committee, was elected and it commanded the full authority and resources of the Organization. Without discussion, it was proposed and approved that compañeros Ángel Pestaña, Juan Peiró, Camilo Piñón, and Narciso Marcó be appointed to it.

[...]

When Ascaso and I returned to Barcelona, I found a message from Pestaña asking me to drop by and see him and trade impressions. [...] He said to me:

—[...] You know the resolutions passed in Besós. [...] we need men of ability, and we need money. We are short of both of those. [...]

—[...] You must form a group to carry out two executions right away: that of the Pretender Don Jaime, commander of the *requetés*, and that of General Martínez Anido. Don Jaime resides in Paris, and Martínez Anido is currently in San Sebastián. The execution of those two individuals might stop our enemies in their tracks.

[...]

—But there is another aspect to the mission, Juan ... We haven't a peseta left. [...]

—We are giving you carte blanche. Put the group together and get money wherever you can. No matter what happens, we will cover your back within the Organization and before the world [...] I put the group together and it became known as *Los Solidarios*[16] [...]. There were a lot of us, nearly too many. [...]

16   García Oliver is playing fast and loose with the truth a little here for, according to Abel Paz in *Durruti en la revolución española* (90), the group had already been set up by October 1922.

The ones that set off for Paris—Durruti and the two others who are still alive—returned to base when carrying out their mission proved impossible. The same was not true of those who headed for San Sebastián—Rafael Torres Escartín, Francisco Ascaso, and Aurelio Fernández. They [...] decided to make a stop-over in Zaragoza [...]. Somebody gave them Cardinal Soldevila's itinerary and they executed him [June 4, 1923]. At the time, the cardinal was the figurehead of the Spanish reaction.

For their part, the guys from León—"Toto" and "Torinto"— [...] executed Regueral, the former governor of Bilbao who had been involved in the bloody crackdown on strikers in the mines and the big metalworking plants.

I was called before the Executive Committee to give an accounting. This time, Pestaña had Peiró with him. [...]

Pestaña opened the conversation:

—"Peiró's presence here relates to the background of the topic we need to address. You know that nothing that we, you and I, agreed upon, hassn't been realized. [...] In contrast, the execution of Regueral in León and of Cardinal Soldevila in Zaragoza wasn't part of what we agreed. And we know for a fact that they were the handiwork of the Los Solidarios group that you put together at our request." [...]

—"You are both right and wrong. True, you pointed me in the direction of the two individuals picked by the Committee. By the time the three group members appointed to the task arrived in Paris, Don Jaime had fled, which would indicate that someone had talked. Likewise, Martínez Anido left San Sebastián just as the three members of the group were arriving. [...] It's true that the execution of Regueral and of the cardinal weren't part of any decision by the Committee. But they weren't the outcome of any decision taken by the Los Solidarios group either. [...] You on the Committee take issue with them. And I, the person charged with liaising between the Committee and that Group, am not happy with it either."

Then Peiró spoke up:

—"So, according to you, the group that you put together is made up of mavericks. They do as they please or do whatever is decided in León and in Zaragoza. And those of us on the Committee are responsible."

—[…] "You are wondering what the repercussions of the execution of Cardinal Soldevila are going to be for you and for the Organization. The blow was delivered so high that, had it been just one more notch higher, and the entire heavenly court would have felt it. They carried it out with the authority of the Committee and of the group. And by going off half-cocked, they did it; they put an end to the white terrorism that was leaving us compañero-less." […]

—"Since you can give no guarantees of your authority over the group, you should disband it. For its part, the Committee too had decided that it should be disbanded." […]

The assassination of Cardinal Soldevila in Zaragoza caused a sensation. The murders of CNT militants stopped and it was as if the gunmen from the "*Libre*" had faded away.[17]

We might add that those politically responsible for that assassination—though they did not actually carry it out themselves—were Francisco Ascaso and Rafael Torres Escartín, and that two other "Los Solidarios" members were convicted in relation to it: Juliana López Máinar and Esteban Eleuterio Salamero Bernard.

For more information, see Miguel Iñíguez (ed.), *Enciclopedia histórica del anarquismo español* (Vitoria: Asociación Isaac Puente, 2008).

{37}
PAGE 113

Even as Antoine was arguing in Barcelona with María Ascaso over militarization, the refractory militia members back in Aragon kept up their protests. The conflict that erupted between one faction of the libertarians and a Popular Front government increasingly under the sway of the PCE and Stalin, would also cleave the anarchist movement. After

17   Juan García Oliver, *El eco de los pasos* (Barcelona: Ruedo Ibérico, 1978), 627–32.

seeing the Durruti Column's declaration of November 1, we could think that Durruti was out of step with García Oliver, Federica Montseny, Abad de Santillán, and, obviously, with María Ascaso. Between October and December 1936, a growing number of militia members were to publish notices of protest. The internationals were all the more responsive for being volunteers, and, being such, they thought that they were free to question the terms of their commitment and to walk away if they chose. The Italians from the Ascaso Column were the first to speak out. On October 10 (on the 30th, according to Prudhommeaux), 1936, on Monte Pelato on the Huesca front,[18] they drafted the following declaration:

> The members of the Ascaso Column's Italian Section are volunteers who come from various countries to make their contribution to the cause of Spanish freedom and so for universal freedom. Having learned of the decree promulgated by the Generalitat Council regarding the overhaul of the makeup of the militias; wish to reaffirm their commitment to the cause which brought them here, and declare the following:
>
> 1. The above-mentioned decree can be binding only for those who are subject to the obligations of a mobilization emanating from the authorities which have made the promulgation [...].
>
> 2. This confirms us in our conviction that that decree cannot apply to us. However, we need to state with absolute clarity, that, in the event that the authorities should deem us liable to implementation of it, we could only consider ourselves released from any moral obligations and reclaim our full freedom of action—the foundation pact of the Section itself being rendered null and void.
>
> On behalf of the Committee:
> Vindice, Mioli, Buleghin, Petacchi, Puntoni.[19]

18   There is no "Monte Pelato" there; in reality, this was just the name the Italian members of the columns had given to one of the hills surrounding Huesca.

19   Fedeli, *Un trentennio di attività anarchica*, 186–87; see also André Prudhommeaux and Dori Prudhommeaux, *La Catalogne libre (1936–1937)* (Paris: Le Combat syndicaliste, 1970), 25.

That was followed by others in which they issued a reminder that "the determination to fight fascism cannot be dissociated from the determination to make revolution" and renewed their "staunch determination to remain miliciens."

Plainly, the Italians were not the only objectors, as the following document testifies:

> The compañeros in charge of the centurias from the Aguiluchos, Ascaso, and Ortiz columns appear in the company of compañero Jover. They have come to speak out against the militarization which the call-up issued is supposed to put into effect. They are resolved not to accept the 10 peseta pay rate and will go naked and unfed, but the fact is they flatly refuse to leave this place, they have weapons and will defend themselves against all comers [...]
>
> The delegate from Los Aguiluchos states that, despite the distances separating them from the other centurias, they have all realized what their needs are and this is why several *responsables* have come to detail them to the organization.
>
> The French delegate voices similar objections to the mobilization order, underlining the dangers that might arise should command over the militias be entrusted to certain individuals, and reminding them of what happened in Russia. He says that if the militia members are militarized, [...] things will be changed beyond all recognition: instead of being the men and women of freedom they might very easily turn into tyrants over their people.
>
> Another delegate says that the problem comes from the organization, that if it had first consulted the front-line comrades, this militarization order would have been dead in the water [...].
>
> The Aguiluchos delegate goes on to say [...] they will not allow anyone, for any reason to disarm them. [...]
>
> Jover demands two hundred men to make up for the losses and for leave to be granted.[20]

The aforementioned protests produced no tangible results, as confirmed shortly thereafter by the Swiss volunteer Albert Minnig, enrolled in the Los Aguiluchos Column since September 6, 1936. On his return

---

20   "Actas de la Reunión de Comités celebrada el día 31 de Octubre de 1936." IISH, CNT 84 D1, reel 265. Brought to the authors' attention by Pere López.

to the Huesca front in late November, he found that his company had been disbanded for lack of machine guns. In fact, he realized that the columns that had refused militarization were particularly under-equipped:

> The republican political parties' newspapers talk about nothing but Russia and the democracies' conditions for their supplying us with arms, munitions, and the provisions needed to put down the fascist rebellion. Loudly, they proclaim that militarization can be embraced on a temporary basis and indeed be adapted to suit our ideas and principles. In return for that concession, they contend, we will receive aircraft, tanks, artillery, and ultra-modern machine guns firing 2,000 rounds a minute and, above all, munitions and food galore. All the delegates are urged to embrace militarization and Stalin has a whole caste of spies laboring shamelessly and relentlessly to get it into the heads of the militia members that we are not going to win this war if we stay like some flock without a shepherd.
>
> [...] rather than be forced into militarization, we would rather apply to join the Italian battalion [of the Ascaso Column], which is determined to retain its autonomy at any price.[21]

{38}
PAGE 115

Camillo Berneri, born in Lodi in 1897 and forced into exile by Mussolini's rule, was "Europe's most expelled anarchist": for years he was dogged and imprisoned by a range of police forces, was banned from residing in Switzerland and, furthermore, the OVRA (Organizzazione di Vigilanza e Repressione dell'Antifascismo) followed his every move. Moreover, the political police systematically tracked all the Italian refugees, especially the anarchist ones, no matter their level of commitment; during the 1930s, the Second Republic in Spain handed a number of them over to Mussolini.

21   Gmür and Minnig, *Pour le bien de la révolution*, 44–45.

Berneri moved to Barcelona in late July 1936 as the USI's pleni-potentiary in dealings with the CNT-FAI, and he oversaw the inser-tion into the confederal columns of many Italian volunteers, whose numbers were later estimated to be about a thousand. Elected by the militia members as their political commissar, he made many trips to the front. Contrary to his wishes, the alliance on the ground with Giustizia e Libertà broke down. Toward the end of November, Carlo Rosselli set up the Giacomo Matteotti centuria, and Antonio Cieri took charge of the Italian Section, who were now mostly anarchists.[22] Cieri was less than twenty years old when the fascist menace took to the streets in Italy. He played his part in the fighting in Ancona and then on the barricades in Parma, heading the *Arditi del Popolo*, which stood fast against fascist attacks. In 1924 he had been forced out and into exile in France. Hounded by the police, and by then a widower with two children to look after, he left for Spain the moment the rev-olution broke out.

In Barcelona, Berneri had no interest in political or military office; and he withdrew from cooperation with the Generalitat's Council of Economy. Berneri was one of the very few anarchist contemporaries to have posed and discussed the theoretical and doctrinal aspects of the phenomenon of power during a revolutionary process, and he would become the leading intellectual among the Italian volunteers. Being of the view that "the anarchist movement should not be looked upon as a propaganda school but rather as a life-centered research and devel-opment bureau," he went on to assume responsibility for a range of propaganda and intelligence functions; over the airwaves of Radio CNT he made broadcasts to Italy and addressed the soldiers Rome was sending to the battlefronts in Spain; he worked on a report on "Mus-solini, out to conquer the Balearics" using archives uncovered in Italy's consulate-general in July 1936; he went on to draft most of the articles for an Italian-language news sheet that was replaced in October 1936 by the newspaper *Guerra di Classe*, which borrowed its title from the USI mouthpiece launched in Bologna back in 1915. That newspaper would have followed in the footsteps of the fugitives because, before Barcelona, it had reappeared in exile in Paris in 1927, then in Brussels in 1929–1933. Staking his claim to the status of "independent critic"

22   See Balestri, *La Section italienne de la colonne Ascaso*, chapter 6, "Dissen-sion—Dissolution," 56–62.

within the libertarian milieu, Berneri repeatedly urged anarchists to work out a strategy that considered an international context. In the article "What Is to Be Done?" on October 24, he offered a pragmatic breakdown of things:

> We need to adopt a vigorous foreign policy centered on Portugal [...] The only course of action therefore is to make a clean break with Portugal by means of the following steps: immediately expelling all Portuguese diplomatic representatives, [...] confiscating all of the assets of Portuguese capitalists who reside in Spain.[23]

And he pushed for the same approach to be adopted vis-a-vis Germany and Italy. He strongly insisted that they needed to ally themselves with Moroccan anticolonialists in concert with the efforts of the IWA's Pierre Besnard; but they ran up against dogged obstruction from Largo Caballero.

Long a supporter of political solutions and the development of "minimum programs," Berneri entirely agreed with the "realistic" and "unitary" options that his Spanish comrades adopt after July 18. In "Warning! A Dangerous Turn," he wrote:

> [...] we must live up to the historic role we have decided to take on.[...] Reconciling the "necessities" of the war, the "will" of the social revolution, and the "aspirations" of anarchism: that is the problem.[24]

On the basis of such views, which he himself characterized as "centrist," Berneri strove to bring a level-headed approach to the militarization issue. However, he was soon portraying the dissolution of the CAMC as a mistake, calling for it to be brought back and voicing opposition to the entry of the anarchists into the central government on November 4, 1936. The latter was a partnership that seemed to hold out little prospect of adequate assurances regarding the prosecution of the revolutionary struggle. In the same article, he wrote:

> Convinced that the Spanish revolution is hurtling toward a

23 *Guerra di Classe*, no. 3, 1.
24 *Guerra di Classe*, no. 4 (November 5, 1936).

dangerous bend in the road, I take up my pen the way I would a revolver or a rifle. With the same determination but also with the same ferocity.[25]

He denounced Madrid's capitulationist outlook and called for the mounting of a military offensive in accordance with some wide-ranging, solid plan:

> The clock is now against us.[...]
>
> Since it is clear that the Madrid government is pursuing a "war policy" capable of guaranteeing its political hegemony and serving as a bulwark against the spread of social revolution, and as it is obvious also that the Communist Party (in the line laid down by Moscow) is tending to become the Foreign Legion of democracy and Spanish liberalism [...], the anarchist press [...] must either be swamped by the unwelcome "Sacred Union" mentality that has whittled political criticism down to an imperceptible minimum. By singing the praises of the USSR's Bolshevik government, *Solidaridad Obrera* has, by the way, attained the high point of political ingenuity. [...]
>
> For some time now—he stated—the CNT and the FAI have adopted an attitude of surrender vis-a-vis the normalization of the revolution.[26]

In follow-up articles up until April 1937, the Italian anarchist would clarify his criticism, while advocating to deepen the revolution as a means to win the war. The fact that he remained in direct, ongoing contact with the militia members on the Aragon front, relaying their views and their grievances, was certainly a crucial factor in this. In a letter addressed to them, Berneri denounces the counterrevolutionary maneuvers of the Spanish and Soviet communists:

> That leaves the matter of the expansion of the Section. The Italian Column in Albacete [home of the International Brigades] numbers a thousand men and there is a two-thousand-strong column of Germans, also organized by the communists. We

25   Ibid.
26   *Guerra di Classe*, no. 4.

know from a reliable source that since the start eight thousand Germans have entered Spain under "Russian officers." Clearly, Madrid is raising its own Tercio; a well-armed and well-officered "Foreign Legion" will be able to ensure order. The boosting of police numbers [Assault Guards and Civil Guards] and the massive influx of Moscow's Moroccans should give us food for thought.[27]

Then his tone grew increasingly alarmist, as in this article entitled "The War and The Revolution":

The French proletariat and the British proletariat are not going to do a thing on behalf of the Spanish proletariat. There is no point in deluding ourselves. [...]

Even now, Spain is caught between two fires: Burgos and Moscow.

[...] There is a whiff of Noske floating in the air. [...] Madrid's policy stands on the brink of success. Hasn't it refused revolutionary Catalonia arms and money in order to court the USSR [...]?

The dilemma—Madrid or Franco?—has Spanish anarchism paralyzed. [...]

But we can yet perform miracles. Trapped between the Prussians and Versailles, the Paris Commune lit a fire that still sheds light upon the world.

Between Burgos and Madrid, there is Barcelona.[28]

Berneri wore himself out penning articles and pamphlets and letters; he was still hopeful:

for among the Spanish anarchists there is no shortage of men of clear vision who understand the need to get back on the straight and narrow as soon as possible.[29]

But at the beginning of February, the CNT suspended funding to

27   Letter undoubtedly dating from October 1936, but first published in *Volontà* of July 19, 1951.

28   *Guerra di Classe*, no. 6 (December 16, 1936).

29   Camillo Berneri, *Guerre de classes en Espagne, 1936–1937 et textes libertaires* (Paris: Spartacus, 1977), 51.

his newspaper, and this was a severe blow to him. As well, the tension with the communists continued to grow: "For some time now, there have been frequent victims in our camp, because of the Stalinists here," he said out in a letter to his partner in January 1937.

This was the backdrop against which he addressed his "Open letter to Compañera Federica Montseny":

Dear compañera,

[…] I cannot forgive you for having written that 'in Russia, it wasn't Lenin who was the real builder of Russia but Stalin, that practical thinker, etc., etc.' And I applauded Voline's reply in *Terre Libre* to your utterly inaccurate claims about the Russian anarchist movement.

[…] In your speech on January 3, you stated:

"The anarchists joined the government in order to prevent the Revolution from deviating and to pursue it beyond the war, as well as to oppose any attempted dictatorship, from whatever source."

Well, *compañera*, in April, after three months of collaboration, we are faced with a situation wherein grave incidents are occurring, even as other, even worse ones are looming up ahead.[30]

He goes on to say:

The time has come to see if the anarchists are in the government just to act as the vestal virgins of a fire that is about to burn out, or whether they are now there just to provide politicians flirting with the enemy with Phrygian caps […].

The dilemma—war versus revolution—is now meaningless. The only dilemma is this: either victory over Franco by means of revolutionary war, or defeat.

The problem for you and for the other comrades is choosing between Thiers's Versailles and the Paris of the Commune, before Thiers and Bismarck can reach their *union sacrée*.

For more detail, see Giovanni C. Cattini, "Anarquistes Italians a l'Espanya republicana. La visió de Giuseppe Ruozi," in *Afers*, no. 37

30 *Guerra di Classe*, No. 12, (April 14, 1937).

(Barcelona: Editorial Afers, 2000), 713–29; Carlos M. Rama, "Camillo Berneri y la revolución española," in Camillo Berneri, *Guerra de clases en España, 1936–1937* (Barcelona: Tusquets, 1977); Gaetano Manfedonia, "Notes sur la participation des anarchistes italiens à la révolution espagnole"; and Miguel Amorós, *Durruti en el laberinto.*

{39}
PAGE 116

From the end of July 1936 onward, communist activists from a range of countries had been spontaneously setting off for Spain without party support. The decision to recruit and marshal and expedite such volunteers was formally agreed upon at a meeting of the Comintern Executive Committee on September 18, 1936. The military and political officerships in the International Brigades—with the exception of the Italian Garibaldi Brigade headed by Randolfo Pacciardi, leader of the Italian Republican Party—were to be vested, the overwhelming majority of them, in Communist Party members. Stalin appointed one of the secretaries of the Communist International, the Frenchman André Marty, to organize the brigades in Albacete. So Comintern cadres and nearly two thousand military advisors trooped through Spain where sundry other "advisors," journalists, and "diplomats" were already at work on the ground.

In a special confidential report dated December 25, 1936, addressed to the CNT and Catalonian Regional and titled "Moral Report," IWA secretary Pierre Besnard brought the following to their attention:

1. The massive influx of foreign and especially French communists across the land borders;
2. Harassment, sanctioning, threats, and disappearances of syndicalist and anarchist personnel posted—unbeknown to them—to international columns controlled by the marxists;
3. Dire material organizational conditions at the [anarchist-occupied] Espartaco barracks;
4. Arrests and detentions of foreign comrades;

5. The existence in Barcelona of a clandestine communist prison.[31]

Later he cited the following details:

(1) [...] Such personnel actually include civil war experts, communist movement leaders from around the world, military experts who make up the cadres of an extremely dangerous and well-armed movement, which may make up a veritable Foreign Legion in the service of the Spanish Marxists and those who lead them. [...]
(4) [...] numerous arrests made, generally of foreign comrades, taking place on the most varied of pretexts and even because of unproven denunciations [...].
Many comrades are presently held in such conditions and have been for quite some time, not knowing precisely what it is that they are accused of. [...]
The best way to resolve this, it seems to us, is to set up a commission that [...] would , perhaps, drop in on holding centers and prisons once a week.
(5) [...] We need not underline for you the danger posed by this. Your militants, those from the IWA's trade union centrals [...] are liable to be abducted and disappeared without us being able to do a thing about it. [...]
From reports supplied to us, this prison may be located in the Sarrià district.
[...] we believe your investigative resources are such that you could uncover it and put it swiftly out of business.[32]

Besnard later makes some observations (late 1937):

Though that Report was not followed up, one immediate consequence of it was that it allowed Galvé and me to visit two of the Barcelona prisons on the same evening: Montjuich and the Modelo Prison.
[...] In the Modelo prison we discovered thirty-five militia members from the international columns: twenty-seven Belgians

31   Pierre Besnard, "Rapport moral," IISH, CNT, package 61 D5, 27.
32   Ibid., 27–29.

and eight French, imprisoned at the behest or on the orders of the Communist Party for having applied for transfer to those confederal columns not yet disbanded.

I drafted a document for the Catalonian Regional beseeching it to intervene [...].

I never got a response to that plea [...].

During my stay, I intervened on several occasions to point out that considerable numbers of communist volunteers were passing [...] whereas the anarchist and anarcho-syndicalist comrades found all manner of obstacles placed in their path, because of the contradictory orders issued by the officials of the CNT [...].

To support this, I reproduce the report from one of our people to show how Stalin's men in Spain conduct themselves.[33]

There followed a report "signed: Léger" (we have mentioned this cook, a member of the Fédération communiste libertaire, who set off on November 28, 1936, along with sixteen others under the auspices of the (CGTU) Cooks' Union, to cater for the International Brigaders on the Madrid front):

In Paris at the Avenue des Mathurins, International Column Recruitment Centre.

Recruitment also from CGT-affiliated unions in which the communists are in the majority.

Recruitment is genuinely effective, for the jobless are promised that their families will receive an allowance higher than unemployment benefit; and that they will be paid 10 pesetas or more in the front lines ...

I have also noticed at the departure from Paris that they were mostly guys who were coming solely for a "beefsteak," those and adventurers, but scarcely any activists.

There were about eight hundred men when we set off from the Austerlitz Station. [...] In Figueras came the first speech.

To summarize: the anarchists and the POUM were not in favor of the international Column; the communist orator said that the anarchists recently barred convoys of communists from crossing the border.

33   Ibid., 29–30.

[...] On the train between Valencia and Albacete, a syndicalist comrade wearing a red-and-black bandana around his neck was ordered by a communist official to take it off.

In Albacete, same speech as in Figueras, that the Spanish organizations are clueless when it comes to organizing the struggle in the front lines, that the soldiers from the International column will be the ones that will defeat fascism.

[...] Every time any objection is made, whether about the food or sleeping arrangements, the political officials say that these are anarchists or Trotskyists trying to infiltrate the international column.[34]

We shall complement this report with more detailed testimony about the same subject, as forwarded to the UA upon his return from Spain:

Comrades [...]

I have therefore summarized things between my departure and when I had to leave unless I wanted to go to prison or perhaps worse. [...]

First off, let me point out that they were only accepting communists or sympathizers, but definitely no anarchists.

[...] out of eight hundred guys, around 750 were tramps, drunks and adventurers turned into fanatics by the Communist Party.

[...] In Albacete, there are about ten thousand men in the International Brigades led entirely by the "bolshies."

Inside the barracks there is a prison, cells for those who do not comply with the discipline. [...]

Positions of command are plainly awarded only to those who have proved their commitment to the Communist Party. I should point out that they appoint corporals galore. Out of every six men, one is a corporal. The guy with the stripes immediately starts taking his role seriously. The communists have no better supporters than these guys whose egos have been flattered.

As I was appointed delegate-spokesman for the kitchens and canteens, they had assigned me two tasks:

34   Ibid., 30.

—Organizing the kitchens and canteens, and listening in on conversations to find out if there were anarchists or Trotskyists around.

Every evening, I had the vile task of reporting back to the commandant, as they had me tapped as 100% "bolshie." [...]

Authentic communists, and they do exist, the ones that realize that they have been misled, are thrown into jail and written off as defeatists and counterrevolutionaries.

Everything is ultra-military.

All the food, and everything coming from Russia, is meant only for the communists.

Everything is going awry because the staff officers are incompetent and untrained. They live high on the hog.

[...] Those returning from the front lines have had their fill, and they let us know that down there, the guys in charge, the officers, have five blankets whereas they themselves frequently have none.

There are some groups paid only 3 pesetas a day rather than 10.

Military hierarchy, different food, massive differences in amount of rations between the men and their officers.

It should be pointed out that the Communist Party demands and confiscates the papers of the boys who sign up to the International Brigades.

[...] There are lots of genuine communists who have requested a transfer to the CNT or the FAI. [...]

In Albacete the communists paid a visit to the local CNT committee to tell them: "Be on your guard against those who leave us to join you; these are fascist personnel." [...]

In my own case, they wanted to throw me in jail as I had been recognized by some "bolshies" from Paris. [...]

[...] I just had time to save myself. [...]

I had to hide out with the Albacete local CNT committee and at 3 o'clock in the morning take the train under escort from four armed friends, because the "bolshies" were turning the town upside down, looking for me.[35]

35   Michel Léger, *De brigades en brigades* (Breuillet: self-published, 2005), 124–27.

Michel Léger goes on to deal with the cases of brigaders mistreated or disappeared, as well as the poor quality of the weaponry, the difficult combat conditions experienced by the brigaders, et cetera. He then brings up the case of another five anarchist cooks who managed to escape from Albacete right after Robert Léger.[36] They wrote up mutually corroborative reports about their time with the International Brigades; their names were Marcel Gautier, Bigot, Wipff, Fassier, and Henri Dubois. Their reports can be found in the Amsterdam archives,[37] along with that by the Polish Moneck, a refugee in France, "member, under the name Henri Martin, of the Communist Party, Cell 305, 3rd Precinct, Paris." Moneck applied to go to Spain through the good offices of "comrade Castro, a member of the same cell." After this had been approved by "comrade Friedman" and "Jacques, of the Jewish (*israélite*) section," Moneck set off for Spain on November 14, 1936, together with a forty other Polish people; he was made politically responsible for them. Sometime in December 1936, while he was serving in Albacete and Almansa in a clerical capacity, Marty, Fein, and Bastien accused him of spying (they knew that he had previously been sympathetic to the anarchists in Belgium and France). His communist pal Fernand Malvergue, who spoke up on his behalf, was also placed under arrest.[38]

These accounts should be read in conjunction with the testimony of Sygmunt Stein and Laurie Lee.[39]

And here is further firsthand testimony, from the Thalmanns:

At this point who should turn up in Pina but our friend Heiri Eichmann, who had asked us back in Zurich to smooth the way to Spain for him, he too being keen to do his bit in the struggle. Since it was not possible for him to set off at the same time as ourselves, we had left him the address of the border checkpoint in Perpignan. We had already been fretting about his absence, but in the end we had concluded that he must have had a change of mind. He showed up in the company of a German émigré and told us what had happened to them.

36   Ibid., 145.
37   IISH, FAI, Pe 17-5.
38   See IISH, CNT, 81B.
39   Sygmunt Stein, *Ma guerre d'Espagne. Brigades Internationales: la fin d'un mythe* (Paris: Seuil, 2012). Laurie Lee, *Instants de guerre (1937–1938)* (Paris: Phébus, 2009).

All unsuspecting, they had fallen into the clutches of the communists who were also monitoring the border crossing and had promptly been dispatched to the Albacete front where the Frenchman André Marty was political commissar to the Brigades. Since they had been found somewhat suspect during the customary debriefing, they were simply confined to barracks instead of being sent directly to the front. Luck for them, Marty, unsparing with those who did not share his own political opinions, had everyone who he felt was suspect locked up. That barracks-turned-prison already held upward of one hundred anarchists, socialists, opposition communists, and volunteers with no party affiliations. The atmosphere in Albacete was explosive, and tit-for-tat attacks and killings between anarchists and communists were proliferating. The eruption came spontaneously. After a brief exchange of gunfire with the communist guards at the prison, the FAI stormed it and rescued all the inmates. Eichmann and Gernsheimer were thereby able to return to Barcelona, where they presented themselves to the DAS and traveled out to join us in Pina.[40]

On November 4, 1936, one might have read in the CNT's daily newspaper, *Solidaridad Obrera*:

At the present moment, the government as the instrument regulating the organs of the State, has ceased being a force for oppression against the working class, just as the State no longer represents the agency that divides society up into classes. Both will have all the more reason to stop oppressing the people now that CNT personnel are coming on board.

Besnard's report shows that the CNT actually was not capable of preventing the spread of the Stalinist terror.

By requiring Spanish and foreign militia members to amalgamate with the new republican army, the officers of which [were] largely communists schooled in hatred of libertarians, and by entering the Madrid government as ministers, the anarchist leadership conjured up unease and anger in the minds of many militants.

40   Thalmann and Thalmann, *Combats pour la liberté*, 140–41.

In Aragon, where Antoine was about to return, the front was stagnating in a war of positions, and the militia members were arguing bitterly over recent developments. In certain columns, the rejection of militarization was about to become the focus of a huge battle against the CNT's new departure. Certain militants were of the mind that the lack of coordination on the front certainly did need rectifying, although they would not be budged from the libertarian movement's traditional stance, starting with the consultation of the rank and file.

{40}
PAGE 117

Antoine was back in Farlete by around October 24, assuming that he stayed in Barcelona as many days as Vagliasindi. Since he doesn't mention Durruti's death in Madrid on November 20, or the consequences this might have had for the column and the International Group (which was in the process of being overhauled), there is reason to think that Antoine actually left for the Sierra de Alcubierre in late October and stayed there for several weeks at least. Whereas the history of the foreign volunteers during Berthomieu's time is beginning to be somewhat better known, thanks to the efforts of Abel Paz, David Berry, and Phil Casoar, "phase two" of the group, post-Perdiguera, remains a little confused. Let us try to pick out a few milestones from the early winter of 1936, which was very eventful.

—The International Group left Pina and was thereafter stationed, turn and turn about, in Farlete, Gelsa, or Velilla de Ebro; a number of factors transformed its profile. Lucio Ruano, who we mentioned when dealing with the battle of Perdiguera,[41] replaced Durruti as head of the part of the Column that remained in Aragon when the rest set off for Madrid; he had help from a whittled-down War Committee. Every other member of the old committee left for Madrid.

—In mid-November, Pablo Vagliasindi and a few of the internationals joined the 1,500 men from the Durruti Column who were

41   See endnote 31 above.

thrown into the defense of the capital. The archives of the Italian political police bear this out: "At present [letter dated November 24, 1936], he has transferred to the central sector of Madrid."[42]

Prior to leaving he would have notified the Italian consul in Spain that it pained him to fight for an ideal that was not his own, but that he held the Italian authorities to blame for that: "I offered myself to you like a whore, but you turned me down. I would have come back to Italy as a simple soldier, but you turned me down. I offered to play the spy for my country, but you turned me down. Now, here I am back as Colonel Vagliasindi fighting at the head of my soldiers."[43]

A core of foreign "veterans" therefore reorganized in Madrid around Pablo: the French were less numerous and a number of them who had stayed on in Aragon shuttled between the International Group and the Sébastien Faure *centuria*, which had also suffered some losses.

In the meantime, in Aragon, the militia members and the front were lapsing back into idleness. Fighting was sporadic, half-hearted, and inconsequential. On November 19, the Durruti and Ortiz columns captured Quinto de Ebro but failed to hold on to it. In the March 15, 1937, edition of *Mi Revista*, a Barcelona movie magazine under anarchist control, we can read an account of the *internacionales'* feats in Quinto de Ebro, in the course of which the Frenchman Georges Monnard, the delegate from the Sébastien Faure *centuria*, lost his life.

A list of International Group fighters suggests that during the attacks on November 19 and 21, eight men were killed or reported missing and that eighteen were wounded, including Saïl Mohamed[44] and Madeleine Gierth.[45] The Durruti Column's last action of any note was the attack on Nuez de Ebro and Villafranca in late November and early December, and there again poor coordination—"*el asincronismo tradicional*"—allowed the enemy to marshal his forces and

---

42   ACS-CPC, 5281 86811.

43   Ibid.

44   Mohamed Saïl returned to France in December 1936. He took part in talks organized by the Union Anarchiste on the accomplishments of the revolution in Spain. Under the Occupation, he was arrested and interned in the camp in Riom, from which he escaped. Up until the Liberation, his specialty was in counterfeiting papers. He resumed his anticolonialist campaigning in *Le Libertaire* from 1946 right up until his death in Bobigny (Seine) in April 1953.

45   IISH, FAI, package 15.

fight off the attackers. After that, the columns gave up on any offensive action and got themselves organized for the winter by fortifying their positions.[46]

Antoine mentions the presence of his friend Otto for the second time here. The arrival of upward of fifty Germans from the Erich Mühsam *centuria* would bolster the group after November 18. In those "Russophile" times, that machine-gunner section published a timely address to the Russian people regarding Zensl Mühsam, the widow of the anarchist Erich Mühsam, murdered by the Nazis in Germany two years earlier, in the Iron Column newspaper *Línea de Fuego* of November 19. Having fled to the USSR, she became a victim of the purges there in 1936 and was sent to the gulag:

> What has become of Zenzel [*sic*] Mühsam, the partner of the man whose name features on our flag? That question is easily answered. Comrade Zenzel is not the only one to have found herself in the clutches of the police in soviet Russia. Countless comrades endure incarceration in the homeland of the proletariat. In the name of the cause of the freedom of the Spanish people, which at present is closely associated with comrade Erich's name, our group calls upon the Russian toilers to see to it that one of the next vessels bound for Spain brings Zenzel Mühsam back to us.[47]

These German anarcho-syndicalists from the DAS would incorporate into their membership lists the militiamen and what few Germanophone militiawomen or nurses there were, as well as volunteers drawn from northern and eastern Europe, many of whom were Swiss. On January 2, 1937, Michaelis sent this letter to a DAS comrade in Barcelona:

> When our Swiss comrades joined the militias, they abandoned their Mercedes-Benz in Barcelona in accordance with an agreement that the DAS group had not strictly honored. Comrades Hermann Höner and Helmut (Hache) then promised the Swiss

46 See Anonyme, *La 26 División*, 21–23.
47 Miguel Amorós, *Durruti dans le labyrinthe* (Paris: Encyclopédie des nuisances, 2007), 70–71.

Edwin Gmür that the DAS would tell the owner of the car [...] information to the effect that it had been seized by some administration or was wrecked in an accident.

[...] Meanwhile, the bourgeois press in Switzerland has spared nothing in order to portray comrades Gmür, Aeppli, and all the other "*Spanienfahrer*" as one big gang of thieves.[48]

The comrades in question were greengrocers Edi Gmür and Emil Kummer, journalist and teacher Jacob Aeppli, and Richard Müggli, a tinsmith. In Zurich, all four had rented a car after leaving a security deposit and had made it to Aragon. Edi Gmür, a thirty-year-old socialist, kept a personal journal, from which the following extracts come:

Barcelona, December 26.

The *miliciano* brought us straight to the Regional Committee. We arrived in an office where we introduced ourselves as volunteers and were assigned to the DAS, which also took control of the car. [...]

December 28, morning.

[...] When we got to the station, a long train was waiting for us. [...] There was an eighteen-strong group of us men under the leadership of Schlegel, a big beanpole of an Austrian who has already seen action with the Grupo Internacional and is just out of hospital where they treated him for a bullet wound in the belly. Among us there are Germans, Swiss, Swedes, Norwegians, and one Pole.[49]

Schlegel had equipped himself with a good supply of wine and nearly all of us had our fill. He was forever encouraging us to sing, which we did, to the great delight of the other passengers. We had to spend all our cash, because they have no use for it at the front.[50]

Gelsa, December 29.

[...] We have at last arrived at our destination. The village is known as Gelsa and lies on the front. When we debussed, a

48   IISH, FAI, 1.

49   Gmür and Minnig, *Pour le bien de la révolution*, 67, 69.

50   Heiner Spiess (Hg.), " ...dass Friede und Glück Europas vom Sieg der spanischen Republik abhängt," in *Schweizer im Spanischen Bürgerkrieg* (Zurich: Limmat Verlag Genossenschaft, 1986), 66.

Left: Edi Gmür and Emil "Migger" Kummer. Right: The International
Group in Velilla de Ebro in December, 1936

machine gun was rattling somewhere out in the darkness. The
Grupo Internacional's delegate arrived to greet us. We were
shown to our quarters. [...]

January 12 [Pina].

We have been assigned to a house that's home to all the militia
members from No 1 and No 2 sections. We cleaned it from top to
bottom and each of the huge rooms accommodates an eleven-man
platoon. At mealtimes, eight-man groups go to the private homes
assigned to them, where the woman of the house does the cooking. I have already made myself a number of Spanish friends.
These are sound guys, all anarchists. [...]

January 16.

[...] In the evening I was invited over by some people who
live across from our quarters, the Casa Carmen. I had great fun.
Three Spaniards played mandolin and lute. They sang superb
Aragonese folk songs and the mother of the family danced a *jota*
with astounding litheness. Nobody thought about the war. I met
Henrique [*sic*], a happy-go-lucky, highly intelligent lad. They
asked my name and where I am from. When I said that I was a
suizo, one elderly *campesino* who can probably neither read nor
write, exclaimed in delight: 'The land of Francisco Ferrer's friend
Henrique [*sic*] Pestalozzi!' Which left me open-mouthed with
surprise. [...] And little Carmen from the house is very pretty.[51]

51   Gmür and Minnig, *Pour le bien de la révolution*, 70, 71, 73, 74.

(Left to right) Vagliasindi, Ruano's partner, Ruano himself, the journalist Caba, and Campón

From the end of November onward, Durruti's death in Madrid and the militarization of the militias sparked a serious crisis in the Durruti Column, one that would bring it to the brink of disintegration. Furthermore, relations between the militia members and headquarters, where Lucio Ruano was behaving like an authoritarian, a brutal warlord, as we shall see, became extremely tense. Vagliasindi returned to Aragon at the end of November or sometime in December. He became the expert military advisor to the column's new War Committee, still based in Bujaraloz. This is the description of him in *Mi Revista*: "Ruano pores over maps and plans with an older man; he has a dry, pale face, a military stiffness, and a penetrating gaze."[52]

The same article reveals the makeup of the War Committee by late December: Lucio Ruano, chairman; Pablo Vagliasindi, military advisor whose service fighting with the International Group has begun; Pedro Campón Rodriguez (founder of the Pina revolutionary committee), secretary; José Espluga, general delegate of the *centurias*.

As for the International Group, it was based in Velilla de Ebro at that point; we do not know who acted as general delegate.

At this point, the young Spanish libertarian Juan Giménez Arenas joined Durruti's *centurias* in Pina de Ebro. Militarization was already an issue, and Ruano (who Arenas wonders how he could ever have risen to a position of such responsibility) seem to be doing everything, according to him, to ensure that militarization became effective. The column met in order to appoint a three-man delegation charged with conveying the message to the high command that the majority of the militia members were out to "make revolution and not war." On reaching HQ they made it clear to Ruano that the *centurias* categorically refused to militarize. Ruano interrupted them in mid-message to tell them:

> "Get back to your *centurias* as fast as you can unless you want me to put you up against the wall. Know this: I give the orders here and what I say, I do." Our answer to him was that he might very well put us up against the wall but that it was going to be his turn in a few hours, since our *centurias* were waiting for a concrete answer from the command. We returned to Pina and reported back. We assessed the situation, which wasn't very encouraging, and a number of us began to have doubts. One night the watchword "Vengeance!" circulated. The following day we learned that Durruti had died in suspicious circumstances.
>
> Manzana showed up from Madrid with an arm injury a few days later. He assembled the *centurias* in Pina, Gelsa, Osera, and Farlete and briefed us on the situation and need to organize along military lines if we were to get to grips with the war situation. At the same time, we would respond to politicians of all kinds who were leading a campaign against the column. From that moment, many of the comrades drifted back into the rearguard to await the mobilization order; among these was a group of Gypsies who stated that, being revolutionaries, they had no desire to become soldiers.[53]

The matter of how Ruano was behaving is raised in the testimony of Antonio Campos Crespo, who spent two months on secondment with the field artillery in Bujaraloz. One day, at the end of November, Sáez, a CNT political commissar, accosted him and told him that some officers had been placed under temporary arrest in a field tent and that he, Campos, was going to have to train his artillery on headquarters in Bujaraloz, some 3.5 kilometers away. If Sáez did not return before 8:00 p.m. with countermanding orders, Campos was to fire on the target.

53   Juan Giménez Arenas, *De la Unión a Banat. Itinerario de una rebeldía* (Madrid: Fundación Anselmo Lorenzo, 1996), 56.

Campos agreed though adjusted his sights to overshoot the HQ, while hoping for counter-orders to come quickly. And they did before the 8:00 p.m. deadline. He later found out the reason for all this: during fighting on November 19, in Fuentes de Ebro, the fascists had gained the upper hand, and the militia members had fallen back in disorder, so much so that one of them lost his rifle:

Headquarters thought this was a mess and it couldn't continue. A written proclamation was issued that pointedly stated, more or less: "We are soldiers of the Republic, we must be disciplined, the abandonment of one's post will be punishable." (Some said that this was followed with "by death.")[54]

The political commissars quickly put their heads together and replied: unless that proclamation was rescinded within eight hours, HQ would come under bombardment. HQ backed down, claiming that it was merely a matter of holding militia members responsible. That incident, attributable to Ruano's uncompromising approach, was obviously only a first attempt, because on December 10 HQ this time carried out its threats by executing two militia members from the machine-gunner section who were guilty of retreating and abandoning their weapons during the previous day's operations. That act created such deep resentment among the militia members towards this War Committee that Ruano was called back to Barcelona to explain himself.

{41}
PAGE 120

Manuel Ramos, who we mentioned earlier, had been in the Sierra de Alcubierre since the battle of Farlete on October 8, 1936. He was undoubtedly a member of the *centuria* that Antoine's group was coming to relieve. He offers this very precise description of the Aragonese militias' months of inactivity through the winter of 1936–1937:

54 Antonio Campos Crespo, *Guerra y cárcel en España 1936–1975* (Barcelona: Virus, 1999), 42.

The weeks followed one after another, and to kill time we used picks and shovels to build fantastic fortifications on the side from which danger might threaten. Fresh food arrived daily on the backs of the mules that made the descent into Farlete. At that altitude, there was no drinkable water [...]. Unfathomably, we remained day after day in those mountain trenches, which were of no strategic value, for, had the fascists attacked, we would have found ourselves without food and water.[55]

Then, at the beginning of 1937, the *centuria* moved out to take up positions in Farlete:

We took possession of the lands, but we cannot say that we were at war [...] rabbits were springing up everywhere [...].

All us comrades set about digging a big pit in the ground that served as the school and the dining room, we cut down lots of trees and piled the trunks on top of each other, which is to say, lashing them together, we covered them with grass and then a thick coating of dirt [...].

What were we doing there? To this day, I just don't get it. In any case, we were training; what else could we do? As we were organized into Libertarian Youth groups, and a congress was due to be held in Pina de Ebro, the centuria appointed a *compañero* [...] and me as delegates to the congress.

[...] We arrived without any intellectual baggage [...] There was a lot of talk there about the evolution of the war and what our role would be as the villages of Spain were liberated. We talked in revolutionary terms because Spain had woken up after centuries of submissiveness and poverty. And, naturally, there was also talk of love, but of a pure love, love for one's fiancée, one's wife, the children, and not the sort of love that gets talked about these days, which consists of getting a woman into bed for a few minutes of pleasure. We argued that we had to throw all our support behind the nascent free women's groups, for the women were still feeling society's mistreatment and men's dark side. We also berated prostitution, which was a hot topic as, at the start of the war, many of those women had signed on with the militia

55   Ramos, *Una vida azarosa*, 54–55.

members and it was said that they were behind a lot of withdraw-
als from the front due to the venereal disease they had carried. Be
that as it may, I remember that many female compañeras traveled
out to the front and that there was no connection between them
and those women.[56]

Ramos must have run across the young Giménez Arenas whose
centuria was stationed in Pina in late November 1936:

There were quite a number of young people in the village and we
decided to organize the JJLL [Libertarian Youth]. I worked to get
us some books. We issued a leaflet inviting youngsters of both
sexes. About thirty of them showed up for the inaugural meeting. We organized a round table discussion; they agreed to set up
a JJLL branch and we started appointing representatives. One of
them said: I propose Such-and-Such, etc. If he was not acceptable,
somebody else was put forward, until eventually the committee
was formed. I was awarded a three-day furlough to go and fetch
books from Barcelona.[57]

{42}

PAGE 120

While Antoine was up in the sierra, the International Group was seething. Let us look at Edi Gmür's testimony:

[Gelsa] December 31.
    [...] The Grupo Internacional is currently made up of about
a hundred men; there are still more on leave. In total, there
are around a hundred German-speaking fighters in this group,

---

56   Ibid., 60–62.
57   Giménez, *De la Unión a Banat*, 55.

most of them emigrés. This afternoon there was a gathering of all the internationals. The topic: militarization. The debate was quite lively. The French and the Spaniards are utterly against militarization of the militias. The Germans and the other internationals are for it, but they stipulate certain conditions. The meeting ended in a screaming match. My comrades and I had a hard time believing that such a pressing necessity could still be up for debate. [...]

January 6.[58]

The internationals who are in favor of militarization left Gelsa today, as we did. The atmosphere is very tense. They came in six cars to take us back to Pina. Our centuria leader ordered the guy sitting in the back of the very last car to keep his rifle at the ready. [...]

[Pina] January 9.

Every day, there is a meeting. Manzana, head of the Durruti Division is calling for militarization with all possible speed.[59] We are no longer referred to as the Grupo Internacional, but rather as the Primera Compañía Internacional. We have been ordered to mount military exercises daily.

January 11.

Today forty-nine men headed back to Barcelona because they don't agree with a real militarization. The political commissar discharged them. A fair number of them have been here from the very beginning and have taken part in several attacks. They left the village, singing.[60]

From this we learn that the International Group had formally been militarized and returned to its post in Pina on January 6, 1937. But those in the group who had rejected militarization stayed on in Gelsa, and on January 8 they posted a notice drafted and endorsed jointly by the militia members from No 4. Agrupación, from the War Delegation and from the "Acción y Alegría" group:

58   Or January 5, according to a document cited below: IISH, FAI 1, package 27. [Giménologues' note.]

59   Manzana was at that time in the throes of ousting Ruano and the entire War Committee. [Giménologues' note.]

60   Gmür and Minnig, *Pour le bien de la révolution*, 71–73.

We have a highly-tuned conception of responsibility, which cannot coexist alongside the military mentality that will inevitably lead to dictatorship; and as conscious, responsible men we must avert that. [...] Winning the war does not mean winning the revolution.[61]

What is more, on January 10, following a general assembly, seventy-six of the internationals who had followed Manzana to Pina drafted a resolution pointing out that the assurances offered by HQ as a means of ensuring a "military reorganization" no longer held. As a result, the signatories made these demands:

1. Every section elects a soldiers' delegate. The four delegates from each company have the following rights:
   a. The right to take part in all of the military and administrative tasks concerning the International Group.
   b. In urgent cases and on the basis of their documents issued by headquarters, they are always entitled to travel to any location to resolve an issue as required.
2. Free election of all officers, except for those cited earlier [regimental commander, staff officers, and column leaders].
3. Equal pay for all fighters from the confederal columns. Here we refer to an article published in *Solidaridad Obrera* on January 9, 1937 about the standardization of pay, with which we are in complete agreement.
4. No requirement to perform the military salute.
5. No requirement to sign on for a fixed duty of service.
6. Those comrades we appoint to put our demands to the Regional Committee shall not be entitled to amend them. They have a duty to return within forty-eight hours, even should they not have received any written response from the relevant Committee in charge. If it fails to respond to our demands, we will take it that they have been rejected.
7. In the event that our just demands are rejected or go unanswered, each of the signatories shall be free to act.[62]

61   IISH, CNT, 94 E, 1, 2.
62   IISH, FAI 1, package 27.

But given that Manzana refused to let these same delegates leave for Barcelona, on January 12 (Gmür says it was the 11th), forty-nine internationals quit the Durruti Column and headed for Barcelona, clutching a fresh statement dated January 13, 1937: "Report for the CNT Regional Committee." They set out that, even though they had agreed to militarization and elected their delegates, those delegates had not been recognized by HQ and that Manzana ordained that he alone was setting the new conditions now. When they objected and said that they were off to Barcelona to make a complaint to the Regional Committee, Manzana's response was: "I *am* Barcelona," adding that any meeting on the subject of militarization was henceforth banned. The militia members' concluded their report:

> According to him, we had only two options: to agree unconditionally to the militarization measures of Manzano [*sic*] or to leave the column. … We saw no option other than resigning in order to put our demands to the Regional Committee, and we have done precisely that.
>
> But this does not mean that we are not prepared to fight.
>
> Quite the opposite. We will even state that we acknowledge the need for reorganization of the columns in order to boost their military efficacy, but we insist that this be done in a revolutionary and federalist spirit, that being the essence of our convictions and the outlook of the CNT.[63]

Now back to Gmür's journal:

[Pina] January 18.

Almost daily, there are discussions and arguments among the anarchists and us three communists. Things took a particularly violent turn today. Heiny was grumbling about inactivity on the Aragon front; according to him, an offensive to take the pressure off Madrid was needed urgently. Moses, the little anarchist, got all excited: "I'd just like to know what arms we might use to go on the attack again? These ancient rifles of ours?" The communists give us no weapons. Russia delivers only to the PSUC. They send us tin cans instead of guns and planes. They agree with

63   Ibid.

Non-intervention. The communists are betraying the revolution here in Spain!' I raised the objection that Russia cannot send arms openly because of the geographical factor. The fascist states are watching like hawks. Anyway, neither England nor France would allow it. To which Moses replied: "That isn't the issue. The communists are out to take power in Spain. But they can only pull that off once the anarchists have been wiped out."[64]

Let us continue with the testimony from Paul and Clara Thalmann who turned up in Pina in January 1937:

There was a motley collection of antifascists from all over the world. Initially the group had been made up of Germans, who had been joined by Dutch and Swedes, Luxembourgers, and a few Spaniards who felt at home in the company of foreigners. [...]

The acting military commander was from the Saar, a First World War veteran.[65] The final choice was due to be made once the reshuffle of the group was complete; Michel Michaelis was the political leader, but we shied away from appointing him commissar. He was by far the best educated and strove to turn his men into real anarchists. And, besides, he was possessed of the sort of moral authority that is alone in conferring prestige and respect. He lived the same as everybody else, with no privileges. Every decision, no matter how trivial, was first subjected to a discussion in which the entire unit had its say before a final vote was cast. [...]

The militia army also adopted the voucher system [which was used previously for paying the peasants], and ten pesetas a day was the going rate. Each day, everyone was issued a pack of cigarettes or tobacco, and anyone who smoked more than that was of course free to use his money to buy more. Wine, on the other hand, was rationed, and one liter per person was the sum total issued.

Since there was nothing in the villages meriting special purchases, the militia members amassed a fair sum, their wages being

---

64   Gmür and Minning, *Pour le bien de la révolution*, 75.
65   Quite possibly Gottfried Schreyer, born in 1895, who arrived in October 1936. [Giménologues' note.]

paid weekly. The itch to spend this money was certainly very strong, but Barcelona was the only place where that was a prospect. Now, furlough arrangements were strictly regulated. Every three months, everyone was entitled to a week off. Anybody wanting more had to justify himself to a special committee made up of the military commander plus three militia members. As a general rule, nobody abused the furlough arrangements.[66]

This testimony confirms that the International Group was still in the throes of reorganization and had only an interim commander. We note too that the Thalmanns thought that the group had been set up by the Germans, such was the extent to which Germans were omnipresent by that point. We might add that in an internal DAS document also it is expressly stated: "The Durruti Column's International Group, now the Durruti Division's 1st International Company, grew out of an initiative of our group [...]."[67]

This demonstrates that the German anarcho-syndicalists were rewriting history somewhat....

As for the front, it was still immobile, the same old causes reproducing the familiar effect. To return to the Thalmanns' account:

Our military training consisted of long marches, shooting practice, training in the use of hand grenades; we also dug trenches along the Ebro. Sightings of the enemy, over on the opposite bank of the river, were rare. Across from Pina, on the enemy side, the Francoist troops had taken over a large white house. We would occasionally fire shots at the invisible occupants of that house. Often we could hear artillery firing in the distance and the occasional sound of air raids. Apart from the sending out of the odd patrol, no military action took place. Besides, military ventures on a larger scale were beyond our capability; that our armaments were very rudimentary ruled that out completely. In our unit, we had four different models of rifles: Czech, Spanish, French, and Mexican, most of them old and in bad shape... One of our daily occupations was sorting the ammunition appropriate for each type of rifle. We had a huge number of egg-shaped grenades at our

66   Thalmann and Thalmann, *Combats pour la liberté*, 138–39.
67   IISH, FAI, package 1/c3.

disposal; the handling of these was not safe and their effectiveness was limited. Our one and only heavy weapon was a Maxim-type submachine gun. [...]

Around the campfires, in the dormitories, and at meetings, there was much talk of how the war was going. Sometimes, Michaelis would chip in with news and observations. The news was bad. The loss of the Basque Country had a catastrophic military and psychological impact. Italian troops were closing on Málaga. There was no denying the growth in communist influence; they opposed the militia armies with all their might and were calling for the raising of a regular army under a single command. Even though many anarchists agreed with the idea, they were not going to have a Bolshevik supreme command at any price. [...]

During the long winter evenings, classes and talks were held for those with any interest. When the talk turned to how the war was progressing, there were often minor altercations, for most of the volunteers were by no means anarchist and were only fighting in that unit as a result of a fluke or out of dislike for the communists. Some twenty-odd professed to be Marxists, and they made up a rather compact bloc.

Some of the militia members used to play cards. When it came to light that they were playing for money, all hell broke loose. A general assembly was given over to this matter and the guilty parties were sentenced to several doses of sentry duty. Just once, we witnessed drinking followed by brawling; the men were cautioned that in the event of a repetition they would be expelled from the militias.[68]

{43}
PAGE 121

Madeleine frequently made trips back to Barcelona to look after both of them. That spring, Hans/Hermann was to rejoin the front following

---

68   Thalmann and Thalmann, *Combats pour la liberté*, 139–41.

several months in hospital, but their son stayed behind in Barcelona, and that turned out to be a matter for the group.

As DAS delegate, Michaelis was in regular correspondence with Helmut Rüdiger, head of the Barcelona branch. Thanks to their preserved exchanges, we have a better understanding of what life was actually like for the militia members. Here is an extract from Rüdiger's March 21, 1937 letter to Michaelis:

> The group's most recent meeting went smoothly, except for one matter: the Gierth family, which is, as you know, on the front, has left its little 12–13-year-old boy here in Barcelona at [Calle] Francoli 57. He is on his own in a large 7–8 room apartment in Barcelona where the power has just been cut off. The boy is penniless; for the first two weeks, another family fed him, hoping that his parents would not forget about him. The youngster can neither read nor write, despite his age. Three letters have been sent to his mother, without reply. Unfortunately, this child has been taken into the emigrants' hostel. Furthermore, he has already begun begging and saying that his parents are with the DAS. One comrade from the group, on whose behalf I am writing, is waiting for you to intervene and get this woman back to look after her child, or find somebody else to do so. It is unacceptable that we have to look after children. The boy could come to a bad end. We hope that you share our opinion, since this child is on the road to ruin.[69]

{44}

PAGE 121

The Thalmanns offer this matter-of-fact description of the living conditions of the collective and its dealings with men in arms:

69 IISH, FAI, 1.

Pina, a typical Aragonese village with a population of around 2,000, sits on the banks of the Ebro. Our unit had moved into two big empty farmhouses. We were bedding down on straw and were entitled to two blankets apiece. Our unit was split up into ten-man groups; each of these groups was assigned to a peasant family with which the men would take their meals. The heads of these groups, elected for a given term of office, would go and fetch foods back from the stores, and on each occasion had to state the numbers in their groups, as well as the members of the peasant family with whom they ate. Every day, three men were selected to prepare the meals with the family. In those massive Aragonese kitchens, meals were cooked in huge fireplaces. The family in question also benefited from this, in that they were eating at the expense of the militias. During the three months we spent in Pina, this arrangement never let us down.

All of the land was collectivized. A committee elected by the peasants orchestrated the work and the distribution of produce. Every morning at 6:00 a.m., the peasants scheduled to work would assemble in the village square with their tools and their donkeys. What work was to be carried out was then decided and entrusted to each of them. The army used to buy up the bulk of the vegetable harvest, wine, potatoes, and olives, as well as a huge amount of mutton, the remainder being marketed in Barcelona or in other smaller towns in the rear guard. The peasants were paid in vouchers recording the hours worked and with these they were able to buy food, wine, tobacco, clothing, and footwear, and even go to the hairdresser. There was also provision for the sick, the children, and the elderly. A small fraction of the wages was paid in cash to cover personal needs; for the purchase of, say, whatever cereals, plants, or vegetables one might have a special fondness for. Of course, cash could also be used to go to Barcelona, for instance, for going to the cinema or restaurants, etc. [...]

There was no fighting going on in our sector, which is why the militia members would often be out in the fields laboring alongside the peasants.[70]

---

70   Thalmann and Thalmann, *Combats pour la liberté*, 138–39.

This testimony offers a description of the situation during January, February, and March 1937. At this time, in the wake of the October 1936 decree—the implementation of which was rather belated in Aragon—the local revolutionary committees were giving way to municipal councils, and the registries were reopening. We know the composition of the municipal councils. In February 1937, Pina's municipal council was made up of nine CNT militants, including the mayor, Pedro Campón. The question of the relationship between the collectives and the municipal councils was discussed at the congress in Caspe on February 14:

> Knowing that the government was our number one adversary and that we were careful to safeguard the social gains that had been achieved, we had said to ourselves that the municipal councils were going to carry on fulfilling their traditional function. However, if they were in our hands, we might protect them against potential maneuvers, by means of our trade unions, strengthened for that very purpose.[71]

{45}
PAGE 123

For those who might have doubts as to the reality of such free love in the Aragonese countryside of 1936, let us look at one of the testimonies collected by the historian Hanneke Willemse. According to one old woman living in Albalate de Cinca, the social revolution brought few changes to the lives of the adult women in that farming town. On the other hand, it really changed the lives of young people. No more priests, no more public authorities to point the finger at unmarried couples! Girls and boys were in each other's company all the time and they shared the same ideas: they were active in the Libertarian Youth.

One former Durruti Column militiaman points out that "from 1933 onward there had been a degree of change in respect to sexual

---

71   Carrasquer, *Les Collectivités d'Aragon*, 64.

relations. The truth is that free love was already a topic of conversation [….] and we were even talking about contraceptives."[72]

He went on to say that they were not able to use these "because the girls would not let us touch them." Then, when he returned from the front in December 1936 to relax in the village, he found that his sister and all his friends were public about their liaisons and were not holding back from sexual relations. He himself slept with his friend, Rosalía. "Now, he says, if her father had known about it he'd have killed me."[73]

To put it another way, and Gimenez opens our eyes to this, mothers might scheme with their daughters in order to keep fathers' noses out of it. It may be that Aragonese youngsters had acquired a degree of confidence in their behavior because the new village community looked upon them pretty much as autonomous individuals. Or maybe it was because they found themselves more left to their own devices because of the upheaval in day-to-day life. Félix Carrasquer, who was actively involved in the Albalate de Cinca peasant collective, touches on the issue in his book:

> As for what is known as the generation gap, we cannot say that there was actually anything of the sort in the collectives, because [...] the traditional tension between one generation and another was never manifest in any systematic way nor was it as radical as it might have been. [...] [For] the authority principle [...] had been undermined by the impact of the collectives, where the relationship model, founded upon free, mutually reliant partnership, acted as a catalyst between the intransigence of the older generation and the rebelliousness of the younger. [...][74]
>
> We took a collaborative approach to work and various plans, and this brought the generations together. The discrimination that women had always been subjected to was becoming less and less stark.
>
> [...] woman being placed on an equal footing within the collective, her independence as far as her husband or parents were concerned was absolutely not determined by any economic

72   Hannecke Willemse, *Pasado compartido, memorias de anarcosindicalistas de Albalate de Cinca, 1928–1938* (Zaragoza: Prensas Universitarias de Zaragoza, 2002), 326.

73   Ibid., 327.

74   Carrasquer, *Les Collectivités d'Aragon*, 139.

factor. We need only remember here the family wage from which every collectivist, man or woman, adult, youngster or child benefited. The allocation due them as a family member was fixed [...] according to a ratio that had been discussed and approved by everyone at an assembly as follows: to each according to needs, from each according to capabilities.

In which case the wife enjoyed the same rights as her husband and, as a full member of the collective to which she belonged, could do with her allocation as she wished. [...]

It should to be pointed out, though, that even if age-old differences between the sexes were beginning to fade, it was not happening as fast as some of us might have liked. [...] So much so that when it came to setting the family wage, the percentage allocated to the women was in the middle, higher than children's but rather less than that allocated to the men. The *Mujeres Libres* groups and the Libertarian Youth took vigorous exception to this arbitrary decision, so that in certain farming collectives and industries, timely amendments were made without too much difficulty. [...]

[...] once they were able to take part in assemblies without restrictions of any sort and once messages started to flood in from all sides favoring the advancement of women, women's interest in social issues began to grow.[75]

But according to Hanneke Willemse's study, among the women she interviewed fifty years on, with only one exception, no young girl or unmarried woman active in the Libertarian Youth could recall having played a part in organizing anything in their villages. The sole meeting the women attended once a month was the general assembly, and none of them had any definite recollection of the contents of the discussions: "The talk was of work and production in the village, and we just chatted among ourselves."[76]

In Albalate, the local Mujeres Libres branch was set up in December 1937.

Nevertheless, for most of the women who gave us their testimony, the most vivid memory remains the enjoyment of unprecedented

75   Ibid., 141–44.
76   Willemse, *Pasado compartido*, 320.

freedom, in that they were no longer "trapped in the home with a broken leg."[77] They could have fun, take off into the fields with their children, dance and enjoy life…

{46}
PAGE 127

Lucio Ruano, an Argentinean member of the Durruti Column's War Committee, was not killed right at the start of the battle for Siétamo as Antoine writes. On the contrary, his continued presence is borne out by the editorial in issue no. 15 (September 19, 1936) of *El Frente*, the Durruti Column's war bulletin:

> Following strenuous resistance from the enemy, our militias stormed the fascists' last remaining forts in Siétamo. The two *agrupaciones* fighting in the Huesca sector under the orders of Ruano and Yoldi have added a page of glory to the record of the Durruti Column. […] The compañeros from the International Group played a very active part in this glorious action by our brave militias.[…] Hats off to these International Group comrades who, along with other militia members, have given up their lives for the cause of the emancipation of the proletariat.

Another article carried in *Mi Revista* (no. 3, November 15, 1936) included a photo of "Ruano (CNT)," identifying him as the man who had commanded Durruti's militia members in the engagement.

That said, but for Antoine's mistake with the chronology, we would by this point in his narrative be in the middle of the winter of 1936–1937, and it may well be that by then some militia members had tried to kill the man who had had their comrades shot in Bujaraloz on December 10. In fact, from then on, despite his reputation as a courageous war chief, Ruano was shunned by a segment of the Durruti Column militia members.

---

77   Ibid., 324.

Durruti and Ruano deep in discussion prior to the attack on Siétamo

If the minutes of the meetings held on December 18, 1936, at the level of the CNT's Regional Committee for Catalonia are to be believed, the matter was beginning to make waves in high places:

> The R[egional] C[ommittee] opens by stating that not only had a delegation come to make a complaint about Ruano and left a report with it, but a delegation from Tarragona has turned up for the same purpose [complaining about Ortiz]. All of this has been passed to War [the RC's War Section] to thrash out a resolution, and this very night a plenum will be held, which Ruano, Jover, and Ortiz will be attending. They will be called upon to explain themselves since it has been noted that the Ruano column is not the only one where executions have been carried out.[78]

Let us dwell upon the minutes of that evening meeting, attended by members from the columns' committees and their leaders. It turns out that Ruano, Jover, and Ortiz drafted and put their signatures to a manifesto on the subject of militarization, remarking upon:

78   IISH, CNT 94 D13, b.265.

the recasting of the columns into divisions and demanding that the characteristics of anarchist ideology be safeguarded. Ten brigades have been set up, with 40,000 men, and there are fears about losing hegemony over command.[79]

Given a reading at the outset of the meeting, this manifesto would be looked upon by some within the CNT as "high treason in the face of History":

It is painful to think that there are comrades who, after five months of struggle [...] are now bridling at a regularization of the army which is required if we are to achieve victory, and this solely because they find the sound of it jarring and because it would not fit in with their libertarian principles.[80]

The three column commanders under criticism replied that the anarchist militias had always been subject to sabotage on the front lines by lack of weapons and munitions, and they objected to the current blackmail by the "Russians" (as relayed by Abad de Santillán), whereby the militia members would be issued modern weapons if they would only embrace militarization.

Ruano asked:

How much longer is it going to be acceptable to ask sacrifices of these thoughtful comrades? [...] Let us be forceful in hoisting the MASSES into the position that is rightfully theirs and steer clear of the pointless or hasty sacrifice of the militants concerned.[81]

Domingo Ascaso declared:

I have been on the front from the very outset, I have witnessed the intent to sabotage and poor command, in the forward positions as well as in the rear guard. I find it inconceivable that one could shoot a comrade stricken with fear at a given point. I have had to call meetings on the front to persuade the comrades that

---

79   Ibid.
80   *Solidaridad Obrera*, January 3, 1937.
81   IISH, CNT 94 D13.

they should be receiving 10 pesetas because many of them were opposed to it, afraid that they might be looked upon as mercenaries […].[82] We must embrace militarization but without imposing an iron discipline. A comrade who lets this get to his head should be set to digging trenches or scrubbing pots.[83]

Ruano retorted:

I have had two people shot but not as specific individuals: what I wanted was to condemn the act per se because if we tolerate certain acts of cowardice, it could result in serious harm to many other compañeros who are in the same perilous situation, or worse, as the ones that cut and ran. Anybody who doesn't like it can exercise his right to leave.[84]

Later he asked council member Germinal Esgleas "to cancel the order whereby pay is doled out on the front, for there is a deliberate Machiavellian and diabolical intention to put money back into the villages, though we have just done away with it."[85]

It may well have been that same night that the decision was made to wind up Ruano's War Committee and to commission Manzana to take charge of the Durruti Column, as he would at the end of the month.

But in order to complete the picture we can outline of Lucio Ruano's rather complex personality, we need to know that complaints of quite a different sort, but equally serious, played their part in this decision. Here we have it: in the archives of the IISH we have come upon small notices signed by the "Peñalba War Delegation—Durruti Column," dated December 2 and 3, 1936. The first one calls upon the population in Peñalba to "surrender short and long arms within twenty four hours, by order of the War Delegation."[86]

The second one demanded: "Insofar as this village has been declared a war zone […] let the population hand over all the cash at its disposal before forty-eight hours have expired."[87]

82   This was the daily pay that went with the militarization. (Giménologues' note.)
83   Ibid.
84   Ibid.
85   Ibid.
86   IISH, CNT 94 E.
87   Ibid.

In addition, from other villages in Aragon (Pina being one) there are several cash receipts, indicating requisitioning on a wide scale, the total being in the region of 90,000 pesetas. This sounds very much like a ransom paid by the population under the aegis of the column's War Committee. Ruano was called to account for this to the CNT at the beginning of January and tried to allege that his trust had been abused: somebody had faked his signature. Nobody believed him, and under Manzana's watchful eye, the Argentinean was forced to hand over cash and valuables that he had commandeered for himself. Various documents attest to this restitution being handed back to the villages wronged.

The closing act: at a meeting of the CNT Regional Committee dated January 27, 1937, the topic was the scandal created "by the moral and monetary issue in the Ruano and Durruti columns." Domingo Ascaso spoke out:

The commission on which I served [...] asked Manzana to insist that Ruano hand over the hundreds of thousands of pesetas inappropriately amassed. As to the moral aspect, Manzana thinks it might be wise not to enforce any reprisals. We have to act with caution in matters of this sort.[88]

Another militant spoke out to say:

This very day there was a meeting held at Metalworking [union], from which came the veiled threat that, some day, without anyone's wanting it to happen, Ruano and Campón will be found lying on some street-corner.[89]

The person reporting the meeting stipulates:

All present are agreed in saying that this must be avoided, that one cannot set oneself up as judge and jury and that if sanctions are merited, the Organization alone should be the one to determine them.[90]

88   IISH, CNT 85, C1.
89   Ibid.
90   IISH, CNT, 85E.

So as we can see there were threats hanging over Ruano's head. Documents show that he was still on the front in late January. Once back in Barcelona, he was the topic of conversation for several reasons, until he was executed by anarchist militants in July 1937.

For more information, see Miguel Amorós, *La revolución traicionada. La verdadera historia de Balius y Los Amigos de Durruti* (Barcelona: Virus, 2003), 151.

{47}

PAGE 128

Given Antoine's mistake with the chronology, we find the International Group outside the village of Siétamo, located eleven kilometers east of Huesca, during the first half of September 1936. Pablo Vagliasindi was definitely there, as we have seen the Italian secret police's report, but he was not still leading the International Group.

Abel Paz explains the importance of capturing that village, which was a real hurdle to be cleared if they were to get at Huesca. He states that the Durruti Column's militias had previously captured Siétamo but that Villalba had failed to hold it. Indeed, as Barrachina tells it,[91] the attack by Barbastro militia members, by the POUM, the Durruti Column, and soldiers led by Medrano had begun on July 26, with support from republican aircraft over the ensuing days. The Nationalists evacuated Siétamo on August 1, but they recaptured it on the 3rd, and Colonel Villalba was forced to run. Between August 3 and 31, the Nationalists had improved the defenses considerably. According to Paz, in mid-August 1936, the Aragon Front's War Committee (in collaboration with the CAMC), based in Sariñena and made up of representatives from the CNT, UGT-PSUC, and POUM columns and republican servicemen, decided to focus its efforts on Huesca.

91   Pedro Barrachina Bolea, "Campaña de 1936. Primeros combates. Alrededores de Huesca," in Luis Alfonso Arcarazo García, Pedro Barrachina Bolea, and Fernando Martínez de Baños Carrillo, *Guerra Civil Aragón. Tomo V. Huesca "el cerco"* (Zaragoza: Delsan, 2007), 90–92, 101.

The Durruti Column en route to Siétamo

According to Amorós, the decision was made to launch a general offensive starting in Estrecho Quinto. Durruti was to create a diversion by attacking Zuera, and Ortiz would attack Belchite. But on August 31, Colonel Villalba—with his three thousand men, based in Barbastro—opted for a different strategy and attacked Siétamo, the furthest location from Huesca and the best defended. On September 1, Villalba again called upon Durruti's militia members, and José Mira attacked Siétamo with several *centurias* on September 4. After having accompanied the International Group and the two *agrupaciones* from his column, led by Yoldi and Ruano as far as Angües, Durruti made for Bujaraloz where the Banda Negra was to attack Fuentes de Ebro and create a diversion.

Using the French anarchist press, let us take a look at the backdrop against which the group operated outside of its usual combat zone. We'll start with Ridel's piece in *Le Libertaire* of September 25:

> Siétamo today is the focus of the Catalan and Aragonese proletariat's attention.
>
> So far, the fascists have managed either to hold on to it or to dislodge the columns that had successfully occupied it.
>
> A detachment from the Durruti Column was dispatched especially to the Huesca front to bring this situation to an end.

These reinforcements consisted of *centurias* plus the antifascist International Group.

In the same edition the paper we read this tribute to the International Group:

> Made up of Swiss, Italians, Germans, Spaniards, and French, it was always at the forefront of the firing line. One of a kind, it makes a centuria with an autonomous internal organization of its own. [...]
>
> Our friend Durruti made no attempt to hide his satisfaction at having this international legion close to him and we know the pain he must have felt when the demands of the situation at one nerve center on the front prompted him to decide to dispatch the shock centuria to the red-hot Huesca front.
>
> We were with Durruti the morning that the International Group boarded trucks and were setting off for Huesca. [...]
>
> Our friends Ridel, Carpentier, Giral, Levysse, and too many whose names we have forgotten were part of the expedition.

For further details, see Abel Paz, *Durruti in the Spanish Revolution* (2007), 513–15; Miguel Amorós, *Durruti en el laberinto*, 72–74; Francisco Escribano Bernal, "¿Un frente tranquillo?," in Francisco Escribano Bernal (ed.), *Guerra Civil Aragón vol. 2, Imagenes* (Zaragoza: Delsan, 2005), 72.

{48}
PAGE 136

The reference here is to a German-speaking Swiss mentioned a number of times by Nic Ulmi and Peter Huber in their book.[92] There we learn that Franz Ritter employed the following aliases: Chnurri, Knurri, and

---

92   Peter Huber and Nic Ulmi, *Les Combatants suisses en Espagne républicaine, 1936–1939* (Lausanne: Antipodes, 2001).

Franz Ritter in 1937 or 1938

Franz Scholl. He was born in the Saint-Gallen canton on May 30, 1914. Living in Zurich, he worked as a cheese-maker and joined the Socialist Youth at the age of fourteen. According to an interview Ritter gave to Hans Peter Onori, this young Swiss was already in Spain by May 1936:

> In 1935 I became acquainted with Dr Fritz Brupbacher and, in Paris, the anarchist educationist [*sic*] Francisco Ferrer who was later killed in what was described as the Barcelona putsch. In May 1936, I made my first trip to Barcelona where I worked for a short time as a cheese-maker. I returned to Switzerland in late June but was unable to find work. That December I made up my mind to go and fight in Spain. Without assistance from any third party, I turned up in Barcelona where I reported to the Durruti Column. At that point the column was 29,000 [*sic*] strong, no more than 600 of whom could read and write. I then took it upon myself to bring over J. Aeppli from the Zurich SP, a reporter with *Volksrecht*, as a tutor for the Durruti comrades.[93]

The date of Ritter's arrival in the Durruti Column (which he generously credits with a greatly exaggerated strength of numbers, though this might be a transcription error) does not match Antoine's account, which refers to his friends being on the front from mid-September onward.

---

93   Hans Peter Onori, "Protokoll des Gesprächs mit Franz Ritter," unpublished paper passed on by Peter Huber, 1.

Besides, Ulmi and Huber found in Ritter's International Brigades file that Ritter had set out from Switzerland for Barcelona in order to take part in the planned antifascist Olympics scheduled for July 19, 1936.

On that date the Catalan capital was expecting six thousand athletes from twenty-two countries, and three hundred of them were Swiss. But the specially chartered train never set off because of the pronunciamento. So a number of the athletes made their own travel arrangements: the bricklayer Otto Götz (a member of the FAUD),[94] the painter Henri Jonzier, housekeeper Käthe Hempel and her fiancé Gerhard Wohlrath, the journalist Vinicio Salati, the carpenter Armin Walter, and the clockmaker Clara Ensner-Thalmann. The last two were to stay in Catalonia and would enlist in the Durruti Column. As for Ritter, he either returned to Switzerland as he claimed, only to return to Spain in November or December 1936 and join the Centuria Internacional (there is a list showing him as having been "mobilized" on December 25, 1936) or he stayed on in Aragon and fought in the very same International Group. He may have had his reasons for not wanting to talk about all this in 1977, or else the International Brigades file is full of concocted information, as is often the case.

In any event, the names of Ritter and his friend Jacob Aeppli turn up in "The Inventory of DAS-supervised compañeros in the militias, drawn up on January 20, 1937."[95] Heiner Spiess has published some letters from Franz Ritter to a Swiss friend of his; they attest to his having been on the Pina front in January, March, and April 1937 then in May he was in Barcelona, where he wasn't shy about his sympathies being with the anarchists.

There were many more spontaneous departures from the Swiss Confederation, even though such departures would be outlawed. Indeed, on August 14, 1936, supposedly neutral Switzerland passed three injunctions outlawing:

1) The export and transiting of war materials bound for Spain;

2) Fund-raising for republican Spain;

3) Citizens leaving "Switzerland for the purpose of taking part in hostilities in Spain."

Such departures would continue, however, via multiple networks, and we have seen that many German-speaking Swiss would swell

---

94 Free German Workers' Union.

95 See Appendix V below.

the ranks of the International Group, which became an International Company in January 1937.

For more information, the reader is referred to the list of Swiss volunteers in Spain at http://gimenologues.org/spip.php?article434.

Furthermore, there is this site, devoted to anarchists in Switzerland: "Cantierre biografico degli Anarchi in Suizzera," http://www.anarca-bolo.ch/cbach/riferimenti.php?php+fr.

{49}
PAGE 136

"Jacques the moviemaker" is the Swiss Adrien Porchet. A member of a whole family of moviemakers, he had been living in Spain since 1931, working there as chief cameraman in full-length features. In July 1936, he was twenty-nine years old and in Barcelona. As he told it himself, in 1981:

> I had no political views at the time [...] I belonged to the CNT as a trade unionist, to its Public Entertainments Union. [...]
>
> I was just finishing off a movie [...] and on the evening of July 19 had no notion that there was a revolution in the offing there [...]. Very shortly after that, some militia members from the Public Entertainments Union dropped by the studio and told us that they needed a cameraman for the front. So they took me there.[96]

Porchet met up with the Durruti Column in Bujaraloz and headed up a moviemaking unit made up of nine militia members:

> One day there was an attack by fascist cavalry and planes about ten kilometers out. I was told: "You're coming with us to the front." To which I replied: "I make my newsreels and movies right here." One of them stuck a revolver in my ribs and warned me: "Either

---

96 Adrien Porchet, *Adrien Porchet, cinéaste sur le front d'Aragon* (Lausanne: Noir, 1997), 1.

you come to the front with us or you remain right here." … And so it was that I arrived in the front lines and set about shooting the fighting live. Gradually, I became accustomed to war. I would be involved in meetings of the command. I remember Durruti gave me a dressing-down, recommending that I set aside my camera and pick up a rifle, but I answered him: "I inspire more courage in your men with my camera than with any rifle!"

I had carte blanche when it came to choosing my subjects. I could even have filmed the executions of fascists or priests, but never had inclination to do so. On the front, I lived the same way as the militia members. There were some very uneventful times and, all in all, a very good atmosphere among the militia members on account of a highly developed sense of self-discipline. The reels were sent back to Barcelona to be developed. […]

What was really tough was having to film friends being wounded or killed. But in times like those, one develops a different mind-set. When Durruti took off in November 1936 for the defense of Madrid along with some personnel from the column, I headed back to life in Barcelona.[97]

Adrien Porchet was in charge of the photography of about ten films on the Aragon front, the four most famous newsreels from the series *Los aguiluchos de la FAI por tierras de Aragón* among them. In the third one, *La toma de Siétamo*, we can see the International Group with, among others, Ridel and Gimenez. The second and fourth of these newsreels show militia members from the 2nd Centuria who captured Pina and Gelsa and then Osera. In them we can spot Louis Berthomieu.

{50}
PAGE 140

Apart from the fact that he describes the incident as having occurred in winter, Antoine is perfectly consistent here with the reporters

97   Ibid., 1, 2.

who covered the capture of Siétamo. The attack dragged out for two weeks, and we can take it that the internationals were involved right from the outset.

Let us take a look at the story of "the Siétamo epic" through the eyes of the Francoist historian Martínez Bande:

> Having been recaptured on August 3, the small village enjoyed few days of relative peace and quiet. By the end of the month it had a 194-man garrison with two 105 field-guns and six machine guns and there was no way of knowing the numbers of the enemy stationed nearby.
>
> On August 31, following intense artillery and air raid preliminaries, a huge mass of attackers overran an infantry section and two machine-gunner sections protecting Siétamo's communications, thereby leaving the town cut off. Successful in that maneuver, the attackers then occupied the cemetery, which was unguarded, and then moved on to attack the town proper.
>
> On September 1, 2, and 3, Siétamo came under continual artillery and aircraft fire, and on the 4th, the attacks resumed, continuing over the ensuing days.
>
> The fighting in the main street started on the 7th, but after bloody combat, the situation calmed.
>
> On the 8th, Villalba's forces brought fresh weapons: flammable liquid, mines, and dynamite, and during the night they managed to set fire to the surrounding barns, while trying, unsuccessfully, to get the flames to spread to the houses.
>
> On the night of the 9th, the enemy slipped into Siétamo and torched several houses. From that point on, the fighting again took a turn for the tough and heroic, with the buildings being defended house-to-house, floor-to-floor, and room-to-room.
>
> A number of Nationalist planes tried to supply the defenders from the air, but such help was limited. Siétamo needed manpower, space, [and] fortifications, and a had a tactical situation that could not be changed.
>
> On the 12th, the last of the defenders withdrew to a line running from the church to the castle, these being the highest defensible buildings.
>
> There, arrangements were made to abandon the village, which by then was one enormous fire. On the morning of the 13th, a

tragic caravan discreetly leaves the last bastion of the castle and joins the defenders of Estrecho Quinto.[98]

The account by Mira, who commanded the *centurias* involved, supports the foregoing account: the push against Siétamo was doggedly pursued in late August and lasted a fortnight. Planes took part, affording cover to the advance of the thousand men from the Durruti Column, abetted by a POUM column under Manuel Grossi.

For further details, here is the follow-up to Ridel's article:

> After five days of bitter fighting, the village fell into our hands. The place had to be taken district by district, street by street, house by house. Every stone concealed an enemy, every building represented a fortress.
>
> Hemmed in on all sides, the fascists were determined to defend their lives dearly.
>
> Around fifty French, Swiss, Italians, and Germans finished them off using grenades and bottle incendiaries.
>
> Two guns were captured, five machine guns, as well as a number of rifles and some munitions. What remained of the civilian population was in a pathetic state, sick with fear and hunger.
>
> In the midst of the fighting, some soldiers who had come over to our side talked to comrades of theirs who had stayed on the other side and persuaded a fair number of them to desert.
>
> The taking of Siétamo—today now no more than a pile of rubble—clears the way to Huesca, the last town defending Zaragoza.[99]

The October 10, 1936 edition of *L'Espagne antifasciste* feature an account by another eye-witness:

> One day Durruti asked that Siétamo, a tiny village that had given us headaches on several occasions, be taken. Our centurias had set foot inside several of the houses, but they had come under sniper fire from the clock tower and from a white house that held the road. Durruti had given us three days to take the village completely.

98   Martínez Bande, *La invasión de Aragón*, 110–11.

99   *Le Libertaire*, no. 515 (September 25, 1936).

[...] That was our third night fighting without any sleep. This attack was the toughest as we had no choice but to advance without cover across the church square. [...]

By daybreak, Siétamo had been taken entirely. We lost thirty-seven out of sixty men (killed, missing or wounded).

Among the dead were two Italian Durruti Columnists. One was Gino (his real name was Agostino) Sette, believed to have been born in Montagna (Padua) on December 5, 1902. According to Fedeli, Sette had been active in the fight against fascism in Venezia. He had left for exile in France in 1924 before moving on to Belgium in 1934. After a time in Marseille where he made contact with the anarchists, he settled in Spain. He had joined the Durruti Column right at the outset of the civil war.[100] The other Italian, from Piedmont, was Giuseppe Lui.

Phil Casoar who collected Carpentier's testimony has provided us with this additional detail:

From Bujaraloz, the International Group traveled to the vicinity of Siétamo in buses. At nightfall on September 9, the Internationals attacked the outlying houses of the village with bottle incendiaries and homemade bombs. Carpentier is injured, alongside Ridel, right at the start of the attack by shrapnel from his own grenades. He was evacuated.

The militia advanced, house by house. After five days of fighting, Siétamo was wholly theirs. [...] Ridel headed off to Barcelona on leave to visit Carpentier who was still convalescing. The pair of them then went to Sitges where they found Simone Weil, still in hospital. With his arm in a sling, Carpentier headed back to Paris, and Ridel set off back to the front.

The outcome of his Spanish adventure was close.[101]

[...] Ridel omits the fact that some Spanish militia members had, on a whim, executed some young men from the village who had been found hiding in cellars after the fighting ended. He also has nothing to say of the bloodthirsty conduct of Sevilla, a Tercio veteran who had been posted to the International Group.[102]

100   See "Agostino Sette," *Anarcopedia*, http://ita.anarchopedia.org/Agostino_Sette.
101   Collectif, *Présence de Louis Mercier*, 15–16.
102   Ibid., 27.

Here Phil Casoar is relying upon a passage in Simone Weil's 1938 letter to Georges Bernanos:

Once more; in a village that had been taken by the reds and by the whites, then lost, recaptured and lost again I know not how many times, the red militia members, having recaptured it once and for all, stumbled upon a handful of haggard, terror-stricken, famished creatures in the cellars, among them three or four young men. Their thinking was as follows: if these men, rather than coming with us the last time we pulled out, chose to stay and wait for the fascists, then they are fascists. So they shot them out of hand, then gave the others some food, and thought themselves very humane.[103]

Apropos of Sevilla, Casoar bases his information on Mathieu Corman's book:

On the evening when I made his acquaintance, he [Sevilla] had just killed fourteen Falangists that the column's court-martial had sentenced to death because they had been captured while bearing arms. That was the evening the castle in Siétamo was taken.

A veteran of the Tercio, a former sergeant with the French Foreign Legion, Sevilla is terrifyingly ugly; his front teeth are all broken, he has a yellowish, bilious complexion, staring eyes, and is misshapen, one shoulder being higher than the other as a result of bearing the weight of a rifle for upward of twenty years.

Sevilla has seen his nearest and dearest perish in Triana [a working-class district of Seville] under Falangist gunfire. He takes his revenge by agreeing to kill anyone the court condemns to death.

I spotted him while he was talking to the prisoners. Of the thirty-eight men captured that day, twenty-four had, in front of a court-martial, found the words needed for their lives to be spared.

Shortly after seeing me, Sevilla came over:

"They're too young to die. But sparing that one there is wrong," he told me, pointing at an intelligent-looking soldier. "It was a mistake to spare him! He was operating the machine gun in the white house. I recognize him! His gun-post was facing my own. He's the one that killed two of my comrades. They didn't sentence him today, but I hope they won't save him a second time…"

Noticing that he was the topic of conversation, the prisoner turned a worried gaze on me. I looked back reassuringly.

Sevilla was determined to explain to me:

"You see, they bring me the die-hards and I have a chat with them and then, just as their mistrust has vanished, I tell them: Turn your head slightly! … Just like that, you see?"

He took my head in his bony hand and pressed the icy barrel of a Colt captured from an Andalusian Falangist, his first victim, against my temple.

There was an ironic glint in his eyes:

"You're not afraid! A man's' life depends on a little hole in the head, however."

At that instant I knew without a shadow of a doubt that I didn't like Sevilla.

"My style of killing is as good as the fascists' own. They may not enjoy it but at least they die without quite knowing about it … They killed two comrades of mine today," he went on between clenched teeth, "and that's going to cost them forty of their own!"

Louis [Berthomieu], the commander of the column's International Group, overheard our conversation. He rebuked Sevilla:

"That's enough of that! No more of your stories, Sevilla! These men fought bravely. You are to leave them in peace …"

Sevilla wandered away, and Louis, turning to me, explains:

"He's exaggerating. The Group absolutely must get rid of that type. We accepted him because he handles the machine gun well, but he exaggerates."

Two days later, I ran into Sevilla in Loporzano, the International Group's new battle station. He was kneeling in the middle of the street near a young boy. They were playing marbles.

Sevilla was the only man from the column playing with the village children.…

That same evening, I heard a gramophone playing Andalusian tunes in a deserted house. I went inside. Sevilla was sitting in one corner, his head in his hands, alone. He lifted his eyes toward the light of the candle as I approached. Big tears welled up in his eyes.

Sevilla was the only man from the column to weep when hearing the melodies of his homeland …

Sevilla was killed outside Madrid in November 1936, manning his machine gun.[104]

Sevilla did not perish in Madrid, however, since the journalist Caba mentions him in an article published in the January 1, 1937, edition of *Mi Revista:*

> Durruti Column militia […] Valentín Puente who escorted me as he was familiar with the men and terrain […] introduced [someone] to me:
>
> This, he said, is the renowned Sevilla, an indefatigable fighter in every operation conducted by our column in Aragon and, not content with that, he went with Durruti to Madrid and fought there the way he knows how, until he was wounded, the day before our caudillo perished; he is off to Bujaraloz to convalesce there.

From Corman's evidence we have confirmation that Berthomieu was indeed in Siétamo. It may be that part of the International Group under Lucio Ruano's command (and including Antoine and Pablo) attacked the village from the northern side, from behind the church, while another part (with Berthomieu, Sevilla, Ridel, and Carpentier) did likewise but from the lower end of the village, facing the famous white house visible in the photograph below [on page 399]. According to Barrachina, the first detail attacked the "Loma Norte" beginning on August 31, while the second attacked the "Loma Sur" from September 4th onward.

Isidro Benet—mentioned earlier in Endnotes 25 and 31—was with Berthomieu and Sevilla's detail. He has supplied us with fresh testimony—and significant testimony, at that. This young Spaniard—together with his cycling friends Salvador Frasquet and Félix Bonells—served with the International Group after this battle, of which he retains very lively memories:

> One night, we had to scramble aboard four or five trucks and a bus bound for the front: "No smoking! Turn off those headlights!"

104   Corman, "Salud, camarada," 53–57.

The street from the church to Siétamo castle, after the fighting

There was about a hundred of us militia members. We wound up in Sipán, ten or twelve kilometers outside of Siétamo. [...] [The following day,] having risen at about 9 o'clock, twenty-five of us militia members set off and arrived at a hill topped by a machine gun. It was El Sevillano [Sevilla], a one-time sergeant with the Legion, who gave us our orders. I didn't like it. [...]

All the Nationalists had left was the machine gun in the church and Aranda castle. The real fighting was about to begin. We had to enter the village, advancing house by house, to within range of the fortified castle. My friends, Félix Bonells and Salvador Frasquet, and I decided that we'd all dart across the street at the same time, the way kids do: "One, two, three. Go!" They opened fire just as we reached the first house on the right-hand side. We warned other militia members against joining us because there was no way the machine gun would miss the next time. I entered the house through the window and found some bread and wine and called Fresco in to share them with me. Then Félix reappeared with a pick and shovel and we attacked the walls in order to burrow through into the house next door.

This was captured in a scene from the [Porchet] movie in which we can be seen swinging the pick against the walls. We had no idea that we were being filmed. Back in Barcelona the entire Les Corts quarter saw it when the movie was screened there, and we saw it ourselves when we were on leave. [...] So we started punching through the houses along what is now the A1219 road. At one point, we stopped in one house that was taller than the rest. I climbed up into the attic, lifted one of the roof-tiles and spotted the machine gun in the clock tower and a small cannon set up in the square. [...] I could also see a house with a whitewashed gable with pop-holes from which the Nationalists were firing. We fired two or three downward shots from a hole cut with a bayonet, then we went back upstairs right away to shoot at the clock tower from the roof. Then, with some mates, we fetched ropes and sheets and material that we set up here and there to screen us as we crossed the last of the streets. But progress was dangerous. All three of us had to spent a day and a half inside that house, taking the occasional shot just to annoy the enemy, and we were passed food and munitions in a basket at the end of a rope. Then we set about smashing through the house walls, and after a day we came to the last house in the village, separated from the rest by a three-meter gap. It was the only whitewashed house. We attacked it, and, overnight, the enemy abandoned it. [...] I don't know if somebody told them to quiet down as things were over, but the two soldiers in the clock tower climbed down and appeared outside the door to surrender with a white hankerchief. We had called out to them to stay under cover as their own guys (Civil Guards) opposite might cut them down. In the meantime, a young lad darted out and made a run for the square to join those soldiers there, but the guys in the castle opened up on him and he fell to the ground, wounded. He dragged himself in our direction but the others kept firing at him until he was dead. Some of his compañeros tried to get him with a rope but all they were able to drag in was his corpse [this too is shown in the film]. Then people appeared out of nowhere, and within seconds the square was filled and everybody was shooting. We made for the dilapidated castle entrance, walking across the rubble [...]. As we reached the castle entrance, we decided to go down and search the cellars. It was dark and at the foot of the staircase, I brushed against a rifle

The southern approach to Siétamo, through which part of the international group has just attacked

at chest height: a soft voice told me that if I cried out I would be shot. I told him what was going on outside. There were three Civil Guards and two civilians there, and I proposed this:

"You Guards stay here and take off your uniforms. The civilians can come out with us as casually as you like and we can head for the pond to join up with our friend who was keeping watch. We'll get you some clothes." Which we did.

The two *fachas* (fascists) washed themselves in the pond and handed us their clothes, plus Félix's. Before we could get back to the cellars we were accosted by a rather elderly militiamen who struck us as intelligent and we told him our story. We were all in perfect agreement: several … would discreetly move off to escort "our" Guards along the route we were going to follow on leaving the castle.

Which is how everything went off; we fetched the Guards some clothing and emerged with them, their rifles slung over their shoulders. Once they had been disarmed, they could be taken away.

This scene calls to mind the situation outlined by Simone Weil in that letter to Bernanos. She refers to "three or four young men" taken from the castle cellars and shot by the militia members. Were they the Civil Guards escorted out so quietly by Isidro and his pals?[105] As they were in civilian dress, some witnesses at the scene may have reckoned that they were villagers, but that is merely a hypothesis.

105   We explore this matter rather more fully in "Retour sur la lettre de Simone Weil à Georges Bernanos": http://gimenologues.org/spip.php?article442.

The "white house" as it look today

At the end of the fighting, part of the Durruti Column set off to take Loporzano. The column then made for Quinto and Fuentes de Ebro in a diversionary move. The fighting for Estrecho Quinto carried on, the escapees from the Siétamo garrison having fled there. The area had been under fire from POUM militias ever since the end of August. The people under siege were in dire straits: all of the Nationalist dispatches refer to desertions on some scale. A lot of people were shot on the Nationalist side; not just the soldiers who had tried to desert but also those of their comrades who had failed to shoot them down. Colonel Villalba eventually captured Monte Aragon and Estrecho Quinto on September 30. It looked as if there was now nothing standing in the way of an attack on Huesca, but no such attack was mounted. Thanks to the resistance from the Nationalists on its outskirts, the town received significant reinforcements, and its fortifications were improved considerably. The siege would last another twenty months. Via the Jaca road, Huesca was connected to the rest of the Francoist zone.[106]

The dearth of arms and munitions so widely decried by the anarchist militia members—and deplored by the communist commander Barrio as well in his October 1936 report—and growing tensions within the republican camp helped keep the Aragon front inactive. As we mentioned in Endnotes 22 and 23 above, the central state—with the assistance of the CNT-FAI—tried to combine militarization with neutralization of the anarchists in this sector. For a start, Colonel Villalba had to be imposed as single commander of the columns. What came next would force Durruti to leave Aragon.

106   Barrachina, "Campaña de 1936," 135–59.

For more details, see Amorós, *Durruti en el laberinto*, 74–79; José del Barrio, *Memorias políticas y militares* (Barcelona: Pasado & Presente, 2013), 157–68.

ENDNOTES 51 TO 82

The War Devours the Revolution

{51}

PAGE 142

On September 27, 1936, the military situation in Madrid became precarious, as Francoist forces were closing rapidly on the capital. Largo Caballero called a meeting of Popular Front representatives as well as representatives from the CNT to discuss the government relocating to Valencia. Horacio Prieto, who had recently returned as CNT national secretary, was against this. Caballero backed off temporarily but then, from mid-October onward entered into negotiations with Horacio Prieto with an eye to bringing some anarchist ministers into his cabinet, while summoning Durruti down to Madrid with his men to defend the endangered capital. Over the ensuing days, Horacio Prieto had no difficulty getting Juan Peiró and Juan López to enter into the government; getting Federica Montseny to agree was rather trickier, and on November 1, he got García Oliver to agree by appealing yet again to his sense of "militant responsibility"; but as far as the transfer of a part of the Durruti Column was concerned, he ran up against problems the very next day, according to Abel Paz, or, according to Horacio Prieto,[1] from October 19 onwards, in the shape of a stubborn refusal by its general delegate who had no more desire to honor that sacred principle, in that he thought it had actually been supplanted by that of "bureaucratic responsibility."[2] He had no desire to leave Aragon at a time when the Regional Defense Council, unrecognized by the CNT, looked upon by communists as "maverick" and ignored by the

---

1   See Horacio M. Prieto, *Utopistas*, unpublished.
2   Paz, *Durruti en la revolución española*, 631.

government, was hovering between life and death. Besides, Durruti's primary interest was in taking Zaragoza.

By November 6, the capital was under siege by Francoist troops, and the government of the Republic, which two days before had added four anarchist ministers, fled Madrid in a hurry and relocated to Valencia. The situation was looking hopeless, and on November 8 a meeting of CNT militants from the Centre region held in Madrid heard from two National Committee members who had made a trip to try to talk Durruti into coming to the aid of Madrid—actually, all they did was pass on a message through Federica Montseny, who they met in Valencia. In the meantime, a military conference called by the Generalitat's Defense Council in Barcelona on November 5 eventually broke through his lingering opposition.

In a top-secret document that the Soviet consul in Barcelona, Antonov-Ovseenko, dispatched to his superiors in November 1936, we read:

> The dispatch of military aid to Madrid is proceeding with difficulty. The question about it was put before the military adviser [Francisco Isgleas] on November 5. The adviser thought it possible to remove the entire Durruti detachment from the front. This unit, along with the Karl Marx Division, is considered to have the greatest fighting value. To put Durruti out of action, a statement [was issued] by the commander of the Karl Marx Division, inspired by us, about sending this division to Madrid (it was difficult to take the division out of battle, and besides, the PSUC did not want to remove it from the Catalan front for political reasons). However, Durruti refused point blank to carry out the order for the entire detachment, or any part of it, to set out for Madrid. Immediately, it was agreed with President Companys and the military adviser to secure the dispatch of the mixed Catalan column (from detachments of various parties). A meeting of the commanders with detachments on the Aragon front was called for November 6, with our participation. After a short report about the situation near Madrid, the commander of the K. Marx Division declared that his division was ready to be sent to Madrid. Durruti was up in arms against sending reinforcements to Madrid, sharply attacking the Madrid government "which was preparing for defeat," calling Madrid's situation hopeless and

concluding that Madrid had a purely political significance—and not a strategic one. This kind of attitude on the part of Durruti, who enjoys exceptional influence over all of anarcho-syndicalist Catalonia that is at the front, must be broken at all costs. It was necessary to intervene in a firm way. And Durruti gave in, declaring that he could give Madrid a thousand select fighters. After a passionate speech by the anarchist Santillán, he agreed to give two thousand and immediately issued an order that his neighbor on the front, Ortiz, give another two thousand, Ascaso another thousand, and the K. Marx Division a thousand.[3]

Durruti was as good as his word and arrived in Madrid with a small part of his column: two *agrupaciones* and three *centurias*, a total of 1,400 men.

As for Ortiz, as far we know, he sent no men; moreover, he put it in writing that he had been unable to attend that meeting:

Federica Montseny confided to the author of *Le bref été de l'anarchie* [Enzensberger] that she was the one who thought that Durruti needed sending to Madrid and had convened a meeting for that purpose. It seems that all the commanders of the confederal columns in Aragon attended it. I didn't make it on time. Whether Jover was there, I cannot say. Had I made it there in time, I would have steadfastly opposed sending Durruti to the slaughter, as my meeting with Largo Caballero [see endnote No 22 above] was still fresh in my mind. In his analysis of the facts, García Oliver is right to believe in an anti-revolutionary conspiracy by self-styled anarchists, or, at least, the torpedoing and obstruction vis à vis the extremists (?) in the name of the politics of the lesser evil—unconquerable fear as an extenuating circumstance …

That was the plot. They flattered Durruti so that he would pay a second visit to Largo Caballero … and the result was equally negative. Then Durruti was sweet-talked so that he would go off to save Madrid and hit the jackpot … and that removed Durruti from his sphere of influence … Catalonia.

3   Mary R. Habeck, Ronald Radosh, and Grigory Sevostianov, *Spain Betrayed: The Soviet Union in the Spanish Civil War* (New Haven: Yale University Press, 2001), 81–82.

Ascaso dead, García Oliver shoved into the quicksands of government, and Durruti dispatched to his doom in Madrid... That is how they exorcised the influence of the Nosotros group over the direction of the Revolution.[4]

In light of these communist intrigues and the matters raised by Antonio Ortiz, it should be emphasized that there is no doubt but that it was of great importance as far as the Soviets were concerned that someone like García Oliver be ousted from the Generalitat's Defense Department where he had oversight of the militias and military affairs. We might note that operations designed to push Durruti out of Aragon only started once García Oliver had accepted a ministerial post and thus relocated to Madrid on November 2.

César M. Lorenzo regards the lines above as "a slanderous innuendo suggesting that the CNT National Committee was in cahoots with the communists. Not to say in their service."[5]

We do not think that it is necessary to resort to conspiracy theories of that sort to explain the growing alignment between the CNT National Committee's choices and the dictates of Soviet diplomacy. One has only to pay careful attention to the facts and take the precise measure of the huge problem that lingering radical options within the anarcho-syndicalist organization posed for all reformists (and the CNT National Committee has to be counted in that camp). Keep in mind here that, on the evening of November 4, Durruti had just delivered a violent speech over Radio Barcelona that was a reminder of the relevance of those options,[6] the emphatic refusal by the militia members to see themselves treated like soldiers and a barely veiled threat to come down to Barcelona to demand an accounting from the sundry bureaucracies jockeying to resurrect republican institutions and the capitalist economy. The only chance of giving such options a first-class funeral was to induce the highest-profiled representative of the radical faction, namely, García Oliver, to join the reformist Spanish

4   Letter to García Oliver, undated, as cited in Gallardo Romero and Márquez Rodríguez, *Ortiz, general sin dios ni amo*, 363.
5   Letter to the authors, December 21, 2005.
6   That speech is reproduced in Morales and Ortega, *El lenguaje de los hechos*, 124–25, the version reported in *Cultura y Acción* on November 7, which undoubtedly comes closer to the original than the remarkably censored version carried by *Solidaridad Obrera* on November 5.

government. Furthermore, the latter was to set out in his *Eco de los pasos* all of the ingredients affording us an insight into the sort of stew being cooked up thereafter in the ministries and high commands, albeit that he painstakingly avoids mentioning the extent to which he himself fell for the charms of the *tovaritchi*.

To complete the picture, it should be remembered that the Soviets, if we are to believe the same document, reprinted by Habeck, Radosh, and Sevostianov, were hell-bent on unleashing a massive attack on Zaragoza ... on November 14, which is to say, just as soon as Durruti's forces had left for Madrid!

{52}
PAGE 142

Antoine tells us that Durruti had set off for Madrid and then that he was killed there. Let us look again at the anarchist column's departure for the besieged capital.

In his book, José Mira relates:

> Durruti asked us all as a matter of urgency to muster 1,500 militia members prepared to give their lives without hesitation.
>
> We immediately put this request to the two *agrupaciones* that had fought to such effect in Siétamo.
>
> The latter were the 1st and the 8th *agrupaciones*, and the 44th, 48th and 52nd *centurias*. Those forces were led by Liberto Roig [Ros] and myself. [...]
>
> By 9 o'clock in the morning, the relief reached the Calabazares Altos y Bajos and deployed cautiously and quickly. Weapons, blankets and warm clothing were issued to the new fighters who had just arrived; [...]
>
> By 1 o'clock that afternoon, we were all in the Plaza Mayor in Bujaraloz. The artillery was already on its way to Lérida and everyone was singing and waving red and black flags.[7]

7   Mira, *Los guerrilleros confederales*, 141–43.

To these 1,300 men, another one or two hundred men joined them en route, including Bonilla's "Asturias" battalion. Young Pina resident Jesús Salillas Artigas's *centuria* (he had signed on with the Durruti Column on August 24) was to set off with them.

Mathieu Corman registered the presence of International Group members in the capital city. They made up a machine-gun detachment: "Ramón's detachment includes the surviving members of Louis Berthomieu's International Group. It was posted to the Puente de los franceses."[8]

Corman monitors, day after day, some of the fighters from this group, including some Germans and an Italian whose dauntlessness greatly impressed him. After a few days of extremely tough fighting in which two International Brigades were bloodied for the first time, the 860 surviving members from the Durruti Column (out of 1,700 fighters, according to Mira) were to be relieved on November 20, the very day that their general delegate perished. They were to stay in Madrid until January 8, 1937, on which date Mira and Manzana returned to Aragon to overhaul the one-time column, now the 26th Division. But, as Mira tells us, they faced great problems: "several comrades of great caliber opted to quit rather than embrace what they looked upon as nonsensical [militarization]."[9]

According to the minutes of the meetings of CNT committees in Barcelona from late November, a sort of a mutiny erupted among the demoralized survivors of the fighting in Madrid who insisted that Durruti had been murdered. At the November 26 meeting of the Regional Committee, this related to:

> some individuals from the Durruti Column who, in spite of everything, refused to listen to anyone or pay any heed to the damage they were doing to the Organization, abandoned the Madrid front. At first, the understanding was that they were not to set foot in Catalonia, and then Ruano was sent for, briefed as to what needed doing [and] invested with wide-ranging powers to compel them to rejoin the front lines, like it or not, [so] that the matter might be resolved.[10]

8   Corman, "Salud camarada!," 202.
9   Mira, *Los guerrilleros confederales*, 194–95.
10   IISH, CNT, 94 D1.

The minutes of the December 2 meeting tell us that those in attendance (the CNT local committee, the Libertarian Youth, and other anarchist groups) were to discuss:

> the deeds and actions of some persons from the Durruti Column who have cravenly abandoned the Madrid front, a move due (according to them) to their having been unfavorably treated here and their intention to hold an assembly to justify their position. [...] Some reckon that they should return to the Aragon front; others think that in order to salvage their honor, which has been slightly besmirched by their actions, they should return to Madrid again; and a few die-hards, luckily few in number, are letting off steam here in immoral activities. The discussion of this matter became heated, with nearly everybody having his say, and opinions differed and the following proposal has been aired: that disciplinary companies be formed to force the undesirables, the traitors, and the cowards to return to the firing lines on the front. Compañeros are to be stationed in the rear guard to monitor them and, should they offend, to punish them severely.[11]

{53}
PAGE 142

The circumstances of Durruti's death are obscure, and to this day no historian has been able to untangle them. Some people may well know the truth or think they do, but they are still keeping it to themselves. The years to come may well bring us some telling testimonies, which will nevertheless have the drawback of being, at best, hearsay evidence.

For a start, let us keep in mind what has been pretty much established, with minor variations depending on the witness concerned.

Durruti arrived in Madrid on November 14, and his men the following morning at around 9:00. They were posted to the front from 2:00 a.m. on November 16.

11   IISH, CNT, 85 C1.

The next two days—November 17 and 18—passed amid ferocious fighting in the University City where the Durruti Column's men were not relieved. On the 18th they were decimated, with no more than four hundred combatants left. At the end of the day, Durruti spoke to José Miaja and Vicente Rojo (chairman of the Madrid Defense Junta and his chief of staff, respectively) at the Ministry of War to arrange to have his men relieved. Miaja and Rojo asked him to hold out for one more day. At around 8:00 p.m. Durruti left the ministry and made his way to his headquarters where he had a word with Eduardo Val, secretary of the CNT Defense Committee in Madrid, about militarization of the militias and communist intrigues designed to capture control of the situation in Madrid. They mentioned a meeting of militants scheduled to deal with the matter the following day, the 19th, around 4:00 p.m. Shortly after this, Cipriano Mera, head of a Madrid anarcho-syndicalist column, arrived. He and Durruti arranged to meet up at 6:00 a.m. the following day at the Durruti Column's HQ in order to set about the capture of the Clinical Hospital, a strategically significant building.

Throughout the morning and until around noon, Mera and Durruti monitored operations, which were such as would allow them to seize control of only part of the Clinic building. Durruti then went to his HQ and it was there that Antonio Bonilla, general delegate of the armored unit, turned up shortly afterward bringing him the latest news about the Clinic where some militia members had been cut off from the rear:

It was 13.00 hours on November 19 when I made up my mind to go and see Durruti to fill him in on what had happened. Lorente drove the car and a very brave Catalan carpenter, Miguel Doga, went with me. When we arrived at the barracks, we saw Durruti's "Packard," which had the engine running, and he was about to leave with Manzana. I briefed him on what was going on and he [Durruti] decided to go and see for himself. I told Julio Graves (his driver) to follow our car, because we had to avoid passing through areas swept by gunfire, and that is just what he did. Manzana, as ever, had his *naranjero* slung over his shoulder and a sling dangling from his neck, and there he would rest his right hand from time to time as he had sustained a finger wound a few weeks previously. Seemingly, Durruti was traveling unarmed, but as usual, he had a Colt .45 under his leather jacket. Their car followed us until we reached some chalets held by our reduced forces. So their car pulled up and we did likewise, twenty meters ahead of it.

Durruti got out to say something to a few militia members who were there taking a bit of the sun, in the lee of a wall. That area was not swept by gunfire. It was there that Durruti was mortally wounded and that the revolution met with the toughest, unimaginable setback.

We were in the other car, some twenty meters further on, and we sat there for three of four minutes. As Durruti climbed back into his car we took off and, glancing behind to make sure they were following us, we saw the "Packard" make a U-turn and accelerate away. I stepped out of the car and asked the youngsters what had happened. They replied that somebody had been hit. I asked them if they knew who they had been speaking with and they answered that they did not. I told Lorente that we had to head back immediately. That was at 14.30 hours.[12]

Durruti's wounded body was taken to the Hotel Ritz, which was being used as the column's hospital facility, and he was immediately rushed into the operating theater where doctors Santamaría and Martínez Fraile rendered first aid. Scared of embarking upon a risky procedure and botching it, they called in an experienced surgeon, Bastos Ansart, who noted the seriousness of the wound and gave his opinion that it would inevitably claim the wounded man's life. So the doctors made no attempt to operate. Durruti then entered upon a lingering death, which claimed him at around 4 o'clock on the following morning.

In the meantime, Bonilla arrived at column HQ:

Manzana greeted me. I asked him where Durruti was and he told me that he was on his way to a National Committee meeting. My response to him was that this was a lie, since the CNT National Committee wasn't in Madrid. His face changed color and he told me that his presence in the column was down to Durruti and to the rest of us, and that if we had lost confidence in him, he would go.

12   Interview given to Pedro Costa Musté for the magazine *Posible*, no. 80 (July 22–28, 1976), quoted in Paz, *Durruti en la revolución española*, 692.

"You lied to me," I told him, "but I am holding you responsible for whatever may have happened, and I urge you to tell me everything some other time."

I had to get back to my men. At 5 o'clock the next morning compañero Mora arrived by motorcycle to tell me of Durruti's death.[13]

We shall not delve at this point into the detail of the various versions of Durruti's death for they are replete with minutiae, most of them fantasy and usually contradictory. Not one of them really stands up to scrutiny, even though Bonilla's is undoubtedly the one that comes closest to the truth, according to Joan Llarch, who has written an entire book on the subject.

All the same, just for the record, we shall briefly summarize the main versions in circulation.

First of all, Manzana's, as reported by Cipriano Mera in his memoirs, published in 1976.[14] At about 5:00 p.m., Mera was in the company of Eduardo Val at the Defense Committee when Manzana turned up and told him the circumstances in which Durruti had been wounded: there had been five of them in the car, Durruti and two couriers, Yoldi and himself. On arrival within range of the Clinic, a bullet fired by the Francoists from a building they controlled, hit Durruti. Having confided in Mera, Manzana asked him to keep the secret lest it damage the morale of the troops. This version forms the basis of the one that the CNT was to elaborate as an official version. And it was to be endorsed by Ricardo Sanz who on November 20 was appointed by the National Committee (in the presence of García Oliver, Mera, and Montseny) to take over from Durruti in Madrid, while Manzana would shortly be dispatched to Aragon to take charge of the remainder of the column, which at that point was seething over the militarization decrees that a majority of the militia members had rejected and because of the belief that Durruti had been killed by the communists.

Regarding the mind-set among the militia members, we can add to our file the evidence of a Swiss militiaman, Edi Gmür, a member of the International Group:

---

13   Ibid., 675.

14   Cipriano Mera Sanz, *Guerra, exilio y cárcel de un anarcosindicalista* (Barcelona and Valencia: CGT-CNT-FSS-Malatesta-Hormiga Roja, 2006).

Moses answered: "The communists want to take power in Spain. But they can only succeed when we anarchists have been annihilated. Yes, they would be delighted if we were to come to some misfortune! But they are mistaken, these blackguards." "There are also blackguards in the anarchist ranks too," exclaimed the Estonian, who was a communist himself. Bortz chose a side: "You have no say. Go join the Brigades in Madrid if you're not happy here!" Moses grumbled: "All communists need killing, for they have murdered our Durruti!" At which I couldn't control myself and roared: "Gang of bastards!" In the end, the political commissar showed up and restored order. All the same, I was furious and depressed. That evening I asked Henrique if it was true that our guys had murdered Durruti. "You can count on it that it was the communists who killed him," he answered. And from his pocket he took a photograph of the murdered Durruti. The naked torso clearly showed the entry point of a bullet aimed straight at his heart. I was very depressed. "Politics!" added Henrique.[15]

Argentinean journalist José Gabriel says much along the same lines:

In Madrid, once the rebels, having regained their strength, advanced through Extremadura, Durruti's presence was demanded so that he might raise a mighty army in a week; but the socialist-communist republican government of Largo Caballero turned a deaf ear to that clamor, even as the Catalan Generalitat, which was of the same political hue, kept the army of the FAI's *caudillo* without weapons, the aim being, on both their parts, to discredit them both.

[…] Nevertheless they all [the unofficial versions of Durruti's death] revealed that the people were not swallowing the official line, any more than they believed it when the Russian consul in Barcelona put in an appearance at the funeral. The fact is that Durruti, shot right through the heart, was murdered by General Kléber's international column, a force "specializing in mopping up the rear guard" (as it unabashedly proclaimed itself), introduced to the Centre front by the republicans and socialist-communists

15   Gmür and Minnig, *Pour le bien de la révolution*, 75–76.

in order to monitor the Spanish people as it defended itself against the rebels. By murdering him, the socialist-communist Republic was dealing a mighty blow on its own behalf and on behalf of England, France, and Russia, to the Spanish working people. Which is not, of course, the truth formally acknowledged by the CNT and the FAI; but officially, circumstances have extracted from the CNT and FAI leadership concessions that not all members of those bodies approve of, as revealed by, among other things, the emergence of the dissident group the 'Friends of Durruti.' With time, we shall see precisely and from the victimizers' own mouths these truths confessed, indeed proclaimed, and many others with them.[16]

Subsequent events have proved him wrong there.

Back now to Sanz who, while on his way to Madrid, stopped off in Valencia on November 21 and there briefly bumped into Manzana who told him: "'Don't go to Madrid: they're going to kill you the way they did him'—he told me as he gestured at Durruti's remains [in transit to Barcelona]."[17]

Not taking the time to press him for a more complete explanation, Sanz arrived in Madrid on the evening of November 23 or 24 and, after formally carrying out a quick on-site investigation (actually he appears not to have questioned any of the direct witnesses), he announced that Durruti had been killed by a bullet fired from the Clinical Hospital a thousand meters away; he stated that there had been seven people in the car—Durruti, Manzana, Yoldi, Graves, a mechanic, and a two-man escort. For around thirty-five years this was the only version of events that was acceptable, even though Sanz was later to come up with a quite different story (see below).

When historians or writers such as Martínez Bande, Enzensberger, or Joan Llarch reexamined the matter, the thesis of an accident caused by Durruti himself came gradually to supplant the notion of a Francoist gunshot because of the improbability of the latter. And so, to

16   Gabriel, *La vida y la muerte en Aragón*, 165–67.

17   Ricardo Sanz "La muerte de Durruti en la batalla de Madrid," in *Boletín de l'Amicale de la 26e Division*, No. 3 (November 20, 1991): 11; Gmür and Minnig *Pour le bien de la révolution*, 75–76; Gabriel, *La vida y la muerte en Aragón*, 165–67; Sanz, "La muerte de Durruti en la batalla de Madrid," 11.

some extent, it has become the official version mark 2, and it would be articulated, for instance, by Diego Abad de Santillán in an interview given in 1977 to Freddy Gomez, Paolo Gobetti, and Paola Olivetti,[18] in which he contends that he had had the truth from Manzana's own lips, namely, that Durruti had fired the fatal shot himself when he had knocked the butt of his *naranjero* against the running-board of the car. Santillán added that Manzana had called him the very same day to apprise him of Durruti's death. But then, why was Manzana telling certain people that it was an enemy bullet and others that it had been an accidental discharge? And as we shall soon see, he even gave Sanz, if Sanz is to be believed, yet another version of what happened!

In order to delve a little deeper into this matter, we can now digest what García Oliver had to say in his 1978 memoirs *El Eco de los pasos*:

I saw Sergeant Manzana and Dr Santamaría, both of them forever by Durruti's side, and they came up to me [on November 22, on the occasion of Durruti's funeral in Barcelona]. [...] Basically whispering in my ear, Manzana told me:

"We'd like to speak with you. Just between us. [...]

"It relates to something about Durruti's death that we covered up. We allowed the story to circulate in Madrid that he was struck by a gunshot, which one might expect since there was so much shooting going on. But that is not true. Durruti did not die the way the rumor suggested. His death was an accident. As he was getting out of the car, he slipped, the butt of his *naranjero* struck the ground and the trigger was released, several shots ensuing, one of which hit him. There was nothing that could be done for him at the hospital. He died."

These details struck me as nonsense, but I kept my cool. [...] The fact of the matter is that the tale of a heroic death facing the enemy was already rampant. There was no way to deny it and there would have been no advantage in doing so. Furthermore, even had inquiries been made, we would never have found the truth, because, in the impassioned Hell that was Spain, everybody would have had his own version to tell, preferably whatever version might do the most moral damage to the anarcho-syndicalists. Our enemies within and without were

18   That interview appears in translation in *À contretemps*, no. 10.

even to go to the lengths of spreading around that the anarchists themselves had murdered him.

[…]

Then as now, some thirty-seven years on, that version of Durruti's death told to me by Sergeant Manzana and Dr. Santamaría strikes me as far-fetched. There was one point that did not fit in what was turning into a sort of a puzzle. What didn't make sense was that on "getting out of the car, he slipped, and the *naranjero* hit the ground, firing the shots."

The fact of the matter is that *naranjeros*, German submachine guns imported by the Civil Guard, were dangerous if they had a full magazine and were knocked against the ground. There had been many accidents.

But the fact is that I never, ever saw Durruti with a *naranjero*. At most, he used to carry a pistol in a holster at his waist. Nor did I ever see a photo showing him with a *naranjero* in his hands. And rest assured that Durruti was photographed in all sorts of poses, and that included while asleep. On the Aragon front he was forever on the move, with Dr Santamaría in tow, just in case he was to be wounded, and a photographer comrade to take his photograph. Given that Manzana and Dr. Santamaría were no lightweights, I always believed that the *naranjero* that went off and hit Durruti must have belonged to one of the comrades from his escort.[19]

These revelations carry over into another passage of his book:

For many years the story of the accidental discharge from the *naranjero* remained unknown. Then, with the passage of time, there were a few, such as Santillán, who revealed it. But not me. I absolutely never acknowledged that version, for Durruti had never traveled around with a *naranjero* or any other weapon in his hand.[20]

From which belated admission we can deduce that García Oliver, in the days following Durruti's death, was told in confidence by Manzana that Durruti had fired the accidental gunshot and that he had not

19   García Oliver, *El Eco de los pasos*, 340–41.
20   Ibid., 529.

believed him … and that he never breathed a word of it to anyone. This last statement is not quite true, though, if we believe what Ortiz was to remind him of in a letter that he sent to him following the publication of his *Eco de los pasos*:

> Where we do not see eye to eye is about what you told me at Durruti's funeral […] that he had killed himself with the *naranjero* that went off on its own.[21]

But Ortiz seized the opportunity to go further:

> The bullet that killed Durruti ENTERED VIA THE SCAPULA AND EXITED UNDER THE NIPPLE ON THE SAME SIDE … which is to say, followed a downward trajectory moving forwards from behind…!
>   The jacket Durruti had been wearing is the best proof of what I am saying … so … why all the assurances and lies … !!??[22]

In an earlier letter to Antonio Téllez, Ortiz had raised the same question and answered it thus: "For reasons of state maybe?"[23]

As we can see, Ortiz had the same suspicions as García Oliver. In the book they wrote about Antonio Ortiz, Gallardo and Márquez have this to say:

> Among the contacts during this time in Paris, we should single out the visit he paid to Émilienne Morin [early 1939], Durruti's partner. […] But the important thing for Ortiz was getting sight of the jacket his friend and compañero (Durruti) had been wearing on the day of his death: "When I saw the jacket, it made me feel queasy, for, obviously, García Oliver's fairy-tale during the burial about the accident that cost Durruti his life didn't hold up … The bullet had entered from behind and one could see the clean hole in the jacket, whereas the larger hole in the front had left the tear characteristic of an exiting bullet."

21   Letter sent from Venezuela, undated but probably in 1979 and reprinted in Gallardo Romero and Márquez Rodríguez, *Ortiz, general sin dios ni amo*, 363.
22   Ibid.
23   Letter dated May 9, 1977, IISH, Téllez archive.

It was then that the notion that he was to entertain for the rest of his life first entered his head: Durruti had been killed and he pointed an accusing finger at Manzana, although he had no way of proving it: "The bullet that cost Durruti his life had entered the left scapula from above and had exited near the floating ribs. Now, an accidental gunshot might have followed a horizontal trajectory or upward trajectory, but never a downward one from behind."[24]

From which it follows that Garcia Oliver was hiding his true motives when he said that he had refused to put forward the thesis of an accident caused by Durruti himself, since that was the version he had put to Ortiz in Barcelona on 22 November. We can only suppose that he was no stranger to the game of differently nuanced confidences—he did the same with Émilienne Morin—depending on whether one was or was not a member of the inner circle of initiates; broadly speaking, as far as the mass of the membership was concerned, it was a hero's death, cut down by an enemy bullet, whereas for members of the circle of militants close to office, it was Durruti who had executed himself unaided, and, for the militants at the very top, well used to all manner of intrigues, it was something else again ... namely, that it was Manzana that had released the gunshot, as Bonilla would disclose later on:

> The bullet that mortally wounded Durruti came from the *naran-jero* that Manzana carried slung over his shoulder. Just as they were preparing to get back in the car to follow us, Manzana opened the door to allow Durruti access to his seat [...]. The *naranjero* slid off his shoulder, the butt striking the car's runningboard, the submachine gun went off by itself and wounded Durruti. [...] I have always kept quiet about the issue of whether the gunshot was accidental or not, for I meant to check it out with Manzana myself, but I never managed to set eyes on him again over the past forty years.[25]

24 Interview with Ortiz on July 26, 1995, in Gallardo Romero and Márquez Rodríguez, *Ortiz, general sin dios ni amo*, 287–88.

25 *Posible*, no. 80, reprinted in Edmundo Marculeta, *Las seis muertes de Durruti* (Barcelona: self-published, 1984), 43–44.

To be more precise on this score, we can take note of some correspondence with the authors from Miguel Amorós on November 23, 2005:

> [Regarding Bonilla's version] I have a confidential document from him. It is a communication passed to me by Piqueras, who is now deceased, entitled "Work toward a get-together of veteran militants, due to take place from November 21 to 26, 1977 in Barcelona." As to Durruti's death, it states: "[Bonilla first rehearses his description of events]. In edition No. 80 of the review *Posible* [...] I state how he was wounded, but three voices spoke up expressing surprise that I should have maintained a forty-year silence regarding the death. Let those three voices, one being that of his French partner, Émilienne, hear this: I have kept quiet these forty years because I was hunting for Manzana in order to kill him. And now, to conclude, I invite those who may have written on the basis of a mistaken version of that death to rectify things no matter what the cost. Because we must not lie about it."

As we can see, the noose is tightening on Manzana. To boost such suspicions somewhat more, we can produce testimony passed to us by César M. Lorenzo.

According to the testimony of one former Durruti Column militian, whose name we now reveal as José Mariño Carballada, Durruti was indeed accompanied only by Manzana and his driver, Graves. Another car, carrying this witness as well as some well-known militants such as Liberto Ros and others, had parked up a little further on, between fifty and two-hundred meters further on, but out of sight of Durruti. A third car carrying, among others, Miguel Yoldi was situated even farther away. On hearing a crack coming from Durruti's location, though the area was calm, the occupants of both these cars arrived on the scene where they found a dumbfounded Manzana who explained that he had just accidentally killed Durruti. According to César M. Lorenzo, who collected the evidence of Liberto Ros and José Mariño, Julio Graves and Manzana had already placed Durruti's body back in the car. Bearing out what Liberto Ros had said, Mariño reiterated to César M. Lorenzo what Manzana had confided to them:

As he opened the door so that his boss could slide into the car, the *naranjero*-type submachine gun he was carrying over his left shoulder knocked against the pavement, releasing a bullet that struck the forward leaning Durruti near the heart.[26]

The witnesses had to think on their feet before carrying away Durruti's body, for he was not dead yet and it was in their haste that the contention about an enemy bullet fired from the Clinic was cobbled together. With the exception of Mariño, they believed Manzana, it seems (certainly Liberto Ros did, as he made the same disclosures to César M. Lorenzo long ago, yet still looked upon Manzana as "decent sort") because of his great closeness to Durruti, especially after the taking of the Atarazanas barracks.

On this point, however, Ortiz

> is emphatic that it is a historical mistake to regard Sergeant Manzana as one of those who sided against the rebel officers. "During a search of the Atarazanas, Manzana was discovered locked inside a cell and was removed to POUM headquarters where Valeriano Gordo later went to secure his release."[27]

Yet, even though the witnesses to Durruti's death had their doubts, they reckoned that the truth could not be told, first of all because Manzana would have been executed and then because anarchists could not make public the deplorable circumstances in which their hero had met his end.

Furthermore, César M. Lorenzo remembered a passage in a text written by his father, Horacio Prieto:

> They said his death was down to a *"paco"* [sniper], one of the many operating in the area; it was also said that his right-hand man, Manzana, was the one who had shot him with a pistol, albeit accidentally; but wagging tongues also said that he had been killed by his very own anarchist friends, because Durruti was gradually coming around to the idea of friendly relations and an arrangement with the communists. There is every chance that it was the *pacos* who killed him [...] whether or not they were aware of who it was they were killing; it might have been the accidental discharge from the gun of Sergeant Manzana who was a pro; but if he did

---

26   César M. Lorenzo, book in preparation, chapter entitled "Tantarantana."
27   Gallardo Romero and Márquez Rodríguez, *Ortiz, general sin dios ni amo*, 101.

it deliberately, who knows what his motives were? And if it was not the handiwork of the *pacos* or some accidental discharge from Manzana's gun that killed him, those who might have hatched a plan to kill Durruti could hardly have been anyone other than people with an interest in the International Brigades' not being overshadowed by the "Durruti" myth. Later on, these people attempted to kidnap Miguel Yoldi, the way they did others whom they eliminated. It is my firm belief that no way was it anarchists who killed Durruti; that he was deliberately killed by someone, or was a random victim. He was too greatly admired and loved by all for anarchists to have carried out such a nonsensical crime.[28]

After forwarding this extract to us, César M. Lorenzo made this additional observation: "What I find striking now is the threefold repetition of the reference to Manzana's gun."[29]

In exile in France in the 1940s, Félix Arcal, a militant from the Bujaraloz CNT and an active member of the CNT-UGT Revolutionary Committee, often spoke of the circumstances of Buenaventura Durruti's death with a close friend (whom we met in 2009). He didn't hesitate to emphatically accuse Manzana who—according to him—had supposedly been acting at the behest of the communists. And he added that every anarchist he knew back in 1936 thought the same thing.

Just after the 1972 publication in France of the first edition of his book *Durruti, le peuple en armes*, Diego Camacho (aka Abel Paz) returned, in a letter to García Oliver dated September 24, 1972, to his presentation of Buenaventura's death:

> My main concern has been to disentangle those versions of Stalinist derivation alleging that Durruti had been murdered by his own *compañeros*. I think I have managed to do that. Now the "mystery" of his death has yet to be sorted out. I have asked Santillán and other *compañeros* on several occasions, but have had no clear answers. [...] Now Germinal Gracia [a member of the "Los Quijotes del Ideal" group, who used the *nom de plume* Víctor García] has published a critique of my book. He is happy with everything

28   Prieto, *Utopistas*, 123.
29   Letter to the authors, August 28, 2004.

except the matter of the death because he reckons that I am betraying History by offering the official version. He says that both you and Santillán provided him with the accident story, but that he does not believe it. He wonders if the theory of an accidental discharge by Manzana might not be closer to the truth. […] Up until now, nobody had mentioned that Manzana hypothesis to me. But I will confess that in the course of my research I have come to be dubious about him. Well, I have looked into the sergeant's record and found out that after Durruti's death the FAI's PC [Peninsular Committee] (Escorza) took him on as a military expert or something of the sort. This startled me because it amounted to making the Stalinists' task easier … I stopped at that point and upheld the official thesis. Was I wrong to do so? I don't think so.[30]

To our knowledge, in all the texts published on the subject, the possible role Manzana played in Durruti's death was first explored in 1972. Reading other letters exchanged between Camacho and García Oliver—between 1970 and 1979, during the years when each of them was drafting his book—we note that the latter was never really willing to help Camacho in his investigation; moreover, he failed to answer Diego as to the circumstances of Durruti's death. Not that that would stop him from suggesting in his autobiography, which came out in 1978, that Manzana might well have accidentally discharged his weapon and thus gone along with Víctor García's version.…

So the most serious leads appear to point to Manzana. But a number of questions then arise: why would he have done this? And on whose behalf? One hypothesis is worth a mention, albeit that it is put forward here only with the utmost caution, for want of sufficient evidence to back it up.

In his memoirs, García Oliver contends that at a meeting of the Supreme Council of War held on November 14, Largo Caballero agreed, at García Oliver's suggestion, to appoint Durruti to head the Madrid Defense Junta as a replacement for Miaja (contingent upon Caballero's precondition that that decision be kept secret for eight days).[31]

30   Diego Camacho correspondence, deposited with the Centre Ascaso-Durruti in Montpellier. Letter reproduced in *Balance: Cuaderno de historia, no. 38* (2014), special issue: *Correspondencia entre Diego Camacho ("Abel Paz") y Juan García Oliver*, 31.

31   García Oliver, *El eco de los pasos*, 326–27. See the extract presented as

If we believe García Oliver on this score and, above all, if we keep in mind that no one on that Council had a very high opinion of Durruti's capabilities, whether in matters military or matters political, we might wonder if such an agreement might not have served as a deadly bait for Durruti. Miaja, who rather prided himself on his position and to some extent regarded himself as Spain's savior (which was why Caballero wanted to dismiss him and was looking around for a replacement) was certainly not going to let himself be dropped so easily. So the initiative might have been left up to him when it came to deciding, in this instance, when and how Durruti would be gotten rid of.

Why not, then, think that Manzana might have been acting at the behest of his superiors, General Miaja and Lieutenant-Colonel Rojo, like the good soldier that he was (remember that he had seen action in the Rif, had been decorated several times, and that all his service records in the army sang his praises)? The hypothesis has already been floated that he was acting at the behest of his military superiors in the Francoist camp,[32] but has any consideration been given to the possibility that he might have been obeying his superiors on the loyalist side?

Consequently, that hypothesis should be construed as a variation on the trail leading to the communists, which was the one most favored among the militia members, as it is plain to see that at the time Miaja and Rojo were largely controlled by the communists and Soviet agents who would soon exploit that ascendancy to the full by placing their people in key positions in the army that was in the throes of being overhauled. If we add to this the fact that Miaja and Rojo had, prior to July 19, 1936, been members of the UME (Unión Militar Española [Spanish Services Union])—a secret organization within the army, whose mission was "throwing up, at the opportune moment, a dike capable of protecting Spain from the Communist tide"[33]—and that the communists knew it, and that was a superb means of their bringing pressure to bear, we can appreciate the extent to which it was crucial for them that the wolf Durruti not be admitted to the republican fold.

Appendix I below.

32 See *El Periódico de Cataluña*, November 24, 2002.

33 Francoist document quoted by Burnett Bolloten, *The Spanish Revolution: The Left and the Struggle for Power during the Civil War* (Chapel Hill: University of North Carolina Press, 1979), 275. It should be pointed out that this accusation is a controversial one: see Julio Aróstegui and Jesús A. Martínez, *La Junta de Defensa de Madrid* (Madrid: Comunidad de Madrid, 1984), 68, 69.

If that hypothesis could be substantiated it would explain why Voline, who was in charge of the editing of the newspaper *L'Espagne antifasciste*, would receive in Paris, on November 21, the following telegram from Barcelona:

Durruti murdered by communist gang on the Madrid front.

And also why, within hours, he also received this rebuttal:

Ignore previous telegram in order to preserve unity of action.[34]

We can take it for granted that the initial reports led the upper echelons of the CNT to the communist trail and that as far as they were concerned such a provocation from their worst enemies was not one to let slide but that further inquiries persuaded them that the trail went beyond that and incriminated Miaja and the entire high command and, further, the government as a whole. At which point, the choice now was between out-and-out confrontation with the entire republican camp ... or letting the matter drop.

Again in the context of that hypothesis, we can try to imagine how the trap closed in around Durruti: several military commanders, Mera for one, noted as early as November 18 that the enemy's forces seemed to have run out of steam and were throwing everything they had into one last attempt to capture Madrid and thereby rack up a significant psychological success and decisive diplomatic victory, as many countries were simply waiting for that before recognizing Franco. When Durruti explained to the high command on the evening of the 18th that his men were spent, the answer he received was that there were no reserves available and he was asked to hold out for another twenty-four hours. We can assume that Miaja was waiting to see if the front would crumble—in which case they would gladly allow Durruti to take charge of the losing Defense Junta—or whether it would hold, in which case he was not going to be allowed to profit from such glorious resistance, and they would resort to anything to be rid of him. All of which may well have been anticipated by Largo Caballero when, the week before, he gave his blessing to this strange promotion for the renowned anarchist.

34   Evidence of his son Léo Voline, dating from 1985 and published in the *Bulletin du CIRA of Marseille*, no. 26–27, 73.

That said, they may very well have settled in advance on a "weak" version of this theory, namely that the purpose was to appoint Durruti to head a junta upon which all of the blame for the debacle could readily be pinned. That was, after all, the main purpose behind the relocation of Durruti and part of his column to the capital: to heap all the blame for the anticipated military setback onto his shoulders and thereby forever discredit the man, the militia members still digging in their heels over their opposition to militarization, and, beyond them, all the radical currents within the anarchist and anarcho-syndicalist movement.

Since tradition has it that, once the indictment has been read, the accused is allowed to have his say, we shall quote what Ricardo Sanz stated at a later date, in a text drafted in 1981 and published in 1991, in which he said that he bumped into Manzana in Barcelona, a year after Durruti's death to be sure, on the occasion of an exhibition put on as a tribute to Durruti. It was then that the former sergeant, who in the interim had been made captain commanding a unit based in Mataró, informed Sanz of the "real" circumstances of his leader's death:

> We climbed out of the car, Durruti and I; we took a few steps towards the forward posts and came upon three youngsters going in the opposite direction. Durruti asked them:
>
> "Where are you going, lads?"
>
> "To fetch some rifles, because we can't find any rifles to fight back with," they replied.
>
> "There are no rifles in the rear guard," Durruti answered. "There are up the line."
>
> "We'll find some," the youngsters persisted.
>
> "Get back to the trenches," Durruti ordered them.
>
> "We're going to look for weapons."
>
> At which Durruti made as if to draw his pistol. One of the youngsters, who was holding a short arm, fired at Durruti and the trio took off running. Durruti did not have time to draw his gun and I gathered up the wounded man and dragged him back to the car, with some difficulty, for I was injured myself at the time.[35]

35   Sanz, "La muerte de Durruti en la batalla de Madrid," 16.

We may legitimately have a few misgivings about this version of events from Manzana, not least because the attackers managed to get away from a crack shot like himself, wounded or not. Moreover, Ricardo Sanz adds: "I must have conveyed the impression that he had not dispelled my doubts about this belated 'confession' of his. We were left like divorced people are left for the remainder of their lives: wondering."[36]

Since we are talking about "wondering," we may also wonder why Ricardo Sanz, forty-five years on (or fifty-five if we go by the date of publication) is offering us this version, which utterly contradicts the one that he had previously always championed (and that he recounted in an interview with Joan Llarch as published in her 1973 book).[37]

By way of a temporary conclusion to this murky affair, we shall, in spite of their being slightly bombastic and empty rabble-rousing, quote these remarks by one informed observer:

> Even as they showered him with flattering remarks, the bourgeois component of the anti-fascist bloc tried cunningly to mount a counterrevolution by restoring the social and governmental status quo and through the reconstitution of the regular Army. It was then that Durruti bared his teeth and threatened the politicians that he, personally, and his front-line comrades with him, would go and put an end to their petty schemes and their dalliances with fascism.
>
> Freedom's enemies in Spain realized that they were dealing with an irreconcilable opponent who would always decline to play ball with the mighty of this world. Their talk was all of capitulation, militarization, diplomacy, strategy, capital, and politics. Durruti's response was revolution. All conversation was impossible. Unable either to break Durruti or to corrupt him, the counterrevolution murdered him.[38]

But before we leave you to pick up your reading where you left off, we must add that we should not, on foot of the clues set out earlier

36   Ibid.
37   Joan Llarch, *La muerte de Durruti* (Barcelona: Edicions 29, 1983).
38   André Prudhommeaux, *Ou va l'Espagne?* (Nîmes: Les Cahiers de Terre Libre, 1937), 41.

in this note, succumb to the temptation to explain everything away by invoking the unseen hand of the Soviets and the Spanish communists, if only on account of counterrevolutionary strategies that the socialists were no slouches in implementing, the best example being the partial control they managed to retain over the dreaded Military Intelligence Service (SIM), despite the communists' strong grip.

And nothing prevents us from believing that the intrigues designed to draw the anarchists into the government were largely instigated and overseen by the socialists, as they first showcased a Largo Caballero surrounded by the aura of some supposedly revolutionary regeneration....

And, finally, nothing prevents us either from thinking that a good part of the CNT and FAI apparatus had every interest in marginalizing individuals like Durruti, who, simply by existing and because of their strong symbolic powers conferred and guaranteed a degree of credibility on radical options looked on as continuing the July revolution—it's not for nothing that certain people will adopt the name Friends of Durruti in order to preserve that legacy and keep those options alive. Opposing them, and for complex reasons that it not for us to demonize on a whim, a good part of the CNT and FAI apparatuses opted to prioritize consensus with the other political forces making up the Popular Front. This progressively led to their racking up setbacks and compromises and even commitments, the most blatant of which were to bring participation in many repressive operations that would soon hit those among the worker and peasant militants who remained faithful to anarchism's principles and the struggle against state and capitalism.

{54}
PAGE 142

In the CNT's document dealing with the history of the 26th Division, we read:

By virtue of the official ordinances militarizing the militias from January 1937 onward, our column changed its name to the

"Durruti Division." The Aragon front continued to be organized into sectors, each one a division answerable to the overall front commander. With his staff, he coordinates the activities of the various sectors. The infantry of the erstwhile Durruti Column is organized into three 4-battalion regiments […].

The conversion was slow and difficult, for the reasons set out above, that is, resistance from most of the militia members to their being turned into soldiers and to the lack of personnel with sufficient military expertise to serve as military instructors.[39]

In order to resolve the command issue, headquarters allowed the soldiers to elect their officers, except for the battalion commanders who were chosen by the divisional commanders, who also picked all their own headquarters staff […]

In the most difficult times, when militia members who did not find militarization acceptable and were abandoning the front, the presence of forces from outside of the division had to be accepted, and some of these were from the Catalan Flying Column, with a total of one thousand men […]

The presence of forces from outside the division brought about something unprecedented: desertions to the enemy, including by erstwhile professional servicemen and soldiers of questionable loyalties.[40]

During the month of January 1937, phase one of the division's military organization, operational activity was virtually nil, since all of the effort was going into the technical training of the units. […] A few reconnaissance patrols did manage to strike deep into the enemy rear in the Villafranca-sector in Villamayor […] Technical direction was entrusted to the enthusiastic and clever international volunteer Karl Einstein, who worked loyally alongside the divisional commander.[41]

Carl Einstein was an art historian who had set aside his pen for a rifle. He arrived in Barcelona in August or September 1936, and his wife Lyda joined him there shortly afterward.

39   Anonyme, *La 26 División*, 42–43.
40   Ibid., 45–46.
41   Ibid., 51.

According to Dieter Nelles, both were members of the DAS.[42] They shared lodgings with Helmut and Dora Rüdiger. Carl signed on with the International Group as a military expert, and he saw active service on part of the front. He felt very close to Durruti, and over the airwaves of Radio CNT-FAI, after the Durruti's funeral, he delivered a speech that he'd written. In it he hailed the organization of the column in these terms:

> The column is not organized along military lines or in a bureaucratic way. It is an organic outgrowth from the trade union movement. It is a social-revolutionary body and not a flock. [...] We despise all war, but we understand it to be an instrument of revolution. We are not pacifists and we fight with gusto. War—that silly anachronism—is justified only by social revolution. [...]
>
> The comrades know that on this occasion they are fighting for the working class and not for the adversary, the capitalist minority. Appreciation of this fact means that they should all abide by a strict self-discipline. The militiamen does not obey: in concert with his compañeros he pursues the realization of his ideal, which is a social necessity. [...]
>
> The revolution requires of the column a discipline even stricter than any that militarization might impose. [...] I do not believe that generals or the military salute would inculcate in us an approach more consistent. In saying that, I am convinced that I am speaking the mind of Durruti and of the comrades.
>
> We do not renounce our old anti-militarism [...]. In the final analysis we are fighting against rebel generals. [...] Militarization [...] has always been a slick means of stunting the proletarian personality.[43]

42   See García, Nelles, Linse, and Piotrowski, *Antifascistas alemanes en Barcelona*, 409, 122.

43   Carl Einstein, *La Columna Durruti y otros artículos y entrevistas de la Guerra Civil española* (Barcelona: Mudito, 2006), 18–21.

{55}

PAGE 143

Since late November, fighters from a number of anarchist columns (the Durruti, Los Aguiluchos, the Ascaso, Tierra y Libertad) had been leaving the front en masse. Some, notably those from the Durruti Column, gathered in Barcelona to orchestrate the fight against militarization and were in continual liaison with members from No. 4 Agrupación and from the International Group back in Gelsa. The voices raised in protest were not solely in the anarchist ranks, for among the foreign volunteers serving in the POUM's Lenin Column the issue was also broached. On October 11, the militia members, gathered in assembly, declared that they would quit the front if forced to militarize. So a military conference was organized in Lérida to thrash out their position on the matter. After securing guarantees that militarization would not be imposed on their unit, the international volunteers set off back to the front. In late October however, militarization was finally imposed from that point onward: after that, the international column would withdraw from the front. The Bordiguists and Trotskyists, which is to say, the vast majority of the French militia members, headed home while others transferred to CNT units (Benjamin Péret being one case in point).[44]

In addition to anger, which was the prevailing mood among militia members, there was huge loss of morale. One of the leaders of the Ascaso Column, Cristóbal Aldabaldetrecu, referred to this at a meeting of the Regional Committee for Catalonia and column commanders on December 18, 1936:

> The impression given by the columns is actually more one of death than of life. [...] What ought to take only a few days drags on for many months [...] and above all, one is forced to retreat for want of munitions. This is the thing that has lowered spirits the most. Watching the corpses of cherished beings dropped. In the wake of a retreat, an advance, finding one's brother, one's friend, wounded or dead, and most often, all because of the higher ranks' incompetency. [...] Unless we really close ranks, our men

---

44   Édouard Sill, "Ni Franco, ni Staline. Les volontaires français de la révolution espagnole," dissertation, (Tours: Université François-Rabelais, 2006), 169–70.

are going to be used up and the "Asiatics" [the Russians] will take over all the strategic posts in order to wipe us out.[45]

In Pina, Manzana's firm hand, shown on January 6, had settled nothing. In his report to the CNT that month, the sergeant doesn't hide that the column's situation was dependent on

> an unhealthy state deriving from the performance of the compañero who was leading it [Ruano] and the issues raised by the militarization of our militias. [...]
>
> If to all that we add the impact among the compañeros of the death of our beloved comrade Durruti, we will have a better idea of the actual situation in which the column found itself—which led about 1,000 comrades, including high-caliber trade union personnel, to express a wish to turn back for Barcelona and to tender their resignations. [...]
>
> To put an end to this entire state of affairs, my first step was to relieve all of the personnel who had aided and abetted the previous War Committee in its nefarious efforts, so that compañeros coming to me with their requirements would not cross paths with the very same people who had been threatening them with their rifles just a few days before.[46]

Next, he toured the trenches to persuade the militia members of the need to militarize, but he was unable to stop the mass resignation of six hundred of them. All at once, he was forced to accept the 850 soldiers dispatched by the Defense Department; they belonged to Estat Català, a party with a dark reputation in the eyes of anarchists, in that its leaders had ferociously persecuted them during their brief term in power in Catalonia in 1933 and 1934. This did nothing to restore trust, especially as the incoming troops turned up well equipped, whereas the fighters had been sleeping on straw for the last six months and lacked even capes when on sentry duty.

On January 16, a new manifesto, drawn up by the recalictrant militia members in Gelsa was circulated through the units. It carried the endorsements of the same sections as its predecessor, including the

45   IISH, CNT, 85 C1.
46   IISH, CNT, 94E.

International Group, which included the Frenchmen Joseph Marin, Raoul Tarrou, Henri Lacroisille, aka Marseille, and Michel Espigulet from the CGT-SR, and people called Moneck Kresch and Blédine.[47] As well, there were signatures from the artillery batteries and the machine-gunner sections. The text reminded the reader that the Aragon front was still short of military hardware and that this was the reason behind the paralysis there. It posited that even if the columns were to militarize, the Madrid government would still not hand over arms to anarchists. Then there was a suggestion for a military structure suited to anarchist beliefs, based upon a single command and soldiers' councils. Reading the successive declarations, it was obvious that the militia members were doing their best to resuscitate the principle of consultation with the rank and file, which the CNT reckoned it could dispense with without too much trouble. And furthermore the authors of the declaration pointed out in passing: "We are not willing to travel any further along the course upon which the

47   Henri Lacroisille. Born in Paris on April 26, 1907, in 1926 he was a member of the CGT-SR-affiliated Amalgamated Construction Union (SUB), demolition section. In the summer of 1930 he was supposedly given a six-month prison sentence for "desertion" (?). In September 1936 he arrived in Spain as a volunteer. Initially he was a militiaman in the Durruti Column's International Group, then with the 26th Division's 120th Mixed Brigade, notably alongside Michel Espigulet. Essentially, he served on the Aragon front. On July 4, 1937, he and Espigulet were arrested for having bothered a Spaniard whom they suspected of being a fascist. Charged with unlawful possession of weapons, he was thrown in the Modelo prison. Henri Lacroisille supposedly returned to France as part of the *retirada* in February 1939. He died in April 1966.

Michel Espigulet, aka "Vidal." A CGT-SR member, he set off for Spain as a volunteer in the summer of 1936. On November 23, 1936, he joined the International Group of the Durruti Column on the front. A member of the CNT and the Iberian Libertarian Youth Federation (FIJL), after militarization he was seconded to the International Shock Battalion of the 120th Mixed Brigade of the 26th Division. At the beginning of July 1937, he was arrested with Henri Lacroisille, charged with unlawful possession of weapons and jailed in the Modelo. He was still an inmate on January 1, 1939.

"Espigulet, Michel" and "Lacroisille, Henri" in *Dictionnaire des militants anarchistes*, militants-anarchistes.info/, as well as François Godicheau, "Répression et ordre public en Catalogne pendant la guerre civile (1936–1939)" (unpublished doctoral thesis, Paris, EHESS, 2001), Annexes, "Liste des 'prisonniers antifascists.'"

A todos los Compañeros : A las Columnas Confederales

El problema de la militarización

Ante la conminación de los Comités Confederales para establecer la militarización en las Columnas del frente de Aragón. Después de escuchadas las razones de éstos y visto el panorama del país, hemos de hacer las siguientes consideraciones en nombre de la totalidad de las centurias de la Columna Durruti. La eficiencia de las centurias no tendrá más importancia combativa, por cuanto los factores que intervienen en el frente aragonés y su estancamiento no son de aspecto de buena o mala organización, de éste u otro sistema, sino de un problema de cantidad y calidad de material bélico, que entendemos que nadie lo ignora. De no haber sido así, hace tiempo que nosotros hubiéramos clamado y en lugar de ser los compañeros de la retaguardia que de manera expresa se apresuran a imponérnoslo, nosotros mismos lo hubiéramos reclamado con la misma fuerza como hemos insistido sobre determinados aspectos que no fuimos asistidos, por aquellas razones que no sabemos su alcance.

De los problemas de la vanguardia no queremos conceder el título de poseerlos a quienes sean ajenos a ellos. No queremos decir con esto que algunas reformas se han de establecer y que ponemos a consideración de la Organización Confederal y Específica. Nosotros entendemos que de su aceptación se resuelven problemas de escrupulosa conciencia de anarquistas y de organización bélica. Podemos afirmar, para acabar con este respecto, que hay columnas militarizadas en el frente aragonés que, si las comparamos a las de organización popular, los resultados se han visto, no queriendo descender a narrar hechos por demasiado enojosos e imprudentes.

Las razones que nos ponen los Comités se enfrentan con solo mirar a los seis meses en curso. Al parecer, el Gobierno condiciona la entrega de material en abundancia si nos militarizamos. No queremos profundizar la cuestión. Hasta hoy, los compañeros de retaguardia, en lo que respecta al material bélico lo han confiado al esfuerzo ajeno: Francia, Rusia y hoy el Gobierno de Madrid. ¿La realidad cuál es? Esto basta para hacernos la firme resolución que sólo nuestro esfuerzo cuenta, que allí donde los compañeros han intensificado con el trabajo la fabricación de material de guerra, y la pasión, es donde podemos contar con algo y nos salvan del peligro. El problema es: ¡Material de guerra! ¡Material de guerra! Lo hemos de construir nosotros con nuestro sudor e iniciativa, venciendo dificultades, perseverando. Al decir de los mismos Comités, no pueden asegurar que ni aun militarizándonos el Gobierno de Madrid nos dará dicho material. Siendo así la transgresión que hacemos de nuestras ideas es tan solo compensada con una vana promesa.

No queremos ahondar más en el camino donde la Organización Confederal se ha comprometido en el mundo de las transgresiones sindicales, políticas y, hoy, de carácter militar, poniendo en pugna nuestra conciencia de anarquistas. Los que partimos para el frente hacia los últimos de Julio, en los compañeros de la retaguardia depositamos ese acerbo de la Organización Confederal, conjunto de anhelos revolucionarios, sacrificios y esperanzas de tantos caídos en la lucha contra el capitalismo. Hoy estos compañeros, al decir de ellos, la militarización es una fatalidad que tenemos que aceptar si no queremos que todo se pierda y que la historia nos juzgue agriamente. A este juicio nos atenemos nosotros y para salvar esta responsabilidad hacemos esta consideraciones ante las generaciones futuras y os ofrecemos el presente proyecto de organización que, de ser aceptado, salvará de este naufragio gran parte de las esencias de nuestras ideas.

DIRECCION Y ESPECIALIDADES DE COMPAÑIAS, REGIMIENTOS, DIVISIONES Y CONSTITUCION DEL MANDO UNICO COLECTIVO DEL FRENTE ARAGONES.

Nosotros, como militantes, proponemos a la organización y a las Columnas Confederales el presente esquema, que creemos se amolda a nuestros pensamientos anarquistas:

Las compañías se constituirán en la forma siguiente:

4 escuadras de 12 hombres = 48, los cuales componen una sección.

4 secciones de 48 hombres = 192, los cuales componen una compañía.

Un batallón se compondrá de 3 compañías de infantería y una de especialidades.

Una compañía de especialidades (ametralladoras, morteros y fusil ametrallador) estará formada por 84 hombres, que juntos con las tres de infantería darán un total de 660 hombres, o una batallón.

Un regimiento estará formado por 3 batallones, que dan un total de 1.980 hombres.

Una brigada se compondrá de 2 regimientos de Infantería, Caballería, Artillería y servicios especializados.

Una división se compondrá de 2 brigadas.

Todas estas unidades serán mandadas por técnicos salidos de las escuelas especiales de guerra. Tendremos el cuidado de que estos cuadros del frente aragonés estén compuestos, en lo posible, por elementos de las escuelas especiales de guerra auspiciadas por las Juventudes Libertarias. En cada una de estas unidades se nombrará un delegado político, nombrado por los componentes de dichas unidades, y que tendrá potestad en la marcha moral y administrativa, dejando para el técnico su peculiar actividad.

No se aceptará ningún distintivo que determine las diferentes posiciones de cada uno de ellos. El técnico podrá ser depuesto a petición de las unidades, depositando las quejas en un tribunal de mando de compañía, batallón, etcétera.

Se formarán Comités de Batallón por delegados de Compañía, de División por los de Regimiento y Comité del mando único del frente aragonés por delegado de las Divisiones.

Teniendo esta garantía de representación desde el mando único del Estado Mayor del frente aragonés hasta la Compañía, las órdenes para realizar operaciones no podrán ser discutidas. Se constituyen tribunales para fallar las faltas de transgresión a la disciplina, si son leves en el seno de la Compañía y si fueren graves en la División. Dichos tribunales estarán compuestos por los delegados políticos. El grado de sanción de dichas faltas se establecerá por normas de la más elevada justicia, aminorando siempre su extrema gravedad.

Por la Columna Durruti:
LA 4.ª AGRUPACION DE GELSA.
GRUPO ACCION Y ALEGRIA.
GRUPO INTERNACIONAL.
BATERIAS DE ARTILLERIA.
SECCIONES DE AMETRALLADORAS Y DEMAS CENTURIAS.

GELSA, 16 de enero de 1937.

Reproduction of the Gelsa Group's challenge to militarization, dated January 16, 1937

Confederation has embarked, a road paved with trade union, political, and now military faux pas."[48]

But most of the leadership of the CNT, FAI, and Libertarian Youth abided by the "circumstantialist" policy of collaborating with the state and with Stalin's emissaries, no doubt thinking that they

48 IISH, FAI, 1.

were strong enough to defy the booby traps and intrigues littering the political swamp. Reading the minutes of the January 27, 1937, meeting of the Catalonian Regional Committee, we find the Confederation growing more and more exasperated, primarily with its own membership:

> "Any column failing to comply will receive neither munitions nor food of any kind; [...] any individual returning from the front shall not be able to return to his employment unless he has lawful discharge papers from the front."[49]

The height of contempt for libertarian principles came, in the eyes of some, when they learned of a speech given by García Oliver at the beginning of January, to the officers of the People's War School, which he headed in Barcelona:

> You must abide by an iron discipline and enforce it on your soldiers who [...] cease to be your comrades once they come on board the military machine of our army."[50]

Despite a number of meetings of officials and delegates in Barcelona and on the front, no agreement was reached, and the militia members, without abandoning either their posts or their weapons, dug their heels in, while suffering enormously from the situation. Resentments grew, as they found that the *centurias*, who had gone along with militarization, were no better armed than usual, whereas the communist brigades and Assault Guards in town were resplendent in their uniforms and brand-new rifles.

Catalan anarcho-syndicalism was racked by a deep-seated crisis, as the minutes of Regional Committee meetings between December 1936 and May 1937 attest. The militants in charge of the new "line" were well aware of the risks they were running. On December 26, Aurelio Fernández noted: "They acknowledge the danger we pose everywhere to statists, and they are out to use every means at their disposal to wipe us out."[51]

---

49   IISH, CNT, 85 C1, b. 232.

50   Amorós, *La revolución traicionada*, 150.

51   IISH, CNT 94 D1.

And they were also well aware that their position on the front lines had been undermined too. Some delegates from Madrid reported the following on January 11:

> The higher echelons of our army corps have a tendency to betray us, which becomes obvious when they bring our militia members down from the hills and dispatch them to hollows and ravines where they are easy targets for the fascists to shoot down at, since they overrun the unmanned hills.[52]

On January 13, Santillán pointed out:

> In the beginning, the CNT and the FAI were the people's cry of hope, but today many believe that they are the cause of all evil, given that they do not love us so much. We have to win back the people's love by carrying out a bit of proselytization.[53]

Marcos Alcón retorted:

> I see things quite differently than Santillán. [...] In reality, the CNT is actually responsible for everything [...]. As it [the PSUC] sees no opposition (because we mount none), [...] it plucks up the courage to launch the slander campaign it is presently mounting. All because we have made too many concessions. [...] Let us bolster the unions and stop dabbling in politics![54]

At the very same sitting, Aurelio Fernández, in charge of Catalonia's Internal Security Department, broached the matter of anarchist involvement in upholding public order:

> Should one party [here Aurelio Fernández is taking a swipe at the communists] provoke demonstrations against a reorganization, and should serious incident ensue, and should the person now speaking to you be faced with a choice between having to take to the streets with the security forces and confronting the people,

52   IISH, CNT, 85 C1.
53   Ibid.
54   Ibid.

with our compañeros in its ranks, I will not do the latter and I would resign first.[55]

During the January 27 meeting, Isgleas pointed out:

The situation we are passing through is extremely worrying. Unrest is still with us, due to the militarization, which is to say, the clash with the ideas. [...] When I saw Largo Caballero I told him: "The Aragon front is too weak to withstand the inevitable offensive, which the fascists, it is obvious, are busily preparing [...]." So our guys must not abandon their weapons. [...] I stress the fact that the Gelsa sector, unlike the rest of them, is the only one where there has been no dumping of weapons.[56]

Another militant, Jesús Trabal, declared shortly after that: "One meeting more, whether we like it or not, the collaboration with the Generalidad has been our ruin."[57]

The final phase of the clash over the militarization issue was to come in Valencia on February 5, 1937. The Iron Column from the Teruel front took the initiative and called a national plenum of the confederal and anarchist column, to which the National Committee of the CNT and the Peninsular Committees of the FAI and Libertarian Youth were also invited. At the end of January, the Iron Column's War Committee issued to its members a report containing these thoughts:

[In the beginning,] the state was a phantom to which no one paid any attention. The working-class organizations of the UGT and the CNT represented the only guarantee for the Spanish people [...] But almost without noticing it, our own dear CNT itself became a sapless and lifeless phantom, having injected into the State its own power and prestige. It is now just another appurtenance of the state and another extinguisher of the flames of the revolution.[58]

55 Ibid.
56 Ibid.
57 Ibid.
58 *Nosotros*, February 16, 1937, reprinted in Bolloten, *The Spanish Revolution*, 316–17.

Ruiz, Ródenas, and Guerra represented the 4th Agrupación from Gelsa, the Velilla sector, and the International Group. But on arrival, they found that another Durruti Column delegation, made up of fighters who had embraced the "militarist" line, had passed itself off as the authentic one, and that they themselves were unable to participate in the proceedings, pending supposed authentication of their mandates.

Despite that, this congress represents one of the last manifestations of internal democracy within the libertarian movement: the grassroots militants had painstakingly gone through the formal procedures in order to force the leadership to come and give a public accounting for the choices it had made over recent months. The representatives from the committees raised procedural quarrels right to the end in order to dodge this but were forced to toe the line. Once the proceedings got under way, a lot of miliciens were harshly critical of them and, notably, leveled charges of indiscipline at them, since the leadership committees were in fact doing their best not to consult the rank and file. The latter noted that, faced with a choice between storming the arsenals or deferring to the government in order to obtain arms, they had chosen the second option and they had to accept the consequences, otherwise the Communist Party was going to seize the army and the direction of the war. Then they labored the point about the Madrid militias having been effectively militarized and invoked the militarization (albeit partial) of the Durruti Column to show the die-hards that they were now nothing but a minority out of step with the rest of the movement.

José Pellicer from the Iron Column answered:

> Willingly or otherwise, the National Committee [...] has played into the hands of the state. [...] we are in the throes of premeditatedly sacrificing our beliefs in order to try to gather up a few crumbs. Isn't that true? We opposed militarization. We want to see if it is possible to put pressure on the government in order to get weapons without going through militarization.[59]

But it was obvious that the CNT's representatives hadn't come to give in on anything, and the tone grew more shrill. Pellicer went so far as to question the supreme authority of the CNT's national bodies:

59 Nestor Romero, *Los Incontrolados. Chronique de la colonne de Fer. Espagne 1936–1937* (La Bussière: Acratie, 1997), 149, 163.

Those of us who are members of the Confederation but who also belong to the columns and have our own personalities, want it made clear that we are neither beneath nor above the committees.[60]

At this point in the conflict either the columns disbanded or they embraced militarization: the plenum was brought to an end on the third day, without general agreement.

Invoking "circumstances," the CNT and FAI increasingly insisted that their rank-and-file members put their trust in the organization, with no discussion, and looked to the prestige enjoyed by libertarian leaders. But any reservations appeared to be lingering, as some miliciens, such as Antoine in this instance, were beginning to talk of "treachery."

Utterly isolated, the Iron Column announce during a final assembly on March 21, that it was disbanding.

In the Gelsa, though, in the wake of the plenum on February 5, the crisis lingered on. On February 12, Manzana reported back to the meeting of the CNT Regional Committee in Barcelona. After pointing out that the opponents of militarization were sticking to their propaganda, he accused them of thievery (of weapons and munitions) and of murder (one of the members of the Hijos de la Noche had turned up dead in Gelsa). Manzana warned that unless this crisis was sorted out it was inevitable that he would tender his resignation and that all of his miliciens would follow suit. At which point tension grew at the meeting: Picas bluntly moved that militarization be imposed at the end of a machine gun. Merino stated that he was unfamiliar with the people in Gelsa and protested such talk, as well as the fact that these militants were being depicted as dangerous offenders, or even traitors to the revolution, whereupon all those present rounded on him. Once calm had been restored, Manzana spoke up again to deliver an inventory of the war materials at his disposal, in anticipation of the inevitable fascist push that was in prospect; he argued that the most serious shortages were in hand bombs, shells, and mortars. All of a sudden, the atmosphere at the meeting grew heated once more. Column leader Domingo Ascaso rose to his feet and exclaimed:

We have to pull out of the government, bring our ministers back to Barcelona whether they like it or not and publish a manifesto stating in capital letters: THE GOVERNMENT WOULD RATHER DELIVER THE PEOPLE UP TO THE FASCISTS THAN TO THE REAL REVOLUTION!!![61]

To the list of problems he was cataloging, Manzana added that he had a sense not only that the Libertarian Youth were organizing in the rear, but that they were also banding together in the trenches and that there was every chance that when the day came for him to give them their orders, such organized youth might not obey him.

It was in these more measured terms the Regional Committees of the CNT, the FAI, and the Local Federation of Anarchist Groups addressed a letter to the Gelsa War Committee on February 14:

> Considering your intransigent refusal to abide by the accords reached by our CNT-FAI organizations regarding militarization of our confederal columns, their responsible committees have gathered and decided to address you one more time to get you to set aside your attitude, lest it hamper the general approach imposed upon us by the circumstances of the war.
>
> Think again, compañeros: [...] you should not become an exception. [...] We insist that four days from now [...] you contact the divisional headquarters, [...] and warn you that those compañeros who put their ideological scruples before the needs of the war will be fast-tracked for demobilization so that they can return to the rear guard.[62]

Those in Gelsa replied, in a letter dated February 17, that they would abandon the front in two weeks. Pablo Ruiz declined the post of commander offered to him, resigned from the War Committee, and, together with a dozen other militia members, returned to Barcelona. In an interview granted to *La Noche* on March 24, he reiterated the demands of the militia members:

> We are in agreement with a restructuring, but the people's army cannot be answerable to the Generalitat or to the central government. It must be controlled by the CNT, which is in the majority

61   IISH, CNT, 85 C1.

62   Amorós, *La revolución traicionada*, 159.

in Catalonia, and the top positions should be filled by competent personnel from the same organization, assisted by experts and all under the direction of political delegates drawn from the centurias themselves, who would look after the management of morale overall.

[...] But they refuse to heed us, which is why seven hundred of us find ourselves obliged to head back to Barcelona, and we are waiting here for whatever solution they have devised for that reorganization, ready at all times to fight against fascism and give our lives for the Revolution.[63]

On March 15, Pablo Ruiz, Francisco Carreño, Félix Martínez, and other ex-miliciens gathered on expropriated premises in the Ramblas with the weapons they had brought back from the front, including two machine guns. With Jaime Balius, they laid the groundwork for the Friends of Durruti group.

As for the International Group, on March 9 in Barcelona it took part in a gathering of all the militia members from the Aragon front. Domingo Ascaso and Augustin Souchy strove to persuade them of the merits of a "properly understood militarization," but to no avail. The militiaman Lovi declared:

We need not get fixated on the question of the war. We should also concern ourselves with the matter of the Revolution. They want to blindfold us and blind us with this "For Madrid, everything! For the children, everything!" There are two capitalisms trying to wipe out every revolutionary movement: home-grown capitalism, represented by the Generalidad, and foreign capitalism, represented by Blum, France, England, America, etc. To us, the CNT is more than just the leaders, the "directors," and we trust the opinion of the CNT. The profession of officer is always dishonorable in our view. And while there may a need for military advisors, the latter should be overseen by the unions' political delegates. But it looks as if care is already being taken to keep the unions at arms' length, as happens in Russia. They are out to crush the revolution, and since that is not possible, they are straining to choke it.[64]

63   Ibid., 160.
64   IISH, FAI, package 17.

French militiaman Raoul Tarrou declared,

that he will be speaking, not as an antifascist, but as an anarchist.
[…] In Gelsa, […] two months ago now, we were presented with
an ultimatum. […] If our suggestion that we reform as a free corps
is not agreed to […], then I am ready to head back to France.[65]

Fernand Fortin, delegate of the CNT's French Section, ordered
them either to submit to militarization or to leave. He promised to
find work for the foreign deserters or draft-dodgers wanted in their
own countries. Some left Spain, others withdrew into the rear or, like
Antoine, stayed on at the front as irregulars with people like Mombiola, a Libertarian Youth militant who had signed on with the Durruti
Column: he declined the command of a battalion and then rejected
militarization and thereafter fought on in a group of *dinamiteros* right
up until the collapse of the Aragon front.[66]

65   Ibid.
66   Ángel Pedro Mombiola y Allue was born in Sariñena (Huesca) on February 6,
     1908. After rejoining his former battalion within the 26th Division, he left for
     exile in France and was interned in a number of camps. In the autumn of 1943,
     he was drafted and, it seems, interned in the Ha fort (Bordeaux). Then, along
     with his partner, María Lozano Mombiola, he took part in the Resistance in
     the Haute-Garonne department. On August 20, 1944, he was shot along with
     two other CNT compañeros, Ricardo García and Francisco Aguado, after
     they were caught by German troops nears Ondes in the act of preparing to
     blow up a bridge over the Garonne. (See http://miitants-anarchistes.info/spip.
     php?article4019.) María Lozano Mombiola, born in Zaragoza on March 3,
     1914, died in Toulouse on February 19, 2000. She had served in the Durruti
     Column as a militiawoman and then been involved in the collectivization in
     Sariñena. Exiled to France in February 1939, she was interned in a camp in the
     Tarn department. After escaping, María Lozano managed to rejoin her partner
     Ángel and joined the Resistance in Haute-Garonne. Come the Liberation, she
     settled in Toulouse where she remained active in both the FIJL and the CNT,
     forever supporting all the *compañeros* belonging to the action groups in Spain.
     In particular, she was a staunch supporter of Francisco Sabaté Llopart, aka
     Quico. In the 1970s, she belonged to the Groupes d'action autonome and was
     actively involved in helping and supporting activists from the Iberian Liber-
     ation Movement (MIL) and the GARI, often making her home available to
     militants on the run and to those newly released from prison. In 1972, she was
     one of the founders of the CRAS libertarian archive in Toulouse. She actively
     campaigned against the nuclear power plant in Golfech.

{56}
PAGE 144

Carl Einstein, then, had been military advisor with the 26th Division since January 1937, and Manzana commanded about two thousand men stationed in Pina. In March, friction arose between Manzana and his men as well as with other veterans from the column. It would appear that the sergeant drew his gun in a conflict with one of Durruti's compañeros, José Mira. As a result, and on account of his repeated absenteeism from the front, Manzana resigned during April. Had possible suspicions regarding his part in Durruti's death generated tensions? Einstein's name was put forward as his replacement, but he refused. In his view "everybody should cultivate his personality, and military experts merely advise, they do not give orders." In May, Ricardo Sanz was to take charge of the division, which would integrate five hundred men from the Durrruti Column freshly returned from Madrid. As for Manzana, he would be made a gunnery captain in Mataró.

Meanwhile, the anarchist division had still not received any weapons. At a plenum held February 21–23, under pressure from its more radical groups, the FAI threatened that it would publicly denounce the government about the sabotaging of the Aragon front and insisted that the anarchist ministers step down if the state didn't come up with war materials within eight days.[67] There was to be no response to that and there was no follow-through to all this bluster.

The libertarian movement's powerlessness was plain to be seen, but Camillo Berneri's suggestion that it switch to reverse gear before it was too late does not seem to have been taken into consideration. At meetings of the Regional Committee in Barcelona, problems were logged but no solutions were devised: there were the food shortages in the rear guard, increasingly serious brushes with the communists inside the Generalitat as well as on the streets, continuing desertions from the front lines. Here the reports from the column leaders indicated that things could only get worse when new officers, anarchists included, treated their men in offhand fashion and destroyed any relationship of trust that had formerly been a feature of the columns; not to mention the questionable elements (unspecified by the antifascist organizations) making up the People's Army.

67   Amorós, *La revolución traicionada*, 162.

Back to No. 1 Company of the 4th Battalion of the Durruti Division's 3rd Infantry Regiment, also known as the International Company, which was still answerable to Carl Einstein according to certain historical sources. The historiographer of the 26th Division records that:

> The erstwhile International Group became a spearhead company. As in every other unit, militarization had a profound impact on the group, and most of the men belonging to it pulled out. But others joined and together with the ones who did embrace militarization they numbered 120 perfectly organized men in all, marshaled and disciplined by the Company's organization. It was the first unit in the 26th Division to introduce the outward display of military discipline, with close order drills, march-pasts, etc. It acquired huge fighting capacity, as it was to prove in future offensive operations to which it was assigned.[68]

Which is not really what Antoine said ... or what we deduce from other sources emanating, essentially, from the Germans of the DAS. According to them, what prevailed among the internationals of Pina de Ebro was a wait-and-see attitude and loss of morale. In a letter dated January 2, 1937, political commissar Michaelis wrote to Rüdiger (one of the staunch backers of CNT policy in Barcelona): "A captain was elected, a Frenchman of the Napoleonic sort. He is very theatrical and we hope that he has some military expertise."[69]

In another letter on February 3:

> To bring an end to the current situation whereby it is captain-less, the Group has appointed a Frenchman as its captain. The man is an ex-serviceman, a French Schreyer maybe, but, being French, a little too French and rather theatrical in his manner.
>
> [...] Our finding ourselves once more grappling with antisocial elements with fractious tendencies in Pina was down to you.[70]

That correspondence closed with a listing of the 104 internationals, broken down on the basis of nationality: "46 Germans; 14 Spaniards;

68 Anonyme, *La 26 División*, 49.
69 IISH, FAI, 1.
70 Ibid.

12 Swiss; 12 French; 4 Dutch; 3 Polish; 2 Austrians; 2 Belgians; 2 Swedes; 1 Norwegian; 1 Finnish; 1 Italian; 1 Yugoslav; 1 Hungarian; 1 Bulgarian; 1 Icelandic.[71]

Some DAS members wrote from Pina de Ebro on March 8, 1937:

The scheduled military exercises have had to be canceled because of a few days of rain. [...] As for ourselves, in the International Company, the immediate future will be occupied exclusively by our military exercises, unless they move us elsewhere.

It is clear, with this inactivity, that nerves are strained. Our company, and it's not the only one, is today a bunch of neurasthenics. Every day, comrades come to see their delegates to indicate their wish be allowed leave or to change division, or quit the militia once and for all, unless the front sees some action soon. Such requests go unanswered by HQ, even though they come from foreigners. It takes all of the persuasive capacity of our company's leading personnel to get all these impatient people to stick to their duty and revolutionary spirit. In this situation, a few conflicts erupt, of which more anon. [...]

In conclusion we really must return to the conflict mentioned above; for the first time in our company's history, it has forced those of a different political outlook to indicate that they feel out of place. This applies to comrades Paul THALMANN, Klara THALMANN, Karl BRAUNER, Ernst GALANTY, Hans WIELAND, Armin WALTER, Heinrich EICHMANN, Willi JOSEPH, and Georg GERNSHEIMER.

A meeting for all the German-speaking comrades, convened by No 2 section, was held on Saturday the 6th of this month. It adopted a stand on personal differences rooted in political disagreements. It emerged that certain DAS members had had repeated clashes with Marxist comrades and that the former had suggested that the latter transfer to a Marxist division. [...] Given all the personal nuances in such quarrels, the main aim of the meeting was to clarify all the objective differences once and for all. The nine comrades named above tried, after exchanging different opinions, to have a vote on a motion permitting the International Company's Marxist comrades to mount propaganda on behalf of

71   Ibid.

their beliefs in the form of the spoken word, images, and writing. The political delegate stepped in to ensure that the motion was not put to a vote [...].

Pursuing the matter later with the political delegate, the nine unanimously decided to leave the Durruti Division.[72]

The Thalmanns have their own version of this episode:

Thirty to forty militia members were regularly taking part in classes and lectures. Besides cultural and artistic matters, the war was our chief concern. Michaelis championed the official anarchist position of the CNT and FAI. His own temperament was such as to place him on the revolutionary side, but in light of the post he held, he was unable to identify with our Marxist critique. His line of argument could be pretty much summed up like this: "In order to secure the support of the Russians, certain compromises have to be made with the communists. As long as we are the masters in the firms, as long as we are based on the soldiers' and peasants' committees, and the militia army is on our side, we can keep the communist influence in check and largely combat it."

Our critique was essentially directed at the inadequate defense and unduly weak political extension of the committees as the basis for the revolutionary social turmoil already embarked upon, and, in our estimation, the entry of anarchists into the Popular Front government was simply delaying and maybe even frustrating such a revolutionary turn. In so doing the anarchist movement was marching in step with the communist line that stated: "First, win the war against Franco, and then start the revolution," which inevitably was an impediment to the revolutionary movement. Now, the only way of winning the war was by recourse to revolutionary methods and objectives. The compromises with communist policy had already overstepped the mark and the revolutionary forces were already so weakened and thrown into disarray that the civil war was slowly but surely turning into a mere imperialist military conflict.

---

72   Hans-Jürgen Degen and Helmut Ahrens, "Wir sin es leid, die Ketten zu tragen," *Antifaschisten im Spanischen Bürgerkrieg* (Berlin: Jakobsohn, 1979), *Dokumente*, 165 and following.

Michaelis, eager to bolster his authority, went off to Barcelona to fetch an anarchist theorist versed in the matter so as to dismantle our critique. The constant defeats at the hands of Francoist troops, the fall of Málaga [February 8, 1937], which came right in the middle of our discussions, gave the debate a shrill tone. One day, Michaelis told us that things could not continue this way. We knew what that meant. He then told us that he could no longer guarantee our safety, following which we put our heads together. Fifteen members of the unit, including ourselves, decided to leave the front. Michaelis welcomed this decision with some satisfaction and did nothing to hinder our departure. [...] Michaelis had most likely been overstating things when he claimed that our lives were in danger; he just wanted to be rid of our, to say the least, irksome criticisms. [...]

We stayed a week in the barracks in Barcelona. Carry on fighting in Spain or give up? That was the question facing each one of us. Willi Joseph, Heiri Eichmann, Armin Walter, and a few others had had enough and decided to leave Spain; others signed on with an anarchist battalion known as the "Death Battalion."[73]

73 Thalmann and Thalmann, *Combats pour la liberté*, 141–43.

According to a report dated December 28, 1936 and forwarded to the Italian police by a correspondent in Barcelona, this assault battalion was made up of hand-picked antifascists, used dagger and bomb, and was organized along the lines of the First World War Italian Arditi.

It was set up and funded by the Generalidad of Catalonia and sponsored by Abad de Santillán in November 1936 as the "First Generalidad Assault Battalion."

Its five hundred volunteer militias, mostly drawn from the CNT-FAI, it seems were broken down into five centurias plus a machine-gun section, and they made a great impression when they paraded in very martial style through Barcelona on March 3, 1937, with their greenish uniforms and black jerkins displaying the death's head symbol with crossed tibias. According to Vicente Guarner, the battalion suffered a defeat in its very first engagement in Almúdevar and Montalbán. It was all but wiped out during the attack on Santa Quiteria (in April 1937). What was left of the battalion then joined the Ascaso Column or returned to France. But according to Arcarazo, Barrachina, and Martínez de Baños, authors of *Guerra Civil Aragón*, vol. 5, 275–79, the battalion first did not see action before April 20, 1937, in the Tardienta sector. In the wake of that setback, it was to be absorbed into the 12th International Brigade.

We are not in a position to say exactly who it was that was in command of the company between January and March; there was talk of someone from the Saar and then of a French captain, or even of its having no commander. But it seems certain that the Frenchman Alexis Cardeur was appointed on March 2, 1937, according to Gmür's diary:

> We have chosen a new captain, a Frenchman by the name of Cardeur. Headquarters suggested him. A majority voted for him, but asked for a probationary period. He didn't agree to that. Either we trust him entirely, as he did us, or he refused to take over the

According to Mimmo Franzinelli, *I tentacoli dell'OVRA* (Turin: Bollati Boringhieri, 1999), 270–71, the battalion's commander was Candido Testa (b. 1900). Like Vagliasindi, he was a dissident former fascist who immigrated to France in 1926 and then to Argentina where he became a journalist with an antifascist newspaper. He arrived in Spain on October 25, 1936, and took charge of the battalion, leaving after a few months. He was an agent of the OVRA (under the code name "Argentino"), operating as a double agent, according to Franzinelli: "A valuable collaborator with the fascist services [who] in the first half of 1938 supplied lots of information of a military nature." He left for France during the summer of 1938, just as his cover was about to be blown; but other collaborators of his stayed in Spain. Interned in the Le Vernet camp in July 1940, he was repatriated and set free.

Miguel Vivancos has left us this reference to him: "After the war end and while in exile in Paris 1945, I learned from Italian exile circles that Testa had been a member of the OVRA and that he had tipped off the secret service about the date of Carlo Rosselli's departure for Paris" (Miguel García Vivancos, *Mémoires inédits*). Carlo Rosselli and his brother Nello were to be murdered in France on Mussolini's orders in Bagnoles-de-l'Orne on June 9, 1937.

The other officer in the battalion was Emilio Strafelini, an Italian anarchist, a "disciple of Malatesta." Born in Rovereto in 1897, he died in Trento in 1964. Strafelini signed on with the Ascaso Column on August 13, 1936 on the Huesca front, where he commanded three centurias before joining the Death Battalion in November or December. He became its second commander. He left it following political disagreements in April 1937. Strafelini then withdrew to Barcelona. Tracked by the Stalinists during the events of May 1937, he managed to hide out. "Out of fear of being killed like Berneri," Strafelini returned to France in October 1937. But he returned to Barcelona where, greatly demoralized, he lived until February 1939. He then crossed into France and was put in a camp. He was repatriated in June 1940, arrested and interned on Ventotene up until 1943.

company. So he was elected definitively. Which pleased me. Cardeur was a colonial officer, around fifty years of age.[74]

In a letter to Einstein on March 6, 1937, Michaelis referred to Manzana's back-and-forth trips to Barcelona in search of weapons:

Our Cardeur is also in the city right now settling financial affairs and moving heaven and earth to get the Company battalion status. And to apply to you for the *Baja definitiva* [final discharge] of a number of "internationals," as they think of themselves "*como voluntaries*" [as volunteers].[75]

Let us finish this review of the troops with a letter from Michaelis to Rüdiger on March 14, 1937:

And then formal notice was received from comrade Manzana, passing on how pleased our *consejeros* [counselors] and headquarters were at the work we had accomplished. My whole antimilitarist sentiment came flooding back (this is for your benefit alone). [...] A military training has its implications; and I do not know if they will ever be surmountable, even after we have won the revolution.

Interestingly, our battalion's No 2 Company, the old "Banda Negra," which was supposed to organize a parade in Osera the way we did in Pina, reacted more sourly than we did. One section flatly refused and took no part in the parade before our *consejeros*. However, like us, they had to show the Generalidad that militarization was being conscientiously applied in our division. (Keep that to yourself too.) [...]

This week we will try to conduct an attack. Where, when, and how, nobody here cares. I hope it turns out to be a success so that we can shrug off this atmosphere of defeat.[76]

This reference to the Banda Negra affords us a better understanding of the sort of unit Antoine found himself in after January 1937.

---

74 Gmür and Minnig, *Pour le bien de la révolution*, 80.
75 IISH, FAI, Pe1.
76 IISH, FAI,1.

Obviously, he was not in Pina with those who had embraced militarization "through clenched teeth," nor was he in Gelsa with the ones who categorically rejected it and who were to return to Barcelona. It seems that a segment of the veteran internationals and those who had belonged to the old Banda Negra guerrilla band had managed to keep a detachment of irregulars up and running, somewhat on the fringes of militarization. Its activities still consisted of raids and reconnaissance patrols, and by virtue of that fact it was highly mobile; but it would also take part in offensives along the line, as we shall see. According to Antoine, Vagliasindi was in command of this brand new Banda Negra (although we have not been able to turn up a single reference to him from this time), in which case he had not been a casualty of the fallout from Ruano's fall from grace in January. Among the old hands from the International Group, Scolari had quit the column with his pal Balart back in December 1936, over the militarization issue. They had moved to Barcelona where Charles Carpentier joined them. In February 1937, the three pals spent some time in Portbou where there was a detachment from the Sébastien Faure *centuria* seconded to Investigaciones, according to the testimony of Robert Léger, the volunteer who had escaped from the communists in Albacete.[77] After he had been smuggled out of Albacete thanks to the CNT-FAI, and after a time with the Ortiz Column with Jean Maillol, Robert Léger helped the Spanish anarchists' investigation service monitor the frontier up until he went back to France in March 1937. So, the numbers of the International Company must have fluctuated a lot due to the variously motivated departures, not forgetting the fact that many Germans and Italians, unable to return home, had ended up being recruited, willingly or otherwise, into the International Brigades.

{57}
PAGE 144

Let us quote the historiographer of the 26th Division once again:

77   Léger, *Entretiens avec Phil Casoar.*

Later on, in order to set up a shock battalion on the basis of the International Company, two other companies were raised, one based on a militia unit called the Banda Negra and another one with personnel drawn from various scouting teams and other small pre-militarization units. But the three companies operated in isolation from time to time, and the battalion could not quite pull this off. In May, after the International Company engaged in operations of its own, it was sent to Barcelona, where an attempt was made there to raise an International Battalion based upon it and fresh volunteers, but, although it was successfully organized and seconded to the division, the battalion proved to be very low-quality, so much so that it bore little resemblance to the old Company; and so it was disbanded by the divisional commander and its men were demobilized.[78]

The operation cited above came on April 12 and was mounted against the enemy positions in the Santa Quiteria hermitage in the Tardienta sector in which

our International Company distinguished itself, fighting with incredible daring, effectively carrying out the planned action. By the time it got back to the division, that Company had sustained 50% losses, stark proof of its fighting spirit.[79]

What the pompous propagandists of the CNT fail to mention is that the anarchist infantry was not supported, as was agreed, from the air force, which was in communist hands, and that the men thought that once again they had been sent into slaughter due to the incompetence—or worse—of the command. This triggered further desertions by the militia members, to the great annoyance of the CNT's regional committee in Barcelona. Minutes of the regional committee meeting of April 19 bear witness to that: on the basis of information provided by Domingo Ascaso, the committee secretary described how, in the course of the most recent operations on the Huesca front:

400 *compañeros* were swayed (according to some reports, by two

78   Anonyme, *La 26 División*, 49–50.
79   Ibid., 52–53.

individuals who have never taken part in any fighting whatsoever) and deserted along with their weapons and hand bombs,
making the trip, willingly or under coercion, back to Barcelona,
with the men in charge of the column unable to do anything to
stop them. To make matters worse, when these men fled from the
front, the comrades from the POUM battalions had to disarm
some of them [...]. At which point an urgent telegram arrived
stating that further deserters from the front had arrived. Given the
threat that this represented, serious steps were taken. For a start,
the compañeros from Defense were awarded our full confidence
and every facility to take the necessary measures. [...] After the
facts had been established, the two people responsible for the first
batch of desertions were to be shot; as to the 400 others, they were
to be arrested that very night in their homes (we had a list sent to
us for that purpose) and they were to be removed to the Montjuich fortress where a commission from the Regional Committee
would register their arrivals. After which the ones with the greatest responsibility were to be dispatched, willingly or under compulsion, to the most dangerous front lines, and the rest advised to
return of their own volition to the place they had abandoned.

Xena asked if the Regional Committee was aware of the
arrest of one of Reyes's assistants and of the men in charge of the
airfield, for most of the front-line *compañeros* reckoned that those
were the persons solely responsible for this whole demoralization.

Ascaso stated that the arrest had indeed been made, but it was
not known by whom.

Xena stated: "I am informed that the air force gave a negative
answer [to the request that it play its part during the battle] and,
through that mischievous act, allowed the enemy to wreak havoc
among our men and carry out a number of maneuvers."

Ascaso said that there was no doubt that the air force was to
blame for the loss of morale. The air force failed to take off, and,
once it did, it caused us the loss of eighteen of our men. And it
wasn't a mistake, for the operation involved our people inside
a wooded area and the enemy on the plain, and our air force
bombed the woods and not the plain. That may have been the
cause of our compañeros' desertion from the Aragon front. [...]

[The] Communications [Union] reported that a relative had
written it a letter indicating that, in his opinion, there were people

in the front lines who had an interest in ensuring that our operations came to grief. […]

Xena stated that much had been said about the Aragon front at the plenum there and it looked as if the government might be right sending our militias nothing, because it believes them to be utterly demoralized.

[…] it is agreed that we shall seek all means of disciplining the Aragon front […].

[…] Barrueso […] [believes that] for our compañeros' peace of mind, we must first try and severely punish the airmen responsible for defeats. That way, our compañeros will see that our justice is even handed and falls where it may.[80]

In his *Mémoires inédits*, Miguel García Vivancos, once a member of Los Solidarios and a CNT member, gives a detailed report of an episode that corroborates and tries to excuse the despicable performance of the Catalonia Regional Committee vis-à-vis the militia members. He even encapsulates this in the chapter entitled "Mutinies." This occurred on April 7, 1937, when Vivancos was in command of the 126th Brigade of the 28th Division (embracing the former Ascaso and Los Aguiluchos columns):

On April 7, 1937, Major Rodríguez, a commander with the 126th Brigade, reported to our HQ in Albero Bajo. […]

"I ran away from Vicién," he answered. "One of the companies from my brigade had left the front line, threatening to kill me if I did not assign them the leave they were due and which I had promised them. Those behind this mutiny were the boys from a different company who I had sent to Barcelona for two weeks leave. They had not come back and had been away for twenty days. I tried to reason with them, but they rejected all my arguments, threatening me again if I was not prepared to order them back to Barcelona right then and there. Seeing that my life was in danger, I ran away and have come to ask you to help me resolve this serious problem."

—Listen, Rodríguez, I told him, you departed from the beginning of militarization, setting an example of indiscipline, just to demonstrate the strength of your convictions, and now you can see the consequences in the ranks of your men who are now paying you back in your own coin. […] So I invite you to head for home with your discharge papers and banish all thoughts of ever asking for the command of a unit in the future, no matter how small. Get out and make sure you don't come back."

[…] I set off […] for Vicién with my driver and my assistant. Arriving in the village square, the car had difficulty getting through due to the crowds there. Most of them were soldiers with rifles slung over their shoulders and some 'Universal' type grenades dangling ostentatiously from their belts. I ordered my driver, Martín, to step on it, sounding the horn until we reached the center of the square. We pulled up and they all gathered around us. I opened the door and stepped out with brusque movements, glowering at them. As they recognized me, they mobbed me, all of them simultaneously putting in their demands. I addressed the ones badgering me:

"We can't all talk at once. Tell your representatives—I'm assuming you've appointed some sort of a commission—that I am on my way to the brigade command post, and there we can all sit down together and calmly sort out the issues bothering you."

With my assistant, I headed for the brigade CP, and, shortly after that, twelve boys arrived. They introduced themselves as the company representatives and as members of the Libertarian Youth. I invited them to take a seat and asked them to fill me in on the grievances that had spurred them into breaching discipline. One of them, the one who was the fastest talker and who seemed to be a bit of a show-off, stood up and, showing me a large sheet of paper, said to me:

"The company's demands are set out here. Read it and you'll know what it's all about."

I got up and took the paper passed to me by the delegate, and without looking at it, folded it several times before tearing it into 1,000 pieces that I tossed away as the startled commission looked on. Then I turned to those twelve representatives:

"You ringleader mutineers came up to the front hell-bent on disrupting the military organization of the militias, which our organization had decided upon at its recent congress. Men with an obligation to the CNT are duty bound to see that militarization

through. By your attitude, you are in revolt against the accords
of our CNT and of the 'specific' (the FAI) and unwittingly favoring the victory of fascism, the victory of the enemies of the Spanish people. Is that what you want? I will never allow the efforts
that have cost us so dearly to be destroyed by you who are only
fake libertarians. We who are answerable to the mandate from
the organization, will not tolerate these acts of rebellion that you
are fomenting, you who purport to be idealists, not realizing that
your task is to help us maintain discipline within our units …
Now we shall work on a resolution of the issue that your clown
of a commander has failed to resolve."

I then turned to the chief of brigade staff who was in attendance:

"Draw me up, immediately, a complete list of names and
addresses of the men from this company on leave in Barcelona.
You have my word that, like it or not, they'll be back here within
two and a half days. And then, I went on, addressing myself to the
commission, your company will get its leave, but not before then."

—"Good solution," said the one who appeared to be the
group's spokesman.

And, addressing himself to me, he asked me to announce the
solution from the balcony.

"No way, *compañero*. Feelings are running high and if one
voice was to ring out above the crowd and oppose my suggestion, it would ruin everything. Given that you have taken on the
responsibility for representing them, it is up to you to play the
hand I am about to deal you. Step out into the square, get the
company to form up in platoons with their respective commanders, tell them that we have thrashed out a resolution, and, once
they are lined up, you will explain the outcome of our meeting,
which is entirely favorable. As I have said, I undertake to honor
my word, and, before three days have passed, you will have your
fortnight's leave."

The delegates endorsed this and stepped into the square, getting the company to form up; in good order, off it went to man
the lines it had abandoned that morning.

We headed back to Albero Bajo and I summoned an officer
from HQ, an officer I trusted implicitly. I handed him the list of
company personnel on leave and ordered him to go down to Barcelona with five trucks and six armed men to round everybody

The slopes leading to the Santa Quiteria hermitage, overlooking the village of Torralba

up for me, during the night or in the early hours, house by house, using force if necessary. I wanted them all back by the next day.

At daybreak the following day, the entire company arrived in Albero Bajo, and, summoning the chief of brigade staff, I made him responsible for dispatching these men into the front lines as relief for the other company and for ferrying its men down to Barcelona in the same trucks. And so this annoying incident, triggered by the ineptitude of the command, was resolved."

Let us look somewhat more closely at the matter of the deserters disarmed by the POUM, using Paul Thalmann's account, which actually appears to relate to this incident (the Thalmanns left the International Company during March):

I was accepted into the POUM without any difficulty, as were two other comrades from Pina [...]. The unit to which we were assigned was an assault unit made up of Germans, Dutch, and some Spaniards. [...] The pay was still 10 pesetas, but officers could claim more; in addition, discipline and the relaying of orders were stricter and closely resembled the practice in the regular army. There was not much left of the anarchist militia arrangement. [...]

In the very first week, there was a night-time alert. Within a quarter of an hour, they had us all on trucks riding like the wind. After quite a short trip, we were unloaded and cordoned off a clearing. A strange sight met our eyes under the pale light of dawn. About two thousand unarmed militia members,[81] dressed in motley FAI uniforms were stretched out in a broad meadow. We were encircling them without even knowing the reason why. In conversation, we discovered that they were a unit of an anarchist column that had refused to serve any longer at the front. After having spent many a long month in the front lines without being relieved even once, they had suffered heavy losses in serious skirmishing. An operation on a larger scale, upon which all the men had agreed, had been a bloody failure, for neither the republican troops nor the communists had come to their aid, as had been arranged. The men from this unit were convinced that this was an act of sabotage. And we had to stand guard over these 'mutineers'? My blood froze. I felt a mixture of shame and anger: I had not come out to the front line to play cop. As the rest of the comrades felt the same as I did, we decided to send one of our number as a delegate to see Reiter, insisting that we be pulled out of that place right away. Naturally, Reiter was not in the know and immediately contacted POUM general headquarters. Half an hour later, we were pulled out. Before we left we made it clear to our anarchist comrades that we supported their action and we parted on friendly terms.[82]

We shall deal in more detail with the course of the battle of Santa Quiteria in the chapter devoted to that, with lots of firsthand testimony.[83] It had great impact on the minds of those who took part in it, and the contingent of internationals sustained heavy losses yet again. Which is why Antoine and others were sent into the rear to rebuild its numbers. According to Gmür, the entire International Company was sent to Barcelona on leave on April 18.

Aldabaldetrecu, the war commissar of the northern precinct at Barbastro HQ, the man who back in December reckoned that everything was going to end badly, offered this assessment of the event in a "Strictly private report" dated April 15, 1937:

Recent days have taught us a terrifying lesson. [...] I think those

---

81   This figure is, of course, an exaggeration. (Giménologue's note).
82   Thalmann and Thalmann, *Combats pour la liberté*, 144–45.
83   See endnote 74 below.

who launched these operations, more or less in support of their political plans or something of the sort, did not believe they would take such a heavy toll of human lives.

The lives lost will be a cruel burden upon their consciences and they will have been driven to such extremes by their rabble-rousing. Time and history will judge them (which is a real shame) as actors in the Confederation's history.

This government crisis, this manpower crisis, this crisis in the Confederation's trajectory, which translates into a huge crisis in the attention paid to problems of the war and thus absolute ignorance as to the course to take, an ignorance that paves the way for the potential slow eradication of our stronger personality. [...]

By not wanting to win the war, we are in the process of losing the revolution. [...]

Point one, the operations mounted in recent days; point two, the deadly outcome produced because of, among other factors, the air force which was pulled out on orders from Valencia in a curious act of sabotage, while our troops were mown down with impunity and, after being decimated, were forced to fall back on Santa Quiteria and Carrascal [...].

And the third point, the rumor peddled in different reports regarding the eradication of our identity as the guiding force on the Aragon front. [...]

This is my call for help. With all the force I can muster, against the struggle unleashed by the espionage services at the highest level to lay a trap for us that will force us to yield. And if there are still some sleepwalkers who deny this fact, they must be taught and made to understand that the threads that blind them, all unbeknown to them, are part of a plan to eliminate us [...].

Rumor has it that in Madrid there are some 30,000 carabineers standing by and that they will show up as soon as we fail on the Aragon front. [...]

But there is a solution to this great problem [...]. We should no longer rely on the Valencia government. [...] The existing war machine does not suit us [...].

There is still time to remedy all these things, still time to come to our senses and make the revolution by winning the war.[84]

84   IISH, CNT, 002 A2.

{58}

For weeks the situation in Barcelona and throughout the rest of republican Spain had been explosive. For months, the communists had been taking charge of various slices of power, capitalizing on the popularity conferred upon them by deliveries of Russian arms and the victorious resistance put up by the International Brigades in Madrid. Within the Generalitat in Catalonia, despite the signed agreements and other pacts of unity between the CNT and the PSUC, the fight between them was becoming obvious. Backed by the Catalanists and relying on the middle classes, who were hoping for a return to the pre-July 1936 status quo, the communists insisted and, in December 1936, successfully ensured that the POUM be removed from the Generalitat cabinet. The PSUC then exploited genuine difficulties with supplies in order to turn the population against the CNT, as a CNT was in charge of the Department of Supply. Some people even suspected Juan Comorera, the new communist department chief who replaced him, of making the shortages worse in order to point the finger at feckless collectivists.[85] Finally, a crisis erupted in the Generalitat cabinet line-up on March 26. On the pretext that there were "uncontrollable" armed civilians posing a threat to public order, the Catalan government decided to disband the Control Patrols made up of a thousand political and trade union activists. Initially the CNT agreed to this but then, its hand forced by its rank and-file membership, it blocked the order's implementation. The Thalmanns, who were in Barcelona at the time, could feel the mounting tension:

> For a long time now, the anarchist and POUM control patrols had been a considerable irritation to the Stalinists. These rear-guard security forces, intended to combat fascist personnel or sabotage, were armed and trained to perfection. [...] Through the Generalitat, the call went out for the disbandment of these patrols, which

85   We shall read about this subject in Agustín Guillamón, *Iborra, La Guerra del pan. Hambre y violencia en la Barcelona revolucionaria. De diciembre de 1936 a mayo de 1937* (Barcelona: Aldarull & Dskontrl, 2014). This book is a detailed catalog of the communists' shitty maneuvers as, under the direction of Comorera, they directly sabotaged the food supply to Barcelona in order to expedite a return to private trade.

they aimed to replace with government police. This undisguised aggression on the last remaining bastions of the revolutionary era stirred up great discontent and heightened tensions. Everyone could sense that the political climate was highly charged and was just waiting for a spark to ignite the gunpowder.[86]

On April 27, and over the ensuing weeks, Catalanist and communist troops ousted the anarchists from control of the border, and there was an upsurge in skirmishes, murders, and acts of provocation. In their reports for *Le Libertaire*, Carpentier and Ridel denounced this state of affairs:

> Let the 3,000 carabineers with their rifles, grenades, and machine guns, who were sent in to protect the border and who are causing unease in Catalonia, be sent up to the front lines since France is no threat at all to our borders.[87]

They also denounced the murder of Antonio Martín from Puigcerdà:

> He was the very first militant we met on Spanish soil on July 29. [...] Tall, thin, dragging a stiff leg behind him, he was cool and calm, but had great energy and a fire that put a twinkle in his eye. Martín was everywhere. [...] In the reactionary press especially, much has been made of the executions carried out in Puigcerdà. These were depicted as murders carried out by *pistolero* gangs against defenseless persons. The reality is quite different. Every expedition exposed the patrols to as many dangers as the enemies whose record of fascist activism made them an adversary to be mercilessly cut down. The revolutionary committees and trade union committees sat in judgment and framed their decisions [...] Today, Puigcerdà is proof that social life rooted in work and freedom is feasible. The big estates have been collectivized, schools are operating in the former monasteries, the stores have become cooperatives, the libraries are open to all and sundry. [...] It took the anarchists to disarm certain local petit bourgeois personnel,

86   Thalmann and Thalmann, *Combats pour la liberté*, 150.
87   Charles Carpentier, "Où va l'Espagne," *Le Libertaire*, May 6, 1937.

whose Catalan republican credentials barely disguised [...] their
nostalgia for commercial and capitalistic profiteering. [...] They
had to combat the return of the forces of repression reorganizing under the aegis of the Valencia government. Martín played
his part in all these activities. And it was in a brush with the
carabineers standing for "order," dispatched by Valencia to end
the revolutionary committees' grip on public life and backed by
speculators, village political personnel, and dispossessed former
property-owners, that he met his death.[88]

We must understand that, by its nature and the practicalities of
implementation, this episode should be seen as presaging the counterrevolutionary happenings of May 1937.[89]

So everything appeared to be proceeding along the same lines;
methodically, the state and the bourgeoisie attacked the gains made
back in July 1936, which the CNT claimed to be promoting and
defending through its participation in the regional and national governments. In addition, UGT and CNT personnel had long been prey
to abduction and torture in the clandestine prisons of the Soviet secret
services or had been turning up, dead, in the streets in several locations
around the peninsula. Many men had been withdrawn from front-line
service for such dirty work and were swelling the ranks of the new
police force that was being raised. Some libertarian militants were
returning blow for blow, as the Thalmanns noted:

> [...] the anarchist youth movement [...] had long since been
> locked in a deadly contest with the PSUC. It responded to every
> murder of one of its members, to every attack targeting its meet-
> ing-places, with attacks on communist officials or Stalinist bar-
> racks. Because of these vigorous and active defensive moves, the
> official [anarchist] leadership had lost all control of the youth

88   Ridel, "La mort d'Antonio Martín," in ibid.
89   For more information about Antonio Martín Escudero and the economic
     policy of the Puigcerdà Committee—which tried to enforce set price uni-
     formity for wheat, milk, and meat throughout the Cerdagne as a counter
     to speculation—see the two-part article by Antonio Gascón and Agustín
     Guillamón in the magazine *Catalunya* (November and December 2014):
     "Martín Escudero, Antonio (1895–1937). El Durruti de la Cerdanya."
     Accessible at www.revistacatalunya.cat.

organization which had swung much further to the left and was ripe for revolutionary action.[90]

We might add that in mid-February 1937, at a Barcelona rally that drew a crowd of fifty thousand people, a "Revolutionary Youth Front" was launched, which united the Libertarian Youth and the POUM youth organization as a counterweight to the "Antifascist Youth Alliance" under Stalinist sponsorship; this constitutes the only tangible instance of collaboration between the anti-Stalinist forces.

The scene was set therefore for the trial of strength that the CNT wanted to avoid at all costs, a civil war within the antifascist camp; but, in keeping with its decision not to create problems for the government, the Regional Committee in Catalonia remained on a defensive footing, though privately seething, for they could plainly see that the politicians were toying with them.

At one meeting in April, Aurelio Fernández pointed out that

PUBLIC ORDER IS IN THE PROCESS OF OVERWHELMING THE REVOLUTION. [...] We used to be the masters and now the petite bourgeoisie is tossing us overboard. [...] We must not trust Companys, the craven politician [...][91]

In another discussion on April 21, CNT personnel noted that the communists had twenty-three companies of carabineers on stand-by and that they were ready to impose their rule, while in Madrid eighty anarchists had been murdered. It was common knowledge who was responsible; it was Galarza, the socialist minister of the Interior, the man who was dispatching the security forces into the villages and killing at a whim. In short, they announced, vigorous action was called for if they were to counter the campaign being waged against the CNT and launch an offensive against fascism in all its guises. It was obvious to them too that there had to be an end of tolerance for the propaganda emanating from the Friends of Durruti, which was grating on their nerves, in that they were speaking out as CNT-FAI members and this was creating waves within the libertarian movement. Furthermore, on May 1, the National Committee issued a circular urging its

90   Thalmann and Thalmann, *Combats pour la liberté*, 149.
91   IISH, CNT, 85 C1.

militants not to launch campaigns in support of libertarian prisoners, since securing their release was more difficult if the spotlight was on them. This unwitting admission of powerlessness added to the anger and bitterness of the militants for whom support for prisoners constituted one of the golden rules of the organization.

Though in the spring of 1937 anarchists were still in the majority in the antifascist camp in Catalonia and Aragon, at any rate, it was obvious that they couldn't defend the "gains of July 1936" as long as they remained part the government, which the CNT-FAI intended. There was an ever-widening rift between the CNT-FAI leadership and a segment of the movement: the Barcelona Local Federation of Groups; the Libertarian Youth of Catalonia; the Food, Transport, and Metalworking unions; the Control Patrols, the collectivists; the militia members opposed to statist militarization. These plus all their newspaper platforms were demanding an explanation of the CNT-FAI's passivity in the face of the sabotage the socialization of industry, the persecution of revolutionary militants and POUM militants, the disarming of the local revolutionary committees, and the neglect of the Aragon front, which the communist press had tagged "the only idle front." At a local plenum of the Barcelona anarchist groups on April 12, 1937, it was noted that the CNT, which had been the embodiment of the aim of revolution, was losing the trust of its base. The young libertarian Juan Santana Calero pointed out that,

> the counterrevolution has taken important positions, despite our collaboration with the government, and that's why he stated that collaboration had proved counterproductive and ineffective.[92]

92   Guillamón, *La guerra del pan*, 428. This book is, in a more general sense, crucial in that, thanks to publication of the minutes of CNT, FAI, Libertarian Youth, and Generalidad meetings, it lifts the lid on the real balance of power between the various component parts of the "republican" camp in Barcelona, notably just prior to the "May events." Out of this comes an appreciation that the latter should no longer be considered a straightforward "Stalinist provocation," as had been the custom thus far, but rather as an inevitable clash that had been prepared and cultivated on both sides. In March 1937, a number of anarcho-syndicalists were stockpiling arms in anticipation of the clashes to come. The fact is, however, that they had been preceded by provocations galore emanating from the Generalidad, within which the greatest malice came from the Stalinists.

In short, these critical militants were reactivating opposition to the Popular Front government, a role that the Confederation had abjured. They were forever sounding the alarm about dangers threatening the movement and the revolution and found themselves written off as uncontrollables, even by the CNT. As François Godicheau put it:

> A "man of action" like Dionisio Eroles, for example, who was called in by his union to come to the aid of its imprisoned members, sided with the CNT leadership in labeling the individuals in question as "uncontrollable" and "thugs": half integrated into the established order, he was actually conceding a degree of legitimacy to the police and prison authorities of the Generalitat and "antifascist government."
>
> We should not be surprised by such legitimacy: it was actually because it existed, even in the eyes of some of the anarchists, that the state was able to pursue its own reconstruction through the Generalitat and its repressive agencies.[93]

In a public address delivered on behalf of the Friends of Durruti on April 20, Carreño distanced himself from the CNT's antifascist ideology and hammered it home that in Spain there were two bourgeoisies, one fascist and one republican, and that the battle was against them both. On May 2, the Friends of Durruti held their second public rally in Barcelona's Goya Theatre:

> Taking into consideration the situation, which has been aggravated by numerous provocations, the Friends of Durruti predict[ed] an imminent attack on the working class, an attack that, according to them, was being hatched in "official circles, where the representatives of supposedly antifascist forces are to be found."[94]

Like Manuel Escorza from the anarchist Investigation Service, therefore, many people were expecting an imminent coup de force by

---

93   Godicheau, *La Guerre d'Espagne*, 169.

94   Hans Schafranek and Werner Wögerbauer, "Nous, 'agents provocateurs et irresponsables.' Esquisse d'une histoire des Amigos de Durruti," in Universitat de Barcelona, Centre per a la investigació dels moviments socials, *La Guerra i la Revolució a Catalunya. Comunicacions. II colloqui internacional sobra la Guerra Civil espanyola* (Barcelona: CEHI, 1986), 160.

the state. The "May events" were to be the logical culmination of a counterrevolutionary process that was already well advanced.

For further information, see Amorós, *La revolución traicionada*, 191–212.

{59}
PAGE 146

In Barcelona, Antoine would run into his countrymen from the erstwhile Italian Section who had left the front, where the atmosphere was not the best. Relations with the CNT were strained. From January 17 onward, grudgingly compliant with the militarization process, the Italian anarchists on the Huesca front set up the Ascaso Division's International Battalion, while holding on to their internal autonomy. On April 7 and 8, they, along with other Spanish battalions, took part in the attack mounted against Carrasacal de Huesca. Nine Italian men were killed—including the battalion commander Antonio Cieri; forty-two more were wounded and twenty missing.

Deeply affected by this, the members of the battalion disbanded; some returned to France and carried on with support activities from there; others transferred to the Durruti Division's International Company. The latter returned to Barcelona where life was just as fraught for them, for several of their compatriots had been disappearing into communist jails for some months by then and—the lucky ones among them—resurfacing in the prison system.

Camillo Berneri unremittingly denounced this witch-hunt against "uncontrollables" and did his damnedest to secure their release, sometimes succeeding with great pains. Some Italian militants had supposedly even threatened the CNT National Committee that they would leave Spain en masse unless it intervened on behalf of their captive countrymen Bibbi, Fontana, and Tommasini. At the time when Antoine was hoping to see Berneri again, the main issue was raising an international brigade for the Aragon front along with Domingo Ascaso and the Italian fighters. But both Berneri and Ascaso would soon be murdered.

For further information, see Cattini, *Anarquistes italiens a l'Espanya republicana*, 726; Fedeli, *Un trentennio di attività anarchica*, 188–93.

{60}
PAGE 146

Let us set out a rough timetable of events in Barcelona. On May 1, tension was running so high in the city that, for fear of provocations, the UGT and CNT unions gave up on holding their joint demonstration. On May 3, the Generalitat unleashed an orchestrated attack on the revolutionary workers' committees. The Catalanist councilor heading up the Internal Security department, Esquerra member Artemio Aguadé, dispatched Barcelona police chief and PSUC member Rodríguez Salas to commandeer the telephone exchange in the Plaza de Cataluña, which had been under CNT control since the previous July. The workers at the exchange promptly resisted this, while the CNT's Defense Committee sprang into action. Within two hours, the residents of the main districts, who had been on the alert for weeks, launched a general strike and erected barricades; many saw the issue as defending the revolution, and towns and villages across Catalonia rose up.[95]

Let us look at the Thalmanns' account, for they happened to be outside the Telefónica [Telephone Exchange] on the day:

> This spontaneous uprising, targeting the Stalinist organizations, broke like a storm over their heads. Throughout Catalonia, the committees seized back power, with the support of the control patrols. People's Army officers strolling through the city streets were disarmed by the crowds and kicked aside. We took part in this game, during which we frequently came across anarchist comrades from Pina. They were actively involved in the disarmament, throwing up barricades, taking over buildings facing

95 There might even have been talk of taking back the revolution, such was the extent to which it had been unmade up to that point!

Stalinist barracks and trading gunfire with the occupants of the latter. That night we could scarcely tell who was shooting at whom, nor tell the friendly barricades from the enemy ones. In the fury of the struggle, loudspeakers broadcast the news and anarchist songs. According to the news bulletins and the rumors that were rife, the revolt had spread to the whole of Catalonia. The parties' premises, as well as the communists' and Civil Guard barracks were encircled and besieged by the insurgents. Units of militia members from the Aragon front were en route to Barcelona. The Valencia government had yet not reacted.[96]

Representatives of the CNT immediately entered into negotiations with the Generalitat president who pretended to be unaware of the police action and promised to rein them in. But on the morning of May 4, Assault Guards took over the courthouse and deployed to every strategic point in the city, while the Nationalists from the Esquerra and Estat Català the membership of the UGT and the PSUC barricaded themselves inside their respective buildings. The bloody battle then shifted to the streets and was tilting in favor of the anarchists and the POUM. The action men from the CNT Defense Committee, like Lucio Ruano, manned the artillery in Montjuich and pointed it on the Generalitat. By May 4, it was a matter of "an all-out attack, and damn the consequences" and of mounting a final assault on the government positions: the Generalitat, the police headquarters, and the Hotel Colón (PSUC headquarters).

At a Regional Committee meeting that same day, certain CNT personnel moved that the CNT's collaboration in government be terminated, but others suggested that four militants be sent to talk with the very people who were labeling them "seditious uncontrollables."

And the political sleight-of-hand continued: the Generalitat's government, with the communists in the forefront, charged the anarchists with rebellion and provocation, resigning en masse and refusing to negotiate, while the population was locked in street fighting with the police. In agreement with the line about not breaking antifascist unity, which would be playing into Franco's hands, or affording the capitalist powers an excuse for intervening (there were British and French warships anchored in the port), the CNT did all it could to

96   Thalmann and Thalmann, *Combats pour la liberté*, 152.

bring calm to the situation.⁹⁷ Whereas, on May 2, it had urged workers to not let themselves be deprived of their weapons, by May 4 and thereafter CNT ministers García Oliver and Federica Montseny issued appeal after appeal over the radio. They pleaded with the defenders of the barricades to call a ceasefire and return to work. Moreover, they ordered militia members, who had left the front lines in Aragon to come to the aid of the Barcelona workers, to go back. This was debated at an extraordinary meeting of the Regional Committee on May 5, at a time when the CNT's own headquarters was surrounded by Assault Guards:

> Jover reports that arrangements had been made at the front, namely that our compañeros are to make sure that government troops are not able to close on Barcelona. And certain centurias

97   Regarding the interest shown by the British in developments in Spain, we might point to a document published in Hilari Raguer, *Carrasco i Formiguera. Un Cristiano nacionalista (1890–1938)* (Madrid: PPC, 2002). It consists of a letter from the British ambassador Sir G. Chilton to the secretary of the Foreign Office regarding a proposal just tabled by Carrasco, the envoy of the Valencia and Barcelona governments to the Basque government in Hendaye on February 23, 1937:

> The idea is that a federal solution is the only one sustaining the remaining prospects of peace for Spain, and he believes that if the great powers, mainly Britain and France, with the possible acquiescence of Russia and Italy, were to back this plan, it might be possible to get Franco to accept it. […] Señor Carrasco and his friend then dwelt at some length on the fearsome obstacle constituted by the CNT and the FAI. They had no thoughts beyond their own aims; they would shrink from nothing in order to achieve them; […] The FAI hobbled the Republic at every opportunity. But […] the Republic is presently in the process of marshaling its forces in order to crush them. It may well not be able to beat Franco, but it will be able to crush, and assuredly will crush, the FAI. As to Barcelona, with moral support from a British cruiser and an Italian one, the thing would be child's play for the FAI would cave in.

> Make no mistake: had the CNT and the FAI not lain down, no counterrevolutionary force would have backed down in the face of a bloodbath in Barcelona … Berneri had already stated that there was a whiff of Noske in the air, and everybody knew that the Stalinists would gladly serve as the bloodhounds.

had proposed coming to Barcelona. This was entirely disapproved by the plenum.[98]

Manuel Ramos confirms this:

[By May 4 or 5] we, the personnel of the centurias, had come to an agreement; half of us would remain at the front and the other half would head for Barcelona, because a number of centurias had left the Huesca front and had reached Lérida by the time the cease-fire order came through. Lots of compañeros were very surprised by our ministers' attitudes, even though the war was lost—though we didn't know it at the time and wouldn't have believed it. The CNT could not fight fascism and communism on its own; I think we should have swooped on Barcelona, and a brand-new phase would have been ushered in, in our favor or to our detriment. As I have stated already, the revolution was a goner right from that audience with the Generalidad president.[99]

In his *Mémoires inédits*, Vivancos recounts how, on May 5, 1937, he supposedly forced the commander of the 127th Mixed Brigade, Máximo Franco, to abandon his plans to head for Barcelona with two battalions, some trucks, and some field guns.

The Thalmanns joined the barricades in the city center, where the Friends of Durruti were fighting:

The first night [May 3] we spent behind the big barricade on the Rambla de la Flores, trading gunshots with a bunch of Assault Guards, who had gathered in the Café Moka. Once the shooting stopped, we chatted with the workers about what the meaning and purpose of the fighting was. They were proud of their spontaneous response and convinced that in Catalonia the Stalinists were on the losing side. [...]

During that first night nobody could tell exactly who was shooting at whom. From time to time shouts would ring out; the people controlling the barricades were stopping passers-by who had been out late and who were desperately trying to find a way

---

98   IISH, CNT, 85 C1.

99   Ramos, *Una vida azarosa*, 65–66.

back home. If these stragglers approached the barricades, they had
to put their hands in the air. Most of them, terrified, would shout
"CNT-FAI!" with all their might to identify themselves as friends
or sympathizers of these organizations. Anybody in possession
of any sort of anarchist documentation was allowed through: on
the other hand, anybody unlucky enough to be carrying a PSUC
or Communist Youth membership card was taken away for questioning.

[...] That evening [May 4] we reached an agreement [with
the Friends of Durruti] on the production of a leaflet that was
to explain the meaning and purpose of these muddled battles. In
essence, it contained the following demands:

– Immediate formation of a Junta de Defensa, Defense Council made up of all the revolutionary elements from the FAI, the
CNT, the POUM, the Juventud Libertaria [Libertarian Youth],
whichever militia members' committees were still extant, and the
control patrols.

– All power to the workers' and peasants' committees and
to the unions; withdrawal of anarchist representatives from the
Valencia government; disarming of Communist Party organizations in the rear guard; a stepping-up of pressure on the central
government with an eye to recognition of a brand-new revolutionary home-rule government in Catalonia.

That appeal went out with the endorsement of the [Friends of
Durruti]. [...]

On the evening of the uprising's third day, Federica Montseny and García Oliver, anarchist members of the Valencia government, spoke on the radio. In tearful, moving tones they begged
the workers to end the fratricidal struggle and go back to work,
as the number one priority was winning the war against Franco.
Some of the anarchist workers at first refused to believe that these
were really their leaders speaking, but when they were forced to
face facts, their disappointment and fury knew no bounds. Out
of anger, shame, and rebelliousness, many FAI and CNT members ripped up their membership cards, tossing them into the fires
behind the barricades, fires on which their soup was often still
heating. In their hundreds, they left their posts, taking their weapons with them in order to keep them safe. This spontaneous and
violent revolt, leaderless and without any commanders, was based

more on the instinct of self-defense than on any real appetite to attack, and it so petered out. The end was near.[100]

And indeed many a militant did pull out of the fight, only to take to the streets the very next day, since the PSUC and the Catalanists did not lay down their arms and were shooting away at the anarchists and tightening the noose on their locals. One can imagine the extent of the exasperation and bewilderment that situation might have generated. In the end, the fighting petered out; it has to be said that the CNT pulled out all the stops to assert its authority. The May 6 edition of *Frente Libertario* read:

> There is but one authority in Spain: the government elected by the people. Those who rebel against it [...] are the accomplices of Hitler, Mussolini, and Franco; they must be dealt with an inexorable hand.[101]

One can only wonder what the staffers at *Frente Libertario* might have come up with had the plan to bombard buildings held by CNT forces been put into effect![102] Companys proposed that plan on May 7, 1937 to the Valencia government, through the PSUC's military secretary, José del Barrio.[103]

No doubt aware of the extreme seriousness of the situation generated by this Catalanist-communist provocation and obliged therefore to play the Valencia government against the Barcelona government, the state anarchists, such as Federica Montseny, but primarily García Oliver, asked the militants in Catalonia's towns and villages not to attack the 5,000 Assault Guards dispatched from Valencia to restore public order in Catalonia. On May 7, the Assault Guards entered Barcelona and encountered no resistance, and after a few days 12,000 men with ultramodern equipment had occupied the region. En route and

---

100   Thalmann and Thalmann, *Combats pour la liberté*, 152–54.
101   Amorós, *La revolución traicionada*, 226.
102   Among these forces were the Spartacus barracks, housing Durruti Column militia members on furlough, the Bakunin barracks, and the erstwhile Escolapios convent, the base of the Defense Committee of the Centre, et cetera.
103   See Agustín Guillamón *Iborra, Barricades à Barcelone. La CNT de la victoire de juillet 1936 à la défaite de mai 1937* (Paris: Spartacus, 2009), 132, 153, 216, 217.

with the aid of local police forces and UGT personnel, they stormed the anarchist locals, murdering workers in Reus, Tortosa, and Tarragona and wrecking the collectives.

A correspondent for *Guerra di Classe* wrote in its no. 22, July 19, 1937, edition, on page 4:

> When the painful incidents in Tortosa occurred, dark pressures were exerted on the Garibaldi Brigade to get it to go along with the 'extermination' of the members of one collective made up of antifascist workers and tried-and-true anarchists, who were represented as counterrevolutionaries, etc. The Garibaldi Brigade refused, due in large part to the pride and integrity of its commander, the republican *compañero* Pacciardi.

While barricades belonging to the communists, police, and Estat Català were allowed to stand, the Telefónica and other strategic buildings were wrested back from the unions, promises or no promises. In the general confusion of battle, and above all afterward, lots of militants, notably the Libertarian Youth, were liquidated with a bullet to the back of the head or "disappeared." Among the working population, the dead numbered somewhere between four hundred and five hundred. Three hundred anarchists, many of whom were executed over the following days, were held as hostages at central police headquarters, while the CNT had freed its Assault Guard captives.

The CNT had called for a return to calm and rejoiced at "renewing [its] association with the Generalitat government and the new Public Order chief sent in by the central government"; but the latter was about to unleash a crackdown on "any individual or organization not part of the armed forces [...] who was found in possession of weapons": the POUM and the anarchists were in the firing line.

Below we reproduce some maps of Barcelona showing the main flash points in the fighting.[104]

---

104   Manuel Cruells, *Mayo sangriento, Barcelona 1937* (Barcelona: Juventud, 1970), 24–25.

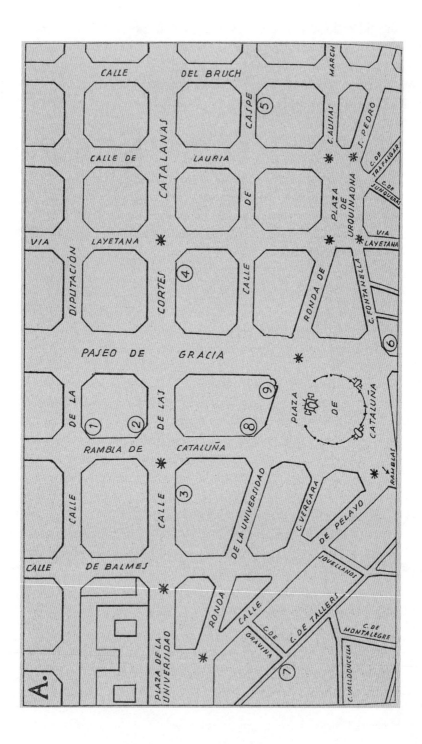

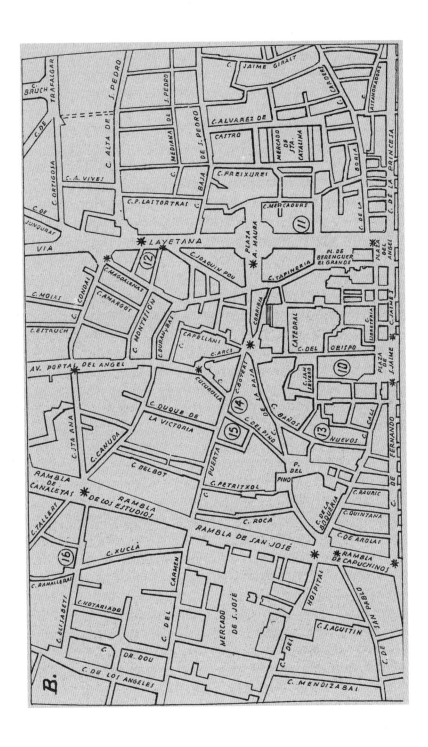

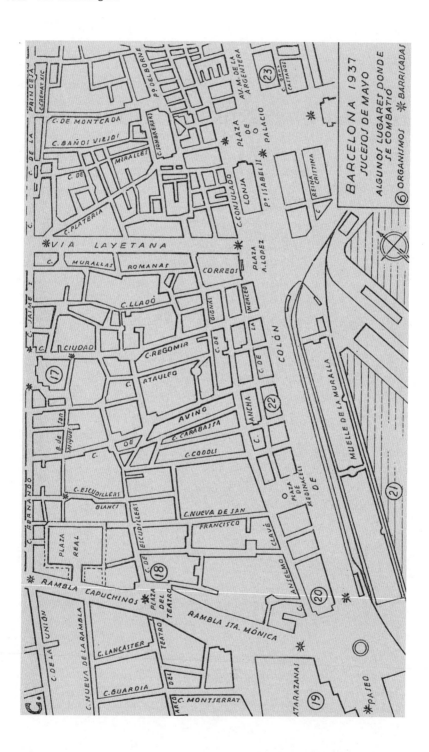

{61}
PAGE 147

In referring to the local of the "Spartacus" group, Antoine is actually referring to the local of the DAS, which occupied the German consulate building at no. 132, Paseo de Gràcia. We know more about this from other testimony, such as that of the German Fred Schröder, one of the founders of the DAS back in 1934; he worked for the CNT press agency and helped dismantle the Nazi organizations in Barcelona:

> Within hours, barricades were thrown up all over Barcelona. Best of all, those barricades were built in such a way as to cordon off the central police headquarters. For our part, we had occupied the German consulate, which occupied a very favorable strategic position, and we had erected our barricades in front of it. The entire German Library was stacked up on the balcony and used as building material for the barricades. The fighting lasted three days. It was a strange sort of fighting. In fact, no attempt was made to capture anything at all, each side being content to fire from its own barricade. At midday there was a pause and a break for lunch. One could move around freely. At two o'clock, the fighting resumed.[105]

Evidence from the Frenchman Marcel Ollivier, who arrived in Barcelona as a reporter and wrote primarily for *La Batalla*, the POUM newspaper, supports this:

> [On May 4] fresh barricades had gone up in the Calle Salmerón [today's Calle Gran de Gràcia] and on all the streets leading from the Diagonal to the working-class Gràcia district. Gangs of young people armed with revolvers and rifles were patrolling. In front of the building housing the erstwhile German consulate, the anarchists from the DAS (a German anarcho-syndicalist group) had built a barricade topped with a machine gun, from where they overlooked the entire length of the Paseo de Gràcia. At the intersection of that street and the Diagonal, one had to

---

105   Degen and Ahrens, "Wir sind es leid, die Ketten zu tragen," 90–91.

pass between the POUM barricade and the Assault Guard barricade and risk taking a bullet that wasn't meant for you.[106]

We might add that lots of German anarcho-syndicalists were arrested during these events and over the months that followed the clashes in Barcelona: Fred Schröder, Willi Paul, Helmut Kirschey, Rudolf Michaelis, and Gustav Doster all came through this alive.

Other foreign volunteers fought in the Spartacus barracks, which had been held by the anarchists ever since July. The Swiss Edi Gmür records that the fighters from the International Company stayed there while on leave in Barcelona. Thanks to the account of the anarchist Aldo Aguzzi, we know the circumstances in which Italian militia members took part in the defense of the barracks on the Avenida Icària near the port of Barceloneta during these events:

[On May 3,] the Spartacus barracks became the main focus of the fighting. At the time it was occupied by nearly 5,000 men, two hundred of them Italians. A few dozen volunteers from other nationalities and members of the Tierra y Libertad Column had twenty artillery pieces, sixteen armored cars, and a single machine gun. The Italians were weaponless. [...]

The committee met in the presence of [...] Sanz, the Durruti Division's commander, who was on leave in Barcelona at the time. [...]

The Italian compañeros were assigned the task of defending the most important position in the barracks. [...]

[On the morning of the 4th,] despite instructions and advice, two Italian compañeros there, namely [Adriano] Ferrari [...] and De Peretti [two twenty-year old-anarchists who had deserted in Italy] made to go outside. They were unarmed, but one of them was wearing a red neckerchief. When they reached the Plaça de l'Àngel, they were stopped and shot by some PSUC members. [...]

With shells still raining down, several telephone calls were made to the communist-held Karl Marx barracks six hundred meters away to get them to stop firing. They responded that they had no idea where the shooting was coming from. [...]

106   Marcel Ollivier, "Les journées sanglantes de Barcelone (3 au 9 mai 1937)," in *Spartacus, cahiers mensuels, nouvelle série*, no. 7 (Paris, 1937), 73.

Meanwhile, other Italian compañeros had dug in in various positions around the city, notably the "Casa Malatesta," the local of the Food Union, the central CNT-FAI headquarters, et cetera. Requests for help were pouring in nonstop from these places, as well as from the seat of the CNT-FAI Regional Committee. On the 4th […] some Italian compañeros grabbed four armored cars. Under hellish gunfire, they crossed the Plaça de l'Àngel, skirting the Generalitat […] and reached the CNT headquarters. […]

On Wednesday morning [May 5], another risky sortie was attempted. Six armored cars left the Spartacus barracks. It took them three hours of standing and fighting to reach the control patrols' seat in the Calle Cortés. […] The Italians who took part in the defense of the building, including Cafiero,[107] Marcon,[108] Zambonini,[109] [and others] fought heroically. Marcon was killed and Zambonini seriously wounded.

To get help to the *compañeros* who had stayed on at the Casa Malatesta, which had in part been overrun by the communists

107   This must be Luigi Cafiero Meucci (1905–1965), a militiaman from the Italian Column; he went back to France during the summer of 1937.

108   Pietro Marcon, born in 1903 in the Treviso region; a member of Giustizia e Libertà and the Italian Column.

109   Enrico Zambonini (b. Reggio Emilia, 1893) had been living in exile in Spain since the 1930s. In July 1936, he was involved in the fighting and enlisted as a militiaman with the Ascaso Column's Italian Section. Taking issue with the militarization, he returned to the rear guard in April 1937 and then was active in the CNT's Foodstuffs Union in Barcelona. Crossing into France at the time of the *retirada*, he was interned in the Argeles concentration camp. In August 1942 he was handed over to the Italian authorities in Mantua and sentenced to five years' internment on Ventotene. Come the downfall of fascism, he, like many other anarchist militants, was not released but transferred to the Renicci di Anghiari concentration camp; during the relocation he refused to go any further and was interned in Arezzo prison from which he would not be released until December 4,1943. He then made contact with the underground movement and the partisans in Emilia. Arrested by the fascists on January 21, 1944, he was brought to the prison in Reggio Emilia. Enrico Zambonini was sentenced to death by a special tribunal and shot on January 30, 1944.

To these May 1937 murders of Italian anarchists we can add that of Mario Luigi Beruti (b. in Turin, 1894). He had been living in Spain for some years and had enlisted with the Iron Column. The Stalinists shot him in Tarragona.

and Assault Guards toward the end of May 4, some armored cars attempted a sortie but were forced to turn back. On the morning of the 5th, another attempt was made. Six armored cars came forth. [...]

The Italian compañeros who had escaped from the Casa Malatesta and the Food Union mostly sought refuge in the Spartacus barracks. They brought with them news of the general situation and the many assassination attempts on the compañeros... [...]

They decided to finish it. An initial sortie led to their occupying all the buildings separating the two barracks. [...]

An assault designed to storm the communist barracks [...] was scheduled for 9 o'clock that evening. [...] But during that day Federica Montseny and García Oliver had mounted propaganda to get the anarchists and CNT personnel to stop the fighting. Commander Ceva, who was on his way to discussions with the CNT Regional Committee, returned late that night with instructions to call off the attack.

[...] The Italian compañeros didn't think they should pass up a chance to strike a decisive blow at the counterrevolution's provocations and intrigues.

Even though CNT and FAI supporters all over the city were—while they were protesting their leaders—starting to leave their barricades, a substantial force of communists and Assault Guards mounted an attack from the Estación de Francia against the Spartacus barracks on the night of May 5–6. The compañeros mobilized to counter this; they threw up barricades in the surrounding area and blocked the way at the Avenida Icària. There were contradictory reports all that day. [...] Two German compañeros ventured very close to the enemy's position and threw hand bombs. Only to perish as they withdrew. [...]

On the 7th, the CNT's order to "cease fire" became even more peremptory. The Spanish leaders at the Spartacus barracks, headed by commandant Sanz, complied and starred pulling back from all strategic points. Overnight, there was further skirmishing, but by the 8th, the anarchists had abandoned all their positions. The Italian compañeros manning the barricade at the Avenida Icària [...] thus withdrew from the last position [...].

The fighting was just about over, [...] Sanz [...] immediately suggested using the Italian personnel, whose handiwork he had seen for himself, to bolster his division's International Battalion, which he didn't entirely trust.[110]

The May events exacerbated the bickering between the Italian and the Spanish anarchists: the former felt more and more alienated by the tactics of the latter. In 1947, Ernesto Bonomini concluded his testimony,[111] entitled "Bloody week," like this: "Despite the passage of time, one cannot help but feel some repugnance at those who, continuing to betray the anarchist movement even today, engage with the ministerial compromises of successive token governments in exile."[112]

The murders of Berneri and Barbieri were the last straw for the column of Italian volunteers in Spain: a large segment of them launched the Spartacus Battalion (in memory, perhaps, of the fighting they did in that barracks) and joined the "Tierra y Libertad" column. Others joined the Durruti Division's International Battalion, and others still Ortiz's 25th Division or the Garibaldi Brigade.

{62}
PAGE 147

The reference here is to the third newsreel in the series entitled *Los aguiluchos de la FAI por las tierras de Aragón*, by Adrien Porchet. On his return to Barcelona, Porchet carried on working for the CNT: he was the chief cameraman on the first full-length movie produced by the union—*Aurora de esperanza*. He then worked on newsreels on the Confederation's behalf, covering demonstrations, congresses, and so on. During the May 1937 events, he had a ringside seat and filmed the fighting at the Telefónica. Porchet left Barcelona shortly before the

110 Fedeli, *Un trentennio di attività anarchica*, 194–98.
111 It is known of Bonomini—among other things—that he gunned down Nicola Bonservizi, Mussolini's personal representative in Paris on February 20, 1924.
112 *Volontà*, No. 11.

Nationalist army entered and did manage to bring some negatives with him. He had emotional memories of Félix Marquet, a militiaman who he had trained as a cameraman at the front.

To quote Ridel's eyewitness account, sent off to *Le Libertaire* and published in its October 9, 1936, edition:

> In the midst of the whirlwind of revolution, the Public Entertainments Union took over the entire entertainments industry; the theaters and the cinemas. Each premises had its own organizing committee on which all of the various staff grades were represented. [...] ticket prices were slashed considerably and tipping eliminated, as was complimentary ticketing; wages were raised considerably, even as working hours were reduced.[113]

After the war, Emmanuel Larraz wrote this:

> The anarcho-syndicalists had immediately grasped the importance of cinema for propaganda purposes and, constantly linking the war to social revolution, they doggedly paired the shooting of films about military operations with films about the changes under way in the rear guard, in the workshops and factories. The anarchist output, which was voluminous (six full-length features plus more than sixty short features) is characterized essentially by a violent anti-clericalism, especially during the early days of the war, by the focus on workers' dignity, and, finally, by a very lively appreciation that the fate of humanity as a whole was then at stake in Spain.[114]

---

113   Quoted in Porchet, *Adrien Porchet, cinéaste sur le front d'Aragon*, 3.

114   Emmanuel Larraz, *Le Cinéma espagnol des origines à nos jours* (Paris: Le Cerf, 1986), 83–84.

{63}
PAGE 147

From Antoine, we know that Carl Einstein was in Barcelona during the events of May 1937 and in the thick of the fighting. The presence and activity of this writer while in Spain remains poorly known and little documented. We should point out that Einstein was not related to Albert Einstein at all. Anyone wishing to learn more about him is referred to the research in progress in France and Germany.

Having served in the front lines for nearly nine months, Einstein took his first break from armed service in late April 1937, at which point he went to Barcelona for treatment. We do know that he continued to serve in the People's Army on the Aragon front, but the theory is that he was progressively sidelined because of his criticisms of the anarchists' strategy, on the one hand, and his growing depression on the other. We would also need to take notice of the battle of Santa Quiteria on April 12, 1937, in which the International Battalion sustained 50% losses. During his time in Barcelona, he wrote an article, which was published on May 1 in *Die Soziale Revolution*, the DAS newspaper published in Stockholm and Paris. Here are a few excerpts from that article, entitled "The Aragon Front":

> Any revolution today necessarily turns into a war. The proletariat's adversaries have their generals and high commands at their disposal. [...] Now, with the aid of international financiers, a more or less disguised intervention is being deployed. [...]
>
> The civil war has thus been turned into a colonial or international war. The war in Spain bears out this contention. It has had a change of face and of political hue: it has been bolstered. The role of the military has been boosted considerably.
>
> [...] Nevertheless, the warfare of the confederal columns meant something other than the doltish, destructive running of the war by the conventional military. The situation and disposition of the Spanish front have been determined not only by geographical or strategic considerations; that front separates two conflicting views of society and of history, of reality and of how it is to be changed.
>
> [...] Outside intervention started to become more visible in Aragon as well. [...] The white aluminum bombs from the

steel plants of the Rhine blasted peaceable peasants, shepherds, and livestock. One can hear the heavy sound of German boots. Despite which the front stayed virtually stagnant; [...]

The comrades standing guard on the Aragon front have long been clamoring for the fighting and the marching to press ahead. No matter the cost, they want to take the pressure off Madrid. But their pleas have gone unanswered. This front sleepwalks behind a dense veil woven of a deceptive silence and imminent weariness. Why the reluctance to pay serious heed to this front and to take some pains with it?

With the militarization and the events of May '37, Einstein's hopes regarding the chances of a global social liberation were diminished. He went through moments of dejection and depression. Despite that, he stuck by the CNT. He was let down by the performance of its leaders, but he kept up his commitment to the People's Army while reverting occasionally to his authorial activities. He was back in Barcelona for treatment at the beginning of 1938, and Rüdiger found him a post with the information bureau. In an interview he gave to *La Vanguardia* in May 1938, he set out his political analysis and his thoughts of the part he thought Spain was playing in that war in European terms. In addition, he had to draft something for the IWA on anarcho-syndicalism in Spain; but by August he had still not delivered it. Carl and Lyda returned to France via Portbou in late January 1939 together with the last of the foreign volunteers, but they were separated following an Italian air raid. Einstein was committed to the Argelès camp but managed to get back to Paris quickly, where his friend Kahnweiler saw him once more on February 15. On February 16, 1939 *Match* carried a very famous photograph of Einstein as an officer, on the terrace of a Perpignan café, as an illustration for a report on refugees from the Spanish war.

In 1940, Carl Einstein was placed in a camp near Bordeaux as part of measures taken by the French government with regard to Germans living in France. Most likely released because of his age, but still depressed, he attempted to take his own life near Mont-de-Marsan in late June. He was rescued and sent to live among the monks of Lestelle-Bétharram abbey. But his hopes were dashed, and he knew that he was still on the Nazis' blacklists and so had no chance of fleeing across the Pyrenees, given his service in Spain, so he threw himself into the Gave de Pau on July 5, 1940.

Sketch of Carl Einstein, illustrating an interview
that appeared in *Fragua Social*, April 13, 1937

For further information, see:"Carl Einstein," http://gimenologues
.org/spip.php?rubrique34; Einstein, *La Columna Durruti y otros
artículos y entrevistas de la Guerra Civil española*; García, Nelles,
Linse, and Piotrowski, *Antifascistas alemanes en Barcelona*; Liliane
Meffre, *Carl Einstein, 1885–1940. Itinéraires d'une pensée moderne*
(Paris: Presses universitaires de Paris-Sorbonne, 2002); Marianne
Kröger, "Carl Einstein im Spanischen Bürgerkrieg" *Archiv für die Ges-
chichte der Widerstandes und der Arbeit*, no. 12 (Fernwald [Annerod]:
Germinal Verlag, 1992); Marianne Kröger and Roland Hubert (Hrsg.),
Carl Einstein im Exil. Kunst und Politik in den 1930er Jahren (Mün-
schen: Wilhelm Fink, 2007).

{64}
PAGE 151

The issue raised here regarding the responsibility of parents for their
children and the need for "womb strikes" typically invokes matters

raised by certain anarchist thinkers. Soledad, educated and rebelling against convention, must undoubtedly have identified with the individualistic and idealistic young libertarians forming affinity groups, which were often tied to neighborhood (*barriadas*). They wrote a lot about issues relating to naturism, medicine, education, women's liberation, anarchist ethics, anti-militarism and pacifism, illegalism, and so forth. In late 1935, in light of the imminent victory of the Popular Front, many individualist anarchists started giving some serious thought to the society of the future. They cautioned themselves against undue idealization of country life and the problems of social coexistence:

> For us to crave an escape from the life of the factory, the office, the shop [...] is a natural, wholesome, legitimate feeling; [...]
> The way to build up every chance of success [...] is a GRADUAL return to country living, keeping up the work that guarantees the wherewithal to live (if we can) and, gradually, relocate ourselves entirely. To think a different way, we have to "act alone" in order to hold on to our independence rather than running the risk of compromising that of others. [115]

Young editors in Barcelona and Valencia published the following notice in the January 1936 edition of the review *Ética-Iniciales*:

> For all those who want to form an association of conscious individuals with a predisposition toward living out anarchism in moral as well as economic terms, as much as current possibilities allow. Every one of us who feels the need to live as much of an anarchist life as we can in the present moment rather than waiting for the problematic achievements of an uncertain future, or waiting for humanity, the great mass of society, to open its eyes to its fatal errors, we all could, "between us," come to some mutual arrangement and help one another.[116]

115   Raoul Odin, "Algo sobre colonias libertarias," *Iniciales*, 7/11, November 1935, 6, as quoted in Xavier Díez, *El anarquismo individualista en España (1923–1938)* (Barcelona: Virus, 2007), 222.

116   Quoted in Dolors Marín, "Han Ryner et la diffusion de sa pensée au sein de l'anarchisme ibérique," in Collectif, *Actes du colloque Han Ryner*, Marseille 28 et 29 septembre 2002 (Marseille: CIRA & Les Amis de Han Ryner, 2003), 93.

This plainly articulates one of anarchism's views, one that holds that thoroughgoing change only works in the long term, through workers' self-education rather than by means of violent, murderous insurrections. So, for such young people like the pacifist Vicente Nebot from Torrasa, who was obliged to go to the front in 1936:

> the war has been fatal to us in that it destroyed the handiwork we were in the process of building; we had been in the throes of molding ourselves as free men for a better society, and the war robbed us of all that. We had been sorely tempted to accelerate the model society that we were after, but people were not ready.[117]

We can sense something of the same sort of loss in Soledad, especially in the wake of May 1937.

{65}
PAGE 152

Back from the Huesca front, Camillo Berneri was resting in Barcelona, at his home at no. 2 in the Plaça Dostoïevsky (Plaça de l'Àngel today), close to the CNT headquarters in the Vía Durruti (currently Vía Laietana). He had written a text about Gramsci and another in defense of the POUM, which had both been broadcast over the CNT-FAI radio station on May 3. He was joined by his friend Barbieri and his companion.

Francesco Barbieri, born in 1895, had immigrated to Argentina in the 1920s, where he had taken part in armed robberies mounted by Di Giovanni's anarchist group. On returning to Italy, he escaped from prison and made for France and then Switzerland before arriving in Spain in October 1935. Denounced by the Italian secret police, who applied to have him extradited, he surreptitiously reentered Switzerland and stayed there up until developments in Barcelona in July 1936. A well-known militant in Catalonia, he ran the Italian Column's security service.

117 Ibid., 96.

From the outbreak of the fighting that May, Berneri's porch was caught in the crossfire coming from the PSUC-manned barricade in the Calle Llibreteria and a UGT local in the Vía Durruti. On May 5, some men in plain clothes and wearing red armbands arrested Berneri and Barbieri. They were accompanied by some police officers, who had dropped in the previous evening, blatantly reconnoitering the place. According to the testimony of Barbieri's wife and another female militant—who asked one police officer to produce his warrant card and who wrote down the number—the apartment was searched and then the two Italians, charged with counter-revolutionary activities, were taken away. Their bullet-riddled bodies were found the following day, one on the Ramblas and the other in the Plaça de la Generalitat.

In 1978, García Oliver wrote:

> Among the May dead, I would like to give due mention to the person and personality of Camillo Berneri, an Italian anarchist murdered in mysterious circumstances during the events of May 1937. [...]
>
> [...] I never met him nor did I associate with the man. And but for his tragic end there is every chance that I would never have heard of his existence. I was unacquainted with him either as an anarchist or as a professor or as a writer. [...] And I am convinced that the same goes for at least 99% of the Spanish anarchist and anarcho-syndicalist compañeros."[118]

So, the "strong man" of the CAMC was unacquainted with one of the founders of the Italian Column, a man who had direct dealings with Santillán. However, the counterrevolution struck down the Italian intellectual just weeks after publication of the "Open Letter" that he'd written to Federica Montseny.[119] We might add that Montseny's parents had, over the years between 1929 and 1934, published lots of articles in support of Berneri in *La Revista Blanca*, the extremely popular anarchist cultural review.

In an interview given to Freddy Gomez in 1977, García Oliver reckoned that: "Berneri's influence was very slight. [...] What interest

118   García Oliver, *El Eco de los pasos*, 431.
119   See endnote 38 above.

could the communists have had in liquidating him? One could understand their trying to kill Marianet or Federica or me, […] but Berneri? No."[120]

Whether his audience was tiny or otherwise, Berneri was definitely one of the staunchest critics of both Mussolini's policies in Spain and of Moscow's, particularly of the way the NKVD (soviet political police) could operate in the country with impunity. He was also one of the few libertarians to publicly disassociate himself from CNT policy after having initially supported it. While the goons who shot him in the back of the head were never found, his murder was not universally "mysterious." Antoine and many another anarchists then and now were and are of the opinion that the murderers were the Stalinists who were, systematically and physically eliminating those anarchists who still subscribed to the social revolution. It would appear therefore that, as in Durruti's death, the thesis of communist responsibility for the murder of the Italian philosopher may be backed by the libertarian rank and file and not by their leaders, those unshakable champions of "safeguarding the unity of antifascist action."

Francisco Madrid did a lot of important research into Berneri, the revolution, and counter-revolution in Europe between 1917 and 1937. He pointed out two documents that support the contention that the Italian intellectual died at the hands of Stalin's thugs. An article from the May 20, 1937 edition in *Il Grido del Popolo*, the Italian CP's mouthpiece in France, stated that:

> Camillo Berneri, one of the leaders of the Friends of Durruti—which, though disowned even by the leadership of the Iberian Anarchist Federation, triggered the bloody uprising against the Popular Front government in Catalonia—has been liquidated by the democratic Revolution, and no antifascist could question its right to act in self-defense.[121]

Which is hard not to construe as a sort of claim of responsibility.

Another article, this time from the communist Palmiro Togliatti and carried in an Italian CP weekly paper on January 15, 1950,

120 "Juan García Oliver 1902–1980," *À contretemps*, no. 17 (2004).
121 Cited in Francisco Madrid Santos, *Camillo Berneri, un anarchico Italiano (1897–1937)* (Pistoia: Archivio Famiglia Berneri, 1985), 387.

is tantamount to what Francisco Madrid has described as "the second murder of Berneri":

> Camillo Berneri was an anarchist, and within the anarchists of Barcelona in April 1937, he was part of the tendency which was, to some extent, akin to the unified socialists, the Catalanists, and the republicans, in that he had opposed, and indeed vigorously opposed the behavior of the notorious uncontrollables and provoked a backlash. That is what the famous Barcelona revolt in May was: a muddled series of bloody street battles fought house to house and from rooftops. Berneri perished in one such clash: that is all....[122]

And so Berneri has been portrayed sometimes as an uncontrollable and sometimes as an enemy of the uncontrollables. Pretty much the same as Durruti had been....

The CNT had lobbied for the funerals not to be turned into public events in order to avoid incidents; the members of the DAS defied the ban and paraded with its flags behind the coffins of Berneri and his three comrades. But the erstwhile internationalist militia members were now going to have to worry about managing on their own ...

For further information, see Fedeli, *Un trentennio di attività anarchica*, 191–201; Rama, "Camillo Berneri y la revolución española," 18–32; Luigi Di Lembo, *Guerra di classe e lotta umana. L'anarchismo in Italia, del biennio rosso alla guerra di Spagna, 1919–1939* (Pisa: Biblioteca Franco Serantini, 2001), 210.

{66}
PAGE 152

Francisco Ferrer was murdered in Barcelona on May 5, 1937. This left its mark on Edi Gmür and some *compañeros* from the International Group:

---

122   Cited in ibid., 388.

May 7.

[...] We left the barracks for the hospital, to pay a final tribute to Francisco Ferrer. He was killed by the Guardia for refusing to be disarmed. He'd been suffering from wounds since Santa Quiteria. He was a good comrade. In the hospital morgue, we first had to search for his corpse. A ghastly stench made us hold our breath. A large hall filled with corpses, packed together like sardines in a tin. Several of them had swollen bellies, grinning faces, and others were folded together, empty eye-sockets and sunken cheeks. How many more victims will this revolution claim? We escorted the coffin as far as the cemetery. Eighteen more coffins overtook us, hurtling past with neither mourners nor wreaths. Nameless victims of the Revolution.[123]

From the second part of the interview with Giuditta carried in *Guerra di Classe* (we have seen part one), we learn how Francisco Ferrer was murdered:

– We would like to have it from your lips how Francisco, the grandson of Francisco Ferrer y Guardia, met his end. We are aware that you knew him.
She replied:
Actually, I was like a mother to him for a long time. I am fifty-two years old. We both set off together with Durruti in July 1936. Like his grandfather, he was kind and generous. Francisco was born in Paris in 1909. After the downfall of the Bourbon monarchy he rushed back to Spain. He could see the social revolution looming ... He could have stayed behind in Barcelona, come the fascist army mutiny. He had a heart complaint and, in addition, held a certificate showing him to be completely unfit for military service on account of an accident at work. Instead, off he went with Durruti and applied to be accepted into the International Assault Group, one of the most heroic units.
– Why was he in Barcelona during the May events?
– Here goes: on April 8, he took part in the so-called Santa Quiteria hermitage operation. He was hospitalized in Barcelona. By late April, his physical condition had improved, but he had

123   Gmür and Minnig, *Pour le bien de la révolution*, 100.

to report almost on a daily basis to the hospital to continue his treatment. We were together on May 5. In the Calle París, we stumbled upon a bunch of soldiers—communists, I suppose. Francisco was wearing his militiaman's uniform and was carrying his revolver in his belt. He had with him a document authorizing him, as a member of the International Assault Group, to go armed anywhere he pleased. The strangers, training their rifles on him, ordered him to hand over the revolver. He refused. He made vociferous objection, stating that he could not allow himself to be disarmed since he needed the weapon for the fight against fascism. He was the object of brutal assailants, who, showering him with all manner of threats and abuse, forced him to produce his papers. When Francisco showed them his CNT card, a voice shrieked: "Kill him!" He was never given the chance to defend himself. He was thrown up against a wall and the bandits opened fire at him simultaneously from a few steps away.

Our comrade paused … She swept a hand across her brow. She had the appalling spectacle still before her eyes: It took him twenty-four hours to die. It was ghastly. One of my arms was slightly wounded.

We asked her: Did they know it was Ferrer y Guardia's grandson that they were killing? And that they were committing against him the very same crime as the infamous monarchy?

– I don't know. They did know that he was a CNT militant, a Durruti volunteer. That was enough for them to murder him!

Our *compañera* who lived through the Italian proletariat's battles of 1919–1922 and through the epic events of July 19 in Barcelona, who looked death in the face in the trenches of Aragon, is overcome with grief. Our hearts ache with the same pain that torments the hearts of every revolutionary, and hers, right now."[124]

---

124 *Guerra di Classe*, no. 22, (July 19, 1937).

{67}

PAGE 152

On May 12, the Generalitat announced the effective decommissioning of the Control Patrols without a word of objection from the CNT. On the pretext of punishing the instigators of the May disturbances, the Barcelona police, riddled with Stalinists and answerable to no one, stepped up the counterrevolutionary offensive. The meeting places of groups and unions critical of the government were laid waste, and outlaws where forced to go into hiding wherever they could in the city. Mysterious squads carried out illegal arrests of foreign militia members belonging to the confederal columns.

The Thalmanns thought it wise to get out of the country altogether:

> Convinced that the revolutionary élan of the Spanish workers and peasants was spent and that the civil war was now no more than a pale imitation of imperialist contradictions, we wondered whether it might not be better to leave Spain. We had no particular desire to be abducted by the Russian secret police and to turn up as unidentifiable corpses![125]

But they were arrested on the ship they had boarded.

> They took us to a huge building located near the city center and led us down a corridor leading to the terrace of an inner courtyard. About a dozen people were shuffling around there, smoking and speaking softly. With amazement and bittersweet delight, we recognized Michel Michaelis and a number of our comrades from Pina.
>
> "Ah, you're here as well?" he greeted us tersely.
>
> "Can you tell us who arrested us?" I asked him.
>
> "The Russians, GPU. They've been holding us here for the past eight days without questioning. There are at least three hundred prisoners here, and we haven't seen the half of it yet. They allow us into the yard for an hour a day. If the FAI doesn't get us out of here, I don't think we'll ever get out."
>
> "What is this place?"

125   Thalmann and Thalmann, *Combats pour la liberté*, 161.

"They call it the Puerta del Ángel (Angel Gate), and it belongs to some Spanish count."

Clara and I looked at each other. So, they had us in their clutches at last.

[...] Every nationality and political persuasion was represented among the prisoners—Spaniards, Germans, French, British, Belgians, Yugoslavs, Italians, and Polish. They belonged to the POUM, to anarchist organizations, and to the Spanish Socialist Party or to the Italian Marxists whose leader was Pietro Nenni. [...]

During one stroll, Michel informed us that he was being held in the garage with forty other comrades. They slept on the bare cement floor without mattresses or blankets.

[...] One group of his *compañeros* decided to start a hunger strike if there was no improvement in their conditions of detention. Neither in the overcrowded garage nor in any of the other cells was there a fascist or monarchist to be found; all these prisoners were antifascists of varying persuasions.

[...] One afternoon, we heard voices coming from the chapel window; I clambered up on the window bars and saw six individuals stretched out on mattresses inside the chapel. Among them, I recognized Fred Hünen, Egon Korsch, and a few other militia members who had served alongside us in Michaelis's centuria. [...]

During my walk, [...] I heard a racket in the corridor. The door to the yard burst open and I saw Michel Michaelis grappling with a soldier who was ordering him to remain in the yard. [...]

"What's going on?" I asked.

"I escaped, then came back of my own volition. This idiot guard refuses to believe me."

"You returned of your own volition?" I asked him, in disbelief.

"Believe me. Last night, the guard forgot to lock the garage door: we could all have escaped. We argued half the night away, deciding what we should do. We were actually afraid that the GPU might take reprisals against any comrades left behind. In the end, by common accord we agreed that I would escape on my own in order to brief the FAI National Committee on the details of this private prison, and that I would come back. So off I went to the FAI; they are now well briefed on the Puerta del Ángel and will spring us out of there. Upon my return, I simply strolled right through the main entrance and now these idiots are refusing to believe me!' That was Michel in a nutshell: absolute solidarity and boundless confidence in his anarchists, all bound up with an unbelievable naiveté and utter incomprehension of the situation. Shortly after that, they came to get him."[126]

After he got out of the Stalinist jails, Rudolf Michaelis took Spanish nationality and joined the army of the Republic. Crossing into France during the retirada, he was then to smuggle himself back into Spain, only to be arrested and sentenced to thirty years in prison. Released in 1944, he would live in Madrid, under police surveillance, up until 1946. He then made his way to Germany and joined the Communist Party in East Berlin. In 1951 he was expelled from that party but stayed on in Eastern Berlin with his family. In 1967, his former partner, Margaret, who had moved away to Australia, visited him, and he corresponded with her up until 1975. He also made contact again with some of his former comrades from the FAUD and gave talks in West Berlin (under an assumed name), notably about the Spanish revolution. Rudolf Michaelis died in 1990.[127]

But the FAI did not step in, and in July 1937 a batch of the prisoners were relocated to Valencia, to the former Santa Úrsula convent, now a prison, under the sole control of the PCE; Comintern agents interrogated and tortured on a nightly basis, and many of the inmates died there:

> In front of our window there was a tall tower with only its walls visible to us. We were forever hearing singing and wild screams coming from that tower, and, by lying down on the floor, we could just about make out a mob of people flailing their arms around in every direction on the platform. My *compañero* explained to me that upward of a hundred anarchist militia members were locked up in the tower, an entire section of a column that had mutinied on the front.
>
> [...] One Dutch socialist who happened to be on the same floor as us, but to whom I hadn't yet spoken, told me one day as

126   Ibid., 163, 165–67, 170–71.

127   See García, Nelles, Linse, and Piotrowski, *Antifascistas alemanes en Barcelona*, 419.

he displayed his toothless mouth: "Look at me, the shits really laid into me, they've broken all my teeth and, take it from me, I'm not the only one. No one knows why they select some people for torture and others escape. Back in my cell there's a Yugoslav they occasionally lock up for twenty-four hours at a time in a cage so tiny that his legs are all swollen and he loses consciousness. And soils his clothing. And I have heard that they have done the same with other comrades."

Pedro had already told me of similar horrors, but I was unable to verify them for myself. Nevertheless, having seen and heard Raab, as well as the Dutch guy, there were no grounds left for doubt.[128]

On August 30, 1937, the Thalmanns were released:

We owe our lives to the effective solidarity campaign mounted by our friends. For we were sure that we were never going to break free of the spider's web that the GPU had woven in Spain.

We had realized too that the comrades who had been tortured and liquidated had all been refugees from fascist countries (many of them Germans, Italians, Yugoslavs, and Polish), serving as volunteers with POUM or FAI units. In their cases, the GPU had no reason to fear intervention by the governments in question.[129]

Alongside such Stalinist persecution, an underlying trend toward the restoration of order, all dressed up as a republican virtue, was triggering a further wave of arrests: between May 1937 and the end of 1938, some 3,700 militants were to bear the brunt of this in Catalonia, over 90% of them libertarians. Let us take a look at the political backdrop against which this was going on. On May 17, the communists brought about the collapse of the Caballero government and joined the representatives of the right wing of the socialists—Indalecio Prieto and Juan Negrín—to form a new government. According to César M. Lorenzo, the CNT-FAI, in defiance of the views of some of its leaders, turned down the ministries offered to them by Negrín. Not that this stopped it from entering the next "Negrín" government in April 1938. For the

128   Thalmann and Thalmann, *Combats pour la liberté*, 173, 181–82.
129   Ibid., 189.

time being, by June 1937, the CNT was no longer represented on the central or regional governments and became the opposition:

> Our role at present is to alert the proletariat marshaled within the Confederation to the fact that it must, now more than ever, abide by the instructions of the accountable committees. Only coherent and concerted action will allow us to thwart the counterrevolution [...]. Let no one play into the hands of the provocateurs! [...] Long live the trade union alliance![130]

In the estimation of François Godicheau, the May gambit had been successful; it had paved the way for the installation of an "authoritarian democratic State," with the Stalinists as its spearhead. And Godicheau also makes this significant point:

> The complete inversion of the balance of political power took place, not just at the time of the clashes [in May] but over the ensuing months. Whereas even at the beginning of May it was the militants of the UGT [the Catalan branch, which was dominated by communists] who were afraid, from July onward, it was CNT members who were in trouble, and hundreds of them had to go into hiding or seek refuge in the front lines. For a year, arrest followed arrest until several thousand individuals were affected, and dozens and dozens of trials were mounted. This is one of the most repressive episodes in the history of the Republic. It targeted the usual "troublemakers," the revolutionary militants from the trade unions. Despite that, these events have remained almost completely unknown, the CNT's official historians, José Peirats in particular, having been very mealy-mouthed about the scale of this wave of repression. The little-known history of this wave of repression needs to be reconstructed.[131]

130   Taken from a National Committee notice released around May 20, and quoted in César M. Lorenzo, *Le Mouvement anarchiste en Espagne. Pouvoir et révolution sociale* (Saint-Georges d'Oléron: Éditions Libertaires, 2006), 349.
131   Godicheau, *La Guerre d'Espagne*, 172–73.

{68}
PAGE 153

Like Antoine, Swiss volunteer Edi Gmür had rejoined the front lines, but he was profoundly troubled:

[Monday] May 10.

A group from our company was chatting in the courtyard of the Spartacus barracks today. I listened in for a bit and made note of what I could gather. "I'm leaving," one of them said, "our cause is a lost. The CNT has failed to lead the fight, the POUM's influence among the toiling masses is too small. The Valencia government has emerged as the winner. It's the most right-wing government since the start of the revolution, and it's a sham government at that, because behind it stand Stalin and his dictatorship. I will not sacrifice myself for some bourgeois state. [...]"

[...]

What is one to think of this? It's a matter for the Spaniards. I came here to fight international fascism, and now we find ourselves faced with the choice of siding with one of the workers' sides against the other. If it's come to that, then obviously bloody clashes lie ahead. With the best will in the world, I didn't know where I stood.[132]

{69}
PAGE 156

The International Company, newly dubbed the International Battalion, left Barcelona on June 7, but Giua was not among them. Antoine has undoubtedly mixed this date up with a different one; or maybe he wasn't aware that his friend from Milan had taken the officer training course that spring at the military training school in Albacete. Made a lieutenant, Lorenzo signed on with the Garibaldi Battalion that May.

132   Gmür and Minnig, *Pour le bien de la revolution*, 101, 103.

As to the International Battalion, Edouard Sill's memoir tells us that it

> was split up into four companies [comprising] a hundred men apiece, plus the high command. By June 1, 1937, it was up to full complement and then stationed in Monegrillo. The captain was Asencio Francisco Rodríguez and the commissar André Patural. No 1 and No 4 companies were entrusted to Frenchmen: Captains Jean Schwartz and Mohamed Sana. The foreigners were spread over three companies (the Nos 1, 2, and 4).[133]

And so, Antoine rejoined the Aragon front. Militarization was now complete. Incorporated into the brand new Army of the East, the anarchist divisions would now have to take orders from General Pozas, who was under the sway of the communists.

Pacciardi recorded in his memoirs:

> Despite calls for a reshuffle of Brigade staffs in light of the recent developments [May 1937], I deliberately held on to two anarchists as part of my staff, my assistant Braccialarghe and signals chief Hortega.
>
> I didn't want to lose excellent fighters, and, above all, I was out to spare the Brigade its first-ever split. Battistelli shared my opinion, so much so that he—he who had quit the anarchist militias for our ranks—promptly wrote a vibrant article paying tribute to the memory of Berneri.[134]

Having arrived in Spain in mid-September 1936, Pacciardi left Spain in late August 1937 with Braccialarghe; they are open about the fact that they had cut ties with the communist organization. [135]

In mid-June the republican divisions launched "diversionary" pushes in Aragon, from Huesca to Teruel, to break Franco's stranglehold on Bilbao. In Huesca, it failed, and a thousand lives were lost, most of them anarchists. Gmür recounts the circumstances in which the

---

133   Sill, *Ni Franco, ni Staline*, 183.
134   Randolfo Pacciardi, *Volontari italiani nella Spagna Republicana. Il Battaglione Garibaldi* (Lugano: Nuove Edizione di Capolago, 1938). Quotation borrowed from *L'Adunata dei Refrattari*, May 14, 1938.
135   See Habeck, Radosh, and Sevostianov, *Spain Betrayed*, 342–44, 352–53.

International Company, with Alexis Cardeur as its new commander, mounted an attack in the Monte Oscuro sector on June 17; there he ran into Antoine and his friends from the Banda Negra flying squad:

[Thursday] June 17

[…] We were told to head down to Monte Oscuro, in a small valley. […] Our Captain told us that we were due to relieve the Banda Negra. They had mounted their attack in the early morning. […] The men we were relieving crossed our path in a straggling line. A number of them were carrying two or three rifles. […] In addition to rifles, we had each been issued with a spade and a pick. There was an adequate supply of grenades on site; but they were the old, primitive hand grenades that the enemy had dumped. My platoon, with Fischer as its lieutenant, took over the main position, the Ermita Santa Cruz. We immediately began fortifying it. Enemy troops had dug a trench and a few machine-gun nests there, but there was no cover against air raids. […] On the other side, at the bottom of a sheer cliff traversed by small streams, sat Perdiguera, where forty-two men from the International Group had died. From our position we could pretty much monitor the village.

I was on sentry duty from 1 o'clock to 4 o'clock. When I arrived, I spotted a large number of trucks entering the village. I reported this immediately to the *sargento*. Two hours later, which is to say at about 3 o'clock, I saw the beginnings of a strong counterattack. Around three thousand men were slowly advancing across a line about 2 kilometers in length. Eight tanks led the way. They were closing slowly but methodically. Suddenly, our position came under ferocious artillery fire from three sides. […] Report of the counterattack had been passed on, and our company and No 1 Company made ready for the attack. […] Our artillery was firing on the enemy but badly, falling short or past them. Rarely getting anywhere close to the tanks. Our *teniente* was in the shelter where the munitions and grenades were stacked up and he was busy cursing. Each of us was issued with six, which were quickly primed. Meanwhile, twelve or sixteen guns were pounding our position. We were lying in the trenches, carrying on with our work. […] But, all of a sudden, we heard the drone of aircraft engines. […] We counted six three-engined bombers drifting majestically across the blue sky. Ten smaller planes appeared

above them, with twelve fighters higher up. Piet looked at me
with a grin, but his cheeks were ashen: "We're not going to make
it!" Which was what I was thinking myself. The *teniente* came
dashing back and ordered us to be ready to attack. Oskar said to
him: "You're crazy. Hold on here with ten men? If reinforcements
don't come, we're goners!" But the *teniente* did not want to hear
that, and several times, in a threatening tone, loud enough to be
heard throughout the trench, he reiterated: "I'll shoot any man
who leaves his post without an order from me!"

[…] We settled into the trenches as best we could and it kicked
off. The ground shook, stones and dust rose from the ground, and
we were deafened. […] The engines' drone grew louder and louder.
Fischer ran into the trench shouting: "*Adelante! Adelante!*" We
grabbed our rifles and grenades, darted out of the trenches and
started hurling our devices. But we couldn't do it for long. A hail
of bombs rained down on us, and everything burst into flames;
the entire mountain and the very ground was on fire. The sleeve
of my jacket even caught fire. It only took a second to tear it off
and toss it away. Piet and I slowly returned to the trenches. We
were swathed in a dense smoke that stung our eyes and threatened
to choke us. We held our bedrolls against our noses. Visibility was
less than five meters. Then the fighter planes went to work, Rrrrr,
Rrrrr. They swooped so low you'd have thought they were scrap-
ing the ground. Bullets were flying left and right and everywhere.
[…] In a moment of calm, I shouted to Piet who was stretched
out in the trench beside me, wiping away the tears drawn by the
smoke: "This is suicide!" […]

Eventually, the planes seemed to be pulling away. We got to
our feet to check on the others. "Look," Piet said, "Fischer has
done a runner!" It was true, and there were three men ahead of
him. So, let's go! Reinforcements hadn't come, and neither had
our planes. We were the last pair to climb out of the trench and
I can still hear the laughter of the fascists who had arrived at the
trench and were shooting at our backs. Halfway down the slope,
I spotted an enemy machine gun off to the right. "No more running!" I thought, and grabbed my weapon, meaning to open fire
on the machine-gun operators, but I only got off a single shot.
The gun wasn't working. It was just then that I spotted a Czech
member of the company who seemed to have fallen from the sky,

and who was on a breathless run. "If he can get out of this, I'm going to have a go as well!" I kept to the side of the hill, as the artillery was still pounding the valley. Once again bullets started flying all around me, but I was no longer bothered. "Go on, fire away," I said to myself, half-demented, and pressed on. I couldn't run any more, so I started walking briskly. Piet was slightly off to my left, and there was a Hungarian scuttling along beside me. Twenty meters away, a number of men popped up and started shooting at us with their handguns. I alerted the Hungarian; there was nothing I could do with my rifle. The Hungarian wheeled around abruptly, there was a burst of gunfire and the first of our pursuers stumbled. He had a long beard and seemed to be trying to call out "*¡Camaradas!*" but the word died on his lips. I also pretended to shoot, and a few of the others dropped to the ground and opened fire. When the fascists realized it, they made a U-turn and headed back toward the mountain.

[...] We set off again, to gather near our former positions. I still had everything, my rifle, my cartridges, my bedroll, and, above all, my life; the only problem being my charred jacket. Fischer couldn't get over it when he laid eyes on me again. He merely said: "Ah, so here you are! I thought you'd stayed there!" He had given the order to retreat, but there was no way we could have heard him. Eventually, the reinforcements turned up, albeit somewhat belatedly. The Hungarian told me: "I served two years in the World War, five years with the Foreign Legion, and four and a half months in Madrid, but I never saw all Hell break loose the way it did just now."[136]

At the same time, on a front line in ferment, the Socialists-communists didn't hesitate to disband the POUMist battalions and place their officers under arrest. In Barcelona on June 16, Soviet agents carried out the arrests of forty POUM members who were charged with "treason" and "Trotsko-fascism." The POUM party's headquarters in the Hotel Falcón were turned into a rat-trap and then a prison. One of the POUM's leading lights, Andrés Nin, was permanently "disappeared." Many others member or party sympathizers were abducted, tortured, and surreptitiously executed.

136 Gmür and Minnig, *Pour le bien de la révolution*, 106–10.

From June 19 onward, the front line stabilized, but all those sacrifices had been in vain, for Bilbao fell on June 22. The Negrín government had decreed that all foreign volunteers were to transfer to the
International Brigades, and there were serious questions hanging over
the future of the International Company. Uncertainty and discontent
prevailed among its personnel. Again we have Gmür's evidence:

June 25
    Our commander Cardeur finally showed up. He delivered a
speech that went, more or less, like this: "You were dispatched to
Monte Oscuro without my knowledge and despite explicit orders
to the contrary. It was utter idiocy to send you there like that and
with these weapons!" The men grumble out loud about his having
lingered in Barcelona too long without coming to the front. He
defends himself, and tells us that tomorrow or the next day we
will head back to Tarrassa to join three other battalions to make
up a shock brigade. We will be issued weapons. The brigade will
also have its own armored artillery and machine-gun companies,
and, indeed, planes. Cardeur appeals to our spirit of comradeship
and to the discipline in the ranks. We'll see what comes of this.
    [...]
[Wednesday] June 30
    [...] Virtually all of the Germans from No 1 Company have
asked to be discharged. I'm also wondering why I should stay
here. We are being sabotaged from two sides and we don't know
what will happen to us in the next attack. We can only think that
the aim is to destroy the International Battalion. In one way or
another. This is the simplest way of getting rid of us. The dead
will be beyond all care. It's a bitter realization. Most of those who
are here came voluntarily to lend a helping hand, they were ready
to put their health and their lives on the line to help the Spanish
proletariat. There can't be many who are not as badly let down as
I am. There are days when I wish I was someone else. Enemies in
front of us, enemies behind.[137]

According to a report on the activities of the French section of the
CNT-FAI propaganda service:

137   Ibid., 111–13.

Cardeur was not in charge of the Battalion very long; in fact, he was charged in July 1937 with having abandoned his men on the front. In August he was arrested in the rear, on suspicion of having embezzled his men's payroll. [...] Nevertheless, he has a number of highly placed connections who ensure that he is simply banished.[138]

Finally, let us add that Alexis Cardeur was tried before a military court and released on December 1, 1937.[139]

{70}

PAGE 169

Edi Gmür witnessed the demise of the Durruti Division's International Battalion, which had been subjected to relentless reshuffles since April:

Evening of July 6

Here we are, reissued with weapons, but they're same old weapons as ever. Our battalion is recognized neither by the People's Army nor by the 26th Division, to which command we are attached [...] The 26th Division's commander, Sanz, declared that he doesn't want any more foreigners among his men. But he hasn't discharged us. Which is not a good omen for the future. The company has been allotted two machine guns. The men were hurriedly gathered together. The Internationals are looking preoccupied. The Spaniards are on the brink of mutiny. What does the future hold? Old rifles that are useless, half-strength companies, lot of green, untrained recruits, nearly everybody demoralized. Who's going to take responsibility for this? For the past three weeks, we've had no clean laundry, lousy food, hardly anything to sleep on, no mattresses and no straw. We'll probably be moving

138   Sill, *Ni Franco ni Staline*, 182.
139   Information supplied to the authors by François Godicheau.

out tonight. This afternoon, twenty enemy aircraft bombed our positions.[140]

Against this backdrop, they moved out again to stage an attack, until they were "hastily" relieved on July 22.

July 22
[...] Anyone wants to can be discharged once and for all. Wages will be paid out in Barcelona. Great excitement and chatter. The battalion was meant to attack Quinto in broad daylight, with no air cover and no artillery overture. It refused to do so, as have four Spanish battalions.[141]

It seems that defiance of orders was proliferating right across the Aragon front. In his memoirs, Manuel Ramos recounts how Ricardo Sanz ordered his men to attack a hill swept by enemy machine-gun fire. When they refused to keep at it, he shipped the recalcitrant, every one of them from the CNT, off to prison in Lérida like common criminals and then to the Montjuich fort, which has a sinister reputation.
Edi Gmür confirms this in his journal:

July 21
Last evening, the whisper at headquarters was that a battalion from the 119th Brigade has mutinied in Pina. People are beginning to take a stand against Mr. Sanz's dictatorship.[142]

The foreign volunteers at least could choose to head for home or stay on by joining the International Brigades. Not without some hesitancy and regret, Gmür decided to leave Spain on August 12:

July 25
The train arrived in the Estación del Este in Barcelona at 5 o'clock in the morning. The battalion made its way to the Espartaco Barracks, but only for a short time. The Cuartel Espartaco [Spartacus Barracks] was no longer a militia barracks, but a police

140   Gmür and Minnig, *Pour le bien de la révolution*, 114–15.
141   Ibid., 125.
142   Ibid.

Guardia Asalto [Assault Guards] barracks. [...] Strict checks are carried out: anybody who cannot produce his militiaman's card runs the risk of arrest. Barcelona has really changed. Fewer people around and, strikingly fewer pedestrians. The factories running at full speed. [...]

July 28

At the police station with Jak and Franz [no doubt Jacob Aeppli and Franz Ritter]. I have been arrested and locked up in a garage. It holds about thirty men, many of them from the POUM. Walter Ullmann tells me that the Thalmanns have been arrested too. [...] I was suspected of having served in the Batallón de Choque [Shock Battalion] formed by the POUM, the Spanish Trotskyite party. I am allowed to go back to the emigrés' hostel to spend the night there. [...]

July 30

Our delegation is back from Lérida. It has managed to get recognition for our battalion and ensured that we foreigners are to be seconded to the 12th Brigade and the Spaniards to the 27th Division. What are we to do, head for home or stay? [...]

[Thursday] August 5

We received our personal discharge papers today: free at last. But I am in no hurry to leave. Be that as it may, my mind is made up that I will not be returning to the front.[143]

In July 1937, Antoine may well have crossed paths one last time with his friend Franz Ritter, in Pina or in Farlete. In any case, following the disbanding of the International Battalion, Franz set off for Switzerland on leave August 3–19, 1937, and then was in France until September 19, 1937. In other words, he signed on with the International Brigades, arriving in Albacete at the end of his leave.

In fact, foreign anarchist or opposition communists unwilling or unable to leave Spain hoped to avoid detection in the International Brigade ranks and kept their political views to themselves. Hans/Hermann Gierth, who seems to have had Trotskyist leanings, obviously tried that gambit. According to the biographical notes on him drawn up by Dieter Nelles, Hermann Gierth, born in Zscherben in 1898, left for exile in France and then on to Spain, settling in Barcelona where he was working in 1934. He joined the Durruti Column back in July 1936. Seriously wounded that December, he spent months in hospital. He joined the International Brigades in June 1937. Wounded again in February 1938, he was pulled out of front-line duty and arrested by the SIM for "Trotskyist sympathies." In the SIM file on him, it states that, "his wife [Madeleine] was a prostitute often spotted in anarchist and POUM units." In France, Hermann would be incarcerated in the camps in Gurs, Saint-Cyprien, and Argelès and then dispatched to the camp in Djelfa until August 1941. He was then handed over to the Gestapo. Interned in Dachau and later Auschwitz, he emerged, alive, in 1945.

As for Magdalena (Madeleine) Geibel, his wife, according to Nelles she died in S'Agaro in Catalonia on February 7, 1939 of an injury sustained at the beginning of the civil war. She was born in 1890 in Saarbrücken and had moved to Barcelona in 1933 with Hermann Gierth and their son, Heinz. She was with the Durruti Column from July 1936 until April 1937.[144]

The twenty Germans from the International Battalion who joined the Brigades were kept under close surveillance by the SIM, the counter-espionage agency launched in August 1937; the Swiss Aeppli and Ritter found themselves in hot water, as we shall see soon. Nelles has consulted the 2,267 files held in the archives of the KPD (German Communist Party) on the German volunteers with the International Brigades. He found that all of those who had worked with the CNT-FAI or the POUM were suspected of having taken part in the May '37 events. Two hundred Germans were arrested by the SIM.[145]

Antoine makes one last reference to Lorenzo Giua's presence in Farlete in July. Maybe their paths crossed when Giua showed up for service with the 12th Brigade? In any event, Lorenzo was wounded for a second time on July 16. After some time spent convalescing, he rejoined the front, only to be wounded a third time outside Zaragoza.

As for Pablo Vagliasindi, according to the police archives in Rome, he was supposedly arrested by the SIM during the summer of 1937, "on political grounds." Notably, he is supposed to have turned down

144   Werner Abel and Enrico Hilbert (Hrsg.), "Sie werden nicht durchkommen!" *Band 1: Deutsche an der Seite der Spanischen Republik und der sozialen Revolution* (Lich: Edition AV, 2015).

145   García, Nelles, Linse, and Piotrowski, *Antifascistas alemanes en Barcelona*, 174–76.

command of detachments pitted against Italian legionaries serving on the Francoist side. The Italian police tracked him down in March 1938, by which time he was a prisoner in the Montjuich fort before being moved to Segorbe near Valencia; they didn't give much for his chances. So it looks like Antoine was mistaken when he spoke of Pablo leading his group in August 1937 and afterward.

Finally, here is the edifying report from one Canadian volunteer, published in September 1937 in *One Big Union*, a monthly mouthpiece of the Industrial Workers of the World (IWW):

> Marseilles, France
> Fellow Worker:
> [...] I am out of Spain. The reasons are numerous. I was not wanted by the government as I was in the Durruti International Shock Battalion. The government sabotaged us since we were formed in May and made it impossible for us to stay at the front. No tobacco unless you had money. All of the time I was in the militia, I received no money. I had to beg money for postage stamps, etc. I was sent back from the front lightly shell-shocked and put in a hospital in Barcelona. When we registered at the hospital I told them I was from the Durruti International Battalion and they wouldn't register me. In fact they told me to go and ask my friends for money for a place to sleep. I explained to them that I was from Canada and had no friends in Barcelona, then they tried to make me a prisoner in the hospital. I called them all the lousy --- I could think of. Anyway, I ran away from the hospital one day to the English section of the CNT-FAI and the people there insisted that I see the British consul for a permit to leave Spain, which I did, though I hated to leave.
> Spain is a wonderful country. At present it reminds me of the stories I have read of the O.G.P.U. [secret police] in Russia. The jails of loyalist Spain are full of volunteers who have more than a single-track mind. I know one of them from Toronto, a member of the L.R.W.P. I wonder if they will bump him off. The Stalinists do not hesitate to kill any of those who do not blindly accept Stalin as a second Christ. [...] Every volunteer in the Communist International Brigade is considered a potential enemy of Stalin. He is checked and double-checked, every damn one. If he utters a word other than commy phrases he is taken "for a ride."

I believe that the IWW has lost some members here, as I doubt if they would keep quiet at the front in view of what is taking place.

It was only through sabotage that the government succeeded in disbanding the International Battalion of Anarchists. Four of our bunch died of starvation in one day. Our arms were rotten, even though the Valencia government has plenty of arms and planes. They know enough not to give arms to the thousands of Anarchists on the Aragon front. We could have driven the fascists out of Huesca and Saragossa had we had the aid of the aviation. But the Anarchists form collectives wherever they advance, and these comrades would rather let Franco have those cities than the CNT-FAI.

[…]

The CNT-FAI seems to have lost all the power they had in the army. There is a good fort on the top of a hill overlooking Barcelona which the anarchists captured from the fascists. When I left for the front it was still in the hands of the FAI but when I came back the communists had it. The workers of Spain are against the communists, but the latter don't care. They are making a play for the support of the bourgeoisie and other racketeers. As far the industries are concerned, the CNT has a lot of power, far more than any other organization.

[…]

I met two more men from the International Brigade this morning. They say many Canadians are in prison in Spain.

[…] *Bill Wood*

Antoine definitely lost touch with most of his international *compañeros*; he attempted to escape to the International Brigades but found himself bounced from one front-line unit to another, caught up in the big offensives that followed one after another in Aragon.

{71}
PAGE 170

Luckily for him, Franz Ritter didn't end up "swallowed up by the shadows" of war, though he did come close. It would appear that he got noticed in the International Brigades. According to a note by the Swiss (communist) cadres agency,

> [he] was, unbeknown to us and without passing through Albacete, accepted into the German No 13 Anti-Aircraft Battery on some wholly incomprehensible grounds [...]. According to reports from comrades from Barcelona and from the 13th AAB, he is a bare-faced Trotskyist who is on good terms with the outlawed POUM.[146]

According to another entry, in December 1937, by the same agency:

> Ritter has even admitted that he is in touch with the POUM and the FAI and is, indeed, proud that the POUM lives on and is still active.[147]

Ulmi and Huber tell the rest of the story:

> Disgusted with the growing surveillance mounted by the communists, Ritter abandoned the battery and in April 1938 prepared to return to Switzerland. Otto Brunner, the head of the International Brigades' Swiss delegation in Barcelona, got wind of these preparations, intercepted Ritter at the Scandinavia Bar and made to arrest him. A shoot-out ensued, in the course of which Brunner killed another volunteer, Karl Romoser (who was wholly unconnected with the incident). Ritter managed to get away, made for the Swiss consulate and secured a ticket to Geneva. Whereupon Brunner alerted the Spanish police, telling them that Ritter had killed Romoser. So Ritter was arrested at the border and jailed

---

146 Comintern Archives, cited by Huber and Ulmi, *Les Combattants suisses en Espagne républicaine*, 206–7.

147 Ibid., 207.

on murder and espionage charges. Thanks to pressures by the Swiss consul [...] and the Swiss Socialist Party [...] the prisoner was eventually brought before a regular court in September 1938. At the end of the trial, he was found innocent and set free. He returned to Switzerland in October.

In order to discredit anything Ritter might say at his court-martial in March 1939, *Freiheit* mounted a campaign to defame him. Producing phony papers purporting to be from the International Brigades, that communist newspaper accused Ritter of having passed weapons to the Nationalist camp. Ritter, who'd made up his mind to say nothing about the incident, lest it damage the Swiss workers' movement, then broke his silence and placed himself at the disposal of the Zurich courts in bringing charges against Brunner. The trial, which didn't get under way until 1942, was a great sensation and was seized upon by the right-wing press, but in the end the charges dropped. In fact, Brunner managed to 'sell' a brand new version of what had happened, according to which the fatal gunshot had been fired accidentally.[148]

In his 1977 interview with Hans Peter Onori, Franz Ritter had this to say of his experiences:

During the supposed "Barcelona putsch" I fought alongside the anarchists. Following the fragile cease-fire between the two workers' factions, strife continued to simmer. Countless people were portrayed as "Trotskyist" traitors and swiftly liquidated. One example was the teacher J. Aeppli, following the intrigues of the Swiss Rudolf F. [Frei] [...]. Rudolf F. had had the benefit of a year's training in Moscow and was an influential agent of the communist police in Spain.

In March 1938, the 13th Anti-Aircraft Battery sustained heavy losses. The men were utterly routed and had to fall back into Catalonia. I wanted to head back to Switzerland because I was due to serve a period of training [military service]. My application for discharge was granted.

[...] Later came the controversial events in the course of which Otto Brunner, who was drunk, negligently killed Romoser. I was

148   Ibid., 207–8.

afraid of being liquidated. I knew how many alleged "Trotskyists" had been shot. [...] Behind the entire affair, in all likelihood, was Rudolf F., who had already shown himself to be utterly unscrupulous when dealing with those who didn't think like him. The murder of J. Aeppli was in all likelihood just another episode in a whole chain of similar happenings that are to be "chalked up to Rudolf F." Rudolf F. was very likely an agent of the GPU.

[...] I found out in prison that I was going to be accused of espionage, treason, and murdering K. Romoser.

Later, when I was moved into *"comunicado"* [incomunicado] untried, armed men turned up several times, wishing to take me to the execution stake. The *"comunicado"* was a prison area where those sentenced to death were moved three days before their execution. On each occasion, I refused to accompany them and stubbornly demanded to speak with somebody from the Swiss consulate. When I was finally brought before the court, it was explained to me that I had been arrested in error. At my express request, I was even issued with an affidavit of my innocence.[149]

On his return to Switzerland, Ritter was sentenced, in February 1939, to three months in a military prison for having served in a foreign army, the sentence received by most other Swiss volunteers. In his account, he alludes to the Zurich-born Jacob Aeppli's having possibly been liquidated by the Stalinists. The twenty-five-year-old teacher Aeppli, a journalist for the socialist press, became a lieutenant and served in the International Brigades. In July 1937, he was denounced as a Trotskyist and arrested, only to be released. And then he vanished. That September, his wife made inquiries about him but to no avail. On December 6, 1937, the news reached her that he had died in an unknown manner.

Franz Ritter died in Zurich on April 12, 1984.

For further information about the Scandinavia Bar incident, see Marianne Enckell's exciting account: "Au Bar Scandanavia," http://gimenologues.org/spip.php?article205.

---

149   Onori, *Protokoll des Gesprächs mit Franz Ritter*, 2–4.

{72}

PAGE 171

Following the battle for Brunete on July 25, 1937, the Francoist air force commanded the skies. With the escalation in the bombing of soldiers and civilians and the 1914–1918-type battles in which tens of thousands of men perished in the trenches, modern warfare was unleashed on Spain. Even as the northern front crumbled, the republican army made preparations for its big push against Zaragoza, scheduled for August 21. Over a number of weeks, a huge contingent of troops—nearly seventy thousand men—gathered around Zuera, Villamayor, Quinto, and Belchite. Part of the Durruti Division was to fight alongside other forces in the Pina sector, the object to cross the river and seize the railway station and the Bonastre hermitage before closing on Quinto. After ten days of fighting involving the 11th, 12th, 13th, and 15th International Brigades, Belchite was overrun on September 6 at the cost of a huge number of dead, especially among the anarchist 25th Division. But the town held out long enough to thwart the taking of Zaragoza.

Under communist command and with modern weaponry previously unseen in Aragon, the People's Army didn't do much better than the much-criticized anarchist militias. In light of the repeated strategic mistakes made by the high command, some commentators have estimated that Stalin's real strategy was to drag out the war in Spain just to keep Hitler busy, and to consolidate his own role as "vital" player in the eyes of Britain and France. Others, such as the PCE leader Jesús Hernández, speculated that:

> Between May and August 1937, he [Stalin] made extraordinary efforts to reach an agreement with Hitler. Naturally the democratic powers were familiar with all these intrigues and yet they shunned all of the overtures he made to them. In light of this situation, they too courted Hitler's friendship.[150]

Still others thought that the battle for Zaragoza was primarily intended to bring "anarchist" Aragon to heel militarily.

One thing is certain; the capitalist democracies watched without protest as Spanish revolutionaries, whose very existence was more

---

150   Jesús Hernández, *La Grande Trahison* (Paris: Fasquelle, 1953), 121.

irksome to them than Hitler's or Stalin's, were killed in the front lines or in the rear.

The next big engagement in Aragon began on December 15 outside Teruel, entered by the republicans on December 24. The Francoist counteroffensive was long and terrible and ended a month later in a landslide victory.

{73}

PAGE 171

On August 10, 1937, shortly before the push against Zaragoza, three divisions, including the one commanded by the communist, Líster, were removed from the front lines by the socialist defense minister and unleashed on the Aragonese collectives. They had carte blanche when it came to pillaging and looting (the harvests had just been gathered in). Collectivists who resisted were executed, and almost a thousand peasants were thrown in prison, including members of the Council of Aragon. At the same time, a decree ordering the dissolution of the Council of Aragon was issued; unelected town councils replaced any local revolutionary committees and, whenever possible, collectivized lands were handed back to their owners. These fresh, large-scale maneuvers by the socialist-communist government were extensions of those already under way in Catalonia. In fact, the crackdown on anarchists had been unrelenting ever since the "May events." How would the CNT react, now that it was in the opposition?

In the June 12 edition of Valencia's *Fragua Social*, we read this view from the CNT National Committee:

> A wave of blood and terror has swept over the communities of Catalonia [...] Our libertarian movement has kept silent ... not out of cowardice but out of discipline and a sense of responsibility [...] With incomparable stoicism, it has endured the assault on the collectives, on the constructive work of the proletariat.[151]

---

151   Quoted in Bolloten, *The Spanish Revolution*, 455, 667.

Not all militants were persuaded by this stance. On July 1, 1937, the underground anarchist newspaper *Anarquía* expressed the view:

> In the face of the serious situation confronting our organization, in face of the barbarous repression unleashed against us, in the face of the assault on and destruction of our collectives and our revolutionary work … we must sound a cry of alarm and urge the militant comrades [that is, the leaders] of the CNT and FAI, who optimistically believe that our revolution is advancing and that we are still a force to be feared and respected … that they should finally open their eyes.[152]

Depicted as an FAI mouthpiece, the paper spent five weeks publishing unsigned articles in defiance of the censor. It complained of the arrests of militants and the conditions in which they were being held. "It had the endorsement of only a part of the Regional Committee and certain political articles querying collaboration created unease."[153]

In Aragon, despite the calls for help coming from the local militants, the CNT and FAI talked the anarchist divisions out of stepping in, precisely as they had done back in May: "Keep calm; your intervention, when it comes, will be only in the eleventh hour and it will be definitive."[154]

We also note from Gimenez's account that news was only reaching the front with difficulty and in a muddled way in late August.

In reality, the Confederation, at national level, was not inclined to stand by the Council of Aragon, which had been launched without its authority; besides, it had not yet given up on getting back into government, and from July onward was even lobbying for precisely that. So, as far as it was concerned, the aim was to look like a responsible partner in the eyes of the reconstituted state, and its protests to the Negrín government were just it going through the motions.

The line that CNT fed its own militants was that it would be better able to defend the collectives from within government, than on the streets. It did nothing until April 1938.…

152   Quoted in ibid., 455.
153   Godicheau, *La Guerre d'Espagne*, 313.
154   Lorenzo, *Le Mouvement anarchiste en Espagne*, 384.

In Pina de Ebro, where the 26th Division's 120th Brigade was headquartered, the so-called forces of public order arrested some leaders of the collective and of the town council unhampered, whereas in Monegrillo they had to beat a retreat in the face of the firm line taken by Belmonte, the commander of the 119th Brigade, who was visibly unwilling to obey the official anarcho-syndicalist line.[155]

It quickly appeared that the mayhem created by the communist troops posed a serious threat to agricultural output. In addition, thousands of men fled to safety in Catalonia, and the collectivists, stripped of their lands, refused to work for the owners. At this point, the minister of agriculture back down, and, for the sake of guaranteeing the forthcoming harvest, started tolerating the collectives again. Peasants promptly resurrected the collectives in Aragon, Catalonia, and elsewhere, though on a smaller scale and, of course, in a greatly altered context. The unspoken tussle between owners, insisting that their assets be handed back, and the collectivists would linger right to the very end of the war, the outcome varying in accordance with the local balance of power. As for the province of Zaragoza, over that autumn, collectives were resurrected in Pina, Bujaraloz, La Almolda, Lécera, Azuara, Sástago, and Gelsa, indicating that part of the population at least was still bridling at statist centralization.

In September 1937, a delegate from the governor-general of Aragon (José Ignacio Mantecón) showed up in Pina to install a town council made up of five UGT members and five members from Izquierda Republicana, replacing the previous anarcho-syndicalist municipal line-up. According to a report dated October 22, we discover that "today, the collective operates autonomously, paying no heed whatsoever to the [new] town council" and that the Pina collective, which "was launched by the entire population's being forced to join,"[156] had retained upward of half of its membership and was still affiliated to the CNT, even though these people had been "liberated." It had a hand in much of the village's production. In conclusion, the writers of the report bemoaned the strength that the 26th Division still enjoyed in the village, in that it encouraged the collective to carry on. It is also reasonable to think that a fair number of *pineros* (Pina residents) were supportive of a way of life that they had finally embraced as their own.

155   See Borrás, *Aragón en la revolución española*, 198–213.
156   Casanova, *Anarquismo y revolución en la sociedad rural aragonesa*, 286.

According to oral sources, it was said in Pina back then "that there were two fronts, one facing Franco and the other between the anarchists and the Republic,"[157] or, in other words, between the collectivists and the "individualists."

Also note that the brand-new municipal team—on which the CNT villagers identified "some of the most suspect and most reactionary personnel" recycled as members of the IR—had a lot of trouble gaining a foothold in the village, so much so that Assault Guards had be brought in from Caspe to impose it.[158] Lastly, toward the end of October "military forces, in obscure collusion with civilian personnel" were behind the disappearance and murder of two republican members of the town council.[159] Such was Pina's bruising response to the arrests of several of its collectivists over the summer.

The fact remains, however, that the counterrevolution had reached an important stage in Aragon. Premises and locals belonging to the trade unions, or groups other than the communists, were wrecked and shut down; anarchist-controlled town councils were done away with; upward of six hundred collective organizers had been jailed, and the CNT now had barely any presence at local level in the province that had been one of its strongholds, alongside Catalonia. On October 22, 1937, the delegation from the Regional Committee for Aragon delivered its report to a plenum of peasant organizations in Valencia:

> Landholdings, draft animals, and plowing tools have been handed over to the members of fascist families [...].
> [...] In certain villages, including Bordón and Calaceite, seeds have were actually taken back from the peasants [...].[160]

The "normalization" of Aragon was pursued through the operations of special courts, if militants did not simply disappear into *checas*. Certain collectivists were left to moulder in the jails up until the Francoists entered Aragon in March 1938, and, at best, would make their escapes with a few hours to spare. Adolfo Ballano from the Aragon Defense Council remained locked in the Montjuich fortress, up until

157 Ledesma, *Los días de llamas de la revolución*, 221.
158 Ibid., 222.
159 Ibid.
160 Leval, *Espagne libertaire*, 375.

January 1939, at which point a rescue party of young libertarians arrived at the eleventh hour to rescue him.

For further information, see Daniel Pinos, *Ni l'arbre, ni la pierre* (Lyon: Atelier de création libertaire, 2001), 59; Gallardo Romero and Márquez Rodríguez, *Ortiz, general sin dios ni amo*, 190–95.

{74}
PAGE 172

The battle for Santa Quiteria has been depicted as a great republican victory. The reality was very different. Here is the testimony of Edi Gmür, based on what he was told by friends:

Evening, April 14

The newspapers tell of a great victory near Tardienta, the capture of the strategically important position of *la ermita* de Santa Quiteria in the Huesca sector. We have taken four guns and twelve machine guns and a stack of gas masks and other gear from the enemy and made 250 prisoners. I cannot go up to the front lines yet as the whereabouts of the company is not known here.

April 17

I am getting ready to move up to the front. At the railway station, I happened upon an ambulance train. Hundreds of weary, ashen faces, bandaged arms and legs, some of them supported by walking sticks, others clinging to crutches, they packed the long train. [...]

[Sunday] April 18

I found my company in Bujaraloz. [...] My comrades greeted me with delight. But fright was still etched on their faces. I finally got a detailed understanding of what had happened. It has the ring of catastrophe about it. The victorious attack took place on the 12th, with an unexpected counter-thrust following on the 13th. They were pounded by fourteen planes and three artillery batteries for six hours. In No 4 Section, only one of thirty-two men made it back. They walked into a dirty fascist trap.

Some of them were screaming "*¡Viva la República!*" and our Pepita, the only woman fighting in our ranks, positioned herself in front of the rifles of our comrades who had misgivings about the situation and wanted to fire. That was her undoing. Pepita was taken prisoner. The others fought on to the end. The next day, a deserter brought the news of Pepita's execution. He also brought his binoculars. She had been ordered to shout "*¡Arriba Espana!,*" but she shouted to the fascist officers: "You are sons of bitches!" So she was killed. Only two hundred men out of a Spanish battalion some eight hundred strong made it back. The whole engagement has cost upward of one thousand lives and nearly three thousand wounded. The fascists have retaken Santa Quiteria after ten hours of fighting, because our airmen failed to intervene, even though there are twenty-one planes ready to take off in Sariñena. The word is that the commanding officer there was shot for sabotage. But it is openly being claimed that it was on Valencia's orders that there was no intervention, to ensure that the anarchist troops would be decimated and total militarization enforced.

Twenty times I heard it said: "You should be glad you weren't there. You wouldn't have been able to do anything, but there is every chance that you would have cried." Viennese Karl says: "That wasn't war any more; it was a slaughterhouse, with us as the livestock!"[161]

We mentioned Rosario-Pepita Inglés before, in endnote 14 above. As to her death during the battle for Santa Quiteria, let us look again at Lola Iturbe's account:

She participated in the fighting in Perdiguera and then in Montes de Villafría and Montes de Vaca. The battle for Quinto, a position of value to the fascists, who defended it with a passion, began on November 19, 1936.

The attack on the Santa Quiteria hermitage, a strategic position atop the Sierra de Alcubierre [on a peak, as it happens], overlooking the flatlands of the same name and communications with Tardienta, took place a few weeks later. It should have been anticipated that the fascists would put up a desperate defense, as was the case.

161 Gmür and Minnig, *Pour le bien de la révolution*, 92–94.

During some ferocious fighting, Pepita Inglés, who was fighting with a squad of militia members, ventured out slightly ahead of them. A group of soldiers showed up from the opposing lines shouting: "Don't shoot, we're coming over to your side!" Pepita Inglés, overjoyed, ran over to meet them. It was a trap. They were fascists, and they disarmed and captured the militiawoman and, prodding her with their bayonets, they ushered her toward their lines. The militia members sized up the situation and rushed out to rescue Pepita. But by then the fascists had reached the safety of their parapets and the effort was doomed.

So, given that rescue of Pepita Inglés was no longer feasible, one militiaman hurled a bomb at the fascist parapet. Once the smoke from the explosion cleared, many dead could be seen sprawled on the ground; the fascist soldiers, the militian who had hurled the bomb, and Pepita Inglés.

So, up in the Sierra de Alcubierre, which within a few days looked like it was blanketed in snow by the *djellabas* of the Moors mown down by our forces' lead, Pepita Inglés was struck down, thereby spared the even more cruel death that the enemy would have had in store for her.[162]

{75}

PAGE 174

Here is the follow-up from Gmür's diary, which bears out Antoine's account of the Calvary of "Swede":

Of the company's 158 men, about 70 are left. Red Nils lost an eye, Jack Vesper a leg. Not until the sixth day did Jack come limping back, one foot with bullet wounds. He had limped five hundred meters every night. By day, he had had to lie still, the entire field being swept by machine-gun fire. He returned with his rifle and ammunition. His leg had to be amputated. Six days without a bite

---

162   Iturbe, *La mujer en la lucha social y en la guerra civil de España*, 122–23.

to eat and nothing to drink under the burning sun. That's crazy! The scariest thing about the attack was that virtually all of the wounded in the forward positions had to be abandoned so, little by little, they came to wretched ends. What horrific warfare![163]

Some Swedes did actually serve in the International Group, under DAS supervision. One of them, Nils Lätt or "Nils the Red" provided the most detailed testimony about what happened to Jack, who was not Swedish, but German. He was in fact Hans Vesper, registered with the DAS group on January 20, 1937.

Helmut Kirschey,[164] another DAS member, arriving from Barcelona where he had worked for the Investigaciones agency, has strong memories of that battle, his first taste of combat:

In mid-April 1937, we were dispatched to mount Santa Criteria [*sic*] to take part in an operation due to be mounted by some five thousand men. We were supposed to sever the rail link between Zaragoza and Huesca so as to stop rail transport and ease the pressure on Madrid. [...]

We were on one side of the tracks and the fascists were on the other. Over on their side there was a small village, around fifty houses that we were to take and hold. When we were given the

---

163   Gmür and Minnig, *Pour le bien de la révolution*, 94.

164   Helmut Kirschey was born on January 22, 1913 in Wuppertal. He became an anarcho-syndicalist in 1931. He served jail time on several occasions between 1932 and 1933. He then left for exile in Amsterdam and joined the DAS. In late July 1936 he set off for Spain with three other Germans. Helmut worked for the CNT-FAI investigation services in Barcelona up until 1937 and then left for the front with the Durruti Column's International Group. In May 1937, he was arrested and incarcerated in Santa Ursula and then moved to Segorbe. He was freed in April 1938. He fled to France at the beginning of 1939, then made his way to Sweden. He broke with the SAC during the 1950s. Helmut joined the Swedish Communist Party in 1968. There was a rapprochement with the SAC during the 1990s and he became a public figure as a German antifascist and veteran of Spain. His memoirs were drafted and published in Swedish in 1998 and in German in 2000. He was unsparing of CNT personnel, including Souchy, who had failed to ensure the release of arrested foreigners. Helmut died in Göteborg on August 23, 2003. (See Garcia, Nelles, Linse, and *Piotrowski Antifascistas alemanes en Barcelona*, 415–16.)

Helmut Kirschey

order to attack, a ferocious shootout ensued, with rifles, machine guns, and cannons, designed to counter the fascists' fire. Then we crossed the tracks. [...]

In the village itself, there was terrible fighting, and we had to proceed from house to house with our grenades. This was my first taste of battle and it was all very troubling. We were very tense and didn't have a lot of time to think things through. People were running all around, our guys as well as the fascists. Afterward we could barely remember the details and confined ourselves to shooting in the hope of coming through safe and sound. The Austrian in my company found a stash of beautiful red sausages in one of the houses we overran; he draped them around his neck and raced on. Scarcely a minute later, the detonation of a grenade went through his neck. Nothing was left of the man or the sausages. When we moved forward again, Nisse Lätt was wounded. We were racing one way and then the other in a street when, all of a sudden, I heard a scream. Nisse had been hit in the eye by shrapnel from a grenade and I brought him to the medics. They quickly dispatched him to the hospital in Tarragona, where his eye was removed.

A little after that I was in a house, firing through the window at the house opposite, when, out of the blue, the order came that we were to fall back to our positions. On the return journey we could hear the screaming of the wounded everywhere. The sky suddenly darkened with German bombers and fighter planes. [...] A single republican plane flew up and it was miraculous to us that the pilot would dare because he must have known that it was pure suicide, being so heavily outgunned. But take off he did and he was immediately shot down.

At the same time as the aerial attack, we could see tanks and a dangerous mass of soldiers bearing down on us from far off. Elite Moroccan troops [...] These were outstanding sharpshooters, but they also carried modern weapons with sights, and everything that we lacked. We knew they took no prisoners; they killed anyone who fell into their clutches. This naturally struck terror into us. Grenades were going off all around us. I have never been so scared in my life; I was so terrified that I shit myself. [...] Our company had withdrawn in good order but on our left and right flanks the Spaniards were fleeing in panic. [...]

Finally, we regrouped in Sariñena [...], having sustained tremendous losses. Of the company's 104 men, only forty-eight remained, the rest killed or wounded. Shock at what had happened got the better of me and there was this relentless feeling of bitterness: 'We have only a few miserable weapons and they have so much more.' It was depressing. [...]

Three days later [...] we were told that a German from our company had been found. He had been recognized by the insignia on his uniform. Rudolf Michaelis asked me to identify him. It was Hans 'Jack' Vesper. From what we were told, he had taken a bullet in one leg and had laid out in no man's land when we fell back. In order to avoid discovery, he had moved only under cover of night. He reached our trenches after three days. [...]

We ferried Jack to Sariñena where we'd set up a temporary field hospital in a pharmacy. A Spanish doctor turned up, examined him, and gave him some painkillers, but they were useless and he was screaming like a wild animal. His wound was teeming with maggots and there was nothing to do but amputate the leg immediately. He was held down by some Spanish medics, who were on hand. Jack had been out in the burning sun for days on end, and by night the temperature plunged to 4 or 5 degrees. In the end, he was taken to Tarragona to the very same hospital that Nisse Lätt was in. I was able to go there and visit. Seeing Jack again, the way he was, was ghastly. He was completely out of it, growling and thinking that he was a bear. But little by little he recovered and made it out to Sweden.[165]

And here, again apropos of the same battle, we have the testimony of the Swede Nils Lätt who mentions the presence of two more Swedes, Norrblom and Andersson:

> We had time to take in our surroundings. They weren't very encouraging. On the left side of the valley, where we found our- selves, there was a plateau, not too high, topped by some tanks. On every side, our troops were starting to fall back toward our positions, which were well constructed and easier to defend. The skies, to which we'd paid little attention, were filled with planes, twin-engined bombers and fighter planes. The latter could swoop very low and target us. Lying on our backs, we opened fire on them but missed. I counted seventeen of them circling the hill- side we were on; a terrifying aerial fleet, even taking their meager operational range into consideration.
>
> Teary-eyed, our political delegate gave the order to retreat. [...]
>
> Our delegate, Michael, was particularly well regarded by all of us. Since we had no "chief" and he was the oldest, he naturally assumed command.
>
> So we retreated in the direction of an area surrounded by stone walls, and from where we had overrun the fascist positions. We were curious to know who was manning it, but we soon had other things to worry about. The fascists had brought up their grenade-launchers, and grenades began to rain down behind us. I was chatting to a German lying alongside me when he fell silent. I could see that he had lost consciousness, or near enough. A Spaniard on my other side had been killed. Michael ordered us to gather up as much gear as we could and to make a prudent with- drawal in the direction of our positions. When we saw that the

---

165   Helmut Kirschey, "A las Barricadas." *Erinnerungen und Einsichten eines Antifaschisten* (Wuppertal: Achterland, 2000), 126–29.

German wasn't dead, we carried him away on the piece of tarp that Michael used as a blanket.

The grenade-thrower who had picked out our squad was throwing six grenades at a time. Then there was a short interval, which gave us the chance to advance another dozen meters before we heard the sound of the whistle made by the grenades as they started to rain down.

Along with Norrblom, Andersson, and a Spanish guy, we carried or dragged the wounded German. But just as we were about to set off on our second or third run, we realized that he was dead. [...]

How many times I was forced to take cover, I cannot say. [...] I counted the strikes and noted that they were closing in on me. It would have been more dangerous breaking into a run than staying put. By my reckoning, the fifth grenade simply had to get me between the shoulders, but I had miscalculated for I heard the fifth blast, but not the sixth.

Tremendous calm swept over me and I was thinking, good, it's all over. But, in a flash, I said to myself: 'If I'm dead and I know it, those bastard priests must be right!' That nonsensical thought brought me to my senses. I stood up on shaky legs ...

All thoughts of cover had evaporated and I set off, bent on reaching our positions, which were close by, and then somebody called out to me: "*Verlass mich nicht!*" [Don't leave me!]. It was a German whose leg had been torn off. I tried to take him on my back but to my astonishment I hadn't the strength for it. Then I caught sight of our *cabo* Juan [most likely Juan Puig, see appendix V below] emerging from a foxhole. I called out: "¡*Venga aquí!*" (Come here!) Over he came and hoisted me onto his shoulder as if I were a feather. But I pulled at his hair and pointed to the German, at which he set me back down. Then Michael and Norrblom turned up. I realized that I was unarmed and I shrieked into Michael's ear: "Where's the damned rifle?" He laughed and answered me; "*Lauf nur schnell!*" [Get out of here, pronto!], an order I carried out with alacrity, galloping off without even trying to take cover, diving into our trench.

I don't remember much else. I found myself back in a long corridor filled with amputees and the wounded in Tarragona military hospital. [...]

The hospital had been set up in a former Catholic seminary. Up until July 19, 1936, care—and indeed, education—had been in the hands of the Catholic Church. Some swift improvisation had been called for. But the work of the girls from the youth organizations, especially the Libertarian Youth, was outstanding and what they lacked in knowledge they made up for in selfless commitment.

I had been hit in the forehead, just above the left eye, which had to be removed. I would rather forget the operation, which took place without anesthesia. Not even local anesthesia.

I don't know if the one our *cabo* had picked up and who stayed behind in the trenches was Jack Wesper. Maybe Juan himself was killed. Be that as it may, Jack was a German sailor, stoker on a steamboat. [...] He plied that badly paid trade in an inferno devised by capitalism-driven lackeys.

So Jack stayed in the trenches with his leg blown off [...]. He stayed there for six ghastly days and nights, up until it struck him that his leg was starting to rot. At night he used to lick the dew from the stones and, because of his fever, was not unduly bothered by hunger. But, come the sixth day, he had reached the limits of human suffering. He reached into his pocket for a grenade and was about to use it on himself when he heard voices. He dumped the grenade and started crawling toward the voices, heedless of his pain—his work on ships' open boilers had hardened him. He said to himself that, even if these were fascists, any tortures that they might make him suffer would pale alongside what he had suffered already.

I bumped into him in hospital in Tarragona and we became friends. Dropping into his room, I thought he was on his deathbed. His leg had been amputated above the knee and the femur was sticking out like the bone from the Christmas ham that my mother used to decorate with a paper rosette. But within two days the bone had been sawn off and his wound covered with a carefully sewn cloth, like the handiwork of some master-sail maker. Over time, my head became less addled and Jack told me his story. [...]

Before leaving hospital, I was visited by the delegate from the Swedish seamen's union [...].

Ring informed me that he was making preparations to have all the wounded Scandinavians repatriated and said that I could have my name added to the list. My response was that I was not yet ready to leave and, while front line service might no longer be an option for me, my heart was set on finding work in some farming collective. I had run across several members of such collectives at the front and I was eager to share in their experience; I needed to sample it at their level to find out for myself the extent to which a CNT worker's life might approximate Kropotkin's ideas.

I told Ring, though, that I did have a comrade, a German sailor who had lost a leg in the same engagement in which I had been injured. I asked if there might be any chance of his joining the evacuation [to Sweden]. Ring replied that I had his word on it and he also reckoned that the Swedish union would add Jack to its books.[166]

Thanks to Marianne Enckell and Editions du Coquelicot we know much more about the Swedish volunteers:

Journalist Axel Österberg just happened to be in Barcelona on July 19, 1936; he immediately sent some reports to the SAC newspaper *Arbetaren*.[167] He stayed there for several months, and oversaw Swedish-language broadcasts over CNT-FAI radio. The station broadcast in several languages and could be picked up on short wave right around Europe. That October, Osterberg published a pamphlet with photo illustrations, *Bakom Barcelonas Barrikader* ("Behind the Barcelona Barricades"), which generated enthusiasm and no doubt encouraged a few young men to set off as volunteers.[168]

166   Nisse Lätt, *En svensk anarchist berättar. Minnesbilder ur Nisse Lätt liv som agitator och kämpe för de frihetsliga idéerna* (Göteborg/Nittorp: Nisse Lätts Minnesfond, 1993), 25–26 and 28–30 of the PDF document (translated from the Swedish by Marianne Enckell, with help from her brother, Pierre).

167   The SAC and its *Arbetraren* newspaper had at least eight correspondents in Spain, a record for the Swedish press. From 1938 on, it carried collections of articles in pamphlet form, plus eyewitness testimony. Several of these books and pamphlets (such as those by Nils Lätt and Ivan Faludi) can be found on the SAC website (www.sac.se) and can easily be downloaded. Ivan Faludi, a journalist of Hungarian extraction, was one of the Swedish anarcho-syndicalist press's correspondents in Spain.

168   Nils Lätt, *Milicien et ouvrier agricole dans une collectivité en Espagne* (Toulouse: Le Coquelicot, 2013), 63.

And in his introduction to the text, Renato Simoni tells us the following:

> Nils "Nisse" Lätt was born on December 30, 1907, in Sweden in Södermanland county. At the age of fifteen, he joined the merchant navy. He soon joined the anarcho-syndicalist SAC (Sveriges Arbetares Central-organization) and began learning Esperanto. In 1934, he contacted the CNT in Bilbao, where his ship had docked—this was shortly after the Asturias uprising. In 1936, having made up his mind to sign on as a militian in Spain, he set off for Paris where he secured a pass for the "Comité anarcho-syndicaliste pour la défense et la libération du prolétariat espagnol." [See the documentary evidence in appendix VI below.] In January 1937, he crossed the Pyrenees and arrived in Barcelona, where put himself in the service of the libertarian movement. For a time, he was assigned to the column led by Antonio Ortiz, then served with the Durruti Column's International Group, joining it in Pina de Ebro (Zaragoza), on the front lines of the war.[169]

After he was discharged from hospital, Nils Lätt wanted to remain in Spain and for a time lived in a collective in Aragon, in Fabara, where he left a deep impression on the village memory and legend. Back in Sweden, he promptly wrote his recollections of that sojourn (published first in 1938 and now available in French). He also wrote his memoirs in 1982, *En svensk anarchist berättar. Minnesbilder ur Nisse Lätt liv som agitator och kämpe för de frihetliga idéerna.* This book was published in a French translation (as *Un anarchiste suedois raconte. Souvenirs de la vie de Nisse Lätt, agitateur et lutteur pour les idées libertaires*) only in 1993. Nils Lätt died in Goteborg on January 14, 1988.

And Marianne Enckell points out:

> Something like 520 Swedes served in the Spanish republican forces as volunteers, most of them serving with the International Brigades. But others signed on with the militias, people such as Olov (Olle) Jansson, the president of the Stockholm Syndicalist Youth (SAC), who spent several months in the front lines, probably from October or November 1936 onward. He is included in

169   Ibid., 1.

the lists of the DAS (Deutsche Anarcho-Syndicalisten) Group as serving with the Durruti Column's International Group in January 1937, alongside Nils Lätt.

At least three other Swedish anarcho-syndicalists were part of the Durruti Column's International Group: Harry Norrblom, Yngve Andersson, and Eilert Hagberg. They sent letters to their friends, and several have been published.

All three came from the working-class areas of Stockholm and belonged to the Socialist Youth, a revolutionary syndicalist-inclined breakaway from the Socialist Party. On February 11, 1937, they left Sweden, sailing for Paris to secure passes for Spain, where they hoped to join a POUM column. But, from what Hagberg has said, they bumped into a communist there who told them that these militias had been disbanded and that they should join the International Brigades. Hagberg unwisely entrusted him with his letter of recommendation from the SAC and never saw it again.

They then caught a special train down to Perpignan, with a thousand communist volunteers. After crossing the border, they had the good fortune to come upon a CNT militant in Port-Bou, who told them how to get to Barcelona. It's there where they met Olle Jansson, who drives them [...]

[During] the awful battle of Santa Quiteria [...], Norrblom [...] sustained a leg wound. Eilert Hagberg threw his arm around Yngve Andersson's neck just as some shells were falling and probably saved his life by so doing: Yngwe took a shrapnel to the neck, and Eilert in the arm, of course. They were transferred to Sariñena by ambulance and ended up in the dispensary in Lérida. Setting off again for the front lines, Yngwe recounts the ensuing battle, which was almost just as fierce.

At the end of May, they were on two weeks' leave in Barcelona [...] Hagberg may have traveled back to Sweden at that point.[170] By then there were just the three of them with the Shock Battalion stationed in Peñalba [...]

170 According to Marianne Enckell, the journalist Ture Nerman stayed in Spain in May–June 1937, and—among other things—interviewed Eilert Hagberg; he published a series of articles in the socialist daily newspaper *Folkets Dagblad*. See the independent website http://marxistarkiv.se. [Giménologues' note.]

They quickly learned [...] the fresh directives coming from the communists who did the damnedest to disarm the anarchist militia members [...] They were considered deserters. Just like Yngve Andersson, who was back in Sweden by the summer of 1937. Just like Harry Norrblom who went back in mid-August, having come under attack in Spain and then in Sweden from the communists. In *Avantgardet*[171] he gave his eyewitness evidence, "How and Why I Left Spain."[172]

As for Franz Ritter, he gave Hans Peter Onori the following details:

On April 14 [*sic*], 1937, incidents occurred outside Huesca that ignited the conflict between anarchists and communists. Catalonia's communist minister of Defense left the column defenseless in the face of enemy aerial attacks, so that Durruti's militias were decimated, reduced to 30% of their original strength, even though soviet fighter planes and artillery had been available at the time.[173]

Let us point out, however, that the Catalan Defense minister was not a communist, being Francisco Isgleas of the CNT. Ritter may have confused him with Alfonso Reyes, the communist commander of the Sariñena air force base who had been shrilly accused of precisely this (See Endnote 57 above). In the "Urgent Report to the Commissar-General for War," dated April 14, 1937, and drafted by R. García Melero, Commissar Inspector for War, it is confirmed that no republican aircraft intervened, despite repeated appeals. He stated that he feared "very grave consequences," since the Luis-Jubert, Durruti, and Ascaso divisions might construe this failure as "political maneuvers against them."[174]

We should point out, though, that the infantry of the UGT-PSUC's Karl Marx Column, plus a "red shock battalion" were also engaged in that same attack and had also come under fire from the enemy air

---

171   According to Marianne Enckell, *Avantgardet* was the newspaper of the Socialist Youth. The paper's main articles about Spain were collected in 2010 into a small anthology: *Avantgardet om Spanienrörelsen* (*The* Avantgardet *Newspaper on the Turmoil in Spain*).

172   Lätt, *Milicien et ouvrier agricole dans une collectivité en Espagne*, 63–66. See also http://gimenologues.org/spip/php?article566.

173   Onori, *Protokoll des Gesprächs mit Franz Ritter*, 2.

174   See http://gimenologues.org/spip.php?article288.

force, sustaining heavy losses. In an April 14 letter addressed to PSUC general secretary Joan Comorera, the head of the communist militias, del Barrio, expressed utter consternation at the failure, particularly because, before the battle, he had made the case that in the absence of aerial support the Santa Quiteria position was untenable.[175]

According to military records, the twelve planes at the Sariñena republican base were out of commission on April 12 and 13 due to wear and tear, and all had to be transferred to Sarrión for repairs....

{76}

PAGE 176

According to an October 1938 FAI Peninsular Committee report, thousands and thousands of *compañeros* admitted that they were much more afraid of being murdered [on the front] by adversaries fighting alongside them than of dying at the hands of the enemy opposite them.[176]

The Libertarian Youth who were sent to the slaughter were the same Libertarian Youth who had stood up to the communists in Barcelona that spring. In Barcelona, the Libertarian Youth fought back as best they could, and printed up handbills urging militants to be discreet about their political affiliations when they joined up. In the front lines also, there were mixed brigades made up of anarchists who had had to enlist in the People's Army. In short, not only had militarization separated the war and the revolution, it had also turned into a weapon of political elimination. This vile fact is illustrated by the fate of the 83rd Brigade, made up of veterans from Valencia's Iron Column. Assigned to a division commanded by a communist—Martínez Cartón—it was posted in late July 1937 to the Albarracín sector to relieve other troops. The entire operation was carried out in great disorder, under intense gunfire, and the departing troops didn't even pass on their weapons. Brigade commander José Pellicer was seriously wounded and evacuated. Losses were numerous, and a lot of men deserted, including Iron Column founders

175   See Barrio, *Memorias políticas y militares*, 246.
176   Bolloten, *The Spanish Revolution*, 470.

Segarra, Cortés, and Rodilla. They were sentenced to thirty-year prison terms and posted to a disciplinary battalion. Pellicer was arrested by the SIM that November on the basis of outlandish allegations (holding on to treasure, aiding and abetting the fascists) and he remained in prison up until August 1938. He was then welcomed back into the army and given command of one battalion of the 129th Mixed Brigade, which became the plaything of the Soviets' military "strategy." Following the battle for Teruel it was so badly used that it was no longer recognizable; the bulk of its men were dead or missing. This spelled the end of the revolutionary Iron Column, well before Franco had actually won.

Persons individually and politically targeted by communist officers were also perishing in the front lines, often in utter anonymity.

As Jesús Hernández tells us of the summer of 1937:

> the order passed on from Moscow to Togliatti and from Togliatti to the [PCE] Politburo and from the Politburo to our mammoth agitational and propaganda apparatus was as follows: recruit 50,000 fresh members to the Party on the various fronts within three months [...]
>
> An out-and-out propaganda mania gripped our men [...] We were recruiting everyone, heedless of their antecedents and employing the foulest methods. Anyone who showed any second thoughts about the Party or Youth application form knew that he was a candidate for the front lines and the assault units. [...]
>
> The [socialist] minister of the Interior, Zugazagoitia, begged Negrín, a friend of his:
>
> "Don Juan, we cannot blank it any longer. At the front, comrades of ours are being murdered for refusing to accept the CP card."[...]
>
> The campaign had been pushed as far as it would go and communist ascendancy was mirrored in every essential military command posting by the spring of 1938.[177]

As for the International Brigades, the republicans used them as spearhead troops up until they ran out of volunteers. And since some officers treated their men very badly, refusals to go up the line or even desertions happened en masse sometimes and were followed by

---

177   Hernández, *La Grande Trahison*, 122–23.

executions. With the opening to historians of the Soviet archives, we now have confirmation that International Brigade deserters, caught by the SIM were shot or locked up in the so-called "reeducation" camp in Albacete. It looks as if several thousand International Brigaders may have been processed there prior to October 1938 and that many of them were never seen again.[178]

{77}

PAGE 176

From June 1937 onward, and as the war went on with its procession of defeats, repressive legislation expedited proceedings, and arbitrary conduct by the police became widespread. Very often it was a case of antifascists hauled before special courts on charges of "defeatism and high treason." And punishments ranging from six years in a labor camp to capital punishment were visited equally on the Barcelona libertarian youth handing out leaflets denouncing the government's policy and on the Gerona railway workers who called a strike over their working conditions. During the same period, arrests were made of fascists who had infiltrated the judiciary ... only for them to be set free. This gave underground Falangist groups a free hand to lay the groundwork for the Francoist purges to come.

From Perpignan prison, Tommaso Serra, a veteran from the erstwhile Italian Section, who had been arrested and then expelled from Spain, wrote to *Le Réveil* newspaper on September 11, 1937:

> The efforts made by the Stalinist gentlemen and their allies to sabotage the war and the revolution are without precedent [...]
>
> The prisons are full; militia members on furlough or even serving ones are arrested without rhyme or reason.
>
> On the other hand, priests have been let go; Masses have been celebrated in Madrid, Valencia, Barcelona in the presence of civil and military bigwigs [...]

178 See Habeck, Radosh, and Sevostianov, *Spain Betrayed*, 454–59, 461–63.

> Despite everything that is going on, the word [from the CNT and from the FAI] is to put up with every provocation so as not to furnish the pretext for some fresh massacre. Yet in the end the clash is going to become inevitable, for no level-headed person could be anything but revolted by all this.

Since the CNT was not really fighting back against the statist terror, and it was restricting its advocacy for prisoners to matters of legal technicality, some libertarians in Barcelona resurrected the *comités pro-presos* [Prisoners' Aid Committees], which had been a familiar part of the organization before 1936. Arrested militants were championed on political grounds as "antifascist prisoners," who looked upon themselves as the victims of "counterrevolutionary" policies.

In particular, the Modelo Comité highlighted the huge scandal of foreign prisoners, who had even less protection than the CNT inmates—especially the Italians and Germans whom the communists were systematically accusing of spying—being left to their own devices. Even Helmut Rüdiger complained in one report that "the CNT remained indifferent to the persecutions visited upon foreign comrades" who were going hungry, whereas the underground organization of the POUM, which was relentlessly persecuted, was managing to get food through to its jailed militants.[179]

Once the central government set up shop in Barcelona on October 28, 1937, the crackdown on the streets was pursued with vast dragnet operations on the boulevards and the raiding of trade union or Libertarian Youth locals. By November, according to a leaflet circulating in Barcelona, there were 15,000 revolutionaries in jail, not counting those who had vanished into clandestine prisons. The Comité Pro-Presos relayed reports of hunger strikes and violent protests followed one after the other inside the Modelo prison, while groups on the outside aided and abetted would-be escapers. So, in order to break the back of the resistance, four hundred Assault Guards poured into the Modelo on December 2, and moved 230 of the inmates to Manresa prison. The CNT, which had not conducted any real newspaper campaign to

---

179 On the prisoners' struggles we have a priceless book (regrettably not available in translation) that publishes their letters: François Godicheau, *No callaron. Las voces de los presos antifascistas de la República (1937–1939)* (Toulouse: Presses universitaires du Mirail, 2012).

focus attention on its imprisoned members' circumstances, didn't protest about this either. Instead, it threatened the prisoners, saying that it wouldn't lift a finger on their behalf unless they calmed down. Certain people therefore ran out of patience, and in the *Alerta* newspaper of December 4 (no. 7), we read:

> Now, we aren't going to put up with this any longer. Beginning today, we will repay provocation with provocation; gun for gun, murder for murder. We shall issue our declaration of war, confident that we will prevail. If we must lose our lives, whether we win the war or lose it at the front, fighting the declared enemy, and in the rear, murdered by "comrades" who bushwhack us, we shall die in the rear guard, giving as good as we get [...]
> Let us defend ourselves first, and then attack![180]

So the defense of prisoners and protests against the criminalization of revolutionaries accused of high treason were the focus of all of the aforementioned grievances regarding the CNT-FAI's strategy; there was an ever-widening gap between the protesters and an anarchist leadership mired in its choices, and leadership didn't hesitate in printing, in the September 9, 1937, edition of *Solidaridad Obrera*, a headline that read: "The world proletariat must actively support the stance of the USSR."

The oppositionist anarchists, many of them members of the CNT's former defense committees, found an outlet in newspapers that had been defying the censors for months: *El Amigo del Pueblo, Anarquía, El Incontrolado, Esfuerzo, Alerta*, et cetera. François Godicheau tells us:

> The anger and outrage of the grassroots membership were considered dangerous by the CNT leadership. Above all, the opposition must not be left a free hand when it comes to the clandestine press.[181]

Godicheau develops his argument like this: in mid-July 1937, up popped *Libertad*. It posed as the mouthpiece of the FAI and greatly resembled *Anarquía*, five editions of which came out between its first edition and July 22, 1937 (see endnote 73 above):

180   Cited in Amorós, *La revolución traicionada*, 340.
181   Godicheau, *La Guerre d'Espagne*, 315.

Very vehement on the prisoners issue but utterly mute on the Confederation's political outlook, *Libertad* was a perfect counterweight to *El Amigo del Pueblo* and perhaps even to *Anarquía*.[182]

That October another very radical clandestine newspaper surfaced: *Alerta!* It was sold on the Aragon front and in the *comarcas* [regions] of Catalonia, energized by ex-members of the CNT Defense Committees, which had been a special target of the repression since March 1937. Officially wrapped up that June, they maintained an underground existence under the designation "CNT-FAI Coordinating and Information Committees." Their grassroots organs were the *barrio* committees. In the November 20 edition of *Alerta!*, there was a headline threatening:

> The proletariat on its feet. For the immediate release of all revolutionary prisoners. If the government does not open the prison gates, the people will storm them.

Another clandestine publication appeared at the end of January 1938: *El incontrolado*. The CNT-FAI deployed all of its propaganda resources to avert its being "overtaken on its left" by this paper: the newspaper *Libertad* switched to weekly publication and grew from four to eight pages. It also tried to control the release of the clandestine handbills that the Libertarian Youth were distributing pretty much all over Catalonia during the summer of 1937. It also published its own, though the content was confined strictly to the prisoners issue. But this triggered great internal tensions due to the lack of homogeneity in the CNT leadership.

The same gulf existed on the other side of the Pyrenees; the Union Anarchiste (UA) and its mouthpiece *Le Libertaire* backed the official stance of the CNT (which was represented in Barcelona by Gaston Leval and the "Mimosa Group," to which Fernand Fortin and Félix Danon belonged), whereas the FAF (French Anarchist Federation) and the CGT-SR (General Confederation of Labor-Revolutionary Syndicalist) opposed it. Pierre Besnard, André Prudhommeaux, and Voline, through their new paper *L'Espagne nouvelle*, now singled out the "government anarchists" with their stinging criticisms.

182   Ibid.

An extraordinary plenum of the IWA in Paris (June 11–13, 1937) led to violent attacks by militants heavily invested in support for revolutionary Spain. The IWA secretary, Pierre Besnard, published a scathing, unsigned editorial in the June 11, 1937 (no. 212) edition of *Le Combat syndicaliste*:

> Such a situation [...] has allowed the politicians who were cast aside after July 19 to recapture the governance of affairs. It has once and for all compromised the social revolution's success by making it subordinate to a war that can only profit international capitalism and its representatives. It has allowed the Spanish Communist Party, which was nonexistent yesterday, to raise the colors of its dictatorship, which it will not fail to take further, under cover of the restoration of the democratic Republic.[183]

Come the UA congress in October, at which Carpentier and Ridel were present, Ridel piped up to say (the secretary's record shows):

> In his estimation, the Spanish movement is in need of criticism because it highlights the shortcomings of every anarchist movement: no economic planning, no program. Class and cabinet collaboration has shown itself to be impotent; Durruti's threat "to seize the money in the Bank of Spain" should have been carried out, he said. Ridel agrees with Daurat [Feuillade]: "We are not antifascists, we are anti-capitalists."[184]

Carpentier, recently returned from Barcelona, where he had fought on the barricades that May, wrote in August 5, 1937's *Le Libertaire*:

183   Quoted in Berthuin, *De l'espoir à la désillusion*, 152.
184   *Le Libertaire*, early November 1937, 4. In the introduction to his book (*La Révolution défaite. Les groupements révolutionnaires parisiens face à la révolution espagnole* [Paris: Noir et Rouge, 2013], 13–14), Daniel Aïache has rightly pointed out that "the term antifascism [...] only became preponderant after it had replaced the term 'revolution,' once the first fissures had appeared inside the republican camp [...] antifascism is a creation and an accessory of the world communist movement [...] antifascism disguises the reality of the clash and opposition between revolution and counterrevolution."

All these facts, all this repression shows that the Negrín government and the communists who are pulling the strings are just
counterrevolutionaries in the hands of Russian, British, or French
imperialism, and that, more than ever, the world proletariat
should come to the aid of the Spanish revolutionaries in their fight
against Franco as well as the Negrín government […].

Less theoretically, Carpentier and Ridel set up an ambush of one
of the instruments of Stalin's policy in Spain, Palmiro Togliatti, while
he was passing through Paris; but they failed in this. The two friends
went on to quit the UA after the congress, which passed a motion of
solidarity with the CNT.

Based on that, *Nosotros*, by now the mouthpiece of the FAI Peninsular Committee in Valencia, carried an article on November 5 entitled, "The Libertarian Movement Abroad."

The recent resolutions of unshakable, bolstered support and
solidarity across the board, which have just been passed by the
French Union Anarchiste congress […] are a stinging rebuke to
those who, even here, brag of support from libertarians from
other countries in continuing their foolishness and devoting their
tiresome scribbling to nit-picking.[185]

The remainder of the article cast this slur, without actually naming
them, on the Spanish groups opposing the policy of collaboration with
the Popular Front government:

If only their like-minded friends in France and around the whole
world were not locked into a passivity that borders on philo-
fascism! […]
    On our side, we have those who have lent a helping hand in
thwarting fascist intrigues in France, whereas the friends of our
traders-in-criticism are allowing and have been allowing fascists,
lurking in ambush in the neighboring democracies, a completely
free hand in stabbing us in the back and, even now, are forcing
antifascists fleeing there to seek shelter in Catalonia.[186]

185   Translated and reproduced in *L'Espagne nouvelle*, no. 34–35 (January 7, 1938), 4.
186   Ibid.

The term "traders-in-criticism" was probably a reference to the Friends of Durruti and other "nongovernmental" groups in Spain and the editors of *L'Espagne nouvelle* in France who backed them. This, published in *L'Espagne nouvelle* on January 7, 1938, was the response from Nadamas (André Prudhommeaux, no doubt) to this derogatory reference:

> That article is designed to bring the weight of French anarchism's disapproval onto those CNT-FAI personnel hostile to collaborationism and militarism [...] Naturally, there are those who would look upon the reaffirmation, amid the social whirl, of anarchism's basic principles and aims as "foolishness." It might also be thought that exposing the fearsome dangers that the Iberian revolution is facing from every quarter (disasters, betrayals, self-aggrandizement, and the ineffable speculation in which individuals and parties are engaged), as reported by the "opposition" groups, which they strive to counter, is no small thing and confers a degree of interest upon the "tiresome scribbling" of the outlaw newspapers [...]
>
> We cannot believe that the comrades from the CNT National Committee and FAI Peninsular Committee can [...] choose over us the dictators and politicians whose portraits and praises are strewn across the official FAI press: the likes of Miaja, Masaryk, Lenin, [...] Azaña, Del Vayo, Roosevelt, Ehrenburg, Dimitroff, etc.[187]

In its "Read in the Spanish proletariat's (clandestine) revolutionary press" column, the same newspaper carried an item from the October 30, 1937, edition of *Alerta*:

WE CHARGE:

The Negrín-Prieto "government of victory" with bearing the chief responsibility for the following crimes against the revolution:

1. having lost Bilbao [...];
2. having lost Santander [...];
3. having lost Gijón [...];
4. persecuting the members of the CNT and FAI in accordance with policy imposed by the Communist Party [...];

187   Ibid.

5. holding in the prisons of loyalist Spain upward of 5,000 revolutionaries, mostly in preventive detention […];

[…]

7. destroying morale on the front lines and in the rear, for the unspeakable purpose of wearying the people of the war and imposing an armistice that would consign authentic revolutionaries to exile or death and plunge the exploited people back into an abyss of poverty and impotence.

For all these reasons, we insist that these people be ousted immediately from the leadership of the country and referred to a revolutionary court as traitors to the cause of the People's freedom.[188]

The conflict's culmination at the international level came during the IWA's extraordinary congress held in December 1937, at which Pierre Besnard was forced to resign; Manuel Mascarell, a henchman of Marianet's, replaced him as general secretary. In other words, the CNT seized the reins. It justified its policy in a report signed by David Antona, José Xena, Mariano R. Vázquez, and Horacio Prieto:

In truth, the CNT had stepped outside of its own jurisdiction and any counter-messaging would have been untimely and ridiculous. We were wholly committed to political action without ever having decided upon it, without having thought it through, without having worked out the implications, without so much as any thought of them. What mattered was defeating fascism and deploying every effort to that end, and we displayed an extraordinary intuition and a mental agility that left other antifascists astounded […]

They looked to us when Madrid was in grave peril of falling into rebel hands. The trespass against doctrine was a fait accompli; the CNT has committed the heresy of which we are unrepentant. Previously we had fought a lonely fight against capitalism and the State. Then, with capitalism overthrown, and being obliged to direct and administer a very considerable portion of the nation's assets, we weren't able to cope without the extraordinary powers of the state in holding on to our gains, regularizing the operation

188   Ibid., 3.

of the factories, collectives, transport, and trade [...] And quite naturally we were compelled to ensconce ourselves in the state. There could be no option of a state within a state with those two states engaging in a hypocritical but, for all that, no less cruel warfare.[189]

Here we see highlighted, unintentionally, the central error in the CNT's conduct: the belief that capitalism had already been overthrown, whereas that had only just begun. Many of the subsequent faux pas must be chalked up to that.

On April 5, 1938, with military defeat looming and Stalin beginning to plan his withdrawal from Spain, the anarchist trade union joined the new Negrin cabinet and, for the first time, the Antifascist Popular Front, thereby linking itself to a completely revamped state that turned its courts into out-and-out war machines.

Morale continued to plummet in the front lines and in the rear, and, according to the Stalinist "El Campesino" (Valentin González), hatred of the communists was running so high among the population that one of the members of the politburo announced:

We cannot back down now; we have to keep moving forward and stay in power at all costs, or we will be cut down in the streets like beasts.[190]

In Catalonia the military and police clampdown eventually triggered a loss of revolutionary engagement, and hunger strikes became rife among the prisoners. Political and social frictions melted into the day-to-day management of sheer survival, and this led men and women to focus solely on their own individual fates. To the great surprise of many, Barcelona, when she fell, did so without a fight.

For further information, see David Berry, "Solidarité internationale antifasciste: les anarchistes français et la guerre civile d'Espagne," in Jean Sagnes and Sylvie Caucanas (eds.), *Les Français et la guerre d'Espagne. Actes du colloque de Perpignan* (Perpignan: Presses universitaires de Perpignan, 1990), 73–78, 85; Amorós, *La revolución traicionada*, 273–346.

189   Quoted in Lorenzo, *Le Mouvement anarchiste en Espagne*, 316.
190   Cited in Bolleten, *La Guerre d'Espagne*, 832.

{78}

Hot on the heels of the recapture of Teruel, Franco made up his mind to finish with Aragon; on March 9, 1938, he launched his offensive, and by April 15 had reached Vinaròs, thereby cutting the republican zone in two. The defeated beat a hurried and disastrous retreat and the plight of the civilian population was even worse. On foot and on horseback, they fled by road and mountain track, dumping everything and seeking refuge in Catalonia. Some of those who were unable or unwilling to flee paid for it with their lives.

On March 22, Yagüe's Moroccan army corps crossed the Ebro. Even though an entire company of the 26th Division was sacrificed, General Monasterio's cavalry entered Pina on the 24th.

The Valero Labarta family fled the village, as did many others. According to what Vicenta remembers, her family members lost contact with each other—her father, herself, and an aunt set off in one direction on a horse-drawn cart, while La Madre, María, and little Jacinto also made for Catalonia but separately. After some nights spent traveling through the darkness to escape the relentless enemy air raids, Vicenta and her father arrived in the Catalan village where they had planned to seek a safe haven. She doesn't remember seeing Antoine and other people from Pina again, as his account has it.

The two brothers, Félix and Vicente, rejoined the front in Valencia, while Vicenta and her father spent some time in Catalonia before crossing the border into France in January 1939. Vicenta's mother and sister, though, decided to make their way back to Pina. Which was brave of them, because, once the Francoists arrived, some members of the population were executed.

José Borrás offers a list of twelve individuals shot in Pina; notable among these were the republican mayor and two teachers.

{79}

PAGE 192

Huber and Ulmi shed some light on this:

> Even as the battle of the Ebro was moving toward its conclusion in a defeat for the republicans, the International Brigades, which were seriously impacted, retained one lingering value in the government's eyes: as a bargaining chip. In one final attempt to use diplomacy to force the withdrawal of Italian and German forces, the leader of the government, Negrín, decided to offer world opinion a spectacular goodwill gesture: on September 21, 1938, he announced his intention to discharge the Internationals. From then on the International Brigaders were stood down and distributed around "muster centers" in Catalonia and in the Valencia region.
>
> [...] André Marty strove to orchestrate the political repatriation of the freedom fighters; an army of soldiers was disbanded and an army of propagandists on behalf of the Spanish cause created [...] To that end, "bad elements" had to be isolated from the rest and expelled one by one as "undesirables."[191]

The last to leave would be the Swiss. Around twenty of those volunteers expressed the desire to be shipped out to Mexico, the only country in the world that had declared a readiness to harbor all former International Brigaders, regardless of nationality. Here, as reported by Fernand Jossevel, is the farewell address given by the "hero of the Black Sea" (Marty) to those fighting men:

> On January 22, 1939 [...] Marty [...] assembled us, asking for volunteers for front-line service. Since the entire battalion declined, he berated us [...] He insulted the [Spanish] women we had married, dismissing them as whores, etc., in front of the entire battalion. The captain later approached him for instructions meant for those who were due to leave for Mexico. His response was [...] that the Swiss were all bandits and thieves who had left their own country and did not dare go back, and that the ones wanting

---

191   Huber and Ulmi, *Les Combattants suisses en Espagne républicaine*, 219.

to head off to Mexico intended to thieve and rape and murder women there [...] We all made up our minds to head back to Switzerland. Furthermore, in the wake of this, our captain was arrested.[192]

The state apparatuses were to discern a lot of "undesirables": several democracies followed Switzerland's example and indicated that they would not oppose the repatriation of their respective countrymen but that they were not about to take in any foreigners, including those who had lived in their countries as refugees prior to moving on to Spain. When Barcelona fell on January 26, 1939, some five thousand International Brigaders found themselves in the dire straits of not being eligible for repatriation. The concentration camp lay in prospect for any of the Germans, Austrians, and Czechs who might try to head for home. The Poles, Yugoslavs, Bulgarians, and any Jews among them who had been stripped of their nationality because of their activity in Spain would have to contend with repression. And so, one last Agrupación Internacional took shape; some 4,500 men strong, it was placed under the command of the 13th (Dombrowski) Brigade's last commanding officer, the Polish Jew Henryk Torunczyk:

> The soldiers from the Agrupación sacrificed themselves to slow down the fascist onslaught and cover the retreat of the civilian population toward France.
>
> One night, a few days before crossing the French border, Marty gave the Agrupación the order to commandeer cars and ambulances in order to "save the cadres"—in short, to abandon the other ranks and to usher only eminent party members across the border. Four Jewish officers, Major Torunczyk foremost among them, spoke up against this plan. Torunczyk, Hibner, Szurek, and Doctor Flato remained with their men right to the end.
>
> The histories of the Spanish Civil War and of the International Brigades make no reference either to this group or to their glorious end. No general study mentions the fact that the International Brigades took part in that closing stage of the war. Likewise, none of the Eastern European communist military histories as a whole have yet managed, to this day, despite the material

192   Cited in ibid., 221.

facilities and documentary sources available to them, to record these events.[193]

Here is an example of how German volunteers were treated after they were demobbed in October 1938. The names of several of them turn up in the list of inmates in the Rieucros camp.[194] Devised in October 1938 by the Daladier government in France within the scope of the decree-law of November 12, 1938, which allowed for the internment of undesirable foreigners ("suspected of breaching public order"), the camp opened its gates near Mende on January 21, 1939.

We learn from a notice identifying "Foreigners in breach of the regulations" that Walter Gierke was born on July 29, 1888, in Mohren, Germany (these days known as Moryn, a Polish village close to the border), and that he was a mechanic. On arrival in France on May 13, 1938, via Cerbère as an "ailing militiamen," his only identification paper was a permit from the Land Army of the Ministry of National Defense. His wife and two children were still in Germany.

Thanks to Dieter Nelles, we know that Gierke was a KPD member.[195] He signed on with the Durruti Column's International Group in September 1936. He was listed as a member of the DAS, from which he was expelled on January 4, 1937. He joined the International Brigades that very month and was assigned to a vehicle depot in Albacete as HGV driver. He was jailed for a month for indiscipline. Initially held in Saint-Hippolyte-du-Fort, he was transferred to the Rieucros camp between February and September 1939. Walter Gierke was probably the creator of the sculpted rock nicknamed "the Spaniards' rock," created to mark the 150th anniversary of the French Revolution. It represents a French combatant standing watch, while above his head there is a wreath of hands like a halo. Walter Gierke's signature appears on a neighboring rock. Gierke asked to be allowed to leave the camp for Paris, Mexico, or Russia.

According to Nelles, Walter Gierke was extradited from France to Germany in April 1941.[196]

---

193   Arno Lüstiger, *"Shalom Libertad!" Les Juifs dans la guerre d'Espagne, 1936–1939* (Paris: Le Cerf, 1991), 38–39.

194   Lozère departmental archives, reference M11121.

195   Abel and Hilbert, "Sie werden nicht durchkommen!"

196   See http://gimenologues.org/spip.php?article392.

{80}
PAGE 193

Lodovico Rossi (aka Enrico Ferranti or "Lo Zoppo") was born in Ravenna on November 18, 1898.

In 1920, the police had him classified as a socialist before changing this to dangerous communist and then anarchist. His partner, whose first name is given by Antoine as Louise, was actually called Prima Poli, born in Ravenna on December 11, 1901. She had a son, Luigi, on December 3, 1922 and took him with her when she left for France in 1923 to escape the fascist repression. Lodovico Rossi, living in exile in Paris that same year, acknowledged the boy, though he was not the biological father. Rossi and his partner were great labor activists, and, after having belonged to the Young Communists and the Arditi del Popolo in 1921, Lodovico joined the left faction of the Communist Party of Italy (PCI) before moving on to an "anarchist-communist" group (1931) connected with the "Dutch Left" (Gorter) current, so-called. In Lyon he served as secretary of that anti-union "workerist" group, which had a membership of about fifteen people.

From late 1932 until July 1936, Rossi lived in Marseilles, where he was prominent in raising money on behalf of the (anarchist) *Comitato pro vittime politiche* (Political Victims Support Committee). As soon as revolution broke out in Spain, he engaged in intensive support activity, notably in concert with Giuseppe Pasotti in Perpignan. He handled correspondence for the Italians from the Garibaldi Brigade in late 1937. The Italian police in Toulouse kept him under surveillance and recorded his activities as a recruiter on behalf of the militias.[197]

Lodovico Rossi arrived in Barcelona and, along with Bonomini, Fantozzi, and Barbieri, he looked after the smuggling of antifascist volunteers into Spain. He crossed into France at the end of 1937 and lived there under a phony identity. With Pasotti he was active on the Comité pour la révolution espagnole. No doubt he made further return trips into Spain. He was interned in the Argelès camp in April 1939 and his name is on the membership list of the Libertà o Morte group. He remained in France throughout the world war and returned to Italy after the Liberation. There he resumed his activism in the ranks of the

197   See ACS-CPC, envelope 3654.

FAI (Italian Anarchist Federation). He died in Bologna in 1970 after a car knocked him down.[198]

{81}

PAGE 193

In the police archives in Rome, in the file on the anarchist Maria Simonetti, there is a note from Italy's embassy in Paris dated February 9, 1931 pointing out that her sister, Eugenia Simonetti (aka Lina Tommasini), born on January 10, 1905, in Castellier d'Istria, was an associate of the anarchist Michele Schirru and had been with him in Paris in August 1930.[199]

According to Luc Nemeth, Lina Simonetti "was an activist of the first order, notably at the time of the Spanish revolution and [she] might even have been induced in that capacity to cosign communiqués from the Ascaso Column's Italian Section."[200]

Lina Simonetti did indeed sign at least two communiqués from the Defense and Assistance Committee addressed to the Barcelona Anarchist Committee in October 1936 and January 1937.[201]

According to one study of Spanish labor conscripts in Corrèze (France), Lina and her son Claude Franchi (born in Italy on December 8, 1924) had sought shelter in May 1939 in Combressol, an area in the Corrèze, before moving on to Ambrugeat on August 7.[202]

The archives of the political police in Rome tell us that Lina then lived in Uzerche on January 14, 1941, and that she was trying to find her husband, Ferdinando Franchi, who had been arrested in 1940.

At some unknown date, Lina must have settled in Marseilles: "Even well outside the anarchist camp there are still some people

198   Antonioli, Berti, Fedele, and Iuso, *Dizionario biografico degli anarchici italiani*.
199   ACS-CPC, envelope 3297.
200   Communication to the authors, 2006.
201   Berneri, *Epistolario inedito*, vol 2, 315, 317.
202   Paul Estrade (ed.), *Les Forçats espagnols des GTE de la Corrèze (1940–1944)* (Treignac: "Les Monedières," 2004), 72–74.

(Left) Francisco Ferrer and (right) Giuditta Zanella with Ilario Margarita

who remember 'Lina the fruit-seller' in Marseilles, where she died on November 7, 1964."[203]

Thanks to further information supplied by Tobia Imperato from Turin, Giuditta has now been identified.[204]

She was Giuditta Maria Zanella, the daughter of Liberale Zanella and Letizia Carrieri, born in Barzola (Varese) on April 26, 1885, according to the profile that the Turin prefecture forwarded to the Italian Interior Ministry on November 10, 1920. At that point, Giuditta was on file as an anarchist who had for several years been associated with the activities of another well-known activist known: Ilario Margarita.

In her file, under the heading "Political Behavior," it is noted that Giuditta had, prior to being an anarchist, been a member of the Socialist Party, and that she was in touch with the Geneva-based *Le Réveil* newspaper; that she mounted active and effective propaganda targeting female workers; that she had taken part in "subversive" demonstrations, and been arrested in 1915 on account of her "obstreperous character."

During the 1920s, Giuditta lived clandestinely with Ilario Margarita in France, Belgium, Cuba, and the United States. They were both arrested in Barcelona in July 1932 and expelled to France on September

203   Luc Nemeth, communication to the authors, 2006.
204   Communications to the authors, July 2008.

20 for "clandestine anarchist gatherings." They returned to Spain, not leaving again until 1939.

One Italian political police document points out that at the time of their arrest in Barcelona on May 7, 1935, Ilario and Giuditta had been living in Francisco Ferrer's home at 104 Calle Galileo for two years.[205] In July 1936, they both took part in the popular uprising in Barcelona. And then set off to fight on the Aragon front, in the Durruti Column in Giuditta's case, as recounted in an article in *Guerra di Classe*.

Giuditta died in Turin in 1962.

So Giuditta Zanella's date of birth and record of activism match what Antoine recorded, except that she was Ilario Margarita's partner and not Francisco Ferrer's.

For further information, see "Notice biographique sur Guiditta Zanella," http://www.gimenologues.org/spip.php?article377.

{82}
PAGE 194

Like thousands of other men, women, and children, Antoine was dumped on the beach at Argelès, in the Pyrénées-Orientales department of France. Simply to keep warm and keep up the spirit of solidarity, which these militants had always acted upon throughout their lives as on-the-runs, 117 Italians, plus a few Yugoslavs no doubt, set up the Libertà o Morte (Liberty or Death) group. A document discovered in the police archives in Rome (see addendum VI below), dated August 8, 1939, lists these men by last and first names. In the list we find a Magnani, a Rossi, and one Gimene [*sic*], Antonio ...

205   ACS-CPC, envelope 5516.

BIOGRAPHICAL NOTES

ANTOINE GIMENEZ (REAL NAME BRUNO SALVADORI)

Antoine Gimenez

Bruno Salvadori was born in Chianni in the province of Pisa, Italy, on December 14, 1910, but his parents, Giuseppe Salvadori and Anna Montagnani, did not register his birth before their wedding in 1915.

Luisa was born to the same parents in 1913 near Reggio di Calabria. Antoine's second sister, Bruna, was born in Livorno in 1917, her father being employed on public works (Bridges and Highways) there. Having served in the army during the 1914–1918 war, he passed

Antoine, his mother, and one of his sisters

away in La Spezia in 1944; Bruno had never made any effort to see him again, judging by what he said in some correspondence with his sisters.

At the age of nine, Antoine was living in Livorno with his mother and his sisters. His father was employed on the postwar reconstruction projects near San Dona di Piave in the province of Venezia. They used to join him there for the holidays.

It was at the age of twelve or thirteen that Antoine became acquainted with the Livorno anarchists, during some scuffles with the Blackshirts. He briefly met Malatesta at this time and was introduced to libertarian ideas.

Let us look at his own account of that episode in his life:

[This was around about 1922.] Fascism was on the rise and poverty was forever growing in Italy. One day, on my way to school with a bunch of friends, we saw one of the girls from our class surrounded by three or four individuals who were chanting: "Castor oil laxative!"

The girl was the daughter of an elected socialist and the boys were Blackshirts.

It wasn't chivalry or political beliefs—I was about twelve years old—but was quite simply that the girl was a student in the same class as us. What was said I can't recall now, but our drawing easels were set against the wall, and our rulers—flat rulers measuring 80 cms long by 5 or 6 cms in width—were drawn and we plunged into the fracas. They had not been expecting us. Surprised, they let go of their prey, who ran off as fast as she could. My friends did likewise and I found myself all alone, pushed up against a wall and facing what struck me at the time as an entire phalanx of vanguardists [fascists] armed with *manganèlli* [truncheons made of hammer shafts fitted with carry-straps]. There was the sound of some cracks, a truncheon shattered my ruler, there was the roar of an engine starting, and further cracks, and my shoulder hurt like hell …

When I came to, I was lying on a camp bed. Two grinning women were looking at me. What appeared to be the older of them hugged me and said: "You scared us!"

I had a terrible headache and my left shoulder was tightly wrapped in bandages. A few moments later, a middle-aged man with a beard stepped inside. I stared at him, taken aback. It was Errico Malatesta. Malatesta, the apostle of Anarchy. A few months before, I had seen him at my school with a bunch of grown-ups. I had been rescued from the Blackshirts' clutches by some anarchists.

He reassured me that everything would be fine. Aside from a lump on the head and a baton blow to the shoulder, which was painful but nothing serious, I was unscathed. While we chatted, Lucia arrived. Lucia was a very young woman from the same village as my mother, married to a traveling salesman; she lived in Livorno. Since her marriage, when her husband was off on his travels, she habitually spent her days at our house and that's where she had been when word reached my mother.

I was taken home between Lucia and a young girl, under a discreet escort from a few young male and female libertarians. Mum was very calm; I had been expecting a real roasting. I was really afraid of seeing her break into tears, or simply being sad … Francesca, the young libertarian girl who had come with me, told her: "*Signora, può essere fiera di suo figlio* [you have a son to be proud of]."

"I know," said Mum. "His pals popped in to check on him; they gave me the complete rundown just after you and Lucia set off to fetch him."

My life altered from that day forth. I would spend whatever spare time my schoolwork left me poring over pamphlets on Thursdays and Sundays and listening to discussions among my new anarchist pals: Malatesta, Gori, Kropotkin, Reclus, Bakunin, pamphlets, newspapers, books, it was all part of the mix. Little by little an ideal trickled through; it was all intuitive aspirations and received notions such as love, liberty, the right to happiness, production as a way of earning the right to consume, and end of man's exploitation of his fellow man. To keep me safe from any potential punitive expedition, my mother had me sleep at Lucia's place when her husband was away. By way of excusing my absence from school, she had written the headmaster that I had fallen down the stairs and she had one of my school-friends bring in a note that was passed on to the history teacher, Mrs Bellucci del Villa. This schoolmistress had a daughter who was a teacher at a different high school and who had helplessly witnessed beatings. The older teacher was in the habit of having students bring history exercise books to her home for marking.

One day, it was my turn. Her daughter opened the door to me, but, after sizing me up, instead of taking the parcel and allowing me to go on my way, she told me to go upstairs. Teacher had something to say to me. The old lady had nothing to say to me at that time, but within five minutes she was showering me with questions. Was it true that I had been in the Piazza Cavour on April 1? And who was it that carried me off? I just giggled and told her over and over again that I had fallen on the stairs. But I was wrong to be on my guard. Seeing that I was sticking by my story, her daughter—whose name escapes me—stood up and said: "That's good. You are right to say nothing, but my mother and I trust you, come!"

She brought me into a room and showed me a portrait wreathed in black ribbons; and told me: "That's my brother. He died on that date in Milan, killed by the Blackshirts: he was a socialist, as am I. Look, here's my party card."

Tears were streaming down the elderly schoolmistress's face as she gazed at her son's photograph. We stepped back into her office. Upset by the old woman's tears, I told my story … Once she was sure that her daughter's trust in me had not been misplaced, she contacted my mother and it was decided that on the days when I had no classes in the morning or afternoon, I would drop by their house for a couple of hours to catch up on my math and drawing. And I have to admit that I was a real dunce in both subjects. Her daughter would give me lessons.…"

Bruno lost his mother to liver disease at some date unknown but most likely around 1928, according to part of his manuscript—the "Perdiguera" chapter. Losing her very traumatic for him and of course may well have had a lot to do with the powerful attachment he felt to La Madre later in Pina de Ebro.

Up until July 1936, Bruno led the life of a *chemineau-trimardeur* (tramping artisan), as he liked to describe himself, and this led to him making several trips to Spain. Once again, he alluded to that life in his manuscript when he talked about having been a smuggler of publications and pamphlets.

At the very beginning of the 1930s, he was living in Marseilles, having moved away to there. During his numerous stays in that city, he made the acquaintances of Jo and Fred who pop up in his *Memories* and with whom he would dabble in a bit of "cat burglary." On July 28, 1930 he was sentenced, by the city's court of corrections, to a year in prison for "attempted theft. Carrying a prohibited weapon. Has yet to perform his military service."

"This foreigner was arrested on June 15, 1930, having entered the apartment of the widow Amar at 45 Boulevard Lonchamp in Marseilles with two accomplices. In addition, he was carrying a ring of twenty-four keys. Given the seriousness of the offenses leading to his conviction and the bad reports gathered regarding him, by my reckoning there are grounds for expelling him from the territory," concluded the Bouches-du-Rhône prefect in a letter dated August 21, 1930, and addressed to the Interior Ministry.

According to the "individual register of arrested foreigners liable to expulsion," which recorded his words, Bruno was a boilermaker by trade and unmarried; he had been in France for four years and was living with his family [?]; he was living at 34 Rue de la Bonneterie in Marseilles: "Says he is not currently working." His conduct was assessed as "bad."

The expulsion order issued against him was dated October 7, 1930, and handed to him when he was committed to the Saint-Pierre prison in Marseilles on October 16. He was eligible for release on June 16, 1931. We can only suppose that he was expelled at that point.

But he must have returned to France pretty quickly, as we know that on July 23, 1931, he was rearrested in Marseilles for thievery and breach of the expulsion order and was sentenced to two months in prison. It was the same story on October 15, 1931, when he copped three months. He reoffended on January 22, 1932, again in Marseilles; and was given six months for handling stolen goods.[1]

We do not know the exact date at which Bruno was "repatriated in order to do his military service" with the Mantua division, as the Italian archives have it. Perhaps he was expelled "under escort" and handed over to the authorities in his homeland. In any event, it was after August 13, 1932, on which date the court of first instance in Bouches-du-Rhône sent a telegram to the Interior Ministry requesting an "extension of the expulsion order" against Bruno Salvadori.

The prefect in Mantua pointed out that "Bruno Salvadori spent little time in this city as part of his military service." And it was as a soldier serving in that division that he was issued with a passport on September 1, 1933, as "he needed it at the time to go spend a year convalescing in Marseilles."

On December 13, 1933, the Bouches-du-Rhône court sent off another telegram to the direction of the Sûreté Générale in Paris, seeking "an extension of the expulsion order" against Bruno Salvadori. Because he had been arrested in Marseilles on December 9, 1933,

> on the Rue des Chapeliers while selling boiler suits, which he dumped right then and there, taking to his heels to evade the police. He was unable to account for the provenance of the clothing, confining himself to claiming that he had been given them by an unknown person to sell. Expelled from France under ministerial order of October 7, 1930. [...] Nîmes, September 5, 1934.

On October 11, 1934 he was briefed once more about the expulsion with an additional "five year residence ban." This time it was the

---

[1]   Archives nationales, Moscow Fund, dossier no. 1994 474/40, "Bruno Salvadori 1930–1935."

prefecture of the Gard department that reported to the Interior Ministry on October 31, 1934, that the fellow had been sentenced by the appeal court in Aix-en-Provence on February 7, 1934, to a year and a day in prison for "receiving goods and breaching the expulsion order." He was committed to the central prison in Nîmes, eligible for release on August 11, 1934.

An umpteenth "personal file" on him mentions that he had "a measure of higher education" but was "of very ill repute in town."...

By March 25, 1935, they had had so much trouble turning the guy away that the decision was made "to issue in the name of this foreigner a free transport voucher valid from Perpignan to Feignies [Nord-Pas-de-Calais, as far as the Belgian border]." They still had to be sure that "the Italian national, once expelled and penniless" had the requisite papers to get him over the border. A safe conduct pass was to be handed to him.

In one last document from the Interior Ministry, dated August 20, 1935 and discovered in his file, we learn that he had a total of six convictions, the most recent (four months) in Perpignan on December 26, 1934, for "infringing an expulsion order, violence, and assault." To complete the picture, there was this: Bruno was arrested in Le Boulou on August 4 that year and on August 22 sentenced by the court in Céret to six months in prison for breaching his expulsion order.

According to the Italian police who had him under close surveillance, he was claiming at the time to be a deserter and an antifascist. According to the court in Perpignan, he had eight convictions under his belt by then, essentially for crossing the border illegally or for vagrancy, which was the charge repeatedly preferred back then against members of the "dangerous classes."

Bruno was increasingly drawn to Spain, and again it is the police who report his presence there. On May 25, 1935, he was apprehended in Barcelona, while attempting to sell his Italian passport, which led to the opening of a file by Mussolini's political police as he was a "subversive element." It is thanks to the opening of that file that we have been able to pick up his trail ... and seen his twenty-five-year-old's mug shot. Purporting to be a "commercial traveler," Bruno was staying at the "Bon temps" guesthouse in Vigatán Street.

Expelled from Spain into Portugal on June 13, 1936, via Valencia de Alcántara, he had supposedly in the interim been hanging around "subversive circles" in Barcelona.

Bruno surreptitiously and rather quickly returned to Spain; he was arrested yet again, and on February 21, 1936 was convicted of "breaching a banning order." He was committed to the Modelo Prison in Barcelona. At which point he began to trade letters with Giuseppe Pasotti from Perpignan. This very active anarchist would soon take charge, on behalf of the FAI, of the Political Investigations Service, which was to carry out the screening of the volunteers, in concert with the corresponding committee in Portbou and an agency of the same name, answerable to the Generalidad and run by Francesco Barbieri. Pasotti set up an effective network for smuggling men and propaganda through the LIDU (Italian Human Rights League) and was supporting militants imprisoned in Spain with some success. Ernesto Tamburini, an informer for the Italian police, who was spying on Pasotti (and would successfully steal his address book) had this to say in his report:

Barcelona, April 20, 1936
Letters from Italian detainees addressed to the local LIDU branch often reach this town from the Modelo prison. [...] Especially after LIDU's victory in the Barbieri affair (see endnote no. 65, above). I believe that I am acceding to your wishes in seeking [...] to obstruct and sabotage LIDU's efforts on behalf of these individuals; [...] allow me to point out that from said prison (and this very week) [a letter] has come [...] from one Salvatori [sic] Bruno, detained since February 7 this year; [...] he arrived here from France carrying a particular recommendation from Pasotti in Perpignan. [...] I will do whatever it takes to prevent any assistance at all from reaching this guy [another Italian detainee], like all the rest.[2]

Having served his sentence, Bruno Salvadori was to be expelled to France via Puigcerdà.

It is from around this time that Antonio Gimenez—holding a CNT membership card in that name—appears and that the police lose track of Bruno Salvadori once and for all. Gimenez quickly turned back for Spain since he was in Alcarràs near Lérida on the eve of the pronunciamento (coup attempt). He worked alongside some friends on the Vallmanya agricultural holding. It was in Alcarràs that his path

2   ACS-CPC, personal files 50, pack 1196.

would cross with that of sixteen-year-old Josep Lladós, a future militiaman who remembered him simply as Tony.

Gimenez then joined the Durruti Column, followed by the International Group of that column, which was set up in Pina de Ebro. He took part in the battles of Siétamo, Farlete, and Perdiguera. Cross-referencing suggests that he served as group delegate prior to the militarization. We have found an identity card (unsigned by the owner) issued by the AMRE (Agrupación Militar de la República Española) in Toulouse in April 1945, crediting him with the rank of infantry lieutenant.

He would meet Antonia Mateo Clavel and her daughter Pilar in Peñalba in Huesca province. They would become his wife and daughter.

Demobbed in October 1938, like the other foreign volunteers, he was spending some time living in Barcelona and then in Montcada i Reixac, a few kilometers to the north. He would work in Barcelona up until the *retirada*. He left Spain via Portbou on February 9, 1939, just a day before Catalonia was overrun completely.

The Italian Ministry of the Interior recorded him in August 1939 under the name Gimene Antonio (no connection being made with Salvadori) as being in the Argelès-sur-mer concentration camp, a member of the Libertà o Morte group, made up of 117 libertarian militants. That group looked to survival and collective protection against all the dangers hanging over them: malnutrition, communist hostility, and ill treatment. They went so far as to use a booby-trapped grenade to cause the death of one Senegalese fusilier as revenge for the brutality displayed by the camp's military guards.

> The impact was immediate; punishment measures, naturally, and old-fashioned funk among the military who took certain precautions after that in their dealings with certain of their "guests."[3]

Drafted into the Foreign Labor Squads (Groupes de travailleurs étrangers/GTE), like many other refugees, Antoine would work for a time on the Atlantic Wall in the Royan sector, where he took part in sabotage and Resistance operations. He then worked as a lumberjack on the banks of the Vézère. It was there that he learned of the death of his International Group friend, Otto the German, who was part of the Resistance around Limoges. Antoine was discharged from the GTE

3   Recollection gathered by Frédéric Alémany.

Antoine, Antonia, an unidentified girl, and Pilar in Treignac, sometime between 1948 and 1951

on October 26, 1944, in Uzerche, where he lived with his family. Our Italian then worked on the Treignac dam construction site in Corrèze, work on which began in 1948. The family lived in Limoges from at least 1948 to 1951. He was eventually offered the option of going to live in Paris or Marseilles. Since Antoine had the offer of a construction job, he chose Marseilles. Antoine was hired by the Société des travaux du Midi on March 2, 1953 as a floor- and panel-layer. He would work there until he took early retirement for health reasons.

In a letter addressed to his sister, Brunetta, in April 1952, he offered a glimpse of the suffering with which he was racked:

> There is one battle I would love to win; the one I have been fight-
> ing for a good year now against Pily's [Antonia's daughter Pilar]
> affliction. I would gladly agree to lose every other one as long as I
> get to see the girl happy and healthy again, with a twinkle of con-
> fidence and intelligence in her eye.
>
> Your girl and mine are both victims; they carry around all the
> worries of the world, all the unsatisfied cravings, all the evapo-
> rated dreams, all the disappointed hopes, all the humiliations
> endured by their sires.
>
> Yes, I know we have done everything that could possibly be
> done for them: we have labored, we have sacrificed our freedom,

we have postponed our most cherished wishes. For their sake, we have swallowed our pride, sacrificed our principles, braved a thousand and one sufferings, accepted all manner of privations [...]. They never asked to be brought into this world. The spell-binding products of a moment's pleasure, even before they were born they were carrying the horrible, inexorable worms gnawing at them, for those worms were in their parents. Those worms lurk deep within us all. Their names are: Fear, Cowardice, Selfishness. They lorded over us, commanded and directed us all at some point in our lives, and, perhaps, even today, they command and direct us despite our refusal to acknowledge the fact. Have we achieved our freedom? Have we pulled off the gigantic effort that would have allowed us to rid ourselves of all our prejudices, all our complexes and all our selfishness? Did we pull off that effort so that we might sit in judgment of these youngsters who wish neither to follow in our footsteps nor pay us any heed? No. We came up with excuses and framed reasons to justify our actions in our own eyes and in the eyes of the world.

Our greenhorn youth, the loss of some beloved guide, the impact of the surroundings in which one has lived, the need to survive. Excuses, pretexts, the cloak we throw down over the real reasons that prompted us to do what we have done all through our lives ... Our Selfishness alone has directed us, shaping our existence in accordance with the sum of our courage and our fears. The fear of blows, of prison, of "what will people say?," of Hell ... and I forget what else.

[...] Before you go telling me in your next letter that I have no idea what it is like to have children, as I have done the needful to ensure that I cannot procreate, let me say this to you: "All the children of the earth are my children, the children of today and those of tomorrow. I have fought, am fighting, and always will fight for their sake." That said, back to my message: our children, the one you have brought into the world and the one I have taken into my household, have reacted differently to life's difficulties: mine has been overwhelmed by fear, initially by the shock inflicted in Spain during the war and then by the wretched existence in the refugee camps. Psychologically weaker, she has shied away from reality. [...] We decry the depravity and the degeneracy of modern youngsters, generously overlooking the fact that

Antoine (center) on building site in Manosque

it has only inherited what we agreed to leave it: a rotten society in which only the most wild-eyed cruelty and selfishness are revered, with hypocrisy raised to the levels of a high art.

Antoine never did go back to Italy. A disinterested sort, he often lived one day at a time, not particularly concerned with material matters. As far as we can make out, he never joined any political organization in all the years that come after the war. A lover of literature, he tried his hand at novellas and poems, blending autobiography and fiction. Between 1974 and 1976, he drafted his *Memories*, relying entirely upon his powers of recollection. That led to a number of mistakes and generalizations in his narrative, but maybe that was the price to pay for an authentic opus. In this text he keeps us permanently abreast of his dealings with others, shunning both bombast and smugness, even during the most intimate moments. His every action is in relation to someone else, his every thought referring to them, in battle and love alike.

His main personality traits shine through all his writings, and foremost among them an unbounded love of women, traceable to his childhood. He grew up surrounded by women, largely on account of the Great War of 1914–1918 and his father's frequent absences from home. Besides, Antoine never spoke about his father. And it is noteworthy that he doesn't mention La Madre's husband in Pina de Ebro, even though he was around throughout his stay there.

It is interesting to read the little text, filled with humor and tenderness, that Antoine wrote following the circulation of a few copies of his *Memories*, a text that opens thus:

For the benefit of the lovers of Freudian theories who will later be trying to delve into the deep-seated reasons behind my outlook on life and the secret springs of my actions, I should offer them a few details about my origins. My great-grandfather, a priest who served in a little Italian parish, spotted a beautiful young worshiper in his congregation; he could, as many another would, have made do with giving her a good 'godding' in the presbytery and then marrying her off to some bold farmer who would have taken pride in being father to his priest's children, just the way that Joseph was father to Our Lord. But, driven by some atavistic proprietorial complex, he wanted her all to himself. He dumped the cassock and took off with the girl. Not being a complete fool, he had thought it through like this: I'm a priest, and the Church is my mother and she is very wealthy, whereas I am very poor. I don't know how he contrived the whole business, but before leaving the parish with his Dulcinea, he was rich and Mother Church a little bit poorer. Not enough to render her broke, but enough to allow him to bring up ten children.

My grandfather was a big farmer; as he set others to the working of his land, he had pastimes to help him while away his time: playing baccarat and chasing skirt. If the gossip in the village where he lived with my uncles and aunts at his left hand is to be believed, he pursued these interests so much and so well that when he gave up the ghost, his entire fortune melted away in the combined heat from his years at the casino and sniffing around Venus's backside, and his offspring were obliged to earn their bread by the sweat of their brow. For all of their sound learning and various qualifications, the vagaries of life drove them apart.

It was as if these pages, entitled "Childhood," were meant for those who had been shocked at the racier pages of his *Memories*....

In 1976, in response to the political curiosity of Viviane, Pilar's daughter and his adoptive granddaughter, he reentered into contact with the libertarian movement, dropping in on the Marseilles group of the Fédération Anarchiste (FA), whose premises back then were located at 72 Boulevard Eugène-Pierre. The FA group relocated shortly after that to 3 Rue Fontaine de Caylus in Le Panier quarter, at the foot of the building where the Gimenez family had its modest apartment.

Antoine died of cancer on December 26, 1982, very much surrounded by all the friends gravitating around the group. His death was

Antoine browsing

registered under his assumed name, for which there is no doubt he was indebted to Pasotti.[4]

4   Born in Conselice (Ravenna) in 1888, Giuseppe Pasotti protested against Italy's intervention in the First World War and was arrested in 1915 for anti-militarism. A mechanic, he became trade union secretary at the Alfa Romeo plant in Milan. In that capacity, he was in the firing line in Italy when the popular upheaval inspired by the Russian revolution erupted there. However, he did not affiliate with the Third International and stayed loyal to his anarchist ideals. Later he opposed fascism and, in 1924, had to flee from Milan, escaping the future Marshal Balbo's goons by the skin of his teeth. He relocated clandestinely to France in 1929, initially to Paris. In 1930, after spending a few months working in Germany, he and his new partner, Maria Linari, settled in Toulouse where Pasotti resumed his activism. He patronized the bookshop run by the teacher Silvio Trentin, a very prominent figure on the Italian antifascist scene. That bookshop was a rallying point for the Italian emigrés in the area. He was one of the correspondents of the anarchist newspapers *L'Adunata dei Refrattari*, which was published in the United States, and the Geneva-based *Il Risveglio anarchico*. On arrival in Perpignan in May 1932, as regional chair of the LIDU, he coordinated the antifascist activities in that part of France. From July 1936 onward, and throughout the entirety of the civil war, he was the intermediary between the Spanish libertarian movement and those Italian *compagni* setting off to fight in Spain. His home became the place where Italian

volunteers (notably Centrone, Girotti, Bifolchi, Perrone, Bonomini, etc.) would be marshaled and smuggled out to Catalonia. Carlo Rosseli, Camillo Berneri, the journalist Luigi Campolonghi, and many others also stayed in his home. In November 1936, the police deemed him one of the ringleaders behind the libertarian movement in the Pyrénées-Orientales department. At the time he was a member of the Perpignan group of the Federation anarchiste du Midi, which, according to the police, numbered "twenty-five members, twenty-one of them foreigners (mainly Spaniards and Italians)." Pasotti would escort Italian volunteers lacking identity papers as far the border at Portbou. He waged a bitter battle against the Italian consular resident who lived in Port-Vendres and who was at the heart of the Francoist conspiracy in Perpignan. The consul was declared persona non grata by the French authorities and expelled. An outrage carried out on March 11, 1937, against the Marseilles-Portbou train brought to light the culpability of Mussolini's agencies, if we are to believe the substantial report by the French police into "terrorist threats" in the south of France (Departmental Archives, Gard, 1M757). Tamburini fell under suspicion. Pasotti was arrested, as was the Spanish militant Melchior Escobar y Moliner in connection with interference with the mail (this involved some letters addressed to Francoist activists at a hotel in the city). He was sentenced on June 2, 1937, to a three-month prison term for "infringement of correspondence." Expelled on August 19, and wanted by the police, he fled to Marseilles. He was arrested again on September 19 for "breaching an expulsion order" and, after a short time in custody, Pasotti hid for a number of weeks in Louis Montgon's home in Perpignan. He continued making regular trips to Spain and doing his support activities. He was able to travel to Tunisia in the spring of 1938, thanks to help from some Marseilles anarchists. Over there, he resumed his political activities and, in concert with the anarchist journalist and writer Luigi Damiani, the spiritual heir of Errico Malatesta, he organized a group of anarchist militants. On April 5, 1939, in the wake of an attack upon a fascist venture, he was picked up as a potential accomplice, only to be quickly released. When Tunisia was overrun by Axis forces in 1943, he slipped into Algeria. Though still an anti-militarist, he enlisted—despite his forty-five years and rather poor health—in the British irregulars, while arguing that his mind was made up and that he would not bear arms. So he was made quartermaster and cook with a bunch of Italian volunteers.

Come the end of the war, Pasotti returned to Italy and was active in the Italian FAI's group in Villadossola. Commissioned to reorganize the libertarian movement in Ferrara province, he moved to Pontelagoscuro at the beginning of 1948, but, let down by the turn taken by developments in his homeland and quickly marginalized in a political situation that no longer had anything revolutionary about it, he made his way back to Tunisia, where he died on April 21, 1951.

For further information, see: the register for the Salvadori family, at the town hall in Chianni (Italy); ACS-CPC, Salvadori, Bruno file, PP *personale, fascicoli* 50, *pacco* 1196; Departmental Archives, Pyrénées-Orientales: 3U 2300 and 2304.

JUSTO BUENO PÉREZ

Justo Bueno, son of Justo and Vicenta, was born in 1907 (sometime between April and October) in Munébrega, about ten kilometers south of Calatayud in Zaragoza province. The family moved to Barcelona when he was still a boy. He worked in the metalworking industry as a lathe-operator-cum-mechanic and joined the CNT in 1933. That very same year he joined the Cuadros de Defensa, together with his fellow metalworker José Martínez Ripoll[1] and the Argentineans Ruano and Vicente Tomé Martín:[2]

> As a *pistoler*, Bueno had been involved in hold-ups, the planting of bombs, and urban guerrilla operations in the Catalan capital. It was said of him that during a tram strike in Barcelona, one that became famous, he was involved in herding the passengers off a tram and then, having set it alight, sending it hurtling down the Calle Muntaner.[3]

The other deed that made him notorious was nothing less than the April 28, 1936, murder of the Badía brothers; the actual target was Miguel Badía, in his capacity as head of the Estat Català party's *escamots* (gangs) and former chief of the forces of Public Order and then

1   There is an entry in Iñiguez's *Enciclopedia histórica del anarquismo español* for one Martín Ripoll, which might well refer to him: he was secretary of the Metalworkers' Union in July 1936; given up for dead at the end of the civil war, he forged some papers in the name of José Parejas in order to dodge the repression and fled to Santander. He died in Zaragoza on January 6, 1983.

2   García Oliver's *El Eco de los pasos* mentions a Tomé having taken part in the fighting at the Atarazanas barracks (page 208). Iñiguez's *Enciclopedia histórica del anarquismo español*, mentions a Vicente Tomé who was active in the Woodworkers' Union and who was jailed in January 1933, which fits in with what García Oliver says. Josep Maria Planes i Martí's *Els gàngsters de Barcelona* ([Barcelona: Proa 2002], 21) mentions a Vicente Torné in the ranks of the FAI's *atracadores* (armed robbers). Later (page 33) he refers to a very celebrated atracador by the name of Vicenç Tomé Martín.

3   Josep Benet, *Domènec Latorre, afusellat per catalanista* (Barcelona: Edicions 62, 2003), 375.

Justo Bueno

of the police force of the home-rule Catalan government in 1933–1934, a man distinguished by the ferocity of his attacks on anarchists.[4] The

---

4   The journalist Planes had published in the April 5, 1934, edition of *La Pub-licitat* a report to the effect that Miguel Badía had been sentenced to death

matter was incorporated into the indictment or *sumarísimo* laid against Bueno by the military authorities between 1941 and 1943:

> Before the beginning of the uprising, together with an Argentinean, an armed robber in his homeland as well as in Spain who was wanted by the Spanish police under the name of Lucio Ruano Segúndez, but whose real name was Rodolfo Prina, and of Vicente Tomé Martín, also an arrival from Argentina, and with José Martínez Ripoll, he gunned down the Badía brothers, an incident etched in the memories of most people from Barcelona, one that led to a scandalous judicial process, in that it triggered the arrest and incarceration of a number of Falangists upon whom an attempt was made to pin the blame for said crime, even though it was known that this was a falsehood.[5]

In a statement made to Quintela the following day, Bueno didn't deny that he was involved:

> It is true that he executed Miguel Badía and that in doing so he was accompanied by Lucio Ruano Segúndez, Vicente Tomé Martín, and José Martínez Ripoll.[6] It was Ruano who killed the second of the Badías, by the way, because they had had no plans to target him, but he was killed for stepping out that day, July 17, 1936, [Bueno has the wrong date here, no doubt deliberately] in the company of Miguel, which ought not to have happened, or, at any rate, that had been the arrangement when the decision was made to end his [Miguel's] life by violence. The idea for the killing had come from the deponent. [...] there was a rumor in Barcelona to

> by FAI personnel a few days before.

5   Eduardo Quintela Bóveda, head of the Barcelona Brigada Político-Social, on June 30, 1941, the day after Bueno's arrest. The indictment was held at the Captaincy-General in Barcelona.

6   From José Mariño we've discovered that also in on the job was one José Pla, who Bueno doesn't name, and neither does Martínez Ripoll in his deposition, and who was president of the Metalworkers' Union and secretary of the Barcelona Local Federation of Trade Unions. Pla will crop up again, when he is mentioned in the outline biography of Ruano. Pere López has told us that this was most certainly José Pla Duch, whose partner was Concha Gallent Lara.

the effect that Miguel Badía was about to take over Public Order in Catalonia again, and, since he had during his time as chief of police ferociously persecuted the workers and perpetrated many abuses, he decided that it would be better if he were murdered so as to preclude a repetition of any such activity; he raised the matter with Ruano who was in agreement with his plan [...] and set about searching for the gear and the wherewithal to carry out the "job." The gear (the car and weapons) were provided to them by Jaime Rier who was later in charge of the Control Patrols operating out of the Calle de Balmes premises,[7] Ruano and the declarant having looked around for two collaborators, Tomé and Martínez Ripoll. [...] The deponent, plus Ruano, took up their positions on the sidewalk, and, at a safe distance, Martínez Ripoll, armed with a submachine gun, had the task of covering their retreat once the shooting began; as for Tomé, he was driving the car in which they had arrived and later escaped [...]. The two brothers emerged, and, once they drew level with those lying in wait for them, Bueno grabbed Miguel by one arm and fired a shot into his head, another into his liver and one more after the victim of the attack had slumped to the ground, doubtless killed by the opening shot. In response to the attack, the dead man's brother rushed the

7   There is an entry for Jaime Riera Arbós in Iñíguez's *Enciclopedia histórica del anarquismo español* in which he is listed as one of the signatories to a manifesto drafted in Barcelona prison in 1932 in opposition to Pestaña. An article in *Mi Revista* of January 1, 1937, refers to Jaime Riera as the head of the Grupo de Investigación Central (Central Investigation Squad) in Barcelona, a subsidiary of the Junta de Orden Público (Public Order Junta). He also held an eminent position, albeit informally, within the Control Patrols, especially in the San Elías prison (see Guillamón, *La Guerra del pan*,115).

   According to a French police document dated April 20, 1937 and found in the Bouches-du-Rhône Departmental Archives (4M2355–200437–2182), Riera was at that point in France: "The subjects named Sergio Sala, Riera François (?), González or Gómez Imperator and Sachs or Saes are Spanish policemen, FAI members based in Barcelona, on temporary detachment in France, having come to Marseilles to monitor the activities of Spanish refugees, most especially, those suspected of being in contact with General Franco's government."

   The aforesaid "Riera François (or Francisco)" had been under surveillance by the police in Marseilles since March 1937. An application was made in September for an expulsion order against him.

gunman, or made to do so, but Ruano intercepted his attempt by also shooting him to death. Martínez Ripoll, meanwhile, stayed in the middle of the street with a submachine gun in his hand, covering the backs of the shooters. With the two brothers gunned down, the trio climbed into the car and made for Sans where they dumped it in a location agreed on with the man who had provided it to them, each of them making off on foot in a different direction; the deponent caught the metro and arrived at the "Rosales" bar fifteen minutes after carrying out the *faena* ["job"].

Josep Benet has said:

The double murder left feelings running very high in Catalonia. The journalists José María Planes[8] and Avel·lí Artís-Gener (Tísner) from the newspapers *La Publicitat* and *La Rambla* respectively, bravely denounced the involvement of Bueno and other FAI personnel in this outrage and revealed a lot of detail. Bueno, José Villagrasa,[9] Ignacio de la Fuente,[10] and Manuel Costas [Costa] were arrested on the instructions of Judge Emili Vilalta, but later, on June 25, they were set free by Judge Márquez Caballero.[11]

In the July 1, 1936, edition of *La Rambla*, Tísner voiced objections to these releases, and over the ensuing days, this was taken up by Planes. They both upbraided the Generalitat for its lack of gumption and urged it to expose the role played by the anarchists. And then, one day, Bueno, no less, showed up, uninvited, at Tísner's office. Initially

8   Planes was well known to the anarchist organization on account of a series of articles published in April and May 1934 in his newspaper *La Publicitat* under the title "The Gangsters of Barcelona. Anarchism's Organization in Catalonia and in Spain"; it was meant to expose the collusion between the libertarians and the underworld. [Giménologues' note.]

9   José Villagrasa Molló was an activist from the Transport Union and took part in the abortive attempt on the life of José Andreu (president of the Court of Cassation). He was sentenced to ten years in prison but escaped, in December 1937, and made it to France. (See Iñíguez, *Enciclopedia histórica del aarquismo español*). [Giménologues' note.]

10   Ignacio de la Fuente was an enthusiastic activist with the Barcelona Transport Union. He played a very active role in the tram strikes under the Republic. (See ibid.) [Giménologues' note.]

11   Benet, *Domènec Latorre, afusellat per catalanista*, 375.

very unctuous, he approached the reporter in order to talk about this and that; and then his tone became harsher: in short, Bueno is supposed to have regaled Tísner with all the details required to confirm the charges he had published regarding the "liquidation" of the Badías but suggested that he keep them to himself and stick to the story that Bueno had a cast-iron alibi. Otherwise Tísner would be a dead man because, come what may, there was nobody about to stand by Tísner and Planes, everybody being scared to death. But despite the advice of his colleagues, over the ensuing days Tísner did publish an account of that meeting with Bueno and incorporated the full details of his participation in the crime.[12] *Solidaridad Obrera* responded rather menacingly to that article, while defending itself (see articles carried on July 7, 9, and 10), and everybody thought that the journalist was a marked man. On July 11, Tísner warned his readers that if anything happened to him, *Soli*'s editorial would have had something to do with it.[13]

What we can add regarding this matter is that it was not a straightforward act of vengeance, the initiative for which supposedly came from the level of Bueno and Ruano's group; in fact, the possible return to power of Miguel Badía posed a distinct threat, even to Companys, who shed no tears over his death. So a political decision was taken by the CNT, or at any rate at the level of Catalonia's Regional Committee, with the acquiescence of Santillán (representing the FAI Peninsular Committee), who was not always opposed to the use of violence.[14]

Finally, it is worth noting that, in order to play down his own culpability in the eyes of the Francoist authorities, Bueno tried to depict the murder in a light that might be to their liking:

> The real reasons that drove him to kill Badía were the latter's activities as an enemy of Spain and it was when the October

---

12 In our previous editions we restricted these claims to the conditional in that we had our doubts as to their veracity. But thanks to our friend Enrique Tudela, who supplied us with the *La Rambla* article in question, we noted that Artís-Gener spelled out none of evidence of Bueno's guilt, which the latter was supposed to have vouchsafed to him, but that Bueno had stuck to the story that he had had nothing to do with matter and had airtight alibis.

13 See Avel·li Artís-Gener, *Viure i veure/1* (Barcelona: Pòrtic, 1989), 56–57.

14 César M. Lorenzo has informed us that, in 1935, Santillán approached Horacio Prieto (then national secretary of the CNT) for funding to organize a string of attacks in Barcelona.

[1934] rebellion came about that he came to the view that he deserved to die!

Obviously that "line" proved insufficient to save him.

When the pronunciamento [army revolt] erupted, and with the backlash by the working population of Barcelona, Bueno took part in the fighting:

> [Outside the Atarazanas barracks] a little assault squad made up of Ascaso, García Oliver, Ortiz, Vivancos, Lucio Gómez, Justo Bueno, Barón, etc. set off on a race against death that had them zigzagging to the secondhand bookstalls [in the center of the Ramblas]....[15]

It was at this point, if we are to credit Caridad Martínez Hernández's deposition (*Sumarísimo*), that an incident encapsulating those fiery, bloody moments occurred:

> On the day the mob overran the Atarazanas barracks, where the military holding the premises held out for quite a long time, about ten officers, either junior or senior officers (no heed being paid to whatever rank they might have held) were taken prisoner and were marched away to the Metalworkers' Union; the deponent had also been summoned there in her capacity as a nurse, to look after any wounded that might arrive, as the initial intention was to convert that union hall for use as a field hospital. Finding herself in one of the corridors there, those prisoners filed past her on the way in, escorted by armed militia members into an internal room where she reckoned they were to be held or tried, but in behind them went Justo Bueno, Lucio Ruano, and I can't recall now if there was anyone else, who shot the prisoners to death. From where she was, she could not see the manner of the killing, but she did hear the gunshots and saw Ruano and Bueno as they emerged, still clutching their pistols, smugly announcing: "That's how the people's justice operates."[16]

15 Abel Paz, *Paradigma de una Revolución* (Barcelona: Flor del Viento, 2005), 179.

16 *Sumarísimo*, Justo Bueno.

Bear in mind that this testimony needs to be treated with caution; for one thing, because it was secured by the police in 1941, and then again because this woman may have had reasons to want to damage Justo Bueno, according to Bueno (see endnote 21 above).

On July 24, Bueno signed on with the Durruti Column, which then left Barcelona, going off to capture Zaragoza and liberate Aragon.

Meanwhile, the two journalists who had exposed the activities of the CNT's action men soon felt that they were under threat:

> Directly threatened by Bueno in the flesh, the journalist Avel·li Artís-Gener (Tísner) managed to escape to Paris, returning only on September 29, when his class (the class of 1934) was called up, heading off immediately for the front to join a PSUC unit where he thought he'd be safer than in the rear. Tísner rose to become one of the officers of the Republic's 60th Division. José Maria Planes, on the other hand, hiding out in an apartment in Barcelona, was found and murdered on August 24. Another victim of FAI personnel in relation to the Badía brothers affair was police officer Jaume Vizern i Salabert. As the head investigator of the matter, he had accused Bueno and his FAI-ist *compañeros* of having carried out the double murder. On September 18, 1936, as Jaume Vizern was having supper at the Velòdrom bar-restaurant situated in the Calle Muntaner, near the Diagonal, he was accosted by someone who told him that he was wanted urgently back at the Captaincy-General, and that, if he wanted, he could drop him there in his car. Vizern accepted the offer. Once in the car he came face to face with some other individuals. And just a few streets further on, in the Calle París, Vizern was shot and his body thrown from the car. One of the bullets fired injured one of the gunmen, Vicente Ferrer Cruzado. Someone who happened to have been inside the Velòdrom stated that the individual who had spoken to Vizern was Martínez Ripoll, one of the members of Bueno's gang. It is virtually certain that Bueno himself was also part of the murder gang. Naturally enough, given the chaotic circumstances of the times, no investigation was held into the crime.[17]

Justo Bueno denied having had any hand in that execution:

17   Benet, *Domènec Latorre, afusellat per catalanista*, 376–77.

He states that he was not kept abreast of developments, but knows that the ones who carried it out are José Martínez Ripoll, Rafael Ginestà,[18] Vicente Ferrer Cruzado,[19] Rafael Sellés, and Antonio Moreno López.[20] [...] A few days after the police officer's death, he happened to bump into Aurelio Fernández (one of the revolution's most prestigious figures) in the street quite by chance, who asked him accusingly if he had been the one that killed the policeman. His answer to him was the same as it is today, which is that he denied having been the perpetrator and named the real killers to his interlocutor."[21]

As we mentioned above, Tísner thought that he was safe and sound at the front in a PSUC unity, but there were a few twists yet to come in the story. In his own words:

I was just coming around a corner and making a sharp right turn when I spotted a tank, one of ours and no mistake, heading straight toward me.[22] We braked and ground to a halt twenty meters from each other. On that narrow road, the two vehicles could not pass one another and it was obvious that going off-road

18   His name appears in a circular issued to prefects. Dated April 7, 1939, it listed "276 foreigners to be kept under watch" (Departmental Archives, Isère, série M paquets 75, 10, 62): "GINESTAR or GENESTAR-RUEDA (Rafaël), born January 30, 1909 in Benimanet (Valencia) [...] metalworker, anarchist, secretary of the Metalworkers' Union. Arrested during the 1933 revolutionary strike for possession of weapons in Barcelona. Arrested in Oran (Algeria) November 18, 1938, under the name of Gitarte (Rafaël), born April 2, 1907, in Pina de Ebro (Spain). Managed to escape. Supposed to be at sea right now on a Greek steamer. Arrested in Brussels in 1937 under the name Genestar-Rueda, Rafaël. [...] No known residence in France. Subject of an extradition application by the Spanish government for murder, under the name Ginestal (Rafaël)."

19   Pepita Carpena claims to have met Vicente Ferrer in Perpignan at the time of the *retirada*, in late January or February 1939, along with Bueno. (See Pepita Carpena, *De toda la vida* (Paris and Brussels: Le Monde libertaire and Alternative libertaire, 2000), 32, 37).

20   He too is mentioned in the file at the Isère Departmental Archives.

21   *Sumarísimo*, Justo Bueno.

22   Tísner had set out to fetch water and was at the steering wheel of a truck, probably sometime in the autumn of 1936. [Giménologues' note.]

and waiting in the vines would pose him no problems, whereas it was extremely difficult for me to throw my big whaler into reverse. [...] There was silence for a while longer, then it was broken by the rattle of metal; the hatch turned and flapped open. At this point, up popped the head of Justo Bueno Fernández [*sic*], the driver of the car used in the murder of the Badía brothers! I recognized him instantly—just the same way as he recognized me after a few seconds, after sizing me up through the grille—and it occurred to me: "What a bloody silly way for one's war to end!," convinced that he was about to kill me and was savoring the cat-and-mouse game that he was about to play with me. Grinning, he climbed down from his machine and, once on the ground, threw his arms wide open and came over to me, all gushing cordiality. He gave me a tight hug and began chatting, without further thought of safety, in light of his display of great effusion.

"Artís-Gener, you old bollocks! What a turn-up for the books!" he exclaimed, shifting from amazement to laughter. "Who'd have thought the two of us would bump into each other here? What's up? You don't seem very happy!"

I gave him an honest answer: "I still haven't gotten over my surprise! After our last meeting, I reckoned that if we ever met up again, it wouldn't be in this light-hearted atmosphere."

"Is that what it is? Don't be afraid, man! We're all fighting for the same cause now! You, driving a truck and me a tank; that's the only difference. In prewar times, things were different, and if I had bumped into you then, I'd have given you a right sorting out, because you had earned it! But things are all different today and now we are friends. Let me tell you one thing, though. If there's one thing my organization has always admired, it's balls! And you must have some balls on you!"

"Man! Thank you so much! Now: we being such friends, why not do me a favor and get that shitty tank off the road? I'm off into the hills to fetch water—the *compañeros* have been without for four days—and with this bastard truck, reversing is out of the question. Whereas you can move over into the vines, no bother."

"Indeed I can! In times like these one finds out who one's friends are. Right you are, *salud* and I hope everything works out for you!"

And he skipped back on board the tank, started her up, and retreated into the vines. As I drew level with him in my tanker truck, he played me a cordial *"nas de barraca"* fanfare with his accelerator and clutch, to which I replied using my horn.[23]

It would have been at roughly that same time that, in order to meet the Durruti Column's requirements, in terms of vehicle parts and car and truck repairs, Justo Bueno and José Martínez Ripoll were charged with the requisitioning of a garage, and that was the origin of the "Durruti garage" in Barcelona, known also as the "Ripoll garage":

The Metalworkers' Union commandeered the Casanovas garage [it was actually the Casanova garage, near the Gran Vía de las Corts], at no. 29 in the street of that name, an establishment that was later placed at the disposal of the Durruti Column [...], and Luis Latorre Mestres, Vicente Ferrer Cruzado, Antonio Moreno López, Rafael Ginestà, Rafael Sellés, José Martínez Ripoll, José Parés,[24] and declarant reported there for work; they were in

23   Artís-Gener, *Viure i veure/1*, 214–16. As we indicated earlier, a reading of the article in *La Rambla* of July 7, 1936, has shown us that Artís-Gener's bravery was sheer invention and that, as a result, he had no reason to fear Bueno's vengeance. What we have here is a fine example of macho self-glorification.

24   His nickname was "El Abisinio," but his real name was Jaime Parés Adán. Born in Barcelona in 1910, he joined the CNT when he was very young and by 1926 was already part of the Confederation's clandestine defense groups. He went on to serve with the Durruti Column and as a member of Eugenio Vallejo's bodyguard (Vallejo was Catalonia's Secretary for Armaments) and he took part in operations mounted to free anarchists imprisoned by the Stalinists. Once the war was over, he signed on with the guerrilla groups, including that of the renowned Sabaté, taking part in numerous operations freeing prisoners, carrying out sabotage and expropriations. He died during one incursion, in a clash with the police on May 9, 1946. We are certain that José Parés and Jaime Parés Adán are one and the same person, for we have found in Catalonia's National Archives a note from special judge Bertrán de Quintana, dated October 5, 1937, ordering that Justo Bueno Pérez and Jaime Parés Adana [*sic*] be held in custody. He is also cited as having been among the prisoners transferred to Manresa on December 2, but we cannot say if he was one of the eleven escapees that day, of the eighteen who escaped on January 3, 1938, or some other escape bid. (See Iñiguez, *Enciclopedia histórica del anarquismo español*; Antonio

charge of storing and repairing the column's vehicles as they arrived from the front, in working order or in need of repairs.[25]

Furthermore, in Bueno's file we find some notes on his private life and alleged sexual preferences:

> He is, besides, a sexual pervert, or one who will perform for money, while at the same time he was exploiting women, including his own woman, by extorting from them the cash they were earning from the practice of prostitution. In a fit of jealousy, the invert known around Barcelona by the nickname "La Joconde" declared when arrested once upon a time that Bueno would pay him good money for his caresses....[26]

On this score, José Mariño has it that Bueno was married but childless, that his wife was not a militant, and that he was a great friend of the CNT jeweler militant nicknamed "La Joconde." He specified also that "La Joconde" back in 1934 had been a member of the same affinity group, made up of about fifteen metalworkers close to or members of the FAI, that his homosexuality was common knowledge, and that no one made any slighting remarks to him because of it.

According to a number of witnesses, it looks as if Bueno may have remained on the front for about six months, beginning July 1936, which is to say, up until December 1936 or January 1937. There is a chance that when Ruano was begged to leave the sector, he went with him.... From then on he remained in Barcelona and would put in plenty of appearances at the "Durruti garage":

> On my return to Barcelona, I reported to the Metalworkers' Union in search of a job placement: I was entrusted with setting up metalworking shops in the Calle Abadal (in Sans)—the Labora workshops. Four months later, more or less, I was summoned to the Metalworkers' Union to be relieved of that assignment and set to mounting and assembling two aircraft engines on a dinghy, a

---

Téllez Solá, *Sabaté. Guérilla urbaine en Espagne (1945–1960)* (Toulouse: Répères-Siléna, 1990).

25   *Sumarísimo*, Justo Bueno.
26   Ibid.

vessel built at the Cardona workshops in the Paseo Nacional (in Barceloneta). [...]

Certain incidents occurred within the Durruti Column at around that point. When the column was under the command of Campón, Manzana, and the Ruano brothers, as a result of Durruti's having died, in the course of one attack mounted by Nationalist troops, they [which is to say the militia members] had been forced to give ground by the enemy's élan; Campón and the Ruano brothers, in order to "make an example," had a number of the militia members shot so that in the future no ground would be yielded on any pretext.

That approach triggered a lot of unhappiness among the column's militia members, and in order to defuse the growing animosity in the ranks, they found themselves obliged to leave the column and return to Barcelona.[27]

This was the point at which something came to pass wherein political activity unmistakably took a back seat to criminal activity. In the wake of the events of May 1937 in Barcelona, the state authorities were to go flat-out for reestablishment of the judicial machinery, the main aim being to rid themselves of revolutionary personnel. It was against that backdrop that a wide-ranging investigation was about to be mounted into the so-called "clandestine cemeteries"; entrusted to Bertrán de Quintana, it was out to jail all those responsible for summary executions, which in most cases been carried out by revolutionaries during the early days of the revolution. So it was that a special court was to get wind of the affair concerned, in which Bueno, together with Ruano, had been implicated.

This is by Don Francisco Tenorio Mariscal, clerk to the number one special judge from the Central Espionage and High Treason Court:

By the order handed down by this Court dated August 23 last [1937], we forwarded the book of evidence regarding the murder of the under-named Frenchman, Jean-Marie Moreau, opened by No 4 Remand Court in this city and numbered as 293 this year,

---

27   Ibid. Here Buenos is referring to the incidents in December 1936, which just goes to show how he had stretched out the work assignments, cited above, just to pad his resumé.

before being referred to the Central Espionage Court, which appointed its No. 4, D. Ángel Romero del Castillo as special supervising magistrate: the aforementioned book of evidence included the complaint and dossiers which read, more or less, literally:

Complaint—to the Remand Court—The prosecution [...] brings a criminal charge [...] relating to the complex offense of robbery and murder of the person of the aforesaid Frenchman, D. Jean-Marie Moreau: a complaint founded upon the following consideration:

Facts –

1. The aforementioned Frenchman Jean-Marie Moreau, pilot, builder, and inventor of a prototype plane of his own manufacture, entered, for the purposes of selling the aforementioned plane into contact with José Martínez Ripoll, Justo Bueno Pérez, and an individual by the name of Roanno [*sic*] who claimed that, being members of the Barcelona Metalworkers' Union, they were authorized to proceed with the purchase of war materials on behalf of the Spanish Republic. These business dealings, which opened on February 25, 1937, through the good offices of the French pilot Raymond de Larvre, led to the acquisition of the plane in question by the aforementioned Martin [sic], Bueno, and Roanno for the sum of three hundred thousand francs, sixty-five thousand of which sum was payable immediately. A contract was signed at a gathering of all the individuals concerned at the Metalworkers' Union local on March 21, once the plane in question had been flown down from France to this city and stored at the Durruti or Ripoll garage, located at 29 Calle Casanova.

2. Monsieur Jean-Marie Moreau, after spending the whole of the morning of March 23, 1937, at the Ripoll garage where the plane was being kept, returned, after lunching with some friends at around three o'clock that afternoon in the company of a certain Coustaing, one of his countrymen, it would appear, to the Majestic Hotel where he was lodging, and when they showed up [...] Bueno and Roanno arrived by car and invited Monsieur Moreau to get into their car so that they could take him to the garage where he would receive the sum agreed. [...] nothing more has ever been heard from him since that moment. There are enough facts and substantial strands of evidence to justify the conclusion

that they brought him swiftly to the garage and, for the sole purpose of not handing over the agreed sum and seizing the plane for which they had yet to pay, did him to death, José Martínez Ripoll having acquiesced in this: they buried the corpse right there in the garage near the western door some fifty meters to the righthand side of the entrance, up against the wall. The plane, which, up until that point, had been in storage at the aforementioned garage, was, without question, dismantled, with only the engine and two turntables left in place, and it seems they are there still.[28]

Those seem like pretty solid charges, but Bueno challenged them, in a letter in his defense written in October 1942:

In this town [Auch in France, late 1937], we [Martínez Ripoll, Latorre, and Bueno] discovered that the Red government was seeking our extradition for the alleged crime of murdering a French airman, whose body had allegedly been discovered in the Durruti garage, which actually belonged to the elder of the Ruanos; since a French airman, who had come to sell a small plane to Catalonia's Red government, had gone missing, they seized upon that pretext in order to bring pressure to bear in support of the extradition request and secure our arrest and surrender to the Negrin authorities.

However, it was public knowledge, as was later proven, that everybody knew that the corpses found in said garage were those of the Ruano brothers and their wives, but the Red government had to cover this up lest the truth come out about what had happened.[29]

It is unlikely that Bueno's argument is true, but be that as it may, we should point out that Jean-Marie Moreau's body does not seem to have been among the corpses buried inside the garage:

After telephone inquiries were made of D. Eudaldo Clotet, medical aide and ambulance-man, whose office answers to the Barcelona mayor's office (he oversaw the business of exhuming the corpses from the Casanova garage), regarding the number of

28   Ibid.
29   Ibid.

corpses found within the Casanovas garage, and of which sex they were, the latter's response was that there had been four, two males and two females.[30]

José Martínez Ripoll's statement was to the same effect:

It is far from certain that Monsieur Moreau's corpse could have turned up at the Calle Casanovas garage, for his firm belief is that the gentleman crossed back over the French border, a belief shared by the French police who spoke with the deponent who was at all times questioned in a witness capacity.[31]

And this was corroborated further by Luis Latorre's statement:

Questioned regarding the disappearance of a French aviator, he stated that it was for that very reason that the Spanish Red government had requested his extradition of the French government and been granted it, but that he knew nothing of the circumstances in which said disappearance occurred. He remembered that one day he found a small plane in the garage and asked Martínez Ripoll what it was doing there and whether the garage was to be converted into a hangar, to which the latter replied that it was the property of a Frenchman who had brought it down to Spain to sell and that this would be a one-off. The name of that aviator was Moreau. He reckons that the demand for his extradition was prompted by his clandestine flight to France the day after the deaths of the Ruanos, in the company of Bueno and Martínez Ripoll. His accusers may well have linked his flight with the disappearance of the French airman, but it had been on account of that of the Ruanos that they had fled from a possible crackdown by the Red police.[32]

Thanks to the investigations carried out by Ricardo Ramos Jiménez, one of the driving forces behind the blog montcadapost.blogspot.com, it looks as if the corpse of the French airman Jean-Marie Moreau

30   Eduardo Quintela, July 2, 1941, ibid.
31   Deposition of José Martínez Ripoll to the Madrid Brigada Político-Social, April 18, 1940, ibid.
32   Eduardo Quintela, July 10, 1941, ibid.

may have been dumped in a mass grave in the cemetery in Montcada i Reixac, near Barcelona. This was a "clandestine burial ground," to borrow the expression of the time. According to Ramos Jiménez, a document at the Montcada district civil registry, dated June 20, 1938, bears this out. An autopsy found that he died of a gunshot.

Moreover, the circumstances of Bueno's arrest in Marseilles are less than crystal clear:

> The widow [of Moreau] [...] made her way back to France and there, some months later, bumped into Bueno in Marseilles and had him arrested, repeating the charges, that he had murdered her husband, that had prompted the extradition request framed by the Negrín government.[33]

Now, in this letter in his own defense in October 1942, Bueno had this to say:

> I worked loading and unloading in the [Marseilles] docks [...] up until arrested, in Marseilles in my own case and, in the case of José Martínez Ripoll, in Aix-en-Provence on March 9, 1939, on the basis of a denunciation by two former Generalitat policemen— Gómez Emperador and Llaneras.

Perhaps it was Bueno himself who came closest to the truth, of course, when he wrote (above) that he was charged with "conniving with the fifth column over the May events," which, in the language of communists hell-bent on a real witch-hunt, meant the members of the CNT defense committees who had not gone along with their dissolution.

We know nothing of what Bueno was up to over the following months, between April and July 1937. For instance, we don't know what he was doing during the May events in Barcelona; but bet that he was involved in the fighting as a member of the defense committees, especially as we know that his friend Ruano played an eminent role in it.

The next episode that we were told about relates to the sad business that would see Bueno occupy a significant part in the elimination

33   Quintela investigation, July 1, 1941, ibid.

of this same friend, Lucio Ruano, on July 15, 1937. For the details we refer the reader to Ruano's biographical note.

Right after that, he left Spain with Luis Latorre and José Martínez Ripoll:

> We arrived in Tremes Aiguas [Tramezaigues] (France) on the 19th of that month and there we reported to the French authorities and were told to report to Tarbes, where the aforementioned authorities assigned the town of Auch as our place of residence. [...]
>
> [On August 31, 1937, an investigation was opened into the murder of Jean-Marie Moreau.] In September that year, I smuggled myself back into Spain and was arrested the very day I arrived by the communist Cheka. I was taken to a police station located in Barcelona docks, and thanks to intervention by a first cousin—Domingo Bueno—to whom I had been able to get a note delivered, I was able to thwart the plans of the communists who wanted to eliminate me. I was locked up and held at the disposition of the Russian Embassy; since they were unable to hold me with all the discretion they might have liked, I was transferred to the Police Headquarters after seventeen days, then incarcerated in Barcelona prison two days later [the 20th].[34]

According to a document dated September 18, 1937, Justo Bueno was arrested at the El Prat airfield in Barcelona on an unspecified date (most likely September 1) following the arrival of a plane from Toulouse. Bueno had on him a false passport made out in the name of Antonio Giménez Nuñez![35]

He would spend two and a half months in Barcelona's Modelo prison where he bumped into lots of his comrades-in-arms (about five hundred of them), since this was when the communist crackdown against the radical anarchists was at its height. There are suspicions regarding certain frictions within the judiciary, for in the National Archives of Catalonia there is a file on Bueno that contains a series of reports insisting that he be held in custody and at the disposition of the DEDIDE, plus others calling for him to be released. On October 30, however, Don Ángel Romero del Castillo, the special magistrate

---

34   Bueno's letter to the judge, October 21, 1942, ibid.
35   Archives of the Courthouse, Barcelona, summary 168.

from the Valencia TEAT [Espionage & High Treason Court] took up Sumario No. 293, relating to the murder of Moreau. The order went out that Ripoll and "Roano" [sic] were to be arrested; clearly the fate of the latter was not yet known at the time.

That October, there were outbreaks of mutiny as prisoners bitterly protested the inactivity by the confederation. Justo Bueno Pérez was prompted to use his writing gifts to compose a grievance letter addressed on November 24, on behalf of Metalworkers' Union prisoners, to the steering committee of the union of which they were members:

> We suggest the following: that some union comrades be appointed to get the files at the courthouse and bring them out into the light, in concert with the comrades from the Jurídica [Legal Commission], and at the same time that a lawyer be found to handle the investigations opened into the imprisoned metalworkers. We have found ourselves obliged to take this decision because there are comrades who have been locked up for the past five months and we still have to lobby the Organization for a lawyer to tell them why this should be the case. We have no doubt but that you will be in agreement with what we are proposing, as it is perfectly logical. Those comrades who are to be appointed, should they have any objection to raise or detail requiring clarification, should approach comrade Justo Bueno, whom the imprisoned metalworkers have appointed for that very purpose.[36]

Faced with the proliferating unrest in the Modelo, the authorities set about transferring sizable batches of prisoners, and this afforded a number of them an opportunity to escape—eleven of them on December 2 (the day of the transfer to Manresa) and eighteen (Justo Bueno being one of these) on January 3, 1938, from the prison in Manresa, where the city officials were still close to the CNT.

Bueno crossed back into France and settled in Marseilles. It seems that he then stepped up his activities as an agent in the service of Manuel Escorza del Val and the CNT's spy network in France:

> During the war, he was often dispatched to France as an agent by the murderer Escorza [sic], whom the CNT-FAI had put in

---

36   Document given to us by François Godicheau.

charge of spying on Nationalist Spain. But he then ran into difficulties and had altercations with the latter [Escorza] who stripped
him of his assignment, meaning that he stopped sending him
money, which was why he had to come back to Barcelona. Once
there, making threats against the CNT, having knowledge of a
number of its unspeakable acts, he secured some subsidies from
that organization for fresh missions in France; but he was so prof-
ligate with the funds available to him that the CNT also wearied
of him and withdrew its trust from him. He was unable to regain
it, despite making a trip back to Barcelona in an effort to do so, an
effort involving threats and attempts at self-justification. In Paris
he was known as "Le Millionaire" because of his ostentatious lifestyle. This is why, when the time came for him to be jailed, he had
nothing left of the thousands of pesetas that had passed through
his hands, and had only a few items of clothing left to remind him
of his "millionaire" days.

He had nothing left come the routing of the Red army, with
which he crossed into France via Bourg-Madame; but there he
heard that the commanders of the Ascaso and Ortiz columns had
likewise crossed over but with a huge treasure, which he meant,
ipso facto, to get his hands on. To that end, bringing his influence
and engaging personality to bear, he arranged for them both to
meet with him in a café in the French town, where he passed them
a cocktail that he had earlier laced with poison. His plan was to
present himself at their home once they were dead and to make
off with the suitcases of treasure. But he miscalculated the poi-
sonous dose so that it made those who drank it sick, albeit seriously sick, and this led to their losing the booty to which they had
staked their claim, and Justo Bueno got none of it. The owner of
the rooms in which they were lodging did, taking off with it to
London and depositing it under his own name in a British bank.[37]

Of Bueno's ostentatiousness in Paris we know nothing; on the
other hand, we do know of the repugnant incident with Ortiz and
Ascaso, which took place in August 1938 and not in 1939 during the
retirada. The book by Gallardo and Márquez has delved deeply the
matter and we propose merely to summarize it.

37   *Sumarísimo*, Justo Bueno, August 1941.

For reasons never entirely clear, Antonio Ortiz, former commander of the 25th Division, and Joaquín Ascaso, former president of the Council of Aragon, and a number of other fighters concluded, in the summer of 1938, that it would be wiser for them to get out of Spain as quickly and discreetly as possible. Ortiz felt that his life was on the line:

> It was at this point [around June 17, 1938] that he received a summons to report to Barcelona's Calle Muntaner where the high command sat: "They were lying in wait for me behind the pine trees in order to turn me into a hero the way Durruti was. But I never started off."[38]

Such "desertion" was viewed very badly at the top of the CNT, and a meeting took place at which it was decided that Ortiz and Ascaso must die; their old friend García Oliver was present at that meeting. And the man commissioned to do the dirty deed was none other than Justo Bueno, abetted in this by a handpicked squad that included his brother José.[39] It seems that Bueno's appetite had been whetted by the supposed existence of a "Council of Aragon treasure" that Ortiz and Ascaso had allegedly managed to haul with them when they left Spain by crossing the mountains! Paradoxically, it was that very supposed treasure that saved their lives, for the would-be hitmen dallied at the last moment in the hope of finding out more about it, so much so that some of them, such as Justo Bueno, pretty much made friends with the intended victims, and the killers could no longer bring themselves to kill them; it looks as if they were torn between the CNT leadership and all the threats that potential failure to accomplish their mission might bring down on their heads, and the flickering flame of their consciences. What followed was a tragicomic poisoning farce in which the dose of arsenic[40] used was deliberately inadequate,

38 Gallardo Romero and Márquez Rodríguez, *Ortiz, general sin dios ni amo*, 241.

39 "Urging that you track them down and plant José in the fugitives' company, in particular Ortiz and Ascaso, as a provocateur, for he has always been considered an unscrupulous adventurer, qualities that operate to the advantage of the matter we have outlined to you and which we regard as vital." (Letter dated July 13, 1938. In the "Red de Espionaje" dossier, IISH, CNT, cited in Ibid., 252–53.)

40 The arsenic had been supplied by Émilienne Morin, Durruti's partner, who naturally was clueless as to the purpose and the person for whom it was

dispatching the poor Ortiz and Ascaso to the hospital for a few days but ultimately saving their lives.[41] The CNT spent a fortune on this venture, and what its dues-paying membership might have thought of it is unknown, for the simple reason that it was never asked. To this day, hardly anybody knows about this dismal parody of Stalinist methodology and would rather Ortiz's reputation remain under a ghastly cloud, for the sole purpose, no doubt, of wiping its own slate clean after that.[42]

Unfortunately, this affair was not enough to cure Bueno of his taste for treasure hunting, although we cannot be sure if he was driven mainly by personal considerations or by a strong sense of activist responsibility. The fact remains that Ortiz remembered that in Paris,

> in May or June 1939, we bumped into a terrified Batlle on the Boulevard Montmartre.[43] I say "bumped into" because I was out strolling along with El Valencia. Batlle told us that he had just got away from Justo Bueno and the others who had abducted him. We welcomed him into our shelter and it was there that he told us about his whole odyssey and his intention to return to Spain. Batlle hadn't a penny left, no more than we had. We brought him to see Andreu i Abelló (who had been president of the Barcelona court) and he, through the good offices of the Esquerra, let Batlle have 4,000 francs, with the oddity that it was Joaquín and I who

intended. She had been asked to procure it by Facundo Roca, the CNT's delegate in France.

41　Gallardo and Márquez contend that the "unwilling murderers" set a trap for Ortiz and Ascaso in the hope of getting them arrested by the French police, so as to "ensure that the physical integrity of the targets was ensured by their being arrested" (ibid., 270). They state that three former Generalidad policemen (Jaime Llaneras, Sergio Sala, and Mariano Gómez) put their signatures to the complaint sent to the Spanish consulate in Marseilles, which forwarded it to the French police.

42　García Oliver would not be the last instrument in this campaign of ostracism, as Octavio Alberola has confided to us.

43　José Batlle Salvat, a very well-known militant from the Woodworkers' Union, had played a prominent part in leading the CNT's Comités pro presos in 1934. He was arrested in Barcelona in July 1941, and was sentenced to death before that was commuted to thirty years in prison. He finally walked free in 1951. [Giménologues' note.]

signed the receipt for it, so as to ward off suspicion ... I subsequently discovered that he had been arrested in Barcelona.[44]

We should point out that the date mentioned by Ortiz may not be correct, since Bueno was being held in custody in Aix-en-Provence on March 9, 1939 (after an application for his extradition that was to be granted on August 11, 1939, and put into effect on March 12, 1940), but let us follow up on Batlle's return to Spain, as described to us by Vázquez Osuna:

Batlle had been in Barcelona since the beginning of 1941 when Franco's police had tracked him down on the basis of intelligence received from France, which indicated that he had come back to Spain to retrieve a "treasure." His *sumarísimo* was to open on June 30 that year, when the CNT's Justo Bueno Pérez was arrested by the police and revealed that in July 1939 "the deponent being at that time in custody in Aix-en-Provence prison, after an extradition application drawn up by the Red Spanish government, which the French government had acceded, José Batlle Salvat, whom he had long known on account of his activities within the extremist CNT, was also detained there for having no identity papers. That Batlle had asked him whether he knew of anyone who might provide him with some means of entering Spain, which by that time was entirely under Nationalist control, as he had considerable swag stashed there, the proceeds of his activities as part of the Justice Committee alongside Barriobero and Devesa. That 'the mother of his children,' a former lover by the name of Dolores Mir, a married woman, was keeping it safe for him; he had entrusted it to her on account of the case brought against Barriobero for smuggling capital abroad ..."

The police picked up Batlle in Barcelona on July 11, 1941. In his deposition, he declared that CNT members who, like himself, had fled to France "had gotten wind of assets he had left behind in Spain and were badgering him by a thousand different means, to the extent of making his life unliveable, for the sole purpose of forcing him to go back and fetch them out, along with his persecutors, with whom he was expected to share them. That he was,

44   Letter to Téllez, May 14, 1978, cited in ibid., 287–88.

therefore, forced into returning to Spain in the company of a certain Roche,[45] whom he had given the slip once back in the country, in order to make his way back to France a few weeks later, flush with money, which he quickly squandered. That the people who had been hoping for a share of this wealth started in again and that he had then explained to them that what he had brought back was a pittance, and that if they would go back with him into Spain, he would provide them with so much that everyone around him might live well without working for years on end, a promise that attracted people by the names of Muñoz and Casterlinas (the latter being, it seems, the brother of a famous Barcelona armed robber),[46] who crossed over the border with Batlle but he managed to shake off once here. [...]"

As we shall see, it looks as if the fact that Batlle dumped his former *compañeros* there was quite simply his way of reporting them to the Francoist police so that he would not have to share his booty with them. It may even be that Batlle made sure they return to Spain so that he might deliver them to the Francoist police, while negotiating his own future prospects with the new dictatorship. Unlike Antonio Ortiz and Joaquín Ascaso who were to "trust [...] the men who were their would-be murderers, that is, José and Justo Bueno, two of the main contacts of the CNT spy network" in France, Batlle did not. In the case of the former, as soon as they became exiles the network began to scheme "how best to get its hands on the few items of value they said they possessed [...] and, above all, to annihilate them, which was the essential point." This was in stark contrast to Batlle's. Batlle played along with the network, and proof of that is the fact that he drove Bueno, Casterlinas, and Muñoz down to Barcelona in order to hand over the treasure to them.[47]

Vázquez Osuna then adds that Batlle was fearful of winding up like Dionisio Eroles,[48] citing the following comments by Ortiz:

45   Might this have been Facundo Roca? [Giménologues' note.]

46   The parentheses have of course been inserted by Vázquez Osuna.

47   Federico Vázquez Osuna, *La rebel·lió dels tribunals. L'Administració de justícia a Catalunya (1931–1953). La judicatura i el ministeri fiscal* (Barcelona: Editiorial Afers, 2005), 230–32.

48   This was a renowned CNT man of action who headed up the Generalitat's

On my return to France (following the end of the World War) I tried to locate Castán[49] to find out what had happened, but was unable to find him. Some time after that, I bumped into one of the members of the aforesaid group and asked him to tell me what had happened. He said that they had taken Eroles out [from the Le Vernet camp where he too had been detained], because they were keen to extract the *moniato* [swag] from him and that [Eroles] had led them a merry dance and told them lots of tales, until he managed to escape from them ... but that they managed to find his hideout after several weeks and grabbed him ... being unable to squeeze any *moniato* out of him, they opted to bury him way up in the Pyrenees.[50]

The Muñoz mentioned by Batlle was part of that wretched incident, but Bueno, on the other hand, could not have been involved in the group since by that point he had been in custody in Aix-en-Provence or awaiting transfer to a Spanish prison.

On the other hand, if what Vázquez Osuna has to say about Batlle is to be believed, Bueno was still active as part of the CNT's spy network between July 30, 1940—on which date he was to be released from Francoist custody in Madrid—and June 29, 1941—on which date he was to be rearrested in Barcelona. It is intriguing to read what Bueno himself had to say about that interval:

Messrs Costa and Quintana[51] asked me to join the Falangist police and combat communism and separatism, an offer that I did not decline, given that at every opportunity that had come along,

Public Order Service until May 1937. See Miquel Izard (ed.), *Entusiastas olvidados* (Barcelona: Descontrol, 2016).

49   A fellow prisoner with Ortiz in the Le Vernet camp in 1940, a team of CNT militia members including Gregorio Muñoz had smuggled him out of the camp—only days before they did the same for Eroles, probably in March 1940. Victorio Castán Guillén died in Bayonne in May 1983.

50   Letter to Téllez, cited in Gallardo Romero and Márquez Rodríguez, *Ortiz, general sin dios ni amo*, 101.

51   In his July 1941 deposition, Bueno refers to them as police chiefs in Barcelona; he even says that the former had harbored him shortly before the revolution, when he was on the run from Catalanist militants (retaliating for the Badía murders perhaps?).

I had done precisely that,[52] but, given the need to earn a livelihood, I joined the Maquinista Terrestre y Marítima firm in San Andrés,[53] where I worked right up until June 29, 1941, when I was arrested leaving my home.[54]

Stepping back a little, in the very same letter we read what Bueno had to say:

We [Martínez Ripoll and Bueno] were handed over to the Nationalist authorities in Port-Bou on March 12, 1940 because of the aforementioned extradition warrant. We were transferred to Figueras prison and from there to Madrid, at the disposition of the General Security Directorate and from there we were transferred to a police station in the Calle Fomento where we remained for a month. We were brought to the courthouse (Las Salesas) where a judge instructed that we were to be detained in the Principe de las Asturias prison, and from where we were moved to Porlier prison and released at the end of July 1940. Martínez stayed in Madrid, and I returned that same day to Barcelona where I started work, manning a marble-cutting machine.[55]

And to conclude with this strange activist who was simultaneously brilliant, likable, unselfish, radical and dour, murderous, violent, and a blackguard who would stoop to anything, here is what Abel Paz had to say of him:

---

52   The possibility that Bueno was a double agent should come as no surprise, especially in Spain where mutual infiltration was common currency....

53   Thanks to a kind communication from Antoni Tomàs Pineda from Barcelona, we know that Justo Bueno was arrested at his place of work, this metalworking form. Antoni has taken the testimony of Jesús Arce, a worker who was fourteen years old at the time and had witnessed him being arrested. From what he says, some policemen showed up at the Maquinista works to arrest him, in the presence of officials from the firm. Justo offered no resistance. A few days later, his father called to pick up his effects and, weeping, stated that they were going to shoot him. Later, from the press, he found out that Bueno had been responsible for the Badía murder.

54   Letter to the judge, dated October 21, 1942, in *Sumarísimo*, Justo Bueno.

55   Ibid.

In the wake of those executions, it fell to us to witness another: that of Esteban Pallarols. Esteban Pallarols returned to Valencia at the end of the war and managed to evade arrest. He went into hiding and, from his hiding place, set about reorganizing the CNT, serving as its first secretary in the clandestine years. A number of documents were forged and used to secure the release of masses of militants from concentration camps and prisons. The groundwork was laid for the underground organization, coordinating the comrades across the whole of Spain. But in the end, in February 1940, all or part of the National Committee fell into police hands. Pallarols, who had adopted the alias Riera, complicated his file, meaning to play for time, by planting doubts about his possibly being a British agent. He managed thereby to delay his execution but not prevent it. When his true identity was discovered, he was claimed by a court-martial in Vic (Barcelona) and then transferred from Valencia to Barcelona for trial on wartime charges. After all that, he was shot in the Campo de la Bota on July 8, 1943, along with other comrades: Eduardo Cura Estiarto, Francisco Ferrer Vilella, José Pla Masana, Agustín Farré Casademunt, and Juan Bernadés Pascual. [...]

Within a few days Esteban Pallarols's execution, it was the turn of another fine militant, Justo Bueno Pérez, and his close pal Luis Latorre. They were both brought in front of a Council of War, and sentenced to death. [...][56]

When Justo Bueno returned from the Council of War and was moved to No. 4 landing, to be placed in the death row cells, a bunch of Estat Català activists on No. 2 landing threw a party to celebrate Justo's death sentence. But the curious thing about that party was that Miguel Arenas Pons, an individual who had served under Badía's command, turned up late for the festivities and missed out on the cigars being smoked by his fellow guests, and had to be content with a blond cigarillo. Nothing out of the ordinary there, so far, aside from Estat Català's bad taste. But here comes the funny part. Miguel Arenas was also hauled in front of the Council of War and sentenced to death, ending up on death row with Justo. But as fate would have it, the order for

56   Apropos of Latorre, Abel Paz is mistaken, since he was given a twenty-year prison term; it is not known if he served it all.

Justo Bueno to be executed arrived on February 11, 1944 [actually it was the 10th], and Miguel Arenas's name, among others, was listed as part of the same group.

Luis Latorre, who was on death row and had said his farewells to Justo Bueno, related that when the latter found himself with Miguel Arenas as a fellow passenger on the one-way trip they were about to take, he said to him: "Friend, on this occasion, you were not able to puff a cigar to celebrate my death sentence; now you can puff on one so that we can celebrate our deaths together." And he gave him one of the choice *puros* he had set aside for that critical moment. Apparently, Arenas's hands were shaking so badly that he could not manage to get it lit, and Justo had to help him light it up. What coincidences and surprises history holds in store for us all!

That morning Justo Bueno, Miguel Arenas, Alfonso Palau Font, Feliciano Blaya Junta, and José Guia Cruceta met their end in the Campo de la Bota.[57]

And later he [Paz] goes on to add:

The day they brought me some books,[58] they capitalized on a momentary distraction on the part of the guard, and signaled toward the toilet by forming their lips into an O shape. I quickly caught on to what they were trying to tell me: the telephone.

It was easy to use this phone. Six cells were connected by the same sewage pipe. One had only to scoop out the water from the bottom of the toilet pan and arrange with another cell to do the same and we could chat quietly, with no need to shout. [...]

After the sharp knock that was the call for silence, I emptied the toilet pan and made ready to begin my "telephone" call, albeit not knowing exactly who it was that I was about to speak with. The voice I heard was Justo Bueno's. [...] As to the "telephone," we used to use it every night at the same time and he signed off by saying that "unless there's an earthquake, we are only in prison for a while." He was an optimist. [...]

57 Paz, *Al pie del muro*, 78–80.
58 At the time, Abel Paz was being held in isolation for two months, up until February 1944. [Giménologues' note.]

I was entitled to my "call" every night and I was up to speed about everything that was going on in the prison and on the streets, for Justo was an excellent reporter.

I had Justo at the other end of the line for nearly a month and a half, but one night the "answer" came, not from him, but from a different comrade. Justo had been shot that very morning, February 11, 1944. Poor Justo! He really wasn't in prison for long. Many times I envied him his fate. He died steadfast in his ideals and his hopes invested in upcoming generations ...

The following night, my "correspondent" briefed me on Justo's execution. He told me that Justo's partner, Flora, having arrived at the prison to pick up his effects, had been told by Sister Josefa—the nun who always attended those on death row—that Justo "had gone to his death reconciled with the Lord, that is, had made his confession and received communion." Flora was having none of it. Quite the opposite, since family members could handle the funeral arrangements and gaze one last time upon those who had gone to their deaths in such circumstances.

Flora made a beeline for the court to check on who should dispose of the corpse, but was told there that "her husband had died like a dog." She then made her way back to the prison to report to Luis Latorre the tall tales being peddled by Sister Josefa.[59]

Justo Bueno's name appears on one of the columns erected at the approach to the mass grave commemorating those shot in the Campo de la Bota. Ever since 2008, it has been regularly scratched out by Estat Català diehards, only to be restored by Barcelona city council.

59   Ibid., 88–89.

CHARLES CARPENTIER

François-Charles Carpentier was born on October 28, 1904, in Reims. His childhood was spent in various places around the Pas de Calais as his father was forever changing jobs. At home, anarchy was even then the keynote:

"We had two cats," Carpentier would say. "One was called Bonnot and the other Valet. In the 1914 elections, I was the one who filled in my father's voting card. He voted for Bonnot."

In January 1915, the family found itself in the occupied zone. Charles and his father were deported to a camp in Germany. Being only ten years old, Charles was repatriated by the Red Cross. Claimed by an uncle, he was back in the Nord by 1916 and started working at the age of twelve in the weaving mills around the area. His father came back from captivity, and together they worked digging up shell casings and filling in trenches. Two years later, Carpentier was trundling small wagons deep in the mines in Bruay-en-Artois. Then he took to the road working as a docker in Rouen and as a packer in the market in Les Halles. In Paris in 1924, Carpentier started his activism and hung out with the anarchists around *Le Libertaire*, which had just switched to publication as a daily.

Called up for military service, on November 10, 1924, he was assigned to the 65th Regiment of Fusiliers in Avesnes and was dispatched to southern Morocco to face Abd-el-Krim's rebels. He ended that campaign as a machine-gunner corporal. Demobilized on May 10, 1926, he returned to Paris and tried his hand at a range of jobs, became secretary of the Saint-Denis libertarian group, and was active in the trade union movement.

By the beginning of 1928, he was living in Aubervilliers, working as a coalman. He bumped into Charles Ridel (aka Louis Mercier Vega) in 1930:

> They struck up an unfailing friendship, within the anarchist organizations and in combat. It was to survive for upward of half a century. [...] [Carpentier] was loyal to his friends, a quality by which anarchists place great store.

594

Carpentier (right) with Odéon (left)

In February 1934, during the fascist riots in France, Ridel and Carpentier spent the night of February 11 standing guard over the Bourse du Travail, guns at the ready. During the days of the Popular Front, they became friendly with Simone Weil during the strike at the Sauter et Harlé plant. And then off they went to Aragon in the summer of 1936....

In the wake of the battle of Perdiguera, Ridel and Carpentier returned to France to orchestrate solidarity activities, and then Charlot, as his friends called him, returned to Barcelona in late 1936 as the UA's delegate to the FAI. He would send articles on the Spanish situation to *Le Libertaire*. Together with Scolari and Balart, he attended the big New Year's rally at which the trio "refused to sing the *Internationale* with bolshies." Thanks to Berthe Ascaso, Carpentier found lodgings in the requisitioned home of a commissar, which may well have been located at the same address as the Pro-Spain Liaison Committee: 47 Calle Rogent in the El Clot district. His partner joined him there after making the trip down by truck with Pierre Odéon. Carpentier also associated in Barcelona with the Basque anarchist Zarategui brothers and the Italian Ernesto Bonomini.

In May 1937, as he told Phil Casoar, Charlot was involved in the showdown: doubtless together with Scolari and Balart, he set up a machine gun on the roof of a Myrurgia soap factory near the Sagrada Familia. He also recalled having made a small sortie by armored car to machine-gun the Estat Català premises not far from there.

Disheartened and disappointed like many others in the wake of the bloody repression, he made his way back to France. He and Ridel had few illusions about the follow-up to the revolutionary experience in Spain, but they carried on collecting weapons that were then smuggled down to Barcelona. They spoke at the UA congress in Paris on October 30–November 1, 1937, before leaving that organization.

When war broke out in Europe, the anarchists were also in a state of disarray; everybody did what they could. Called up in 1939, Carpentier and his regiment were surrounded by German troops, but he managed to escape.

By 1943, he was working for the Comité ouvrier de secours immédiat (Workers' Emergency Aid Committee), a Vichyist body, alongside his comrade Guyard, and they criss-crossed France. That fact testifies to his sometimes prioritizing his workers' solidarity instincts over any political analysis.

After the war, he carried on as a jack-of-all-trades and eventually set up a haulage business. He ran into Ridel-Mercier again in 1946.

In the 1980s, he gladly answered questions put to him by David Berry and Phil Casoar, thanks to whom we have priceless details about his role in the fighting in Spain.

Charlot died on March 21, 1988.

"As far as I was concerned, there was family, there were friends, and there was anarchy. And that was it."

The quotations above have been lifted from Casoar and Feuillade, "Itinéraire François-Charles Carpentier," as well as Phil Casoar's conversation with Carpentier in the 1980s.

For further information, see Éphéméride anarchiste, www.ephemanar.net/; see also the entry for "Carpentier, Charles" in Maitron, *Dictionnaire biographique du mouvement ouvrier français*.

LORENZO GIUA

Lorenzo Giua was born in Milan on March 13, 1914, into a Sardinian family that moved to Turin by the time he was six years old.

It was in Turin that he received all of his education, being taught by Augusto Monti at the Liceo Azeglio, and quickly, in accordance with family tradition, came into contact with antifascist circles in the Piedmontese capital. His father, Michele, a leading chemist who had previously been assistant to the anarchist Ettore Molinari, was one of the university lecturers who refused to pledge loyalty to the fascist regime and in 1936 would be given a fifteen-year prison sentence.

In January 1932, when he was still in his last year of schooling, Lorenzo was prosecuted for subversive activities but, after spending four months in prison, was acquitted by the Special State Protection Court on grounds of insufficient evidence and on account of his age.

In 1934, now a student in the Faculty of Letters, he crossed into France in order to avert being arrested a second time.

In "Destino spagnolo (Ricordo di Renzo Giua)," Massimo Mila testifies about those times when they knocked around together in Milan, where Giua's attraction to Spain was highlighted:

> Our association with Renzo—he was at university and we had formally left by then, but were still connected to it by lots of ties—lasted about eight months. Twice-weekly meetings under Monti's chairmanship in some café or other, which was greatly honored to have been selected to play host to us; those Saturday meals at the Nazionale with the obligatory *agnolotti*; the evening cinema visits; the extra-mural excursions; the Po with its prowed boats; and, Renzo and I, the mountains, the boxing matches, the concerts. All of these habits were interrupted, like a lightning flash in a clear sky, by the events of March 1934: the Ponte Tresa incident, Mario Levi escaping by night by crossing the Swiss border, Sion Segre arrested with a carload of GL material, the big wave of arrests in Turin: Ginzburg, Monti, Carlo Levi, Allason, and all her "salon," Renzo being one of her regulars. In very timely fashion, his parents sent him off to the mountains to await developments

Three views of Giua

in the Balme area that was so familiar to him and from where, at a given signal, if things started to move on apace for him, he might, albeit not without considerable difficulties at that time of year, get across the border.

Over the ensuing days, Giua was not on the police wanted list, whether deliberately so or out of carelessness. But, without waiting for the signal, he made a dash out of Balme, crossing the mountains, through the Val de Viù, to Malciaussia, from where he sent one more letter, seemingly sentimental and quirky, to a young girl, but really to pass on his news; then he skied across a col 3,000 meters above sea level, l'Autaret perhaps or maybe Arnas, battling against the storms and spending one or possibly two nights under canvas and then on to France. The GL crowd—Rosselli, Garosci, Lussu, Tarchiani—watched as he arrived in Paris in a ski suit, his face burnt by the sun's reflection from the glaciers, his eyes twinkling with excitement. [...]

This apparently hurried decision was actually the opposite: a step in the direction of fulfillment of a destiny that was ripening harmoniously, a step taken with that far-sighted, knowing lucidity of one who answers an inner calling that no one else can hear. The same odd but firm determination as when he had picked his special subject: Hispanic studies.[1]

---

[1]   Massimo Mila, "Destino spagnolo (Ricordo di Renzo Giua)," in *La Rassegna d'Italia,* dossier 6 to 10, June–October 1947 (Milan: Tip. G. Colombi & C.),

In Paris, he made contact with the Giustizia e Libertà (GL) social-ist movement, becoming an active propagandist on its behalf. He quickly earned the trust of its founder, Carlo Rosselli, even though some reports suggest that certain strains and disagreements later sur-faced between them. In 1935, Ursula Hirschmann—a young Berlin antifascist who had fled to France—mingled with the Italian antifascist militants, including Lorenzo Giua. Like many others, she was struck by his personality and, long afterwards, Ursula, in her autobiography, offered this splendid testimonial to Renzo:

> The memory of our meeting is bound up with that of his smile, which he couldn't contain. He was a good-looking boy, steel gray eyes, short eyelashes, and gleaming teeth. He would laugh at everything: the questions I asked, my pronunciation, my shyness. His laughter was automatic, out of sheer amusement, and then I'd laugh as well, for no reason, shyness all gone. Thus disarmed, we put our first questions to each other, regarding, of course, the reasons why we were antifascists, the groups to which we each belonged, our ideas and our plans for the future. [...]
>
> I was struck by Renzo Giua's personality and he became important to me, precisely because he was so different from the other people I knew. Through his laughter, Renzo forced me to own up to certain philistine aspects of our moral stance: the sham activism, the lack of courage on the one hand and unduly opti-mistic propaganda on the other, the persistence with nonsensical polemics between socialists and communists, married to the care we invested in steering clear of more profound revision.[2]
>
> Renzo's casual questioning touched me deeply, without his even noticing it, perhaps. Because there was nothing more foreign to him than trying to talk anyone around. He had this way about him that was persuasive. [...]
>
> Each of us had become antifascists for different reasons, but we nearly shared the knowledge that we were leaving behind, sometimes a sensibility of the weight of the decision we had made and at the same time the austere moral commitment that

13–14.

2   Ursula Hirschmann, *Nous, sans patrie* (Paris: Les Belles Lettres, 2009), 149–52.

drove us to carry on down the path we had chosen. Renzo, by contrast, was not antifascist on the basis of reasoning or on the basis of moral purity. He was that way because of his vitality, because he could not be anything else; in a way, he got involved in it, *noblesse oblige*.[3]

The Italian political police reckoned around 1936 that Giua was dabbling in anarchism and, as a result, had resigned from the movement, but they then disclaimed their own report. According to whoever drew up the biographical note in the Italian version of Gimenez's memoirs, Lorenzo in late 1935 was effectively part of the "new dissidents" and had broken with Giustizia e Libertà. He moved to Annemasse where he bumped into Nino Napolitano, to whom he confided that Malatesta's thinking intrigued him. It was in Geneva, to where he fled next, that he found out about the civil war that had erupted in Spain. By July 24, 1936, he was in Barcelona with Francesco Barbieri, Fosca Corsinovi, and other refugees who had set off from Switzerland:

> Yet again, Spain was the irresistible lure that drew him from beyond the Alps: Paris being just one stopover on the road to the Pyrenees, one stitch in the gradual tapestry of his life.[4]

He went there to volunteer, undoubtedly during the first few days of August, and served in the Durruti Column (International Group). As had Simone Weil who, in August 1936, wrote to her parents from Barcelona:

> Everything is as calm as can be—nobody is being killed [...] I am off to spend a few days studying socialized production. [...] Think of me as unwinding peaceably in sunny climes.[5]

According to Massimo Mila, Lorenzo Giua sent a reassuring letter to his mother, playing it cool:

3   Ibid., 155–56. The entirety of the passage about Giua can be found at http://gimenologues.org/spip.php?article419.

4   Mila, "Destino spagnolo (Ricordo di Renzo Giua)," 14.

5   Simone Weil, *Oeuvres complètes*, vol. VII, *Correspondance* (Paris: Gallimard, 2012), 193.

"I'm here for a few days' holiday … It seems that we have a big war going on here and I have secured for myself a 'ringside seat' from which to watch." On 20 August, he carried on, without any great conviction, trying to hide from his mother why he had come to Spain, and this time he tried a tongue-in-cheek tone that now has a rather different ring to it. "I suppose you'll be asking me: what do you mean to do there? An odd question … […] In reality, what I am actually doing here, amid all this nonsense and metaphor, is getting a bit of rest in a social setting in which I can unwind … You would be wrong to fret: you should get it into your head that I would have a hard time doing any better … Or perhaps your motherly selfishness would rather I were at some address surrounded by Swiss hosts, rather than know that I am without an address in the shade of a sombrero?"[6]

He was first wounded in September 1936 outside Huesca. That was during the famous battle of Siétamo, which Gimenez has told us about. Giua spoke of it in some detail from hospital in Barbastro, in a letter dated September 10, 1936 to his friend Mario Levi:

My dear Mario, here I am in hospital with just a slight wound and with a nurse so gorgeous that the blood pumps gently through my veins. I didn't write to you recently because we were with the more than glorious International Group on its expedition from here to there; for some days, we were in Siétamo, a village a few kilometers outside Huesca […]. The fascists were dug in in the upper part of the village, the tower, the church, the barracks—in short, everywhere except for a line of little houses in which the great ferocity with which they defended the position could not stop a mere infantry centuria from entering. Those little houses are separated from the center of the village by an esplanade over-looked—and, luckily, screened—by machine guns and some very eagle-eyed fascist sharpshooters (one of them, a Civil Guard in his seventies, who will go down in history: everything he spot-ted became a target. Plus he is the one who got me.). The houses in question, occupied by our guys, were undefendable; but the fascists were not attacking, and neither were our guys. This way

6   Mila, "Destino spagnolo (Ricordo di Renzo Giua)," 22.

that combatants have of shielding themselves by firing from long range is certainly a handy way of making war, and we often come across it. Up comes the German-French-Italian-Iberian International Group, led by an outstanding fellow, a great warrior. Our way of making war is the other way around; we attack with grenades and incendiary bombs. Which is the approach we adopted in Siétamo, by taking over several fascist houses and putting several others to the torch, rattling the enemy defenders who are not used to such forceful methods. I was involved in the entire attack and come daybreak, covering some open ground, I was hit in the thigh by some shrapnel. I'll be back at my post in two or three days. For the time being, I unwind by having a chat and a quiet read.[7]

It would seem that he then moved abroad.

We cannot be sure exactly where he was assigned upon his return to Spain at the beginning of December 1936.

A document from the Comité de défense de la révolution espagnole antifasciste (Committee to Defend the Spanish Antifascist Revolution) delivered in Perpignan a collective pass, dated December 6, 1936, and among those listed is a certain "Guia." This, no doubt, was Lorenzo Giua. Dispatched by the Paris anarcho-syndicalist Committee, those listed were directed to the Pedralbes barracks and the Italian Section.

In a letter to Emilio Lussu, Giua wrote:

On I go, from one wound to the next, from one battle to the next, guided by the sure-footed instinct of not wasting a single hour of this war. [...] Even should I have to perish, my account will still be in credit when it is closed.[8]

In late December 1936 or early January 1937, he made another trip to Geneva.

On returning to Spain in March 1937 (we can't tell if he had made another round trip in the interval), he was posted to Albacete to the International Brigades staff officer training school, graduating as a

7   Ibid., 22–23.
8   Ibid.

lieutenant. The Italian police also detected his presence in the Teruel area.

In May 1937, after finding himself with Gimenez in Barcelona, he was incorporated into the Garibaldi Brigade. Gimenez refers to Lorenzo being left in Farlete that July. On the 16th, he was wounded a second time. After some time spent convalescing, he was then off again to the front and wounded a third time outside Zaragoza.

In October 1937, he was promoted to captain of No. 3 Company of the Garibaldi Brigade's 2nd Battalion.

During an attack on the night of February 16–17, 1938, on the Extremadura front, Giua assumed command after the battalion commander was killed, and he too was killed, shot through the abdomen.

We shall leave the last word to Ursula Hirschmann:

> By the time Renzo was killed in Spain, I was already in Italy. The circumstances of his death I know not, and any time I might have been able to ask questions about them, many years later on, I did not. But in his death, the features of his personality traits are blended inside me with an image of great beauty. [...]
>
> He had fought briefly in Spain against the Falangists and the fascists with the light-heartedness of an aristocratic hero; and there he had certainly learned to laugh irreverently at the antifascist bigwigs who stayed behind in Paris, just as, while in Paris, he had earlier poked fun at those po-faced antifascists writing bombastic letters from prison to their wives, pleading with them to stow them safely for posterity. Then he had soared into the heavens, skirting a slightly too garishly pink cloud, forever laughing from here on, his heart torn asunder by a Falangist bomb.[9]

For further information, see ACS-CPC, envelope 13361; Centro Studi P. Gobetti and AICVAS, *Antifascisti piemontesi e valdostani nella Guerra di Spagna*.

9   Hirschmann, *Nous, sans patrie*, 155–56.

GEORGETTE KOKOCZYNSKI ANGO, AKA "MIMOSA"

"This civil war is a mistake, on both sides,
but who will dare admit it?"

—MIMOSA'S JOURNAL[1]

This information we have borrowed from Lola Iturbe:

> I never knew her personally. But those who had dealings with her
> assure me that she was very pretty and highly educated. A cere-
> bral Frenchwoman and a strong character.
>
> Drawn from a middle-class family, she couldn't get along
> with her relatives and, at the age of sixteen, she left the parental
> home. She frequented communist circles, but didn't fit in. In 1924,
> she was welcomed into the home of André Colomer, who did
> so by protecting her from her parents' harassment. At the time,
> Colomer was an editor with the anarchist *Le Libertaire* newspa-
> per. Colomer's partner [Magdeleine], who shared his views, took
> Georgette under her wing and introduced her to libertarian think-
> ing. [...] She found work and lived freely. Montmartre was her
> favorite district, and she hung out in the cabarets there, listening
> to the poetry and songs. [...]
>
> By 1925, she had entered into a free union with the anarchist
> Fortin, and was working with the Éducation Sociale group that
> Fortin had set up in the Tours area. From then on she participated
> in meetings and festivals.
>
> On returning to Paris in 1928, she cultivated and asserted her
> artistic bent. An outstanding performer, she was one of a troupe of
> enthusiasts that toured the Paris area entertaining audiences with
> poems and songs and plays, while setting up anarchist groups.

[1] We have published the journal just as it came to us, complete with the page
numbering, pages missing, and the abrupt ending, as appendix 7 below.

Mimosa made a name for herself and was well thought of in artistic and libertarian circles. [...] Once she had finished a recital, she would step out into the room and sell *La Revue Anarchiste*, to which she was a contributor.

At the time she was training to become a nurse and earned her diploma.[2]

Thanks to information passed on by Éric Coulaud, we now know that Georgette was born in Paris on August 16, 1907, to Léontine Brivady, a maid, and an unnamed father. On November 14, 1908, her mother married Robert Ango, aged twenty-eight, a house-painter, and the couple acknowledged and legitimized Georgette. Following Robert Ango's death, Leontione remarried on April 15, 1919, this time to Abel Perriau, who turned out to be a violent alcoholic. He was the person to whom Gimenez was referring, though Antoine confused him with Georgette's own husband. The rest is as Lola Iturbe recorded it.

In 1931, Georgette left Fernand Fortin and married Miecsezslaw Kokoczynski, the son of Polish refugees. He belonged to the No. 14 Paris branch of the SFIO, and during the war and the Resistance he used an alias that he took as his real name once the war was over. That was a time when Mimosa was frequenting "far left socialist circles, not that that stopped her from keeping up her dealings with some of her former comrades," wrote Lola Iturbe in a tribute to Georgette-Mimosa, drafted in 1937.[3]

Georgette set off for Spain on September 18, 1936, and ended up in Pina de Ebro as part of the Durruti Column's International Group on October 4. Lola Iturbe says that, from a reading of Georgette's personal journal, it's obvious how steadfast she was in her determination to fight in the front lines rather than serve in the rear guard. That journal was rediscovered in 2007 at the IISH (in the FAI archives) by Édouard Sill who kindly passed it on to us. Here are a few extracts, the first of which sort of bears out what Lola Iturbe said:

The die is cast and I too am on my way to the front, as I expressly requested. I reckon I will not be coming back, but that doesn't

---

2   Iturbe, *La mujer en la lucha social y en la guerra civil de España*, 126–27.
3   IISH, FAI, package 50.

Georgette Kokoczynski Ango

matter, my life having always been sour, and there is no such thing as happiness. […]

I want to be off, to go where maybe everything is forgotten about, where mine can be the rescuing hand and where I might perhaps be loved a little.

Such thoughts show us how badly Georgette was suffering already, even as she arrived in Spain. In the last page we have, which comes to an abrupt end in mid-sentence, she describes the palpable tension by which she was surrounded in that society of armed men:

Rain. We sleep in haphazard heaps. I have found myself a mattress, alone in a room, hoping for some peace and quiet, but it is not long before I am disappointed and soon there comes a scratching at the door; I have barricaded myself inside with everything I could find.

Everything repugnant that Man has about him is in…

[*here the Journal ends*]

Her time on the Aragon front was brief, since she met her death there on October 16, 1936, in Perdiguera.

Here, again from the pen of Lola Iturbe in 1937, is one version of how she met her end:

There are a number of versions in circulation. According to certain prisoners, and as Durruti himself believed for a time, she was shot by the fascists, along with three other comrades on the expedition. According to the Military Health Council's version, she was shot and her body dumped in a barn, which Franco's men then set fire to. The precise details of her death we will never know, for the nearest witnesses were a long way from the site of the tragedy. One thing is certain: she was murdered by fascists in an atrocious way.

So perished Mimosa at the age of twenty-eight.[4] The comrades who knew her launched an FAI group in Barcelona that took her name, and she symbolizes the sacrifices made by the foreign women who perished for the sake of antifascist Spain.[5]

4   In reality, she was twenty-nine. [Giménologues' note.]
5   Ibid.

JOSEP LLADÓS TARRAGÓ

Josep Lladós currently lives in the Périgord in France and has published his own memoirs. Here is a little extract:[1]

> In the village, unbeknown to me, there was a union affiliated with the National Confederation of Labor [CNT]. It was made up of a bunch of impatient youngsters between twenty and forty years of age. As everybody in Alcarràs knew everybody else at that time, one of them contacted me and invited me to drop in at the union local. There, there were books, magazines, and other reading materials but no alcohol, and there were next to no smokers. I realized that the ambiance there was more wholesome than in any inn or café. I dropped in at the union one night when I couldn't think of anywhere else I could go without having to spend a cent. Those who were there gave me a friendly welcome and told me: "Look! On the table, we have newspapers, magazines, and books!" Flicking through them inquisitively, I came upon an article in one magazine dealing with sexuality. There I discovered how many diseases one could catch from frequenting whorehouses. Reading that article has stayed with me for life, so I have never had dealings with people of that sort since then. In those days, there were lots of cafés and even more taverns. I never heard tell of a library! What I learned at the union, without anyone forcing me to learn it, has stood me in good stead for life. Such was the anarcho-syndicalist cultural impact wherever the CNT had a presence. Not that that stopped its adversaries from criticizing it. Unlike the taverns and cafés where smoke and alcohol created an unbreathable atmosphere, at the union I was in wholesome surroundings where I could read and learn things I never knew. So I took out a CNT card and that too has not left my side since.[2]

1   In 1935, he joined the CNT in his village. It was at that point that his path crossed that of Antoine Gimenez.
2   Lladós, *Guerre et exil d'un Républicain Espagnol, 23 ans, apatride*, 23.

Josep Lladós Tarragó

Josep Lladós was born on February 6, 1920, in Alcarràs near Lérida. He was the second of three children in a family of smallholders. At the end of September 1936, at the age of sixteen years and seven months, he joined the Durruti Column's 11th Centuria, near Osera. Billeted in an under-equipped *paridera*, his main duty was standing guard. After some time on Monte Alfajarín, his *centuria* returned to Osera, opposite Villafranca. He left the column when militarization was imposed and returned to Alcarràs where he was appointed secretary of the Libertarian Youth.

In April 1938, he spontaneously joined his class in Barcelona when it was called up. Incorporated, for want of proper information, at the Karl Marx barracks, he was then assigned to the 34th Division under the command of Trueba; 104th Brigade, 15th Battalion, No. 2 Company, No. 2 Section.

On August 25, 1938, Josep Lladós took part in the battle for San Cornelio as his baptism of fire and was one of just four survivors from his group. Antoine mentions in his account how the Libertarian Youth, under communist command, were used as cannon fodder in battles. In the rear too the Libertarian Youth printed up leaflets urging militants to be discreet about their political affiliations when they were signing up. They warned that most of the communist officers sent the anarchists out into the firing line. For a long time, his unit camped in Tavascán way up high in the Pyrenees—up until the summer of 1938.

After the disorganized displacements of the general retreat in the winter of 1939, he crossed into France via Prats-de-Mollo. Imprisoned in No. 1 camp in Agde and later in Saint-Cyprien up until December 1939, he found himself seconded to the 684th CTE (Foreign Labor Company) posted to Haute-Vienne until France was defeated. His CTE then withdrew to Bergerac in the Dordogne. He was hired out, with others, to the local farmers, and then to the Germans once they opened a flying school at the Roumanières aerodrome in 1942, up until they pulled out in August 1944. He then met up with the "Alexandrie" resistance group and was put in charge of guarding Russian, German, and Polish prisoners.

Josep Lladós was discharged from the GTE in late 1944. After some professional training in 1947, he settled once and for all in the Dordogne. He went on to marry and have six children. Having worked as a journeyman-plasterer up until 1967, he set up shop as an artisan until he retired in 1985.

LOUIS MERCIER VEGA, AKA CHARLES RIDEL

Charles Cortvrint was born on May 6, 1914 in Brussels. From the age of sixteen, he was active in the anarchist movement. Dodging his military service, he moved to Paris and joined the Union Anarchiste, serving as its delegate to the Orléans congress of 1933. One after another, he worked as a laborer in Les Halles, leather-worker, street-hawker, and proofreader. After offering *Le Libertaire* articles written under a variety of pen names (Couramy, Liégeois) in 1933–1934, he became a regular contributor under the nom de plume Charles Ridel between June 1936 and October 1937. He also penned a few articles for *La Révolution prolétarienne*, notably a report on the CNT congress that he attended in Zaragoza in May 1936.

During his Paris years, Ridel hung out with a small band of anarchist pals who had styled themselves the "Moules-à-gauffre" [Waffle-irons]. These included Charles Carpentier, Félix Guyard, Robert Léger, and Lucien Feuillade.

> Within the Union anarchiste [...], Ridel and his pals from the Jeunesses [Youth] belonged to the libertarian-communist faction that set up factory-based groups, and were not content with antifascist sloganizing and posited an economic and political program as an alternative to the Popular Front. [...] Revolution? "This year or never," as he told Simone Weil [in 1936] [...].[1]

As early as July 1936, he headed for Barcelona with his friend Charles Carpentier. He threw himself into the anarchist militias on the Aragon front and, together with Berthomieu and Carpentier, he launched the Durruti Column's International Group.

Following the battle of Perdiguera in October 1936, his comrades persuaded him to return to France and embark upon a massive publicity program on behalf of revolutionary Spain. In its October 9 edition, *Le Libertaire* announced a series of talks complete with film

---

1   Marianne Enckell, in Louis Mercier Vega, *La Chevauchée anonyme* (Marseilles: Agone, 2006), 218.

Louis Mercier Vega, aka Charles Ridel

screenings on events in Spain, with the proceeds going to the feeding of Spain's antifascist militias. Up until February 1937, therefore, Ridel was criss-crossing France with Porchet's films like *Los Aguiluchos de la FAI*, and it was in the course of this tour that he met his future wife, Sarah.

> [In 1938] even as revolutionary Spain was going through its death throes, anarchist belief was slowly turning into an enthusiasm for war; in which case, it was better to let oneself be written off as a coward and deserter and be in a position to proclaim the truth: "That truth is negative, impotent, and pessimistic, but it is a truth stark and cruel and one that we shall proclaim in the face of all who live on the back of the—antifascist—war: yoking the sacrifices of revolutionaries to the defense of Negrín and bourgeois democracy would shatter the hopes of their being resurrected in the struggles yet to come. We are aware that we can say on behalf of those who perished as miliciens of social revolution: 'That it was not for this that they perished,' and forbid the clowns of *la sociale* [the revolution] from despoiling their corpses," read the May 1938 editorial in *Révision*, a little review with a provocative title, run by Ridel, Marie-Louise Berneri, Lucien Feuillade, Jean Rabaut, and a handful of others.[2]

2   Ibid., 220.

In *L'Espagne nouvelle* in the summer of 1939, Ridel wrote one final article headlined "Pour repartir" [Beginning Afresh], in which he gave free rein to all his cold wrath:

> Once it becomes possible to sit in judgment of the conduct of the Spanish militants and organizations of every persuasion over the years '36 to '39, onlookers will find it hard to believe that such a massive and thriving movement should have concealed so many weaknesses, betrayals and ignorance.
>
> [...] Even exile has not opened the mouths of those who know, mouths that so often gaped wide to peddle huge untruths for propaganda purposes. [...]
>
> Yet there are so many mysteries that require unveiling, so many situations in need of clarification, so many contradictions to be unraveled. But above all else, that would require that the moral principles essential to any collective effort should stir in those who have so blithely forgotten them in the throes of revolution.
>
> Because that is precisely where the Iberian revolution has fallen down [...].
>
> Over and above the labels, the tendencies, and the jargon, the Spanish workers' movement has succumbed to the usual vices: *arrivisme*, feathering one's own nest, contempt for the masses, and scorn for the ideas that drive them.
>
> We have seen anarchist individualists becoming staunch supporters of government, libertarians ensconcing themselves in ministerial armchairs, wild-eyed advocates of class struggle questing anxiously after support from bourgeois republicans, internationalists singing paeans to the peculiar genius of Spaniards [...]. Yet such weird about-turns might be thrashed out if we were dealing with an evolution in the face of brand-new phenomena, but that is far from being the case. A remarkable intellectual dishonesty covered up for every retreat, every act of treachery was accompanied by eloquent invocations of traditional principles.
>
> The libertarian movement's leaders did not even have the benefit of being out-and-out adventurers or members of coup d'état squads. Intoxicated by their own speechifying, admiring themselves in the mirror in their general's outfit, playing the big wheels in peasant villages, they were gulled by the old foxes of traditional cronyism and made to toe the line by the Stalinist

checas. García Oliver was poring over the Code even as the GPU was committing murders. Federica Montseny was watching over Hygiene! All of the sub-Olivers and mini-Montsenys prattled on about *trayectorias históricas* [historical trajectories], even as the Bank of Spain's gold was making a beeline for the USSR or the United States. [...] And the hapless militiaman found himself shot for having pocketed a ring found in some village [...].

Throughout the months of revolution and war, the National Committee, the delegates from the lost Regions, and the Peninsular Committee operated and made decisions, unsupervised and unpublicized. The Regionals fed off themselves. At no point was there any broad discussion about the most significant issues. [...]

The old habits of allying oneself with the left republicans, dating back into the last century, the habitual contacts with anti-government, regionalist, pro-coup factions impacted upon the subsequent performance of the leaders. [...]

Thousands of rank-and-file believers, still fiercely attached to their notion of libertarian, egalitarian socialism watched as day by day they turned into the pawns in a game, the direction of which was increasingly slipping from their grasp.

Instead of searching for formulas that might have made it possible to tackle situations without hobbling the march of revolution, propaganda peddled the slogans offering the most rabble-rousing cover possible for opportunism and counter-revolution.

At the time of the Munich crisis, Ridel crossed into Switzerland with Jean Bernier because, as an editorial in *Révision* (No 3, April 1938) announced: "the only betrayal would be to march." In September 1939, he traveled to Marseilles, only to find that the city was hardly the best place through which to leave France. Off he went to northern Europe that October, via Belgium and Hem Day's house. That November he boarded a cargo ship bound for Argentina, under the assumed name Carlo Manni. His book *La Chevauchée anonyme* retraces the period between 1939 and 1941. Mercier recounts this crucial time in his life through the characters Parrain and Danton. This was the point at which Ridel evaporated, turning ever after into Luis Mercier Vega, Chilean. He then switched to Africa, to Brazzaville, where, on June 26, 1942, he signed up with the Free French forces.

Demobilized in October 1945, he was hired by *Le Dauphiné libéré* in Grenoble as an editor. He penned articles for *La Révolution prolétarienne*: in No. 333, new series No. 32 in November 1949 in which he registered "the almost utter non-existence of the proletariat [...] as a candidate in the succession to capitalism" and yearned for a "de facto international, linking all who have not lost hope."[3]

At the beginning of the 1950s, Mercier Vega became a member of the Amis de la liberté, the militant French chapter of the Congress for Cultural Freedom, an international organization, an umbrella for anti-totalitarian intellectuals launched in Berlin in June 1950. Certain anarchists took him soundly to task for his collaboration with the Congress and its publication, *Preuves*, on the basis that the organization was subsidised by the CIA.

In 1957–1958, having realized from his breadth of international contacts that there was "an urgent need for the establishment of a network of ongoing relations between libertarian personnel and revolutionary syndicalists from different countries," he set up the Commission internationale de liaison ouvrière [CILO/International Worker Liaison Commission] and played an active part in editing its four-language bulletin, which would be replaced by the international anarchist research review, *Interrogations*. The very first issue of *Interrogations* appeared in December 1974 with this preliminary announcement:

"No longer can anarchism make do with repeating what was true yesterday. It has to come up with whatever corresponds to its mission today."

His book *L'Increvable Anarchisme* appeared in 1970 with a dedication to his International Group "compañeros from the *chevauchée anonyme*" [nameless cavalcade].[4] It was to be a landmark publication.

After three years of intense activity, Ridel-Mercier took his own life in Collioure on November 20, 1977 (in memory of that fateful November 20 in 1936 when Buenaventura Durruti was killed?), and it was Carpentier that was charged with passing the news on to old friends.

---

3   Cited in Collectif, *Présence de Louis Mercier*, 75.

4   *L'Increvable Anarchisme* (UGE, 1970), republished by Analis in 1988 (from which edition that dedication was strangely dropped).

LUCIO RUANO

After some months of investigation, we have reconstructed the story of this complex man who held a position of responsibility within the libertarian movement yet was largely forgotten in the anarchist historiography. But, as in lots of other facets of the Spanish Civil War, some questions remain unanswered, starting with the true identity of Ruano as well as his brother's identity.

Phase One:
Argentina 1931–Barcelona, July 1936

According to a report of June 30, 1941, from police officer Eduardo Quintela,[1] Lucio Ruano's real name was supposedly "Rodolfo Prina, Argentinean, a hold-up man in his homeland and in Spain, registered by the police under the name Lucio Ruano Segúndez." There was also a brother, Julio.[2] Be that as it may, Lucio Ruano was indeed Argentinean. In 1930, he was a member of a band of anarchist expropriators mounting armed raids on banks on behalf of the movement, plus attacks on their police pursuers. Following up the "Prina" trail, we find some interesting detail in Osvaldo Bayer's book, *The Anarchist Expropriators*. They were Julio and Toni Prina. Here are some extracts (the operation in question was mounted in 1931 in Avellaneda, Argentina, at a point when Morán's anarchist group, hounded by Major Rosasco's police, decided to hit back):

> In this contest, the only factor in the anarchists' favor could be the element of surprise. The expropriators acceded to Morán's proposal. Julio Prina, a philosophy student, would come down from La Plata. "Nene" Lacunza would also be at Morán's side. The only son of a peasant from San Pedro, he'd had his baptism of fire alongside Severino Di Giovanni and Emilio Uriondo in the raid on

---

1   *Sumarísimo*, Justo Bueno.
2   On the basis of Bueno's statements, we have reason to believe that Lucio Ruano was actually Julio Prina and that Rodolfo was the younger brother.

La Central Bus Company. The third man to accompany Moran as his driver was a Spaniard, González, whose picturesque life was to peak in 1944 when he entered a liberated Paris aboard a tank belonging to the Leclerc Division. Finally, he had backing from "The Engineer," one of the most intriguing members of the group. Though personally opposed to violence—because he believed the bourgeoisie could be fought using other more ingenious methods—"The Engineer," when invited by his comrades, was up for any of the most dangerous and risky operations.

On the evening of June 12, 1931, Major Rosasco, accompanied by the deputy mayor of Avellaneda, Eloy Prieto, left police headquarters to go to dinner in the "Checchin" restaurant 150 meters away. Rosasco was very happy, having just rounded up forty-four anarchists, including some youths who had been distributing leaflets that read: "Death to Rosasco!" To tell the truth, those kids were about to lose their taste for printing, even if they were only printing "Little Red Riding Hood"!

Rosasco had summoned the press to announce that he had thwarted yet another anarchist plot.

They stepped inside the restaurant and ordered their first course, which they wolfed down with a good appetite. Once the first course was finished, "five respectably dressed individuals" climbed out of a car. One of them sat at a table beside the door, and the other four walked to the back of the dining room, as if making their way to the yard.

Some wisecrack had just drawn gales of laughter from Major Rosasco when, all of a sudden, the four individuals stooped down in front of his table. One of them stepped forward. He had the look of a *criollo* about him and seemed as strong as an ox. He moved towards Rosasco and shouted at him: "Dirty pig!" Rosasco stood up slowly, his eyes bulging. The stranger, who was none other than Juan Antonio Morán, drew, equally slowly, a Colt .45 and fired five shots, all of them deadly.

The five men then took to their heels and, to cover them, Julio Prina fired some more shots that inflicted slight injuries upon a young man and Prieto.

At this point, the drama reached its second act: as he fled, one of the anarchists stumbled and crashed through a plate glass window. By then, his colleagues were back in the car waiting for him: they thought it must just be a slight accident, but this wasn't the case. The young man—Lacunza—never got up again. He was dead. The anarchists quickly retraced their steps to retrieve their comrade's body. They managed to bundle it into the car, and raced off. [...]

The assassination was a gauntlet flung down by the subversive anarchists in front of the government, army, and police. And the police in charge of inquiries would enjoy carte blanche: woe betide the anarchist that fell into the hands of the authorities just then! [...]

The police never did manage to find out who killed Rosasco, though they always suspected the steersman Juan Antonio Morán. He was, moreover, sentenced to death in absentia.

What we have published here for the very first time is the actual story of how Major Rosasco was assassinated and the names and persons involved. [...]

In spite of the repression and their casualties, the anarchist expropriator movement was still showing signs of strength in 1932 and 1933, mainly in La Plata, in Avellaneda, and in the capital [...]

Armed raids and attempts to break people out of prison were carried on at the same pace. [...] the Prina brothers from La Plata (Julio and Toni) were active with Juan Antonio Morán, Daniel Ramón Molina (who worked at the docks), Julio Tarragona, Ángel Maure, Pedro Blanco, and Victor Muñoz Recio. These were two small groups but they fought to the bitter end.

At the end of 1932, at the instigation of Rafael Laverello and with help from Morán, Prina, Molina, and Gatti, a new tunnel was dug. This time it started from an apartment near the jail, and it was designed to secure the release of Emilio Uriondo and other anarchists. It was even better thought out than the Punta Carretas tunnel. It was fifty-eight meters long and went right up to the prison laundry. But after they had dug the first twenty-three meters, they had to call it off because the police were closely watching all of the men involved. And besides that, they were starting to run out of money.

Then came a series of blows dealt by the unrelenting Inspector Bazán. [...] The Prina brothers fled to Spain. On June 28, a police squad cordoned off a house in Mitre Avenue in Avellaneda and caught Juan Antonio Morán asleep. [...]

It was all over now. There was no one to work for the freedom of those in jail.[3]

According to the preamble to the verdict handed down by the Barcelona court on January 28, 1935, on "Lucio Ruano Segúndez, the thirty-three year-old, Valladolid-born, unmarried son of José and Romana, a dye-worker living in Badalona, educated, with no nickname and no prior criminal record, held in preventive detention for assault and battery," Ruano had been under police surveillance and tailed by Elías Cano Barahona, a policemen disguised as a workman. On May 31, 1933, Ruano ambushed him on a street corner and attacked him, stealing his gun. He was given a sentence of two months and one day and had to pay a fine.

Many other Argentineans, Spaniards, and Italians fled Buenos Aires, and most of them ended up in Spain. No matter what his identity, Lucio Ruano must have followed much the same course as Julio Prina. According to the CNT's Jacinto Toryho, outstanding among the young anarchists arriving from Argentina in 1933 and promptly embarking upon risky hold-up activities were two brothers who— according to Paz—were the Ruanos.[4]

Lucio Ruano fit in quite quickly into the Catalan anarchists' Defense cadres and committees. These recently founded underground groups were very pro-active and highly mobile and went into action in the event of a general strike, uprising, or hardening of repression, when not engaged in intelligence-gathering. The CNT had lived most of its life underground, and, at given points in its history, it had to stand alone against horrific repression. "Defense groups" connected to it and specializing in the fight against the bosses' *pistoleros* [gunmen], had been up and running since the 1920s and, as we have seen (see endnote 36 above),[5]

3   Osvaldo Bayer, *The Anarchist Expropriators* (Oakland: AK Press/KSL, 2015), 120–22, 123, 127–29.

4   Paz, *Durruti en la revolución española*, 425.

5   In which we refer to the setting up of the Los Solidarios group in 1922, charged by the CNT with executing members of the upper echelons of the state. Disbanded following its initial operations, it was pretty much reactivated through the creation of another combat group, the Nosotros group, which replaced it in 1933. Made up essentially of the same men of action— Durruti, Ascaso, Jover, and many more besides—it also carried out hold-ups to finance the libertarian movement.

units made up of action men could strike when needed under the more or less disguised supervision of the Confederation. The defense cadres and committees acted as a liaison between the CNT and the FAI and shouldered the responsibility for offensive and defensive operations (uprisings, outrages, sabotage attacks, strike support, boycotts). According to César M. Lorenzo, they operated in utter secrecy, even with regard to official trade union bodies (be it the National Committee or regional committees) and were autonomous, which was not to the liking of everyone within the organization. In 1933, in the view of García Oliver, that great lover of "revolutionary gymnastics," nothing looked more important than bolstering these action groups, which had the capability of handling the inevitable showdown with the reaction.

In 1934, together with the Argentinean Tomé Martín or the Spaniards Martínez Ripoll and Justo Bueno, Ruano was a member of such action groups recruited from among the *militancia* [membership], while carrying on with *atracos* [hold-ups], individual expropriations, or armed robberies, in order to fund the organization. As it happened, in April and May that year, the mouthpiece of the Catalanist Acció Catalana organization, *La Publicitat*, carried two series of articles entitled *"Els gàngsters de Barcelona"* and *"L'organització de l'anarquisme a Catalunya i a Espanya."* The author, reporter Josep Maria Planes, had thrown down a gauntlet to the CNT. On an almost daily basis, readers learned that the gangsters had allegedly been bolstered considerably in Barcelona by the arrival of upward of three hundred Spanish anarchists, home from Argentina. Ruano was mentioned, with Pau Fabrès i Murlé, as having planted bombs and carried out sabotage attacks. In addition, Planes credited him with the executions of two police informers.

That all-out attack on the CNT was bound to have consequences. There actually were more and more armed robbers in Barcelona. And they weren't all of the same integrity as Durruti or his *compañeros*, and certain militants used the bulk of their swag for personal ends. This was so much the case that Ascaso once declared: "We must have done with armed robberies, or armed robberies will do for us!"

Thus, in May 1935, at an underground meeting in Barcelona, Durruti and Ascaso spelled out to the action men in attendance—including the Ruano brothers and many other young Argentineans—the need to cut out the expropriations and other individual acts of violence. Durruti spoke up to emphasize that the proliferating hold-ups

Luciano Ruano

were a menace to the organizational unity of the anarchist movement and, above all, that they could ruin the organization's standing in the eyes of the population. In the course of the discussion, Durruti found himself being chided by Ruano—a young anarchist subscribing to "weird *sociological* theories as regards 'expropriation'"[6]—for condemning activities of which he himself (Durruti) had previously been an exponent. Durruti blithely replied that times had changed and that hundreds of thousands of workers affiliated with the CNT looked forward to getting on with the "great collective expropriation" and that there was no place now for individual acts, which had become counterproductive and obsolete. Those eager to carry on with such practices needed to get out of the organization now. Ruano was described by Jose Mariño as being very attached to Durruti, and he ended up coming around to his point of view. Little by little the *atracos* [hold-ups] died out.[7]

6   Jacinto Toryho, *No eramos tan malos* (Madrid: G. del Toro, 1975), 70.
7   See Paz, *Durruti en la revolución española*, 425–26.

On the other hand, outrages were still on the agenda, notably in the context of the strategy put in place to counter the coup d'état that many could see coming. And there too the CNT sought to control the situation. At the time, relations between the Confederation and the Estat Català Catalanists were very strained: the latter's *escamots*, or support groups, had stepped in on several occasions to help break CNT strikes such as the 1933 transport strike.[8] Once the *escamots'* boss, Miguel Badía, returned from exile to join the Generalitat government, the CNT defense committees decided it was time for him to be killed. According to the evidence of José Mariño, Badía and his brother were executed on April 28, 1936, on the Calle Muntaner by Justo Bueno and Lucio Ruano. The other two people involved, meant to provide covering fire, were José Martínez Ripoll and José Pla, militants from the Metalworkers' Union.[9] The outrage rattled the Catalan capital[10]: the press (and above all Josep Maria Planes and

8   Discerning certain fascistic leanings in that organization, in 1934 the Nosotros group had made an unsuccessful attempt on the life of its leader, Josep Dencàs, who was none other than the Generalidad's Public Order counsellor, at whose instructions Badía operated as chief of police. (See Gallardo and Márquez, *Ortiz, general sin dios ni amo*, 78–80). Dencàs fled to Mussolini's Italy following the failure of the October 1934 uprising. Returning to Spain in February 1936, he left for Italy once again just before July. During the first few months of the revolution, Dencàs plotted against the established authorities in Catalonia (See García Oliver, *El eco de los pasos*, 159, 177, 254, 581).

9   Some years ago, the son of a certain Manolo, who was one of the CNT's action men back then, contacted us to pass on to us the testimony of his father, recorded in 1976. In it, he provides a detailed account of that execution, in which he says he was involved. He confirms that Bueno and Ruano were the killers of the Badía brothers but makes no mention of Tomé Martín or that Pla was part of the gang. He does, though, mention a certain Fernández from the Metalworkers' Union, who acted as driver; this might be Pla under an assumed name. He does confirm that there was another man there, armed with a machine pistol, to provide cover, though he doesn't give his name (this was probably Martínez Ripoll).

10 To this day many books and newspaper articles rehash this matter, and Catalanists continue to settle their scores with the anarchists. See Josep Maria Solé Sabaté and Joan Villarroya (eds.) *La guerra civil a Catalunya*, vol. 1 (Barcelona: Edicions 62, 2004); Jaume Ros i Serra, *Miquel Badia. Un defensor oblidat de Catalunya* (Barcelona: Mediterrània, 1996); and Benet, *Domènec Latorre, afusellat per catalanista*.

Avel·li Artís-Gener) pointed to Justo Bueno and other militants as
having been behind the attack. The latter were arrested, jailed, and
then released on June 25. And then, on July 18, the generals' pronunciamento arrived.

Phase Two: July 1936–November 1936

Intelligence gathering by the defense cadres[11] and the establishment
of an organization capable of taking on the military bore fruit in Barcelona on July 19, 1936.[12] Among the mob of militants who set out
to storm the Atarazanas barracks and crush the army revolt, García
Oliver, Ascaso, Durruti, Jover, Ortiz, Fernández, Sanz, Carreño,
Bueno, Ruano, and many others who paid the ultimate price took the
lead. These men were to pop up again in positions of responsibility
during the revolution, in the front lines or in the rear guard, on the
back of the prestige they earned. Some of the members of the Catalan defense cadres would join Escorza's Investigaciones teams, whereas
others would serve in the Control Patrols or on the various columns'
war committees.[13]

As we know, Lucio Ruano set off for the Aragon front with
Durruti and served on the War Committee of his column. He handled several offensives successfully, up until he took over from Buenaventura at the head of the column in mid-November 1936 when
Durruti moved to the Madrid front. In the minutes of the meeting of

11   The CNT's action men struck up close relations with conscripts, leading
      to the formation of defense cadres even within the barracks, and these had
      the sympathy of young officers who would help crush the rebellion in July
      1936.

12   At that point, no organization as effective was to be found in Seville, La
      Coruña, or Zaragoza.

13   In Madrid, the Defense Committees had also been kept going through the
      revolution. It was Eduardo Val who organized them on a district-by-district
      basis. This proved useful in October 1936 in the defense of the city and the
      prevention of a complete communist takeover of the city. The CNT's men
      of action would also play a preponderant role during the events of May 1937
      and afterward, since anarchists were again to become the State's bête noire.
      That June, the CNT ordered the dissolution of the Defense Committees,
      but certain militants would lead them again, though in a different format.
      See Godicheau, *La guerre d'Espagne. République et révolution en Cata-
      logne (1936–1939)*, 316.

the Committees on November 11, 1936, in Barcelona, the report writer noted, in essence, that those of the Durruti Column who were left in Aragon would be under the command of Ruano and Campón. Abad de Santillán, who had lived in Argentina for quite some time and bore a grudge against anarchist expropriators, suggested that Ruano be replaced by somebody else, because, he argued, he was temperamentally authoritarian and abrasive. Ricardo Sanz's name was put forward, even though it was known that he would not be as federalist in outlook as Durruti, who knew how to keep the column cohesive. In the end, a communiqué from the newspaper *El Frente* (no. 43, November 13, 1936) confirmed the formal appointment of Ruano, assisted by a War Committee made up of *compañeros* Campón, Bargalló, Cuba, Pablo [Vagliasindi], "Esplugas" [Espluga], and Busquets.

Phase Three: From the death of Durruti to Ruano's death

Let us begin with an extract from Joan Llarch's book, *The Death of Durruti*:

> Among the *responsables* who did not leave for Madrid along with Durruti in November 1936 were the two Ruano brothers […]. The Ruanos were two of those undesirable types who habitually crop up in every movement and organization, and who bring the circles in which they move into disrepute. The only law they recognized was expropriation for their own benefit, and they used the revolver to get their way every time. The Ruanos' father had protected Durruti from prosecution by the Argentinean courts during the latter's activities in Argentina, when, together with Francisco Ascaso and Gregorio Jover, he had carried out the robbery of the San Martin bank. Buenaventura Durruti was not a man to forget services rendered; […] The welcome he reserved for the Ruano brothers in Aragon, placing his full confidence in them, was due recompense for the help he had received from their father. He looked upon them both as particular friends, the equals of his inseparable *compañeros*: Antonio [José] Mira, Pedro Mora, Mariño, Liberto Ros, and others […]
>
> While Durruti was in Madrid, the two Ruanos, like so many others of the same breed, laid down their own laws and nobody dared challenge them on it. Durruti had taken his best men with

him and left behind in Aragon a contingent of decent miliciens peppered with questionable individuals [...].

The two [...] operated without either scruple or restraint.[14]

This picture bears out what we mentioned in endnotes 40 and 46 above: Ruano treated his militia members brutally and had two of them shot, eventually bringing a wave of resentment down on his own head. Many thought that it was only after Durruti's death that the Argentinean let loose his disposition to violence and bullying. According to José Mariño, Durruti never had a fighter from his column shot for retreating in the face of the enemy or for desertion, contrary to what certain slanderers would claim. There was no need, if one may say so, because he managed to sustain a high degree of cohesion among his miliciens and most of them had every confidence in him. Ruano, on the other hand, was not in control of the situation and lacked stature. He never managed to fill Durruti's shoes.

In this instance, we should add, it cannot be ruled out that the executions blamed on Durruti should have been chalked up to Ruano. Moreover, on a date unknown to us, and again according to Mariño, he had shot a young militiaman who had left the front without permission to seek out his family. The Libertarian Youth swore to avenge him, but Ruano was not afraid of them and just laughed at their threat: "Let them come! The moment they see me they'll take to their heels like rabbits!"

It should be pointed out that Ruano was not on his own; there were several members of the defense cadres operating in the Durruti Column's theater of operations—Justo Bueno, for one. Both his accomplices are described as tall, well-built men, highly effective militarily, and their practice of cutting corners inspired tremendous fear.

To complete the picture, let us remember that Ruano lined his pockets at the front, and he couldn't have been the only one.[15] This

14   Llarch, *La muerte de Durruti*, 34–35. Regrettably, Llarch cites none of his sources; we have no idea from where he gleaned his information about the Ruanos's father.

15   We might add that he also had Jaime Boguña, the one-time delegate from the Statistics Section—or, to put it another way, the column's bookkeeper—shot for having siphoned the pay of several miliciens. The official execution announcement, dated December 8, 1936, and endorsed by the War Committee, closed with these words: "Nevertheless we affirm our uncompromising stance vis à vis those who abuse the trust we place in them and try to

was done at the expense of arrested and executed "fascists," as well as of the villagers. The scale of the phenomenon is something we cannot gauge, any more than the proportion of veteran militants who indulged in it. The issue is whether or not such individualistic behavior, riding roughshod over anarchist morality, should be linked with Durruti's death and the obvious setback to the revolutionary process.[16]

Be that as it may, Ruano left the front, most likely in late January 1937, following some sort of a trial involving him being held in Sariñena on January 26, at which it was determined that he return to the villagers everything that he had stolen from them. His presence and activity in Barcelona during the incidents in May suggest that there was still a place for him within the movement and that he was still serving on the defense committees.[17] Now it looks as if he carried on mounting lucrative ventures in concert with other former armed robbers, revolving around the Durruti Column garage, which had been commandeered by the Metalworkers' Union. As we explained in the biographical note on Justo Bueno, that machine workshop was used as a warehouse for assets requisitioned by the little gang[18] and was the scene of the murder of the French aviator Jean-Marie Moreau, for which Bueno and Ruano were reputedly responsible.

line their pockets at the expense of their compañeros." (IISH, CNT, 94E.) Ruano had some nerve.

16 See García Oliver's view regarding "the role of the conscious revolutionary, capable of reacting against the breakdown of restraints," who comes to the fore in a revolutionary process (*À contretemps*, no. 17, 24).

17 Severino Campos's article in *Le Combat syndicaliste* of December 23, 1976, harks back to the May 1937 events: "[On the afternoon of May 5,] Julián Merino [...] called a big meeting [...]; Aurelio Fernández was there, with the Ruano brothers in tow. [...] The predominant option was 'mount an all-out attack, no matter what it brings.' The decision was made to form two commissions, one that would operate in the city center and the other on the Paralelo, near the Plaça de Espanya. It was not easy for the commission chosen to get to the Paralelo to get through the door of the Casa CNT-FAI [the PSUC across the street had its machine guns trained on them]. [...] Given this situation, the older Ruano asked us if we wanted to get out of there quickly; when we replied in the affirmative, he requested some hand bombs and, with masterful aplomb (which he deployed also against the libertarians on the front lines), he opened up a path for us with those bombs and delivered the commission to its destination."

18 Essentially, the CNT had intended these to be used for arms purchases.

Let us leave it to Josep Benet to recount how events panned out, again on the basis of the same court file:

> One day, though, Bueno discovered that the Ruano brothers [...] were getting ready to flee the country by yacht, together with their respective mistresses, and meant to take with them the swag that they had accumulated, leaving him behind. Treacherously, Bueno invited each of the Ruano brothers, separately, at different times and together with their lovers, to drop by the garage to see him. With the connivance of his pal Martínez Ripoll, he then murdered all four of them.[19]

In an October 1942 letter to the judge, Bueno offered his own version of the whole affair: miliciens had long been coming to the garage with the idea of silencing Ruano. On one such visit, they learned that the brothers were due to drop by the garage an hour later. Realizing what was bound to happen, Bueno made himself scarce, doing nothing to warn the Argentinean. The following day, he found out that these miliciens had killed the Ruano brothers as well as their partners.[20] He further stipulated that Ruano had amassed a pretty penny for his own personal benefit and that he was intending to escape with it, after buying a boat. His younger brother was supposed to have applied to the Argentinean embassy for a passport to this end.[21]

That said, Bueno, in his deposition to Quintela in July 1941, offered a different version: the brothers "were already in the process of packing their suitcases to join the 'yacht' in which they had prepared a hiding place for the treasure, when the deponent [Bueno] and his pals at the garage found out everything and agreed to kill the two brothers. [...] The deponent stayed outside and the others positioned themselves inside [the garage], weapons at the ready; Rodolfo was the first to show up with his partner [...]. Since Julio, the erstwhile column commander and actual perpetrator of the thievery, turned up three minutes later, with his partner in tow as well," all four of them were killed and their bodies buried on site.[22]

19   Benet, *Domènec Latorre, afusellat per catalanista*, 378.
20   Lucio had seduced the wife of column commander Cristóbal Aldabaldetrecu, and the latter was, for that reason, also looking for him to settle scores.
21   *Sumarísimo*, Justo Bueno.
22   Ibid.

Let us close with one further piece of the puzzle, supplied by José Mariño, who knew Ruano and Bueno well. From the latter, he received information that we now summarize, insofar as we have been able to piece it together:

Ruano was planning to leave for the Far East with ten other militants belonging to the Foodstuffs Union and Metalworkers' Union, among them José Pla. Ruano informed Bueno—who would also be taking the trip—of his plans; once the boat had set sail, he intended to kill the ten others and scoop up their money and make off with Pla's woman, whom he fancied but who had refused him. At most, Bueno is supposed to have agreed as far as the Foodstuffs workers were concerned, as he regarded them as small-time thugs, but murdering a well-known militant like Pla, for whom he had great respect, wasn't happening.[23] Despite his friendship with Ruano, he went and disclosed the whole affair to the intended victims. At a meeting in July 1937, they all decided to have done with Ruano as well as his brother, who followed him around everywhere like his shadow. By the same token, it was agreed also that their partners would be eliminated, in that there was the threat of denunciation or revenge by them. Bueno then cooked up a scheme to get the Ruanos to the "Durruti" garage before backing out of the operation, not wanting to play any direct part in the hit on his friend. On July 15, it was four Metalwork Union militants who executed the four victims.[24] The elimination of the Ruanos had not been determined in secret by militants acting independently, or by Escorza, but it had the acquiescence of the CNT—at regional committee level at any rate (as in fact the words uttered at the Regional Committee meeting on January 27, 1937, suggested).

23   It was from José Mariño that we learned that José Pla had featured prominently in the elimination of the Ruano brothers and the execution of the Badía brothers; and, by the way, we should point out that Bueno was very careful never to disclose Pla's name in any of his statements.

24   Let us add the following information: according to the deposition made by Luis Latorre, Bueno's co-accused, on July 10, 1941, there were more than four executioners; "the deponent saw the perpetrators of the crime leave and among them recalls Liberto Ros Garro, José Mariño Carballada, a certain Gómez who was president of the Metalworkers' Union, known by the nickname 'Gómez the Terrible,' Rafael Sellés, Vicente Ferrer Cruzado, José Martínez Ripoll, and José Parés, and those are all he can remember." (*Sumarísimo*, Justo Bueno.)

The very next day, Bueno, Martínez Ripoll, and Latorre left Spain. Of course, there are still a few pieces of the puzzle missing before we can conclude finally. In any event, Ruano had become an irritant to everyone and had probably over-stepped the mark, even in the eyes of his own friends. We should therefore add, now that we can reveal that the "Militiaman X," who we cited in previous editions of this book, was the late José Mariño Carballada and that the latter was best placed to authenticate this last version of the murders of the Ruano brothers and their partners....

Having said that, a letter from Antonio Ortiz to Antonio Téllez on February 26, 1980, cast a rather different light, revealing that Ruano had not lost all of his friends:

And sotto voce, the rumor spread ... that Escorza had had Ruano, Pili [Ruano's partner], Ruano's brother, and a young girl who was with him, killed[25]... and the executioner was none other than Justo Bueno, with others. The murder had taken place in the 26th Division's garage (in Barcelona) where Justo Bueno had invited all four to discuss and thrash out some agreement to smooth over their differences, which had arisen following the death of the French airman and a number of batches of gold and gems that had not been declared. This was not the first instance of an execution by the gang around Escorza with the acquiescence of Marianet and Federica.

In spite of everything, Ruano had worked his way into the good books of some *compañeros*, with whom he had done things and who were outraged by the manner in which the murder, not

25 A hint that Escorza was responsible for the elimination of the Ruanos has been provided by Nuri Escorza, his daughter, who passed on some papers to Adolf Bertrán, the producer of the "Sentits" program on Radio Catalunya, as part of a special broadcast devoted to Manuel Escorza del Val and those close to him, on May 10, 2012. Those papers bear witness that Liberato Minué, Escorza's brother-in-law, a refugee in Belgium at the time, secured five visas for Chile in the names of Manuel Escorza, his wife Aurora Balaschs, his own [Minué's] wife, Manuel's sister Dolores Escorza, and probably Dionisio Eroles. The phony identity used by Minué was none other than that of one Rodolfo Enrique Prina, a Cuban national! Eroles having been unable or unwilling to join them, the four of them sailed for Chile on board the *Copiapó* on June 5, 1939.

just of the men, but also of the women, had been carried out. One of them, Alfonso,[26] spelled out to me the sinister modus operandi of Escorza and his gang, and raised the possibility of doing them all in. I did not dismiss the idea … better still, I told Alfonso that they could always number me among their friends if they were to bump off these irksome animals … Alfonso, or one of the others, had a word with another *compañero* about this plan, and the latter, scandalized, condemned the idea, pointing out that, if carried out, it would result in great upheaval as far as the organization was concerned … and things were left like that. […]

That was why Justo Bueno disappeared from Barcelona. A *compañero* from the Woodworkers' [Union], a good friend of mine, then reported to me that Justo Bueno had taken off for France after a big fallout with Escorza and certain of his acolytes, in the course of which guns had been drawn.[27]

It is hard therefore to reach a conclusion about this character, but our thinking is that he should not be looked upon as a mere criminal, the way Agustín Guillamón depicts him,[28] but rather as a hero, as a revolutionary who got caught up in the mafia-like atmosphere that came flooding back, especially after May 1937, with the reconstruction of the state and the relentlessly counterrevolutionary approach espoused by the CNT.

26   One Alfonso Martínez Blanco turned up in another letter, dated April 5, 1980, from Ortiz to Téllez: "I had a pistol left over from the collection at the archbishop's […] and Alfonso Martínez Blanco and Ruano were the ones who had presented it to me. This would have been sometime around July 21, [1936]." In another letter, dated February 26, he had already mentioned this matter: "On July 19, Ruano and some others—Argentineans—were alongside the Nosotros group in the shooting and—along with Durruti—he was one of the ones who seized the archbishop's treasure, before handing it over to the Generalidad."

27   IISH, Téllez Archive, 425.

28   Guillamón, *La Guerra del pan*, 28, 46, 400.

CARLO SCOLARI

Carlo Scolari was born in Val Marchirolo (Varese) on October 8, 1898, the product of the union of Luigi Scolari and Maria Colombo.

He spent his first fifteen years in Val Marchirolo before setting off with his father to work in the building trade in Zurich.

In 1914 they were repatriated, and Carlo did his military service with the Artillery. He enlisted but never took part in any of the fighting, because of a deformed left hand.

He was demobilized in 1919 and returned to his trade as a bricklayer.

In 1926, after a few seasonal sojourns in France, he settled there, in the Pyrenees. Then, in 1930, after some time spent in Algiers, he moved to Toulon and remained there until the spring of 1936. Scolari had been surveilled by the Italian police since 1933, when the consulate in Toulon had cited him as "one of unruliest and most active subversives" in the city. At the time, he was regarded as an anarchist. At that point his parents returned to Italy, and he moved to La Seyne-sur-Mer.[1] It was there that he became acquainted with a certain Balard, who he claimed, under questioning in December 1941, was a Spaniard, with the first name Michele (most likely an Italianized version of Miguel: notably, other documents show this Balard as being French). Together they set off for Spain on August 28, 1936. The moment he arrived in Barcelona, he and Balard were taken under the wing of the Durruti Column and dispatched to Pina. According to what he told police in December 1941, he fought for only three months, then moved back to Barcelona to work in a food distribution cooperative and later as a carpenter's helper in the docks. There are grounds for suspecting that he lied to the police, as there are two reports mentioning that he passed

---

[1] A group of Italian anarchists was very active back then in the Var department: they included Giuseppe Casabona, Gaetano Berti, Romualdo del Papa (see http://militants-anarchistes.info/spip.php?article1173), and Mario Bellini (the "Mario" to whom Antoine refers?). Most of these set off for Spain in the summer of 1936 and went on to serve in the Durruti Column: *La Vanguardia* (July 29, 1936) hailed the arrival in Barcelona of eleven Italian anarchists from Toulon.

through Toulon in late 1936 or early 1937 and again in December 1938, having come seeking treatment for his wounds. Besides, thanks to Robert Léger's testimony in 1984, we know that for several weeks he served with the (anarchist-controlled) Investigations agency monitoring the frontier in Portbou. In the 1980s, Leger still had very warm memories of Scolari, "an Italian who was working in Turin," and of his friend, whose name he had forgotten. They were "good guys, terrific, idealists."[2]

An article in *Le Libertaire* of July 15, 1937, signed by Ridel and Carpentier, paid tribute to "trois miliciens" who they had known well in the Durruti Column's International Group: Alexandre Staradolz, Carlo Tornari, and Manuel Aracil. Alexandre and Manuel had died in action in Perdiguera (see endnote no. 32 above). It is almost certain that the sole survivor of the three, "Tornari," was in fact Scolari. According to Carpentier's account as collected by Phil Casoar, Scolari and Balard had, along with Ridel, Berthomieu, and Carpentier, become the mainstays of the International Group up until the end of October 1936. Scolari and Balard left the column in December 1936 over militarization, and moved to Barcelona, where Carpentier would join them. In July 1937, Scolari was still fighting in Spain, hence the change of name:

> Among the Italian anarchists, there are many categories: Carlo embodied the sort of anarchist that should be pointed out to anarchism's enemies so as to demolish their prejudices. […] In Toulon, where had been working for a long time, the communist workers used to say that if all anarchists [had] been like him, no one [would have] dared proclaim himself their adversary. Tornari had a sense of social fairness that would countenance no trespass, and an unfair distribution of food would leave him glum the whole livelong day. And with it there was an unshakable determination to win. During street fighting in a town on the outskirts of Huesca, good old Carlo spent an hour taking aim at a fascist soldier whose head appeared at a window from time to time. […] The shot was fired […] the soldier gave a grunt and slumped, struck right in the forehead. […] Pulled back into the rear, he carried on his work as a militant on the CNT's defense committees in Barcelona. The May events found him lying in wait on the barricades. The counterrevolution tore

2 Léger, *Entretiens avec Phil Casoar.*

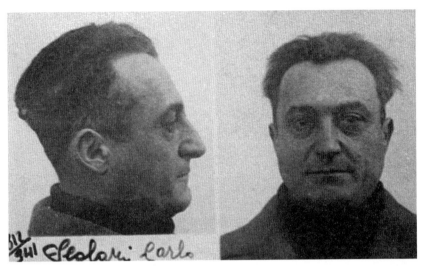

Carlo Scolari

the heart out of him, but, being ready for battle and determined to fight, he was up for any attempt to correct the course. Men might turn traitor and experiments might fail, but Carlo remains and shall remain faithful to his conception of the new Society.

In March 1940, and again in October the same year, he was reported by the consulate in Toulon as being an inmate in the Sainte-Catherine fort "in company with other subversives." Under questioning, Scolari omitted any mention of this, and claimed to have moved away to Bordeaux where he was supposedly working from July 1939 to September 1941, at which time he applied to the local consulate for repatriation. On November 23, 1941, he arrived in Bardonnecchia, where he was arrested and questioned. On December 29, he was sentenced to five years' banishment to Ventotene. It is noteworthy that during the questioning he gave the names of three of his countrymen who had fought alongside him, but it should also be noted that the first of these, Mario Castellani, was probably using an assumed name, in that he could not be identified by the police (he was probably the Mario mentioned in the manuscript), and that the second, Raineri, was probably Pietro Ranieri, who had perished in Farlete on October 4, 1936, and the third, Lorenzo Giua, had by then died in action, as Scolari must have known, since Gimenez himself mentions the fact.

For further details, see ACS-CPC, envelope 131947.

PIETRO PAOLO VAGLIASINDI, WHO APPEARS IN ANTOINE GIMENEZ'S MEMOIRS AS *PABLO*

According to the records of the political police in Rome, Pietro Vagli-asindi was born in Bergamo on September 21, 1889, the son of Casi-miro Vagliasindi and Marina Battisti. His father was the general of an army division.

Here is a glimpse of the political and military career of this curious individual, as reconstructed from reports of Mussolini's political police,[1] and papers impounded by the Spanish anarchists in 1936.[2]

Pietro Vagliasindi became an officer during his military service in 1911, then took part in the World War. He followed D'Annunzio in the Fiume incident and became a renowned aviator.[3] Then he moved to Milan, settling into bourgeois life. Being on very good terms with the royal family and the fascist hierarchy, he had direct dealings with Mussolini. But it appears that he took issue with the 1924 murder of the lawyer Matteotti, the general secretary of the PSI [Italian Socialist Party]. As a result he was forced to leave Italy and set off for East Africa as a pioneer.

After various interventions in western Arabia, Vagliasindi carried out intelligence work in France from 1924 onward, mingling with dissident fascist circles. He was also a habitué of the casinos and gambling dens. In 1925 he was spotted in Monte Carlo and then in Paris, where, through the good offices of police inspector Sabbatini and Italy's ambassador, Baron Romano Avezzana, he was entrusted with a political assignment: sounding out the intentions of the dissident Carlo

---

1   See ACS-CPC, PP B 5281, which contains two fat files, No 86811. These bear the stamp "Antifascist" and appear to have been opened in 1927. The last report about him dates from August 28, 1943. Before and during the Spanish civil war, Vagliasindi would be regularly approached by the Italian secret services.

2   See IISH, FAI, package 44 B9, microfilm no. 91.

3   Fiume is the old name for Rijeka: now in Croatia, this port was claimed by Italy and by Yugoslavia after the First World War. It was occupied in 1919 by troops raised by D'Annunzio and, although made a free city under the 1922 Treaty of Rapallo, it reverted to Italy in 1924.

Bazzi. It would appear that Vagliasindi had his reservations in accepting this assignment.

In fact, since 1925 he had become Mussolini's personal enemy. In the very same year that Vagliasindi was promoted to lieutenant-colonel in the army, a disciplinary inquiry was mounted against him, which infuriated him. So, from 1927 onward, he began to shut himself off from fascist circles, notably in Brussels, where he moved in order to link up with the Italian consul, Giuriati, who supported him.

Meanwhile, Vagliasindi had been expelled from France on February 10, 1927, for military espionage. The French press reported the matter, stressing that the status of this Italian serviceman was ambiguous. They stipulated that in the Garibaldian circles in which he hung out, he was considered an antifascist but that he had received money from the Italian Embassy in Paris for very specific services rendered.

Back in Italy, his circumstances continued to worsen. On July 28, 1928, a warrant was issued for Vagliasindi's arrest, and his file was stamped "subversive." The colonel was eventually demoted to infantryman in 1929 on the grounds of "indiscipline." In the end he was forced to leave Italy because of his "clashes of opinion with Mussolini," and he fled to Belgium. The entirely personal nature of the clash between Vagliasindi and the fascist government was plainly laid out in his will, dated July 30, 1928:

> In the event of my death, the blame lies wholly and solely with Benito Mussolini, given that I have no personal enemy other than him and that he is the only person with a substantial interest and reasons for wanting to see me done in.

In December 1929 and January 1930, Vagliasindi had plans to launch a huge press campaign targeting Mussolini. But he restricted himself to having a series of articles (drafted by the dissident fascist Carlo Bazzi) published in the Brussels daily *Le Soir*, for the dual purpose of hitting out at the leaders of the antifascist emigrés and taking his revenge on Mussolini.

In 1931, France agreed to play host to him again; two or three times a week he would travel to Argenteuil to test a flying boat with his aviator friends. It seems that he wanted to sponsor the setting up of an association of Italian antifascist aviators prepared to take action. Various Italian police documents dating from 1933 report on Vagliasindi's activities in Nice, Monte Carlo, and so on. He was now regarded as an antifascist. In one report, it was noted that he had gone to Spain "for reasons unknown."

In April 1933, the ex-colonel was a lodger in a Barcelona boarding house. Leading what was by then a "retired and mysterious" existence, he wore war medals on his lapel. He tried to ingratiate himself with the crew of the Italian-owned Genoa-Barcelona airline by showing an interest in the features of its aircraft.

In 1934, Vagliasindi was living with a Belgian countess in a villa in Sitges in Catalonia. He had a comfortable existence, owning a stamp collection that he would sell off to philatelists. On August 21, 1934, he wrote to someone named Faldella—the Italian vice-consul in Barcelona, one of the bosses of the OVRA (the fascists' secret police)—a mysterious letter regarding negotiations as to how he might be of service to his country, a "matter of the utmost importance, that he must handle with great skill." On August 22, Faldella answered him in equally sibylline language.

During 1935, the Italian-Abyssinian war gave him an opportunity to apply for readmission into the army. From Spain Vagliasindi then took a number of steps to place himself "under the orders of king and country." But at the same time, he regarded the war in East Africa as "silly and ruinous," and in his correspondence he carried on labeling Mussolini a murderer and thief. On April 28, 1936, the Italian consul-general in Barcelona notified Vagliasindi that the Ministry of War had rejected his request to serve in East Africa.

A report, dated September 1935, points out that, while in Spain, Vagliasindi had had certain dealings with one Antonio Carniato, a republican. Another report, dated June 1, 1936, mentioned that Bruno Castaldi, an opponent of the regime, was among his associates.

It seems obvious that, throughout these years, Vagliasindi was hedging his bets. There is no question that he was working for the Italian services and feeding them military and political intelligence. He made overtures to antifascist and dissident fascist circles. It might be thought from his contacts with the latter that he had become a fascist dissident himself and that for a time he was playing a double game vis-à-vis the Italian state. In view of his enduring political and military disgrace, his moving to Spain in 1933 seems to have been his own idea; but Spain also happened to be the place where many Italian antifascists were, and he plainly sought out their company. Was he still working on behalf of the fascist intelligence agency, still playing a double game, or had he some scheme of his own in mind? It seems astonishing that a military man like him didn't throw in his lot with the Francoists before July 18, 1936.

With the outbreak of the Spanish revolution—so the reports from Mussolini's police recount—he refused to take part in the unrest by the "Reds," but he then joined the Catalan antifascist militias in which he distinguished himself as a ranking officer in combat. Camillo Berneri had Vagliasindi pegged as a spy, but an investigation by the anarchists turned up nothing.

According to a document dated October 9, 1936, and emanating from the Italian consulate-general in Barcelona (which had withdrawn to Saint-Jean-de-Luz), the anarchists had forced Vagliasindi to work for them, but he had then been overcome by an enthusiasm for that war. Approached by someone trusted by the consulate, he had expressed his resentment toward his homeland, which had washed its hands of him. He reckoned that he'd stumbled upon a fresh opportunity to pursue his military career. A police report of October 24 spoke of Vagliasindi's frame of mind as he mingled with the "Reds": on September 27, he had traveled out to the Caspe front with Bruno Castaldi "in charge of the stopover where the Italian columns and the Durruti Column were fed."[4]

A few months later, his file had been reclassified under "Frontier, search and arrest"; by then, the services regarded the ex-colonel as "a dangerous antifascist," and they forwarded his file to the Italian

---

4   ACS-CPC, No 26453. We might also mention these details: "Bruno Castaldi, aged around forty, was an officer in a battalion in charge of revictualling in Letux. He stayed in a house on the square [in Letux], near the blacksmith's, beside the hostel. [...] Castaldi had signed on with the Ortiz Column at the end of July 1936. He went on to become political delegate for the "Luz y Vida" centuria. Wounded on the Aragon front, he then looked after food supplies of the columns and especially of the Durruti Column. On November 10, 1936, the Letux Antifascist Militia Oversight Committee announced in a statement carried in *Solidaridad Obrera* in Barcelona that it had, "thanks to compañero Bruno Castaldi," taken delivery of produce offered to the militias by the residents of Sitges. Castaldi was still present in Letux that December, when he enjoyed a measure of prestige in the eyes of the antifascist volunteers. He "handled the command of three companies nominated for fortification work and belonged to the 2nd [*sic*] 'Jubert Hijar' [*sic*] Division, with the rank of captain.'" In Giménologues *¡À Zaragoza o al charco!* For a fuller profile, see http://gimenologues.org/spip.php?article358.

Military Investigation Service [SIM]. In June 1937, his entire file was forwarded to the Ministry of War.

Thanks to Gimenez, we know something of Pablo's military activities with the Durruti Column on the Zaragoza front. According to Antoine, the Italian fascists had apparently arrested Pablo during a battle on the Aragon front late in 1938.

There is a reference to Paolo Vagliasindi in a document drawn from the Comintern archives; written in German, there is a chapter relating to tracking down Abwehr spies: "Paolo Vagliasindi. Handled personally by Gen. Fedeli, forwarded to Albacete." The Italian Interior Ministry eventually discovered that "Vagliasindi was arrested by the Red SIM during the summer of 1937 for political reasons": he was placed in Montjuich and then in prison in Segorbe. Actually, Vagliasindi was arrested before then: in a list of republican prisoners drawn up by François Godicheau, we find that on May 20, 1937, he was jailed in Segorbe, near Valencia. The same source reports that his "acolyte," Castaldi, was on record as an inmate in the Modelo prison in Barcelona on November 10, 1937. Charged with working for the fascists, Castaldi had been placed under arrest on the orders of the Negrín government in August 1937.

On March 24, 1938, following Franco's overrunning of Aragon, Vagliasindi was supposedly detained near Gerona. Shortly before Gerona was occupied by Nationalist troops in January 1939, he crossed into France with other political prisoners.

Oddly enough, Vagliasindi then decided to go back to Spain, confident that he would have no problems. He crossed over the border at Le Perthus but was recognized during a stopover in Gerona in February or April 1939 and then thrown in prison. "He had been condemned to death by the Reds for having bluntly refused to lead units against the Italian legionaries. Now he stands accused of having fought against the Nationalists," the writers of the Italian reports noted.

On October 25, 1939, Vagliasindi was made available to the Supreme Headquarters of the Servicio Nacional de Seguridad y Orden Público [National Security and Public Order Agency] in Madrid. On March 29, 1940, he was sentenced to life imprisonment by a council of war in Barcelona, for "having technically aided and advised the Durruti Column and taken part in activities on the Aragon front from August 1936 until February 1937. For two months he worked in the manufacture of hand bombs with the Pole Vladimir Zaglowa, on behalf of the Red Army."

Pietro Vagliasindi

In July 1940, his sentence was commuted to a twenty-year jail term, and he remained in the Modelo prison, Barcelona, for political reasons.

On December 8, 1940, a *Pro memoria* was presented to the Duce reviewing the adventures of the former(?) fascist, and, for his own part, Vagliasindi sent letters to his remaining friends in Italy: he seemed to hold out hopes for his rehabilitation.

An Italian army major, Ottavio Zoppi made overtures to secure his release, but, according to a document dated January 25, 1942, withdrawal of Vagliasindi's Italian nationality would have come into it. There is every reason to think that the Duce left him to rot.

In police headquarters in Bergamo, Gianpiero Bottinelli discovered a wanted notice for one Pietro Vagliasindi; dated November 27, 1946, it shows that inquiries were at a standstill due to the reorganization of the political police's files.[5]

To date, we have not come up with Pietro Vagliasindi's file in the Modelo archives in Barcelona or those of the Barcelona court-martial. His file (and he himself?) must have been switched to some other prison: Salamanca, Guadalajara, Alcalá de Henares. So we do not know what became of Pablo.

As for Bruno Castaldi, after rotting in prison until January 1939, he was to be released from Montjuich just ahead of the fall of Barcelona and was able to cross into France.[6]

---

5   Antoine Gimenez, *Amori e rivoluzione. Ricordi di un miliziano in Spagna (1936–1939)* (Lugano: La Baronata, 2007), 239.

6   Antonioli, Berti, Fedele, and Iuso, *Dizionario biografico degli anarchici italiani*, 341.

THE VALERO LABARTA FAMILY OF PINA DE EBRO

"From that day on, I knew that I had found myself a family."

The real name of La Madre, also known as Tía Pascuala, was Pascuala Labarta Uson. We have two snapshots of her, passed on by her granddaughter Concha Valero. Everyone is agreed that she was a forceful personality. La Madre died in Pina on June 11, 1961, at the age of seventy.[1]

Her husband was Vicente Valero Labarta, and he doesn't appear in Gimenez's narrative, even though his children remember the pair of them often chatting the evenings away, once Vicente came home from the fields. His family describe him as a very kindly man. We have two photographs of him, thanks to his granddaughter, María Jesús. He passed away in Pina ten years after his wife, on May 9, 1971, at the age of eighty-nine.

Pascuala and Vicente had four children, the oldest being María Valero Labarta, born on April 9, 1913. Before the war, she married Manuel (whom Antoine took to be one of Pascuala's sons) who died young of throat cancer, at some date we do not know. In 1937, they had a son, given the name Jacinto. After the war, María lived in Barcelona; she had a daughter from a second marriage (we have a snapshot of her as a young communicant, with her grandfather.) She died in Barcelona on May 2, 1964. Her niece, María Jesús, remembers that she used to tell lots of stories about the war. María had moved around quite a lot, working in a number of locations (Barcelona, Palma de Mallorca, etc.).

The second born was Félix (Antoine calls him "Paco"). He stayed in Pina through the first three months of war, then was mobilized on the front between Teruel and Belchite, whereas Antoine and his unit were operating in the Sierra de Alcubierre. After the war, Félix was arrested, then detained in a slave labor camp in the Teruel sector for twenty months. He is loath to speak of these matters in a family setting, but, when asked if he remembers Antoine, he talks about him as if it were yesterday. He retains warm feelings for him as a great friend,

---

[1]   This profile is based on conversations and mail exchanged with several members of the Valero family in 2003 and 2005.

always up for a laugh. According to Félix, Antoine was one of a band of irregulars who ventured beyond the enemy lines to gather intelligence. They were known as the Banda Negra, on account of their operations being at night. He was over ninety years old when he died in Pina on January 14, 2008. He was very well thought of in the village.

Of the third-born, Vicente, we know, thanks to his grandson Ivan Ballabriga Valero that he,

> was the most "revolutionary" of the siblings; thus he signed on as a volunteer with the Durruti Column at the age of seventeen and set off immediately for the Alcubierre front where he took part in the earliest skirmishes with the Falangists and fascist troops, as well as in the early offensives against Huesca with the regiment that the Durruti Column dispatched into the "Carrrascal" area, where he was miraculously spared, having come face to face with "Moors," rather than the raw replacement soldiers of earlier engagements. […]
>
> Well into the war, and because of the "May events," the Durruti Column was militarized that same month and, along with the first Durruti regiment (all volunteers from the very early days), which was part of the division of that name set up in April 1937, the 119th Mixed Brigade (the one Vicente was attached to) was formed, making up, together with the 121st and 120th Mixed Brigades, the brand new 26th Division, which the communists, who were eager to erase the slightest trace of anarchism from the brand-new sovietized People's Army, stripped of the label "Durruti." My grandfather's adventures continued between one trench and the next, from Huesca to Alcubierre and Monte Oscuro, until, fed up and disappointed with life in the front lines, he tried to find himself somewhere safer, signing up for an Assault Guard course onto which he was accepted (he could read and was very tall at the time); he was sent to the academy in Benicassim, and came out a Guard three months later. He was posted to Caspe where he was caught up in the March 1938 retreat, withdrawing little by little as far as the coast, finally settling in the Valencia area, though not before he had been wounded in an air raid in Maella. Vicente finished his war back in the front lines again, since the Assault Guards were regarded as fine shock troops and very loyal to the Republic. On April 1, 1939, he surrendered himself in

La Madre standing at her front door, with one of her grandsons

Valencia and was sent to Pina where, on arrival, he was denounced and jailed in the "Torrero" prison, notoriously one of the harshest back then. After spending some time there, he was transferred to the convict camp in Belchite and later to a labor battalion in Africa, from where he returned to Pina at last in 1945, after six years inside.

My grandfather never spoke to me about Antoine Gimenez, maybe because he would not have been in his mother's house at the same times as him, given the tough and lengthy conditions he experience during the war and which I have already mentioned. Maybe it also had something to do with the fact that he was very reserved and didn't like talking about those times.[2]

Vicente then lived in Pina until he died on May 16, 1998, at the age of seventy-nine.

The fourth-born and youngest child answers to the name Vicenta. She was born on January 20, 1924, so she was somewhere between twelve and fourteen when Antoine was commuting between the front and Pina (August 1936–March 1938). He was very affectionate with her and very familiar, and they used to play together. She tends to say that

---

2   Letter to the authors in the summer of 2009.

she was only young at the time, and in those days fun was in the forefront of her mind, but she remembers a lot. Her husband died a few years back, and she has recently been staying with her children, turn and turn about; she had two sons living in Pina and a daughter in Zaragoza.

Here are a few glimpses of our interview with her and her daughter María Jesús Alfonso Calvo in May 2005 in Zaragoza. Vicenta was then reading the Spanish-language version of Antoine's *Memories*. "No mean feat," her daughter commented, "for she was never a reader."

By contrast, her daughter María Jesús is an avid reader and has long had an interest in histories of the war and her village. From quite an early age, she would bombard her father or her paternal uncle with questions about the war, the CNT, and so on, and invariably the answer would be: "That's none of your affair, political matters like those; that's men's business!"

Her uncle, exiled in France, fought in the French army and was taken prisoner. It appears that he was then deported to a German concentration camp (Mauthausen or Dachau). Luckily, he made it back and married in France. He made his first visit back to Pina thirty years after the war. He chatted a lot with the old folks, but she was not allowed to eavesdrop or remain in the company when they got together. "They carried their tales of the war with them, inside," says María Jesús. All in all, country folk are not much given to talking. Some people dropped by the village to collect their testimony but with no great success. "We need to talk about the whole thing now," she adds.

Vicenta told us about her impressions of the time the anarchists showed up in Pina back in August 1936 and of what followed. She gladly recounts how things were at home with Antoine, how he became "one more son" (see endnotes 3, 4, 6, and 27 above). She has an outstanding recollection of the war, as Pina was right on the front line on the Ebro and came under repeated shelling. Besides, the main church was largely destroyed that way; only the spire survives. Sometimes there were endless air raids, or they were pounded by artillery ensconced on the far side of the river. It was dangerous to venture along the river; so the inhabitants used well water for everything. During alerts, the family would scurry off to the shelter of a foxhole dug in the garden. They lined it with straw and, together with the neighbors, old and young, would while away their time there. Vicenta says that they survived because not a single shell ever fell on them, for their "shelter" would not have withstood the test.

Vicente Valero Labarta. Photo taken in Valencia in 1938 or 1939

In March 1938, the family left Pina, bound for France: Vicenta and her father took one route by horse-drawn cart, and they lost contact with the remainder of the family; La Madre, María, and her little one took a different route. She didn't see Gimenez and the other refugees on Catalan soil at that time. Once in France, they were held in the Argelès camp, where her father would languish for some time thereafter, whereas she made her way back to Pina with another family after a month. She was scared, as the talk was that the Falangists were mistreating the wives of republicans and shaving their heads. But it all went well, though they went hungry.

Tía Pascuala also returned to Pina, but she wasn't able to go to her own home, as she had to provide proof that the house was hers;

Vicenta Valero Labarta, at age twenty

according to her granddaughter Concha, she had kept the deeds to the house with her all the same. The red tape took quite a while to get through, but she was able to return to her home along with Vicenta and María. The whole place had been cleared out and ransacked; even the shutters had been removed. Her husband also came back from France, but he was reported by persons unknown and jailed for five months. "I was just happy they didn't kill him!" It has to be said that the house was known as the *"la casa del maquis"* [maquis house]. He was released from prison in December 1939. María Jesús tells us that Auntie María told her: "Pascuala Labarta traveled up to Zaragoza to ask an officer that the death sentence hanging over her husband be commuted."

She remembers how her grandmother was an intrepid sort, afraid of no one and well able to stand up to the priest, the mayor, or the Civil Guard. And then it was her son Vicente's turn to be arrested, at a time when his father was still behind bars, and he served a lot of time before he was freed and returned home. As for Félix, after the war, he was sentenced to hard labor in a camp in Teruel for twenty months. María, by then a widow, set off for Barcelona to work. Vicenta and her mother worked hard in the fields to "fend off starvation": "Lucky for them, they still had the garden to help them feed themselves; other folks in the village suffered even worse!" María Jesús adds.

For a while it had been hard to assert their title to their land since the registers had been burnt, and then matters were settled. Everything

Vicenta with her granddaughter on her right, her niece Concha on her left and her grand-niece behind her at a memorable launch of En Busca de *Los Hijos de la Noche* in Pina de Ebro in 2009

that could be sold off was: hens, eggs, pig; they fed on whatever was left—bacon fat and potatoes. "And so life went on … and now here we are," Vicenta concludes.

In response to our questioning, Vicenta says that La Madre never again mentioned Antoine's name at home.

All of this information is additional to the interviews that Frédéric had with Concepción (aka Concha) Valero Gómez, Félix's daughter, and her husband Rubén in Pina back in 2003. Concha had previously written to Frédéric to tell him how moved she had been on reading extracts about themselves from Antoine's manuscript:

"This is our history, though we have a tendency to forget it […]. It brings me great joy to know that my grandmother was remembered after all these years. I have lots of childhood memories of her. She passed away when I was eleven. I remember her as a very industrious person of strong character."

Vicenta Labarta passed away in Zaragoza in 2012: she was buried with her brothers and sisters in Pina.

AFTERWORD

Revolution or Reform?

"This is what has happened in Spain. After what I have seen
in Spain, I have come to the conclusion that it is futile to
be 'anti-Fascist' while attempting to preserve capitalism.
Fascism, after all, is only a development of capitalism, and the
mildest democracy, so-called, is liable to turn into Fascism
when the pinch comes [...] I do not see how one can oppose
Fascism except by working for the overthrow of capitalism,
starting, of course, in one's own country. If one collaborates
with a capitalist-imperialist government in a struggle 'against
Fascism,' i.e. against a rival imperialism, one is simply
letting Fascism in by the back door. The whole struggle in
Spain, on the Government side, has turned upon this."

GEORGE ORWELL, LETTER TO
GEOFFREY GORER, SEPTEMBER 15, 1937[1]

In any revolution, the die is cast in the first few days, for it *very
quickly* becomes the case that unless maximum effort is made, and the
decision to *take over everything* made immediately, ancient identities
and old drivers regain the upper hand. The *restoration* may well style
itself "revolution" and mouth radical, inflammatory jargon, but, even
at that point, it will nonetheless be at its handiwork, with guns at its
disposal.

Many a man has been ready to effect a radical change in his life,
as long as he can be sure that everybody will join in of their own volition; despite any distances in time and space, this is the very yardstick
by which the far-reaching radicality of the *socialization* experience of
the Spanish revolution of 1936 can be measured. The collectives established in Aragon and in Catalonia stood in stark contrast to what the
Soviet Union's authoritarian experience had been. Yet, at first glance,
both these styles of collectivization might seem related, and this

---

1   George Orwell, *The Collected Essays, Journalism and Letters of George
     Orwell*, vol. 4 edited by Sonia Orwell and Ian Angus (London: Secker &
     Warburg, 1968), 284–85.

looking-glass effect has misled more than one person, starting with the many anarchists who, throughout the growing bureaucratization of the "revolution," failed to weather the runaway bolshevization of their minds. Antoine Gimenez testifies to this more than once, in his naïve way, when he reports conversations that he had with the communist political commissar Cathala who occasionally tripped him up by getting him to believe that they were both referring to the same thing when they talked about collectives.

Nevertheless, it should not be thought that this aspect of the collectivization experience in Spain was anything more than a draft of an escape from capitalism:

> Ever since the First International, anarchism has counterposed the collective appropriation of the means of production to Social Democratic statism. Both visions, nonetheless, have the same starting point: the need for collective management. The problem is: management of what? Of course, what Social Democracy carried out from above, bureaucratically, the Spanish proletarians practised at the base, armed, with each individual responsible to everyone, thereby taking the land and the factories away from a minority specialized in the organizing and exploitation of others; the opposite, in short, of the co-management of the Coal Board by socialist or Stalinist union officials. Nevertheless, the fact is that a collectivity, rather than a state or a bureaucracy, takes the production of its material life into its own hands and does not by itself do away with the capitalist character of that life.[2]

And from the same source comes this:

---

2   Gilles Dauvé, *When Insurrections Die*, Endnotes ed., 68–69 (see https://libcom.org/library/when-insurrections-die. Let us be clear that the reader should not infer from our quoting from Gilles Dauvé in our afterword that we follow him in everything. While the comments concerned here regarding the reasons for the failure of the revolution in Spain struck us as sufficiently illuminating for us to repeat them, the same doesn't necessarily hold true for other things he has written. In particular, we wash our hands of certain of his remarks as contained in the texts he published in 1979 in *La Guerre sociale* and shortly afterward in *La Banquise*, remarks relating to the Nazi concentration camps and the destruction of European Jewry.

The Spanish Civil War proved both the revolutionary vigor of communitarian bonds and the forms that have been penetrated by capital but that are not yet daily reproduced by capital, and also their impotence, taken by themselves, in bringing off a revolution. The absence of an assault against the state condemned the establishment of different relationships to a fragmentary self-management preserving the content and often the forms of capitalism, notably money and the division of activities by individual enterprises.[3]

Besides, far from seeking solace in some sort of naturalistic Rousseau-ism, we can discern in people some tremendous aptitudes for generosity, goodwill, and bigheartedness; what greater pleasure could there be, indeed, than losing oneself in *the other*? That experience, which, ordinarily, we access only through love, was lived and relived time and again, no offense to the Finkielkrauts who twist themselves into knots these days equating the craving for revolution and the Bolshevik terror, or, according to one recent definition, the urge to escape and planned suicide in the modern settings of banishment and "pogrom." [The use of the term "pogrom" harkens back to something said by the French writer Alain Finkielkraut who likened the suburban riots of November 2005 to an "anti-republican" pogrom.]

Unfortunately, we are obliged to concede that such rewriting of history has the wind in its sails, primarily in Spain: a host of professional historians, super-documented and hyper-published, is presently busy revisiting the period of the Second Republic and Spanish Civil War.[4] For those with the courage to read them, there will be a mass of interesting things to be learned, but, if they look no further than that, they will miss the essence, for these people's knowledge of the libertarian movement is often acquired at a distance, as academics. The likes of Ucelay Da Cal, Santos Juliá, and Julián Casanova can only chase up what the cold archives serve up to them, which is to say, reports and briefings that are mostly from police or court sources and that are bereft of the sap, which is the only thing that can afford them an understanding of what the times were like in a Spain liberated, for once,

3   Ibid., 64.
4   See appendix 2 below for extracts from Gutiérrez Molina's essay on the subject.

from the coldest of cold monsters. So, the hobbyhorse of these salaried historians/researchers is the supposed terror that anarchist militia members allegedly enforced wherever they went, simply to impose their pipedreams. If you believe them, the collectives were established only under the yoke of these *pistoleros*. There we are dealing with the updated version of one of the classical mechanisms for the Stalinist rewriting of history, according to which there never was any Spanish revolution, for the simple reason that the Stalinists wanted none of it.

Lots of testimonials, of which Gimenez's is but one of many on this count, bear witness to the self-management experiment's having been precisely that, an experiment. Nobody really knew what needed doing, aside from the fact that no longer was a peasant proprietor to be allowed to work any more land than his own unaided efforts could manage, for instance, or that the old bonds of deference that underpinned the caciques were to be done away with, but the interesting thing about the libertarian approach is that it allowed us to draw a distinction between the point at which those old relations were abolished and the devising of new relationships agreed upon. Even though lots of experienced militants within the CNT and the FAI had definite ideas as to what libertarian communism should look like, at no point was any enlightened Bolshevik-style leadership, persuaded of its own omniscience, set up to organize the collectives from on high; one has only to see the diversity of the arrangements implemented here and there. In one location, money might be abolished outright, whereas somewhere else it was retained, albeit under the supervision of some elected revolutionary committee, and somewhere else again, a voucher system might be introduced to cover certain types of produce, et cetera. In short, the search was on for the way ahead and, had Líster's communist troops not vandalized the collectives in Aragon in the summer of 1937, we might well have found it, based on the fact that it is not enough just to abolish money as a concrete resource in order to have done once and for all with the sort of relationships it expresses and sustains within capitalist society.

For the fact is that the Spanish anarchists, while outstanding in terms of their human qualities of courage and their empathy with their fellow human beings, were not always very conversant with the relationships at work within capitalist society. This being due in part, no doubt, to those very same human qualities that screened whole aspects of that reality from their view.

It strikes us that here we ought to point out a significant contradiction in the anarchist discourse and ideology. The separate critique of money and the charge leveled against it, that it is a source of *evil*, point to an unduly superficial anticapitalism, which believes that in money— and, often, in those who have it—it has identified the factor with the capacity to pervert *sound*, labor-based economics capable of generating wealth.

So work is construed as man's generic ahistorical endeavor by means of a "metabolism with nature" (Marx). And, as for money, it looks like it has been grafted on to the former for the purposes of exploiting and lording it over him, so it would seem that its abolition might be enough to bring about the advent of a fairer society, released from the capitalist yoke.

But work is not the human endeavor by means of which man sets out to perpetuate himself, but, instead, the specific effort he devotes to producing commodities. Commodities are not random goods but the material embodiment of the time required for their production, their value. Their use value merely serves as their carrier. And in the end, money turns out to be "the queen of commodities," operating as the equivalent to all the rest. So what is traded on the market is units of work-time. The shift in value is this ongoing conversion of capital (money) into more money by means of labor and commodity. Being, of itself, the accumulation of expended labor, capitalism grows through being valorized by being channeled through live labor. Capitalist production is only ever aimed at the greatest possible production of commodities, without ever querying whether society needs it. That only becomes a consideration when it comes to the disposal of commodities, which is why, in a capitalist society, production takes precedence over needs, rather than needs determining production.

Historically, the term "labor" initially referred to the exertions of slaves, which is to say, those who produce under compulsion from others. There has been a migration away from such a blatantly coercion-based definition toward the mirage of a free pursuit that might involve expenditure of a morsel of one's labor power in return for the wherewithal to survive. The freedom concerned is the freedom of the absence of further ties. Labor is still "random toil": the practicalities of it—say, the baking of bread or the construction of tanks—are simply the material embodiment of their abstract aspect, the "deployment of brawn, nerve, or brain" (Marx) over a given unit of time. That unit makes up the value of the commodity and finds expression in the form of money. Money being the only means by which two entirely different commodities can be measured, one against the other.

Trying to do away with money while preserving labor's dignity, as Antoine puts it in many a place in his memoirs, is therefore a nonsense not susceptible to practical implementation and has recourse to ersatz devices that are assuredly even more coercive than money: numbered tokens spelling out the value of labor performed, accounting practices taking precise account of the time taken by production, which is to say, everything that goes to sustain a "soviet"-style economics purporting to mirror value and redistribute it with greater fairness. Calling into question not value but merely "theft of the surplus value."

Implicit in labor is the human being as something separate from the community and the effort one expends as an alienated constraint existing outside of oneself. This is an entirely modern worldview that would have seemed nonsensical to members of premodern societies, to whom belonging to a community (albeit not freely chosen) was basic.[5]

But let it not be thought that this flaw in theory was specific to anarchists alone: it is interesting, on this score, to stress the commonality between them and other workers' movement tendencies ("party" communists or "council" communists, social democrats, utopians, etc.), all of whom, for all their mutual invective, sang the praises of labor and, in so doing, made themselves members, albeit unwilling ones, of the great family of modernizers and "progressives," even though we need not turn a blind eye to such *marginal* and often unsolicited moments that were beyond the ken of ideology, for which very reason we are out to uncover their tracks these days.

Since we have our eyes trained on the margins, we might first remind ourselves of this famous passage in the letter that Mikhail Bakunin wrote to Sergei Nechayev on June 2, 1870:

> In our people's life and thought there are two principles, two facts on which we can build: frequent riots and free economic community. There is a third principle, a third fact: this is the Cossacks and the world of brigands and thieves which includes both protest

---

5   To anyone wishing to know more about this core element in our discourse, we can only recommend that they read Anselm Jappe, *Aventures de la marchandise* (Paris: Denoël, 2003).

against oppression by the state and by the patriarchal society and incorporates, so to say, the first two features. [...]

If the villages do not revolt more often this is due to fear or to a realization of their weakness. This awareness comes from the disunity of peasant communes, from the lack of real solidarity among them. If each village knew that when it rises, all others would rise, one could not say for certain that there is no village in Russia that would not revolt. Hence it follows that the first duty, purpose, and aim of a secret organization is to awaken in all peasant communities a realization of their inevitable solidarity and thus to arouse the Russian people to a consciousness of their power—in other words, to merge the multitude of private peasants revolts into one general all-people's revolt.

One of the main means for the achievement of this aim, I am deeply convinced, must and should be our free Cossacks, our innumerable saintly and not so saintly tramps (*brodiagy*), pilgrims, members of '*beguny*' sects, thieves, and brigands—this whole wide and numerous underground world which from time immemorial has protested against the state and statism and against the Teutonic civilization of the whip. [...]

The world of Cossacks, thieves, brigands, and tramps played the role of a catalyst and unifier of separate revolts under Stenka Razine and under Pugachev. The tramping fraternity are the best and truest conductors of people's revolution, promoters of general popular unrest, this precursor of popular revolt. Who does not know that tramps, given the opportunity, easily turn into thieves and brigands? [...] That is why I am on the side of popular brigandage and see in it one of the most essential tools for the future people's revolution in Russia. [...]

It is not easy to use the world of brigandage as a weapon of the people's revolution, as a catalyst of separate popular revolts; I recognize the necessity, but, at the same time, am fully conscious of my incapacity for this task. In order to undertake it and bring it to a conclusion, one must be equipped with strong nerves, the strength of a giant, passionate conviction, and iron will. You might find such people in your ranks. But people of our generation and with our upbringing are incapable of it. To join the brigaes does not mean becoming wholly one of them, sharing with them all their unquiet passions, misfortunes, frequently ignoble aims, feelings and actions; but it does mean giving them new souls and arousing within them a new, truly popular aim. These wild and cruelly coarse people have a fresh, strong, untried and unused nature which is open to lively propaganda, obviously only if the propaganda is lively and not doctrinaire and is capable of reaching them.[6]

For a start, Bakunin displays his insightfulness here on the subject of these vagabonds, thieves, and beggars, and little consideration has been given to their role in the hatching of the Spanish revolution. Yet tens of thousands of vagabonds, which lots of *leyes de vagos y maleantes* (vagrants and miscreants laws) were forever looking to monitor and crack down on, tramped the highways and byways of Spain, in search of a job or of some "stroke" to pull. Antoine himself is not very forthcoming on this subject, but he was one of them, part farm laborer and part petty thief, a real "tramping artisan," as he liked to describe himself (see his biographical note). And among the contraband goods that he had occasion to traffic across the French border was anarchist propaganda.

These wanderers cannot help but call to mind the famous hobos of 1930s America who were also carriers of emancipation and freedom. As with their trans-Atlantic counterparts, one also finds among them unbelievable levels of hospitality and generosity (which had all but evaporated from the wider society of employees that modern capitalism was in the process of embedding in Europe and the United States) and—to borrow the language of the criminologist (the sworn enemy of the Gimenologist)—of "social perilousness."

It is interesting to learn that in Spain, the CNT's "intelligence services," in concert with the renowned action groups, were mainly organized around staff drawn from cafés and hotels, where the *camareros* (waiters) would cock an ear and eavesdrop on the conversations of the *señoritos* (little lordlings) who were plotting against the workers' organizations. Vagabonds and brigands were also closely in touch with such junior staff, and, deep down, the two communities were one and the same. In such circles none could have been unaware of what the ruling classes thought of the poor and what steps they were ready to take against them.

6   Mikhail Bakunin, *Bakunin on Violence. Letter to S. Nechayev* (New York: Unity Press, New York, 19--), 18–21. The letter in question was written from Locarno on June 2, 1870.

Unless one keeps in mind the amount of suffering that such an impoverished existence entailed, with its unrelenting harassment from the Civil Guard, there is simply no understanding of why, right from the start of the revolution, vicious and cruel violence targeted *personas de orden* (the old regime's "respectable folk") who had, with the crassest stupidity, always championed a system in which the sheer struggle to survive might provoke even a child into extreme measures. In *The Thief's Journal*, Jean Genet, for instance, describes how Pépé, a young gypsy from the Barrio Chino, stuck his knife into the belly of a card-player over a handful of pesetas. And Laurie Lee, in *As I Walked Out One Midsummer Morning*, refers to the persistence of money-grubbing prostitution in flea-bitten hovels.

In his letter, Bakunin is not at all fascinated by the world of the thugs, in that he acknowledges "their often odious motives," but he declares that there is a chance of "arousing in them [the need] for a different purpose!" To be sure, and even though he guards against it, there is still a modicum of "playing to the gallery" and "propagandism" in Bakunin's argument, but he puts his finger on what Antoine himself would try to describe: prior to the revolution, Antoine had been merely a vague rebel and, by dint of the extraordinary encounters thrown his way by the fabulous summer of 1936, he was to remain, for the rest of his days, an enthusiast for utter emancipation from the State and from Capital.

Unfortunately, good intentions alone are not enough:

> Anarchism overestimates state power by regarding authority as the main enemy, and at the same time underestimates the state's force of inertia. The state is the guarantor, but not the creator, of social relationships. It represents and unifies capital. It is neither capital's motor nor its centerpiece. From the undeniable fact that the Spanish masses were armed after July 1936, anarchism deduced that the state was losing its substance. But the substance of the state resides not in institutional forms, but in its unifying function. The state ensures the tie, which human beings cannot and dare not create among themselves, and creates a web of services which are both parasitic and real.

In the summer of 1936, the state apparatus may have seemed derelict in republican Spain, because it only subsisted as a potential framework capable of picking up the pieces of capitalist society and rearranging them one day. In the meantime, it continued to live, in social hibernation. Then it gained new strength when the relations opened up by subversion were loosened or torn apart. It revived its organs, and, the occasion permitting, assumed control over those bodies that subversion had caused to emerge. What had been seen as an empty shell showed itself capable not only of revival but also of actually emptying out the parallel forms of power in which the revolution thought it had best embodied itself.[7]

And, before that, we read:

> In the same way, the integration of Spanish anarchism in the state of 1936 is only surprising if one forgets its nature: the CNT was a union, an original union undoubtedly but a union all the same, and there is no such thing as an anti-union union. Function transforms the organ. Whatever its original ideals, every permanent organism for defending wage-labourers as such becomes a mediator, and then a conciliator. Even when it is in the hands of radicals, even when it is repressed, the institution is bound to escape control of the base and to turn into a moderating instrument. Anarchist union though it may have been, the CNT was a union before it was anarchist. A world separated the rank-and-file from the leader seated at the bosses' table, but the CNT as a whole was little different from the UGT. Both of them worked to modernise and rationally manage the economy: in a word, to socialise capitalism. A single thread connects the socialist vote for war credits in August 1914 to the participation in the government of the anarchist leaders, first in Catalonia (September '36) and then in the Spanish Republic (November '36). [...] in 1914, Malatesta had called those of his comrades (including Kropotkin) who had accepted national defense "government anarchists."
>
> The CNT had long been both institutionalised and subversive. The contradiction ended in the 1931 general election, when the CNT gave up its anti-parliamentary stand, asking the masses to vote for Republican candidates. The anarchist organisation was turning into "a union aspiring to the conquest of power" that would "inevitably lead to a dictatorship over the proletariat" (*PIC*, German edition, December 1931).

7 Dauvé, *When Insurrections Die*, 59–61.

From one compromise to the next, the CNT wound up renouncing the anti-statism which was its raison d'être, even after the Republic and its Russian ally or master had shown their real faces in May '37, not to mention everything that followed, in the jails and secret cellars. Like the POUM, the CNT was effective in disarming proletarians, calling on them to give up their struggle against the official and Stalinist police bent on finishing them off. As the GIC put it "… the CNT was among those chiefly responsible for the crushing of the insurrection. It demoralised the proletariat at a time when the latter was moving against democratic reactionaries" (*Räte-Korrespondenz*, organ of the Dutch GIC, June 1937).[8]

The second last of these quotations, the one from the *PIC*, is interesting, for it was a very early flagging up of the political stance that would become the CNT's line later, in 1936, but above all in 1937 and 1938. But it is also indicative of the sort of critique expounded by the tiny ultra-left groups of the day. Unlike, say, a Prudhommeaux who was very quick to detect the CNT's tendency to drift in the direction of antifascism and alliance with leftist or republican forces, but who entered the lists alongside Spanish and international proletarians anyway, those tiny groups never managed to move beyond criticism, convinced that they had said all there was to say about events in Spain. From the lofty heights of that truth, though varying according to the oracular pronouncements of some theoretician or another, the revolutionary process under way following the advent of the Republic in 1931 was boiled down to certain determinants or certain directives emanating from one quarter, from what we might term the "realist" or rather, reformist quarter of the trade union confederation. Furthermore, the dismissal of the revolutionary experience as doomed to predictable failure, insofar as that dynamic supposedly had failed or simply refused to *"get with the program"* fails to take account of the scale of what was a revolutionary transformation not ordained by decrees but growing out of the grassroots of society.

If we agree that the CNT was a trade union different from the others, then we have to concede that genuinely revolutionary forces found expression within its ranks, in spite of the—sometimes

8   Ibid., 57–58.

At the Le Panier Hostel in the Montée des Accoules in Marseilles, circa 2008

wobbly—choices made by certain of its leaders: in appendix 2, we reprint some extracts from Gutiérrez Molina's essay pointing this out.

On the other hand, though, we should be capable of acknowledging the deep split that emerged within its ranks following the first few months of revolution *put to the test*; after November 1936, there was an out-and-out divorce splitting the CNT into reformist and radical strands, a split that was to widen right up until the incidents of May 1937, which exposed just how far it had gone, and from then on, much of the efforts of the organization were devoted to hiding it from view. Anarchist historians, for the most part, would aid and abet this effort over the ensuing decades.

That said, we may perhaps be a little better equipped to appreciate how that formidable and tragic eruption in the Spanish summer of 1936 managed, after the first few days of vengeance had passed, to trigger countless manifestations of the setting aside of resentments, as exemplified by that storybook encounter between Justo Bueno and his erstwhile enemy Tísner in the Aragonese countryside. And we are willing to bet that that sort of new beginning will be the hallmark of revolutions to come....

The Giménologues

APPENDICES

APPENDIX I

The Appointment of Durruti as a Replacement for Miaja

Off-handedly, as if dealing with some run-of-the-mill matter, Largo Caballero [...] tabled the explosive issue. According to him it related to General Miaja, chairman of the Madrid Defense Junta, who, according to reports from the Minister of War [i.e., Caballero], was openly defying the prime minister-cum-Minister of War. He was behaving, not like the head of a Junta with delegated authority, established by the government to act on its behalf, but quite the opposite: he was forwarding no information of any description. Resorting to lots of demagogy, he was busy trying to persuade the members of the Defense Junta to think of themselves as the government, not merely of Madrid, but of the whole of Spain. And that could not be tolerated.

"As a matter of urgency we have to come up with a suitable replacement, somebody not tempted to imagine himself as leader of the Republic's government as well. Who would you suggest?"

Silence followed and this time it was quite lengthy and burdensome. This was something that had caught us by surprise. I ventured to speak again:

"It would seem that we need to come up with somebody who, while not a serviceman, is not lacking in talent for military leadership and who, being a civilian, is not tempted to pass himself off as the head of the government. Allow me to nominate Durruti who was briefed on Madrid's problems a few days ago and who, from what I have learned this morning, is right now in the front lines with his column."

"I have no desire to belittle the Justice Minister's suggestion," Prieto declared. "But before I say anything and, given the complicated nature of the matter, I should like to know the opinion of the leader of the government."

Irujo remained silent. The other members of the Higher War Council went along with what Prieto had said.

Largo Caballero spoke up:

"I think that our comrade the Justice Minister's suggestion is still the right one. [...] I will go along with it and agree to appoint Durruti. The only thing is that I must ask that this be kept wholly confidential, for we must allow eight days to pass to give Durruti time to make himself known in Madrid and for me to have a chance to travel up there, both to talk with him and to appoint him to his post. What do you think of that?"

We were all in agreement.[1]

1   García Oliver, *El eco de los pasos*, 326–27.

APPENDIX II

Anarcho-syndicalism in the Historiography of the Second Republic and the 1936–1939 War

We thought it might be of interest to include a few extracts from José Luis Gutiérrez Molina's afterword to Abel Paz's *Durruti in the Spanish Revolution* (Oakland: AK Press, 2007, 720–22, 725–27, and 728–30.

A significant portion of contemporary Spanish historical literature emerged from a specific moment—the 1970s and the establishment of the present regime [...]

Historians had a significant role to play during this time of accelerated change, when new social and political structures were being born: their task was to establish historical memory and set up standards of political legitimacy that would buttress the system being constructed. It is not accidental that studies of the workers' movement predominated among the pieces released, although there were also significant works on electoral sociology [...] It was during this period that many important studies appeared on one of the taboo subjects of Franco's regime: the Second Republic and the so-called *Civil War*.

[...] Their job was to provide an intellectual justification for the emerging democracy in a society that had seen the dictator die in bed. It was necessary to replace the rancid, anti-liberal historiography of Franco's regime with a new, social one. Researchers focused on two major topics: Spanish society in the thirties (relevant as an example of the democracy that people now aspired toward) and the causes and course of the civil conflict (which had been the origin of the dictatorial regime).

As noted historian Julián Casanova indicated, there was a need for a new conceptual apparatus.[1] The discussion began in the second half

1   Julián Casanova, *La historia social y los historiadores* (Barcelona: Crítica, 1991) 159–60.

of the 1970s and was bolstered by debates in other countries on topics such as the transition from feudalism to capitalism and the bourgeois revolutions. It was then that Marxist methodology lodged itself in Spanish historical studies. It was a Marxism more connected to the West, primarily to British Marxist historiography and the Annales school than to the historical sciences in the officially Communist world. It is important to bear this in mind in order to understand the fate of Spanish anarchism and anarcho-syndicalism in the historical literature.

These overwhelmingly young and "progressive" historians enthusiastically set out to scrutinize the inner workings of the Republican regime, document the vicissitudes of the proletarian organizations and analyse the trajectory of the armed conflict. It was during this time that what are today seen as historical truths emerged. They ended up establishing a consensus—another concept closely linked to the 1970s—that stressed the democratic role of the Republican government, as a promoter of the country's modernization and that characterized the so-called *Civil War* as a conflict fought in defense of those bourgeois, democratic values.

Historians found the conclusion they were looking for: they argued that pressure from right and left-wing extremists prevented the Republican regime from instituting its democratic reforms. This pressure inevitably resulted in the fratricidal struggle that stained the Iberian soil with blood for nearly three years and brought Spain into the long tunnel from which it was just beginning to emerge.

[...]

In the 1970s and 1980s, like now, the memory of the 1936–1939 war served as an antidote to any attempt to question the new regime that was consolidating itself. [...]

The rains brought mud. Contemporary Spanish historiography must accept responsibility for its role in the decline of the humanities. Its position towards the study of social movements in general and reduction of history to a mere contingency in which utopia and scepticism disappear, makes it an accomplice to the present dilemma. Intellectuals who embrace a historical perspective shaped by the needs of the *Spanish transition* are incapable of studying social movements coherently. [...] Historians frequently forget, minimize, and even ridicule the significant presence of anarchists in Spain. They have applied labels such as "irrational," "messianic," "utopian" (in the pejorative sense), "terrorist," and "criminal" to anarchist organizations and individuals. If urban anarcho-syndicalists were anachronistic in the context of the new industrial modes of production, the CNT's peasant unions rested on a *millenarian* outlook based on forms of life that were disappearing.

[...]

Spain's Second Republic emerged with enthusiastic popular support and the widespread hope that the new regime would institute the changes that its leaders had promised. Historian Santos Juliá described it as a *popular revolution* in which the progressive, enlightened bourgeoisie tried to transform Spanish society by changing the political regime. It relied on the workers in the Socialist Party and the UGT to do so, whose support was ratified in the August 1930 Pact of San Sebastián.

The fall of the Bourbon monarchy not only produced a formal regime change, but also a subversion of the dominant social norms. To an extent, the fear of the master, of the cacique and of religion disappeared. The popular classes demanded their signs of identity, society entered into a process of secularization and customs *relaxed*. [...] The rebel anarcho-syndicalism of the 1920s reappeared and declared its desire to militantly transform society. The new rulers would have to take this into account.

But the rulers did not and were unable to carry out their promises or resolve the country's social and economic problems. [...] when historians say that the CNT is a revolutionary organization, they also mean that it subjected the Republican regime to devastating pressure and imply that the 1936–1939 war was a consequence of right and left wing extremists who made an intermediate path impossible. But this is a half-truth. During the first year of the Republic, from April 1931 to May 1932, it is inaccurate to characterize the CNT as a revolutionary organization.

[...] However, after the proclamation of the Republic [...] the government responded as if it was facing a revolutionary threat [...] Why?

In the first place, it did so in the interests of its foreign policy which required that it offer a reassuring image to international capitalists; and, second, because it was obsessed with *erasing anarcho-syndicalism from the map*. The Socialists worried as they saw the CNT rebuild itself and gain ground among workers that the UGT had previously controlled, like telephone and railway workers. Socialist ministers mounted an aggressive anti-CNT campaign, particularly Largo Caballero, head of the Ministry of Labor. [...]

Instead of satisfying the transformative expectations, they merely tried to silence their critics with the same coercive methods that the monarchy had used (like deportation and imprisonment). There were also highly radicalized groups that didn't hesitate to call into doubt the state's monopoly on the use of violence. [...]

Casas Viejas, one of the most violent events in the Republican-CNT confrontation, caused both the collapse of the public's faith in the Republicans' reformist capacity and the beginning of the center-right offensive. The Republic began to lose worker support and to weaken the few improvements that the proletariat had won in the preceding months. Politically speaking, it also paved the way for increasingly right-wing governments after the November elections.

After the Socialists' departure from the government and the defeat of the CNT's insurrections in 1933, the two strategies that had defined the labor movement up until then began to sink into discredit. Spanish Socialists felt betrayed after their expulsion from the government and adopted a more radical posture. Largo Caballero was the most well-known representative of this tendency and his most dramatic act was the failed uprising in October 1934. For its part, the CNT was struggling to survive as an organization and voices began to arise within it that questioned its insurrectional strategy.

An element appeared on the horizon in late 1933 that would have great importance for 1936–1939 conflict: a feeling of unity among the working class. [...]

The CNT collaborated with the UGT in labor conflicts on numerous occasions in 1934. This occurred in Madrid, Salamanca, Santander, Zaragoza and in Sevilla during the UGT's national peasant strike. The CNT and UGT signed an accord in Sevilla that became the model for widespread local agreements in the succeeding years. Finally, the May CNT congress in Zaragoza approved some foundations of a CNT-UGT pact.

The repression unleashed after the revolutionary events of October 1934 forced workers' and Left Republican organizations underground. The government persecuted the anarcho-syndicalists as if they were responsible for the uprising and they also had to endure harassment from the Socialists and Communists, who accused them of betrayal because they hadn't participated in the rebellion.[...] After the Popular

Front victory in February 1936, the CNT began to surpass the UGT in its traditional strongholds like Madrid. Its proposal for a Revolutionary Workers' Alliance at the Zaragoza congress made it seem like the promoter of proletarian unity.

[...] This year, two decades have passed since the death of the victor of the 1936–1939 war. The mass media in Spain and elsewhere have run endless analyses and criticisms of the Spanish "transition," all focused on establishing the "historical truth" about the country's recent decades. Most commentaries depict contemporary Spain as the happy consequence of the resolution of the problems that caused the "civil" war. According to this theory, the present 1979 Constitution marks the definitive end of the fratricidal confrontation.

These formulations assume that the Spanish conflict was a struggle between "brothers," whose tensions were exasperated by the Second Republic, the uniquely conflicted European 1930s, "primitive" influences like anarchism and the country's "delayed" modernization. One cannot forget that international public opinion received the Spanish conflict with great excitement because it was considered the first act in an increasingly more certain conflict with fascism. Nevertheless, its existence as a "social war" has been forgotten, when not deliberately concealed; a conflict in which those fighting one another were not brothers, parents, or cousins but rather partisans of opposing visions of social life. Indeed, many historians also forget that thousands of Europeans and Americans saw the events in Spain as a struggle for genuine social transformation.

One can argue that it was such a struggle until the "events of May 1937." The Spaniards who confronted the military rebels in July 1936 were not trying to stop German fascism or settle old family grudges, but to create a system of social relations distinct from the "Old Regime" and the Republicans' "formal democracy." Curiously, on this point, liberal as well as Marxist historians coincide in concealing the revolutionary implications of the Spanish war [...]

For example, Alejandro Díez Torre notes that historian "Julián Casanova gives precedence to the top regional Communist leader José Duque Cuadrado ... who when the conflict was already over ... wrote a very personal and ... self-serving account." Casanova believes that this is "the only thorough study—errors and groundless accusations against the libertarians aside—of events in Aragon after the military uprising and before the dissolution of the Council." Díez Torre asserts that his work is not even "minimally resistant to verification against other primary sources."[2]

The result is that many historians accept the idea—which therefore becomes "truth"—that the collectivizations in Aragon and, by implication, those elsewhere, were not as deep nor did they affect as much of the population as claimed [...]

While we mustn't avoid difficult questions or write hagiographies, we also cannot stop questioning frameworks that conceal what is most meaningful about the Spanish conflict in the 1930s: its revolutionary achievements.

2   For the critique of Casanova, see Alejandro Díaz Torre, *Crisis regional y regionalización. El Consejo de Aragón*, doctral thesis (Department of Contemporary History at UNED, Madrid), 19, and notes 10–13 of the introductory chapter. Díez Torre borrowed the quotation from Casanova from *Anarquismo y revolución en la sociedad rural aragonesa, 1936–1938* (Madrid: Siglo XXI, 1985), 142.

Appendix III

Document Lifted from David Berry's "French Anarchist Volunteers in Spain, 1936–1939."[1]

Thirty four of the French libertarians who signed on as volunteers with the anarchist militias perished in Spain.

Badard/Baudart, Roger—d. Perdiguera, October 17, 1936

Baudard/Baudart, Juliette—d. Perdiguera, October 17, 1936

Bégué/Béguez, Jean—d. Belchite, September, 1936

Berard, Mario—d. Perdiguera, October 17, 1936

Berge/Bergé, Raymond—d. Perdiguera, October 17, 1936

Berthomieu/Berthonnieux—d. Perdiguera, October 17, 1936

Boff, Émile—d. Casa del Campo, November 12, 1936

Boudoux—d. Pediguera, October 17, 1936

Casteu, Eugénie—d. 1937

Charrang[eau?], Georges—d. Perdiguera, October 17, 1936

Chatelain, Lucien—d. March 1937

Colombet, Philippe—d. Codo, August 1937

Cottin, Émile—d. Farlete, September 8, 1936

Coyne, Sénateur [?]—d. Barcelona (air raid)

Delalain, Jean—d. Perdiguera, October 17, 1936

Delaruelle, Henri—d. Perdiguera, October 17, 1936

Détang, Max—vanished, Albacete, December 1936

Ferrand, Jean—d. Barna, May 5, 1937

Fons—d. Santa Quiteria, April 1937

Galissot, René—d. Perdiguera, October 17, 1936

Gérard, Marcel—missing, Teruel, December 1936

Gessaume, Georges—missing, Tortosa, July 26, 1938

---

1   See Berry, "French Anarchist Volunteers in Spain, 1936–39: Contribution to a Collective Biography of the French Anarchist Movement." Berry gives the date as October 17, but it was actually the 16th. [Giménologues' note.]

Giral/Giralt, Jean—d. Perdiguera, October 17, 1936
Greffier, Marcel—d. Cuesta de la Reina
Hans, Suzanne—Farlete, November 1936
Kokoczinski, Georgette—d. Perdiguera, October 17, 1936
Lemère—d. Farlete, September 8, 1936
Meller, Bernard—missing, Huesca, November 1936
Monnard, Georges—d. Quinto, December 1936
R????s [?], Yves—d. Perdiguera, October 17, 1936
Rajaud, Maurice—nothing else known
Recoulis[?les/ls], Louis—d. Farlete, November 1936
Trontin, Jean—d. Perdiguera, October 17, 1936
Vitrac, Yves—d. Perdiguera, October 17, 1936

Fifteen members of the Durruti Column's International Group were killed during the Nationalist attack on Perdiguera on October 17, 1936.[2]

Badard, Baudard, Roger—nothing else known.
Baudard/ Baudart, Juliette—nothing else known.
Berard, Mario—nothing else known.
Berge/Bergé, Raymond: Berge/Bergé set off for Spain in September 1936.
Berthomieu/Berthonnieux: "Delegate-general" of the International Group from its inception, he had served in the Great War as an artillery captain and had been living in Barcelona for some time.
Boudoux: perished alongside several other members of the Saint-Denis anarchist group, about whom we know nothing.
Charrang[eau?], Georges: nothing else known. Could this be the Chaffaugeon from the Communist Youth of Lyon who was also a member of the International Group and who perished in the same battle?[3]

2   About 170 members of the International Group met their death in Perdiguera. How many of the (about) 155 others who were left were French is not known. (Remember that we thought we had established that the total number of dead was somewhere between forty and fifty.) [Giménologues' note.]

3   See Charles Ridel, "À ceux qui sont tombés" in *Le Libertaire* (October 23, 1936). That article and other texts sent by Ridel (Mercier-vega) from the front lines have been collected and republished as Louis Mercier, *En route pour Saragosse avec la colonne Durruti.*

Delalain, Jean: nothing else known.

Delaruelle, Henri: actually a member of the "Italian Column," according to one document, whereas another document records him as having perished in Perdiguera.

Galissot, René : nothing else known.

Giral/Giralt; Jean Giral/Giralt was a member of the Durruti Column's International Group right from the outset. He took part in the capture of Siétamo and was hospitalized in Barcelona. His death in Perdiguera was reported in *Le Combat syndicaliste*, which hints that he was member of the CGT-SR. According to Ridel, Giralt was a member of the JEUNES (Youngsters) of Paris and "reckoned that he had taken the lead in his group."[4]

Kokoczinski, Georgette: "Georgette," as she was known, was captured and executed by the Francoists. She had served as a nurse with the Durruti Column but also took part in raids behind the Nationalist lines alongside the *Hijos de la Noche* (Sons of Night).[5] According to Paz, she was "a sort of a mascot for the Column." She was well known to people involved in *Le Libertaire*, *L'Insurge*, and *L'En-Dehors* and, especially, *La Revue anarchiste*. She had performed at anarchist "galas" under the name Mimosa.

R????s [?], Yves [?}: Name illegible. Nothing else known.

Trontin, Jean: Trontin was a supporter of Pivert's Gauche revolutionnaire and a member of the Oyonnax (Ain) Socialist Section, even though he lived in Colombes (Seine department) and was occasionally active in Lyon.[6]

Vitrac, Yves: nothing else known.

4 Ridel, "À ceux qui sont tombés" (To the Fallen), in *Le Libertaire* (October 23, 1936).

5 Paz, *Durruti: The People Armed* (New York: Black Rose Books, 1977), 276–77. According to Paz, Émile Cottin—the French anarchist famous for having attempted Clemenceau's life—allegedly also perished in Perdiguera. A machine-gunner with the Durruti Column's International Group, he actually died in a successful counterattack in Farlete on September 8, 1936. See Berry, *French Anarchists in Spain, 1936–1939*, 447.

6 *Dictionnaire biographique du movement ouvrier français*; Charles Ridel, "À ceux qui sont tombés."

Appendix IV

List of Those Killed in Perdiguera on October 16, 1936[1]

Jean GARCIA[2] (Spanish or French)
Pedro MARTINEZ
Lorenzo BENZO
Francois LOPEZ GLOIRE, or GLORI (French)
Francisco GIL
Charles SPOHU [or SPOH: French]
Julio ZORITA PEREZ (Spanish)
Yves VITRAC (French)
Roger BAUDARD (French)
Bernard MELLER (French)
Jean DELALAIN (French)
Suzanne GIRBE (French)
Louis RECOULES [or RECOULIS: French]
Andre LESAFFRE (French)
Rene GALISSOT (French)
Jean ALBERTINI (French)
Émile BOFF[3] (French)
Manuel HERNANDEZ
Santos TANS
Jean FERRET
Juliette BAUDARD (French)
Jean TRONTIN (French)
Louis BERTHOMIEU (French)
Augusta MARX (German)

1   See IISH, FAI, package 50, box 521.
2   Said to have fought as part of the Durruti Column and as a member of the Sébastien Faure centuria.
3   According to Berry, he perished in Madrid on November 12, 1936.

Jean GIRALT (French)
Simon LACALLE
Alexandre STARADONZY (Russian)
Teodor BARRADO
Eugenio RUIZ
Georges CHAFFANGEON (French)
Carlos CONTE[4] (Italian)
Estanislas CRIBALLES
Manuel ARACIL (Spanish)
Jose SEGURA
Remy BOUDOU[5] (French)
Georgette KOKOCZYNSKI (French)
Pedro FERNANDEZ (Spanish)

Dave Berry's list of "French anarchist volunteers in Spain" includes the names of a further four Frenchmen who he states perished in Perdiguera: Mario Bérard, Raymond Bergé (who arrived in Spain in September 1936), Henri Delaruelle and R...s(?), Yves.

In another "Liste des morts aux combats de Perdiguerras [*sic*] [...] le 11 [*sic*]-10-36"[6] the name Gabaoloff is also included. For our part, we would also add: "Pietro Ranieri, killed in Perdiguera on October 16, 1936," according to Antonioli, Berti, Fedele, and Iusao (eds.) *Dizionario biografico degli anarchici italiani*. As to the German who Antoine Gimenez claims committed suicide in the hayloft, we have not been able to identify him.

---

4   No doubt Carlo Conti, an Italian anarchist from Le Marche. Cited in Fedeli, *Un trentennio di attività anarchica 1914–1945*, 186, as being a member of the Durruti Column and recorded as having perished in Perdiguera. Perhaps this was Durruti's Italian friend who had been smuggled out of Zaragoza by Isidro Benet. See Giménologues, *¡A Zaragoza o al charco!*

5   The reference is to Francis Boudoux, but this is a mistake, as he survived: see http://militants-anarchistes.info/spip.php?article6486.

6   IISH, FAI, PE 15.

Appendix V

Lists of DAS Militia Members Compiled in January 1937

1) List of comrades under DAS supervision who set off for the front with the International Group and who are no longer there.[1] List compiled at the end of the latest round of furloughs. Possible mistakes cannot be ruled out.

BARTLING, Kurt: has apparently joined the 'Todesbatallion" [an Italian Battalion, The Battaglione della Morte].

SCHREYER, Gottfried: wounded for at least a month.

GORG, Karl: D.U. gone to France.

HEILIGER, Franz: wounded.

KOKES, Alfred: expelled.

WIENHOLD, August: in the old people's home for emigrants.

ZIMMERMANN, Walter: refused to rejoin the International Group. Involved in further bickering and is in a military hospital.

KOKES, Léopoldine: expelled.

LASSEN, Alfred: has supposedly left for another unit.

THOMA, Hans: on leave in France. Does not care to return.

LIPFERT, Fritz: wounded in the foot in Barcelona.

EBERHARDT, Ernst: very ill, undergoing treatment.

WEBER, Fritz: D.U. in France

KAISER, Karl: receiving treatment in Barcelona (A).

GIERKE, Walter: expelled.

PALULAT, Hermann: lost.

BOEHM, Karl: expelled to France.

BENNER, Fritz: left the front, ill.

LOESAUS, Karl: gone.

GIERHT [*sic*], Madeleine: in Barcelona.

1   IISH, FAI 1 (translated from the German by the Giménologues).

UHRBAN, Philipp: wounded, in Barcelona.

OHR, Willi: unknown posting.

HONECKER, Rudolf: left for France, never came back.

WETTLAUFER, Albert: barred from the front on political grounds.

HEINZ, Oskar: wounded, in Barcelona.

TESCHKE, Alfons: wounded, in Bacelona.

BOROSTOWSKI, Willi: wounded, in Barcelona.

RUDOLF, Paul: works in the Group's restaurant.

LEHMAN, Werner: D.U., never returned from Belgium.

VOLKERT, Georg: left, destination unknown.

SCHOBER, Martin: ditto.

HANEL, Wenzel: ditto.

v.d. LOHE, Anton: ditto.

CHOQUETTE, Simon: killed on the front.

STERNHEIM, Lazar: left without notice to join the International Brigades.

MIKENAUER, Mischa: no explanation.

GIESKE, Werner: has asked to leave.

SCHWIENTECK, Hermann: left for another section.

HAENDEL, Hans: sick, in Barcelona.

Barcelona January 4 [1937]

2) Inventory of compañeros under DAS Group supervision in the militias. Drawn up January 20, 1937.

DURRUTI DIVISION INTERNATIONAL GROUP

AEPPLI, Jacob (Swiss)
BADER, Alois (German)
BAHLKE, Henri (German)
BERGER, Alfred
BERNAUER, Theodor
BOEHME, Kurt
BORTZ, Heinrich
BRAUNER, Karl
BRINKMANN, Georg
BRUHNS, Helmuth

EICHMANN, Heinrich (Swiss)
EY, Edgar [name lined out] in Gelsa[2]
EY, Harry [name lined out] in Gelsa
FISCHER, Emanuel (German)
GALANTY, Ernst (German)
GERNSHEIMER, Georg
GIERTH, Hermann (German)
GILLOT, Regis (French)
GMUER, Edwin (Swiss)
GOERTEMAKER, Dietrich
GROECHENIG, Alois (German)
GRYALVO, Fernando (Spanish)
GUERNDT, Paul
HAAG, Theodor
HAMANN. Karl
HAMELINK, Peter (Dutch)
HARLEY, Ralph (English)
HOPF, Primus
JANSSON, Oloff (Swedish)
JOSEPH, Willi
KLEMENT, Ernst
KRAFFT, Waldemar
KUMMER, Emil (Swiss)
KWANT, Herbert (name lined out), *vermisst* (vanished)
LAMOTTE, Christian (Louis)
LATT, Nisse (Swedish)
LEDERMANN, Hans (Swiss)
LORK, Willi
LUDWIG, Heinz
LUSTICA, Antonio (Spanish)
LAJEWSKI, Otto (German)
MARSCHL, Franz (Austrian)
MICHAELIS, Michel (German)
MUGGLI, Richard (Swiss)
OSTROGA, Kurt (German)

---

2   "*In Gelsa*" indicates that they had rejected militarization of the International Group and did not move with it into its new quarters in Pina. (Giménologues' note.)

PIKK, Hermann (Estonian)
PUIG, Juan? (Spanish)[3]
RAU, Heinrich
RAUSCH, Hugo (name lined out), Grupo de Ingenieros a Gelsa (Sappers' Group in Gelsa)
RAUSCHENBERGER, Norbert
REITMEYER, Franz
RITTER, Franz (Swiss)
RYBKA, Oskar (German)
SANER, Ernst (Swiss)
SCHEUNGRAB, Josef
SCHMEIDEL, Paul
SCHREIBER, Robert
SCHREIZ, Anton (German?)
SCHWARZ, Christian (name lined out), *Aufenhalt unbekannt* (whereabouts unknown)
SCHWARZ, Jean
STOCK, Jules
TARGOWNIK, Liejbus (*Staatenlos*/stateless)
THALMANN, Klara (Swiss)
THALMANN, Paul (Swiss)
TOEWE, Otto
VESPER, Hans (German)[4]
VOGT, Fritz (name lined out, *Kaballerie in Montegrillo* (Cavalry in Montegrillo)
WALTER, Armin (Swiss)
WIELAND, Hans
WIESE, Franz
WITTFOHT, Walter
ZIMMERMANN, Oskar (German)

3   One document refers to him as the delegate from the Durruti Column's "Hijos de la Noche" long-range scouts. CMDH, PS Barcelona-Generalitat 336, 11.
4   The amputee "Swede" mentioned by Kirschey and Lätt, who give his first name as Jack.

Appendix VI

List of members of the *"Libertà o Morte"* [Liberty or Death] group

Confidential
Ministry of the interior

Copy of a list of libertarian militants from the "Libertà o Morte" group (Argelès-sur-mer Camp, France)

1. Dupuys, Marcello (12384)
2. Castellani, Dario (20543)
3. Bruschi, Angelo (79430)
4. Ragni, Cesare (15643)
5. Volontè, Giuseppe (18637)
6. Carelli, Giuseppe (7513)
7. Borgo, Enrico
8. Ortega, Arquinio
9. Maran, Valentino (127330)
10. Lopez, Alberto
11. Magnani, Pio (129106)
12. Giovinazzi, Francesco
13. Rosso, Giuseppe
14. Calderoni, Mario (120861)
15. Venanzi, Ercole (114052)
16. Bellon, Bruno (129021)
17. Marconi, Mario
18. Osio, Lelio
19. Corradi, Costantino (13889)
20. Della Torre, Oreste (127015)
21. Renzi, Trentino (133874)
22. Vigano, Angelo (115448)
23. Domi, Aldo
24. Bonfanti, Enrico (44003)
25. Martini, Giovanni (112242)

26. Baglioni, Mariano (78101)
27. Mascherini, Mario
28. Batelli, Corrado (132714)
29. Luisi, Pietro
30. Pavesi, Ruggero (129028)
31. Motta, Adamastorio (112055)
32. Corali, Uggero
33. Colombo, Filippo (5726)
34. Bonafede, Eugenio
35. Gorini, Pietro
36. Diana, Pietro (127760)
37. Pisani, Santiago (18410)
38. Rubini, Giuseppe
39. Landini, Enea (98359)
40. Amorini, Carlo
41, Canale, Aurelio (126889)
42. Diano, Consolato
43. Donati, Enzo (127587)
44. Braga, Fausto (11968)
45. Ercolani, Enrico (8344)
46. Calderara, Giuseppe
47. Fantoni, Luciano (128048)
48. Bandinelli, Rinaldo
49. Nannucci, Guglielmo (124712)
50. Donadio, Aristide
51. Bientinesi, Armando (111988)
52. Dardanelli, Matteo (22352)
53. Crespi, Enrico (3636
54. Levi, Gualtiero
55. Gramsci, Gennaro (47095)
56. Sabbatini, Sergio (3599)
57. Clerico, Liberato (123682)
58. Coldra, Giacomo
59. Neri, Ermanno (125092)
60. **Gimene, Antonio** [*sic*]
61. Mantovani, Angelo (18601)
62. Martinet, Giovanni
63. Rossi, Lodovico (3654)
64. Seles, Antonio

65. Paoli, Antonio (83180)
66. Gabbani, Giuseppe (125752)
67. Milani, Giacomo
68. Pavese, Ruggero (129028)
69. Benussi, Carlo (75978)
70. Rosati, Domenico (25538)
71. Ardemagni, Massimo (136350)
72. Sestan, Lodovico
73. Rolando, Pietro (132925)
74. Zazzu, Giovanni (57318)
75. Margarita, Ilario (23274)
76. Mengati, Ettore
77. Vezzulli, Giovanni (42719)
78. Primi, Enrico (131607)
79. Querin, Umberto (64195)
80. Aldighieri, Carlo
81. Bertola, Ernesto
82. Sternini, Rolando
83. Scanziani, Romeo
84. Giusti, Lorenzo (93756)
85. Franchi, Ferdinando (3964)
86. Massera, Pietro
87. Montacci, Angelo (115962)
88. Bregoli, Dino
89. Checchi, Luigi (p8297)
90. Martini, Giovanni (112242)
91. Montresor, Gaetano
92. Tortolini, Corrado (112493)
93. Giuduci, Mario (125560)
94. Pedrazzini, Enrico (120029)
95. Di Pompeo, Vincenzo
96. Premoli, Piero (129109)
97. Matteuzzi, Carlo
98. Minzoni, Cesare (135763)
99. Virgilio, Giovanni
100. Mangraviti, Placido (124421)
101. Wladimiro Dabichevich
102. Frossini, Adolfo
103. Frossini, Luciano

104. Frossini, Guglielmo
105. Frossini, Roberto
106. Frossini, Guerino
107. Frossini, Carlo
108. Rizzotto, Leonardo
109. Cetin, Pietro (135012)
110. Chervatin, Fernando (121144)
111. Valcica, Biagio
112. Giacomelli, Cornelio (43314)
113. Guerrieri Settimo (86102)
114. Vautero (38704)
115. Tosi Muzio (79759)
116. Pesce, Giuseppe
117. Zambonini, Enrico (31376)

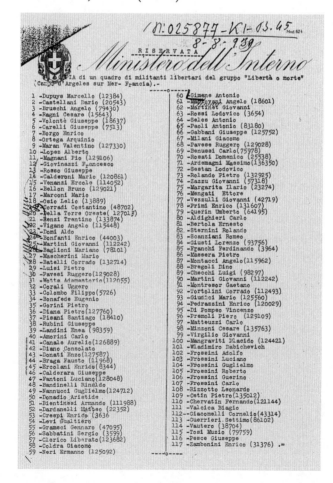

Appendix VII

MIMOSA'S JOURNAL

My Campaign Diary.
Thoughts to Remain Unspoken,
Letters to Remain Unsent.
Poems. Musings...

Friday, September 18, 1936. [Pages 2–6 are missing]

7.

My comrades! These are my comrades ... I wanted my soul
unblemished ... do I like them, though? Is it them that I like? No, it is
life, the life force for which they do not display enough respect.

My comrades! This swarm that gets intoxicated on noisy music,
dresses up in tawdry jewelry and douses itself in cheap scent! ... How
we have to love these crazies shrieking the "Internationale," though,
and teach them kindness ... and the other side too if possible, but, alas,
the other side are wild beasts ... as well.

How many lives will come to an untimely end because of this taste
for hymns from which they all drink so deeply?

My heart is moved to pity for them all; may my soul be forgiving
and let us reach out to them with healing hands and calming words ...
And words of courage.

9/21/36

8.

Departure.
Overcast, unsettled weather. We set off. Paris still sleeping. Not off

685

to some gilded future or to the great inner forests that ennoble men's souls and thoughts; so what does lie ahead of us? My comrades do not even pose the question; they are racing flat out simply because Man is an animate being like all the rest. These guys are communists, not especially less intelligent than the rest (mmm, communists and intelligence?!), but they have been turned into fanatics by orders handed down but never questioned, they have soaked up the message of their leaders like some harmful drug and are blinded by ignorance.

On we race, our car laden down with the accoutrements of life and death, items that heal and items that kill. The latter are weighty and all the weightier to my mind and to my heart, for they lie heavy upon my mind, which craves mercy and kindness.

9.

The other side carries contraptions for killing a people that do not believe as they believe, people that will never submit the way that they have done and, let us hope, will never become what they represent today. The others, the communists, the titans of the revolution in the USSR, do they know the satisfaction of things done well, a soul at peace? And will they summon up strength tomorrow? Revolutions do not honor their promises, revolutionaries sell out, apostles are murdered ... On we roll as I think about all that, about you, G. Meyer, my dear great friend, about you, Michel, my *compagnon*, my husband, all lucid and vast intelligence. On we race ... Did I do the right thing, leaving everything behind, did I do right? I'd like to think so, but I have my doubts. By Perpignan we are already in the revolutionary zone; Liaison Committee, Surveillance Committee, questioning, scrutinizing papers. The comrades are committed, full of energy, diffident, cordial ... We have passed muster.

10.

A female militant, comrade Lucie Golliard, a face of great kindness, consumed by the fire of conviction, by weariness as well, and then again, there is infinite sadness in that high-browed face with its onyx eyes, sunken cheeks, and over-wide weary mouth. She too, as she admits to me, has her doubts, but she carries on with the fight nevertheless. *La bonne* Louise, *la grande*, must have borne a resemblance to her. Finally, someone who will understand, someone I can talk to, who will not laugh, the good comrade.

We pull out of Perpignan, darkness falls, it is raining and dismal; the sun has set in a swift fiery glow and we are a lot more sensible of worrisome things, by contrast. We press on cautiously, the road being greasy and our cargo dangerous. This time we have some Perpignan comrades along with us; one of them knows the customs officials; we will be crossing the border ...

11.

Long, half-whispered conversations, scrutiny of papers, a station under the falling rain and an arrangement is arrived at and we are on Spanish soil; the first house on the far side of the border is a café; we step inside to toast our arrival with an aperitif. The French customs officer keeps us company and appears to have a soft spot for the taste of the stronger absinthes (but let us not speak ill of that, for he is a comrade). We are worn out and the storm rumbles on, yet off we go again.

Our French comrades are still escorting us; we are in a land in ferment and precautions must be taken; the talk here is more vigorous and we know that speechifying is no counter to an unanswered ... unanswerable ... gunshot. We press slowly onward, the darkness rent by lightning bolts, the rain pelting down on the roof and the raindrops rolling down the windows like pearls.

We really do look as if we are on the run.

12.

Are we evil-doers? ... maybe so ... we shall see.

Militiamen keep watch along the roads from roadblocks made of bags filled with earth and stones and erected at 25–30 kilometer intervals.

We know the passwords and the signal: headlights extinguished and flashed three times, three toots on the horn. We pass through little villages as pretty as scenery, so old and curious you would say they were imperturbable miniature fortresses. They do not appear to have suffered; the militia keeps watch anyway. It won't take us long to learn this. The rain has stopped and we proceed somewhat more quickly. A roadblock that we had failed to spot, some shouting and we are surprised to find ourselves being arrested, interrogated and held at gunpoint by the owner of a superb Browning. Meanwhile, gallantry still has its place and the magnificent human animal beside me forgets the cause,

13.

the revolution and everything else so as to gesture that he means to be pleasant to me. To be honest, his timing was very poor and I am consumed by annoyance and anxiety. However, all that evening this delightful suitor was to bombard me with choice compliments and every consideration.

We finally reached Figueras where we were going to sleep. We were greeted there by the revolutionary committee, by the war committee, and we bumped into a number of French comrades. They all but threw a party for us.

We will be setting off again tomorrow morning for Barcelona, our journey's end. A militia will escort us and we'll pass through many more roadblocks.

Between Figueras and Barcelona our eyes drink in the magnificent scenery. We skirt the coast; on our

14.

right, the mountains with their pine trees and saw palmettos, and, here and there, red-earthed fields with gnarled, twisted olive trees, tortured by the wind.

Finally we are there. The revolution has passed this way! God of Mercy, you do not exist!

The Generalitat palace is a teeming anthill; we drop by for visitors' passes and make a thousand acquaintances. How busy things are, here in the workshop of slaughter! We go from office to office and eventually to the CNT headquarters in the mansion that once belonged to the well-known economist, Cambó. It is a real palace, radiating a beauty and harmony that no longer serve any purpose. All this wealth is still respected and the mansion is open to the wide-eyed populace. Its splendor commands respect and they are filled with wonder … and fears … their dreams were less beautiful.

15.

1st day in Barcelona.

I saw nothing last evening, nothing … ! Behold! However, it is terrifying, houses emptied of everything, bereft of doors and windows, gutted, smoke stains on the façades, and white trails like worm-casts; bullets made those marks.

Everything has either shut down or been commandeered. This Monday, the city is dead. Only toward evening do the Ramblas liven up momentarily. The Spain that only wakes up in the evenings is now asleep from 11:30; the cafés are closed, the lights extinguished, there is no music, no theater, nothing … nothing. Or yes, there is the radio, blaring out news that I cannot fathom and trumpeting the "Internationale."

The only cars circulating, banners fluttering in the breeze, are in the service of the organizations; no private vehicles. Soldiers set off for the Zaragoza front, they sing

16.

and lots of them will perish there, they sing the anthem of revolutions, they are brave and fierce. Will Mercy some time have its day in this world?

I chat at length with some militiamen. What they have told me is so horrifying, how can I dare set it down in writing? These men are sound, it is said, but they horrify me; they have blood on their hands and I shudder as I offer them mine. They have killed, every one of these men has killed … lest they be killed. I am going crazy, yet I do not want for courage.

The die has been cast and I too am on my way to the front, as I expressly requested. I reckon I may never come back, but that is of no matter, my life having always been sour, and there is no such thing as happiness. Happiness has no face, no store cupboards and no colors and I have never been able to find it.

I had treasures of tenderness, desires

17.

that did not consist of the suffering of others and I was never able to give enough and have been given nothing, more's the pity!

Am I to teach all these hotheads that they are scorning the only thing that is real, the only thing! ... Living, breathing life, the sort that watches the opening of the buds, the rising of the sun and the stars in the heavens?

Happiness! You can have no idea how I have quested after it; I can scarcely remember myself; in serious books, in questionable beds, in the simplicity of things. At last I am to set off, happiness?! Is it perhaps the repose of burned out souls?

18.

2nd day.

I have looked again at the ancient locations, the promenades, the churches, the works of art. Tombs and rubble strewn in my path. Here and there, on the ground, heaps of already mouldering flowers: Here perished Juan Fernández, here Ascaso, here somebody else. And the looming great skeletons of the churches. The soul has been driven out. Whether this is a good thing, tomorrow will tell. What I know right now is that it is not good to overthink, yet in my head this ferments like it was a brand new bin and despite all the countless demands problems arise that have no possible solution. I mingle with the people, with the simple fellow, eager to learn and compare; what they tell me is terrifying, nightmarish and I am morally sickened in a sort of a mental hangover.

19.

Some French miliciens, smug, proud, and self-satisfied, tell me: at night, in Barcelona city, people are being lifted who are barely suspect and, without a trial, being executed. Twenty people died that way only a few days ago, having been taken out toward Tibidabo. Another three individuals were shot in the Calle Córcega. On the night of July 19–20, the prison gates were thrown open and the men newly released were armed. Alas, they did not understand and did not do what was expected of them but headed back to their haunts in the Barrio Chino. After which there were some carry-ons, orgies. The newly freed and armed underworld carried out lots of bloody deeds and those who had yearned to see these creatures set free had to cut them down like mad dogs. Barcelona,

20.

freed from the fascist gangs, was forced to fight against the human dregs it had planned to save. In the Barrio Chino, there were three days of executions.

Other miliciens talked to me and told me lots of other even more hateful tales. In both camps, it is kill, kill, and a human life is worth no more than the life of an insect.

I spotted my old friend Ferry again, an old acquaintance; he knows everything and everybody knows him and he can access all areas, he has the gift of the gab and knows a thousand and one odd things, he's a liar but means well, full of heart and fire but not that brave; he's the typical gallant lover one finds everywhere, as ugly as a monkey and he loves me like a lap-dog. Two years on and he hasn't forgotten me. He discovered that I was here and within ten minutes he was at my side. He's a

21.

delightful friend who talks a lot and takes the utmost care of me. So I will be tolerant of his shortcomings. My old pal Ferry grants my every whim, showing me around the hospital, introducing me and acting as my interpreter, walking me around and explaining things to me and he also gets a kick out of scaring me with his tales of fire and blood, true stories, alas!

We also visited some warships—waging war is all the men think about—and put out to sea at dusk. The port is dismal, the light fading and someone had thrown a vast veil over the whole earth. I am sick, weary, drained and we talked and argued too much. Evolution, barbarism, revolution, philosophy, continuity, race spirit ... Yes, we talked far too much and I am still drunk from it ... True, Ferry does take the greatest care of me. I feel

22

as I have been left dangling and must get some sleep or I'm done for.

3rd Day

Arthur. You may not know who Arthur is; he's a Parisian chum I bumped into here quite by accident. A not very likable chum! A swaggering liar of no significance and quite cowardly. He's off back to France tomorrow. I spent the morning with him ... a stroll, making observations and sorting out papers. I'm filled with mistrust and this bird who I have known a long time has nothing good to tell me. We visit an artist friend of his. Simple-minded, bourgeois, honest, humane. I get an invitation and I will be back; all I have seen are wild beasts and this guy is not one of them, yet already I am warming to this mediocrity.

I am waiting for my travel warrant. God but it is awful, living in expectation of uncertain tomorrows. The comrades are off in columns, fists raised, minds at ease, no hint of doubt in their minds. Many

23.

set off to fight the way one would set off on a stroll, or to the running of the bulls, and besides, the mentality is often the same; ferociousness beginning to stir itself. The love of stop-start, the taste for paroxysm, the cruelty without hate ... are these not the features of this Spanish people which is nothing but refinement contrasted against vulgarity, laziness and sensuality; a blend of good taste and kitsch, idleness and violence clashing with each other.

I am very uneasy and I'd like to write to Paris. I left behind me there two creatures who I cherish for different reasons, two men that I love, to own up to a thousand thoughts to the two halves of my heart. I can expect no answers and I can provide no return address as I will be leaving tomorrow or in three days' time and cherished letters go astray.

24.

One can get used to anything and the horrors that are spoken about are starting to turn, for me, into the sort of stories one reads; I have adopted a literary stance and am applying myself to the belief that I dreamed all this and committed it to paper. I am not very proud of myself. However, I thought I had more gumption. Ferry and I are becoming inseparable; he is as infatuated as an old tomcat and still deliciously agreeable. We have had lunch together and this evening he brought me out to the suburbs for a Basque handball championship; he played, but mascot I am not and he lost the match!

I am not cut out for resolving certain problems that crop up indiscreetly and, morally, I am snagged in a barbed wire

25.

net.

There was a funeral march playing below my window today and bodies retrieved from the front lines were paraded through the town; the army and the crowd walked behind. These are people that want to better themselves, yet like half-savages they parade their dead, under the usual colors and come to pray over human remains.

Now I know, and I have properly understood that this civil war horror is going to continue right down to the last drop of blood, right down to the last breath of the last man in one camp or the other.

There are a lot of French hereabouts. Some are believers, others adventurers and the rest are communists, which is to say, nothing at all and unduly aggressive with it.

At the hotel, the nosiest of them

26.

if not the most pleasant a guy who is twice a marquis, twice a baron and a count, an cultivated adventurer, member of the C[ommunist] P[arty], with an anarchist way about him; he must have a lot of dead bodies on his conscience, he is cynical and I feel very uneasy when he takes my hand in his. However, he appears to have taken a bit of a shine to me—which is undeserved and I don't trust him—and wants to train me to manufacture airplane bombs, he being in charge of that here. Everything here is two-faced, everything lies and that includes things themselves. How is one to get a handle on the true meaning of things ... nothing is true, not a thing and my head is dizzy looking for the essence and interpreting things; but I cannot find the essence and, what is worse, I cannot get my bearings at all. I think I am becoming seriously ill. There are no

27.

specific symptoms and everything is very vague and as unfathomable as my life and my thoughts; the world surrounding me I perceive only through a veil of mist and everything is a blur. I am weary and becoming as skittish as a mouse. Everything deceives me here, everything.

28.

Friday–Sunday.

More than a week now since I left Paris, my Dianoute, and my Mitzou [*her cats*], and for seven days I have been leading this silly, woeful life in a vacant and useless luxury hotel.

I am sick, that much is certain, and weak and weary; languor has fallen out of fashion and these days one is no longer allowed to die of that affliction; however, I must cling to life for what I hope are specific and imminent purposes. I have failed to weather a storm of feelings. Once everything has been said and all my goodbyes are done, I am left with nothing, other than the sour taste of regrets and having to drag this corpse of mine around with me.

I want to be off, to go where maybe everything is forgotten about, where mine can be the rescuing hand and where I might perhaps be loved a little.

29.

Last evening, Ferry, his partner, and a few friends threw me a party ... why, I have no idea. They made me drink and smoke, and I am drinking far too much at present to go on without contradicting myself—and the outcome is a disaster.

30.

The rebels sow terror. They have resurrected the Inquisition. The miliciens are leaving for the front: long live the soldiers of the CNT and FAI.

For the very first time the State is run by a revolutionary organization. Will it bring forth errors as the old arrangements did? The new Spain is bent on success and on conjuring up a brand new consciousness; schooling with a taste for Humanity, for Emancipation.

No compromise between the parties; one side or the other has to win. The choice is between the old regime and the new constructive fire.

Franco declares that, should he be facing defeat, he will trigger an incident out of which world war will come.

31.

Do you know what Spain was before the revolution came along? A luxury accommodation for the career military. A mighty church in cahoots with the official authorities.

The people have overthrown that order by banding together into the CNT and against the Church, capitalism, and militarism.

The Republic is straining to take shape. The initiative in the fight does not come from the working class; the ones behind July 19 are out to establish a dictatorship by pitting their troops against the people. The CNT scorned the danger and carried people along. Ascaso perished near the port facing the sea. Barcelona, Valencia, Asturias in the people's hands. The reaction beaten. Franco declares that he will have half the womenfolk shot if that is the price of victory.

32.

After all that was said
The supreme things said
Why suffer on?

I thought I was going to die
Once the words of farewell had been uttered
Yet my breathing has not ceased.

I have carried the despair of many another
Who lived before me
My brain, when it remembers, hurts.

My overlong fingernails and my moist eyelashes
Say that a lot of time has gone by
That was merely suffering at drawing breath far from you.

Others have come and I have shown them my giftless hands
And my heart, beating solely to remember.
Fine summer's mornings are always gray to me.

33.

One day in the succession of days.

Dear God, I shudder, I turn red and then ashen, then green, like a watermelon, and all aquiver; but, sure, didn't I volunteer, wasn't I drawn here? So have I long been anything other than an empty shell, a pained soul bereft of hope, and does the dead weight of illusions not weigh heavily enough upon my chest for me to want to be rid of them?

Yes, I am keen to go and now I am afraid, I knew that I loved the life that made me ill … I did not know, I did not believe that I loved it quite this much.

Who will there be to think as I do, who will remember me when I am no longer

[Pages 34 and 35 are missing here]

36.

One day like any other.

Oh! To sleep, to sleep! No more to see the overflowing sewer spilling into the things I once loved and admired; no more to see crassness, ugliness, ignorance and hate ensconcing themselves the masters' plush armchairs; no more to listen to the prattle of the self-satisfied and the sordid. Oh! to sleep, weary as I am, to forget that I ever came here, to forget that elsewhere there are lives different from the one I lead here! To forget, to forget, can it be done?

Today I wanted to run away and head for home, to love and be loved by a pure being, and two silly creatures, Diane and Mitzou. The comrades?! beg me to stay a while longer but soon I will be off and I will be useful: suffering souls are shortly going to be in need of someone to plead for their lives, lay

37.

down the law and watch over them.

For now, I have nothing to do and shuttle between one office and the next. I have my sight and I languish in sadness;

I arrived here full of courage and goodwill … Alas! What became of all that? Such a loss of heart!

They are looking for a French woman, a blonde, a spy; I have been followed, kept under surveillance, arrested … now that was worth the living.

Before I leave, I am going to live at the barracks like all who serve. In a splendid prison or barracks; much the same thing. All brand-new, immense, with crenellated walls, white, three stories high and splendid pompous names for the whole thing and perimeter walls to guard the mind against itself.

38.

A splendid barracks resembling a perfect fortified castle. We shall laugh, we shall laugh and dance sarabandes in the hope that the end is very nigh.

The revolution!! There is too much talk of it. That it should exist as it does is already too much; it is the only thing that is ever spoken of, that and songs glorifying heroes (they need to be seen from close up) niggle me. This civil war is a mistake on both sides, but who will dare admit it? I have had my fill of the lies justifying and glorifying everything through legends that are embroidered upon with every passing day. There is one hard and incontrovertible fact: everything gives off the stench of putrefaction released by the charnel houses opened up one after the other.

Who is going to say it loud and clear and who is going to set down the truth in writing about the women who left for the front lines; the newspapers talk about them respectfully. Yet on the streets there are misgivings. They just about know already. This is the greatest, the gravest defeat. This problem that I cannot

39.

resolve here raises another question of significance for those who have taken no sides: Who made the revolution? There is, alas, but one very sad answer to that question, but dare I speak it even here on my sole say-so? The very least I could say of it is that it was the ignoramuses, the pretentious, the half-baked, the adventurers and, among that bunch, only the malcontents and tail-ending workers have a case to argue. The prisons have opened and those emerging from them spotted the solution in a life that they had neither loved nor chosen.

There has been much talk of the female militiawomen. They are the sisters of Belleville's Lulu and the *midinettes'* Marilou, cruder and more cruel than the men. Ah! More anon about the graciousness, delicacy and beauty of women ... But where, in all that, is the belief, the grandeur, the good faith of a people out to build upon love and justice

40.

Tuesday, October 4

I haven't made an entry here for the past several days; what was the point? I had only too many dismal matters upon which to make observations. Today, though, I must have my say if I am some day to remind myself of the horrifying aspect of what we are living through.

Saturday, we set off from the Pedralbes barracks; forty of us. Black scarf with the anarchist motto "Neither God nor master" roughly daubed in white with a death's head just like the pirates of the high seas used to display on the prows of their ships. Those of my friends who will be reading this, can you remember the trainloads of men on furlough and the leave-taking back in 1914? We set off as all troops do, under the colors of vulgarity and crassness. My *compañeros* are noisy, drunk, filthy and bereft of any trace of moral decency, a vile debauchery. Every one speaking in Anarchy's name and not one knowing the meaning of the word. As far as they are all concerned, it stands for their self-interest which often consists

41.

of not caring a damn for that of one's neighbor, even should that neighbor be wronged. They are brute beasts. Many have fled France, being escapees, liable to arrest, thieves, murderers and fraudsters. All the dregs make up our column. I have seen what I believe to be the scum of the earth. How can one cling to one's faith in the wake of that? It's dangerous being a woman and I can see it in their looks laden with unsettling feelings, hear it in their obscene talk and indeed in the barely veiled threats directed at me.

We caught the Lérida train. It was nighttime and they were singing, swapping dirty talk, getting drunk and throwing up; I feigned sleep and thereby dodged provocations and having to refuse the favors offered to me. I must not accept anything from these wolves, I need to command respect. In Lérida we had dinner in a former seminary and then it was a stroll into town in search of a billet for the night. We are to leave the city by lorry for Pina de Ebro at seven o'clock in the morning. Come the morning, we were not able to leave, as the lorry

42.

did not show up, adding to the impression of a shambles. We're going to have to hang around outside the railway station all morning. In the end, we set off by coach for the front line, having received neither the arms nor the equipment we were promised … are promises the only weapons we have?!!

We have two hundred kilometers to cover, all packed together and I cannot sit on anyone's knee so am forced to clamber onto the roof of the bus.

After leaving Lérida behind, we can sense that we are in a war zone, with houses demolished and wrecked vehicles … On we roll beneath a sky too blue over a stony wasteland, the road like a gray ribbon, across a white mountain, zig-zagging with dangerous sharp turns across sixty kilometers.

We can feel the front line coming nearer and we are all calm, suddenly impressed and becoming almost fearful. Finally we reach Pina. Once upon a time it was a pretty, whitewashed little village, but there was fighting there recently and there are some [houses] from which smoke, dogs and cats escape.

43.

Pina del [*sic*] Ebro.

We have arrived; the residents have nearly all fled and the ones that remain display great warmth towards us: real or feigned? There has been such a lot of shooting around here! We are billeted in an old house in the square. Miliciens circulate everywhere and we can hear all sort of languages spoken; all the men are looking at me, as are the older peasant women who are rooted to the spot, astounded to see me and looking as if they are taking me to task.

No sooner have I arrived than I make for the hospital, to acquaint myself with the doctors and medical attendants and await my orders.

I am to move up to the front; personnel shortages on the line. I find it hard, though, to drag myself away from the hospital where I was received with such courtesy and indeed kindness.

On the front lines we immediately set about our excavations, building our casemates. Naturally, no one is willing to help me build the pharmacy that will also be serving as my quarters. Like

44.

everybody else, therefore, I help build this ancient ur-village; I have to compete with the men in terms of strength and match them and work as fast as they do and make all of them forget that I am a woman. I set to it as best I can for already the provocations are coming thick and fast, resentments are festering and while it was looking as if keeping my distance and being on friendly terms with everyone might be enough, alas, I am the lone woman and there are two hundred of them!!

It rained that night and on the front we could not bed down, as our huts were not yet finished, so we headed back to the village, leaving some armed comrades to watch over our positions.

At the time of writing, there is the thunder of cannon fire and shells have just exploded 150 meters from my house; our little village has been under shelling for the past two days. We are getting ready to reply here and on the front, where the attack is to be mounted this evening or tomorrow; we await our rifles and munitions. The very first line lies two kilometers from the village; the countryside is beautiful, green and lush,

45.

the mutilation of it is under way, though; here and there the fruit trees have been cut down, the rose beds uprooted, the vegetables and crops trampled. But for the cannon booming nearby and the miliciens scuttling around shouting out, the war might be imaginary, a bad dream and the injuries to the soil barely visible.

Rain. We sleep in haphazard heaps. I have found myself a mattress, alone in a room, hoping for some peace and quiet but it is not long before I am disappointed and soon there comes a scratching at the door; I have barricaded myself inside with everything I could find.

Everything repugnant that Man has about him, in ...

[Document ends]

CHRONOLOGY

1936

July 17
Pronunciamento and mutiny by the Army of Morocco.

July 18
Part of the army revolts across the peninsula. Government leader Casares Quiroga resigns.

July 19
The CNT calls a general strike. The Martínez Barrio government refuses to arm the people and is forced to resign.

July 20
The government makes up its mind to arm the people. José Giral sends a telegram to Léon Blum asking him for weapons. Envoys from Companys turn up that afternoon at a plenum of the Barcelona Local Federation of the CNT: later there is an audience between a CNT delegation (García Oliver, Durruti, Santillán, etc.) in Companys's office; the delegation proposes establishing a revolutionary committee in concert with socialists, communists, Catalanists, the POUM, etc. This marks the inception of the Central Antifascist Militias Committee (CAMC).

July 21
In Barcelona there is a regional plenum of local and sub-regional CNT federations convened by the CNT's Regional Committee for Catalonia; with the exception of the Bajo Llobregat *comarcal* [county] federation, which backed García Oliver's motion that they "go for broke," the decision is made to collaborate and to set up the Antifascist Militias Committee, as well as to postpone the implementation of libertarian communism until after victory over the rebel camp. That evening, right after the CNT plenum, the Central Antifascist Militias Committee is launched; representation on it is as follows: CNT, 3; FAI, 2; UGT, 3; what will shortly become the PSUC, 1; POUM, 1; Esquerra, 3; Rabassaires Union, 1; and Acció Catalana, 1.

July 22
The CAMC meets at the Yacht Club, where it is decided that the task of setting off to attack Zaragoza should be entrusted to Durruti.

July 23
The Nosotros group holds a meeting in the evening, during which García Oliver moves that the deployment of troops under Durruti's orders the following day might be a good opportunity to storm the premises of the

authorities. Durruti speaks out against this and the matter is relegated until after the capture of Zaragoza.

July 24

The Durruti Column leaves Barcelona at 10:00 a.m., bound for Zaragoza, and, en route, liberates a number of places in Aragon. The Sur-Ebro Column, led by Antonio Ortiz also sets off.

July 25

The Ascaso Column moves out with Domingo Ascaso, Gregorio Jover, and Cristóbal Aldabaldetrecu.

The CAMC meets that morning, hearing reports from the Durruti Column, which would have passed Lérida on its way to Zaragoza.

In the wake of talks between Blum and Baldwin, the French government issues its first nonintervention announcement.

August 2

A new Generalidad government is formed, under the chairmanship of Juan Casanovas.

August 5

The Majorca expedition gets under way: upward of five thousand men are committed.

Late August

A plenum of the libertarian movement's Catalonian local and *comarcal* federations meets in Catalonia; the choice between collaboration or "dictatorship" is once again mooted by García Oliver who is all for the CNT's seizing power. The majority opposes this and pushes for collaboration and for participation in the Generalidad, in line with Santillán's recommendation. The FAI Peninsular Committee is in attendance in an observer capacity and the plenum is held in secret.

September 3

The Majorca expedition ends in serious failure.

September 4

The Giral cabinet steps down. Caballero forms a new government. Spearheaded by Mira's *agrupación* and the International Group, the push against Siétamo begins.

September 12

Siétamo is captured.

September 15

A national plenum of CNT Regionals is held in Madrid, at which the proposal is put forth that a National Defense Council based on the CNT and UGT be formed.

September 16

With a view to setting up some sort of coordinating body for the 420 Aragonese collectives, a meeting is held in Bujaraloz, with Durruti and Ortiz in attendance.

September 17

Loporzano, Estrecho Quinto, and Monte Aragón are overrun in the wake of the fall of Siétamo.

September 24–26

A regional plenum of the CNT's *sindicatos únicos* meets in Barcelona. The CNT's entry into the Generalidad government (redubbed the "Generalidad Council") is finally endorsed in a decision kept secret until the 27th.

September 27

The Generalidad Council takes shape. The CNT joins the Catalan government with three "councilors" (Juan Fábregas, José Doménech, and Antonio García Birlán). The CNT national secretary, Horacio Prieto, is called to the Ministry of War by Caballero, who addresses the assembled representatives of the Popular Front on the necessity of the government's leaving Madrid. Prieto is against this, and the matter is put off until a later date.

October 1

The Generalidad disbands the CAMC. García Oliver is appointed general secretary of defense.

October 6

In Bujaraloz, the CNT in Aragon holds an extraordinary plenum of its unions, plus representatives from the confederation's columns. The decision is made to set up an Aragonese Regional Defense Council, based in Fraga. Military matters remain under the remit of the Generalidad.

October 8

The Generalidad's Defense Council holds a meeting designed to establish a high command for Aragon: Díaz Sandino, Durruti, Villalba, del Barrio, Ortiz, Rovira, and Pérez Salas attend.

October 10

An order establishes the People's Army. Largo Caballero is made supreme commander.

October 18

In Madrid, Largo Caballero calls a meeting of Popular Front representatives, plus the CNT (which is represented by Horacio Prieto). The matter of the government's leaving Madrid is raised again, but Horacio Prieto is still opposed to this. In the wake of this meeting there are discreet talks between Largo Caballero and Horacio Prieto to finalize the entry into the government of four anarchist ministers, the CNT imposing its right to choose its ministerial appointees, conditional upon Durruti's being sent to Madrid. That evening, after a national plenum has just given its endorsement to the principle of anarchists joining the government, Horacio Prieto, Juan López, and Pedro Falomir pay Caballero a visit to inform him of that decision.

October 19

Horacio Prieto travels to Barcelona to smooth over the lingering reluctance of the Catalan anarchists to endorse the resolution passed by the previous day's plenum. He meets Durruti, who refuses to go to Madrid. The first International Brigade volunteers arrive in Albacete.

October 22

A united action agreement is signed between the anarchists and communists (CNT-FAI-UGT-PSUC) in Catalonia. The two movements commit to bolstering the authority of the Generalidad and to the elimination of "gangs of uncontrollables (*incontrolados*)."

October 23

Plenum of CNT Regionals meets in Madrid. The CNT sues for a place in the government, provided the conditions set by the September 15 plenum of Regionals can be met. It threatens to blockade the capital in the event that it is rejected. The issue is the establishment of a National War Committee as a prelude to unification of the Catalonia, Aragon, Levante, and Andalusia fronts and mobilization of the confederal forces, as many as 100,000 men.

October 24

The Generalidad passes decrees designed to provide a framework for collectivization and to impose militarization on the militias.

October 25

The Spanish government ships 510 tons of gold to the USSR; this amounts to two-thirds of the Bank of Spain's gold reserves.

November 1

The Generalidad's militarization decree comes into effect. Durruti signs a document opposing militarization.

November 4

The CNT joins the government of the Republic. García Oliver becomes minister of justice, and his place on the secretariat of the Generalidad's Defense Department passes to Juanel.

4:00 p.m. A cabinet meeting is held at the War Ministry where Largo Caballero announces that the government is to leave Madrid for Valencia.

Durruti delivers an important radio address to the workers of Spain; it is severely censored by the press, including the CNT press.

November 5–6

The Generalidad calls an extraordinary meeting of column commanders in Barcelona. Durruti agrees to lead a column that is to be sent to Madrid's aid.

November 6

The government relocates to Valencia, and General Miaja is left in charge of the capital's defenses as the head of a brand new defense junta; overnight, Vicente Rojo is appointed as chief of staff.

November 7

Madrid puts up an expectedly fierce resistance, spurred on by the pugnaciousness of the people of Madrid. Combatants fleeing from the front lines gather in Madrid and dig in.

November 8

At around 6 o'clock in the morning, a thousand-strong column of anarcho-syndicalist volunteers, with Cipriano Mera as its political delegate, arrives in Madrid from Cuenca.

November 9

Mera's men move up to the firing line. In Valencia, a Supreme Council of War is established, being a handpicked cabinet to handle military affairs.

November 12
The International Brigades enter the fray in Madrid.
November 13
Part of the Durruti Column (its 1st *Agrupación* under the command of José Mira, the 8th under Liberto Ros, and three *centurias*, about 1,400 men in all) pass through Barcelona en route to the Madrid front.
November 15
The Durruti Column, with a War Committee made up of Miguel Yoldi and Ricardo Rionda, assisted by José Manzana and Francisco Mora, arrives in Madrid during the morning.
November 18
A national plenum of CNT Regionals meets in Valencia, where Horacio Prieto tenders his resignation. His place is taken by Mariano Rodríguez Vázquez.
November 19
Durruti is seriously wounded in the vicinity of the Clinical Hospital this afternoon.
November 20
Durruti dies in Madrid at around 4 o'clock in the morning. Ricardo Sanz is appointed to take over from him in Madrid, while Manzana is to replace him in Aragon. But really it is Ruano who will take charge there.
December 12
Andrés Nin, the Generalidad's minister of Justice, steps down.
December 13
The Generalidad is thrown into crisis for the first time.
December 25
The Council of Aragon is legislated into existence.
December 28
Justice minister García Oliver passes a decree establishing labor camps.

1937

January 15
The Council of Aragon orders the establishment of a people's court in Caspe.
February 5
At the invitation of the Iron Column, there is a get-together of confederal columns.
February 14–15
A congress convened by the CNT regional Committee meets in Caspe. A Regional Federation of Collectives is established alongside the Council of

Aragon, which is deemed unduly governmental. José Mavilla is elected as its secretary.

March 15–16

The Aragon CNT holds a regional plenum; a revolutionary minority is critical of the disproportionate representation accorded to the political parties within the Council of Aragon and the negative role of its departments for economy and agriculture. The Cinca *comarcal* federation (represented by José Alberola) calls for the dissolution of the Council.

April 12

The Barcelona anarchist groups hold a local plenum, with the CNT Defense Groups and the Libertarian Youth taking part. The decision is made to lobby the CNT's representatives to walk out of the Generalidad government and to establish a Revolutionary Council by federating all the Defense Groups. The plenum further decides to place all of them on alert.

April 21

Madrid's Delegate Defense Junta steps down.

April 27

Negrín's carabineers recover control of the borders from the CNT militia members. In Bellver in Cerdanya there is confrontation, and Antonio Martín, the driving force behind collectivization in the area, is murdered.

May 3–7

Bloodshed in Barcelona. Communists, Catalanists, and the forces of public order on the one hand, clash with the *barrio* Defense Committees *(Barriadas)*, CNT-FAI militia members returned from the front, and groups from the POUM on the other.

May 15

The government of Valencia is plunged into crisis. The communists insist that the POUM be disbanded. Largo Caballero refuses this and is forced into resigning in the face of hostility from the supporters of Juan Negrín and Indalecio Prieto.

May 17

Juan Negrín takes over the government. The CNT, standing by Largo Caballero, declines to join the cabinet (having been offered only two ministries).

June 3

The CNT performs a U turn, waiting in vain to be invited back into the government.

June 5

The Control Patrols are effectively wound up.

June 29

The CNT refuses a place in the new Catalan government.

August 9

Indalecio Prieto sets up the SIM, placing the republican Sayagües in charge, who is then replaced by the socialist Uribarry.

August 11

The Council of Aragon is dissolved. The Líster Column attacks the collectives and the Council of Aragon.

September 21
The CNT Defense Committees are effectively disbanded.

1938

March 7
The Francoists push through Aragon, bound for the Mediterranean coast.
April 6
The CNT returns to government, represented by Segundo Blanco as minister of public education.
April 15
The "Nationalists" reach the Medieterranean at Viñaroz, cutting the Republic's territory into two zones.
September 21
Juan Negrín, addressing the League of Nations, moves that all foreigners fighting in Spain be withdrawn.
October
A communist show trial of the leadership of the POUM gets under way. The International Brigades begin their withdrawal.
November 15
The International Brigades formally leave Spain. There is a farewell parade through Barcelona.

1939

January 26
Barcelona is captured. The populace makes for the French border.
February 9
Antoine Gimenez leaves Spain via Portbou.
February 10
Catalonia is entirely overrun by the Francoists.
March 5–6
Establishment of a National Defense Council in Madrid under the leadership of Casado, with support from the CNT of the Center region.
April 1
Franco proclaims that the war is over.

BIBLIOGRAPHY

BOOKS AND REVIEWS

Listed here are only those publications that we ourselves have used, but anyone in search of a more panoramic viewpoint is referred to Salvador Gurruchari's very useful *Bibliografía del anarquismo español, 1869–1975* (Barcelona: La Rosa de Foc, 2004).

À contretemps, no. 8 (June 2002), "Louis Mercier 1914–1977."
À contretemps, no. 10 (December 2002), "Diego Abad de Santillán 1987–1983."
À contretemps, no. 14–15 (December 2003), "Georges Navel 1904–1993."
À contretemps, no. 17 (July 2004), "Juan García Oliver 1902–1980."
À contretemps, no. 21 (October 2005), "Nietzsche et l'anarchisme."
Abel, Werner, and Enrico (Hrsg.) Hilbert. *"Sie werden nicht durchkommen!" Band 1: Deutsche an der Seite der Spanischen Republik under sozialen Revolution.* Lich: Edition AV, 2015.
Acciai, Enrico. *Viaggio attraverso dell'antifascismo. Volontariato internazionale e Guerra civile spagnola: la Sezione Italiana della Colonna Ascaso.* Unversità degli Studi della Tuscia: Viterbo, 2010. See http://unitus-distu.academia.edu/EnricoAcciai.
Ackelsberg, Martha A. *Free Women of Spain: Anarchism and the Struggle for the Emancipation of Women.* AK Press; Oakland, 2005.
Aïache, Daniel. *La Révolution défaite. Les groupements révolutionnaires parisiens face à la révolution espagnole.* Paris: Noir et Rouge, 2013.
Alba, Víctor. *Los colectivizadores.* Barcelona: Laertes, 2001.
Amorós, Miguel. *La revolución traicionada. La verdadera historia de Balius y Los Amigos de Durruti.* Barcelona: Virus, 2003.
———. *Durruti dans le labyrinthe.* Paris: Encyclopédie des Nuisances, 2007.
———. *Durruti en el laberinto.* Barcelona: Virus, 2014 (an expanded Spanish version of the above).
———. *Francisco Carreño, el arduo y largo camino de la anarquía.* Montevideo, Uruguay: La Turba Ediciones, 2014.

————. *Pablo Ruiz de Galarreta, un sastre navarro en la revolución anarquista.* Vitoria: Asociación Isaac Puente, 2004.

Anonyme (José Mira Martínez). *La 26 División.* Barcelona: Sindicato de la Metalurgia, CNT, 1938.

Antonioli, Maurizio, Giampiero Berti, Santi Fedele, and Pasquale Iusa, eds. *Dizionario biografico degli anarchici italiani*, vols. 1–2. Pisa: Biblioteca Franco Serantini, 2003 and 2004.

Arcarazo García, Luis Alfonso, Pedro Barrachina Bolea, Fernando Martínez de Baños Carrilo. *Guerra Civil Aragón*, vol. 5, *Huesca "el cerco."* Zaragoza: Delsan, 2007.

Arnal Pena, Jesús. *Yo fuí secretario de Durruti.* Andorra: Mirador del Pirineu, 1972.

Aróstegui, Julio, and Jesús A. Martinez. *La Junta de Defensa de Madrid.* Madrid: Comunidad de Madrid, 1984.

Artís-Gener, Avel·li. *Viure i veure/1.* Barcelona: Pòrtic, 1989.

Bakunin, Mikhail. *Bakunin on Violence. Letter to S. Nechayev.* New York: Unity Press, 19–.

Balance: Cuaderno de historia, no. 38 (2014): Special Issue: "Correspondencia entre Diego Camacho ("Abel Paz") y Juan García Oliver." Barcelona: September 2014.

Balestri, Alba. *La Section italienne de la colonne Ascaso.* Saint-Georges d'Oléron: Éditions Libertaires, 2015.

Barrachina Bolea, Pedro. "Campaña de 1936. Primeros combates. Alrededores de Huesca." In *Guerra Civil Aragón*, vol. 5, *Huesca "El cerco,"* edited by Luis Alfonso Arcarazo García, Pedro Barrachina Bolea, and Fernando Martínez de Baños Carrillo. Zaragoza: Delsan, 2007.

————. "La Guerra de columnas en el frente de Zaragoza (verano e invierno de 1936)" in *Guerra Civil Aragón*, vol. 7, *Zaragoza*, edited by FernandoMartínez de Baños Carrillo. Zaragoza: Delsan, 2010.

Barrio, José del. *Memorias políticas y militares.* Barcelona: Pasado & Presente, 2013.

Bayer, Osvaldo. *The Anarchist Expropriators.* AK Press/KSL: Oakland, 2015.

Benet, Josep. *Domènec Latorre, afusellat per catalanista.* Barcelona: Edicions 62, 2003.

Berner, Rudolf. *Die unsichtbare Front: Bericht über die illegal Arbeit in Deutschland (1937).* Berlin: Libertad Verlag, 1997.

Berneri, Camillo. *Epistolario inedito, volume secondo.* Pistoia: Archivio Familia Berneri, 1984.

————. *Guerra de clases en España, 1936–1937.* Barcelona: Tusquets, 1977.

————. *Guerre de classes en Espagne 1936–1937 et textes libertaires.* Paris: Spartacus, 1977.

Berry, David. "French Anarchists in Spain, 1936–1937," in *French History*, 3, no. 4 (1989), 427–65.

———. "French Anarchist Volunteers in Spain, 1936–39: Contribution to a Collective Biography of the French Anarchist Movement." At http://raforum.site/spip.php?article2721.

———. *A History of the French Anarchist Movement 1917–1945*. London, Greenwood Press, 2002.

———. *A History of the French Anarchist Movement 1917 to 1945*. Oakland: AK Press, 2009. An expanded version of the above.

———. *Le Mouvement anarchiste en France, 1917–1945*. Saint-Georges d'Oléron and Paris: Éditions Libertaires and Noir et Rouge, 2014. A French translation of the 2009 edition above.

———. "Solidarité internationale antifasciste: les anarchistes français et la guerre civile d'Espagne." In *Les Français et la guerre d'Espagne. Actes du colloque de Perpignan*, edited by Jeans Sagnes and Sylvie Caucanas, 73–78. Perpignan: Presses Universitaires de Perpignan, 1990.

Berthuin, Jérémie. *De l'espoir a la désillusion. La CGT-SR et la révolution espagnole. Juillet 1935–Décembre 1937*. Paris: CNT-RP, 2000.

Besnard, Pierre. "Rapport moral" *[présenté par le secrétaire de l'AIT au Congrès extraordinaire de l'AIT à Paris, décembre 1937]*. unpublished. IISH, CNT, package 61 D5.

Bolloten, Burnett. *The Spanish Revolution: The Left and the Struggle for Power during the Civil War*. Chapel Hill: University of North Carolina Press, 1978.

Borrás, José. *Aragón en la revolución española*. Barcelona: César Viguera, 1983.

Broué, Pierre. *Staline et la révolution. Le cas espagnol (1936–1939)*. Paris: Fayard, 1993.

Camacho, Ariel, and Phil Casoar. "Le petit phalangiste." *Revue XXI*, no. 12 (Autumn 2010).

Campos Crespo, Antonio. *Guerra y Cárcel en España, 1936–1975*. Barcelona; Virus, 1999.

Carpena, Pepita. *De toda la vida. Mémoires*. Paris & Brussels: Le Monde libertaire and Alternative libertaire, 2000.

Carrasquer, Félix. *Les Collectivités d'Aragon. Espagne 36–39*. Paris: CNT-RP, 2003.

Casanova, Julián. *Anarquismo y revolución en la sociedad rural aragonesa, 1936–1938*. Madrid: Siglo XXI, 1985, reissued 2006.

Casoar, Phil, and Lucien Feuillade. "Itinéraire François-Charles Carpentier." *Le Monde libertaire*, no. 708 (May 19, 1988).

Cattini, Giovanni C. "Anarquistes italiens a l'Espanya republicana. La visió di Giuseppe Ruozi." *Afers*, no. 37 (2000): 713–29.

Centro Studi P. Gobetti and AICVAS (Associazione Italiana Combattenti

Volontari Antifascisti in Spagna) Sez. Piemontese. *Antifascisti piemontesi e valdostani nella Guerra di Spagna.* Guanda: Parma, 1975. With introductory note by Anello Poma.

Colera Vidal, José. *La Guerre d'Espagne vue de Barcelone. Mémoires d'un garde civil républicain (1936–1939).* Paris: Cygne, 2008.

Collectif. *Actes du colloque Han Ryner, Marseille 28 et 29 septembre* 2002. Marseilles: CIRA and Les Amis de Han Ryner, 2003.

———. *Présence de Louis Mercier.* Lyon: Atelier de création libertaire, 1999.

Corman, Mathieu. *"Salud camaradas!" Cinq mois sur les fronts d'Espagne.* Paris: Tribord, 1937. (Republished Brussels: Aden, 2010.)

Cruells, Manuel. *Mayo sangriento, Barcelona 1937.* Barcelona: Juventud, 1970.

Dauvé, Gilles. *When Insurrections Die* (London: Antagonism Press, 1999), https://libcom.org/library/when-insurrections-die.[1]

Degen, Hans-Jurgen, and Helmut Ahrens. "Wir sind es leid, die Ketten zu tragen." In *Antifaschisten im Spanische Bürgerkrieg.* Berlin: Jakobsohn, 1979.

Delperrié de Bayac, Jacques. *Les Brigades internationals.* Marabout: 1985. Initially published in 1968 by Fayard.

Di Lembo, Luigi. "La sezione italiana della Colonna Francisco Ascaso." *Revista storica dell'anarchismo,* no. 2 (2001).

———. *Guerra di classe et lotta umana. L'anarchismo in Italia, del biennio rosso alla Guerra di Spagna, 1919–1939.* Pisa: Biblioteca Franco Serantini, 2001.

Díez, Xavier. *El anarquismo individualista en España (1923–1938).* Barcelona: Virus, 2007.

Díez Torre, Alejandro. *Orígenes del cambio regional y turno del pueblo Aragón, 1900–1938,* 2 vols. Madrid and Zaragoza: UNED & Universidad de Zaragoza, 2003.

Einstein, Carl. *La Columna Durruti y otros artículos y entrevistas de la Guerra Civil española.* Barcelona: Mudito, 2006.

Einstein, Carl, and Henry Kahnweiler. *Correspondance, 1921–1939.*

---

[1] The text we have used is a version dating from 1999, but revised and expanded as compared with the 1998 ADEL edition, which was itself a wholly revamped version of Gilles Dauvé's foreword to Jean Barrot, *Bilan, Contre-révolution en Espagne 1936–1939,* 10/18 (Paris: UGE, 1979), under the nom de plume Jean Barrot. The text is an interesting one, but marred by a few roughnesses, notably where certain statements credited to Durruti are concerned. And then there are the sweeping statements that prevent us from grasping how reality appeared to the men and women committed to that revolution and its actual conflicts.

Marseilles: André Dimanche, 1993.

Enzensberger, Hans Magnus. *Le Bref Été de l'anarchie. La vie et la mort de Buenaventura Durruti.* Paris: Gallimard, 1980. First French publication in 1975 and original German edition in 1972.

Escribano Bernal, Francisco. "¿Un frente tranquillo?" In *Guerra Civil Aragón*, vol. 2, *Imagenes*, edited by Francisco Escribano Bernal. Zaragoza: Delsan, 2005.

———. ed. *Guerra Civil Aragón*, vol. 2, *Imagenes*. Zaragoza: Delsan, 2005.

Estrade, Paul, ed. *Les Forçats espagnols des GTE de la Corrèze (1940–1944).* Treignac: "Les Monédières," 2004.

Fedeli, Ugo. *Un trentennio di attività anarchica 1914–1945.* Cesena (Forli): Edizioni L'Antistato, 1953.

Franzinelli, Mimmo. *I tentacoli dell'OVRA.* Turin: Bollati Boringhieri, 1999.

Gabriel, José. *La vida y la muerte en Aragón.* Buenos Aires: Ediciones Imán, 1938.

Gallardo Romero, Juan José, and José Manual Márquez Rodríguez. *Ortiz, general sin dios ni amo.* Barcelona: Hacer, 1999.

García García, Miguel. *Miguel García's Story.* Orkney: Cienfuegos Press, 1982.

García Oliver, Juan. *El eco de los pasos.* Paris and Barcelona: Ruedo Ibérico, 1978.

García Velasco, Carlos, Harald Piotrowski, and Sergi Rosés Cordovilla. *Barcelona, mayo 1937. Testimonis desde las barricadas.* Barcelona: Alikornio, 2006.

García Velasco, Carlos, Dieter Nelles, Ulrich Linse, and Harald Piotrowski. *Antifascistas alemanas en Barcelona (1933–1939). El Grupo DAS: sus actividades contra la red nazi y en el frente de Aragón.* Barcelona: Sintra, 2010.

Gimenez, Antoine. *Amori e rivoluzione. Ricirdi di un miliziano in Spagna (1936–1939).* Lugano: La Baronata, 2007.

———. *Del amor, la Guerra y la revolución. Recuerdos de la Guerra de España: del 19 de julio de 1936 al 9 de febrero de 1939.* Logroño: Pepitas de Calabaza, 2004.

Gimenez, Antoine, and Los Gimenólogos. *Del amor, la Guerra y la revolución. Recuerdos de la Guerra de España: del 19 de julio de 1936 al 9 de febrero de 1939,* followed by *En busca de los Hijos de la Noche. Notas sobre los* Recuerdos de la Guerra de España *de Antoine Gimenez.* Logroño: Pepitas de Calabaza, 2009.

Giménez Arenas, Juan. *De la Unión a Banat. Itinerario de una rebeldía.* Madrid: Fundación Anselmo Lorenzo, 1996.

Les Giménologues. *¡A Zaragoza or al charco!* Montreuil and Lagarde: L'Insomniaque and Les Giménologues, 2016.

Gmür, Edi, and Albert Minnig. *"Pour le bien de la révolution": Deux volontaires suisses miliciens en Espagne, 1936–1937.* Lausanne: CIRA, 2006. Translated and introduced by Marianne Enckell.

Godicheau, François. *La Guerre d'Espagne. République et révolution en Catalogne (1936–1939).* Paris: Odile Jacob, 2004.

———. *No Callaron. Las voces de los presos antifascistas de la República (1937–1939).* Toulouse: Presses universitaires du Mirail, 2012.[2]

———. "Répression et ordre public en Catalogne pendant la Guerre Civile (1936–1939)." Unpublished doctoral thesis. Paris: EHESS, 2001.

Graf, Andreas, and Dieter Nelles. *Widerstand und Exil deutscher Anarchisten/Anarchosyndikalisten.* In *Die unsichtbare Front: Bericht über die illegal Arbeit in Deutschland (1937)*, edited by Rudolf Berner. Berlin: Libertad Verlag, 1997.

Grossi Mier, Manuel. *Cartas de Grossi.* Sariñena: Sariñena Editorial, 2009.

Guillamón Iborra, Agustín. *Barricades à Barcelone. La CNT de la victoire de juillet 1936 a la défaite de mai 1937.* Paris: Spartacus, 2009.

———. *Los comités de defensa de la CNT en Barcelona (1933–1938).* Barcelona: Aldarull, 2011. A fourth amended edition was published in 2013. (A French edition was published by Le Coquelicot in 2014.) See also the English-language edition: *Ready for Revolution: The CNT Defense Committees in Barcelona (1933–38).* Oakland: AK Press, 2014.

———. *La Guerra del pan. Hambre y violencia en la Barcelona revolucionaria. De diciembre de 1936 a mayo de 1937.* Barcelona: Aldarull & Descontrol, 2014.

———. *La revolución de los comités. Hambre y violencia en la Barcelona revolucionaria. De julio a diciembre de 1936.* Barcelona: Aldarull and El grillo libertario, 2012.

Habeck, Mary, Ronald Radosh, and Grigory Sevostionov. *Spain Betrayed: The Soviet Union in the Spanish Civil War.* New Haven: Yale University Press, 2001.

Hernández, Jesús. *La Grande Trahison.* Paris: Fasquelle, 1953.

Hirschmann, Ursula. *Nous, sans patrie.* Paris: Les Belles Lettres, 2009.

Huber, Peter, and Nic Ulmi. *Les Combattants suisses en Espagne républicaine, 1936–1939.* Lausanne: Antipodes, 2001.

Inglada, Jesús. "Jesús Salillas Artigas: Un joven de Pina que ha vivido a contarlo." Pina de Ebro. Unpublished.

---

2   Both these books have been reviewed by a Giménologue; the first review appeared in the book review bulletin *À contretemps*, no. 21, and the second on our website.

Iñiguez, Miguel, *Enciclopedia histórica del anarquismo español*. Vitoria: Asociación Isaac Puente, 2008.

Iturbe Arizcuren, Dolores (Lola). *La mujer en la lucha social y en la Guerra civil de España*. Canary Islands and Madrid: Tierra y Fuego and La Malatesta, 2012. First published in 1974.

Izard, Miquel, *Entusiastas olvidados*. Barcelona: Descontrol, 2016.

Jacquier, Charles, *Simone Weil. L'expérience de la vie et le travail de la pensée*. Arles: Sulliver, 1998.

Jimenez de Aberasturi, Luis. *Casilda miliciana. Historia de un sentiment.* Donostia-San Sebastián: Txertoa, 2012. First published in 1985.

Juliá, Santos, *Víctimas de la Guerra civil*. Madrid: Temas de hoy, 1999, reprinted 2004.

Kelsey, Graham. *Anarcosindicalismo y estado en Aragón, 1930–1938*. Madrid: Fundación Salvador Seguí, 1994.

———. "El mito de Buenaventura Durruti." In *El lenguaje de los hechos: ocho ensayos en torno a Buenaventura Durruti*, edited by Antonio Morales Toro and Javier Ortega Perez, 82–85. Madrid: Libros de la Catarata, 1996.

Kirschey, Helmut. *"A las barricadas." Erinnerung und Einsichten eines Antifaschisten.*Wuppertal: Achterland, 2000.

Kröger, Marianne. "Carl Einstein im Spanischen Bürgerkrieg." *Archiv für die Geschichte des Widerstandes und der Arbeit*, no. 12 (1992).

Kröger, Marianne and Roland (Hrsg) Hubert. *Carl Einstein im Exil. Kinst und Politik in den 1930er Jahren*. Münschen: Wilhelm Fink, 2007.

Larraz, Emmanuel. *Le Cinéma espagnol des origines à nos jours*. Paris: Le Cerf, 1986.

Lätt, Nisse. *En svensk anarchist berättar. Minnesbilder ur Nisse Lätt liv som agitator och kämpe för de frihetliga idéerna*. Göteborg/Nittorp: Nisse Lätts Minnesfond, 1993. Manuscript written in Göteborg in 1982.

———. *Milicien et ouvrier agricole dans un collectivité en Espagne*. Toulouse: Le Coquelicot, 2013.

Ledesma, José Luis. *Los días de llamas de la revolución*. Zaragoza: Institución "Fernando el Católico," 2003.

Lee, Laurie. *As I Walked Out One Midsummer Morning*. Boston: Nonpareil Books, 2011.

Léger, Robert. *Entretiens avec Phil Casoar*. Sound recording, Paris: 1984.

Léger, Michel. *De Brigades en brigades*. Breuillet: self-published, 2005.

Leval, Gaston. *Espagne libertaire*. Paris: Éditions du Monde Libertaire, 1983. First published in 1971.

Lladós Tarragó, Josep. *Guerre et exil d'un républicain espagnol, 23 ans, apatride*. Bergerac: self-published, 2010.

————. *Mémoires et entretiens avec Frédéric Alemany, 2005.* Available on our website: http://gimenologues.org/spip.php?article308.

Llarch, Joan. *La muerte de Durruti.* Barcelona: Aura, 1973. This book was reissued in an amended version, by Edicions 29 in Barcelona in 1983: it is the "must read" version.

López Carvajal, Jesús. "Mémoires de ma vie. Mémoires d'un ouvrier anarcho-syndicaliste dans l'Espagne du XXe siècle." Unpublished.

Lorenzo, César M. *Le Mouvement anarchiste en Espagne. Pouvoir et révolution sociale.* (Saint-Georges d'Oléron: Éditions Libertaires, 2006).

Low, Mary, and Juan Brea. *Red Spanish Notebook.* London: Martin Secker & Warburg, 1937. www.marxists.org/history/pain/writers/low-brea/red_spanish_notebook.html.

Lüstiger, Arno. *"Shalom Libertad!" Les Juifs dans la guerre d'Espagne, 1936–1939.* Paris: Le Cerf, 1991.

Madrid Santos, Francisco. *Camillo Berneri, un anarchicio italiano (1897–1937).* Pistoia: Archivio Famiglia Berneri, 1985.

Maitron, Jean, ed. *Dictionnaire biographique du movement ouvrier français.* Paris: Éditions de l'Atelier.

Manfredonia, Gaetano. "Notes sur la participation des anarchistes italiens à la revolution espagnole." *La Rue,* No. 37 (1986).

Marco Pérez, Emilio. *Entretiens avec les auteurs.* Tours: sound recording.

Marculeta, Edmundo. *Las seis muertes de Durruti.* Barcelona: self-published, 1984.

Marín, Ángel. "Hombres y hechos de la Guerra civil española." In *Lo que Dante no pudo imaginar. Mauthausen-Gusen 1940–45,* edited by Amedo Sinca Vendrell, 51–58. Self-published, 1980.

Marín, Dolors. "Han Ryner et la diffusion de sa pensée au sein de l'anarchisme ibérique." In *Actes du colloque Han Ryner, Marseille 28 et 29 septembre 2002,* edited by Collectif. Marseilles: CIRA and Les Amis de Han Ryner, 2003.

Martínez Bande, José Manuel. *La invasion de Aragón y el desembarco en Mallorca.* Madrid: Editorial San Martín, 1989.

Martínez de Baños Carrillo, Fernando, ed. *Guerra Civil Aragón,* vol. 7, *Zaragoza.* Zaragoza: Delsan, 2010.

Meffre, Liliane. *Carl Einstein, 1885–1940. Itinéraires d'une pensée modern.* Paris: Presses universitaires de Paris-Sorbonne, 2002.

Mera Sanz, Cipriano. *Guerra, exilio y cárcel de un anarcosindicalista.* Paris: Ruedo Ibérico, 1976. Reprint: Madrid: CGT-CNT-FSS-Malatesta-Hormiga Roja, 2006. Available in French as *Guerre, exile et prison d'un anarcho-syndicaliste.* Toulouse: Le Coquelicot, 2012.

Mercier, Louis. *La Chevauchée anonyme.* Marseilles: Agone, 2006.

————. "Lettre à Jean-Paul Samson." *Témoins* 3, no. 8 (1955): 51–53.

————. *En route pour Saragosse avec la colonne Durruti*. Lausanne: Ed. Noir, 1997.

————. "Simone Weil sur le front d'Aragon." In *Les Écrivains et la guerre d'Espagne*, edited by Marc Hanrez. Paris: Cahiers de l'Herne, 1975.

Mila, Massimo. "Destino spagnolo (Ricordo di Renzo Giua)." *La Rassegna d'Italia*, nos. 6–10 (June–October 1947).

Mintz, Frank, and Miguel Peciña. *Los Amigos de Durruti, los trotsquistas y los sucesos de mayo*. Madrid: Campo Abierto, 1978.

Mira Martínez, José. *Los guerrilleros confederales. Un hombre: Durruti*. Barcelona: Comité Regional de la CNT, 1938.

Morales Toro, Antonio, and Javier Ortega Pérez, eds. *El lenguaje de los hechos: ocho ensayos en torno a Buenaventura Durruti*. Madrid: Libros de la Catarata, 1996.

Nash, Mary. *Rojas. Las mujeres republicanas en la Guerra Civil*. Madrid: Taurus, 1999.

Ollivier, Marcel. "Les journées sanglantes de Barcelone (3 au 9 mai 1937)." *Spartacus, cahiers mensuels*, nouvelle série, no. 7 (1937). Reprinted in Groupe Das and Marcel Ollivier. *Révolutionnaires en Catalogne*. Paris: Spartacus, 2006.

Onori, Hans Peter. *Protokoll des Gesprächs mit Franz Ritter*. Unpublished document shared by Peter Huber.

Orwell, George. *The Collected Essays, Journalism and Letters of George Orwell*, 4 volumes. Edited by Sonia Orwell and Ian King. London: Secker & Warburg, 1968.

Österberg, Axel. *Derrière les barricades de Barcelone*. Toulouse: Le Coquelicot, 2015. Translation by Jacqueline Cortes Coumerly.

Pacciardi, Randolfo. *Volontari Italiani nella Spagna Repubblicana. Il Battaglione Garibaldi*. Lugano: Nuove Edizioni di Capolago, 1938.

Pagés i Blanch, Pelai. *La presó model de Barcelona. Història d'un centre penitenciari en temps de guerra (1936–1939)* Barcelona: Publicacions de l'Abadia de Montserrat, 1996.

Paz, Abel. *Chronique passionnée de la colonne de Fer*. Paris: Nautilus, 2002.

————. *Crónica de la columna de hierro*, 2nd ed. Barcelona: Virus, 2004. The first edition appeared in 2001. In English it is *The Story of the Iron Column*. Oakland: AK Press/KSL, 2011.

————. *Durruti en la revolución española*. Madrid: Fundación Anselmo Lorenzo, 1996; reprinted 2004.[3] Published in English as *Durruti in the*

3   A French-language version of this text does exist, but we hesitate to recommend it due to its shortcomings: poor translation, plentiful mistakes, flaws that have not been made good over the two reprints by Quai Voltaire in 1993 and Éditions de Paris in 2000. Readers should be informed

Spanish Revolution. Oakland: AK Press, 2007.

———. *Paradigma de una Revolución*. Barcelona: Flor del Viento, 2005. The first publication was by AIT (Paris: 1967).

———. *Al pie del muro (1942–1954)*. Barcelona: Tot Editorial, 1991.

———. *Viaje al pasado (1936–1939)*. Barcelona: Fundación Anselmo Lorenzo, 1995. A French translation of this was published in 2001 by La Digitale as *Barcelone 1936. Un adolescent au coeur de la révolution espagnole.*

Pinós, Daniel. *Ni l'arbre, ni la pierre*. Lyon: Atelier de création libertaire, 2001.

Planes i Martí, Josep Maria. *Els gàngsters de Barcelona*. Barcelona: Proa, 2002.

Pons Prades, Eduardo. "Verano de 1936 ¿por que no se tomó Zaragoza?" *Nueva Historia*, no. 26 (1979).

Porchet, Adrien. *Adrien Porchet, cinéaste sur le front d'Aragon*. Lausanne: Noir, 1997.

Pozo González, Josep Antoni. *El poder revolucionari a Catalunya durant els mesos de juliol a octubre de 1936/Crisi I recomposició de l'Estat*. Unpublished thesis, accessible on the web.

Prudhommeaux, André. *Où va l'Espagne?* Nîmes: Les Cahiers de Terre Libre, 1937.

Prudhommeaux, André, and Dori Prudhommeaux. *La Catalogne libre (1936–1937)*. Paris: Le Combat syndicaliste, 1970.

Raguer, Hilari. *Carrasco i Formiguera. Un Cristiano nacionalista (1890–1938)*. Madrid: PPC, 2002.

Rama, Carlos M. "Camillo Berneri y la revolución española." In *Guerra de clases en España (1936–1939)*, by Camillo Berneri. Barcelona: Tusquets, 1977.

Ramos, Manuel. *Una vida azarosa*. Self-published, 1993.

that the very first French edition was issued in 1972 by La Tête de Feuille, and, widely expanded and amended, it was used as the basis for the first Spanish-language edition by Bruguera in 1978. When, in his introduction to the Spanish republication in 1996, José Luis Gutiérrez Molina states that "and so the Spanish public will enjoy the same ready access to Abel Paz's book as the French and Germans enjoy today," he is mistaken, for whereas Germans actually do have access—thanks to translator Luis Bredlow and the Hamburg-based publishers Nautilus—to a full version of the text, the same certainly cannot be said of the French public, particularly with regard to the documentation relating to Durruti's death. The same historian is also mistaken when he asserts later that "furthermore, a new edition in French came out in 1993, *Un anarchiste espagnol: Durruti* (Quai Voltaire, Paris), based, this time, on the 1978 Spanish edition."

Romero, Nestor. *Los Incontrolados. Chronique de la colonne de Fer. Espagne 1936–1937.* La Bussière: Acratie, 1997.

Ros i Serra, Jaume. *Miquel Badía. Un defensor oblidat de Catalunya.* Barcelona: Mediterrània, 1996.

Rosell, Thyde. "Femmes libertaires, femmes en lutte, femmes libres!" *Alternative libertaire,* no. 23 (November 2000).

Roselló, Josep Maria. *La Vuelta a la naturaleza.* Barcelona: Virus, 2003.

Rufat, Ramón. *Espions de la République. Mémoires d'un agent secret pendant la guerre d'Espagne.* Paris: Allia, 1990. Translated from the Spanish by Alain Pecunia. The original title was *Entre los Hijos de la Noche* (unpublished, in Spanish).

Sagnes, Jean, and Sylvie Caucanas, eds. *Les Français et la guerre d'Espagne. Actes du colloque de Perpignan.* Perpignan: Presses universitaires de Perpignan, 1990. Reprinted 2004.

Sanz, Ricardo. "La muerte de Durruti en la batalla de Madrid." *Boletín de l'Amicale de la 26e división,* no. 3 (November 20, 1991).

Sanz Martínez, Juan. *Vida y luchas de un idealista.* Valencia: Tétragrama, 1998.

Schafranek, Hans, and Werner Wogerbauer. "Nous, 'agents provocateurs et irresponsables' Esquisse d'une histoire des Amigos de Durruti." In *La Guerra i la Revolució a Catalunya. Comunicacions. II Colloqui internacional sobra la Guerra Civil espanyola,* edited by Universitat de Barcelona, Centre per la investigacio dels moviments socials. Barcelona: CEHI, 1986.

Schröder, Fred "'... alles war Schwarz/rot.' Als Zensor und CNT/FAI-Info-Dienst-Herausgaber in Barcelona." In *"Wir sind des leid, die Ketten zu tragen" Antifaschisten im Spanischen Bürgerkrieg,* edited by Hans-Jürgen Degen and Helmut Ahrens. Barlin: Jakonsohn, 1979.

Semprún Maura, Carlos. *Révolution et contre-révolution en Catalogne.* Paris: Les Nuits rouges, 2002. First published by Mame in 1974.

Sill, Édouard. *"Ni Franco, ni Staline. Les volontaires français de la révolution espagnole."* Dissertation, Université François-Rabelais, 2006.

Sinca Vendrell, Amedeo. *Lo que Dante no pudó imaginar. Mauthausen-Gusen 1940–45.* Self-published, 1980.

Solé Sabaté, Josep Maria, and Joan Villarroya, eds. *La Guerra civil a Catalunya.* 4 vols. Barcelona: Edicions 62, 2004.

Sossenko, Georges. *Aventurero idealista.* Cuenca: Universidad de Castilla-La Mancha, 2004.

Soteras Marín, Alejandro. *Mis memorias.* Gurrea de Gállego: Asociación Casa Libertad, 2003.

Spiess, Heiner (Hg.). *"Dass Friede und Gluck Europas von Sieg der spanischen Republik abhängt." Schweizer in Spanischen Bürgerkrieg.*

Zurich: Limmat Verlag Genossenschaft, 1986.

Stein, Sygmunt. *Ma guerre d'Espagne. Brigades internationals: la fin d'un mythe.* Paris: Seuil, 2012.

Strobl, Ingrid. *Partisanas.* Oakland: AK Press, 2008.

Tasis, Rafael. *Les presons dels altres. Records d'un escarceller d'ocasió.* Barcelona: Pòrtic, 1990.

Téllez Solà, Antonio. *Facerías: Urban Guerrilla Warfare (1939–1957).* Hastings: Christie Books, 2011.

————.*Sabaté: Guerrilla Extraordinary.* Sanday: Cienfuegos Press, 1974.

Thalmann, Pavel, and Clara Thalmann. *Combats pour la liberté.* Quimperle: La Digitale, 1983. Republished 1997.

Toryho, Jacinto. *No eramos tan males.* Madrid: G del Toro, 1975.

Valero Labarta, Vicenta. *Entretien avec Vicenta à Saragosse.* Sound recording. May 11, 2005.

Vázquez Osuna, Federico. *La rebel·lió dels tribunals. L'Administració de justicia a Catalunya (1931–1953). La judicature i el ministeri fiscal.* Barcelona: Editorial Afers, 2005.

Vivancos, Miguel García. *Mémoires inédits.* Given to the authors by the translator, Alain Pecunia, who no longer holds the originals.

Weil, Simone. "Journal d'Espagne" in "Écrits politiques et historiques." In *Oeuvres complètes*, vol. 2, 374–82. Paris: Gallimard, 1991.

————. "Lettre à Georges Bernanos," *Témoins* 2, no. 7 (1954): 2–6.

————. *Oeuvres complètes*, vol. 7, *Correspondance.* Paris: Gallimard, 2012.

Willemse, Hanneke. *Pasado compartido, memorias de anarcosindicalistas de Albalate de Cinca, 1928–1938.* Zaragoza: Prensas Universitarias de Zaragoza, 2002.

Zur Mühlen, Patrick von. *Spanien war ihre Hoffnung: die deutsche Linke in Spanischen Bürgerkrieg 1936 bis 1939.* Bonn: Verlag Neue Gesellschaft, 1983.

ARCHIVAL CENTERS

ACS-CPC (Archivio Centrale dello Stato, Casellario Politico Centrale, Rome) Italian Central State Archives, Central Political Register, Rome

AGMA (Archivo General Militar de Ávila) General Military Archive, Ávila

ANC (Arxiu Nacional de Catalunya, San Cugat del Vallés) Catalonian National Archives, San Cugat del Vallés

Archives nationales, Pierrefitte (French National Archives in Pierrefitte)

Archivo Histórico Nacional (National History Archives), Salamanca

Capitanía General (Captaincy-General), Barcelona

CIRA (Centre International de Recherches sur l'Anarchisme) International Center for Research on Anarchism, Lausanne

CIRA (Centre International de Recherches sur l'Anarchisme) International Center for Research on Anarchism, Marseilles

Hemeroteca de l'Ajuntament de Barcelona (Barcelona City Council Newspaper Library)

IISH (Internationaal Instituut voor Sociale Geschiedenis/International Institute for Social History) Amsterdam

INDEX

Page numbers in *italic* refer to illustrations. "Passim" (literally "scattered") indicates intermittent discussion of a topic over a cluster of pages.

Mavilla Villa, José, 706
Mayol, Juan. *See* Maillol Ballester, Jean ("Juan Mayol")
Meller, Bernard, 672
Mera Sanz, Cipriano, 408, 410, 422, 704
Mercier Vega, Luis (Charles Ridel), 1–7 passim, 15, 213, 219–25 passim, 231–34 passim, 533, 632; Badía execution and, 304; Carpentier and, 231–33, 302, 457–58, 594–96 passim, 611; on cinemas, 478; on Durruti Column's International Group, 243–46 passim, 259–61, 276; on execution of prisoners and militiamen, 75n2, 246–47; on *El Frente*, 257; Gimenez meeting of, 51; meeting of Carpentier, 594; on murders and acts of provocation, 457–58; name changes and pseudonyms, 15n10, 611, 614; in newsreel, 389; Perdiguera, 316–8 passim, 322, 323; Pina, 71–73 passim, 225; reference to Vagliasindi, 331; Siétamo, 384–85, 391, 392, 395; Weil and, 53, 234, 247, 261–64 passim
Merino, Martínez, Julían, 436, 626n17
Miaja Menant, José, 408, 420–22 passim, 535, 663, 704
Michaelis, Rudolf ("Miguel"), 238, 241, 359–60, 370, 372, 441–46 passim, 489–91, 519–21 passim
Michel, Louise, 114, 186
Mila, Massimo, 597–98, 600
Mimosa. *See* Kokoczinski, Georgette (Mimosa)
Minnig, Albert, 343–44
Minué, Liberato, 629n25
Mioli, Giuseppe, 342
Mir, Dolores, 587
Mira, José, 265–66, 384, 391, 405, 406, 440, 702, 705
Molina, Daniel Ramón, 618
Molina Mateo, Juan Manuel ("Juanel"), 704
Molinari, Ettore, 597
Mombiola y Allue, Ángel Pedro, 439
Monasterio Ituarte, José, 538
Monnard, Georges, 358, 672
Montagnani, Anna, 549, 550, 551–53
Montés, Francisco, 290
Montgon, Louis, 563
Monti, Augusto, 597
Montseny, Federica, 143, 147, 280, 342, 401–3 passim, 465–68 passim, 476, 485, 629; Berneri and, 349, 484; Fábregas and, 281; Ridel on, 614; Sanz appointment, 410
Mora, Francisco, 220, 705

Morán, Juan Antonio, 616–18 passim
Moreau, Jean-Marie, 577–83 passim, 626
Moreno López, Antonio, 573, 575
Morin, Émilienne, 243, 283, 415, 416, 417, 585–86n40
Müggli, Richard, 360
Mühsam, Erich, 359
Mühsam, Zensl, 359
Muñoz Recio, Victor, 618
Muñoz Vela, Victor (or Gregorio), 588, 589
Mussolini, Benito, 31, 108, 109, 159, 331, 333, 344, 345; Berneri views, 485; Bonservizi and, 477n111; Rosselli murders and, 445; Vagliasindi and, 635, 636, 639

N

Napolitano, Nino, 600
Navel, Georges, 231
Nebot, Vicente, 483
Negrín López, Juan, 171, 492, 528, 539, 706
Nelles, Dieter, 502, 503, 541
Nemeth, Luc, 543
Nenni, Pietro, 490
Nerman, Ture, 525n170
Nin Pérez, Andrés, 168, 498, 705
Norrblom, Harry, 520, 521, 525, 526
Noske, Gustav, 348, 465
Núñez de Prado, Miguel, 293

O

Odéon, Pierre, 302, 313–4, 595, *595*
Ollivier, Marcel, 473–74
Onori, Hans Peter, 507, 526
Ortega, Arduino, 495
Ortiz, Antonio, 253–56 passim, 277, 379, 384, 403–4, 571, 629–30; Bueno and, 584–89 passim; Durruti death and, 415, 416, 418; on "liberation" of livestock, 233–34; militiawomen and, 239–40; in time line, 702, 703
Orwell, George, 5, 20, 649
Österberg, Axel, 523
"Otto," 72, 116, 132, 144, 158, 163, 182, 192, 359; conjectural identity, 139n1; death, 557; Siétamo, 128–32 passim, 138–40 passim; Tardienta, 171

P

"Pablo." *See* Vagliasindi, Pietro ("Pablo")
Pacciardi, Randolfo, 350, 469, 495
Palau Font, Alfonso, 592
Pallarols Xirgu, Esteban, 591
Papa, Romualdo del, 631n1
Parés Adan, Jaime (or José), 575, 628n24

What is the Kate Sharpley Library?

The Kate Sharpley Library is a library, archive, publishing outfit and affinity group. We preserve and promote anarchist history.

What we've got

Our collection includes anarchist books, pamphlets, newspapers and leaflets from the nineteenth century to the present in over twenty languages. The collection includes manuscripts, badges, audio and video recordings, and photographs, as well as the work of historians and other writers who have documented the anarchist movement.

What we do

We promote the history of anarchism by reprinting original documents from our collection, and translating or publishing new works on anarchism and its history. These appear in our quarterly bulletin or regularly published pamphlets. We have also provided manuscripts to other anarchist publishers. People come and research in the library, or we can send out a limited amount of photocopies.

Why we do it

We don't say one strand of class-struggle anarchism has all the answers. We don't think anarchism can be understood by looking at 'thinkers' in isolation. We do think that what previous generations thought and did, what they wanted and how they tried to get it, is relevant today. We encourage the anarchist movement to think about its own history—not to live on past glories but to get an extra perspective on current and future dangers and opportunities.

How we do it

Everything at the Kate Sharpley Library—acquisitions, cataloguing, preservation work, publishing, answering inquiries is done by volunteers. All our running costs are met by donations (from members of the collective or our subscribers and supporters) or by the small income we make through publishing.

How you can help

Please subscribe to our bulletin to keep up with what we're doing. There are four issues of the Bulletin a year. Or become a Friend, a KSL FRIEND subscription gets you the *Bulletin* and all our publications as they come out.

You can send us anarchist material that you don't need any more (from books to badges)—we can pay postage for large loads, but it doesn't have to be large. A couple of pamphlets will be as gratefully received as anything. Even if you send us duplicates we can trade with other archives for material we do not have. If you publish anarchist material, please add us to your mailing list!

You can send us money too. Details are on our website at: http://www.kate sharpleylibrary.net/doc/donations

Keep in touch!

WWW.KATESHARPLEYLIBRARY.NET | WWW.FACEBOOK.COM/KATESHARPLEYLIBRARY

KATE SHARPLEY LIBRARY
BM HURRICANE
LONDON, WC1N 3XX

AK Press is small, in terms of staff and resources, but we also manage to be one of the world's most productive anarchist publishing houses. We publish close to twenty books every year, and distribute thousands of other titles published by like-minded independent presses and projects from around the globe. We're entirely worker-run and democratically managed. We operate without a corporate structure—no boss, no managers, no bullshit.

The Friends of AK program is a way you can directly contribute to the continued existence of AK Press, and ensure that we're able to keep publishing books like this one! Friends pay $25 a month directly into our publishing account ($30 for Canada, $35 for international), and receive a copy of every book AK Press publishes for the duration of their membership! Friends also receive a discount on anything they order from our website or buy at a table: 50% on AK titles, and 20% on everything else. We have a Friends of AK ebook program as well: $15 a month gets you an electronic copy of every book we publish for the duration of your membership. You can even sponsor a very discounted membership for someone in prison.

Email FRIENDSOFAK@AKPRESS.ORG for more info, or visit the Friends of AK Press website: HTTPS://WWW.AKPRESS.ORG/FRIENDS.HTML.

There are always great book projects in the works—so sign up now to become a Friend of AK Press, and let the presses roll!